MONEY, INFORMATION AND UNCERTAINTY

by C. A. E. Goodhart

The MIT Press
Cambridge, Massachusetts

This book was printed and bound in the United States of America.

Library of Congress Cataloging-in-Publication Data
Goodhart, C. A. E. (Charles Albert Eric)
    Money, information, and uncertainty / Charles Goodhart. – 2nd ed.
        p.   cm
    Bibliography: p.
    Includes index.
    ISBN 978-0-262-07122-2 (hc.:alk. paper) ISBN 978-0-262-57075-6 (pb.:alk. paper)
    1. Money. I. Title
HG221.G674   1989
332.4–dc19   88–38611
                                                            CIP

Contents

Preface to the Second Edition, 1989

Much has changed in the subject matter covered by this book since it was first drafted in 1973. In the policy field, for example, the Bretton Woods system of pegged, but adjustable, exchange rates was succeeded by a period of, more or less managed, floating exchange rates, whose misbehaviour became an increasing subject of concern by the mid-1980s. Associated with these external developments, domestic monetary policy switched from primary concern with maintaining interest rates in order to balance the (conflicting) requirements of external stability and internal full employment towards primary concern with achieving quantitative monetary targets in order to reduce inflation and/or *nominal* incomes: then, as the prior predictability of the relationships between nominal income and (the target) monetary aggregates collapsed in many countries in the 1980s while at the same time inflation had been brought back to more acceptable rates, so the pendulum swung back towards the earlier policy approach.

The course of monetary history, and of monetary policy changes, both reflected and shaped developments in monetary theory. The main battlefield in the 1970s was contested by Monetarists and Keynesians. The apogee of influence of the Monetarists was achieved sometime around 1979–80, with the election of governments in the UK and USA committed to free markets, including notably freely floating foreign exchange rates, and to monetary targetry. Events since then have led to some practical disillusion with the precepts of the Monetarist school.

Whereas this has simply reconfirmed some more traditional Keynesians in the belief that they were correct all along, the newer, and perhaps more influential, school of neo-classical economists in the USA, (e.g., Lucas, Sargent, Wallace), claimed that the breakdown of the stability of the so-called 'structural equations', notably the demand-for-money function, on which the Monetarists had placed so much weight, was an inevitable result of changes in the policy regimes in operation and of changes in underlying structure of the economy itself. In some part these changes occurred as a result of the recommendations of the Monetarists themselves.

These neo-classical economists have criticised both the Keynesian and earlier Monetarist economists for basing their analyses insecurely on *ad hoc* micro-economic foundations. They have claimed that a macro-economic superstructure can be erected only on a firm basis of sufficiently rigorous micro-economic analysis. In one respect I fully agree with this. Most of the interesting, and fruitful, developments in the field of money and banking currently seem to me to be at the micro level – e.g., on the theory of the role of banks (Chapter 5), on credit rationing (Chapter 7), on the working of financial markets and of market makers within them (Chapter 1) – whereas macro-level policy thinking, both on the domestic front (Chapter 15) and internationally (Chapter 18), has currently reached an exhausted impasse.

Yet the neo-classical economists have, it seems to me, chosen to pursue the wrong micro-level paradigm. Because the Walrasian, perfect-clearing markets paradigm is both rigorous, tractable, mathematically elegant, and the main heuristic system used in micro-economics, the neo-classical economists have used it generally as the basis for their macro-models. My belief is that perfect, instantaneous clearing markets are not a general feature of the 'real world' and, moreover, that many – perhaps most – of the conditions that monetary economists wish to explore (e.g., the role of money and of banks) would simply have no place in a world characterised by perfect, instantaneously clearing markets. It is no accident that in many of the latest studies of 'real business cycles' money plays no essential role.

Rather than reach for some set of prior assumptions about the way markets work, economists ought to study them in practice. I believe that this is now increasingly happening, which is why, despite the current failure to present a coherent *macro-economic* set of theories, explanations and policy precepts, I find the current developments in this field at the *micro-theoretical* level extremely exciting.

Because of the importance that I believe needs to be attached to establishing with complete clarity the micro-level basis on which the subsequent macro-level analysis is based, this revised edition starts with an entirely new chapter on 'The Nature of Markets'.

In this, I explain what the conditions and circumstances are that lead market makers to adjust prices at varying speeds, in some cases fast, in others sluggishly, so that the adjustment to shocks and to 'news' is taken in part in quantity adjustments and in part in price adjustments.

For reasons that I believe can be established in a properly rigorous form – though I would *not* claim to do that here – the real economy adjusts relatively slowly, with both prices and quantities in goods and labour markets adjusting slowly, and exhibiting inertia, in response to shocks. If there is, for example, a monetary shock, and certain markets, for labour and goods, react sluggishly, whereas financial markets react much more quickly, then it can be shown that there could be expected to be a tendency for asset prices in such markets (e.g., foreign exchange rates, interest rates) to 'overshoot' on the occasion of such shocks. This is, for example, the basis of the Dornbusch 'overshooting' hypothesis in the foreign exchange market, but the analysis can be, and has been, applied more widely.

My impression of the historical data for asset prices is, however, that they do not exhibit a pattern over time consistent with 'overshooting' in response to shocks and 'news'. My explanation of this is that people do not like to be on the receiving end of shocks, and have established various buffering devices to reduce the extent of such shocks. Prominent among such mechanisms is the willingness of agents to allow their monetary holding to act as a buffer, temporarily expanding or declining in response to (unforeseen) shifts in monetary flows.

Thus, in addition to my other various idiosyncrasies, some of which are mentioned in the Preface to the first edition, I have a clearly established position in monetary economics, as a sticky-price, buffer-stock theorist. Although there are a few other economists who take this view, notably David Laidler, it is not widely popular. The neo-classicists dispute the existence, or the importance, of sticky prices; many of the Keynesians and the earlier Monetarists, who would accept that some markets do adjust slowly, have not seen any need to complement that view with a buffer stock approach. Readers should be aware of, and aim off for, my own idiosyncrasies.

For the rest I hope that I am reasonably mainstream. As earlier noted, in some areas, especially on the micro side, this stream has been moving rapidly in recent years; in some other areas there has been little progress. Accordingly my strategy has been to leave whole chapters or sections unchanged from the first edition, in those areas where little development has occurred, but to introduce completely new material, chapters and sections, where warranted. This may cause some unevenness in the book, but it certainly saved an enormous amount of time.

Thus the bulk of the opening chapters in the earlier edition have been retained (after the insertion of the new Chapter on 'The Nature of Markets'), but a new section has been added on in each case describing recent developments, in Chapters 2–4. The next chapters, on financial intermediation and the supply of money, Chapters 5–6, involve a reordering of earlier material, plus a section on recent theoretical analyses of the functions of banks in the economy. The next three chapters, on 'Credit Rationing', on the 'Need for a Central Bank', and 'Financial Regulation', are new, and spring from the growing interest in some of the micro, structural issues in this general area.

Chapters 1–9 cover essentially micro issues; Chapters 10–18 cover mainly macro issues. Chapter 10 is new, and covers that perennial subject of complexity and discord, 'The Determination of Interest Rates'. This leads on to a chapter on 'The Term Structure', where again an additional section has been added to the earlier material. Chapters 12 and 13, covering the transmission mechanism of monetary effects onto nominal incomes, output and prices, involve a more complex interweaving of old and new material; again the opening sections are mostly old, though much rearranged, while the final sections are mainly new. Turning then to the sections on macro policy, first domestic then international, the chapters from the first edition, coming now as Chapters 14, 16 and 17, have been left virtually untouched, while a further chapter in each case, Chapters 15 and 18, has been added, taking the story of the history and analysis of monetary policies on from 1973 to the mid-1980s.

Once again I should emphasise that, while my view of such policy changes was undoubtedly assisted by my ring side seat in the Bank of England until mid-1985, the judgements on them expressed here remain absolutely my own. One of the benefits of returning to academic life was that it gave me time (though not enough) and an opportunity to carry out this revision. But in the midst of trying to re-establish my teaching and research programme, and helping with Mervyn King to found the LSE Financial Markets Group, this extra work seemed a heavy load indeed. I could not have done it without help from many friends, and the tolerance of my family.

In particular I must mention Mark Mullins, who helped me greatly on the editorial side, and Lesley Spencer and Kim Frame, who bore the brunt of the secretarial work.

C. A. E. G.

Preface to the First Edition, 1975

In recent years there has been a spreading movement among economists to re-examine and to explore the fundamental insights into the working of the real economy which Keynes expressed so vividly. These are, shortly, that the world is filled with uncertainty, that actions are based on insecure expectations, that accurate information is at a premium, and that mistakes are constantly being made, so that our system lurches from one short-term period of disequilibrium to another.

This view of the central message of Keynes's work, maintained by Shackle over many years, revivified by Leijonhufvud and further advanced in recent years by economists such as Alchian and Clower, leads on to the interpretation of the role of money as an informational device made necessary by the enfolding uncertainties of a complex economy. This approach, of course, stands in clear contrast to the construction of general equilibrium systems (à la Walras) in which it is often hard to see what necessary functions money plays at all. So, conceptually, the main theme of this book is the critical importance of uncertainty for understanding the working of the monetary system.

The increasing appreciation of the validity of Keynes's emphasis on the importance of uncertainty, expectations and information costs has, however, been accompanied by a continuing criticism of several of the analytical moulds into which Keynesian theory was simplified and subsequently rigidified. Pre-eminent among these formulations is the *IS/LM* model initially constructed by Hicks. And there are certain other parts of Keynesian analysis which have remained in their simplified moulds, for example the analysis of the determination of the money supply in terms of a multiplier relationship between the monetary base and the money stock. Indeed, one touchstone of areas in macro-economics where analysis has failed to advance has been those that rely on mechanical multiplier relationships between aggregates, rather than relate adjustments to behavioural responses to changes in market signals, usually in the form of shifts in relative prices. In the field of monetary economics the greatest steps forward in this latter direction have been taken by Tobin and the Yale school, particularly in their development of the analysis of portfolio adjustment. Analytically, portfolio adjustment is the main descriptive tool used in the following chapters to examine the working of the monetary system.

In any case, these and many other developments that have taken place in recent years have led to a growing divergence between the substance of current research work appearing in the journals and the contents of many of the existing textbooks. Therefore, there appeared to be something of a gap to be filled by an intermediate textbook which could cover the space between the contents of existing introductory textbooks and the state of current theoretical analysis. What is meant by the term 'intermediate' is that it is assumed that all readers already have a firm grounding in standard Keynesian macro-economic analysis, in particular the *IS/LM* paradigm, and also have had at least an introductory course in money and banking. It is primarily intended for undergraduates in their final year and graduate students who are specialising in monetary economics.

The objective of the book is to advance as far as practically possible into the conceptual framework that lies behind recent analytical developments in monetary economics. In that respect it enters into some fairly complicated fields. On the other hand, it includes virtually no mathematical or econometric analysis, so it requires very little in the way of prior technical skill from the reader. This is partly intended, in order to encourage readers to find out what current monetary economics is all about without slogging through thickets of equations, and partly imposed by my own technical limitations.

Within the framework of the general structure of the book, and in most sub-sections, I have normally tended to start with the micro-economic aspects of the subject at hand, dealing with these on a fairly abstract theoretical level. Then we move on towards the macro-economic, practical and even policy-oriented areas of the subject. In this context I have consciously pointed out in several places the political forces and constraints that bear on monetary economics. Our subject has been rightly called 'political economy', and those who choose to leave out the politics in the pursuit of rigour, or the avoidance of value judgements, or whatever, are to my mind losing too much that is important for the relevance and the immediacy of the subject.

Writing a textbook, mainly consisting of interpretations of the work of others, is a humble, even a humbling, task. Yet perhaps readers should be warned that at certain points the analysis presented here is individualistic, and does not represent an attempt merely to produce and to interpret the accepted work of leading monetary economists. In particular the chapter on the determination of the stock of money and the working of the financial system, with its concentration on the portfolio adjustment approach and its rejection of multiplier analysis, is out of sympathy with the mainstream of current work in this field.

Moreover, even when one is trying to do no more than to extract the central elements of accepted analysis, one's selection process, deciding what is important and what is not, is inevitably biased by one's views and background experience. Here I hope that my own background of working, both as an academic economist and as an adviser in government and in the Bank of England, has helped to give some grasp of which areas of theoretical analysis have a practical relevance, and which do not.

I have learnt much during my work in the Bank. Nevertheless the views, and errors, expressed in this book are very much my own, and no one should attribute anything here to a Bank view, if indeed such a stable, monolithic entity can ever be truly said to exist. This book was written, though, in time which the Bank allowed me to take away from my regular duties, and for this I am very grateful. In this respect I have a special debt of gratitude to Leslie Dicks-Mireaux who arranged that this could be possible.

There would have been many more errors and quirky views contained in this book but for the great help which I received from colleagues and friends in the course of its preparation. Among those whose comments and criticisms on earlier drafts of the book were particularly helpful, I should like to mention Bill Allen, Andrew Bain, Peter Burman, Vicky Chick, Tony Coleby, Andrew Crockett, David Laidler, Kit McMahon, Robin Marris, Rainer Masera, Allan Meltzer, Marcus Miller, Steve Nickell, Bill Poole, Lionel Price, David Sheppard, Case Sprenkle, Michael Thornton, Geof Willetts, John Williamson and Geof Wood. I should, perhaps, add that often the most helpful and trenchant comments and criticisms came from those who do not share my viewpoint on monetary economics.

In addition I had much needed mathematical support from Peter Burman, Mike Clements and David Williams. The figures were drawn under the kindly aegis of Miss Crosby. The main weight of typing, and retyping, the drafts in their various stages fell upon Gill Brewster, with support from Val Carter and Christine Stokes. I am very grateful to them all.

But perhaps the main burden falls upon an author's family, who ceased in this case to see much of me at weekends for over a year. To them I can only apologise for selfishly pursuing the urge to write this book.

C. A. E. G.

Acknowledgements

The author and publishers wish to thank the following for permission to use copyright material.

Bank of England for Table 6.2 from *Bank of England Quarterly Bulletin*, vol.28, no.3, August 1988, table 12.1.

The Brookings Institution for Figure 1.1 from Okun, *Prices and Quantities*, 1981, fig. 4.1, p. 146.

The Controller of Her Majesty's Stationery Office for Table 13.2 from *Financial Statistics, 1987*, table 39, CSO.

The John Hopkins University Press for Figure 15.7 from Campbell and Dougan (eds), *Alternative Monetary Regimes*, 1986, p. 184.

OECD, Paris, for Table 13.1 from Chouraqui chi Driscoll, 'The Effects of Monetary Policy', 1987.

Oxford University Press for Figure 15.8 from Goodhart, 'Financial Innovation and Monetary Control', in *Oxford Review of Economic Policy*, 1986, p. 82.

The University of Chicago Press for Figure 15.4 from Kydland and Prescott, 'Rules rather than Discretion: The Inconsistency of Optimal Plans', *Journal of Political Economy*, vol.85, no.3, 1977.

Every effort has been made to trace all the copyright-holders, but if any have been inadvertently overlooked the publishers will be pleased to make the necessary arrangements at the first opportunity.

I
The Nature of Markets

Summary

Time is the ultimate constraint on mortals. Lack of time contributes also to limited information. Shortage of time and information make it harder for agents to achieve Pareto equilibrium matchings of wants with endowments. This had led, as described in Section 1, to the evolution of several social artifacts to relax such constraints, namely the establishment of both organised markets and money.

If markets are only held at infrequent discrete occasions, potential buyers and sellers lose the advantage of immediacy, a term coined by Demsetz. On the other hand, the flow of new orders into a continuously functioning market may be small and relatively unbalanced in any short period. One common response to this problem has been for certain market participants to assume the function of market making, acting as principals and quoting prices at which they will buy or sell the good or asset being traded.

There are considerable resource costs involved in establishing a market. In practice, many (perhaps most) agents who act as market makers – e.g., retailers – also provide associated functions. Nevertheless, one can abstract from the costs arising from such associated functions and enquire as to the nature of the particular costs involved in market making itself, and how those costs will be reflected in the size of the margin, or spread, between the bid and ask price. This forms the subject of Section 2. There are two such main costs. The first involves resource costs, including the costs of carrying inventory necessary to fulfil the role of market maker. The second follows from the fact that the market maker's quoted prices make him the potential victim of anyone with 'inside information' whether the likely future price is liable to lie outside the quoted price spread.

Despite the fact that new order flows themselves carry information about future prices, one can observe that market makers do not always adjust prices instantaneously. There is a whole spectrum of speeds of price adjustment in differing markets, ranging from very fast indeed in standardised asset markets – e.g., the foreign exchange market – to comparatively very slow in labour markets. In Section 3 we ask what determines the speed with which market makers adjust prices. This remains a conceptually difficult subject. We conclude that the main considerations are:

1. The costs/risks involved in absorbing inventory fluctuations in each market.
2. The extent and distribution of information about the asset, good or service being traded in each market.
3. The relative risk aversions, and hence preference for insurance, among traders and market makers.

There are economies of scale in the establishment of markets. Moreover, as noted in Section 2, the higher the ratio of regular traders to those with 'inside information' about future price levels, the lower will be the spread that the market maker can quote; these low spreads induce more trading and therefore support the continued existence of markets. There are thus centripetal tendencies towards the centralisation of trading through successful markets, although there is the possibility, as noted in Section 4, that markets may collapse and disappear through lack of support.

It is perhaps unusual to commence a book on money with an explicit account of the market micro-structure being assumed throughout the rest of the book. I argue, in Section 5, not only that the system described here of market makers adjusting their quoted prices is more realistic than the alternative Arrow–Debreu Walrasian auctioneer paradigm, but also that many practical aspects of monetary phenomena can be properly analysed only against such a more realistic background.

1. Market Structure

It is, perhaps, a sign of increasing age when one comes to appreciate with greater clarity that shortage of time represents the true economic constraint. In many analytical studies in the field of economics, wealth is used as the budget constraint; however, if time were unlimited and costless, wealth could always be augmented by more work. Furthermore, certain analytical approaches involve agents operating on the basis of information which is less complete than theoretically possible. For example, search theories describe a context in which agents have to decide whether to go on sampling the market in order to acquire more information about prices and qualities or, alternatively, to settle for the best bargain still available; this type of analysis depends on time being limited and, hence, valuable.[1] Similarly, much recent macro-economic analysis ascribes deviations from equilibrium to failure in differentiating between relative and general price adjustments.[2] The main constraint on the acquisition of information in these models is the time involved in that exercise; if time were unlimited and costless, then there would be no reason for agents to fail to gather, and act on the basis of, all available information. In this sense imperfect information derives from the time constraint. Mortals must optimally allocate their scarce time on a continuous basis between the various functions of life, including work, leisure and information gathering.

Gathering information, or shopping, is time consuming (though some may find certain aspects relatively pleasurable and hence devote more time to that exercise). If we had to rely on barter, involving not only a double coincidence of wants but also a double coincidence of timing of those wants, it would take an eternity to be able to reach a general equilibrium solution described by Pareto optimal allocations in all markets. We do not have the time for this. In practice, of course, ultimate buyers of products rarely go directly to ultimate producers at all. A car buyer does not tour car factories, nor does a purchaser of meat visit a selection of farms. Instead, a set of social artifacts have evolved over time in order, primarily to relax the constraints imposed by time and, hence, information.

One such development is the distribution network, whereby wholesalers and retailers purchase products from producers and present them in a more convenient fashion for consumers. This role is well understood and needs no further discussion

---

[1] See Rothschild (1973) pp. 1283–1308; see also Lippman and McCall (1976) Part 1, pp. 155–89 and Part 2, pp. 347–68 and High (1983–4) pp. 252–64.

[2] For example, Lucas (1972) pp. 103–24; Lucas (1983) pp. 197–9.

here. The next two social artifacts which evolved to relax the related time/information constraints are, however, central to the study of monetary phenomena: they are money itself, and organised markets. The role of *money* will be explored in greater detail in Chapter 2. For the time being we need only note that *market* transactions require an exchange in which both sides believe that they will benefit from obtaining from the other party something of greater or equal value to whatever they have given up. The use of money relaxes two informational constraints. The first constraint relates to the potential value of goods in the course of barter (note that the term 'good' is applied to anything that people wish to buy or sell, not only physical, but also services, assets, real and financial, and also factors of production). As Brunner and Meltzer[1] and Jones[2] demonstrate, an exchange of goods for goods will either require the unlikely occurrence of the double coincidences noted above or leave one party to the exchange holding a good which that party will want to exchange later for some other good. The advantage of developing a standardised store of value and means of payment to ease the information/time constraint inherent in this latter option is obvious, and money has generally emerged in the past in a specialised commodity form – e.g., gold, silver, cattle, cowrie shells, etc. – in response to this need.

More discussion on the essential functions of money now revolves, however, around the second constraint, that its use can relax the need for information or trust in the credit worthiness of the counter-party to an exchange. In the absence of a need for trust, exchanges would not necessarily involve an exchange of existing physical assets but could be based entirely on credit; the recipient of the physical good would meet the debt at some future date by promising payment of equivalent present value. Given multilateral credit clearing, a complete set of markets insuring all contingencies and complete honesty, there would be little need for money. In practice, of course, it is the lack of trust in the counterparty's willingness and ability to make promised future payments that makes sellers of spot goods require immediate payment.

Because sellers of goods or services will often be unwilling to extend credit, or accept other goods as a means of payment, buyers may face a liquidity (cash in advance) constraint in which only the availability of money enables them to buy goods. Analysis of such constraints was initiated by Clower[3] and has been continued by economists such as Svensson.[4] It is, however, important to bed such analysis *firmly* in a model in which time – information is limited and costly. Without such an assumption, the constraints imposed by the cash in advance requirement may prevent agents undertaking some transactions which, with the use of time and energy, they could carry out through barter.

Models incorporating the assumption that time is costless will actually produce the counterfactual result that a barter economy is *more* efficient than a monetary economy!

The second social artifact, which has emerged alongside money to help relax time and information constraints, involves the development of organised markets, or trading posts, at which buyers and sellers can gather at prearranged times and places.

---

[1] Brunner and Meltzer (1971) pp. 784–805.
[2] Jones (1976) pp. 757–75.
[3] Clower (1967) pp. 1–8.
[4] Svensson (1985) pp. 919–44.

Knowledge of the existence and timing of such markets clearly relaxes the limitations of time–information of agents, but there still remains a question of how the market should work. In some theoretical abstract models agents are allowed to recontract earlier deals if new information makes them believe that such deals represented a sub-optimum outcome. In practice, recontracting is very time consuming and agents are therefore generally bound by the commitments that they make, even if they shortly thereafter regret them. A basic form of market structure involves open outcry, whereby prospective buyers (sellers) call out bid (ask) prices for some stated (or predetermined) quantity of the object in question; these announcements hold good for some predetermined period of time and can be accepted by a seller (buyer) with the result that a deal is struck.

In practice few people will be confident enough to specify *publicly* prices at which they will buy or sell unless they have reasonably strong convictions (perhaps arising from good information), about the future price evolution of the objects in the market place. Open outcry markets are thus likely to be limited to those where there are a large number of expert dealers. Given that dealing itself involves costs which have to be recouped from profits, this implies that such markets require a considerable volume of trade to succeed.

In other circumstances, markets will require some more structure to function efficiently. A standard approach is for the market to be organised by an auctioneer. The auctioneer will arrange the flow of objects to be sold and organise the bidding for each object in turn. Although the auctioneer will not act as a principal to buy or sell for his own book, he will frequently provide the site of the trading post and arrange information diffusion and the handling process on behalf of both buyers and sellers. All this consumes considerable resources, and payment for auctioneer's costs and profit margins generally runs to a significant percentage of the value of the transactions made through such markets.

In most cases, the flow of new orders to buy or sell a good or asset in any short period of time, say 30 minutes, would be both small and stochastic – i.e., subject to random variation. Consequently, if an auctioneer tried to operate continuously, he would be using his own time and the trading post space to complete a small number of deals, which would be expensive. Moreover, the stochastic variation would lead on occasions to an absence of buyers, and at other times to an absence of sellers, resulting in an endemic volatility in prices caused not by any shift in the underlying equilibrium price but simply by the chance arrival of buyers and sellers.

Accordingly, most auction markets take place at discrete prearranged times; for example, the Exeter market for lambs and cattle for slaughter is on every Tuesday morning, the Banbury market for store calves is held Wednesday mornings and Christie's sales of antique furniture occur at 2 p.m. on Thursdays. The discrete timing of the market allows potential buyers and sellers to bunch together less expensively, and the bunching provides a broader, more stable market.

The problem with such occasional auctions is that both buyers and sellers lose the opportunity to deal as and when they want; they lose immediacy, to use the phrase coined by Demsetz.[1] People value the ability to make transactions when they want and not just on the occasional dates when markets may be open. Access to continuous markets reduces the time and cost (including excess inventories) of having to fit one's own schedule to that of the time pattern of market opening.

This, however, raises the question of how to deal with the irregular, stochastic and

---

[1] Demsetz (1968) pp. 33–53.

often small flow of new orders. The general answer to this, adopted in the majority of markets, is that some market participant(s) take on the function of market making, perhaps while also performing other functions at the same time. The specialist market maker then interposes himself as a principal in the market by offsetting the fluctuating imbalances in demand and supply with purchases or sales for his own account. When there is a temporary excess supply in the market, the market maker will buy for his own account at his announced bid price, thus increasing his inventory of the object being sold, and when there is temporary excess demand, the market maker will sell out of his inventory at his ask price.[1] By this process, the market maker smoothes the stochastic variation of prices and, therefore, encourages potential buyers and sellers to maintain a market for the object.

One may, perhaps, usefully distinguish two aspects of market making. The first is the readiness to quote a price at which deals can be struck. The second is to absorb short-term imbalances in order flow through adjustments to one's own position. The second function, which is critical to a well-functioning liquid market place, may also be performed by other short-term traders who need not be market makers themselves. But these latter are consciously and voluntarily taking up speculative positions, whereas the market maker stands ready – in the very short term, at least – to absorb such imbalances quasi-automatically as a result of the trading decisions of others.

Some of the fluctuations in new order flow, however, will *not* be purely stochastic, but will represent changes in underlying demand and supply conditions. In those cases where the market maker *can* perceive clearly what the new situation implies he can change the bid–ask quotes in line with the new information and proceed as before. More often, the market maker will not be privy to such information and will have to attempt to differentiate between temporary and permanent imbalances between demand and supply on the basis of the evidence of the new order flow arrival itself, together with other evidence such as changes in prices quoted by competing market makers. This subject is covered further in Section 2, where we analyse the determinants of the size of the spread between the bid (purchase) and ask (sale) prices.

When we think of market makers, we usually have in mind specialist market makers operating in financial markets. This mode of analysis can, however, be usefully extended far further. For example, a retail distributor may bid a price for good x from his suppliers and ask a price from his customers; whether the retailer is a price (market) maker, or price taker, in the supply market for good x will, of course, depend on the structure of the market. Assuming that the retailer has some degree of pricing discretion, the retailer acts in effect as a market maker in that good, presenting bid prices to potential sellers and ask prices to customers. This function will be carried out in conjunction with other distributional functions – e.g., the presentation, handling, and information diffusion of the goods in question; it should be noted that these functions are not strictly independent since holding inventory is part of both market making and these other tasks. Similarly banks can be regarded as market makers in money, making bids on known terms for funds from depositors and offering loans on known terms to those needing to borrow money. In this case the bid–ask price spread is represented by the spread between the interest rates offered

---

[1] In highly developed markets for non-perishable assets, the existence of facilities to borrow (or swap) inventories makes it necessary to distinguish between the market maker's *position* and his *inventory*.

and charged.[1] Again, of course, banks provide additional conjoint functions besides market making – e.g., operating the payments system, maturity transformation and specialisation in credit risk assessment, which will be addressed in Chapter 5.

The transformation of inputs into outputs normally entails markets being made in those entities. The institution undertaking the transformation may act as market maker in both its input and output markets, or as price taker in both, or as market maker in some of its markets but not in all of them. In so far as an institution is, say, a price taker in its input market and a price maker in its output market, it still has to decide on the spread between its given input price and the ask price which it chooses. Only if the institution is a price taker in all its markets will the quantity to be produced be its only choice variable. Few medium or large companies are in this latter position. As noted earlier, it needs reasonable confidence that one does have comparatively good information on underlying market conditions to set announced prices. Accordingly, the market maker is likely to be the player in the market with access to good information sources on conditions in that market, whether by virtue of position and market power or for some other reason.

2. Determination of the Size of the Spread

The simplest case of transforming inputs into outputs occurs with a market maker who stands ready to buy some asset at a quoted bid price and to sell that same asset at a higher ask price. As Demsetz[2] noted, the market maker is providing the joint service of immediacy and insurance against price fluctuations arising from stochastic order flows. Even then, the market maker will incur certain resource costs to fulfil his role; these include labour (dealers and backroom office staff), rent of office space, entry costs into the market, communications equipment (computers, etc.), and so on. As was noted earlier, even the auctioneer, who acts as an organiser rather than a market maker, normally charges some considerable fee for services rendered.

Most market makers in goods or services markets who quote prices for their outputs or inputs normally carry out considerable additional functions. For example, a retailer will transport goods from the producer, or wholesale depot, to a shop more convenient to the shopper, break bulk into smaller, more convenient volumes, advertise the availability, quality and price of the goods, present them in a convenient way for inspection or absorb the risk of being left with perishable or damaged goods. A bank will provide payments services, investment advice, maturity transformation, portfolio management or credit risk assessment, in addition to market making in money. In some cases such extra services can be charged for separately: stock brokers can charge a fee, or commission, in addition to the cost to the buyer of paying the higher ask price for a security. More frequently, perhaps, the costs of providing the various services are bundled together and recouped in the margins between output and input prices. For instance, the shopper does not pay individually for the cost to the retailer of transporting, unpacking, advertising and presenting the individual can of soup; instead, the shop charges an ask price for the can well above its bid price.

An important example of this cost bundling in the banking industry arises from the operation of the payments system, involving billions of cheques which have to be dealt with by a combination of people and equipment. It would be possible – and,

---

[1] See, for example, Stoll (1985) pp. 67–91 and Ho and Saunders (1981) pp. 581–600.
[2] Demsetz (1968).

indeed, economically more efficient – to unbundle charges for this service from banks' other role of making a market in money. It would be more efficient because the cost of cheque payments is underpriced and, hence, over-used; the net result means that resources are wasted. In addition, this underpricing serves as a barrier to the introduction of more efficient payments systems, such as electronic funds transfer systems (EFTS), whose relative advantage to potential consumers in terms of lower transactions costs is thus hidden. Furthermore, the spread between the interest offered on at least some classes of deposits – e.g., non-interest-bearing demand deposits – and loans must widen to recoup such resource costs, and such widening will, as described later, act to reduce the volume of intermediation (loans and deposits) below the optimal level. In this instance, one key reason for the bundling together of service costs lies in the tax system: specific interest payments are taxable while bank charges for operating costs are not deductible. If the operating costs of the payments' system can be offset against interest payments in a manner acceptable to the tax inspector, then both banks and bank customers can benefit at the expense of all other tax payers.

To recap, the market maker's spread will have to be wide enough to recoup the resource costs involved in providing market making services; these costs include the normal rate of profit on such capital required to encourage entrepreneurs to continue operating plus the extra costs required to finance the provision of associated functions, payment for which is bundled together in fixing the bid–ask spread. In addition, of course, market makers enjoying a degree of monopoly will charge a larger spread. While all these factors are important, and may in many cases represent the larger part of the actual spread, they are in a sense ancillary to the key elements involved in market making which determine the bid–ask spread in a world in which transactions costs, monopoly powers and associated functions may be assumed away.

In order to honour commitments to buy an asset or good, the market maker has to have access to a means of payments. In order to honour commitments to sell an asset or good, the market maker has to have access to a sufficient volume of that asset or good. The market maker can either hold an inventory of money and assets himself or he can have facilities to borrow them when needed. In either case, there will be some cost involved (particularly, of course, if the good is perishable or depreciates in the course of time). The interest rate available for cash on call, or at short notice, will generally be below that available on longer term riskless assets: there will be some charge for credit facilities available but undrawn, and actual borrowing will be expensive. On the other hand, the running return from holding inventories of assets may be greater, or less, than the implicit cost of capital employed in financing such inventory. In the case of goods, especially perishable goods, the running costs of holding inventory can be very large.

In the case of durables and assets, however, the running cost of holding an inventory is obviously less. In this case, the main concern to the market maker will not be the running cost of his inventory position[1] but the risk that he will make a capital loss through unforeseen changes in the underlying equilibrium value of the asset in which he is market making. Indeed, his position virtually ensures that he will suffer some such loss. Since the market maker publicly announces bid–ask prices at which he will deal, and assuming for the moment that there is no spread between bid

---

[1] Once again the qualification needs to be added that facilities that enable market makers to borrow or to swap inventories enable them to divorce their *position* from changes in their *inventories*.

and ask prices, then it will be the case that any upward shift in demand (downward shift in supply) will cause people to buy inventory from the market maker. As his own inventory is reduced, the market maker will have to buy in more assets at a higher price in order to rebuild his inventory.[1] Similarly, a fall in demand (rise in supply) will leave the market maker exposed to holding a larger volume of lower priced assets. Of course, the market maker will adjust his bid–ask prices to any information that he obtains – e.g., from the pattern of order flow itself – about the likely changes in the equilibrium price of the asset or good in which he is dealing. However, some of the relevant information – e.g., changes in tastes of consumers, changes in production possibilities, etc. – will be private information known only to the dealers coming to him and will not, therefore, be publicly available. Exposed to such informed trading, the market maker is liable to lose money by finding his inventory of assets rising relative to his inventory of cash when asset prices fall (relative to the monetary numeraire), and vice versa.[2]

Market makers must charge a higher spread on the regular, but stochastic, flow of buy–sell orders for any asset or good in order to offset the loss that they will make when dealing with 'inside' traders whose orders arise from private information; this information heralds a shift in the fundamental value of the asset which cannot be observed beforehand by market makers from publicly available information.[3] To take an example, a market maker in some metal will face a stochastic flow of orders from buyers and sellers which will continue in the absence of any change in the underlying demand – supply context, together with orders that do represent a change in that context. Similarly in the asset market, the accumulation and decumulation of assets over the life cycle will lead to a stochastic flow of orders from regular (liquidity) traders, in addition to the flow of orders from dealers with some private inside information on fundamental values (information traders). There may also be some significant volume of traders who believe, incorrectly, that they possess some special

---

[1] In practice, market makers will not be as passive as suggested here. They will accommodate the order flow, but by trading out of a position that each market maker regards as consistent with the immediate short-term trend. Even in a market in which market makers cannot initiate positions directly (by trading on someone else's prices), they can in most circumstances attain the positions which they want by aggressive pricing. I am indebted to J. Hettich for this and several other helpful and pertinent comments on the contents of this chapter.

[2] Partly for this very reason, however, those market participants willing to take on the exposed position of market making are likely to be those with particularly good access to sources of relevant information themselves.

[3] This sentence is put into the plural tense for a particular reason. When a market maker deals privately with an informed client, he may obtain, in turn, access to private information before the rest of the market. In the foreign exchange market, where there is adequate liquidity to adjust large positions, maybe involving hundreds of millions of dollars in a single currency, in a matter of minutes, it is often the practice of dealers at major banks to quote especially fine spreads on large accounts to customers whom they believe to possess privileged information. They do this precisely to take advantage of the informational value of this business for their own positioning, even at the risk of getting 'caught' on the original trade. But while the first such market maker may be able to share in the profits arising from private (inside) information in this way, the set of market makers will find it much harder to do so, unless they can use the information contained in the order flow to adjust their positions, as a group, with their other regular customers before the private information becomes publicly announced 'news'. Absent such possibilities, market makers as a group will lose money from dealing with traders with private (inside) information and will have to raise spreads to compensate.

information on fundamental asset values. Their trades can be aggregated with other regular traders since they do not possess true inside information.

Due to the fact that the market maker will lose money to the trader with inside information, the market maker has to charge a higher spread on his deal with his regular (liquidity) customers. The larger the volume of such regular customers relative to those with inside information, the lower the spread need be to balance the losses to the insiders. Thus, as Glosten and Milgrom[1] demonstrate in their paper (on page 89):

> For any given time t, the ask price A_t increases and the bid price B_t decreases when, other things being equal,
> (i) the insiders' information at time t becomes better (i.e., finer),
> (ii) the ratio of informed to uninformed arrival rates at t is increased.

The market maker faces not only a stochastic order flow from regular traders but also flows that may arise from informed traders; his realised return from the spread charged will, therefore, be less than the apparent return. Stoll, 'Alternative Views of Market Making', especially pp. 83–4, puts this point very well. If there were no systematic tendency for *subsequent* bid and ask prices to change after a market maker had intervened to buy or sell, then the market maker's (dealer's) realised spread would equal, on average, his quoted spread. On the other hand if bid–ask prices have a tendency to fall after a dealer purchase (and, vice versa, to rise after a dealer sale), then the realised spread will fall short of the quoted spread. Thus if, when a market maker sells and reduces his inventory, there is a tendency for prices subsequently to rise, so that he can restore his initial inventory position only by bidding at a now higher price, the actual realised spread will fall below the quoted spread.

Obviously, when the market maker is dealing with informed traders, there will be a tendency for his purchase (sale) to be followed by lower (higher) prices, because it was the informed traders' (subjective) knowledge that the appropriate fundamental price of the object being traded ought to be below (above) the current market maker's bid (ask) price that led to the deal in the first place; indeed, the conclusion of the transaction will itself help to disseminate information about the 'true' price of the object being traded.

Moreover, even in the absence of informed traders, and thus of information about 'true' prices being partially revealed through the time path of trades, there would still be some tendency for market prices to move systematically against market makers. As Stoll notes, 'As risk bearer, the market maker lowers both P^a [the ask price] and P^b [the bid price] after a dealer purchase because he is less anxious to buy additional shares, which would increase his inventory position; and he is more anxious to sell those shares he has just acquired. Similarly he raises P^a and P^b after a dealer sale because he is less eager to increase his short position and more eager to buy so as to cover the existing short position he has just taken'.

So both these views of the position of the market maker – as risk bearer and as victim of information traders – suggest that bid and ask prices will change in a systematic way to reduce the market maker's realised spread below his quoted

---

[1] Glosten and Milgrom (1985) pp. 71–100. See also Copeland and Galai (1983) pp. 1457–69.

spread.[1] Note, however, that both the bid and the ask prices are changing in the same direction as new information arrives (or as the risk of being long or short, of the object being traded shifts) so that the spread between the bid and ask price may remain unchanged over time, even though the bid and ask prices are changing continuously.

Obviously, the market maker will fix his bid price below, and his ask price above, what he believes to be the likely future value[2] of the asset or good in which he is dealing. Glosten and Milgrom, in 'Bid, Ask and Transaction Prices' go on to show that, in a model in which inventory and other dealing costs are zero, the market maker would revise both his bid and ask prices in the light of the probability of a change in such future values occasioned by the information inherent in the new order flow, until the expectation of a subsequent purchase is equal to that of a subsequent sale. In this case, 'the prices at which transactions actually occur [would] form a martingale'. In practice, inventory costs would normally make a dealer keener to induce a sale following a prior purchase and vice versa: this, together with the need to recoup other costs in a wider spread, generally leads to negative serial correlation between observed dealing prices in very high frequency micro data; Glosten and Milgrom have described this as 'the vibration of transactions between the bid and ask prices'.

This completes our enumeration of the main factors affecting the size of the spread – resource costs, associated functions, competitiveness, inventory costs, volume of regular (liquidity) traders, extent of exposure to informed insiders and risk of being caught by an unobservable shift in underlying value. The resulting size of spread – the cost of transacting – can be large. Obviously, when the trader expects to be involved in frequent transactions over relatively short time periods, the size of the spread will be a major factor influencing the chosen trading strategy. Even when the buyer intends to be a long-term holder, the margin between the ask price and the mean of the bid–ask spread can represent a significant proportion of the purchase price. The size of the spread in turn will influence the volume of trading going through that market, as indeed the spread charged by retailers influences the pattern of shopping, and the spread by banks and other financial intermediaries affects the pattern of financial flows. This subject will be considered further in Section 4 covering the question of market success and failure. First, however, we turn to Section 3, which addresses the question of the speed with which market makers adjust prices.

---

[1]This tendency can be expressed, again following Stoll (1985), in notational format as follows, assuming that the market maker can reverse a position in one period: then,

$$P^a_{t+1} - P^b_t < P^a_t - P^b_t$$

and

$$P^a_t - P^b_{t+1} < P^a_t - P^b_t$$

where:

$P^a_t - P^b_t$ = quoted spread at time t

$P^a_t - P^b_{t+1}$ = realised spread, dealer sale followed by dealer purchase

$P^a_{t+1} - P^b_t$ = realised spread, dealer purchase followed by dealer sale

[2] In a liquid market the likely future value of relevance to the market maker will be that ruling in the immediate future, which may well bear little relation to a longer-term 'fundamental' value. The market maker's major concern will be how the market is expected to move within the time frame in which he can adjust his position.

3. Price Adjustments

Many markets create contracts lasting for a period of time, whereby, after an initial bargaining negotiation, a price – perhaps a wage or an interest rate – is agreed; this price may be held fixed over the period or varied in relation to some publicly observable contingency – e.g., change in the rate of inflation or change in the Minimum Lending Rate. Labour markets and some financial markets – e.g., mortgages – are examples of markets where prices are fixed over a period of time. During this period, workers may apply to join or quit the firm, and subject to the terms of the loan, the borrower may be able to draw up to some maximum amount or, alternatively, to repay the loan. In other words, during this period the agent on one side of the bargain acts as a price maker who keeps his price fixed throughout, so that adjustments to unforeseen developments – other than those specifically negotiated in the contract terms to affect the price – on the part of both parties must take the form of quantity adjustments.

At the other end of the scale, most markets for *standardised* goods and assets are effectively organised around specialist market makers who publicly announce bid and ask prices; these prices are held fixed only for a very short time before being readjusted in line with changing circumstances. Even so, while those quotations remain operational, they *are* fixed and they can be 'hit', or acted upon, by other traders. While there do remain a relatively few pure auction markets where price changes respond nearly instantaneously to changing market conditions, these represent the exception and, therefore, for most practical purposes the concept of the auction as the basic market structure can be put aside.

In place of the auction, we should *generally* think of markets being run through specialist market makers who quote publicly announced prices. An interesting question then is what causes the market maker to adjust those quoted prices. Sir John Hicks originated the distinction between flex-price and fix-price markets.[1] This has often been associated with the difference between auction and long-term contract markets. While these concepts have proved useful and illuminating, the bifurcation is too stark and may even serve to deter analysis of the factors determining the speed of price adjustment. Instead, I believe that a more promising approach is to view most markets as being operated via specialist market makers. There is then a possible continuum between those markets in which specialists revise prices very rapidly to incoming news, and those in which the specialists adjust prices more slowly, at the limit holding prices constant for several years. What, then, causes these differences in adjustment speeds?

Across the pricing spectrum, one may think of a market maker in an equity market revising his quotes every few minutes; a market maker in some perishable goods market revising prices every hour; a market maker in a retail store revising prices every few days for some lines of goods and every few weeks for other types of goods; a market maker in high-price durable goods or services revising prices only after a lapse of some months; and, finally, market makers in the labour and some retail financial markets, where contracts may be revised only after a period of a year or even longer.

The question of what determines the speed with which a price maker adjusts his quotes is not easy to answer; part of the reason for this is that too little theoretical or empirical attention has been paid by economists to this real issue, owing to concentration on the artificial paradigm of the Walrasian auctioneer. A simple

---

[1] Hicks (1965); see especially Chapter 5.

answer to this question is that prices will be adjusted only when the costs of changing prices are less than the costs of maintaining a misaligned price quote. The costs involved in having such a misaligned price quote are relatively easy to comprehend. Subject to the price maker's ability to restrict the quantity in which he deals, the maintenance of a misaligned price will lead the price maker to absorb a large volume of inventory of the good or asset if the price quoted for the good is too high, or of cash if the price quoted is too low. This allows one to consider a range of factors that will influence such costs. The less (more) able the market maker is to restrict the quantities in which he will deal at his quoted price, the greater (less) will be his inducement to vary the price quoted. The greater the risk involved in carrying an unintended position, because its price can alter rapidly in a very short time – as in the case of perishable goods such as soft fruit or in asset markets, which respond sensitively to 'news' – the greater the likelihood of the market maker adopting relatively rapid defensive price changes.

There will always be *some* costs involved in maintaining a misaligned price. Why, then, do not market makers adjust instantaneously to all incoming information to change their prices? One approach, emphasised in several articles by Brunner, Cukierman and Meltzer,[1] stresses the difficulty that market makers may have in distinguishing temporary from permanent changes in market conditions. While their approach does offer some insights, especially at the macro level, it is not sufficient by itself to explain price stickiness at the micro level. As Glosten and Milgrom (1985) demonstrate the inflow of new buy–sell orders will, under all circumstances, provide *some* information on the probability of a change in the underlying market equilibrium. Even if the market characteristics were such that the flow of orders provided relatively little information, the market maker should still respond by changing the price a little, unless there were costs involved in changing that price. What are these costs?

The first, and most obvious, expense is the actual physical costs involved in such price adjustments. In many cases these are trivial – e.g., keying a new quote into the electronic display system or simply quoting different prices in the market place. Also, changing price stickers on a good is hardly expensive. Greater expense may be incurred when potential buyers need to be informed of the new price – e.g., by advertisements in the Press; such expense may not, however, even be incurred by the market maker when price dissemination is carried out by others – e.g., by the market, as in the case of Stock Exchange prices, and by newspapers. All in all, it seems implausible that the physical costs of making price changes, even including the cost of making such information more widely observable, is a prime contributor to price stickiness.

Instead, other aspects of time–information costs seem more likely candidates. In particular, where goods or assets are not standardised but vary according to their quality, place and time at which available, one cannot define the value of the good simply in terms of the price; the information required by the prospective purchaser-seller to decide whether a buy–sell transaction is desirable will have to include other considerations besides knowledge of the price quoted. Under those circumstances, the prospective trader will have to search for the information about price–quality-place availabilities. Such search will take scarce time and will be costly for the searcher. There is now a considerable literature on the issue of when a prospective

---

[1] (1983) pp. 281–319.

searcher should cease investing in more search time–information gathering and select the best option from the available sample.[1]

There may well be differences in quality characteristics on both sides, for both price makers and takers. In the case of a theatre, or hotel, for example, the price taking customer will be intensely concerned with the quality, location and date, as well as the price of the service purchased, whereas the price making owner will have little need to differentiate, or discriminate, between customers; as long as the theatre seats are filled, one bottom is as good as another. That is not true in the case of labour markets; here, the businessman will be as concerned with the quality of the worker, as the worker is in the characteristics (including wages) of the job offered. Moreover, there may often be learning processes involved whereby the worker becomes more proficient and productive simply from doing the same job, or working in the same firm, for a longer period. Repetition may allow economies and benefits in other markets besides the labour market: customers learn what they can expect of service and retail outlets, while the price makers learn to anticipate the preference of their clients.

Since search has a cost and repetition has a learning value, it is reasonable to assume that those who have already completed an initial search for a good and have settled with a particular price maker will, when it comes to seeking repeat business, sample that 'acceptable' price maker again first. So long as the terms offered by the original price maker have not deteriorated in the meantime, he is likely to obtain the repeat business. Okun, in *Prices and Quantities* (pp. 45–6),[2] emphasises how the tendency for existing workers (customers) to sample their previous employer (seller) first, under conditions of expensive search reinforced by learning costs, will cause price stickiness.

If a firm, for example, faces what it perceives as a temporary fall in demand, it would not cut its wage rates to the level that would reduce the labour supply to the *immediately* optimal lower level, because that would cause the stock of continuing available (and trained) labour to contract. So when the expected bounce-back in demand came, a firm, which had discouraged its existing work force by lower wages in the meantime, would find it would then have to pay more (than the firm which had kept a constant wage rate–work force throughout) to attract (and train) new applicants.

This same line of analysis can easily be extended beyond the labour market to other markets, especially those in which quality differences are not instantaneously and/or costlessly revealed, so that search costs and repeat buying from the same producer are likely to be involved. In such cases, as Okun, (*Prices and Quantities*, pp. 145–8) describes, the demand curve facing the producer is likely to be kinked. Discussing the demand for hotel rooms, Okun thus notes that, 'The elasticity of demand of these repeaters to an individual firm is likely to be discontinuous. It is bound to be low with respect to price reductions because presumably the repeat callers were ready to rent a room for the same price that they paid the last time. But the elasticity may be substantial at higher prices because the repeaters are responsive to price levels that exceed what they experienced previously or reasonably expected when they made their enquiries'.

With the demand curve for repeat buyers being, therefore, kinked, whereas the

---

[1] See Rothschild (1973), Hirshleifer and Riley (1979) pp. 1394–1403, and Stiglitz (1985a) pp. 595–618.
[2] Okun (1981).

Disaggregated demand curves of shoppers

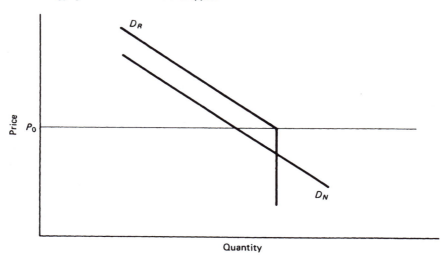

Declining occupancy from sticky prices during a slump

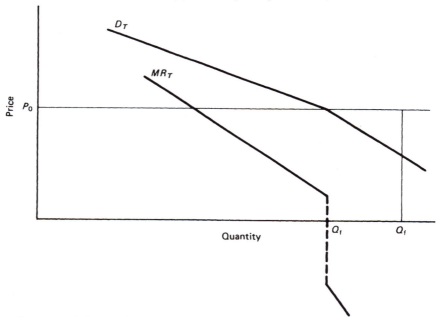

D_R = demand of repeat shoppers; D_N = demand of new (random) shoppers; D_T = total demand; MR_T = marginal revenue; P_0 = previous price; and Q_f = full occupancy.

FIG. 1.1

demand curve for new (random) shoppers has, presumably, a constant elasticity, the total demand curve will also be kinked, as illustrated diagrammatically here in Figure 1.1, reproducing Okun's Figure 4.1 (*Prices and Quantities*, p. 146). The kink in the total demand curve causes a discontinuity in the marginal revenue curve, and this, as is well known theoretically, can lead to prices being held constant as the demand curve declines below the full capacity (all rooms filled) level over a range whose width depends on the extent of the discontinuity. Okun describes this, as follows:

> Suppose that the demand curve had intersected the full-occupancy Q_f with positive marginal revenue at that point and the firm had been operating for a considerable period with full occupancy achieved at a price P_o. Now, the economy experiences a slump, and both components of demand shift to the left in a manner that maintains the elasticity at each price, except for the fact that the angle in the demand curve of the repeaters remains at P_o, the price that had become customary to them. The demand curve and the discontinuous marginal revenue curve of the slump are illustrated in the figure. The firm would then maximize short-run profits when a decline in demand occurred by accepting a reduction in occupancy and holding its price at P_o. The firm cannot attract additional business from repeaters with lower price, and that creates an asymmetry and an 'inflationary bias' because any isoelastic shift upward in demand will raise the short-run profit-maximizing price.

Okun then qualifies this line of argument, which he describes as 'myopic', by noting that a random shopper attracted today by a lower price may become tomorrow's repeat buyer. The long-term effect of cutting prices in a slump, to maintain full occupancy (full capacity utilisation), may thus be somewhat more beneficial than would appear from the single period analysis. Against that, the potential need to raise prices again, once the temporary slump ends, may not only drive away the 'bargain hunters', who had taken advantage of the temporary downturn in demand to drive a hard bargain, but may also disturb the previous solid repeat buyers who would have stayed if prices had been unchanged throughout. Search costs and, thence, inertia in buying habits, can thus (rationally) generate a modicum of stickiness in the process of price adjustment.

It is in this context, perhaps, that the importance of the reputation of a firm arises. A good reputation is akin to favourable information provided costlessly. It raises the probability both that existing customers will repeat business and that new searchers will sample that firm at an early stage. Reputation shifts the demand curve for the service being sold outward and tends to make it less elastic, providing the possessor of such a reputation with the monopoly profits inherent in that desirable position. A firm's reputation depends, however, on continuing to provide satisfactory combinations of price, quality, location and other desirable characteristics. Accordingly, its reputation amd its pricing behaviour are simultaneously determined endogenous variables.

The next question is, then: what features of price behaviour are likely to generate a good reputation and, hence, an increased order flow? Clearly, relatively low prices, good value for money, will be crucial. There is, however, another aspect of pricing behaviour that adds to reputation. Earlier in Section 1, we argued that a market maker provided immediacy; this immediacy can occur, however, even in the absence of an operational market maker since any seller (buyer) can induce a buyer (seller) to deal with him by offering a sufficiently large decrease (increase) in price from the subjective equilibrium price. The dual role of the market maker thus lies in providing insurance to traders that their immediate transactions will not involve unnecessarily wide stochastic fluctuations in price.

The greater the demand by customers for such insurance, the higher will be the reputation of, and the larger will be the resulting bid–ask spread available to, the market maker that maintains stable prices; this also implies that the market maker will be required to absorb increased fluctuations in demand–supply conditions by inventory adjustments. Under what circumstances are customers likely to demand insurance? This is likely to be most important to the customer when the deal represents a sizeable commitment of time–wealth and, thus, has a major influence on utility. Examples are holiday bookings, purchases of large durables and wage settlements where the price taker has to plan and make an important commitment. During the decision process and during some 'reasonable' length of time after purchase, the purchaser will want to feel insured both against the risk that the price to be paid will rise stochastically just before the final commitment is made, *or* will fall sharply just after the deal has been struck; in each case, the *ex post* preferences of the purchaser will not be reflected in the agreed contract.

In some cases, the price maker may make an explicit contract with the price taker to hold prices constant over some set period, except under stated circumstances. This, however, has a number of potential problems. First, it is impossible to foresee all possible contingencies or to list, monitor and negotiate all those contingencies that can be foreseen. Second, the fact of explicit insurance may lead to moral hazard problems: this problem is related to the first since it may be impossible adequately to monitor the behaviour of the insured.

Okun (*Prices and Quantities*, pp. 87–90) analyses this subject within the context of the labour market. Thus he states, 'In particular, because reduced risk and uncertainty about pay and tenure are valuable to the worker, the firm may find it worthwhile to assume binding obligations for a specified period of time about some components of the compensation package'. He goes on to argue that the firm cannot guarantee both the wage level *and* a fixed, certain length of employment – i.e., to guarantee the level of nominal incomes over a period, since, unless that period was quite short, (so that the question of the possible non-renewal of the contract acted as the spur), there would be little incentive to the worker to perform efficiently (moral hazard arising from income insurance) and, of course, the employer would bear all the risks from exogenous (demand) shocks.

Such considerations limit the scope for contracts guaranteeing total nominal incomes and lead instead usually to wage negotiations in which the firm guarantees the hourly wage rate but not the amount of employment. As Okun notes:

> The employer is telling the worker: 'I cannot promise how much employment I will offer you, but I do promise to pay you so much per hour to the extent that I do employ you'. That pledge looks empty at first glance; but it does mean something. After all, that is the basic character of the typical contractual wage arrangement under collective bargaining. In fact, employers are constraining their own behavior by such a pledge. They are promising not to hire another worker in that worker's place during the term of the contract. Such firms sacrifice the opportunity to take advantage of bargains that may arise in the labour market and, in particular, commit themselves not to initiate layoffs while still recruiting new workers. On the other hand, the workers accept a mild constraint on their behavior in return for the contractual obligation; they must refrain from strikes or slowdowns or heartrending pleas to management to raise their pay during the term of the contract.

There are some examples of the other possible alternative contract, in which employment is guaranteed, but not the wage rate; the award of tenure to university professors, teachers and civil servants comes into this category. As Okun notes, this amounts in effect to a right of first refusal to continue work at the offered wage, and thus 'is more readily applicable to individuals or selected groups of workers than to an entire work force'.

In view of the problems inherent in providing a guarantee for the provision of total nominal incomes, in conditions where it may nevertheless be advantageous for a firm to establish a good reputation as a 'caring', reliable employer, firms may try to influence the expectations and attitudes of their work force by various types of statements about intentions and policies. Okun terms the kinds of implicit contracts, going beyond the (formal) wage negotiation, that may result as representing an 'invisible handshake'.

This line of analysis has been developed further, particularly in studies of the labour market under the general heading of the implicit contract theory.[1] There is, however, a general problem with this line of theory. As described by Okun, the firm or price maker generally cannot guarantee both the price (wage) *and* quantity of goods (services, employment) which it will be prepared to provide without risking excessive fluctuations in profits. Accordingly, even if the firm is less risk averse than the price taker, it will generally be prepared to give a guarantee only of either price or of quantity stability over some fixed future period, reserving the right to vary the other parameter (quantity or price) in response to unforeseen shocks.

It is not immediately obvious why a purchaser should prefer a contract in which the price is held stable but access to the good is rationed by the quantity which the price maker feels able to make available at that given price, to a contract in which the quantity is always available but access to it is rationed by price adjustments. Yet in practice, it is the first kind of contract that we see overwhelmingly adopted in markets which involve heterogeneous quality, search costs, repetition and a desire for insurance on the part of price takers; given this fact, it is somewhat difficult to explain why micro-economic theorists focus on the second kind of contract with demand and supply equated solely through price adjustment.

Indeed, the reasons for this general preference for price stability (quantity rationing) have not been sufficiently studied. There may be a general social view that people are inherently equal whereas the endowment of wealth is not. Quantity rationing, especially when it involves the use of time in queuing, discriminates less against the poor than price adjustments which allow the wealthy to purchase all the goods, services, etc. in excess demand.

A more pervasive explanation for the generalised preference for price stability (despite the risk of quantity rationing) may well lie in information asymmetries. As already noted in Section 2, the profitability of a market maker depends on the proportion of insiders to uninformed agents with which he is dealing. Accordingly, there is an incentive for market makers to become relatively well informed, or for those already comparatively well informed to become market makers. Hence, the market maker is likely to know considerably more about fundamental market conditions in his own markets than price takers; the firm will know more about market conditions than the worker, the hotel keeper will know more about the demand–supply conditions for rooms than the tourist, and so on. Under these circumstances, where the market maker has an informational advantage concerning the true market conditions, there will be some incentive to the price maker to misrepresent what the market conditions actually are. The firm will tell its workers

[1] Azariadis and Stiglitz (1983) pp. 1–22 and Hart (1983) pp. 3–35.

that times are bad, the hotel will indicate that every room in town has been already booked, and the professional will indicate that not only does he already face a huge demand for his services, but also that your need for his services is urgent.

If the uninformed trader recognises that such informational asymmetries exist, the trader will seek to construct the contract in such a way as to provide an incentive to the market maker to reveal the true state of affairs. As already indicated, if access to the good is rationed only by price, there will be an incentive to the price maker to dissemble. Indeed, it is arguable that without repetition, and, hence, reputation, affecting the outcome, there can be no equilibrium or viable market. Gould and Verrecchia analyse a model where a specialist market maker has more information on the likely outcome of a risky asset than the ordinary, uninformed trader. Gould and Verrecchia demonstrate that in such cases the market maker would have to incorporate some random 'noise' into the price in order to establish an equilibrium.[1]

The example of Gould and Verrecchia, in which not all private information known by market makers is directly incorporated in prices, is in some cases taken to the limit where prices remain stable and do not, therefore, reflect *any* such private information. This limiting case has the advantage to traders that the market maker is induced to reveal information honestly. Since lay-offs prevent the firm producing as much, the firm will only claim that times are bad when its only option is to sack workers (and not to lower wages). The hotel operator will have no incentive to exaggerate the occupancy rate if his only recourse is to turn away the guest (and not to charge a higher price for the room). A stable price–quantity rationing contract may, therefore, prove to be preferred in conditions of information asymmetry; we shall return to this subject in Chapter 7 on credit rationing.

The greater this asymmetry in information, and the greater the preference for the trader for insurance, the more likely is the preferred contract to be of the fixed price–variable quantity form. The more the product is characterised by standardisation, lower unit costs and higher public recognition, and the more competitive the market makers, the more rapid will be the adjustment of prices; such price fluctuations will also be the main mechanism for clearing the market. In the former case, where heterogeneity, search costs and information asymmetries lead to a preference for stable prices and rationing, the price maker will, despite his ability to enforce certain quantity adjustments, nevertheless face a larger risk of adverse inventory fluctuations.

---

[1] Gould and Verrecchia (1985) pp. 66–83. They argue:

Suppose that the trader conjectures that the price offered by the specialist contains information. If there is very little noise, . . . the trader puts much weight on what price he is quoted as a signal of the realization of the risky asset. For example, if a high price is quoted, the trader believes that the realization will be large and therefore demands a good deal of the risky asset. Thus, independent of his private information, the specialist's incentive is to select a high exchange rate, since if he can sell even a little bit of the risky asset at a very high price, the specialist makes a big profit. But if the specialist selects a high exchange rate *independent* of what he knows, price cannot contain information, so the trader's conjecture is false. Suppose, on the other hand, that the trader conjectures that price contains no information (i.e., he ignores price as a source of information). Then the (expected-utility-maximizing) exchange rate the specialist selects will depend on his private information, so the trader's conjecture is false once again. In short, there is no conjecture the trader can make that is fulfilled until noise passes beyond some threshold, which lessens the weight he puts on price as a source of information.

What often happens then is that the form of the contract allows the market maker to vary price *not* on the basis of private information but on the basis of publicly available information which is germane. Interest rate contracts may thus be related to a publicly observed rate administered by the authorities, certain prices–wages may be adjusted in line with a published price index, or sales prices may be varied in line with known changes in wages and input costs; the latter example demonstrates that mark-up pricing may have the advantage to the customer of being based on public – not private – information.

A further problem facing market makers is how to rid themselves of unwanted inventories (other than cash) accumulated by holding the stable price at too high a fixed level. Reductions in prices may give an unwanted signal of lower quality and may also establish a bench mark from which it would be difficult to raise prices subsequently without losing reputation. One solution to this difficulty that has been adopted in many cases is to combine regular stable prices with occasional clearance sales in which certain excess lines of stock are cleared out at prices which are advertised and accepted to be special and non-repeatable.

Thus price stickiness, induced in part by the concern of traders in facing market makers with private information, may be loosened by relating price changes to publicly observable information. Even so, price stickiness will still involve greater inventory costs/risks and, hence, require a higher bid–ask spread if the market maker is to earn a normal profit.

It is now finally possible to summarise the factors likely to lead to faster/slower price adjustment. These are:

1. The costs–risks involved in absorbing inventory fluctuations in each market.
2. The extent and distribution of information about the object (asset, good, service) being traded in each market.
3. The relative risk aversion and, hence, preference for insurance among traders and market makers.

4. Market Existence: Success or Failure?

There are considerable economies of scale in the establishment of markets. As already noted, there are sizeable fixed costs involved in the organisation of markets; even simple auction markets require arranging a place, hiring auctioneers to hold the auction and making arrangements for noting bids and contracts and ensuring settlements. The process of disseminating information about the time, place and contents of future auctions, and of the outcome of past auctions, is also likely to involve a high proportion of fixed costs relative to those that vary with the additional potential trader reached.

Furthermore, the volume of trading will respond inversely with the cost of transacting. For example, following the removal of fixed commissions on the New York Stock Exchange in 1975, the value of turnover on the Exchange improved sharply. A similar surge of transactions also occurred on the London Stock Exchange following the removal of fixed commissions and the encouragement of competition among market makers after October 1986.

As already described, the extent of the bid–ask spread depends on the volume of transactions from uninformed regular (liquidity) dealers, from whom market makers gain, compared with the volume of deals put through by insider dealers, from whom market makers lose money. As the volume of uninformed regular deals rises, the profits obtainable to market makers from a given bid–ask spread increases; competition among market makers should then force down the size of the spread, thus reducing the cost of transacting and encouraging more regular (liquidity) dealers to trade. This process will not affect insider trading since, by definition, insiders have greater knowledge of the 'true' equilibrium value and will, therefore, trade anyhow so long as they have reason to believe that the equilibrium value lies outside the market makers bid–ask spread.

Success will thus tend to be self-reinforcing; the more successful markets will tend to draw custom and business from the less successful, subject to the limits on the elasticity of uninformed dealer response to relative transaction costs. This elasticity will depend primarily on such factors as information and communication costs. The reduction in such costs over recent decades, owing to technological advances, is increasing the international elasticity of trader response to relative transaction costs and is leading to a centripetal tendency in international money and capital markets. At the same time, however, these same technological advances are making it possible to dispense with a physical market place for financial assets, allowing trading by telephone and electronic link-up.

By the same token that market success tends to be self-reinforcing, owing to the elastic response of liquidity traders to relative transaction costs, it is possible for an adverse spiral (higher spreads, leading to fewer trades, leading to higher spreads) to develop which ultimately leads to market failure. Glosten and Milgrom (1985) (p. 74, also see pp. 84–5), state:

> One of the interesting features of our model is that there can be occasions on which the market shuts down. Indeed, if the insiders are too numerous or their information is too good relative to the elasticity of liquidity traders' supplies and demands, there will be no bid and ask prices at which trading can occur and the specialist can break even. Then, the equilibrium bid price is set so low and the ask price so high as to preclude any trade. A situation like this feeds on itself. Insiders have information that results in a wide spread that precludes trade that prevents insiders from revealing their information through their trading behavior. Since trade itself brings information into the market, this shutting down of the market may worsen subsequent adverse selection problems and cause the next bid price to be lower and the next ask price to be higher than would otherwise be the case. Furthermore, a market, once closed will stay closed until the insiders go away or their information is at least partly disseminated to market participants from some other information source.

There are certain markets in which the objects traded have a homogeneous, standardised quality, whether imposed or whether of an intrinsic nature; an example of the former are contracts in the financial futures markets, which are in effect standardised forward deals relating to the value of a particular asset on a particular future date. Those markets in which standard objects are traded and in which most information is publicly available are likely to be successful, with competing market makers quoting low bid–ask spreads. Government bond markets, money markets and some commodity markets meet these conditions and are successful in the sense defined above.

In most other cases, there will be informational asymmetries. The question that then arises is how markets can flourish in the presence of such asymmetries, especially since market making is itself an expensive activity. One approach – e.g., in securities' markets – is to try to lower transactions costs by limiting insider trading directly; this is, however, difficult to do since the definition of what does, and does not, represent true inside knowledge is imprecise, and the monitoring and regulatory costs of trying to restrict insider trading can be considerable.

A further approach, as already indicated, is to induce those with better information to become market makers themselves and to structure the implicit (or explicit) contract in such a way that the market maker is induced to reveal his information truly. Price stability, or price movements related to publicly available information, and quantity adjustments provide such an incentive compatible market strategy in many cases where the market maker has more private information than the price taker. Even so, this really works only when repetition, and hence reputation, is involved.

If the quality is heterogeneous and uncertain, and buyers and/or sellers trades are predominantly once-for-all or only very occasional, as in the case of second-hand fixed assets such as houses, cars and capital equipment, it will be difficult and more expensive to establish a market.[1] If the market maker is less well informed, he will make losses. If he is better informed about the quality and the buyer is not a potential repeater, the market maker's incentive is to act so as to exaggerate the true quality of the product and to raise the price commensurately.

In such cases, the potential trader can either accept the potential loss, refuse to trade, or reduce the informational asymmetry at some expense – e.g., by hiring an independent expert to check out the quality of the product. The first two options are those facing tourists. The latter option is that usually adopted in high-value asset markets, such as housing and automobiles. In cases where the extra cost of such independent testing is too high relative to the value of the product and repetition is infrequent, markets will tend to be fragile and highly imperfect with prices diverging frequently from their underlying value, wide bid–ask spreads (or occasional auctions at discrete intervals), and frequent market failure (antique markets, for example).

It is often said that markets for assets which provide no services in use other than their expected pecuniary return are driven by two emotions, fear and greed; observations of such markets indicate that both of these emotions feed on price volatility. While it is certainly the case that liquidity traders will trade more if transactions costs are cut, it also seems to be the case that market volatility can *encourage* a larger volume of trade in asset markets, even among the uninformed. Both uninformed speculation and defensive hedging tend to be encouraged by volatility. Expected stability in prices can thus cause the failure of markets linking the future to the present – e.g., asset markets and commodity futures markets – whereas in other cases contingencies may be too remote or uncertain to generate sufficient potential trading to warrant meeting the costs of establishing a market.

To conclude this section, the main determinant of the form, structure and success of a market is the nature of the information sets of the respective potential participants. Where such information is good and publicly available, efficient and successful markets can be established, though in some cases they work even better with more inherent price volatility. Where information is relatively poor, due to, say, heterogeneous quality, and unevenly distributed, markets will not work perfectly. In those markets where repetition and reputation matter, such conditions will tend to lead to adjustment through quantity, rather than price, changes. In those markets where most traders only enter at rare intervals, the markets will be augmented by information-purveying specialists and/or the markets will tend to be high cost and fragile.

---

[1] Akerlof demonstrated this (1970, pp. 488–500).

5. Money and Markets: What is the Best Approach?

Money is a social artifact which evolved to facilitate market trading between individual agents who were not so otherwise bound together by family, tribal or social ties that an immediate exchange of equivalent values in a trade was unnecessary. In order to understand the role and functions which money plays, it is therefore necessary to appreciate the nature and form of markets in which money is used. There have been considerable advances in recent years in analysing the way in which markets, notably financial markets, actually do work. It is, I believe, important to implant monetary analysis firmly within the context of this new, and more realistic, micro-economic market structure.

This approach stands in conscious contrast to the older attempt to integrate monetary theory into the general equilibrium Arrow–Debreu Walrasian paradigm. While the latter has many advantages, its basic assumptions, generally involving recontracting, or an auctioneer with perfect knowledge, and a complete set of markets covering all possible contingencies, imply such a total relaxation of the innate limitations of time, and hence of information, that it becomes exceedingly difficult to integrate money and monetary phenomena into such a world. Since the Walrasian world does not actually exist, it is hard to see the practical value of the difficult task of trying to integrate real institutions, such as money and banks, into such an artificial construct. The exercise *can* be done, sometimes with great elegance and technical skill,[1] but even then many of the insights into the role of money are based on market imperfections, such as a lack of trust between traders, that are tacked on to the Walrasian model rather than which occur as an inevitable consequence of the fundamental constraints of time and information.[2]

So it would seem a superior strategy to start with an account of the structure and working of actual markets and then to relate monetary phenomena to this real world, thus avoiding altogether the need to explore whether and what would be the role of money in an imaginary context. This type of analysis of the workings of markets and market makers leads on naturally to an assessment of the role of money, the topic of Chapter 2. The importance of inventory adjustments for traders in markets is linked to the analysis of the inventory demand for money, and thence to the buffer-stock approach to the monetary transmission mechanism in Chapter 3. Meanwhile, emphasis on the existence of information asymmetries within markets helps to illuminate the role of financial intermediaries in Chapter 5 and the modern analysis of credit rationing in Chapter 7.

One of the main issues in this chapter concerns the speed with which market makers adjust prices and the conditions under which prices will exhibit stickiness. Such considerations are of particular importance for an analysis of (short-term) macro-economic adjustments, and play a major role in the discussions in the later, more macro-economic, Chapters 10–18, but are less central to the immediately succeeding micro-economic chapters. Even here, however, it will be useful to keep the assumed underlying market structure, as set out in this chapter, in mind as the background for the analysis of the behaviour of the individual agents.

Almost as important, starting with an explicit analysis of the structure of markets, market makers, and price adjustment of varying speed, allows us to dispense with having to deal at any great length with certain jejune areas of monetary analysis.

---

[1] As for example by Gale (1982 and 1983).

[2] See Gale (1982 and 1983), Chapter 5, Part 1, and Chapter 6, Part 1.

There is no possibility of money being 'neutral' in this real world, nor is there any need to spend much time on 'Overlapping Generations' models which actually throw more light on life cycle savings than on monetary phenomena proper. Finally, in the real world many markets do *not* clear perfectly and instantaneously, even though market agents behave rationally and efficiently with regards to the formation of expectations under conditions of imperfect and costly acquisition of information. In short, an assumption of rational, efficient market agents does *not* also validate an assumption of perfectly clearing markets.

II
The Role of Money

Summary

In Section 1, it is argued that the need for money as a means of payment is caused by the existence of uncertainty. A distinction is drawn between the narrower concept of a means of payment and the broader concept of a medium of exchange. A medium of exchange, but not a means of payment, would be needed even in an economy where everyone was certain of future events. In Section 2, the lack of personal information on the credit standing of the prospective purchaser is put forward as the main uncertainty that forces us to use a means of payment rather than rely on credit arrangements. Once forced into using a means of payment, the use of money is much more efficient than barter in a market context, though the range of transactions which do not pass through markets at all but are internalised in social groups is often underestimated. In order to serve as a means of payment, an object should embody sufficient information to make it generally acceptable without detailed and costly investigation. As is shown in Section 3, fiat currency can serve this purpose since its value is based on the power of the state. This power enables the authorities to enjoy seignorage, the margin between the nominal value of the notes and coin issued and the costs of their production. Since these production costs are very low, the authorities could in theory issue sufficient fiat money to buy up any additional quantities of goods and assets required. They are held in check in practice by the political unpopularity of the ensuing inflation. The existence of a gap between the real costs of issuing financial liabilities and their value makes it worthwhile for intermediaries (banks) to bid for deposits of currency by offering attractive substitute assets. During the nineteenth century transfers between current accounts (demand deposits) of banks became accepted as final payment, and so these deposits should also be included in the definition of money, as argued in Section 4. But the instrument that sets the payment transmission process in motion, the cheque payment, does not contain full information about the payer's credit standing, etc., so that the transfer process contains more credit elements than in the case of cash payment.

The recent experience of inflation, a monetary phenomenon, has raised the question whether existing institutions – e.g., the government monopoly in the provision of fiat currency – have been partly responsible. Hayek has advocated more competition in the provision of currency, and other proposals for structural change and rules to determine the form and growth of the monetary base have been mooted. It has been suggested that it is unnecessary, and possibly undesirable, for the Government even to define the form of dominant base money and that banks could compete in the provision of alternative monetary units. It has also been suggested that the authorities present ability to influence monetary conditions lies precisely in their legal ability to restrict any such competition in the provision of currency. These various novel ideas are assessed in Section 5.

1. Certainty and Uncertainty

Money can be and has been defined in many ways. For statistical purposes, the stock of money is often defined in terms of certain clearly distinguishable, but analytically arbitrary,[1] institutional dividing lines; for example, the stock of money is often defined as including the sight or short-notice liabilities, notes and coin and deposits of a short maturity, of certain sectors in the economy, usually the Central Bank and the banking sector. Such definitions can, however, become increasingly fragile at times of major financial innovation and structural change. In the mid-nineteenth century, for example, the growing use of bank deposits, and of payment by cheque transfer, led to a gradual shift from a definition of money that encompassed only currency, notes and coin, to a wider definition including such bank deposits. Currently in the 1980s we appear to be in the midst of another round of structural change with the functional dividing lines between different intermediaries, such as banks, building societies and capital market institutions crumbling, at the same time as the degree of international financial competition is becoming greater. The effects of such structural changes on the forms and definitions of money are still in progress.

Alternatively, the choice of assets[2] to be included in the definition of money may be taken on pragmatic and empirical grounds. For example, money might be defined as that set of liquid financial assets which has both a close correlation with the development of the economy, and which is potentially subject to the control of the authorities. Attention then becomes focused on the fluctuations of that set of assets giving the clearest indications of the development of the economy and of the authorites' efforts to influence that development.

Here again, however, the form of the econometric relationships between certain monetary assets and economic developments may depend on the institutional and structural arrangements in the country, and also on the policy regime adopted by the authorities. If these change, previous apparently stable relationships may crumble. The dependence of most estimated macro-economic statistical relationships on more fundamental structural and behavioural conditions has been emphasised in recent years by Lucas, with the well-known 'Lucas critique'.[3]

But if we are to understand why, with a given institutional framework, the stock of money may vary with economic conditions, why it is held at all, then it is necessary to begin by enquiring what functions money fulfils. The primary definition of money, from which the other definitions emerge, is thus functional. What role does money play?

---

[1] Among the statistical issues which require decision in order to reach a definition of the money stock are the following: What is a bank? What is a deposit? Are the sight and short-term liabilities of public-sector institutions, such as the Post Office and Local Authorities, to be included in the money stock? Are non-resident holdings of domestic money balances to be included, or resident holdings of foreign money balances?

[2] In common parlance, 'money' is sometimes used as a general term to cover all financial assets. The term, 'he is rolling in money' thus does not usually mean that the man keeps a lot of banknotes in his bedroom, but that he is wealthy. In some cases, people drawing up home-made wills fell foul of this difference in terminology, since a will leaving 'all my money to my dearest nephew' would provide him with Aunt's cash balances only, while the securities, not being mentioned, would be gobbled up by the State. Although, following Humpty-Dumpty (In *Alice through the Looking-Glass*, Chapter 6), a word can mean whatever you want it to mean, it is often more important to know what it will mean to other people.

[3] Lucas (1976) and Sargent (1982) pp. 388–9.

There are a number of functions which money is traditionally seen as having. The most important is that it acts as a specialised means of payment. Final payment is made whenever a seller of a good, or service, or another asset, receives sometimes of equal value from the purchaser, which leaves the seller with no further claim on the buyer. Money is the asset which specialises in this role, being used generally for the settlement of transactions. As such it must, be definition, be a store of value and, in general, it proves most efficient to treat the means of payments as the unit of account.[1]

Yet another approach to the definition of money is to examine the cross-elasticities of demand and supply between monetary and other assets. This is the normal method that an economist would use to define a particular commodity, or industry, and has the advantage of combining aspects of both the pragmatic and the functional approaches. Only if a definition is chosen where these cross-elasticities are low will there be a close correlation between the growth of the money stock so defined and of the economy, and will this growth be subject to the control of the authorities. Otherwise, the process of substitution, either on the demand or the supply side, would weaken the empirical links between movements in the stock of money and in money incomes. Again, of course, structural change may well lead to changes in such elasticities in the course of time.

However, if one probes further to ask why there should be a low cross-elasticity of demand between money and other assets, it is ultimately necessary to revert to enquiring what special, necessary functions money carries out. Money, in fact, carries out several general functions, serving as a store of value, unit of account, means of payments, etc. and many specialised functions;[2] for example, only certain coins can be used to operate a pay telephone box. The most important general function is, however, to serve as a means of payment.

It is important to note that the functional definition of money as 'a means of payment' is different from, and narrower than, the concept of an asset as a 'medium of exchange'.[3] A medium of exchange includes those assets, or claims, whose transfer to the seller will commonly allow a sale to proceed. The distinction is that when the seller receives a medium of exchange, which is not a means of payment, in return for his sale, he will feel that he still has a valid claim for future payment against the buyer, or even more generally against some other group on whom the buyer has provided him with a claim. As Professor Shackle insisted, 'Payment is in some sense final'. Many, perhaps even most, transactions are, however, carried out on a credit basis,

---

[1] That it is not necessary, but efficient, to treat the means of payment as the unit of account can be observed easily by examining the habit of certain conservative professions of expressing their bills in 'guineas', an obsolete coin. A guinea is not a means of payment, so the receipt of such bills requires the recipients to undertake some tiresome arithmetic to work out how much to pay.

Even so the value of the guinea is at least fixed in terms of the means of payment. Worse problems occur when alternative means of payment may vary in relative value amongst themselves, for example fluctuations between gold and silver in a bi-metallic system.

[2] Cars and trains serve the same transportation function and for some purposes we might want to define a 'transportation services' good. But for other purposes we will want to distinguish between cars and trains. The same argument can be applied to money. We define it above as providing a 'means of payment' service, but for some purposes we may want to distinguish currency and demand deposits with banks.

[3] This distinction has been emphasised by Professor Shackle, for example, in his comments on Professor Clower's paper at the Sheffield seminar on money in 1970, reported in Clayton, Gilbert and Sedgwick (eds) (1971) pp. 32–4.

trade credit, or a personal charge account at the store. Such credit does represent a medium of exchange, but not a means of payment.

This distinction is important because the conditions that will require a medium of exchange are more general and wider than those that will generate a means of payment. It is, therefore, possible to specify the functions of a means of payment in an economy rather more precisely. In fact, a medium of exchange will be desirable in any economy with a time dimension. Because of differences between people in tastes, endowments, etc. exchanges will occur. Because of the existence of time, these deals will not all take the form of contemporaneous exchanges of goods or services – i.e., barter. So the process of exchange must involve the extension of credits and debits – i.e., there will be a medium of exchange through which current goods will be exchanged for future claims to payment.[1] But in a world of certainty, without transactions costs, there is no reason why the ultimate payment need be made in the form of a specialised means of payment. Person A could sell goods to person B at time t, confident in the knowledge that his claim on goods in return will be met by a transfer from person C at time $t+n$, while B may extinguish his debt by selling services at some other time to some other person.

In such a world of certainty the whole time path of the economy is effectively determined at the outset with both present and all future markets cleared at known relative prices. No one can default on an obligation or purchase goods and services which over the course of time exceed the value of the goods and services which he can proffer in return, through the employment of his initial endowment of physical and human capital (plus transfer payments). Under these circumstances everyone knows to whom to send his products and where to pick up his own consumable goods in return. As Professor Meltzer noted, in a discussion on the subject of 'Is there an optimal money supply?', 'in the economy under discussion all market exchange ratios are known, all price changes are correctly foreseen and the only service of money is to serve as an inventory. In the economy, why can't the inventory gap be closed by holding verbal promises to pay, produced whenever they are required without any trips to the bank?'[2]

So the main function of money, defined as a specialised means of payment, is to meet and alleviate problems of exchange under conditions of uncertainty, for otherwise a generalised claim on future goods would suffice. In a world of certainty, market exchange ratios (i.e., relative prices) are fixed at the very outset of the system, in period 1. From then on activities, production, consumption, proceed along prearranged lines. Whenever all market activity can be collapsed in this way into the initial period, there will be no need for money. Such a condition is, of course, unrealistic. Nevertheless, perfect certainty is not the only state in which all market activity could, in theory, be simultaneously arranged in the initial period. If marketing transactions were costless (and required no time to complete), then in principle it would be possible for the members of the economy to prepare themselves for *all* possible uncertain outcomes by exchanging claims on contingent commodities (i.e., a claim for x to good y if state of the world z could occur).[3] Transactors can, in these circumstances, arrange their affairs to take into account all possibilities at the

---

[1] These claims will bear an interest rate dependent on the real forces of time preference and time productivity, even in a world of complete certainty. For an excellent, thorough, but difficult analysis of interest rates under conditions of certainty, see Hirshleifer (1970) Part I.

[2] (1970) p. 452.

[3] See Hahn (1973) pp. 230–42.

outset. Exactly as in the case of a certainty economy, all market decisions, all relative prices (for each possible path of the economy) could be fixed in the first period.[1] Although consumption and production take place over time, all planning and decisions on the allocation of resources, all market activity, could still be collapsed into the first period. Whichever path the economy took, depending on uncertain developments such as weather, health, technology, etc. the pattern of transfers of resources and goods could have been predetermined. Such an economy can be described as having a certainty-equivalent form.[2] In such an economy, presumably, no money would be needed because people would know in advance, for each possible path of the economy, what transfers of goods and services would take place, and also that such transfers would satisfy the conditions that, ultimately, everyone had obtained equal value in goods and services for those that he had sold.

Yet the assumption of a world of uncertainty without transactions costs is so strained that it soon runs into practical difficulties.[3] For example, what happens if some of the transactors are dishonest? Perhaps it would be possible to cope with this by widening the set of states of the world still further to encompass the various subjective probabilities of each of the other various transactors honouring his contracts.[4] In a sense trust – or, rather, lack of trust – in personal honesty lies close to the heart of the rationale for the use of money.[5] If it was possible to believe that IOUs, personal acceptances of indebtedness, would always be strictly honoured, then it would be feasible to envisage a credit economy, even in face of uncertainty and transactions costs. Of course, the issuer of the IOU would have to be able to protect herself against the occurrence of adverse states of the world – e.g., sickness and death, which might otherwise prevent him or her from honouring the IOU. While that should normally be feasible, there might be some non-diversifiable risks (e.g., war) that could limit the extent of available insurance. But there are in any case, even without worrying about honesty in dealing, a virtually infinite number of possible states of the world in any future period, let alone sequence of periods, and to establish a complete set of contingent prices – and transfers at such prices – for all goods and services in all such states is clearly impossible. It would take for ever. Time is a scarce resource also, and the use of time represents an opportunity cost.

It is also arguable that it is superfluous to specify both uncertainty and transactions costs as necessary conditions for the existence of money,[6] since uncertainty will entail

---

[1] If marketing processes were costless, presumably it would be possible to arrange for *tâtonnement*, recontracting marketing arrangements which would allow this. In practice, of course, marketing involves participants having to make commitments, either simultaneously or sequentially, which cannot be recontracted. This will, in general, prevent all marketing decisions being taken in the first period.

[2] An excellent analysis of an economy of this type is provided by Hirschleifer (1970) Part II.

[3] Even though in this context we are not including among transactions costs those transportation expenses that must be incurred, even in a certainty world, in shipping goods from *A* to *B*.

[4] Though this might lead, perhaps, to the reintroduction of 'money' into an economy of this form if, for example, all commodities were subject to physical decay and some transactors were regarded as more trustworthy than others. Then, under conditions of subjective uncertainty over honesty, it might be of general benefit to arrange for payment in the liabilities of the trustworthy transactor.

[5] See Gale (1982a and 1982b) Chapter 5, Part 1, and Chapter 6, Part 1.

[6] These conditions of uncertainty and transactions costs are, it may be of interest to note, exactly the same as R. H. Coase regarded as required to establish a rationale for the existence for firms, see his paper on 'The Nature of the Firm' (1937, pp. 331–51). Otherwise, the functions

transactions costs.[1] Certainly transactions costs mainly, if not entirely, reflect the cost of obtaining information (i.e., of reducing uncertainty). Costs are involved in learning the demand and supply schedules for tradeable goods in the economy and in discovering the prices bid and offered. Setting up physical markets, which in itself involves a resources cost, is a means of trying to reduce such search costs. Once a seller has made a sale he will need information, either on the honesty and worth of the purchaser – should the purchaser offer deferred payment – or on the value and characteristics of the asset or good offered in exchange, which of course leads on directly to the specialised role of money as a device for more simply providing the requisite information necessary to consummate an exchange.

Despite its patent unreality, the abandonment of a certainty, or a certainty-equivalent, economy as the main paradigm of the system causes serious difficulty for economic analysis. Most of the studies of market behaviour, price determination, equilibrium and Pareto optimal conditions have been undertaken within the context of a system[2] which can be collapsed into one period, in an important sense in a timeless system. The rigorous analysis of an economy in which market decisions under incomplete information take place in sequence – described as a 'sequence economy' in the growing literature – has only been recently undertaken, and has proven on the whole to be too complex to provide much illumination, as yet, for more practical and policy-oriented economists.

As described in Chapter 1, however, there is now developing from various sources a new micro-economics of the working of markets that is emerging from the starting point of actual observation of market processes, rather than being based on the Walrasian paradigm of auctions under conditions of certainty or certainty equivalence. The more realistic the micro-foundations of economics become, the easier it will be to analyse the functional role of money within such a system. For the time being, however, it is not surprising that economists such as Clower[3] express doubts whether the theoretical foundations of monetary analysis have yet been firmly established.

2. Money, Information and Markets

In a world of certainty there is no need for the physical existence of markets or for

---

of a firm, essentially the organisation and combination of factors of production for the provision of certain goods and services, could have been undertaken through the market mechanism.

[1] If, as suggested, transactions costs are a function of uncertainty, it is not entirely logical to investigate systems of uncertainty without transactions costs or of certainty with transactions costs. Yet there has been some academic interest in such hypothetical situations, especially in the case of uncertainty without transactions costs. Studies of the other situation, where there are transactions costs but no uncertainty, are less common; indeed it does seem to represent an even more artificial and less interesting framework. Nevertheless, some analyses of an economy of this kind have also been attempted, for example, by D. A. Starrett in a paper on 'Inefficiency and the Demand for "Money" in a Sequence Economy' (1973, pp. 437–48).

[2] Basically the Walrasian system, as extended and developed by Arrow and Debreu.

[3] R. W. Clower has written several papers which touch on this general subject. Among them see 'Theoretical Foundations of Monetary Policy' (1971). Also see his Collected Essays (1984).

money. So uncertainty, a condition which would also seem to imply the existence of transactions costs, is a *necessary* condition for a monetary system, defined as one which generally uses some specialised means of payment to implement exchanges. Is uncertainty also a *sufficient* condition to require a monetary system?

The answer is probably not, if the roles of the various participants in the social system can be established with sufficient overall order and coherence. There are usually, for example, no monetary transactions within a monastery. To take a somewhat wider example, once a contract has been agreed between employer and employee, the employer can, within the terms of that contract, direct the employee to allocate his labour services first on this project, then on that. No money passes hands in the often long intervals between pay-days. The price mechanism is *not* being used to ensure that the worker is so employed at every moment of the working day as to equate his marginal revenue product with his wage.[1] If the system of employment works in a fashion that causes the price mechanism to be in abeyance for most of the time over a large range of economic activity (e.g., university professors do not get paid per lecture, nor professional footballers per tackle – indeed, there is much imprecision about the marginal productivity of workers), one can easily enough conceive of a system in which the price mechanism is not used at all and the allocation of goods and resources is by central direction. No money would then be required.

In a system where the role of each participant is laid down by agreement and/or by custom – for example the family, the commune, religious communities – transactions between individuals will generally not take the form of exchanges of stores of value. It would represent an inefficient way of achieving the goals of the group, as any allocative benefits of a monetary system would be outweighed by the extra marketing and transactions costs in these cases. Indeed, considering the very large range of our activities in any day, all of which in principle could be organised through the price mechanism and involve monetary transfers, it is remarkable what a very large proportion are internalised in social groups such as the firm,[2] or the family, or even informal groups of friends.

Nevertheless, the complete suppression of the price mechanism, and the allocation of goods and resources by direction, somehow organised internally, would require a more authoritarian society than most people would desire, particularly since the difficulty of maintaining harmony in any group beyond some small size is notorious. In any such system the wishes of some of its members would therefore tend to be overridden. These problems imply that in the majority of those cases which involve relationships between large numbers of participants, economic transactions must be

---

[1] See Coase (1937) and also Alchian and Demsetz (1972) pp. 777–95, for a discussion of this point.

[2] Oliver Williamson noted in his paper on 'Management Discretion, Organisation Form, and the Multi-division Hypothesis', Chapter 11 in Marris and Wood (eds) (1971) that 'Internal resource allocation can be regarded both as a market substitute and an internal control technique'. As the unitary firm expands, however, the internal information network becomes overloaded with resulting control loss. In order to cope with this, firms tend to develop multi-divisional forms which make more use of the price mechanism and monetary transfers to allocate resources between divisions. Allocation of resources between the constituent quasi-firms of the multi-divisional firm is based on objective financial results separately calculated rather than on subjective information on relative productivity, as in the case of the unitary firm.

seen to be to the personal advantage of each individual, rather than adding to the social welfare of the group.[1]

Many economists, seeking to explain the existence of money, consider that the development of a monetary economy results from the availability of transaction economies in a marketing context.[2] This is certainly an important element in the story, but it is not the initial key, since it already assumes the existence of a market economy and, although virtually all economies do include both markets and money, it remains true that most activities are internalised within social groups rather than organised through markets. The analysis of such non-market transactions, and the determinants of which transactions shall be internalised and which arranged through the price mechanism has on the whole been ignored by economists, except for the literature dealing with internalisation within (large, multi-national) corporations.

Given, however, a system in which exchange transactions take place between individuals, each seeking to maximise his own personal welfare, though each may obtain utility or lose it through seeing others better off, through benevolence or envy – the question then becomes: how can each individual assess when a transaction will be to his advantage? This is largely a matter of the adequacy of information. If you have no information about the behaviour of the opposite number to a transaction – e.g., a casual purchaser at your stall – then the risk that he will abscond or default, if he does not pay on the spot, is high. The only way to minimise risk sufficiently to enable a transaction to go forward to the benefit of both is to exchange physical stores of value.[3] If, however, the seller has more information about the buyer – e.g., a local farmer comes to buy at the stall, so that there is both information on his balance-sheet position and sanctions against default[4] (e.g., by informing all the other traders), then the seller may be prepared to exchange his goods for credit, involving, perhaps, an interest payment. The debtor will, however, still have to extinguish this

---

[1] It is partly a question of perception. The distribution of welfare in a competitive system is arbitrary, without ethical content, and certainly violates the wishes of some of the members. But it has the advantage of not requiring conscious agreement, and seems to distribute welfare by act of God rather than of authority, whereas in an uncertain, decentralised and complex world it is very hard to obtain an altruistic consensus.

[2] For example, cf. Clower (1971) p. 20; Brunner (1971) pp. 7–13; Niehans (1969) pp. 706–26.

[3] 'One way or another, we must see to it that nobody can get something for nothing', Niehans (1969, p. 707). Also see the section on 'Trust, Rationality and Noncooperative Solutions', in Shubik (1973, pp. 36–7). He notes that:

> As the general equilibrium model of the economy is nonstrategic [i.e., participants do not have trading strategies], it is natural for a modeler to implicitly ignore the problem of how strangers in a market economy can trade together efficiently and more or less impersonally with a minimal need for trust. When the economy is modeled as a non-cooperative game, this problem must be faced. If individuals trust only cash and there is no banking system, then although it is highly likely that optimality in trade cannot be attained without credit, at least all trades that are made are made for immediate value received by both parties.

[4] On this point see the paper by J. M. Ostroy on 'The Informational Efficiency of Monetary Exchange' (1973) pp. 597–610. Ostroy's key point is that 'Sellers, by requiring payment in money, are guaranteeing a steady flow of information such that the monetary authority, and it alone, is able to monitor trading behaviour'. In this case, the monetary authority can provide sanctions against failure to maintain overall budgetary balance.

debt in due course by the transfer to the creditor of a store of value acting as a means of payment.

If market information improves still further, so that there is complete, or virtually complete, information on the standing and behaviour of all the participants, then there is no need even for bilateral clearing of debits and credits.[1] Instead we have returned most of the way to a certainty world, in which transactions will give rise to credit and debit balances which can be settled multilaterally without the need for a monetary asset as a means of payment. The extent to which transactions in any economy are settled by exchanges of stores of value, or by bilateral credit arrangements, or by multilateral credit arrangements (non-monetary sub-systems), depends on the availability of information on the parties to each transaction. The proportion of transactions settled through monetary exchanges will, however, rise with the growing complexity and dispersion of the economy, because of the greater likelihood of *not* having adequate information on the behaviour of the counterparty to the transaction, and will decline with the development of methods to increase the information available about the participants. Seen in this light credit and cheque guarantee cards are, of course, an information-augmenting device. Reductions in the use of money, as a means of payment, depend on increases in personal information.[2] Indeed, the use of cash as an anonymous means of payment is often a way of hiding information, being used in the 'black economy' to evade taxation, in crime, prostitution, etc. Typically, surveys of cash holdings can account for only a small proportion of the value known to be outstanding.

If, however, the extent of personal information on the credit standing of the prospective purchaser is not adequate, transactions will take place only on the basis of a physical exchange of stores of value. When one good is exchanged for another, say apples for haircuts, the nature of the transaction – the transactions technology to use a jargon term – is called 'barter'. It is sometimes said that barter requires a joint coincidence of wants and endowments,[3] finding a person with apples wanting a haircut meeting up with a barber who is feeling that he might appreciate an apple. Certainly there would normally be little likelihood of finding such a joint coincidence of wants, even when the process is facilitated by the development of markets which provide an occasion for all prospective buyers and sellers to assemble in one place. Indeed, the search costs involved in overcoming the need for a joint coincidence of wants are so considerable that barter rarely takes that form.[4] Instead, one or other of

---

[1] Thus the degree to which 'the bilateral balance requirement' holds (c.f. Niehans, 1969) is a function of information. With little information it holds both by transaction and time. As information increases the time constraint will be loosened. With full information, the requirement will cease to hold at all.

[2] David Peretz (1971, pp. 349–56) has noted (p. 353) that 'Cash is basically a decentralised information system; possession of cash is an indicator of entitlement to resources to the holder, and to those who sell to him; but cash itself provides no means of centralising (and then analysing) information about all holders and all transactions'.

[3] 'The well-known problem of a barter economy reflects the necessity for a double coincidence of wants before any exchange can take place and the resulting high search costs which this implies. A problem which has not received as much attention is that a barter economy also involves the necessity for a double coincidence of timing of transactions', Perlman (1971) p. 234.

[4] Except, perhaps, among schoolboys swapping treasures. Even then it is noticeable how some frequently used, standardised treasure, such as marbles or football cards, becomes the common basis for exchange and valuation, and, moreover, is prized for its use in exchange. Even if my son already has a Leeds United picture, he will welcome another for its swap value.

the parties to the deal will take in exchange a good which he does not want himself with a view to subsequent resale, with the intention of moving towards his desired position through a chain of sales and purchases.

It is, therefore, possible to overcome the double coincidence of wants if one of the parties to the deal will accept in payment some good that he does not directly want. But why should he do so? He is still left holding a good, which he wants to sell, and with wants, which he would like to satisfy, and he still faces uncertainty whether, and on what conditions, he can market his new good.

One answer is that there are some goods which have a broader and more stable market than others. If a person is offered salt, or corn, or cows in payment for some sale, he is more likely to find a wide group of transactors, offering a large variety of products, wishing to buy this product at a reasonably stable price, than if he was offered a fishing rod, or roses, or a bowl of goldfish. There will thus be a tendency for people to move towards the general use of one or more goods (assets) as a common means of payment, in order to avoid the inefficiencies of barter,[1] in a system where uncertainty requires the use of means of payment.

Following the illuminating analysis of Professor Brunner,[2] such inefficiency derives mainly from two sources. First, the length of the transaction chain necessary to complete the desired exchange (of good A for good X) will commonly be elongated by barter (in order to overcome the double coincidence of wants and time in a barter context), and secondly each link in the chain involves uncertainty. Assume a chain of the form $A\ B\ C\ i\ X$. When making each step, the participant has to assess the quality and value of the good offered in exchange. In this case, to get from A to X the participant either has to bear considerable risk or obtain a good deal of information (on the characteristics and marketing prospects) on goods B, C and i. If then a good can be found which embodies desirable information qualities, there will be a tendency to use it as the counterpart of all trades, both to reduce the length of the transactions chain and to limit the extent of uncertainty involved at each step.

There are two main pieces of information which people need to learn about goods if they are to accept them as a step in their transactions chain.[3] First, has the object

---

[1] These inefficiencies arise from the enormous transaction costs involved in the process of barter. If these are assumed away, then a barter economy may seem to be potentially *more* efficient than a monetary economy, because in the latter some potential, utility-improving, trades may not be possible since the prospective purchaser may not have command over money at the time when the trading opportunity becomes available, see Ostroy (1973). Models of payments' systems which assume away transactions costs are not, however, realistic.

[2] (1971, pp. 7–19). Also see Brunner and Meltzer (1971) pp. 784–805, where they develop their ideas further. This is, in my view, by far the best article on the uses and nature of money to be found in the literature. See also Jones (1976) pp. 757–75.

[3] Niehans has shown that, under certain assumed conditions, some commodities with relatively low transactions costs may emerge 'automatically' as means of payment, as a result of optimisation processes to minimise transactions costs: 'The adoption of money requires neither law nor convention, nor can it be attributed to an "invention"; it is simply the effect of market forces'.

In my view, however, Niehans's commodity, which becomes used as a means of payment, is not *initially* to be described as money, any more than any other commodity. After a period during which it has been used as a means of payment, this process will, however, alter the information about its characteristics, in particular the existence of good markets where it can be swapped on. This accretion of information will result in falling transaction costs for this commodity, and turn it into a general 'means of payment', *money*. The development of money by this route should thus be seen as a dynamic process, not settled by relative transactions costs at a point of time.

got satisfactory physical characteristics? Think of the difficulties of using cars or furniture as money! Secondly, is there a good market for the object where it can be swapped on? It will be easiest to use as money some object whose precise physical attributes do not require continuous and skilled checking (otherwise each transaction will necessitate the cost and time involved in checking out the state of the means of payment as well as the object being sold), and whose acceptance is guaranteed.

3. What Makes Currency Serve as Money?

There have been two common forms of answer adopted by societies to the problem of finding some standard means of payment, embodying sufficient information to make it generally acceptable without detailed physical checking. The first has been to use objects of varying intrinsic use-value – sometimes very little – which also symbolise some esteemed abstract value, often status, prestige or power. If your standing in the group is determined by the number of cows, pigs or cowrie shells you possess, rather than the precise physical state of these objects, then they can be accepted in payment irrespective of minor physical differences between them, so long as they count recognisably as a member of the set possessing the desired quality. The second has been to have some external authority provide the information on the monetary object, by stamping it or marking it in a manner that signifies information to potential users about the characteristics of the object.

There has long been a debate between those who argued that the use of currency was based essentially on its symbolism of the *power* of the issuing authority (Cartalists) – i.e., that currency becomes money because the coins are struck with the insignia of majesty, not because they happen to be made of gold, silver or copper, and those who argued that the value of currency depended on the intrinsic value of the metal, with the role of the authorities (e.g., minting) restricted to the nevertheless vital function of providing the necessary information[1] on the characteristics of the metal in the currency (Metallists). The substitution of fiat, paper money, for metallic coin as the main component of currency in the last 200 years provides strong support for the Cartalist view that the monetary essence of currency can rest upon the power of the issuer and not upon the intrinsic value of the object so used.[2]

In practice, however, the main transactions costs would seem to be related to information costs. So exogenous factors affecting such information (role of the State, religion, custom, conventions, etc.) are likely to be as, or more, potent than physical characteristics in determining what is used as money. On this point see Niehan's 'Money in a Static Theory' (1969), and also a further development of a similar approach in 'Money and Barter in General Equilibrium with Transactions Costs' (1971) pp. 773–830.

---

[1] Precious metals in an unworked state have been used as a means of payment in exchanges only under very special circumstances – e.g., in the various gold rushes in California and Klondike – and even then the picture, immortalised, for example, in a film by Charlie Chaplin, of merchants and bar tenders weighing and checking the gold dust before accepting it in payment, suggests that payment in unworked precious metals has more in common with barter than with a monetary payment.

[2] There are definite overtones of this debate in the recurrent discussions about the reform of the international monetary system. There are those who would seek to base the international monetary system upon some object, gold, with characteristics that make it a suitable monetary object, and those who recognise that, *au fond*, the establishment of an international monetary system must be based on the realities of international power.

But if it is the stamp of authority rather than their metallic content that makes coins money, why then did the kingdoms of earlier years cast their more valuable coins out of precious metals, gold and silver, thus seemingly reducing their seignorage – i.e., the difference between the value of the resources which could be obtained in exchange for the coin and the cost of its production? If the value of coins was derived, *ab initio*, from the fiat of the government that the coin should be accepted as being worth a certain sum, why not then make the coins out of the cheapest material possible, thus maximising the seignorage.[1] There are a number of reasons for this. First there was, and indeed remains, the problem of discouraging counterfeiting. If the techniques for stamping the emblem of power on to currency are crude and easily copied, then it will be necessary to reduce the profits of counterfeiting (by reducing the seignorage) and to raise the penalties in order to prevent this.

Second, the power of the earlier kingdoms was quite limited, both absolutely in their own areas and geographically. If the coins had little intrinsic value they could not be used in trade across the borders of the kingdom: Gresham's law would come into operation. The population would tend to hold and to hoard the foreign coin of greater intrinsic value and would use the local coin for paying taxes, thus returning them to the authorities. And if the authorities sought to re-issue them at an exchange rate *vis-à-vis* goods that was different from their exchange rate in foreign trade, the population would become resentful at being exploited. Finally, the localised nature of the early economies meant that the bulk of transactions in them could be undertaken without much use of money, owing to good local information, and such trade as went on was often with participants in neighbouring principalities or areas of power. Under such circumstances, it would be difficult to induce the population to hold and to use the local currency, especially if the power of the authorities was considered to be of possibly short duration. In order to increase the attractions and to lower the risk of money holding, the early authorities had to give a proportionately high intrinsic value to their coins. In short, they could not gain much seignorage because they did not have much power.

A related problem arises in abstract monetary models, where the economy has a known, fixed terminal date. If the money stock has no intrinsic consumption value – e.g., paper currency – then no one wants to be left holding it at the terminal date. Rational people, realising this, do not want to hold currency that would then depreciate in value in the period *before* the terminal date; they prefer to hold goods instead. With rational expectations, this terminal problem works back to the present, causing the economy to revert back from a monetary to a barter system. There is a real, practical analogue to this. If it was known with certainty that the world was coming to an end in the year AD 2000, or that the present government would be replaced by another in N years time which would *not* honour claims on the previous government, then it would cause immediate and serious problems for the usage and general acceptance of fiat currency. Fortunately, perfect foresight is not a common attribute and uncertainty about the future eliminates the problems otherwise caused by terminal conditions.

One of the problems before the authorities in these early kingdoms was the percentage seignorage to be incorporated in the currency. An increase in this percentage – often described as 'debasing the currency' – would bring in a higher

---

[1] Coins could hardly ever become worth less than their intrinsic metallic value, for otherwise they would be melted down for their metallic content; but they are frequently worth much more.

return per unit in circulation but would, on the other hand, lead to an increasing unwillingness among the community to hold the currency, and to a growing preference for substitutes.

As the power of the state increased, and with the technical developments of printing providing more protection against forgers, so it became possible for the authorities to lower the intrinsic metallic value and to raise the seignorage obtained from the issue of currency.[1] The use of such state-issued fiat currency was supported by several factors. First, the state levies taxes and can insist that these be paid in state-issued money. This ensures that such fiat currency will have some value. The larger is the ratio of tax payments to total incomes the more important this becomes as a reason for employing the same money in private transactions. Second, state-issued fiat money may have superior characteristics, especially with respect to risk, to the notes of small, private institutions; for example, wildcat banking in the United States was so called because only a wildcat could find its way to the issuing bank to redeem their issued notes in legal tender (though see further Section 5 at the end of this chapter). Third, the authorities could place legal barriers against the use of currency substitutes – e.g., through the definition of legal tender and prohibition on the holding by private citizens of potential substitutes such as foreign currencies and gold. This gave them an even stronger monopoly position.

Given that the authorities can use their power to import a fiat value on a virtually costless piece of paper, the question – a serious one – then needs to be asked why the authorities do not use their power to buy up everything in sight for their own benefit. The answer to this comes in two parts, the first being more of a technical qualification while the second is more fundamental. First, the issue of currency by the government, for the object of buying up goods and assets, will raise prices (as supply constraints are encountered), and the increase of prices will normally lead to expectations of further inflation (the role of monetary expansion in causing inflation is discussed further in Chapter 13). If people hold currency during periods of inflation, the real value of that currency will be declining.

So the expectation of inflation should cause people to wish to hold less currency. Moreover, the costs inevitably involved during major inflations, either from holding currency or in undertaking transactions more frequently in order to divest oneself of unwanted currency, will make the use of currency in transactions as a means of payment increasingly expensive. Despite the monopoly power of the authorities, people would turn to other forms of means of payment – e.g., foreign currencies.[2]

---

[1] Interestingly enough, a similar sort of development may be taking place on the international front with the attempt to replace, or at least to supplement, gold with SDRs. Analogy with the history of the development of local currencies would, however, suggest that the extent of seignorage which the issuing organisation can achieve from the issue of currency of any form is strictly proportional to its political power. If an organisation has little political power, then the intrinsic attraction, perhaps in the form of interest payment on its currency, has to be equivalent to that obtainable on other assets in order to ensure that it is held. The 'link' proposal, whereby SDRs would be provided to the less-developed countries, represents a most interesting innovation, an attempt to provide the seignorage from currency issue to a group with need but not power. It is hard to think of an analogy in domestic national policies, except perhaps in the old English custom of issuing Maundy money, distributed to certain specific needy groups.

[2] Though people are reluctant to change their accustomed means of payment as inflation takes hold, partly owing to the inconvenience involved, partly to 'lingering confidence in its future value'. Cagan's study of seven hyperinflations showed that in no case did the flight from

Because the use of an object as a means of payment depends on information and familiarity with its characteristics, such a move towards an alternative would tend to cumulate over time. Although one can imagine the government printing sufficient money to buy up all the goods and assets in the economy at present prices, prices in terms of this currency would adjust so fast to the attempt to do so that the authorities would not succeed. Given the relationship between the demand for currency and the expected rate of inflation, there will be some rate of monetary expansion which would maximise steady-state government revenue.[1] Any faster constant rate of monetary expansion would cause a proportionately faster rate of inflation, given the disinclination of people to hold money under such conditions, and thus lower real government revenues.

The first point is thus that the rate of monetary expansion that would maximise the steady-state ability of the authorities to extract resources from the rest of the economy is bounded by the ability of the public to economise on money holdings, and find money substitutes as inflation takes hold. The more fundamental reason, however, why the authorities do not behave in this way is that their power is limited by the consent of the governed, and that for the most part their own objectives include the welfare and happiness of the general public. Given that inflation is disliked (the question of the costs and benefits to the economy of differing rates of inflation is discussed further in Chapter 13), the issue of additional money to obtain command over resources, leading to a faster rate of inflation, involves a political cost. The authorities have various ways of obtaining command over real resources, expropriation, taxes, bond issues and the issue of currency. They have to balance the benefits (to themselves and/or to society in general) of diverting resources to public use against the (political and economic) costs of the various methods of doing so. This is the fundamental reason why inflation is intimately connected with war and civil unrest, when the benefits to the authorities of additional command over resources rise relative to the political costs of inflation (or price controls and rationing), *and* when the options for raising funds by other means – e.g., taxes or bond issues – may have become restricted.

Professor Ahmad has pointed out that the process of optimisation requires that the marginal disutility to the authorities of all forms of obtaining command over real resources should be equal at the margin. He writes, 'To be in equilibrium the government's negative marginal return from the issue of bonds must equal the negative marginal return (imputed) from the issue of money'.[2] What Professor Ahmad failed to recognise, however, is that his calculus is basically political rather than economic. Assuming a democracy, this approach would suggest that the authorities would be in equilibrium when the marginal addition to votes arising out

---

money accelerate sufficiently to make price increases self-generating, see 'The Monetary Dynamics of Hyperinflation' (1956) pp. 25–117, especially p. 88.

---

[1] A number of economists have now considered the question of the 'optimal' behaviour of the authorities in deciding on the volume of currency to issue. For example, in his thesis, as described in the abstract of his doctoral dissertation (1971, pp. 786–7), Barro 'extends the model by viewing inflation as a vehicle for generating government revenue. The earlier results on demand for money are used to derive the rate of monetary expansion which maximises steady-state government revenue. If the government presses the rate of monetary expansion beyond this "optimal" rate, steady-state revenues decline'. In a similar vein see Friedman's article on 'Government Revenue from Inflation' (1971, pp. 846–56), and note the references (p. 856) to previous articles on this subject.

[2] (1970) pp. 357–61.

of additional public expenditures was equal to the marginal cost in votes of each alternative form of obtaining resources to finance that revenue. In the light of the political unpopularity of inflation[1] – and of the earlier dodge of debasing the currency – the rate of monetary expansion which maximises government revenue is not likely to lead to a 'steady-state', politically speaking. In their own political interests, which depend directly or indirectly on the pleasure of the public, the authorities are thus led to restrict the issue of fiat money at a point where the market value of assets, which could be bought with the currency, still far exceeds the marginal cost of producing the notes and coin.

4. Bank Deposits, Cheque Payments and the Definition of Money

In view of this gap between the marginal cost of production of fiat money, and the market value of assets which can be bought with it, there would seem to be a clear profit to be gained by producing a money substitute, albeit at a higher real cost, which people would be prepared to hold instead of state-issued fiat currency. An asset which could be transformed easily, at a known constant exchange ratio, on demand, and without much cost into legal tender currency would serve as very close substitute, even though it was not backed by the power of the state. As is well known from the early history of banking, the precursors of modern bankers, money-lenders, gold-smiths, etc.[2] discovered that they could virtually guarantee ready transformation (convertibility) back into gold, or legal tender fiat currency, of such currency placed with them, while holding only a relatively small proportion of currency reserves against their own note and deposit liabilities. So long as confidence in their ability to maintain convertibility continued, only a small proportion of their customers would be likely to want to withdraw their deposits or to redeem their notes on any one day, so only a relatively small reserve requirement would be needed to meet the occasional excesses of withdrawals over new deposits. The remainder of the currency which they attracted could be lent out to customers, thus gaining a return on the margin between the yield on the assets purchased and the various costs of inducing people to deposit their currency with them.

In the earlier part of the nineteenth century banks, both in the United Kingdom and in the United States, customarily had the greater part of their liabilities outstanding in note form; the increase in deposit liabilities occurred in the latter part of the nineteenth century, partly owing to increasing constraints on private sector note issue, partly to the growing convenience and greater safety of the deposit/cheque payment system as compared with note holding. In the course of the nineteenth century the ability of ordinary commercial banks to issue their own bank-notes was thus first restricted, for example by Peel's Bank Charter Act 1844, and then progressively abolished.[3] There is no indication from the historical records that this

---

[1] This political unpopularity, however, probably occurs most strongly in response to an unexpected change in the rate of inflation away from the norm, so the authorities may have some slight leeway to change the rate of monetary expansion, and inflation, gradually over some long period without incurring general public resentment.

[2] The occupational origins of the early bankers were, however, quite diverse, see, for example, Cameron (1967) Chapter 2, 'England', which also gives references to more detailed sources of information on the occupations of these early bankers.

[3] A few vestiges remain. The Scottish banks, for instance, issue their own notes in place of, but equivalently backed by, Bank of England notes.

was motivated by a desire on the part of the authorities to increase their revenue from seignorage by monopolising the issue of currency, though the issue was unlikely to be of great importance in any case under gold-standard conditions, because the value of notes that would be issued would be restricted by the need to maintain the exchange rate with gold. Instead, the main objective was to strengthen the power of the Central Bank to control monetary conditions within the economy. So long as private bank-notes could be freely substituted for state (or Central Bank) issued currency, the Central Bank must have more difficulty in restraining monetary expansion during booms, and holders of both the note and deposit liabilities of private banks would be the more likely to be injured by defaults when the boom broke. The solution to this problem was to prohibit commercial banks from competing freely with the Central Bank in the provision of notes, and to require them to hold a (prudential) reserve of currency and deposits with the Central Bank against their deposit liabilities. These bank-deposit liabilities are close substitutes for currency in many, or most, circum-stances, but by this means the Central Bank enhanced its power to control the growth of such substitutes.

Not only can a deposit with a bank be readily and quickly converted back into currency, into legal tender, but also keeping a deposit with a bank has certain advantages in the form of safe-keeping, convenience, attendant book-keeping ser-vices, etc. People, therefore, came to accept that the transfer of a credit to their current account at a bank represented a satisfactory final payment. The willingness to accept a transfer to one's account with a bank as a means of payment depends, however, not only on the characteristics of that account – i.e., safe, convertible, etc. – but also on the costs and ease of using that deposit subsequently to make transfers to others. So, in addition to offering safe-keeping, interest payments, financial advice, etc. to depositors, the banks have operated a payments transmission service to facilitate such transfers. The costs involved in this process are very sizeable, but the provision of adequate transmission facilities, thereby enabling bank customers to make payments[1] by drawing cheques on their banks, plays an integral role in maintaining the attraction of holding and using bank deposits as a means of payment.

In practice, in the UK at least, the sizeable resource costs of making payments through paper (cheque) transfers are not fully passed on to the payer (or payee) in the form of charges for such services. Service charges commonly only cover a small proportion of the true economic cost of operating this payment system. There are several reasons for this. First, the tax system encourages a shift in the remuneration of bank customers from explicit interest payments (taxable) towards rebates against bank charges (not allowable against tax). Second, the public remains largely unaware of the true costs of operating the payments' system, and banks have tended to use the

---

[1] There are so many transactions in which either currency or cheque can be used that clearly demand deposits and currency will be very close substitutes overall. The price ratio of a cheque for £10 and £10 in currency thus hardly ever deviates from unity, though it can do so: cheques passed at a discount, for example, in the United States in the aftermath of the 1907 banking crisis. Now the price ratio between currency and a range of other fixed nominal value assets – e.g., certain forms of public sector non-marketable debt, building-society deposits, etc. – is also fixed at unity. Yet there is less substitution between those assets and currency than between demand deposits and currency. This is because of the greater transfer costs involved in using those other assets to make or to receive payment. It is, therefore, the provision of adequate transmission facilities, as well as the fixed price ratio, that makes demand deposits a substitute means of payment alongside currency.

lure of low charges as loss-leaders in aggressive marketing campaigns. This comparative subsidisation of cheque payment may have had certain advantages when the alternative means of payment was currency since not all the costs of widespread currency usage – e.g., robbery and offsetting security measures, or the benefits of a greater use of the banking network – could always be internalised, (e.g., there may have been externalities involved in promoting greater use of the banking system). Now that potentially cheaper and more efficient methods of payments are becoming technically available – e.g., electronic funds transfers (EFTs) – this mispricing is becoming much more serious; the existing mispricing reduces the potential incentive of reductions in charges being available to customers using the new methods, which are not only unfamiliar but would also reduce 'float' – i.e., the period between the cheque being written and presented for payment at one's bank.

Despite its usual acceptability, the transfer of assets through the banking system will not *always* be acceptable as a method of payment. There is the well-known pub sign, 'We have an agreement with our bank. We do not cash cheques, they do not sell beer'. People without bank accounts may stipulate payment in cash, since the transfer costs of cashing a cheque may be relatively high for them. Moreover, the means of payment is the actual transfer on the banks' books, but the medium of exchange at the time of the sale (the transaction) takes the form of writing out a cheque, an order to the bank to make this transfer.

It is sometimes overlooked that handing over a signed cheque to the seller of a good does *not* complete the payment; it is not a means of final payment, in the sense that handing over currency or the transfer of other goods (barter) does represent a means of payment. A cheque merely represents an order to a third party, the banker, to complete the final payment to the creditor. The process of payment through the banking system, put into motion by drawing the cheque, therefore involves several credit relationships, requiring the establishment of a state of personal trust dependent on adequate information. This is not the case with payment by barter (or, perhaps, with currency, whose value, though, does reside in the public's confidence in the continuing power of the issuing authority).

In the case of cheque transfers, there are two main inherent credit relationships. First, the seller (creditor) has to trust that the buyer (debtor) has sufficient credit with the third party, the banker, so that the cheque will be honoured by him. It does not matter how large your current account may be in fact; if the shopkeeper should come to the conclusion that you look a shifty, untrustworthy character, he may not feel able to afford the risk of advancing you credit by selling you merchandise in exchange for a cheque which may not be met. Nevertheless, shopkeepers and other traders are loath to lose profitable business owing to worries of the risk involved in accepting cheque payment from strangers. The natural solution is to try to invent means of reducing the uncertainty (increasing the informational content) for the seller. This is, perhaps, the main function of the credit and cheque guarantee card. It allows bank deposits to be used in place of currency in circumstances where the seller has little information about the purchaser.

In order to accept payment by cheque, the crucial information which the seller needs is whether the bank, to whom the order is addressed, will honour the payment order.[1] This does not depend solely on the state of the payer's current account credit

---

[1] Moreover, the experience of the Irish bank strikes, during which the banks were shut for several months, suggests that the inability of a bank to honour such an order immediately, in this case because of physical constraints, will not prevent the use of cheques as a medium of

balance. As Professor Shackle has noted, 'I cannot write a cheque on my deposit account, but I can write one on my current account which, even if that account is empty, will be honoured if covered by my deposit balance'.[1] In addition, 'A man can just as well make a payment by increasing his overdraft (if he has his banker's permission to do so) as by reducing a credit balance'.[2]

Even if the drawer of the cheque is completely sure of the value of payment orders which the bankers will honour (and he often may not be), the payee does not possess this information. Unlike the transfer of currency, or barter, the payee is, in a sense, extending credit to the payer until the cheque has been cleared.[3] Indeed, the distinction between accepting a cheque and accepting trade credit is not entirely clear-cut. Both involve the extension of credit until final payment is completed.

Moreover, the extension of credit by the payee to the payer, until the payer's cheque is honoured by the bank, is not the only credit relationship involved in the transfer process. Both payer and payee have to trust that the bank will honour its obligation to make the payment.[4] If the bank should fail, or close for some other reason, both drawer and payee[5] stand to lose. So in the payment process, set in motion by making out the cheque, the payee has to trust the payer, and both have to trust the bank. Since none of the parties, including the bank, has complete information on the behaviour of the others, this will involve some risk. And in some cases the risk may seem so considerable that cheques will not be acceptable.

The use of cheques as a medium of exchange does, therefore, involve certain credit relationships which are virtually absent when currency is used in payment. This qualitative distinction has aroused, at different times, three separable but related questions about the monetary role of bank deposits. First, cheques may sometimes be declined as a medium of exchange, either because the payee does not want to accept payment in the form of a transfer to his credit within the banking system, or because the payee does not trust that acceptance of the cheque will, in fact, provide the stated credit transfer. On these grounds, particularly before the banking system is fully mature and established, it may be argued that bank current account deposits do not count as money at all.[6]

---

exchange, so long as the payee is confident that the payer, or some intermediary endorser, will in due course be able, if required, to make payment in legal tender. There is a very interesting unpublished paper on this episode by Murphy on 'The Nature of Money – with Particular Reference to the Irish Bank Closure' (1972).

---

[1] Discussion of Clower's paper (1971, p. 33).

[2] Clower (1971, p. 33).

[3] In practice the payee's account will be credited with the value of the cheque paid in while in transit. This reduces the cost to the payee of the extension of credit to the payer, but so long as there remains a finite probability of the cheque bouncing – i.e., until it is finally cleared – the process still essentially involves an extension of credit.

[4] In order to lessen the risks involved in using the banking system, banks need to maintain asset portfolios and adopt behavioural patterns (e.g., paying for deposit insurance, accepting the rules of the game as laid down by the authorities, etc.), which will be seen to reduce their chances of being forced into defaulting on their obligations.

[5] The payee will still have a valid claim of the drawer, but the latter may no longer have the funds to meet that claim if his bank has closed its doors.

[6] In the nineteenth century, this was a subject of considerable dispute being, for example, one element in the celebrated debate between the Currency and the Banking Schools in the United Kingdom. On this point see D. Laidler's papers on 'Thomas Tooke on Monetary Reform' (1972a) pp. 168–86, especially pp. 172–7.

Second, since the acceptance of cheques is akin to the acceptance of trade credit, in that both involve some extension of credit, it has been argued that a bank balance, which is in a sense an immediately available unused credit facility, is fulfilling basically the same function as any other source of unused credit, which could be used as a medium of exchange. On this argument the definition of 'money' would have to be widely extended to cover overdraft facilities, trade credit facilities and loan facilities from all sources.[1].

Third, a bank customer does not have to hold a positive current account (demand deposit) balance in order to have his order to complete the payment honoured by his bank. Payment may be made from unused overdraft facilities[2] or by a semi-automatic transfer from time deposits. The means to complete the requisite payment may be established by holding time deposits or by having access to unused overdraft facilities in a bank. On these grounds it may be argued that the definition of money, while not encompassing all credit facilities, should at least include all bank deposits and, perhaps, unused overdraft facilities with banks.

The first question is pragmatic. It is certainly true that under some conditions payment by cheque may be refused, but then under other conditions payment by cheque may be much preferred to payment in currency. You will not be allowed to pay your taxes by dumping a lorry-load of pennies in the front lobby of the Inland Revenue. There are dangers, of loss or theft in carrying high-value notes, so most large transactions (at least those that are legal) are carried out by preference through cheque payments. Even by the end of the nineteenth century, the greater bulk of total transfers, in value terms, passed through the banking system.[3] People in fact do generally accept that a credit transfer to their current account with a bank represents final payment, and that makes current accounts a means of payment. If people widely accepted transfers to their accounts with other financial intermediaries, such as building societies, as a form of final payment, this would make such accounts serve *de facto* as money. This latter case may happen now that the Building Societies Act, 1986, has enabled the societies to provide their customers with more comprehensive payments facilities.

The second issue is based on a confusion between the general need for instruments to serve as a medium of exchange and the more specialised role of money as a means of payment. There is, indeed, no fundamental difference between accepting a cheque or accepting any other form of credit as a medium of exchange allowing the transaction to take place. The fundamental difference occurs later, when the transmission process initiated by drawing the instrument has been completed. When the current accounts of the payer and payee have been respectively debited and credited by their banks, the payment is completed; nothing further needs to be done.

---

[1] This argument is favoured by Laffer in his article 'Trade Credit and the Money Market' (1970) pp. 239–67. He argues that 'the empirical counterpart of the classical concept of money must include unutilised trade credit available along with demand deposits and currency'. Clower also agrees that trade credit should be included in the definitions of money, c.f. (1971) p. 18.

[2] Examination of the variations in bank 'float' suggest that in the United Kingdom, where reliance on overdrafts is widespread, about 60 per cent of items in transit will result in a reduction in gross deposits and about 40 per cent will lead to an increase in advances. The proportions are, however, not very clearly determined. In other countries, where overdrafts are less used, a higher proportion of payments will be made from deposit balances.

[3] See the survey by D. Kinley reported in (1901) pp. 72–93.

When trade credits and debits are written in the books, or when loans have been negotiated to finance the original payment, an obligation remains to be settled; the process is not completed.[1]

Similarly, the argument that unused bank overdraft facilities serve as a means of payment fails on the same grounds.[2] If A owes B money, but gets C to pay B, then A has merely substituted a debt to C for a debt to B. At some stage, the debt has to be paid off. B may regard the transfer as completed, but it is not, since A has yet to make the final payment. Whether C, who steps in to finance A's payment to B, is a person, a bank, or some other financial intermediary is irrelevant.

A much more difficult question is whether to include time deposits with banks, along with current accounts, in the definition of money. Although the process may be somewhat costly and time consuming, holders of time deposits can use these to make payments. The transfer of funds from A to B by debiting A's time deposit and crediting B's current account will complete the payment for both A and B.[3] There would seem no very strong basis on theoretical grounds for excluding time deposits from the definition of money. The issue should, perhaps, be again decided on pragmatic grounds. If the turnover of current accounts is much higher than that of time deposits, one could conclude that there is a real difference in the usage of these assets as a means of payment. The degree to which the various types of deposit serve as money could be calculated approximately by the figures for relative turnover.[4] Unfortunately, in the United Kingdom such data are not available, but in Holland monetary assets are indeed classified on the basis of their relative turnover. Even though it might be possible to construct a theoretically preferable monetary series, with assets entering weighted by their relative turnover, this would inevitably seem an artificial and complex concept. In the meantime it is probably best to think of the total of currency and bank-demand deposits as an operationally useful approxima-

---

[1] For a somewhat similar approach to the definition of money, see Newlyn (1962) especially Chapter 1 on 'Definitions and Classifications', and also his paper on 'The Supply of Money and its Control' (1964) pp. 327–46, especially pp. 334–9. However, in addition to the above condition that the transfer of the asset must complete the payment for the payer and payee, Newlyn also requires 'the consequential adjustments in the financial system [to] have a zero sum'. This seems unnecessarily restrictive; as noted in footnote 3 below shifts in the composition in which the public prefer to hold their money balances will cause adjustments in the financial system. See the criticism of Newlyn's approach by Friedman and Schwartz in their paper on 'The Definition of Money' (1969) pp. 1–14.

[2] In addition, there is the practical, operational problem of obtaining adequate estimates of the total of unused credit facilities. It is dubious whether this is possible even in principle. Attempts by Laffer (1970) to do so were remarkable for their heroism.

[3] The banks' balance sheet position will have altered. But it will also alter, and more drastically, if A pays B by cheque and B draws the money out of the bank in cash. A shift in the composition in which the public holds their money balances between cash, current accounts, and time deposits may have major consequences for the financial system, but this fact is hardly relevant to the question of what assets serve as means of payment.

[4] D. Laidler addresses the same question, whether time deposits should be counted as part of the money stock (1969, pp. 508–25). Laidler agrees that the test should be empirical and pragmatic. My preferred test, however, is to examine whether time deposits do serve as a means of payment; his preferred test is to examine whether current accounts and time deposits appear to be close substitutes in econometric studies of demand for money functions. The two approaches are quite closely related (i.e., if time deposits are not used as a means of payment they are less likely to be a close substitute for current accounts), but they might give somewhat differing results.

tion to the total means of payment in the economy, on the grounds that most surveys show a very much higher turnover for current accounts than for time deposits.

Another approach towards weighting the relative 'moneyness' of various liquid assets has been recently attempted. This relies on the theoretical presumption that at the margin the perceived yields on all existing assets must be same. Thus, if one fixed-nominal-value asset has a lower yield than another, and is still held in portfolios, it must make up for its relatively low explicit interest return with a higher (implicit) yield in the form of the provision of liquidity services. This implies that the relative moneyness of an asset can be estimated by the extent that its yield falls *below* that of some benchmark non-monetary asset. Estimates of the rate of growth of the domestic money stock employing such a weighting method in the form of a 'Divisia' index have been made for the USA by Barnett and Spindt and for the UK by Mills.[1] While there are considerable advantages in such a measure, particularly at times when financial innovations lead to changes in the interest terms offered on deposits and to the development of a range of new deposit instruments with varying characteristics, the complexity (and apparent artificiality) of such weighted constructs has limited their adoption for practical, public use.

5. Alternative Currencies

In Section 3 above, we described certain aspects of the process that resulted in state-issued fiat money becoming the currency, into which local bank deposits would need to be convertible, for virtually all developed countries. In recent decades, however, at least up till the 1980s, the first systematic inflation to occur in peace-time intensified from cycle peak to cycle peak. Since it is widely argued (as will be further discussed in Chapter 13), that inflation is a monetary ailment, this led to attention becoming redirected at the fundamental institutional arrangements determining the stock of money, and a variety of proposals have been put forward to reform and improve such arrangements. In particular, F. A. Hayek in his various writings[2] argued that the monopoly control of currency imposed temptations and pressures on governments to abuse that monopoly, in order to gain command over resources. His proposal was to open up the provision of the monetary base, of currencies to competition both from the private sector and from foreign issuers of currency.

While the fact of recent inflation is undeniable, the source of pressure on governments consciously to debase the currency is somewhat less clear. Governments have alternative sources of command over resources: taxes, bond issues, even expropriation. Given the comparatively limited amount of cash in circulation compared with holdings of bank deposits, expansion of the currency base would, in a political sense, seem a relatively unattractive way of raising funds. It is notable that the authoritarian countries of the Socialist bloc have had the lowest inflation rates, which implies, I believe, that a government with particularly strong powers would *not* choose inflation as a means of raising additional resources. Moreover, in so far as the link between monetary expansion and subsequent inflation becomes established in the public mind, one would expect that those voters in democratic societies who found the inflation tax more unpleasant than other forms of taxation would vote for

---

[1] Mills (1983a) and Barnett and Spindt (1982).

[2] Notably *Denationalisation of Money* (1976) and *Denationalisation of Money – The Argument Refined* (1978b).

those parties which provided a credible promise of checking inflation, presumably involving tighter monetary control. There is no doubt that there have been times and conditions when governments have been unable to raise funds from other non-inflationary sources and yet have been able to prevent the arrival of an alternative, stronger government with a mandate to do so; in such situations, inflation *can* be attributed directly to the parlous condition of government finance. It is dubious, however, whether the worsening inflationary conditions of the 1970s sprang from this source, affecting as it did virtually all the powerful, democratic countries of the West which had fully adequate access to other sources of government finance.

A further, rather curious, strand in the literature on institutional monetary reform is to be found in a group of articles which have suggested that bureaucratic incentives acting on the Central Bank itself were partly to blame for the recent global inflation.[1] The argument is made that incentives to expand their bureaucratic empire made Central Bankers keen to obfuscate the exercise of monetary management, and to accommodate inflationary impulses arising elsewhere, because that made their role seem difficult and necessary while not at the same time causing any political enemies. Such gems of truth as may exist in this approach strike me as hard to find.

There is, however, a much more plausible explanation of the slowness of the authorities to control inflation that has been recently developed in the literature on 'Rules vs Discretion' and 'Time Inconsistency'.[2] In this context, we begin by noting that wages and prices are sticky for the reasons explained in Chapter 1. Accordingly, there is considerable inertia in the inflationary process at any time, which means that the initial impact of monetary policy changes falls on real output and employment. In the longer run, however, as prices and wages adjust to clear markets, any monetary expansion or acceleration will come through in a higher price level or inflation without having any clear-cut effect on long-term output trends.[3]

At any time, then, the authorities are faced with a position in which inflation and inflationary expectations are largely predetermined, whereas the effects of monetary policy on output are immediate and those on future inflation are considerably delayed. Particularly in conjunction with the political electoral cycle,[4] this imposes great pressures on the authorities to use such policy to raise the current level of output and employment and to look for some other instrument, such as incomes policy, to hold back inflation in the meantime. In the long run, however, such short-run policies cannot, subject to the previous footnote, raise the long-term growth of output, but will lead to potentially far worse inflation. In the long run, supportive myopic short-run policies just cause worse problems.

A solution to this problem is for the authorities to adopt a long term *rule* to constrain monetary growth to some stable, non-inflationary growth path and to eschew contra-cyclical monetary policies. There are, however, several problems

---

[1] See, for example, Acheson and Chant (1973) pp. 637–55 and Shughart and Tollison (1983) pp. 291–304.

[2] See on this Barro (1986b) pp. 23–37 and Leijonhufvud (1984).

[3] As described further in Chapter 13, faster monetary growth may either *raise* the long-term rate of growth of output, as a result of the beneficial effect of the initial surge in output, or *lower* it, as a result of the adverse effect of variable inflation on the ability to make long-term plans, or have no effect. Whereas earlier economists (e.g., Kaldor) thought that mild inflation could be beneficial to growth, recent experience appears now to suggest the opposite, see further Chapter 13.

[4] See for example Nordhaus (1975) pp. 169–90.

about this. First, the authorities will always be under severe short-term political and macro-economic pressures to break their own rule in support of short-term desirable objectives; the incentive to renege on previous commitments is referred to as a problem of time inconsistency. Second, the public, aware of such frailties, may doubt the credibility of such a commitment. Consequently, expectations of future inflation would *not* be revised downwards by the very fact of the adoption of the rule, and so the initial disinflationary impact would still fall on output and employment. Although not put precisely in these terms, this was largely the rationale for M. Friedman's advocacy of a constant (4 per cent) monetary growth rate.[1]

Meanwhile, the growing unpopularity of inflation in the mid-1970s was leading the monetary authorities in most Western countries to adopt published monetary growth targets as an affirmation of their commitment to combat inflation. While most of these targets only covered a 12-month horizon, the UK government in its 1980 Budget adopted a Medium Term Financial Strategy (MTFS) setting out declining monetary targets for £M3 over the next four years. The experience of such targetry has been mixed. While the policies adopted have succeeded in reducing inflation sharply, at the expense of extremely high unemployment, the relationships between the chosen monetary aggregate targetted and nominal incomes seemed to break down in many countries. The same inflationary pressures that led to monetary targetting as a response also brought about conditions – e.g., high and variable interest rates – that were conducive to major financial innovations. These innovations so altered the form and characteristics of monetary assets that the relationships between monetary growth and nominal incomes (the velocity of money) became comparatively unstable.[2] This led to growing scepticism, not least among the monetary authorities, as to whether it would be possible to select and adhere to some targetted rate of growth for a chosen monetary aggregate that would be proof against current far-reaching structural change.[3]

The appreciation that the monetary authorities would not – or perhaps should not – stick firmly to Friedman-type monetary growth rules led other economists, particularly those deeply concerned with inflation, to explore more fundamental, Hayekian-type institutional changes in which the provision of the monetary base is removed altogether from government control.

One set of proposals, as advanced for example by Yeager and Thompson,[4] would be to define the monetary unit in terms of a set of goods in such a way as to provide an incentive for private-sector banks to maintain convertibility between their notes and deposits and the defined commodity set. The authorities would accept payment only in instruments that were convertible at par into such a commodity set.[5] If a bank

---

[1] Friedman (1969a) p. 46.

[2] See Podolski (1986).

[3] See Goodhart (1986c).

[4] Yeager (1985) and Thompson (1986). Also Greenfield and Yeager (1983) pp. 302–15.

[5] A further set of papers, which have certain features in common with those advocating a non-fiat currency monetary base, explores the operation of a financial system in which information/trust have reached a stage at which anonymous means of payment (i.e., currency) are no longer needed. While these studies are strictly academic, in the sense that they are based on assumed conditions which are counter-factual, their study does, nevertheless, illuminate certain crucial features of the working of financial systems.

The key paper in this branch of the literature is by Fama, 'Banking in the Theory of Finance' (1980) pp. 39–57, and useful surveys have been written by McCallum (1985) and White (1984a) pp. 699–712.

behaved in such a way as to risk its convertibility (e.g., by expanding its earning assets too fast), it would be disciplined by its creditors asking to redeem the bank's liabilities in return for the basic goods.

Clearly, the Gold Standard was a member of the set of such commodity standards, and there was sufficient interest in the USA for the President to establish a Gold Standard Commission to examine proposals for a return to this system in 1982.[1] Tying the monetary unit to a single commodity, with particular supply–demand conditions (and thus fluctuations in gold – other good price ratios), has, however, certain drawbacks. The acknowledgement of such drawbacks has, as already noted, generated a range of proposals for redefining the monetary unit in terms of a basket of commodities, or even in Thompson's case in terms of a 'standard' labour hour.

The gold standard worked; though in its prime in the 1870s to 1914, its operation was supported by the interventions of major European Central Banks. There is no reason to believe that a commodity standard is technically unworkable. Nevertheless, the likelihood of a return to such a system is slim. Although the revenue obtained from seignorage is comparatively small, it does provide a final source of funds in a real crisis.[2] Also, a commodity standard does involve resource costs, since stocks of such commodities will have to be provided to act as monetary reserves. More important, perhaps, the national currency is a symbol of political autonomy and sovereignty, and attempts to replace it with private or foreign bank notes are apt to run into widespread political opposition. It will be interesting to see whether proposals to establish a single European currency, and Central Bank, can overcome nationalist instincts.

Furthermore, the experience of private banking systems under gold standard conditions demonstrated that competing private sector banks would often be tempted into periods of overexpansion during cyclical upswings, followed by a financial crisis and subsequent periods of excessive retrenchment, despite the constraints imposed on their actions by the need to maintain convertibility. The subject of the incentives on bankers to take risks, and of the costs of bank failure, are considered further in Chapters 5, 8 and 9. For the time being, it is enough to note that the historical records show that the system of private sector banking within the context of gold or silver standards evolved into a system whereby both the gold standard and the banking system became *managed* by Central Banks. While some may feel that separate Deposit Insurance institutions (see Chapters 8 and 9) may lessen the need for a Central Bank within a commodity system, such historical evidence as we possess argues against that.[3] If so, return to a commodity system would probably not lead to the disappearance of Central Banks, discretionary monetary management, national moneys, *et al*. Given all the short-term political and macro-economic pressures that exist and the historical example of the breakdown of the Gold Standard, the likelihood of a commitment to such a system being maintained through periods of pressure is not great.

---

[1] *Report to the Congress of the Commission on the Role of Gold in the Domestic and International Monetary Systems* (1982). The disputes between the advocates of differing kinds of monetary reform – e.g., Friedman-type targets, gold standard, wider commodity standard, free banking, etc. – were so intense that no consensus about which new road to take emerged despite general agreement that the present system was imperfect.

[2] See Glasner (1983).

[3] On all this, see Goodhart (1985). For a most excellent contrary view about the working of banking systems without a Central Bank, see White (1984b) and Timberlake (1978).

Another set of proposals would not even have the government define the monetary unit (e.g., in terms of a set of commodities), but would allow competing private sector banks to define their own liabilities, notes and deposits, in terms of whatever collection of goods or assets they invididually wish. Such a system was studied by Klein[1] and is advocated by Hayek on the grounds that competition for funds would make banks adopt conservative policies and, hence, lead to a sounder monetary system than occurs with the present government control over the currency system. This system does not necessarily produce a sounder result, since banks offering convertibility into assets which are expected to appreciate less can balance that by offering higher interest rates on their deposit liabilities. Competition enforces *ex ante* equality of expected returns at the margin on all competitive deposits, but it is not clear whether the incentives and information structure would lead to more or less risk taking and expansionary policies under such conditions. It could depend on other institutional arrangements then in place, such as the costs involved in bankruptcy, the extent of limitation of liability for bank stockholders, etc.

What does, however, seem clear is that the proliferation of notes, each convertible into different commodities–assets and issued by banks with differing portfolios, assessed riskiness, etc. would severely impair the information and transactional advantages that gives money its main functional role.[2] Natural incentives would arise to standardise on a single commodity set as a base and/or to make the liabilities of smaller banks convertible at par into those of some dominant bank. The system would automatically tend to evolve back towards those that we have historically experienced.

Thus, I claim, the present system, where private sector banks define their deposit liabilities and make them convertible into a single dominant base money, with the support of a Central Bank, is a result of natural evolution. This claim has, however, been challenged on yet another front by a group of neo-classical economists who argue that the role and power of a Central Bank rests precisely on the narrow basis of a legal *prohibition* on competition from private banks in the provision of notes.

The argument runs as follows: bank liabilities, whether notes or deposits, can be used for payments; this gives them a use, a value to their holders, which is not matched by an equivalent production cost to the banks providing them. Under these circumstances, banks can raise funds by issuing liabilities at rates below the riskless market interest rate and use such funds to buy higher yielding assets. Assume for the moment that the rate of interest payable on such monetary liabilities is fixed at zero. It would then seem to be profitable for banks to expand their books by buying assets and paying for them by issuing liabilities – at zero yields – on themselves until the nominal market rate is forced down to such a low level that it balances the cost of production of such liabilities. Since it costs no more to issue a £1 million note, or to inscribe £1 million in the deposit register, than it does to issue or to register £1, this seems to suggest that under these assumed conditions, and without other official external constraints, extreme monetary expansion and hyperinflation would ensue.

This was the spectre raised by Wallace, though he restricted his analysis to a consideration of what might happen if commercial banks were free to issue zero-yielding notes.[3]

---

[1] (1974) pp. 423–53.

[2] See White (1984a) and the discussion in Section 2 above.

[3] In his paper 'A Legal Restrictions Theory of the Demand for "Money" and the Role of Monetary Policy' (1983) pp. 1–7. His analysis was repeated, and restated, by Kareken (1984) pp. 405–55 and by Jao (1984) pp. 1–24.

Thus Wallace states (1983, p. 3) that:

> Since the revenue for this intermediation business comes from buying default-free securities at a discount and issuing bearer notes at par, in an equilibrium with free entry the discount on default-free securities like Treasury bills must be small enough so that it is not profitable to expand this activity . . . In other words, in a laissez-faire system in which Federal Reserve notes and default-free securities like Treasury bills co-exist, the yield or nominal rate of return on the latter is bounded above by the least costly way of operating such a financial intermediation business.

Accordingly (p. 4):

> Thus far my argument says that if Federal Reserve notes and default-free securities like Treasury bills co-exist under laissez-faire, then nominal interest rates are close to zero.

Moreover, so long as laissez-faire is maintained, it is argued that there is nothing that the authorities (the Central Bank) can do about this state of affairs. Thus, Jao (1984, p. 13) writes:

> Now suppose that government monopoly of currency issue and reserve requirement no longer exist, and a common constant-cost technology for the production and distribution of small-denomination bearer notes is available to the government as well as to private intermediaries. Consider the same open market operation again, whereby the purchase of Treasury bills is made by the issue of currency notes. This time, however, there is no increase in the money stock. For the private intermediaries simply scale down their note-issuing operations, offsetting one-for-one the government issue in the open market operation. The resources thus released from private intermediaries are employed by the government to produce and maintain a larger stock of government currency. Said open market operation merely changes the location of a particular economic activity. Otherwise, nothing else is affected: neither interest rates, nor the price level, nor the level of economic activity . . . The re-interpretation and extension of the Modigliani–Miller theorem undermines the monetarist case in two ways. First, the theorem demonstrates that it is neither necessary nor possible to control bank intermediation and hence bank deposits. Second, government exogenous control of the money stock is an illusion, an illusion made possible only by an uncritical acceptance of a host of binding legal restrictions.

Strong words! Is hyperinflation inevitable, and monetary control impossible, without a host of binding legal restrictions?

The answer, I believe, is that this danger is illusory.[1] If banks are free to offer interest rates – e.g., on their deposit liabilities – then the forces of competition will force such interest rates up to the point where only normal profits are made from intermediation. Even if we assume that technical problems prevent the payment of interest on notes, the banks issuing them still have to make these convertible into dominant base currency in order to ensure that they remain acceptable. This not only assures a stable demand for base money, and thus provides a platform for the Central Bank's open market operations, but also means that any bank trying to expand faster than average will lose reserves at the clearing and will have to bid for funds to make up such losses; the overall potential rate of expansion of the national banking system is limited in a gold standard world by an external drain of gold and in a fiat currency world by the Central Bank's management of the cash base and interest rates.

In this analysis, I have stressed the practical and historical importance of the banks' guarantee of convertibility at par of their liabilities into the dominant base

---

[1] See Goodhart (1986b).

money. A possible future development, however, could be the provision of payments' facilities, transactions services, based on asset holdings which are not fixed in nominal terms in relation to the dominant base money but which may, for example, vary nominally in line with the value of the intermediary's assets. This is already happening and could spread further.[1] If the provision of payments' services on non-deposit-type assets becomes more widespread, it may have no adverse connotations for the Central Bank's ability to control interest rates but it will confuse and blur the definition of 'money' even further.

---

[1] I have explored this possibility in Goodhart (1987a).

III
Micro-Economic Foundations of the Demand for Money

Summary

At the individual, or micro, level demand for money balances will be a function (i) of the differential between the perceived yield on money and on other assets; (ii) of the costs of transferring between money and other assets; (iii) of the price uncertainty of assets; and (iv) of the expected pattern of expenditures and receipts. In practice, analysis of the demand for money as a function of all these variables simultaneously has proved difficult to handle, and so the analysis has been artificially segmented into two main parts. First, consideration of asset-price uncertainty is suppressed and the 'transactions' demand for money is studied, involving minimisation of the costs of undertaking expenditures. Then the 'speculative' demand for money is analysed specifically incorporating asset-price uncertainty, but usually involving drastic simplifying assumptions about transfer costs and/or the time pattern of expenditures. This dichotomy is not valid; nevertheless the tradition of examining these two aspects of the demand for money separately is followed here, since this approach has been so common that the development, and literature, of the subject cannot be appreciated otherwise.

We concentrate on the inventory-theoretic analysis of the transactions demand for money, starting with Baumol's simplified initial model – which largely abstracts from uncertainty – but moving on to the more complex but more realistic models, developed for example by Orr, in which there is uncertainty about the future flow of cash payments. Once such uncertainty is introduced it is difficult to distinguish the 'transactions' from the 'precautionary' motives for holding money. Section 1 then ends with a short summary of the attack made on this approach by Sprenkle. He claims, on empirical grounds, that the money holdings of companies, for example, are far larger than can be explained by the inventory theory, and on practical grounds that these models have overlooked many of the important institutional features of the monetary system.

In Section 2, we begin with the restatement of Tobin's classic analysis of 'Liquidity Preference as Behaviour towards Risk' within a system with one safe and one risky asset in a single period context, an analysis which is compared and contrasted with Keynes's analysis of the speculative demand for money. The approach is then extended to deal with the more general situation where the investor is confronted with an assortment of risky assets, touching here on modern portfolio analysis. Finally, some of the problems of moving from a single-period to a multi-period analysis are presented, though hardly solved.

In Section 3, we return to the inventory-theoretic approach, describing how this strand of analysis has been extended during the last decade into a new, more macro-economic, form, namely the 'buffer-stock' or 'disequilibrium' theory of money holding. There are several versions of this latter approach, and we assess these separately. It is noted how closely this inventory-theoretic, buffer-stock approach coheres with the paradigm of micro-markets outlined in Chapter 1, with market makers holding inventories of both cash and goods.

1. The Transactions Demand for Money

Because of uncertainty, especially owing to a lack of personal information as a result of which A cannot be sure of B's creditworthiness, and vice versa, there will be a demand for some instrument which will obviate the need either for such personal information or for barter in the course of exchange transactions and will thereby serve as a specialised means of payment. In Chapter 2, Section 3, we saw how a government can issue monetary instruments of this kind in the form of liabilities upon itself – even at a zero interest rate. Although the government can command, or delegate – say to the Central Bank – monopoly control over the issue of legal tender within its own demesne, financial intermediaries (banks) can provide liabilities which will act as close substitutes for legal tender – i.e., as monetary liabilities fulfilling the function of a means of payment. But banks could make their liabilities into close substitutes for currency only by ensuring the maintenance of convertibility between their deposit liabilities and legal tender and also by providing certain payment transmission facilities that enhance the attractiveness of cheque payment.[1]

The maintenance of sufficient reserves of legal tender to ensure instantaneous convertibility and the provision of payment transmission services are expensive. It, therefore, follows that private-sector financial intermediaries will have to offer a lower rate of interest on demand deposits than on liabilities which are not immediately exchangeable at a fixed rate into a legal tender (e.g., marketable assets), or which are only exchangeable into legal tender at a fixed rate after a period of notice or on an appointed date. In the latter case, there would be certain penalties, or transactions costs, incurred should the asset holder attempt to switch back into legal tender, or into demand deposits, before the due date. There can thus be a whole spectrum of interest rates on private-sector liabilities; the intermediary is able to offer a higher rate on those assets which it is not committed to redeem at short notice into monetary liabilities at a fixed rate and which have a lower frequency of withdrawal, since it can then deploy its earning assets in a higher yielding portfolio and provide fewer transmission services; the investor, in turn, will demand a higher mean expected yield to make up for the additional risk of variations in the nominal price of marketable assets and/or the extra transaction costs of switching between non-monetary financial assets and money.

Likewise, the public sector can also issue a range of marketable debt, not exchangeable at a fixed rate into legal tender, and non-marketable fixed-price debt, the convertibility of which into means of payment is limited by institutional constraints or by transactions costs. Despite its ability to gain command over real resources by issuing zero-interest fiat money, the authorities may prefer to issue higher interest debt for that purpose, because the effect on the economy (and thus on

---

[1] In Section 5 of Chapter 2, we did consider briefly whether other financial intermediaries could provide payments' services on the basis of liabilities (assets to their holders) *not* convertible at a fixed par into legal tender, but with a varying nominal value. I believe that this development may become more widespread, and in so doing confuse further the definition of 'money', but it is as yet a relatively small-scale phenomenon.

their own popularity), especially the consequences for price inflation, may be preferable. Although the power of the government, which supports the value of its fiat currency, also stands behind its other debt, the characteristics of such debt – e.g., asset-price uncertainty,[1] limitations or costs on convertibility – prevent bonds and savings certificates being used as a means of payment, in exact analogy to the reasons why the bonds or savings certificates issued by banks (or other intermediaries) will not normally be used as a means of payment.[2]

When analysing the development of the economy as a whole, at the macro-level, it is reasonable to assume that the authorities are influencing the overall supplies of various forms of public-sector debt in their monetary and debt management operations; if this is so, it is interest differentials (given transaction costs and asset-price uncertainties) that adjust to clear the market. At the individual, or *micro*-level, the pattern of relative interest rates appears instead as a market parameter inducing the individual person or company to adjust the proportions (to their total wealth) in which they wish to hold their assets. So at this level the analysis becomes turned around to express the micro-level demand for money as a function:

1. of the observed interest-rate differential between the yield for money on the one hand and on other assets;
2. of the transfer costs between money and these other assets;
3. of the price uncertainty on other assets; and
4. of the expected pattern of expenditures and receipts requiring the use of means of payment.

Analysis of the individual, micro-level demand for money function has traditionally (following Keynes's exposition) been, somewhat artificially, segmented. First, the third argument above, asset-price uncertainty, is suppressed, eliminated from the analysis, so that the demand for money is treated as a function of interest differentials (1), transfer costs (2) and the pattern of payments (4). This is generally termed the 'transactions demand for money', the demand that would still occur even if there was no asset-price uncertainty. The next stage is to reformulate the analysis to include asset-price uncertainty (3) as an argument, but dropping transfer costs (2) from the analysis. This is usually described as the 'speculative demand for money', the demand that would still occur even if transfer costs were relatively unimportant.

It is inappropriate, as noted also in Chapter 4, to regard the overall demand for money as the simple arithmetical sum of these two separated components of the demand for money, the transactions and speculative motives.[3] Nevertheless, despite the invalidity of attempting to distinguish, at the aggregate macro-level, between

---

[1] It is not the uncertainty about the money price of marketable securities, whether in the form of public or private-sector debt, that is of greatest importance, for this is only the reciprocal of the 'security price of money', which is equally uncertain. It is rather the fact that the money price of a bundle of goods, and assets, tends to be relatively sticky, whereas the 'security prices of goods' are less so. During periods of volatility in general price levels, however – e.g., during hyperinflations – other assets – e.g., foreign currencies, real assets – may be found to provide more value security, and may become used as substitutes for domestic money.

[2] L. H. White has provided the best, and most accessible, analysis of these issues, see his papers 'Competitive Payments Systems and the Unit of Account' (1984a) and 'Accounting for Non-Interest-Bearing Currency: A Critique of the "Legal Restrictions" Theory of Money' (1986). Also see Goodhart (1986b).

[3] Balances held for one motive may also go to satisfy the need to hold money for the other purpose. On this point, see Friedman (1956) clause 14.

balances held for transactions and for speculative purposes, a complication which has not deterred generations of economists from trying to draw this distinction in applied, empirical work,[1] this distinction between the two motives has been so widely followed, and presumably fruitful, in the literature, especially at the micro-level, that it would be very difficult to comprehend analytical developments in this area without following the same dichotomy.[2] Accordingly, in the remainder of this section we shall review the analysis of the transactions demand for money, abstracting from asset-price uncertainty, and pass on to the analysis of the speculative demand for money in the second section, before returning to recent developments in the inventory-theoretic approach in the final section.

One feature that is common to the analysis of both the transactions and the speculative demand for money is that the (subjective probability distribution of the expected) timing pattern of expenditures and receipts on goods and services is usually taken as given, an external parameter in the light of which the individual adjusts his desired money balances (in part by varying the timing pattern of his transfers between money holdings and other financial assets). This is not strictly accurate. Individuals will have some flexibility in adjusting the timing of their own expenditures, for example by altering their shopping habits, though the periodicity of income payments is usually institutionally fixed in the short run. Firms can, however, vary the timing of their expenditures on bought-in materials and components, even if not on labour.

So if the opportunity cost of holding money rather than other assets, in the form of interest foregone, is high, but the transfer costs of switching between money and assets are also considerable, people could react by altering their expenditure habits. Examples can be observed during periods of hyperinflation, when income recipients try to accelerate their expenditures immediately after their receipt of incomes, to avoid holding depreciating money balances.[3] During more normal times, however, it is generally assumed that the (expected) pattern of expenditures and receipts is set by institutional custom and habit and is relatively insensitive to those fluctuations in interest rates and transfer costs that occur in normal conditions. There have, in any case, been very few empirical studies of the interaction of payment habits and of the demand for money[4] to changes in financial conditions, except for crisis periods such as hyperinflations and breakdowns of the payments system – e.g., periods of bank closures in the United States in 1907[5] and in 1933. This treatment of the pattern of payments as a parameter determining the demand for money balances rather than as a jointly determined variable is thus usually defended on the grounds that it is largely institutionally determined.

---

[1] See, for example, Tobin's early work on 'Liquidity Preference and Monetary Policy' (1947) pp. 124–31 and Bronfenbrenner and Mayer (1960) pp. 810–34. These studies were the ones noted by H. G. Johnson in his majestic review article on 'Monetary Theory and Policy' (1962) pp. 335–84, reproduced as Chapter 1 in Thorn (ed.) (1966).

[2] Nevertheless, the dichotomy remains invalid. This is one of the loose ends of the subject that remains to be tidied up. It would seem, however, that the complexity of handling a formal model which incorporates asset-price uncertainty, uncertainty over the timing and size of future expenditures and receipts, and transfer costs, all at the same time, has been too much to be tackled effectively as yet.

[3] See Barro (1970) pp. 1228–63.

[4] Some theoretical studies of the optimum quantity of money have, however, incorporated explicit consideration of the costs of exchanges between goods (and services) and money into their analysis, c.f. Perlman (1971) and Feige and Parkin (1971) pp. 335–49.

[5] For example, Andrew (1908) pp. 497–516.

With the (expected) pattern of expenditures given, and abstracting from asset-price uncertainty, individuals might be expected to wish to hold that amount of money that enables them to make these payments with the minimum cost. There is an opportunity cost in interest forgone from holding low-yielding money rather than alternative higher-yielding assets, and this has to be balanced by the cost of switching between these assets and money, to provide the cash when it is needed to make payments, in order to find that system of cash management that minimises costs.

Conceptually the problem is simple. In practice, the mathematical solution of the cost-minimisation problem can become quite complex. For example, the optimal cash-management system, which minimises costs, appears to be quite sensitive to the form of the transfer costs between money and higher-yielding assets, whether those are fixed per transfer or some function of the size of the transfer. The problem, moreover, becomes considerably more complex when the realistic assumption is made that future payment (and receipt) patterns are not known for sure but have instead some subjective probability distribution. The search for cost-minimising cash-management policies under a range of alternative assumptions about the functional form of transfer costs and payments patterns has developed into a field for the use of mathematical operations research techniques[1] which have an undoubted intellectual appeal in themselves but have, perhaps, only a limited interest to the more general monetary theorist.

This general approach to the analysis of the transactions demand for money is often described as the inventory theory of the (transactions) demand for money, because of its similarity to the more general analysis of the demand for inventories which had been developed previously. Baumol[2] constructed the first monetary model along these lines. The particular features of his model include a known stream of expenditures, amounting to T in a given period, which have to be paid for in cash. This is obtained by withdrawals from assets, bearing a constant known interest rate i, at a fixed cost per withdrawal of b.[3] If the individual withdraws M each time his balance reaches zero, his average money balance will be $M/2$ and brokerage costs bT/M, so total costs in a given period amount to:

$$C = \frac{bT}{M} + \frac{iM}{2}$$

The objective is to minimise C, and the value of M (the size of withdrawal and therefore the average money balance $M/2$) which achieves this can be found by calculus (setting the derivative of the above with respect to M equal to zero). This reveals that the optimal withdrawal size (twice the average balance) is given by:

$$M^* = \sqrt{\frac{2bT}{i}}$$

[1] See, for example, Orr (1970).

[2] Baumol (1952) pp. 545–56.

[3] The conditions of this model, including a known pattern of expenditure, known asset prices, etc. abstract from all those facets of uncertainty which give money its essential role as a means of payment, as argued in Chapters 1 and 2. Given the artificial nature of its basic assumptions, this particular model can hardly be expected to throw much light on behaviour in the real world. It is none the less worth studying, because it has an important place in the development, and literature, of the subject. Subsequently other economists, as will be seen, have extended this approach, relaxing the assumptions of known expenditure patterns, etc. and replacing them with uncertain, stochastic expectations.

So in this situation the individual should desire to hold money in relation to the square root of the value of transactions; the elasticities of demand for money with respect to real expenditures[1] and interest rates are respectively $+\frac{1}{2}$ and $-\frac{1}{2}$. The time path of the money balance in this case follows a saw-tooth pattern, as shown in Figure 3.1.

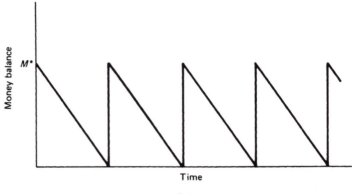

FIG. 3.1

An immediate extension of this model is to consider the case where the steady expenditures are financed, not out of an inexhaustible stock of earning assets, but from periodic receipts (income payments), where expenditures are treated as exhausting income.[2] Let the income payment be Y, and let the cost of transfers be a linear function of the sum withdrawn (or invested) with a constant, fixed element and a proportional element, so that:

$$D = b + km$$

where D is the transfer cost, b the fixed element, k the proportional element and m the sum transferred.

Then the individual has the choice between holding his receipts all in cash form while awaiting expenditures, which would involve an interest penalty of $iY/2$, or of investing some of the cash at the start in higher-yielding assets (e.g. bonds) and drawing this down over the rest of the period. If he invests and then replenishes his cash balances by $n-1$ equal sales, so that his total transfers amount to n (one purchase followed by $n-1$ sales), his total costs would amount to:

$$C = \frac{iY}{2n} + nb + 2kY\left(\frac{n-1}{n}\right)$$

The third term includes the ratio $(n-1/n)$, since at the start of the period $1/n$ of the

---

[1] Note, however, that a once-for-all doubling of all prices would also presumably double transactions costs, b, but would leave i unchanged, assuming that expectations were for prices to remain constant at their new level – so that the demand for money would double following a once-for-all doubling of prices.

[2] Any interest receipts may be assumed to be paid over with income at the start of each subsequent period.

income receipts will be held in cash for immediate expenditures. Again the procedure is to find the value of n that minimises C; n can equal zero,[1] but not 1 – which would represent a purchase without a subsequent sale – and has to be an integer. In the simple case where $k = 0$, and assuming that the values of b and i are such as to make any investment worthwhile, the optimal number of transactions is given by the expression:

$$n^* = \sqrt{\frac{iY}{2b}}$$

and the average cash balance

$$M^* = \sqrt{\frac{bY}{2i}}$$

so that the previous elasticities with respect to (real) incomes and interest rates still hold.

Even while maintaining the restrictive assumption of a known future path of income and expenditures, a considerable range of variations can be played on this general theme. The form of the transfer-cost functions can be varied and the costs of investing and withdrawing funds distinguished separately. In particular, it should be noted that the value of the elasticities obtained by Baumol do depend on the particular assumptions of his model. As Professor Orr notes, 'A proper choice of departure from the Baumol model can generate elasticity predictions that differ significantly from his'.[2] There is no inherent square-root law built into the transactions demand for money

The conditions, indeed, that must hold if *any* temporary investment of the periodic income is to be advantageous are quite severe. Reverting to the previous example, with $k = 0$, Professor Orr shows that, with an annual interest rate (i) of 6 per cent, and fixed costs per transaction (b) of \$2,[3] it would require a monthly salary of about \$1600 in order for it to be economical for the individual to engage in any temporary purchase and resale.[4] If it is not economical to do so, the average balance becomes simply $Y/2$, involving a (nominal) income elasticity of unity (with respect to both incomes and prices) and an interest elasticity of zero.

The general circumstances of this kind of model, involving regular, predictable

---

[1] If $n = 0$, the above formula for C does not apply. Instead $C = (iY/2)$, as stated earlier.

[2] Orr (1970) p. 47. Also see the paper by Brunner and Meltzer (1967) pp. 422–36. In this article, the authors argue that plausible values for the parameters of the model (e.g., for the transfer-cost functions) would result in a unitary value for the income elasticity of demand for money.

[3] \$2 may seem rather a high charge for switching out of demand deposits into, say, a savings account or an account with some other intermediary. And so it probably is, in terms of purely pecuniary costs. But there are other costs in terms of time and effort involved, and these may well appear to rise with increasing affluence. Most of us may always stay below the point at which temporary investment of a monthly salary would seem worthwhile.

[4] Orr (1970) p. 136. Sprenkle has pointed out that the frequency of income receipts over the planning interval will also be important in determining whether it is profitable to undertake switches between money and bonds, see his paper on 'The Uselessness of Transactions Demand Models' (1969, pp. 838–41). The higher the frequency of receipts – i.e., the less that they are bunched, with a given total income – the less will be the return from switches between money and other short-term securities.

sequences of incomes and expenditures is probably most nearly met in the household sector. Yet here transactions costs would seem to make cash management unrewarding except for the very rich; so for this sector the model implies income elasticities near unity and interest elasticities near zero, rather than $\pm \frac{1}{2}$ per cent. Firms on the other hand are more often in a position to command balances of a size that will make cash management profitable, despite transactions costs. It is, however, very dubious whether a model involving certainty of the time of payments is appropriate to any examination of the cash-management problem of firms.

Models which allow for some uncertainty in the future pattern of cash payments[1] tend, however, to be considerably more complex. Optimal cash-management procedures in certain specified conditions of uncertainty over the timing of payments have been formally analysed by Orr[2] and Miller.[3] Orr's basic model has the following conditions:

1. There are two assets available, zero-yielding money and interest-bearing assets (bonds) which have a yield of n per £ per day.
2. A transfer between the two assets involves a fixed cost per transfer unrelated to the size of transfer, of g. These transfers can be put through instantaneously.
3. Cash balances cannot go below zero. There are no overdraft facilities (or alternatively these are always more expensive to use as a method of replenishing cash balances than sales of interest-bearing assets).
4. Cash flows are completely stochastic, and 'behave as if generated by a stationary Gaussian random walk'. In setting out his basic model, Orr assumes that in any short period (t) (e.g., 1 hour) there is a 50 per cent probability, p ($p = 0.5$), of the balance rising by £m and an equal probability, $q = 1 - p$ ($q = 0.5$), of it falling by £m.[1] With t periods in a day, over an interval of x days, the distribution of changes in the cash balance will be binomial with mean:

$$\mu_x = xtm(p - q) = 0$$

and variance:

$$\sigma^2 x = 4xtpqm^2 = xtm^2$$

Since there are costs involved in making a transfer between cash and interest-bearing assets, the cash manager will not make continuous transfers, but will wait until the cash balance reaches its lower permissible limit (zero, given instantaneous transactions between cash and other assets) or an upper permissible limit, determined by the relative expense of transfers compared with the interest yield forgone on cash. If the cash balance reaches one of these limits, the cash manager then has to choose at what level within these limits to restore the balance. The problem for the cash manager is to

---

[1] Some economists would describe cash held to meet possible uncertain fluctuations in payments flows as being required for 'precautionary' rather than transactions purposes. In conditions when payments flows are not known for sure, it is hard to make any clear distinction between transactions and precautionary motives.

[2] (1970) see especially Chapter III.

[3] Miller and Orr (1966) pp. 413–35 and (1968) pp. 735–59.

[4] Orr extends his model in Chapter IV to deal with cases of drift, where $p \neq q \neq 0.5$, that is where the individual (person or firm) is systematically gaining or losing money over some time interval. He argues that his basic model can be used successfully, 'so long as systematic movements in the cash flow persist over a time interval that is long compared to the mean elapsed time between transfers to adjust the cash balance' (1970, p. 73).

select an upper bound, h, and a return point, z, so that the costs of managing the balance (which can be described as:

$$E(c) = gP(T) + nE(M)$$

where $E(c)$ are the expected costs, $P(T)$ the probability of transfers and $E(M)$ the expected average cash balance), are minimised.

The solution to this can be found mathematically,[1] to give an optimal return point:

$$z^* = \left(\frac{3gm^2t}{4n}\right)^{1/3}$$

and an optimal upper bound, $h^* = 3z^*$, so that the average balance becomes:

$$\bar{M} = \frac{4}{3}\left(\frac{3gm^2t}{4n}\right)^{1/3}$$

Policies of this kind give rise to a time path of cash balances that will look somewhat like that shown in Figure 3.2.

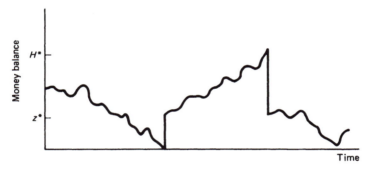

FIG. 3.2

An immediate point of interest is why the return point is not halfway between the bounds, but only one-third of the way to the upper bound. The basic reason for this is that the expected transfer cost is a symmetric function of the distance of the return point from the bounds, while the interest forgone is an increasing function of the average size of balance, see Figure 3.3.[2]

As with the simpler fixed-payments Baumol model, the demand for money depends on relative transfer and interest costs. The most interesting feature of this model with uncertain payments is that the demand for money is related not to the *level* of transactions but to the *variance* of transactions, m^2t. What then would this model[3] predict about the income elasticity of demand for money? This would depend how increases in incomes brought about changes in the frequency of transactions, t, as compared with the average size m. If the size remained constant as incomes rose, but

[1] Orr (1970) pp. 58–63.

[2] See Orr (1970) Figure VIII, p. 63.

[3] The model is, however, constructed at the micro, individual level. There could be serious aggregation problems involved in trying to draw conclusions about macro-economic behaviour from the working of this micro-economic model.

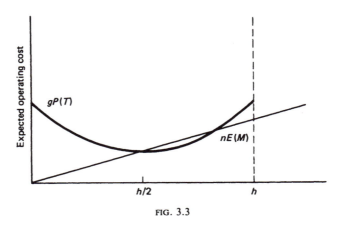

FIG. 3.3

the frequency increased, the elasticity would be as low as 1/3, the same absolute value as the predicted negative interest elasticity of demand. If transactions frequency remained constant, but the size of all transactions increased pro rata with incomes, then the income elasticity would be 2/3.

Indeed, the possible range for the income elasticity in this model is even greater. The ineluctable limits on time, together with the growing demands on that time that will be made as opportunities rise with incomes, mean that increasing efforts will be made to economise on time-consuming activities as the economy grows more affluent. So the number of separate transactions[1] – e.g., shopping trips – may even fall as incomes rise, leading to a rise in the average value of individual transactions proportionately larger than the increase in incomes and expenditures.

The actual mathematical formulae for h^* and z^* shown above depend on the postulated assumptions of the model. The form of the optimal cash-management policy in practice will be a function of the actual probability distribution of cash flows, the particular form of transactions costs between assets and money, the costs of delaying payments, the time taken during asset transactions, etc. Any manager of large cash balances would be well advised to call in specialist operations-research advice to help tailor a policy to meet his own individual requirements. For example, the policy of restoring cash balances to a return point $z = 1/3h$ after it reaches one of the bounds $(0,h)$ is a consequence of the assumption of fixed, lumpy transfer costs. If transfer costs were proportional to the size of transfers, with no fixed element, then the optimal procedure would be to restore the cash balance to the bound which it had

---

[1] Exchanges between money and alternative financial assets are also time-consuming. So the opportunity costs of brokerage, of transfers, will rise with incomes. If this is not specifically allowed for, it could lead to an upwards bias in the long-run estimates of the income elasticity, see for example, Khan, 'A Note on the Secular Behaviour of Velocity within the Context of the Inventory-Theoretic Model of Demand for Money' (1973) pp. 207–13. By an interesting coincidence exactly the same point was made at virtually the same moment by Dutton and Gramm (1973, pp. 652–65). And a further exposition of the same general issue was provided by Karni (1973, pp. 1216–25). Finally on this point see Barro and Santomero (1972, pp. 397–413, especially pp. 406–11).

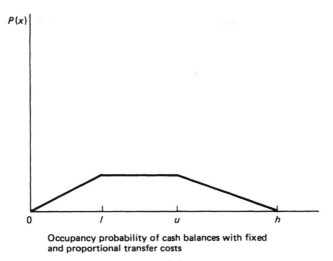

Occupancy probability of cash balances with fixed
and proportional transfer costs

FIG. 3.4

passed (assuming instantaneous transactions) but no further.[1] If transfer costs were some combination of fixed and proportional costs, then it would be preferable to restore cash balances after hitting the lower bound to a point, l, and after hitting the upper bound to a point, u, where $h - u > l - 0$, and the length $u - l$ depends on the relative weights of fixed and proportional transfer costs. The probability distribution of the cash balance occupying a value between 0 and h would then look as shown in Figure 3.4.[2]

Precautionary balances are held to protect the individual (company or person) against uncertain fluctuations in the timing of receipts and expenditures. It is, therefore, natural that such balances should be a function of the expected variance, rather than the level, of cash flows. Companies[3] and individuals with very erratic cash flows, such as art dealers, car dealers and bookmakers, will tend to have relatively large cash balances. It is, however, likely to be difficult to observe systematic changes in the variance of cash flows from macro-economic aggregate data. As incomes rise, the variance of cash flows may either rise or fall depending on the effect of increasing affluence on transaction frequency. Depending on the relationship between rising incomes and the variance of cash flows, this model would allow for quite a wide range of income elasticities of demand for money, ranging from quite low values of 1/3 up

---

[1] In this case the optimal upper limit (H), assuming that all the other initial assumptions hold, would be given by the formula:

$$H + 1 = \left(\frac{2dm^2t}{n} \right)^{1/2}$$

where d is the transfer cost per £ transferred. The average balance is simply $H/2$, Orr (1970) p. 104.

[2] Orr (1970) Figure XII, p. 108.

[3] If large companies can, however, *forecast* future variations in cash flows, they should normally find it worthwhile to take steps to employ any sizeable prospective cash balances in the money market. For large firms the appropriate determinant of the size of cash balances should then be the standard error in *forecasting* the variations in cash flows, rather than the *actual* variance of such flows. I am grateful to Professor C. Sprenkle for pointing this out to me.

towards unity. Furthermore, the assumption of instantaneous transfers between cash and other assets holds only at the limit. If it takes time to obtain additional balances, or if extra speed involves extra cost, there will need to be a further layer of cash to enable payments to be carried out as and when desired. There will always remain a risk that money will not be available – or only on exorbitant terms – to carry out some unforeseen large purchasing opportunity. Perhaps as investors become wealthier, they become prepared to forego more interest receipts in order to avoid such risks. So, besides a positive income elasticity of demand for money for transactions purposes, there could be a positive wealth elasticity also on this account.

Although the 'inventory theory' of the transactions demand for money has been developed in a most impressive manner, with the help of accomplished mathematical techniques, there have been criticisms that the theory fails to account for the observed data of money holdings, particularly of balances held by large firms, and also that its adherents have overlooked, or ignored, some key institutional features of the banking system, lacunae which may invalidate much of the usefulness of these models for explaining the real world.[1] Thus Sprenkle finds that the percentage of the actual cash balances held by large firms that can be explained by the simple Baumol model is miniscule (of the order of $2\frac{1}{2}$ per cent of the total)[2] and notes that other research[3] shows that state and local governments in the United States also appear to hold far larger money balances than the Baumol model would suggest.

The standard versions of the 'inventory theory' imply that cash balances must be maintained above zero at all times. In fact, the state of bank customers' cash balances is not continuously observed throughout each business day, but is monitored only at the close of business on each day. This means that operational constraints on the management of their balances, in the form of, say, maintaining a minimum, non-zero balance at the bank, apply only to a firm's closing balance. So long as firms, or other institutions with access to large amounts of liquid assets, can make day-to-day money-market loans at the end of business on each day, they should never hold in their closing bank balances more than the minimum size for which such short-term market loans can be profitably arranged. In so far as this minimum size of loan is mainly dependent on institutional arrangements in the financial market, the income elasticity of demand for transactions balances by large firms (with sufficient access to funds to enter the short-term money market on a regular basis) should be zero and the interest elasticity very low (in absolute terms), nearer 0 than -0.5.[4]

What, then, explains the observed data of 'close of business' money holdings of large firms? The standard versions of the 'inventory theory' usually incorporate the implicit assumption that each bank customer, person, firm, or institution, will have only one centralised bank balance. This is not the case for large firms and institutions. For several reasons – e.g., ease and security of handling currency, local autonomy, increasing speed of collections and disbursements – large firms and institutions will tend to have a number of bank balances in conjunction with their major centres for cash payments (e.g., at factories) or receipts (e.g., at sales outlets). Optimal cash

---

[1] The main proponent of this contrary view is Professor C. Sprenkle (1969) pp. 835–47; (1972) pp. 261–7.

[2] (1969) pp. 843–7.

[3] Aronson (1968) pp. 499–508.

[4] Thus for large firms the rather striking result is that the demand for money depends neither on income nor on interest rates, but is simply a constant depending on the minimal overnight trading unit (Sprenkle, 1972, p. 265).

management will require that balances be remitted to the centralised head-office account when the return to be made from the use of the funds by the financial manager at head office outweighs the transfer costs, subject to any operational constraints on each balance – for example that (close of business) balances shall not fall below zero. Uncertainty over the flow of receipts and disbursements, the variance of the cash flow, may require a sizeable balance to be maintained in each account if there are any difficulties or delays involved in replenishing the balance, to ensure that it meets the required greater-than-zero constraints. If, however, there are (automatic) overdraft facilities available for each separate account, then this constraint also is relaxed. The mean expected cash balance which the firm plans to maintain in each account (and around which the actual observed balance will vary), should then be a function of the differential between the overdraft rate(s) being charged and the rate available on funds remitted to head office, or otherwise employed, see further Chapter 4 on the importance of the differential, or spread, for the demand for money.

Such decentralisation of cash management, with a resulting multiplication of separate bank accounts, especially in view of the likelihood that many of these separate balances may be too small to make careful cash management worthwhile, can explain some part of the larger observed money balances. Sprenkle, however, claims that such factors are still insufficient to explain a large part of corporate money holdings, at least in the United States where his evidence shows that the ratio of these balances (cash plus demand deposits) to turnover is several times higher than in the United Kingdom. He argues that the main reason for such large balances in the United States is the tradition there of holding compensating balances with banks partly as a form of payment for banking services.[1] In short, Sprenkle argues that the standard versions of the 'inventory theory' overlook several of the crucial institutional features of the monetary system, and thus fail to provide an adequate explanation of actual behaviour. Certainly his criticisms of currently accepted theory have considerable force.

2. Asset Price Uncertainty and the Speculative Demand for Money

As noted in Section 1, borrowers can offer a higher mean expected yield on their liabilities if they are not committed to redeeming them on demand at a fixed money value, since this gives them the freedom in turn to invest in a higher yielding but riskier portfolio of assets. Equally lenders – at least those investors exhibiting normal risk aversion – will require a premium, a positive differential in rates, in order to induce them to hold riskier assets. Asset-price uncertainty is thus one determinant of the yield differential between capital-certain assets such as money, and risky assets, whose nominal value in the market place may vary. Put the other way round, with yield differentials given, such uncertainty is one of the factors determining the relative proportions of 'safe' and risky assets which each investor will want to hold in his own portfolio. Having abstracted from such uncertainty in Section 1, in order to concentrate upon the analysis of the transactions demand for money, the objective in this section is to examine how such asset-price uncertainty affects the portfolio

---

[1] For a discussion of the role, rationale and development of compensating balances, see Hodgman (1963).

distribution between risky and safe assets, and within the set of safe assets how it affects, in particular, the demand for money.

For there is, at least in all financially developed countries, quite a wide assortment of alternative 'safe', capital-certain assets, besides money, available for investors to hold. There are even some assets – e.g., national savings bonds – which are certain in the sense that both the interest payment and the capital value on that asset is fixed over their complete life. A somewhat larger group of assets, including most forms of deposits with financial intermediaries, have fixed, certain capital values, but their interest payments can be varied from time to time as in the case, for example, of the rate payable on time deposits at banks; there will be uncertainty about the prospective fluctuations in such rates. There would, however, be no cost to the investor in failing to predict these variations, so long as he was able to observe them and to respond by adjusting his holdings from one asset to another quickly and without expense. If information is sparse, say because the investor is going to be out of the country, or if it is costly and time-consuming to shift from one capital-certain asset to another, the investor might diversify his holdings even among capital-certain assets to reduce the resultant risks of variations in rates. But these potential costs to the investor, resulting from unforeseen changes in the interest offered on capital-certain assets, arise from frictions and costs in the adjustment process. All funds invested in such assets would be placed in the currently highest-yielding form but for the presence of transactions costs.[1] We may describe all such capital-certain assets, diversification among which depends on the balance between transfer costs and yield differentials, as 'safe' assets.[2]

Moreover, when the length of time over which it is intended to hold financial assets before their realisation to provide funds to purchase goods and services or to give to someone else – i.e., the holding period – is known for sure, it will generally prove possible to find a marketable asset which matures towards the end of that period. This will then be a quasi-safe asset since its capital value when required will be certain. However, there will still be uncertainty over the rates at which the periodic coupon payments of interest may be reinvested in the intervening period,[3] and any attempt to switch out of the asset before redemption, say because some other safe asset was offering a higher yield, would expose the investor to capital risk of having to sell at a depressed market value.

So there is generally a selection of safe, or quasi-safe assets, whose nominal return

---

[1] See the paper by Parkin, with Barrett and Gray, 'The Demand for Financial Assets by the Personal Sector of the U.K. Economy' in Renton (ed.) (1975). Also see Parkin and Gray on 'Portfolio Diversification as Optimal Precautionary Behaviour', Chapter 12 in Morishima *et al.* (eds) *Theory of Demand: Real and Monetary* (1973).

[2] While there is a sizeable set of such 'safe' assets in most developed countries, in the sense that their capital value is fixed in nominal terms, all such assets will have fluctuating real values, as price levels change in inflationary conditions. In these circumstances it is surprising that there has been little evolution of assets that are 'safe' in real terms – i.e., whose nominal capital value is indexed to some general price index. This topic, indexation, is considered at greater length later in the Appendix to Chapter 13.

[3] This cause of uncertainty can be circumvented under certain circumstances by the innovation of coupon stripping, whereby a coupon bond can be repackaged with all the associated payments – i.e., each coupon payment and the final repayment of principal – sold independently as individual pure discount bonds. With such zero-coupon, pure discount bonds an investor can fix a final nominal receipt for a given date and avoid all uncertainty about intermediate reinvestment rates.

till the end of the holding period is virtually certain, which an investor can choose. The choice within the set of safe assets will depend on the balance between transactions costs and yields, along the lines already examined. Transactions costs, however, become relatively less important, compared with prospective yields, the longer the intended holding period. So investors requiring a temporary safe haven for funds, say for a week or so, will tend to keep them in cash, current accounts. If the holding period is to be a month or more, depending on the size of the funds, the interest rate offered and the transactions costs, it may pay the investor to place such funds in time deposits, certificates of deposit, etc. As the holding period lengthens, the range of assets that can be treated as 'safe' widens and, with transactions costs becoming a lesser consideration, short-dated marketable assets, Treasury bills and short-dated government bonds will become receptacles for investors seeking to avoid asset-price uncertainty.[1] Given known holding period(s),[2] the certain yields over these period(s) and the schedule of transactions costs, the choice of assets within the set of safe assets can, therefore, be treated as an extension of the analysis in Section 1. The next question is: what determines the division of the portfolio between the set of safe assets with virtually certain returns and the set of risky asset, where the return over the holding period is uncertain, in particular because their capital values will change in line with uncertain future changes in market yields? To simplify the analysis, consider the case of one safe asset, which may or may not be money, and therefore may or may not have a positive nominal return during the period, and one risky asset.

The return from this risky asset will not be exactly predictable, but each investor can imagine a subjective probability distribution of its likely return.[3] Following Tobin,[4] we shall assume that the investor concentrates his attention on the first two moments of this distribution, the mean and standard deviation, and ignores higher moments, skewness, etc. One can try to justify this assumption, either on the grounds that the subjective probability distribution of returns is completely described by the first two moments, as in the case of the normal distribution, or that the investor's utility function takes a form, quadratic over the relevant range, which depends only on the level and variance of incomes (returns). Whether justification on these grounds is actually possible has been the subject of some advanced theoretical disputation.[5] In any case, both assumptions seem unrealistic. There is virtually always a non-zero possibility of default on any asset, but, except on such assets as lottery tickets and premium bonds, virtually no chance of some equally large prize. Many assets – e.g., bonds – could thus have a negatively-skewed distribution, while others – e.g., equities – may exhibit positive skewness. Furthermore, the prevalence of behaviour such as gambling, which suggests some enjoyment of risk among individuals who in most

---

[1] As the holding period lengthens, however, people will become more concerned with uncertainty about future prices of goods – i.e., about the prospective rate of inflation. So, beyond some horizon, the concept of 'safety' will depend less on asset price certainty in nominal terms, and depend more on the prospective maintenance of real purchasing power.

[2] Though, in reality, the length of the holding period(s) will also be uncertain.

[3] This is a standard assumption and would appear rational. Yet Shackle has queried whether expectations are really formed in this manner (1949 and 1955); one should not, perhaps, overlook the time and effort involved in trying to construct a subjective – and admittedly fallible – probability distribution.

[4] (1958) pp. 65–86.

[5] See the series of articles in the 1969 *Review of Economic Studies* on this issue – e.g., the articles by Borch, Feldstein and Tobin in Vol. 36 (1), No. 105 (January) pp. 1–15, and Samuelson in (1970) Vol. 37 (4), No. 112 (October) pp. 537–42.

other respects appear to be risk averters, for example in taking out insurance policies, makes the assumption that the utility of income (or wealth) can be described by some simple quadratic linear function, such as $U(Y) = (1+b)Y + bY^2$ (where $0 < b < 1$ for a risk seeker, and $-1 < b < 0$ for a risk averter), doubtful.[1] None the less, the assumption that investors concentrate only on the mean and variance of expected returns from their asset portfolio can be regarded as a helpful and fruitful simplification for analytical purposes, which does not seem to be seriously misleading in the various applications to which it has been put.

With two assets, the first a safe asset with zero variance and the second a risky asset, one can plot how the mean expected return and variance of the portfolio changes as the proportion of the total portfolio invested in the risky asset is increased.

---

[1] An individual who has a declining marginal utility of income with a utility function that is concave downwards, as shown in Figure 3.5 below, will be a risk averter. Given the chance to play a fair game with a 50 per cent chance of obtaining an income of $X+1$ or $X-1$, he will always prefer a certain return of X. Given his preferences he should insure, but not gamble, especially not in the usual situation where the odds are loaded against the punter since the organiser of the game – e.g., the bookie, will take his rake-off before distributing the winnings. In practice, however, gambling amongst most risk averters is restricted to wagering fairly small proportionate sums in relation to their overall wealth. This suggests that even those with a declining marginal utility of income may find that a limited, controlled risk adds utility, a certain savour, to an otherwise humdrum life. Furthermore, such gambling frequently takes the form of gambles offering a very small proportionate chance of fabulous wins – e.g., football pools, lotteries, premium bonds. It may be, as Professor Shackle would contend, that the dramatic nature of successes in such games (and indeed the dramatic nature of certain disasters – e.g., air crashes, fire, premature death of the breadwinner) makes one tend to focus so much on these outcomes that the subjective probability distribution is distorted out of true. Alternatively, such positively-skew gambles may provide utility in themselves by allowing us to dream about what might be, while insurance against negatively-skewed disaster situations enables us to avoid the morbid worries about them that their dramatic intensity would otherwise cause. Furthermore, Tsiang in his paper on 'The Rationale of the Mean-Standard Deviation Analysis, Skewness Preference, and the Demand for Money' (1972, pp. 354–71) argues (p. 359) that 'skewness-preference . . . is certainly not necessarily a mark of an inveterate gambler, but a common trait of a risk-averse person with decreasing or constant absolute risk-aversion'.

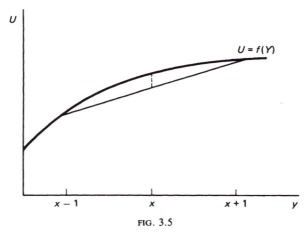

FIG. 3.5

In Figure 3.6, the assumption is made that the mean expected return on the risky asset is higher than that on the safe asset. Otherwise no risk averters would hold the risky asset, and unless there were a sizeable number of risk lovers in the system, buying the risky asset, its price would have to fall until its return rose sufficiently to attract risk averters into holding the asset.

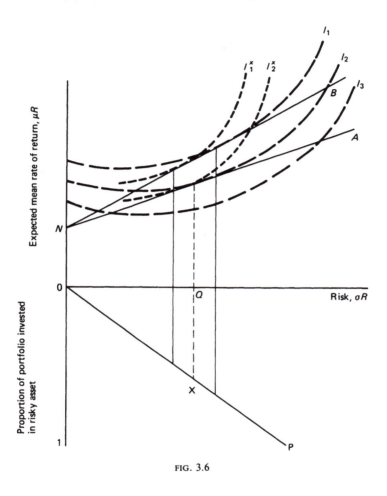

FIG. 3.6

The available combinations of risk and return are shown lying along the line NA. The point on this line where the investor arrives depends on the proportionate division of his portfolio into holdings of the safe and risky asset respectively, traced out along the schedule OP. The investor will select that combination which offers the most utility – i.e., that point on the line NA touching the highest indifference curve. In Figure 3.6, the dashed indifference curves, I_1–I_3, are drawn concave upwards, which implies that the investor requires a continuously increasing incentive in mean expected return to take on additional risk – i.e., that he is a risk averter.[1] As depicted, the investor will reach the optimum portfolio balance at Q, with OX of his portfolio in the risky asset and XP in the safe asset.

If the expected mean return increases, say because of a growing expectation of some capital gain on the risky asset, then the risk–return combination line will shift upwards from NA to NB, as shown in Figure 3.6. With the indifference curves, as shown by the longer dashed lines ($I_1 - I_3$), this rise in expected yields causes the investor to raise the proportion of his portfolio in the risky asset: the shape of the indifference curves might, however, be such, as marked by the shorter dashed curves, $I_1^x - I_2^x$, that he would reduce the proportion held in risky assets.[2] In this case, the 'income effect' of a rise in yields, leading the investor to seek an increase in his security from risk as conditions allow improved risk–return combinations to be achieved, outweighs the 'substitution effect', as the mean expected rate on the risky asset rises relative to the rate on the safe asset. As the expected yield on the risky asset declines, relative to the yield on the safe asset, the theory implies an increasing (negative) interest elasticity of demand for the safe asset as the yield differential approaches zero, but there does remain some ambiguity about the sign of the relationship between the demand for the safe asset and relative yields, in circum-

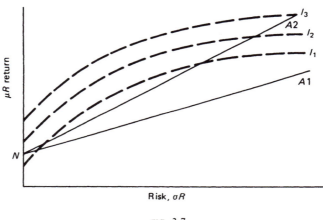

FIG. 3.7

---

[1] If the investor was a risk lover or a plunger, who required a diminishing incentive in extra mean expected return to take on additional risk – i.e., with indifference curves which were concave downwards – he would not distribute his portfolio between the two assets but would plunge all his funds in one or the other asset, depending on the slope of the risk–return combination available and the shape of his indifference curve. In Figure 3.7, if the risk–return combination was $NA1$, the plunger would hold all his assets in the safe asset; with combination $NA2$, he would place them all in the risky asset.

Risk assumption on this scale, placing all one's funds into one asset or the other is, however, rarely seen, and may be regarded as a pathological phenomenon. Absolute risk preference, where the indifference curves slope downwards and all funds are placed in the riskier asset (as long as it provides an equal or larger mean expected return), is even rarer.

[2] Though it is doubtful whether the extreme risk aversion represented by such steeply rising indifference curves is plausible, see on this subject Tsiang (1972) pp. 362–8.

stances when the expected yield on the risky asset rises sharply above the yield on the safe asset.

The great advantage of Tobin's reformulation of the theory of liquidity preference is that he linked it firmly to uncertainty about future asset prices,[1] and thus provided a rationale for portfolio diversification, beyond the existence of transactions costs (which are in turn basically a function of another form of uncertainty). In previous Keynesian analysis of liquidity preference, and of the speculative demand for money, investors were treated as holding completely confident expectations of the future yield on the risky asset. Each investor would then hold all his assets either in the risky asset or in the safe asset depending on which offered more, so there was no explanation of portfolio diversification at the individual level. The existence of a downward sloping aggregate liquidity-preference schedule relating the demand for the safe asset (money) to the yield differential between the risky and the safe asset (with the rate on money being zero) depended on differing expectations between investors (all confidently held!) and an assumption that investors would generally expect some 'normal' rate of return to be re-established on risky assets. These two assumptions together imply that a fall in interest rates on the risky asset below the 'normal' level would induce a growing proportion of investors confidently to expect a future rise in rates, and thus capital losses on holding risky assets, and so switch all their funds into the safe asset. Apart from the obvious inconsistency in the assumption of confident expectations in circumstances where most predictions would always be off target, this analysis rested on a particular assumption about the generation of expectations of future prices in this market. There was no good theoretical reason for expectations to be regressive in this manner; Keynes did not extend the same assumption about expectations to other markets – e.g., the goods and labour markets;[2] in practice, monetary authorities tend to be more concerned with the possibility of extrapolative expectations in financial markets – i.e., price movements feeding on themselves and becoming excessively volatile. Finally, market views of what constitutes a 'normal' level of rates presumably depend on past experience, so that the existence of fixed views on the likely normal level must be a short-term phenomenon, though perhaps long enough for practical, policy purposes.

Tobin's reformulation allowed a much more general and plausible interpretation of the theory of liquidity preference. Portfolio diversification was given a justification at the individual level. This diversification is consistent with differing investors holding a range of expectations of future mean yields on the risky asset.[3] Moreover,

---

[1] One could argue, with Shackle and P. Davidson, that Tobin has merely replaced the implausible assumption that investors act as if certain of the future level of prices and rates of return on risky assets with an almost equally implausible assumption that they act as if certain of the future probability distribution of returns. It is, perhaps, a matter of judgement how much closer to reality Tobin's reformulation has taken the analysis.

[2] If people expected pre-depression price and wage levels to be 'normal' levels, to which they would return, expenditures and the demand for labour should respond directly to reductions in money wages and prices, even if nominal interest rates were sustained by the liquidity preference of investors.

[3] The range is not, however, unbounded. Unless there is considerable risk preference in the community, the yield on the risky asset cannot fall below the yield on the safe asset. At the other end of the spectrum Tsiang (1972) pp. 368–70, has shown that, given the limitation upon the upward slope of the indifference curves (less than 45°) which theory suggests, it will be worthwhile to replace zero-yielding cash completely by further holdings of the risky asset, so long as the expected return on the risky asset is greater than the standard deviation of that yield.

the holding of safe assets, other than for 'transactions purposes', does not depend on some people confidently expecting future falls in risky asset prices.[1]

Furthermore this approach, based on the assessment of portfolios in terms of their mean–variance configuration, can be – and has been – extended from analysis of the selection of a portfolio consisting of one safe asset and one risky asset, to the much broader analysis of portfolio choice where the investor is confronted with a range of risky assets (and possibly, but not necessarily, a safe asset as well). Consider the case where the investor can choose to distribute some funds between two risky assets, X and Y. In situation 1, let there be two possible outcomes (states of nature). If outcome (i) occurs, X pays £6 and Y pays £3; if outcome (ii) occurs, X pays £0 and Y pays £1. The mean expected value of X is £3, of Y £2, the standard deviation of X, defined as $\sqrt{(1/n)(x - \bar{x})^2}$, is £3, of Y is £1. If all the portfolio is held in asset Y, then the risk-return combination is that shown at point A in Figure 3.8. If the portfolio is held entirely in asset X, the risk-return combination obtained is plotted at point B.

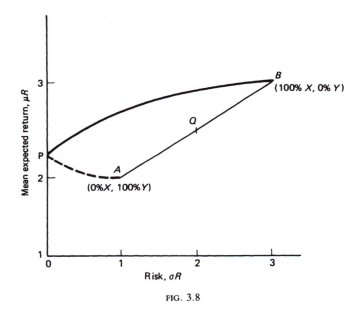

FIG. 3.8

The existence of such assets, and Tsiang argues that 'there must be a host of assets in modern financial markets, e.g., savings deposits and Treasury bills, that would satisfy these requirements', 'would eliminate all demand for cash for the portfolio balance purpose'.

---

[1] Indeed, the more common assumption now in portfolio analysis is to treat all individuals as having identical subjective expectations. This can be, certainly, a useful simplifying assumption for analytic purposes, but is hardly a reasonable representation of the real world and may be seriously misleading in some respects. See, for example, the comments of Stiglitz (1972, pp. 458–82, especially p. 459).

The out-turns for X and Y have perfect positive correlation,[1] of $+1$, since they vary exactly together. If the investor then decides to hold 50 per cent of his assets in X and 50 per cent in Y, the expected mean value of his portfolio will be £2.50, and the standard deviation will be £2: the mean and standard deviation of this combination lies, at point Q, half-way along a straight line joining A and B. All portfolios of X and Y in differing proportions will exhibit risk–return combinations lying along this line.[2]

In case 2, the mean and variance of X and Y remain as above, but in outcome (i) X pays £6 and Y pays £1, while in outcome (ii) X pays £0 and Y pays £3. In this circumstance with perfect negative correlation, of -1, a particular combination of X and Y can be chosen, in this case with 1/4 of the portfolio in X and 3/4 in Y, which will provide a mean return at £2.25, which is higher than the mean expected return on holdings of Y, with absolute certainty whatever the outcome. In this case the opportunities[3] open to the investor lie along the line APB. Obviously the segment PB is preferable in all respects to the segment AP, since it is possible to find points along PB which have a higher mean expected return with similar variance, in comparison with the points on AP. The segment PB may, therefore, be entitled the efficient frontier of the portfolio, since it dominates all other available combinations.

Next take a situation where asset X, say, pays £3, £4, £4 and £5 when possible outcomes (i)–(iv) respectively occur, while asset Y pays £2, £1.50, £2.50 and £2 in the same outcomes. The respective means and standard deviations are £4 and £0.71 for X and £2 and £0.35 for Y. The covariance between the two assets, and thus the correlation also, has been constructed to be zero. In this case also it is possible to reduce the overall variance of the portfolio by a policy of diversification, at the same time as raising the mean expected return above the level, £2, obtainable when all the assets are invested in Y. Thus if half of the available funds are invested in X and half in Y, the mean return on the portfolios is £3 and the standard deviation is £0.39; if 2/3 of the funds are placed in Y and 1/3 in X, the mean return and standard deviation are

---

[1] Defined as:

$$r_{xy} = \frac{\text{Covariance}}{\sigma_x, \sigma_y}(xy) = \frac{1}{n}\frac{\sum(x - \bar{x})(y - \bar{y})}{\sqrt{\frac{1}{n}(x - \bar{x})^2}\ \sqrt{\frac{1}{n}(y - \bar{y})^2}}$$

In this case

$$\frac{3}{3 \times 1} = +1$$

[2] With a portfolio consisting of asset X with mean expected return μ_x and variance σ_x^2, and asset Y with mean μ_y and variance σ_y^2, the formulae for obtaining the mean and variance of the overall portfolio in a combination in which asset X takes up a fraction of the portfolio h and asset Y, $1 - h$, are as follows:

$Z = hX + (1 - h)Y$
$\mu_z = E(Z) = h\mu_x + (1 - h)\mu_y$
$\sigma_z^2 = \text{var}(Z) = h^2\sigma_x^2 + (1 - h)^2\sigma_y^2 + 2h(1 - h)r\sigma_x\sigma_y$

where r is the correlation between X and Y.

[3] The opportunity loci for two asset portfolios are hyperbolas, except in special cases – e.g., where $r = +1$ or when σ_x or σ_y is zero, when the loci degenerate into straight lines. See Tobin (1965) pp. 29–30.

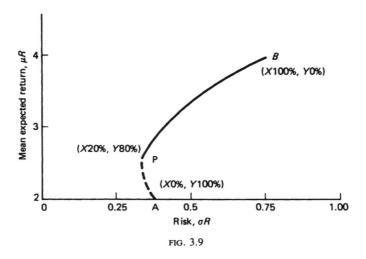

FIG. 3.9

£2.66 and £0.33 respectively. The available combinations, the line APB, are traced out in Figure 3.9. The minimum variance at point P is £0.32 with 4/5 of the portfolio invested in asset Y, and mean return £2.40.[1]

Clearly diversification is an effective method of reducing risk, so long as the risky assets exhibit low or negative covariance (and correlations). Consider, for example, a situation where the investor can divide his funds equally between n assets, which have zero covariance. In this case, the mean return will be $1/n(\mu_1 \ldots \mu_n)$, and the variance of his portfolio will be $1/n^2(\sigma_1^2 + \sigma_2^2 \ldots + \sigma_n^2)$. As n becomes large, the variance of this portfolio drops towards zero. So if one could find sufficient risky assets whose outcomes were nevertheless independent, with zero covariance, it would be possible to combine them to obtain a virtually riskless portfolio. In practice, this cannot be achieved. There tends to be a systematic risk, with general positive covariances, among all risky assets. All assets represent, directly or indirectly, claims upon future economic resources, so that forces that affect the future development of the economy are likely to impinge in a similar fashion over wide groups of risky assets. Imagine an entrepreneur who wanted to take advantage of the demand for diversification and offered to the public an asset with the characteristics that its market value went up when market interest rates rose, and vice versa. How could he invest his funds so as to remain solvent during periods when interest rates rise? He could do so only by levying a charge for this insurance against market risks,[2] offering such a low return that a

---

[1] The formulae for finding the variance of the minimum-risk portfolio and the shares of the two assets in this are given by Tobin (1965) pp. 29–30.

[2] Such events as increases in market interest rates do not have a well defined actuarial probability. It would, therefore, be even more difficult for a private-sector intermediary to offer insurance against them at rates that could allow the intermediary an acceptable risk–return configuration on his own business.

An entrepreneur might, however, consider inviting subscriptions to an intermediary set up to borrow long and lend short. An intermediary run in this way would have exhibited a considerable growth in equity value over the last two decades. I am indebted to A. D. Crockett for this suggestion.

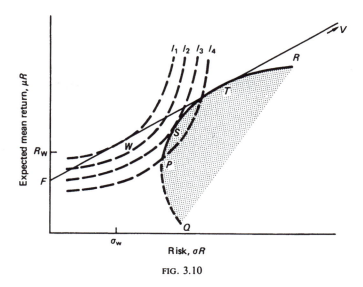

FIG. 3.10

combination of this asset with other risky assets would offer no greater return with the same variance as already existing 'safe' assets.

When the investor was considering selecting between one safe and one risky asset, the attributes of the risky asset which were relevant to this decision, under the particular assumptions set out previously, were the expected mean return and variance of the asset. When the investor is considering adding a risky asset to a portfolio containing other risky assets the critical issue is how much the addition of a unit of the risky asset will add to the overall return and risk of the portfolio as a whole.[1] The various combinations of risky assets, which the investor could hold, will then provide a set of possible configurations for risk and return for the whole portfolio, which can be depicted by the shaded area in Figure 3.10. The upper envelope of this set, the line joining P and R, gives the efficient frontier of portfolio combinations dominating all the other options. Drawing in the indifference curves for a risk averter, assuming that only risky assets may be held, the investor will choose portfolio S. However, there is no good reason why the investor should not be able to invest also in a safe asset and so, analogously to the previous case of one safe and one risky asset, one can assume that the investor can choose some combination of a safe asset and a portfolio of risky assets. Clearly the combinations offering the greatest potential utility must be of the safe asset and of market portfolio T, where T

---

[1] The marginal impact of the jth asset on the standard deviation of the market portfolio (consisting of an investment in every asset outstanding in proportion to its total value) is proportional to the covariance between the returns on the jth asset and the market portfolio. Thus:

$$\frac{\partial \sigma(R_m)}{\partial X_j} = \frac{\text{cov}(R_j, R_m)}{\sigma(R_m)}$$

where R_m represents the expected return on the market portfolio, $\sigma(R_m)$ the standard deviation of that return and X_j the weight which asset j receives in the market portfolio.

See Jensen (1972, pp. 357–98, especially pp. 362–3) and Fama (1971) pp. 30–55.

is the point at which the line from F (the point showing the available yield on the risk-free asset) tangentially touches the envelope enclosing the opportunity set of portfolios of risky assets. If the investor can also borrow, as well as lend, at the riskless rate of interest, the line FT can be extended onwards, indefinitely, towards V.[1] In this example, the investor will achieve his greatest possible utility at point W, with a combination of the safe asset and the portfolio of risky assets offering the expected yield R_w and the subjective standard deviation (risk) of outcomes σ_w.

If all investors have identical expectations, and assuming that the outstanding quantities of all the risky assets are given, then the prices on such assets must shift until each investor holds all the available assets in proportion to their outstanding quantities in his own preferred portfolio, at T. Abstracting from complications caused by taxes, limited marketability of some assets, etc. these assumptions allow one to specify the equilibrium expected return on any asset. This will be greater than the risk-free rate by the extent of a premium which is the product of the general market risk premium per unit of risk (measured by the slope of the line FTV), multiplied by the actual addition to risk that the addition of this asset to the portfolio (in exchange for an equivalent amount of the market portfolio) brings about (which is basically a function of the covariance of the returns on this asset with those on the whole market portfolio).[2]

This analysis has a wide range of practical applications. For example, so long as the assumptions on which the analysis is based hold true, it can be used in a normative manner to suggest how an efficient portfolio should be selected. It can also be used in a positive way to observe whether relative yields on differing assets have varied as the theory would suggest, a process which inevitably involves further extensions and revisions of the basic theory in order to account for the empirically observed discrepancies between actual market conditions and those predicted by the theory. Indeed, an enormous literature on this subject has appeared in the last two decades. To pursue this fascinating, but quite complicated, subject further would, however, take us too far from the main theme of this chapter, the relationship between various aspects of uncertainty and the demand for money.[3]

This examination of the micro-economic determinants of the demand for money

---

[1] This implies that a plunger might try to borrow at the riskless rate of interest enough to buy up all the risky assets in the system. In practice, a number of factors would prevent this. Differing expectations within the economy would lead to prices being forced against him (higher prices on the risky assets, rising borrowing rates). Even though the borrowing would be covered by the collateral of the risky assets, the lenders would become increasingly chary of lending to this plunger as the possibility of his becoming bankrupt increased.

[2] The formula is:

$$E(R_j) = R_F + \frac{(E(R_M) - R_F)}{(RM)} \cdot \frac{\text{cov}(R_j, R_M)}{\sigma(R_M)}$$

where R_F is the riskless rate of interest and R_j is the return on the jth asset; $E(R_j)$ is the expected return on the jth asset. See Jensen (1972) pp. 358–63.

[3] Readers who wish to delve further into the expanding subject and literature on Capital Asset Pricing Models (CAPM) and Portfolio Risk Assessment (PRA) might like to read the following papers:

CAPM

Leroy (1982) pp. 185–217; Dhrymes *et al.* (1984) pp. 323–50.

PRA

Levy and Sarnat (1984) p. 747; Corner and Mayes (1983) p. 253.

leaves us, however, with an awkward conclusion. This is that it is not easy to explain or to account at the individual level for the amount of money balances held. Companies, and other corporate bodies such as local authorities, appear to hold much larger balances than inventory-theoretic transactions demand models show to be optimal. And money should be dominated by other interest-paying capital-certain assets in the role of providing a safe asset in portfolios. We explained in Chapter 1 why money would be demanded and held, but further micro-economic analysis in this chapter suggests that there is, perhaps, something of a puzzle still to explain why such large balances are held.

3. Buffer-stock Models of Money Holding

As noted earlier, the Miller–Orr micro-level inventory-theoretic analysis of the transactions demand for money remains useful as a starting framework for companies, and other large cash-holders, to plan to minimise the costs of holding inventories of cash, though the approach can be subsumed in the wider literature of (operational-research) inventory management. Their work has not, however, succeeded in generating much further empirical work by economists on micro-data to explore and to refine their study. So, there has not been much further development, for the purpose of economic analysis, of this micro-level inventory-theoretic approach.

One important reason for this has been a dearth of suitable data sets for studying such micro-level behaviour. Individual money holdings and income and expenditure flows, both in currency form,[1] where they can be used to hide 'black economy' and illegal transactions, and at banks, which are subject to strict customer confidentiality, are not normally publicly revealed or available to a research worker. Moreover, even in the unlikely case that a research worker were to obtain access to individual customer bank accounts, the researcher could not be sure that the customer did not hold other bank accounts, nor could he or she relate such monetary flows to incomes, expenditures, investments, etc. without having complete access to the books and accounts of each individual bank customer.

Few individuals or firms will give a research worker *carte blanche* access to their complete accounts. Moreover, the accounts of a firm or an individual form a large data set. An economist wishing to undertake research on the basis of the *raw* data in this area is, therefore, almost bound to be working with extremely small samples, and a sample which, because it will be self-selected in a highly confidential area, may well be biased.

Probably the most hopeful line of advance in this study of micro-level money holding behaviour is to study the cross-section balance sheet data, or personal asset-holding surveys, that are available – e.g., in compliance with company regulations. There has been some recent interesting work on company liquid asset holdings,[2] but

---

[1] A survey undertaken by the Federal Reserve Board in 1985 was able to account for only about 25 per cent of the total value of US currency outstanding. Indeed in many countries, (especially those with currencies perceived as stable in real value and with available high denomination notes – e.g., West Germany, Switzerland), the ratio of the outstanding value of currency to GNP provides a calculable average holding per resident that appears implausibly high.

[2] E.g., Chowdhury, Green and Miles (1986).

balance sheet data are subject to various limitations for this purpose, being a posed snap-shot, subject to window-dressing, as are the various asset holding surveys, where frequently an attempt to gross up estimates to compare the survey with the known aggregate value indicates major remaining data deficiencies.

Despite this inability to take micro-level empirical or theoretical analysis of the inventory-theoretic model much further than Miller and Orr achieved at the end of the 1960s, this *general approach* towards an appreciation of monetary phenomena has recently enjoyed a revival of interest. The basic reason for this, however, is a negative one: the standard *macro-economic* asset demand functions that have been more generally estimated at the macro-level with aggregate data, have, as will be described at length in Chapter 4, been failing to exhibit the stability previously predicted for them – i.e., they have been breaking down.

On a variety of occasions in recent years the failure of the demand function for (some definition of) the aggregate money supply to behave as had been previously predicted was associated with some kind of 'supply shock', whereby either the banks or the authorities behaved in such a (novel) way as to cause an apparently exogenous change in the volume of money. An outstanding example of such a supply shock took place in the UK in 1971–3, when the adoption of a new policy regime in September 1971, entitled 'Competition and Credit Control', removed direct credit controls and encouraged the banks to compete more aggressively. As recounted by Spencer,[1] this led to a huge surge in bank lending, financed in some large part by the new technique of liability management, whereby banks bid for additional funds on the wholesale money market, when their ordinary retail deposits were not sufficient to fund their loan books. Anyhow, the resulting explosive growth in UK broad money, £M3, took this far over the level that could be explained on the basis of current and previous values of real incomes, prices, interest rates, etc. (i.e., the arguments in the standard aggregate demand-for-money function, as outlined in Chapter 4). This was, perhaps, the most dramatic monetary phenomenon in the UK in the post-war period.

In order to explain such monetary disturbances, Artis and Lewis[2] initiated the idea that the stock of money actually held could be driven away from the level that would be normally (or in an 'underlying' fashion) held, given the values of the arguments in the demand function, by such 'exogenous shocks'. Initially this was at times termed the 'disequilibrium money' approach (see Goodhart (1984a) chapter X, 'Disequilibrium Money – A Note') on the grounds that supply shocks were deemed to be causing disequilibrium between the actual supply and the 'underlying' demand. This terminology was, however, soon dropped. Certain neo-classical economists object to the concept of disequilibrium as such, on the grounds that rational agents will take immediate steps, via efficiently working markets, to eliminate any such disequilibrium. More importantly, it has been argued that agents rationally choose to use their money balances as an inventory, or buffer stock, to absorb unforeseen transactions in the markets in which they operate, as described in Chapter 1. While the parameters – i.e., the limits and return point – for monetary holdings may be determined for each agent by the parameters in the demand for money function, actual money holdings may fluctuate within such limits as a buffer to unforeseen monetary shocks. The terminology used by Laidler, 'The "Buffer Stock" Notion in Monetary Economics' (1984) pp. 17–34, has become standard.

Although the breakdown of the standard macro-economic asset demand func-

---

[1] (1986) and Goodhart (1984a) Chapters II and IV.
[2] Artis and Lewis (1976) pp. 147–81.

tion(s) for money has been the dominant reason for reviving interest in the buffer-stock notion as a useful macro-economic concept, there have been other unsatisfactory features of the standard model. In particular, the standard function generally incorporated a lagged dependent variable in the estimating equation which commonly had a large and significant coefficient, seemingly implying the existence of long lags; it was never easy to account for such lags. If the lags were to be ascribed in some fashion to the generation of expectations of future ('permanent') levels of prices, real incomes and interest rates, then the lag profiles generally did *not* correspond to those that a rational investor trying to forecast the future on the basis of available information would have adopted. If the lags were to be ascribed to adjustment costs, then the problem is that money is chosen as a means of payment precisely since the transfer–adjustment costs into it are lowest (see Chapter 2). Either way, the existence of such long lags in the demand for money function seemed anomalous and implausible.

Apart from the difficulty of providing any realistic explanation of the derivation of such estimated lags, their existence would indicate that at least some of the arguments in the demand for money function should exhibit severe volatility (overshooting) in face of supply shocks, on the standard assumption that money demanded equals money supply at all times. Thus, if the demand for money is a function of a lagged distribution of incomes – e.g., $M_{dt} = f(Y_{t-1}, \ldots Y_{t-n})$, with all coefficients taking positive values (as would be expected) – then the initial change in Y following a monetary disturbance – i.e., a change in M_s, will be greater than the long-run, steady-state response. Furthermore, the subsequent path of incomes may well be cyclical, depending on the coefficients on the current and lagged income terms.[1] Indeed it is easily possible to imagine a plausible set of values for the coefficients in the demand for money function that would cause the system to lose stability and explode after a monetary disturbance.

Consider, for example, demand for money functions taking the values

(i) $M_{dt} = 0.7Y_t + 0.2Y_{t-1} + 0.1Y_{t-2}$
(ii) $M_{dt} = 0.2Y_t + 0.6Y_{t-1} + 0.2Y_{t-2}$

If, then, M_s increases by one unit, the subsequent path of Y_t in the two cases would be:

TIME PERIOD

	1	2	3	4	5	6	7
(i)	1.43	1.02	0.93	1.02	1.00	1.00	1.00
(ii)	5.00	− 10.00	30.00	− 75.00	200.00	− 520.00	1365.00

Indeed, the length of lag commonly found in demand for money functions is so long that one would expect to find severe overshooting in at least one of the arguments if the demand for money was always to be equated to a partially exogenous supply. With movements in incomes and prices exhibiting some inertia, for reasons explored in Chapter 1, this would suggest dramatic overshooting in interest rates. This does not appear to happen. One reason for this, discussed in

---

[1] For a more extended analysis of this subject, see A. Walters's paper 'Professor Friedman on the Demand for Money' (1965) pp. 545–51.

Chapter 10, is that the authorities take care not to let such financial instability emerge by adjusting their operational techniques in such a way as to dampen such potential instability. Another reason is that monetary supply side shocks may be absorbed in shifts in buffer stock holdings in the shorter run, while in the longer run the determinants of demand will alter the parameters – i.e., the limits and return points – within which such buffer holdings can fluctuate.

The 'buffer stock' notion, therefore, attractively ties up a lot of loose ends in monetary theory. It provides a bridge again between macro-economic empirical and policy-oriented studies and the micro-level inventory-theoretic analysis of the role and demand for money. It helps to explain some part of the recent instabilities in demand for money functions, especially in the face of a variety of supply shocks. It helps to explain both how findings of long lags may be obtained in misspecified single equations, *and* also why economies do *not* appear to suffer overshooting of interest rates in the face of supply shocks. Finally, as discussed in Chapter 12, the buffer stock concept can help to provide a better account of the transmission mechanism from monetary shocks to the economy at large than can either the more extreme forms of Keynesian or Monetarist theory.

Despite such putative advantages, the buffer stock concept has had only partial acceptance as the primary paradigm outside of North America, and little acceptance in the USA and Canada. There are several reasons why this is so and a number of grounds on which the buffer stock notion can be criticised. Perhaps the most startling is that the basic link between the buffer stock notion at the individual level and in the aggregate has not really been firmly established. It may seem intuitively likely that, if everyone uses their money holding as a buffer, a generalised aggregate macro supply shock will raise aggregate buffer holdings, but this is not necessarily so. Indeed, certain theorists who have done most to maintain the inventory-theoretic approach at the micro-level, notably Akerlof and Milbourne, have been most critical of the attempt to jump to the macro-level buffer stock approach.

Following Milbourne[1] and using the notation of Miller and Orr from Section 1, with $h, 0, Z$ being the upper, lower limits and return point respectively, and their assumption of continuous and costless monitoring of cash balances and instantaneous transfers being available at all time, then one can show that most of any unanticipated increase in money balances would very quickly be transferred out of buffer stock holdings. Milbourne notes (pp. 131–2) that:

> Buffer stock theorists argue that any unexpected inflow of money will accumulate in this scenario. It is indeed true that excess money will remain in the account until the next portfolio adjustment if the initial balance was in the lower part of the $(0.h)$ range. However, for an individual who is near the top threshold, h, an inflow causes him to exceed the upper threshold and thus *lower* his money balance to z, transferring the balance to a time deposit or some other asset. That is, an increase in money triggers a portfolio adjustment which lower his money holdings. In aggregate the effect is likely to be very small. For an economy with individuals whose money holdings are uniformly distributed between 1 and h in unit amounts, a £1 given to each person will raise the holdings of $(h-1)/h$ of the population by £1, and lower the holdings of $1/h$ of the population by $h-z$. In aggregate, the increase is $(z-1)/h$. If $z = h/2$, the aggregate response is $\frac{1}{2} - 1/h$. That is, more than one half of the initial increase is immediately transferred out; this process will continue until the distribution converges back to its equilibrium. Since buffer stock theorists argue that the price level, interest rates and

even income respond slowly, so that thresholds do not change, any injection of money will be quickly transferred away in the short run unless individuals *wish* to hold it.[1]

While the formal demonstrations of this argument are certainly correct, I do not believe that they undermine the general macro-level buffer stock notion because they depend, in part, on maintained assumptions about cash balance control as earlier noted – i.e., continuous, costless monitoring and instantaneous transfer. There *are* some large institutions, companies, sovereign bodies, etc. whose Treasurers maintain continuous central surveillance of central cash flow positions for whom these assumptions approximate to reality. But, as noted earlier in Section 1, p. 62, footnote 4, Sprenkle has already described how their observed end-of-day balances will simply depend on the 'minimal overnight trading unit'. For the rest of us, monitoring cash balances can be expensive and we, therefore, tend to defer such monitoring until the costs of gathering information are matched by our subjective perceptions about the likelihood of facing extra costs from being beyond our chosen limits. Moreover, information costs can vary depending on the arrival of bank statements, etc. For all these reasons, an unanticipated inflow of money may be such as to make the recipient want to undertake transactions that will restore the cash balance to the return point, but is *not* necessarily likely to lead to this transaction occurring *instantaneously*, as is assumed in the Miller–Orr model.

Although an individual will generally incur costs in trying to monitor cash balance positions continually, such costs will be far less for banks, which can introduce electronic systems to do so. Account holders should, therefore, be able to arrange standard arrangements for their bank to make certain automatic transfers between lower-yielding chequable deposits and higher-yielding time deposits whenever certain agreed limits are reached. More generally, the costs of organising transfers between the elements of M3 money balances (sight deposits, M1 balances, and time deposits) would seem to be generally so low that unanticipated monetary inflows may be absorbed into broad money holdings but are unlikely to remain in M1 balances. This latter argument has been advanced more forcefully in those countries, such as the UK and Australia, where both the targets, the supply-side shocks and the fragilities in the demand-for-money function have concentrated in the broad money aggregates, than in the US where the target and demand function breakdowns have related to M1.

Unforeseen monetary inflows need not only go to raise monetary balances. They can be used, especially in countries where bank customers maintain overdrafts, to reduce the level of bank borrowing. For example, in the course of trying to allocate 'float', cheques in the course of being collected, the Bank of England has estimated that 60 per cent will normally add to deposit balances and 40 per cent reduce advances. Of any unanticipated exogenous increase in money supply – e.g., caused by government action or change in banks' lending policy – some sizeable proportion will thus naturally be endogenously offset by a reduction in bank lending. Critics of both monetarism, and of the buffer-stock concept,[2] have argued that the endogenous offset from such adjustments is so large that supply-side shocks to real money balances must be relatively unimportant in an overdraft system. While there is no question that such endogenous offsets exist, nevertheless the *ex post* data on total bank lending, which are net of any such offsets, at times of lending surges in the UK following regime changes in 1971–3, and again in the early 1980s, do provide a strong *a priori*

---

[1] Further and more formal demonstrations of this same point are to be found in Milbourne (1987) and Akerlof (1979).

[2] Such as White (1981) and Kaldor (1980).

case that such supply-side shocks can, and do, have a powerful aggregate influence *despite* the endogenous offset.

When the costs of bank intermediation, represented by the spread between deposit and lending rates (see Chapters 1 and 4) fall far enough, it will often benefit those large customers who can negotiate such small spreads to run simultaneously both positive cash balances *and* debit (overdrawn) balances with banks.[1] In such cases, and perhaps more generally, the set of assets which such agents regard as their financial buffer consists of their *net* liquid assets – i.e., those net of bank borrowing. Again the argument about ease and low cost of transfer can be advanced to argue that it is not M3 but a wider set of liquid financial assets which agents regard as their buffer, while transfers within this set remain determined by standard cost minimisation considerations.[2]

It seems, therefore, that even amongst those who accept the intuitive concept of financial, or monetary, buffers, there is no general agreement about which sets of assets represent such a buffer; there does exist some appreciation, however, that differing groups of economic agents, who face, for example, different degrees of imperfections and costs of intermediation in financial markets, may well utilise differing sets of assets as their main financial buffer.

With so little *a priori* agreement about which set of assets represents the financial buffer, there has been a wide range of empirical models set up to examine the concept. In the USA most attention has been paid to possible supply shocks to M1. Whereas Judd and Scadding[3] have related such supply shocks to fluctuations in bank lending, the best known work in this vein has been by Carr and Darby.[4] Following Barro, who estimated the anticipated money stock as that which a rational observer would predict on the basis of available information,[5] Carr and Darby see the money shock as the difference between the actual money stock and the thus-calculated anticipated money stock. They then estimate an equation of the form:

$$(m - p)_t = B'X_t + b(m - m^a)_t + u_t$$

where m_t is log of the money stock at time t, m^a is anticipated money, p_t is the price level, X is a vector of determining exogenous variables, B an accompanying coefficient vector and u is a random error term.

This formulation ran into criticism on econometric grounds, because random fluctuations in m_t are bound to be correlated with fluctuations in $(m - m^a)$.[6] The current state of this econometric disputation is summarised in Cuthbertson and Taylor, 'Buffer Stock Money: An Appraisal', Chapter 5 in Goodhart, Currie and Llewellyn (eds) (1987).

The basic approach to modelling buffer stock money has been quite different in those countries, such as Australia and the UK, who equate such buffers with a broad money aggregate. In this latter case, the approach has been to use the credit counterparts approach to the supply of money, which employs the identities that bank assets equal bank liabilities and that bank lending to the public sector is equal to

---

[1] See Miller and Sprenkle (1980).

[2] This latter position has, for example, been adopted by economists in HM Treasury, see Bennett and Grice (1984) and Spencer (1986).

[3] Judd and Scadding (1981) pp. 21–44.

[4] Carr and Darby (1981) pp. 183–99.

[5] See, for example, Barro (1977) pp. 101–15.

[6] For example, from MacKinnon and Milbourne (1984) 263–74.

its borrowing requirement less its borrowing from all other non-bank sectors, to model (the change in) the money stock in any period as the sum of the public sector borrowing requirement, debt sales to the non-bank public, bank lending to the private sector and external flows. The gap between the money stock, thus estimated from the supply side, and an estimated 'underlying' demand for money, then represents the current buffer, or 'disequilibrium', money holding (which can, of course, be negative as well as positive), which in turn can enter as an explanatory variable in all the other behavioural equations in the system. Such models have been estimated for Australia and the United Kingdom, but tend to be rather complex, involving testable cross equation constraints.[1] Further discussion of this latter approach is deferred, however, until Chapters 10 and 12.

[1] See Jonson, Moses and Wymer (1977), and Davidson, 'Disequilibrium Money: Some Further Results with a Monetary Model of the UK', Chapter 6 in Goodhart, Currie and Llewellyn (eds) (1987).

IV
Macro-Economic Analysis of the Demand for Money

Summary

The factors which would determine the demand for money at the micro, individual level – it was argued in chapter 3 – were largely expectational considerations of the future level and variance of cash flows, of asset prices, etc. It has not been easy to find quantitative counterparts, at least at the macro-economic level, of such behavioural factors. The tendency has been to turn instead for the study of behaviour at the aggregate level to a rather more generalised, simpler theory of asset demand, relating the demand for each asset to total wealth (as the budget constraint), relative interest rates and other variables, such as the level of incomes, which affect the demand for the specific services of the various assets. This gives a demand for money function of the form:

$$M_d = f(Y, r_i, W)$$

However, wealth is the capitalisation of present and future incomes, so the above explanatory variables are not fully independent. The normal procedure is to omit either W or Y from the estimating equation. Much of the controversy between 'monetarists' and 'Keynesians' (or 'fiscalists') has focused on the particular form of the demand for money function, whether it was stable and predictable, and whether the interest elasticity of demand for money (determining the response of holders of money balances to changes in yields on alternative liquid financial assets) was high or low. The question of the (real) income elasticity of demand for money, though of interest in itself, has engendered less heat, since no crucial point of theory rests on this issue. Monetarists took the view that the demand for money function is relatively stable and predictable, and the interest elasticity of demand for money relatively low (at least in comparison with the interest elasticity of demand for goods); Keynesians argued the opposite.

The results of putting these hypotheses to empirical test are described in Section 2. The question of the interest elasticity of the demand for money has been satisfactorily resolved with the finding of significant but quite low values. Econometric results and views concerning the stability of the demand for-money function have, however, changed over the years as the passage of time generated new data. Earlier studies prior to 1973 suggested stability, but during the disturbed years 1973–6, such demand-for-money functions predicted quite poorly. This failure was attributed to financial innovation and temporary supply shocks. Nevertheless, the more general relationships between accelerations and decelerations in monetary growth and in nominal incomes held up well and most monetary authorities adopted monetary targetting. After 1979, however, the combination of a switch in policy with further supply shocks led to more serious breakdowns in the stability of the relationships between money, incomes and interest rates. Previous single-equation estimates of the demand-for-money have not been able to take adequate account of these supply shocks, policy regime changes or more fundamental structural changes. Such changes are breaking down the functional divisions between financial intermediaries and may even be putting into greater question the clarity of definition of 'money' itself.

1.   The Transition from Micro- to Macro-studies of the Demand for Money

In Chapter 3, it was argued that there are two main reasons why people hold money balances. First, in its role as a specialist means of payment, people want to hold money balances against known, or possible, future transaction requirements, even though there might be a higher certain yield on some other alternative asset. For money and an alternative asset with a higher, certain yield to coexist, there must be costs involved in transfers into, or out of, the other asset. This leads on to the general conclusion that the demand for such transaction balances will be a function of the probability distribution of cash payments, the level of the 'certain' yield on the alternative asset, and the transfer costs of switching between that asset and money.

Second, money is itself an asset with a certain yield – at least in nominal terms. People want to hold safe assets even with a lower, even zero, mean expected yield, in conjunction with their portfolio of risky assets, in order to obtain a preferred combination of risk and return. However, it was noted that there is a range of alternative safe, or quasi-safe, assets, so that demand deposits would certainly, and time deposits (and certificates of deposits) would often, be dominated by other safe assets offering higher, but equally certain yields,[1] except over short planning periods when transactions costs became a relatively more important consideration.

It is thus possible to distinguish between the transactions (or exchange uncertainty) motive for holding money and the speculative (or asset-price uncertainty) motive. This does not, however, imply that the overall demand for money of an investor is an additive function of these distinct functions. Money balances held, say, as a safe asset over short planning periods to achieve the optimal risk – return configuration for the asset portfolio will also be available for use if some unforeseen expenditure opportunity should crop up. If individuals facing relatively high transfer costs, or very variable cash flows, feel the need to hold large money balances, their asset portfolio will then include on this account a large proportion of low-yielding safe assets, so that the choice of asset holding over the remainder of the portfolio will be influenced by that fact.

One can draw an analogy, for example, with the demand for jewellery, which provides some services of beautiful adornment and some conspicuous status-enhancing services. Jewellery is also an asset which may rise or fall in value over time, and there is an expected probability distribution of monetary return on holding jewellery. In some circumstances – e.g., of severe political instability – jewellery may be a safer asset, in terms of the probability distribution of real returns, than money. Jewellery, therefore, has a profile of characteristics which endow it with a range of services to its holder. It would not, however, be a sensible procedure to estimate the demand for jewellery by analysing the demand for each service separately, and then adding them up to together. These various services are provided jointly. If more

---

[1] Niehans argues that the speculative demand for money can be ignored on broadly similar grounds.

jewellery is held as a good investment, it will also be available as a potential adornment.

In analysing the demand for the joint services of jewellery, one would consider a range of factors bearing on the demand for such services, such as the longer-run shifts in institutional and social factors (e.g., the custom of giving engagement rings, and various social prescriptions on personal adornment and conspicuous status symbols), and shorter-run changes in the probability distribution of risk and return from holding jewellery. But the analysis would cover the demand for jewellery as a single asset, not for the separate individual services of jewellery. In the same vein, the various services for money are, in the main, provided jointly. It is not, therefore, appropriate to seek to identify, say, the transactions demand for money apart from the speculative demand and then add the separate functional relationships together in order to obtain an aggregate demand function.

A study of the various services provided by money balances, as undertaken in the previous chapters, should, however, give a firmer basis of deciding which variables are likely to affect the aggregate demand for money. Factors which have been already mentioned as likely to affect desired money balances include the extent and nature of transfer costs, the availability of alternative 'safe' assets, the length of planning and holding periods, expectations and uncertainty about the pace of future inflation, the level of wealth, the level and variance of income and expenditure flows, and expectations about the relative yields to be obtained on money balances and alternative assets.

Some of these factors are likely to change only relatively slowly over the longer term. Thus transfer costs are largely determined by the technology of the payments transmission mechanism. The pattern of expenditure and income flows is constrained over the short run by social customs (e.g., the weekly wage packet, the monthly salary cheque) which inhibit flexibility in adjusting the form and frequency of cash flows to changing circumstances.[1] Our statistical records are so short and insufficient, and so many variables move together over the long run, that it is very difficult to distinguish the effects of the several longer-run factors upon the velocity of money. These include technological improvements in the payments transmission mechanism, the increasing availability of alternative 'safe' liquid assets, changes in the structural characteristics of the economy (e.g., urbanisation), and increases in income and wealth.[2]

Moreover, some of the variables influencing the demand for money balances can be measured only with difficulty, if at all. Transfer costs will vary between individuals, and companies, depending on their precise situation, and are not well documented. Feelings of uncertainty about future events are by their nature hard to capture in statistical form. The portfolio choice depends on the relative real yields that are

---

[1] In the longer run, however, payment periods and practices will adjust to the costs of holding and transferring money. 'Surely, the increase in the average cash balance over the past century in this country that has occurred for other reasons has been a factor producing a lengthening of pay periods and not the otherway around', quotation from Friedman's 'The Quantity Theory of Money – A Restatement', Chapter 11 in Friedman (ed.) (1956), from clause 11.

[2] Some economists, for example Garvy and Blyn (1969) have emphasised the role of technological advances in money transmission and cash management techniques in affecting the demand for money; others, for example Gurley and Shaw (1960) and the authors of the Radcliffe Report (1959) Chapter IV and para. 392, have stressed the growing availability of alternative liquid assets; others, for example, Friedman and Schwartz (1963), Chapter 12 – especially, have argued that increases in income have been the main determinant of long-run trends in the velocity of money.

expected to hold on money and alternative assets over some *unknown future* planning period.

Faced with the problem of trying to provide some empirical, factual clothing to the corpus of theory, the tendency has been to use observable, objective, *ex post* data as proxies for subjective, *ex ante* expectations, wherever possible, and to despatch those variables which have no obvious *ex post* quantitative counterpart, such as transactions costs and uncertainty, to that statistical limbo of being represented by a constant, a trend term or some other 'dummy' variable in the usual regression analysis. The most common form of demand for money function which is tested empirically thus relates aggregate money holding (sometimes deflated by a price index and some measure of population on to a *per capita* real balance basis) to nominal incomes (again often deflated into real terms by a price index, or divided into real and price components) and to the current market rate of interest (the yield to redemption on a marketable asset) on one or more assets which are taken as an alternative holding to money. Despite the emphasis on uncertainty, on the variance of the probability distribution of expected returns or of cash flows, on the unknown length of holding period, in the theoretical analysis of the demand for money it is extremely difficult to incorporate such subjective, *ex ante* elements in any statistical tests,[1] and they are virtually universally excluded from consideration in the macro-economic empirical work.

Even when data can be found to serve as proxies for expectational variables that actually influence individual behaviour, the approximation may in practice be subject to considerable error. In particular the *ex post* yield on alternative assets, or the calculated yields to maturity, may often be a poor guide to expectations of yield over the individual's planning period. If a rise in market interest rates induces only a small reduction in money balances, how can one distinguish between the hypothesis that the interest elasticity of demand for money is low and the hypothesis that the rise in market rates had led to a much smaller increase in the expected yield on that asset over the planning period, perhaps because market rates are expected to rise (and prices to fall)[2] yet further in future periods? Only if the planning period and the

---

[1] Moreover, these factors influence the demand for money balances at the individual, micro-level. There are aggregation problems to be faced in the process of deriving an aggregate, macro-economic relationship from the multitude of micro-level functions, a problem noted, for example, by D. Laidler in his review of Orr's 'Cash Management and the Demand for Money', (1972).

[2] Current asset prices should reflect the market's expectations about the future; otherwise the structure of current prices would allow opportunities for profitable speculation by rational investors. Nevertheless, future expected short rates do not have to be the same as current actual short rates. There is no good reason why some change in information should not cause revisions to expectations of future rates as large as, or greater than, the change in current short rates. The postulate that markets make rational and efficient use of information does not imply that market prices can never be expected to change from their current values, as Sargent notes. In his paper on 'Rational Expectations and the Term Structure of Interest Rates' (1972), Sargent tests two hypotheses about the behaviour of the term structure of interest rates. 'The first hypothesis is the "expectations hypothesis", which states that forward rates of interest are forced into equality with the short rates that investors expect to prevail in subsequent periods. The second hypothesis is that the expectations of investors are rational in the sense of Muth (1961): 'By this we mean that investors' expectations are equivalent with the optimal forecasts of statistical theory for a certain specified class of statistical models' (p. 74). Subsequently (p. 85) Sargent notes that these two hypotheses 'do not imply things that are commonly thought to be their

maturity of the marketable asset – the assumed alternative investment to money – should be the same will the yield to maturity become identical with the expected yield.

If behaviour depends on expectational variables which cannot be observed at all clearly, then empirical exercises using available *ex post* statistics will provide only very broad brush tests of the theoretical hypotheses. In recent years, however, some studies of the demand for money,[1] have adopted the rational expectations hypothesis in order to seek to give such expectational, forward-looking variables a firmer foundation. The rational expectations hypothesis, already briefly described in foot-note 2 on page 85,[2] claims that 'rational' individuals will use all information already available to them to construct forecasts of future variables of concern to them using optimal forecasting methods.[3] Thus, in studies of the demand for money, a two stage process may now be undertaken. At stage one estimates of expected future values of incomes, prices and other relevant variables may be constructed on the basis of forecasts using currently available information. Then, at stage two, such constructed expectational variables may be entered into the demand for money function, this procedure allows the restoration of somewhat closer links between the micro-theoretical basis of the demand for money and the form of the macro-models used for empirical testing at the aggregate level.

This forward-looking approach to estimating the demand for money has not, however, had that much impact; the reason for this is that its recent introduction has coincided with structural and other phenomena that have been causing more general fragility and breakdowns in demand for money functions, and thus diverting attention from such (minor and technical) improvements in the estimation of these functions.

---

implications. Thus, they do not imply that the spot one-period rate, R', follows a random walk, which would mean that $R_t - R_{t-1}$ is serially uncorrelated. They do not imply that the j-period spot rate follows a random walk for any finite j. Moreover the "fair game" property built into the model clearly does not mean that spot rates cannot be described by a stable stochastic difference equation'. Sargent does, however, note that there is disagreement about the implications of the efficient market hypothesis, and quotes other authors (e.g., Granger and Rees) who have presented contrary views.

Subsequent empirical work exploring price movements in asset markets has, on occasions, identified (somewhat minor) systematic deviations from market efficiency. See, for example, Baillie and McMahon, 'Rational Forecasts in Models of the Term Structure of Interest Rates', Chapter 8 in Goodhart, Currie and Llewellyn (eds) (1987) in a comment on Sargent's original work. Such deviations may indicate some lapses in the efficiency with which past, available information is utilised to determine current prices; or may simply suggest that the relative costs of collecting and utilising such information are greater than the extra returns, after adjustment for risk, to be obtained from undertaking such speculative activity.

---

[1] Notably Lane (1984) and Cuthbertson and Taylor, 'Buffer Stock Money: An Appraisal', Chapter 5 in Goodhart, Currie and Llewellyn (eds) (1987).

[2] This hypothesis is certainly more attractive than previous, largely *ad hoc*, ways of positing the formation of expectations, methods which often (implicitly) involved the assumption that agents would maintain expectations generating methods that led to systematic errors. Even so, this improved hypothesis leaves a lot of loose ends. For example, what determines how much information an agent actually has, or should seek? Obtaining extra information is expensive in time and effort. What would represent an optimal forecasting method for utilising available information? Using information to pursue a speculative gain may expose an agent to added risk; is it necessarily optimal always to use information to eliminate the margin between a forward (future) market price and the current best expectation of that price, if that exercise should increase the agent's risk exposure?

Anyhow, mainly because of the need to make do with the limited observable data available, the theory of the demand for money, which was set out in Chapter 3 at the micro-level largely in terms of uncertainty and transactions costs, thus undergoes a transformation at the macro-level. The functional forms which are examined in the macro-level empirical exercises usually do not include such factors directly at all. How far, then, these macro-level, aggregative statistical studies can be regarded as a test of, or compatible with, the underlying micro-level theoretical hypotheses is debatable. It is, however, necessary for practical, policy purposes to estimate such macro-economic functions. Even if the functional forms which can be estimated from the data do not correspond very closely to the micro-economic theoretical rationale for money holding, it is possible for theory to provide *some* guidance both on the (statistically available) variables that are likely to influence the demand for money and on the values of the coefficients of such variables that would accord with theory.

Alternatively, it is possible to regard the usual form in which the demand for money function is estimasted as deriving from a rather more generalised, simple theory of asset demand. In this, the demand for any asset is estimated as a function of wealth, acting as the budget constraint, of the relative expected monetary return, or yield, on each asset relative to that available on alternative assets, and of variables which affect the demand for the specific services of the asset, other than its monetary return. In the case of money, which provides specific services in its role as a means of payment, the level of income acts as a broad proxy both for the level of transactions, and perhaps also for the variance of cash flows. Other forms of uncertainty and transactions costs are treated as constant (or incorporated into a time trend), and thus omitted from specific analysis.

The general form of the asset-demand function that results from this approach is

$$M_d = f(Y, r_i, W)$$

where M_d is the demand for money, Y the level of income, r_i the observed monetary yield on the ith asset, i covers all assets, o to n, *including* money itself, and W represents total (non-human)[1] wealth.

The monetary yield on money, narrowly defined as currency and demand deposits at banks, was normally taken to be zero until recently,[2] so that variations in the

---

[1] Human capital cannot be bought and sold in a market in the same way as non-human capital. If the present value of one's human capital rises – e.g., because one's particular skill comes into greater demand – one cannot sell part of it in order to buy financial or real assets and thus maintain a desired portfolio distribution. One can, however, borrow against one's expected higher future income to effect that same diversification. But the uncertainty about future income streams, and the cost to the lender of obtaining an informed view of these likely future income streams, raises the cost of borrowing against future incomes earned from human capital. So the imperfections (basically of information) in the capital market are likely to introduce a differing response in asset holding to changes in human and non-human wealth.

[2] In the United States, legal regulations prevent any explicit payment of interest on demand deposits. In the United Kingdom until 1971 the clearing bank cartel maintained an agreement not to pay interest on current accounts. But there is no essential reason why banks should not make such interest payments, especially in inflationary conditions: indeed in Chapter 2 it is argued tht it would be desirable if such payments were made. Even though explicit payments of interest on demand deposits may be prevented, but see below, the banks can still compete for current-account funds by varying the additional banking services offered (book-keeping, investment advice, loan facilities, etc.) or the charges for banking services (e.g., for operating the payment-transmission system) in the light of the (average) balance maintained. It has never

monetary yield on other assets also provided a measure of variations in the *relative* yield as compared with monetary balances.[1]

In practice, this relationship is usually simplified even further by omitting W, the wealth term. Wealth can be defined as the capitalisation of current and future income streams. The functional form above, however, includes a variable representing income streams, and a yield (r_i), a capitalisation rate applicable to some asset over some holding period. There is, therefore, likely to be considerable multi-collinearity between the variables Y and r on the one hand and W on the other; indeed the three variables are not independent of one another. Moreover, in most countries wealth data are either unavailable or include a generous proportion of uncertain estimation, informed guesswork; for example, data on the market value of real property, land and houses, can only be described as rickety. In the UK, the times series for wealth has been trend dominated and the apparent variations of the data around the trend are of dubious reliability. The income and interest rate series are at least more accurately measured, even if they do not necessarily closely approximate to the underlying factors (e.g., the level and variance of cash flows; the level, variance and covariances of expected yields over the relevant planning periods) which determine the demand for money.

Furthermore, the wealth elasticity of demand for money, when narrowly defined, should be very low. Since money has not, at least until recently, borne a competitive rate of interest, the objective has been to minimise the opportunity costs involved in holding money for transactions purposes – subject to the level of transfer costs. Thus if wealth should be higher, but the volume of incomes (transactions) and the yield on alternative assets – and the level of transfer costs – were unchanged, then exactly the

---

been, therefore, strictly accurate to treat the monetary yield on means of payment as zero, and some studies incorporated an attempt to take account of this, especially the various cross-section studies of the demand for money in the United States, mostly using data from the separate states. See, for example, Feige (1964); Cohen (1976); Lee (1966). These studies used data of service charges on demand deposits as a proxy for the (negative) rate of interest on such deposits. This procedure is not without its drawbacks, as noted by Laidler in his paper on 'The Definition of Money' (1969a) p. 522. Finally on this subject see Barro and Santomero (1972).

During the course of the 1970s and into the 1980s, the high nominal interest rates that accompanied the worsened inflation in that period made the constraint on interest payments on demand deposits, whether self- or legally imposed, more financially burdensome. This led to (competitive) pressures to avoid such constraints. In the US, this primarily took the form of the developing use of deposit instruments – e.g., deposits with Money Market Mutual Funds (MMFs), NOW and Super NOW accounts, and Money Market Deposit Accounts (MMDAs) – that could be used for current payments transactions – (subject to certain limitations in some cases), but were not hindered by the legal prohibition on interest payment. In the UK, competitive pressures led to a widening range of banks, including the main Clearing banks from about 1984 onwards, offering (a range of) interest-bearing current accounts, with the interest rate in many cases varying with market interest rates, see Goodhart (1987). By the latter half of the 1980s, a sizeable, and rapidly growing, proportion of M1 deposit balances in both the USA and UK was interest bearing. The implications of this structural change are considered further in Chapter 10.

[1] When the alternative asset has a fixed nominal capital value the comparison between monetary yields over the appropriate period will also provide an estimate of relative *real* yields since inflation will affect the purchasing power of both assets equally. If, however, real assets, as well as financial assets with fixed nominal values, are substitutes for money, the expected rate of inflation should enter the demand for money function as a separate argument since it will affect the expected relative yield on real assets *vis-à-vis* money holdings.

same volume of money holdings would be demanded. The wealth elasticity of transactions balances should be zero. So long as planning periods are not extremely short some other capital-certain asset is likely to dominate zero interest-bearing money as a 'safe' asset in portfolios. Therefore, the volume of 'narrow' money balances held for such 'speculative' purposes is likely to have been very small anyhow. It is still, however, too early to assess fully how the demand for current accounts will respond to the payment of market-related interest on such balances. It is possible, moreover, that the volume of money held for precautionary purposes, to prevent the risk of unforeseen expenditure opportunities slipping away, responds positively to changes in wealth. Nevertheless, taken all in all, the micro-level analysis suggests that narrowly defined money balances would not have been responsive to changes in wealth, certainly much less than to changes in income, interest rates or transfer costs. Whether that will continue to hold true now that market-related interest rates are being paid on sight deposits remains to be seen.

The same conclusion does not hold, however, with respect to interest-bearing time deposits or certificates of deposits (CDs) issued by banks, which are generally included in broader definitions of the money stock. So long as the banks are not prevented by regulation (Regulation Q in the United States, for example) or by cartel agreement, they will presumably pay a competitive interest rate on time deposits and CDs. Indeed banks should be in an extremely strong position to compete for funds, which investors want to place in 'safe' assets, since their joint role in providing a means of payment offers some attractions to investors – e.g., ease and low cost of transfer into a means of payment, economy in management – which other interme-diaries or other assets – e.g., National Savings – cannot match. There is no reason to believe that time deposits or CDs need be dominated by other capital-certain assets as repositories for that part of their wealth which investors wish to keep in relatively safe form.[1]

Nevertheless, partly because of the difficulty of measuring wealth, the demand for money function in the economy is usually expressed as a function only of incomes (Y) and interest rates on alternative assets (r_i). Movements in nominal incomes are, however, usually divided into two separate components, changes in the price level (P) and in real output (y) respectively, on the grounds that there is reason to believe that the demand for money balances might respond differently depending on which of these components of nominal income varies. With given nominal interest rates a uniform higher level of all prices, including transfer costs, should theoretically lead to an exactly proportional increase in desired money balances – i.e., money holding should be homogeneous of degree one in prices.[2] Unless there is some form of money illusion, investors should be concerned to achieve their desired level of real money balances. This consideration has led some economists to relate the real level of money balances, M/P, to real output y, and relative interest rates. This is probably not the correct econometric procedure. In the first place, the homogeneity of money balances with respect to prices is an hypothesis, albeit a strong one, which still needs testing. In

---

[1] Moreover security, like convenience, may well be something of a luxury. As people get richer, they may be prepared to give up relatively more expected yield in order to be sure of retaining what they already possess. Fat cats are relatively more defensive than hungry cats. If so, the wealth elasticity of interest-bearing deposits could be greater than unity. In any case if (non-human) wealth was higher, but incomes, interest rates, etc. remained unchanged, one would expect investors to place part of this additional wealth with banks, in time deposits or CDs.

[2] C.f. Orr (1970, p. 197).

practice, however, this hypothesis does usually receive support in empirical tests. Rather more important, demand for money functions, certainly when estimated with quarterly data, are usually shown to involve lagged reactions to changes in the explanatory variables. These lags represent adjustment costs, delays in recognition of changing circumstances, etc. but taking M/P as the dependent variable usually involves the implicit assumption that the response of money balances to price changes is *instantaneous*, whereas responses to output changes and to changing interest rates are distributed over time.

Changes in real incomes (y) are not so likely to have an equi-proportionate effect on the demand for money. As real incomes *per capita* rise, transfer costs should not rise at the same rate, unless the technical progress responsible for the rise in real incomes has completely by-passed the payment-transmission mechanism. In reality, many of the most dramatic technical advances of recent decades have been in the field of data handling, the key technology in the payments process; the relative costs of making transfers should thus have declined compared with the average cost of goods and services in recent decades. Moreover, as incomes rise more companies (and wealthy individuals) will pass the point that makes it worthwhile for them to pay closer attention to cash management. With increasing transactions, as incomes rise, the law of large numbers should lead to economies of scale in cash management, so one would expect that the income elasticity of demand for money for transactions purposes would be less than unity, though this effect may be offset to some extent by greater affluence reducing the frequency with which people will find it 'convenient' to make transactions, whether between assets and money or goods and money.[1] This desired reduction in the frequency of transactions could raise both transactions and precautionary money balances, in the latter case because the reduction in the frequency of transaction will raise the variance of the cash flow. Even so, it seems difficult to believe that this effect would be sufficient to outweigh the available economies of scale in cash management as real incomes increase, so that the income elasticity of demand for money should be less than unity.

The various econometric studies of the demand for money, at least those under-taken using post-1945 data, virtually all show a lower income elasticity of demand for a narrow definition of money than for a broad definition including time deposits. Moreover, the estimates of the income elasticity of demand for money (even on a long-run basis after allowance for lagged responses), narrowly defined, are frequently lower than unity, implying some economies of scale. Estimates of the (long-run) income elasticity of demand for money, more broadly defined, on the other hand are frequently well in excess of unity. There is, however, no convincing reason why the *income* elasticity of time deposits or certificates of deposit should be so high: indeed, why should it be higher than the income elasticity of demand deposits? If wealth and interest rates were constant, while transactions and incomes in real terms were higher, there would presumably be a greater demand for time deposits as a second-line precautionary balance, but it is not immediately obvious why this second-line precautionary balance should show a great elasticity than demand deposits. The greater likelihood is that the estimated higher income elasticity of time deposits really is a reflection of a much higher *wealth* elasticity, and that the basic income elasticities of both monetary definitions are less than unity.

There have been controversies in the literature over the likely size of the income

---

[1] One of the distinguishing features of a rich society is how much less time is devoted to shopping, at least by those members of the society who have anything much else to do.

elasticity of demand, and over the associated question of the factors responsible for the long-period trends in the income velocity of money. Insistence that the income elasticity of demand for money is greater than unity[1] is hard, though not impossible, to reconcile with the basic micro-level theories about why people hold money – as distinct from the more reasonable argument that the wealth elasticity of 'safe' assets, especially those interest-bearing assets which dominate non-interest-bearing money balances, may be greater than unity. Nevertheless, no crucial point of macro-economic analysis rests on this issue. And monetary policy can be equally effective whether the income elasticity of demand for money is greater or less than unity, so long as the functional relationship is stable and predictable.

In contrast, the issue of the elasticity of demand-for-money balances in response to changes in yields on other assets has been a focal point for dispute between major schools of macro-economic theorists, between 'Keynesians' and 'Monetarists'. The main area of contention is whether money balances are particularly close substitutes – i.e., have a high interest elasticity – with a sub-set of alternative liquid financial assets, or whether money is a widely generalised substitute for all other assets, including real assets, goods, and so a close substitute with no single one of them. As discussed further in Chapter 12 on the transmission mechanism, there was wide-spread agreement in the earlier debates between 'Monetarists' and 'Keynesians' that monetary policy worked by causing changes in asset yields, thus inducing a divergence between the calculated present value of real assets and their cost of construction. But if money balances were a particularly close substitute for some subset of other financial assets, the implication would be that a monetary disturbance would have its initial effect in altering the yields, interest rates, on these assets, without much, or any, direct effect in changing the yields and prices of other assets (e.g., real assets) which were less good substitutes. So the effect on real demand would depend on the initial change in yields on such financial assets being transmitted in turn, via purchases of somewhat less liquid assets, further along the liquidity spectrum:

> The effect of a change in the money supply is seen to be like a ripple passing along the range of financial assets, diminishing in amplitude and in predictability as it proceeds farther away from the initial disturbance. This 'ripple' eventually reaches to the long end of the financial market, causing a change in yields, which will bring about a divergence between the cost of capital and the return on capital.[2]

The ultimate effect upon the demand for real assets was then, on this view, regarded as the final stage of a chain of responses to relative price adjustments, working outwards from money via substitute financial assets. The extent of this effect depended on the relative elasticity of the response of financial interest rates to the initial monetary disturbance, and of the response of the demand for goods and assets to changes in those rates. Furthermore, reasons were suggested why in some circumstances the transmission of monetary stimuli along the chain might be prevented or retarded. The classic example is to be found in the supposed possibility of a 'liquidity trap', a spectre raised by Keynes, which has been reformulated by Leijonhufvud[3] in terms of possible difficulties in forcing long rates in some cases to

---

[1] As Friedman maintained, for example in his paper 'The Demand for Money: Some Theoretical and Empirical Results' (1959a).

[2] Goodhart and Crockett (1970, pp. 159–98), quotation from p. 161).

[3] (1968); see, on this subject chapter IV; 5, V: 3 and VI: 2.

respond to movements in short rates that have been generated by monetary operations. More generally the length of this chain, and the flexibility of the links along the way, would reduce the stability and predictability of the relationship between money incomes and the money stock.

On the other hand, monetarists believe that money is not a close substitute just for a small range of paper financial assets. Instead money is thought to be an asset with certain unique characteristics, which cause it to be a substitute, not for any one small class of assets, but more generally for all assets alike, real or financial. Thus:

> the crucial issue that corresponds to the distinction between the 'credit' [Keynesian] and 'monetary' [monetarist] effects of monetary policy is not whether changes in the stock of money operate through interest rates but rather the range of interest rates considered. On the 'credit' view, monetary policy impinges on a narrow and well-defined range of capital assets and a correspondingly narrow range of associated expenditures ... On the 'monetary' view monetary policy impinges on a much broader range of capital assets and correspondingly broader range of associated expenditures.[1]

In simple terms, this means that if someone feels himself to be short of money balances he is just as likely to adjust to his equilibrium position by forgoing some planned expenditure on goods or services as by selling some financial asset. In this case, the interest elasticity of demand for money with respect to any one asset, or particular group of assets, is likely to be low, because money is no more, or less, a substitute for that asset – real or financial – than for any other. If the interest elasticity of demand for money is very low:

$$\left(\frac{dM}{di} \simeq 0\right)$$

then the macro-economic demand function for money is further reduced to the simple form, $M_d = f(Y)$. The implication of this is simple, that a monetary disturbance causing a disequilibrium between the supply of money (M_s) – assumed to be given and fixed by the authorities, but see further Chapters 6 and 10 – and the demand for money (M_d), must lead to an adjustment in nominal incomes[2] until equilibrium is restored.[3] Moreover, if the impact of monetary changes on the demand for real assets occurs by direct substitution, and not via a whole chain of substitution links involving a specified subset of financial assets (such as bonds and equities), then the

---

[1] Friedman and Meiselman, 'The Relative Stability of Monetary Velocity and the Investment Multiplier in the United States, 1897–1958', Research Study Two in *Stabilization Policies*, a series of research studies prepared by E. Cary Brown and others for the Commission on Money and Credit (1964). This passage (p. 217) provides an excellent statement of the theoretical basis of the monetarist viewpoint.

[2] The division of this change in nominal incomes into its components of changes in real incomes and changes in the price level is considered further in Chapter 13.

[3] Recall, however, the account from Chapter 3, Section 3, describing the problems that the empirical finding of long lags (i.e., large coefficients on the lagged dependent variable in the demand for money function) presented for this analytical approach – e.g., it should have led to severe short-term overshooting in incomes or interest rates.

Each individual member of the private sector will treat the expected level of expenditures and the yields on alternative assets as parameters, and adjust money balances to these in accordance with his demand for money function. At the macro-economic aggregate level, however, the authorities can, in principle, set the level of the money stock and force subsequent adjustments in interest rates and money incomes upon the economy. In this case the appropriate, single-effect of monetary policy on the demand for assets and goods cannot be approximately measured by the relative interest elasticities of the demand for money and for assets respectively (nor alternatively in terms of the relative slopes of the *IS* and *LM* curves).

Clearly, therefore, the form of substitution between money and other assets is of crucial importance in determining the role of money within the economy. Again, one's attitudes to this matter will be influenced both by *a priori* theoretical arguments and by the econometric findings. In my own opinion the *a priori* arguments give somewhat more support to the Keynesian than to the monetarist position. The monetarists argue that money can be distinguished from all other assets by its unique characteristics. Indeed, money does have certain special attributes as an asset, but then all assets have their own particular mix of characteristics–building society deposits, unit-trusts units, insurance policies, equities, houses, cars, factories, etc. have their own particular attractions. Moreover, time deposits, or certificates of desposits held with banks, are species of a rather broad genus of interest-bearing, liquid, capital-certain assets, including in the UK deposits with building societies, finance companies, local authorities and national savings. There are a number of alternative capital-certain 'temporary abodes of purchasing power.' Indeed, one could even claim on institutional grounds that time deposits had more close substitutes than many other types of asset. 'In a highly developed financial system (such as the United Kingdom system) . . ., there are many highly liquid assets which are close substitutes for money, as good to hold and only inferior when the actual moment for a payment arrives.[1]

If there was only one 'safe' asset available, money, then portfolio theory, as set out in Chapter 3, would suggest that the quantity of money held would depend on its own rate relative to the return and risk on the market portfolio of all risky assets, which would in turn be a function of the rates on all risky assets available and the covariances between them. In such circumstances, the elasticity of the demand for

---

equation relationship to estimate statistically would not be a macro-economic demand for money function, but a relationship linking movements in interest rates and/or money incomes, as the dependent variable, to current and past movements in the money stock; on this point see Sims, (1972). This concern that the structure of the empirically estimated relationship should accord with the direction of causality – i.e. whether the aggregate money stock should enter as a dependent or independent variable – does not itself have any bearing on the wider issues separating Keynesians and monetarists. Keynesians would not deny that the authorities could, in principle, control the money stock, but they would in such circumstances expect the direction of causation to run first through induced changes in interest rates on a subset of financial assets, and only subsequently to changes in money incomes. Thus, if the money stock was being autonomously controlled by the authorities, a Keynesian would tend to estimate a relationship with interest rates as the dependent variable, while monetarists would go straight to a money multiplier, relating changes in money incomes to current and past changes in the money stock.

Even though it does not cast light directly on the controversy between monetarists and Keynesians, the question whether the money stock is, in fact, autonomously determined by the authorities (so that estimating demand for money functions becomes inappropriate), is of much interest in itself. This is further considered in Section 2 and in Chapters 6 and 10. To anticipate these latter passages, the authorities, both in the UK and in most other industrialised countries, at least until recently, have mostly operated to control interest rates, and this does make the money stock, at least partly, endogenous, and a demand for money function, with money as the dependent variable, generally appropriate.

---

[1] Radcliffe Report, para. 392.

money to changes in the yield on any one other asset, assuming that each asset formed a fairly small proportion of the total portfolio, would indeed be low. But this is not the situation in fact. There are a number of capital-certain assets, competing for inclusion in the investor's holding of safe assets, and the degree of substitution between them should be relatively high.

The special characteristics of money stand out in greater clarity when money is narrowly defined as a means of payment. Other assets have not usurped money's role in providing a means of payment.[1] Nevertheless, the inventory theories, described in Chapter 3, suggest that the demand for money in its special role as a means of payment will not be insensitive to relative interest rates, though the interest elasticity of demand implied by such theory is well below unity, in the range from 0 to −0.5. This, however, still leaves open the question whether the elasticity is higher with respect to some subset of liquid financial assets than to the generality of assets, real and financial. Switches between money and other assets, in order to minimise the costs of cash management, will naturally take place with those other assets where transfer costs are lowest, for example bank time deposits, local authority call money, etc. This would suggest intuitively that the demand for money, narrowly defined, should be most sensitive to interest rates on such liquid, alternative assets and less sensitive, if at all, to interest rates on other riskier, illiquid assets with high transfer costs and imperfect markets.

In his study on *Cash Management and the Demand for Money*[2] Daniel Orr has challenged this widespread view. Assume a three-asset world, cash, some alternative, 'safe', liquid asset, and an earning risky asset (say the market portfolio). Then if transfer costs between assets are fixed (lumpy in Orr's phrase) irrespective of the size of transfer, 'the two accounts, cash and shorts [the alternative liquid asset], may in effect be managed independently of each other without significant departure from optimality'. In this case, 'the relevant interest measure [for cash management] is the "long" or "cost of capital" rate.' When transfer costs are proportional to the size of the transfer, however, which is the more normal case, 'the decision rule parameters for [managing] the shorts account and the cash account are interdependent,' and in this case, 'cash will be sensitive to both interest rates'. This analysis is, as Orr notes, of major interest since it gives some theoretical substance to the argument that the demand for money, at least narrowly defined, might be a general function of yields on longer, earning assets rather than a function on yields on other liquid short-term assets.

The *a priori* arguments would, therefore, suggest that bank time deposits should be relatively close substitutes with other capital-certain, interest-bearing assets. The interest elasticity of demand for sight deposits and currency might be expected to be considerably less, and the question of which interest rates are relevant for cash management decisions was reopened by Orr after years in which the consensus view had been that the yields on alternative liquid assets would be the appropriate measure.

Many of the issues discussed in the course of this Section appear capable of

---

[1] The set of assets which is acceptable as payment for transactions is not, however, immutable over time; it has changed in the past and could so again in the future. If people should find it economically advantageous to accept, and to proffer, other financial claims in payment for transactions, then the set of assets which is to be described as money will alter. See further Section 2 and Chapter 2.

[2] Chapter 6. (1970).

resolution by empirical examination – e.g., whether the demand for money function is stable and predictable, whether the interest elasticity of demand for money is low, or high. Most of the empirical exercises to examine these issues have taken the form of running a single equation relating the stock of money, as the dependent variable, to various alternative series of interest rates, nominal incomes, real output, price indices, wealth, etc. as explanatory variables. I had earlier hoped that stronger empirical tests of these hypotheses, about the form of the demand for money function, might be achieved by giving explicit recognition to the fact that money balances represent one asset among many within the total asset portfolio; by examining the simultaneous response of sets of assets, including money balances, to disturbances, it is possible to impose and to test additional constraints upon the values that the coefficients in the system should take. Given the difficulty of discerning clearly from econometric exercises between alternative hypotheses in a system where most variables tend to move together and the available time series are quite short,[1] procedures that allow more searching empirical tests to be undertaken have attractions.

In the first edition of this book, I included a lengthy Appendix setting out how such portfolio adjustment models might be set up and estimated. In the event, alas, the additional insights provided by such simultaneous equation modelling of portfolio adjustment have been more limited than I had earlier hoped, and most further empirical work in this area, as we shall see, has continued to be done on the basis of single-equation estimates.

2.   The Progressive Collapse of Stability in the Demand-for-Money Function

As the discussion in Section 1 indicated, a number of crucial issues, with important implications for both theory and policy, were at stake in the estimation of demand-for-money functions at the macro-economic, aggregate level. Some of these issues, which had figured prominently in the literature before the barrage of econometric testing took place, largely in the 1960s and 1970s, appear to have been resolved to most people's satisfaction. In particular, there has been a general consensus in the empirical findings that the demand for (narrow) money is significantly inversely related to interest rates on altenative financial assets, but that this elasticity is well below unity. Accordingly, neither an extreme 'Monetarist' position, which posited a possible zero interest elasticity, nor an extreme 'Keynesian' position, which hypothe-sised that money was a very close substitute for other financial assets, were supported by the facts.

On the other hand, with respect to certain other crucial issues in this field, empirical findings and opinion seem to have shifted over the course of the last fifteen years, as the passage of time brought forth new data. One such crucial issue concerns the stability of the demand for money. Judd and Scadding begin their review article on 'The Search for a Stable Money Demand Function: A Survey of the Post-1973 Literature' (1982) with an account of why this issue is so important.

---

[1] One aspect of this problem may be illustrated by reference to the difficulty of distinguishing, for example, between different versions of the consumption function. In their paper, for instance, on 'Short-run Consumption Functions for the UK, 1955–66' Chapter 3 in Hilton and Heathfield (eds) (1970), Hilton and Crossfield set out a number of alternative variants of this function, the majority of which have R^2 values above 0.995.

They state that the desideratum is 'a set of necessary conditions for money to exert a predictable influence on the economy so that the central bank's control of the money supply can be a useful instrument of economic policy'. For this to be so, they argue, the demand for money function should exhibit three characteristics. First, it should be highly predictable in a statistical sense, involving criteria of goodness-of-fit, stability, out-of-sample forecasting powers, etc. Second, the function should be relatively simple, with few arguments. Finally, the variables that do appear as arguments in the function should embody significant linkages between the monetary sector and spending and activity in the real economy.

From the time, in the 1950s and early 1960s, when Milton Friedman[1] put the issue of the nature of the relationship between movements in the money stock and in nominal incomes back at the top of the agenda for macro-economic analysis and study, a massive amount of effort has been expended in the study of the empirical relationships between movements in the money stock, prices, output and interest rates, many, perhaps most, of these in the form of demand-for-money single-equation estimates. An account of many of the earlier studies is given in Laidler (1969) and, with more emphasis on UK results, in Goodhart and Crockett (1970). However, the *locus classicus* for finding a lucid description of the state-of-the-art approach to modelling the demand for money in this earlier period is Stephen Goldfeld's paper, 'The Demand for Money Revisited' (1973).

In this paper, Goldfeld examines a large number of alternative formulations of this function, but concludes that a relatively simple and conventional form of the function fits the data most satisfactorily. This is:

$$\ln m_t = a + b \ln y_t + c \ln r_t + d \ln m_{t-1}$$

where '$m = M/p$, assumed to be noninterest bearing – [is fitted] to "the" interest rate, r, and some measure of economic activity such as real GNP – $y = Y/p$, where M = money holdings, P = price level, and Y = gross national product' (1973, p. 580).

After a somewhat exhaustive examination of alternative formulations, Goldfeld's main conclusion was that:

> Perhaps most interesting is the apparent sturdiness of a quite conventional formulation of the money demand function, however scrutinized. More particularly, such a function yields sensible interest and income elasticities. The income elasticity appears to be significantly less than unity and can be pinned down reasonably well on the basis of quarterly data. In addition, the conventional equation exhibits no marked instabilities, in either the short run or the long run. Finally, the conventional equation yields a reasonable speed of adjustment to changes in income or interest rates, with patterns and magnitudes of adjustment that are generally similar in the Koyck and Almon specifications (p. 632).

Indeed, on several occasions Goldfeld records how stable the function appears to be. Thus (on p. 590) he comments that 'On the whole, the money demand function does not exhibit marked short-run instability'; again (p. 592):

> On balance, then, the evidence does not seem to suggest any need to estimate the money demand equation over separate subsamples of the postwar period.

Nor was Goldfeld atypical, or isolated, in his view that a stable relationship in the

---

[1] Key works include 'The Quantity Theory of Money – A Restatement', in Friedman (ed.) (1956); Friedman and Meiselman (1964); Friedman and Schwartz (1963).

form of a demand-for-money function had been empirically established, as can be seen by reference to the 1970 work of Laidler and of Goodhart and Crockett (1970).

Considering the careful academic qualifications expressed by Goldfeld, it would be hard to accuse him, or most of his colleagues in the field, of hubris in reporting his finding of a stable relationship. Yet fate, virtually instantaneously, began to upset that conclusion. Thus, Judd and Scadding note, (1982, p. 994) that:

> Prior to 1973, the evidence that had accumulated from the large body of research done over the postwar period was interpreted as showing that a stable demand function for money did, in fact, exist.

They go on (p. 995):

> But starting in 1974, forecasts from this equation [Goldfeld's preferred 1973 equation] began to seriously overpredict real money balances.

This failure of M1 balances to rise as fast as predicted in the USA over the years 1974–76 became known, in the title of Goldfeld's subsequent paper (1976, pp. 683–739), as 'The Case of the Missing Money'.

Judd and Scadding (1982) provide an exhaustive review of the studies, primarily on US data and in the form of single equation, demand-for-money functions, that attempted to explain this initial lapse from prior stability. The most common explanation was financial innovation. The argument was that rising interest rates during the inflationary period following the first oil shock had made holding zero-yielding monetary balances more expensive. It then became worthwhile to overcome learning and set-up costs to organise more efficient ways of handling and minimising such balances – e.g., by overnight security repurchase agreements (RPs). Since there were a variety of such innovations, some of whose effects were unquantifiable, research workers tried to proxy their effects by including interest rate ratchet variables, on the grounds that each new peak in interest rates triggers off further innovations, whose effect, once learnt, is irreversible. Other economists[1] argued that with alternative, 'better', specifications of the demand-for-money function, much of the apparent forecasting error using Goldfeld's original equation could be explained away.

By the time that Judd and Scadding were assessing the reasons for such instability, one of the promising areas for future inquiry that they considered was whether the relationships between money, incomes, interest rates, etc. were best modelled as a single-equation demand-for-money function. Thus, they raised the question of 'money supply exogeneity' and suggested that:

> the correct dynamic specification is not independent of the direction of causation between the quantity of money on the one hand, and the arguments of the money demand function – interest rates, income and prices – on the other (p. 1012).

Single-equation modelling of the demand-for-money function would thus seem to involve the assumptions *both* that the authorities allow the stock of money to adjust quite passively in response to the demand from the public, which in turn depends on the arguments in the demand-for-money function; and that there are no shocks to the *supply* of money (independent of shifts in demand), that would in turn feed back to nominal incomes, interest rates, etc. The first assumption would obviously fail during periods when the authorities were trying to hit monetary aggregate targets – e.g., in

---

[1] Such as Hamburger (1977).

the years 1979–82 – but would be consistent with the earlier practice of the authorities of trying to select, over short periods, an appropriate level of interest rates, and then providing whatever quantity of money was demanded by the public at that level of interest rates.

But even if the authorities were pegging interest rates, there still remains the possibility of independent shocks to the supply of money, i.e. the second assumption above might fail. Brunner and Meltzer (1976) noted that pegging interest rates also accommodated changes in the demand for (bank) *credit*. Changes in the demand for credit are not synonymous with changes in the demand for money, so fluctuations in the demand for bank loans could lead to changes in the supply of money under this policy regime not matched by an increase in the demand for it. Hence a policy of pegging interest rates does not preclude instances when the demand for money must adjust to changes in supply, rather than vice versa.

This latter consideration was particularly important in the UK. For various reasons,[1] a broad monetary aggregate, M3, rather than the narrow aggregate, M1, had become the main focus of concern in the UK. Following the introduction of a more competitive regime, 'Competition and Credit Control', which swept away direct ceilings on bank lending in 1971, there was an upsurge, an explosion, in bank lending to the private sector, largely funded by liability management, which raised M3 far above the level that would have been predicted on the basis of current and past incomes and interest rates. Attempts to incorporate the effects of such liability management in the demand-for-money function by adding variables representing the own-rate of interest and also some measure of the spread between the own-rate on wholesale deposits and bank lending rates were generally successful, in the sense that such coefficients were found to be significant, but did not serve to eliminate the greater part of the forecasting error in the period 1972–5.[2]

The consensus, then and subsequently, was that the prior stability of the demand-for-money function had broken down under pressure from a major money *supply* shock. Moreover, subsequent explorations of demand-for-money functions for M3 (and the later revised definition £M3) have, almost universally, continued to report that no stable function has re-appeared since; (unlike M1, for which a stable demand function could be estimated until 1984–5, at which time a rapid increase in the volume of newly available interest-bearing sight deposits undermined the previously esti-mated function). But, if the main direction of causation ran from, partly exogenous, fluctuations in the money stock to incomes, interest rates, etc. then a money demand equation was not the appropriate functional form to fit. Artis and Lewis[3] were the first to seize on this point, and responded by transforming the single-equation demand function for money into a single equation with 'the' interest rate as the dependent variable. This had a number of problematical aspects; for example, why should one assume that the variable adjusting to monetary supply shocks was the level of interest rates[4] rather than output or prices? Again, since interest rates in such

---

[1] Briefly outlined in Goodhart (1986c).

[2] See Hacche (1974).

[3] Artis and Lewis (1976).

[4] There has been some tendency in the US literature to regard *the* variable that adjusts to money supply shocks as being the price level. With the dependent variable in most US studies of the demand-for-money function being *real* money balances (i.e., log M-log P) it is possible to reinterpret these equations *not* as demand-for-money functions at all, but as a rather convoluted and curious form of price adjustment equation, see Carr, Darby and Thornton

equations also appeared to adjust slowly, this implied that during the adjustment process following a money supply shock, money holdings would be forced out of line with underlying demand. These considerations led, in the UK and in some other countries, towards the adoption of the buffer stock approach to money holdings, as already outlined in Chapter 3, Section 3. In this latter approach, supply shocks cause actual money holdings to deviate from the long-term underlying level demanded, since individual agents treat their money holdings as buffer stocks; this deviation of actual from underlying demand thereafter influences *all* expenditure and portfolio decisions, a form of real balance effect, potentially affecting financial portfolios, interest rates, and expenditures on goods, output, prices and nominal incomes simultaneously.[1]

The predictive failings of the econometrically estimated demand-for-money functions in the years 1973–6 took place, however, during a most disturbed period of severe supply shocks – e.g., the first oil shock. Moreover, the more general, policy-directed claims of monetarists, that an acceleration (deceleration) in money growth would be followed by a short-term expansion (recession) in output, in turn succeeded by a more permanent accompanying increase (decrease) in the rate of inflation, appeared to receive strong support in the configuration of the world cyclical, inflationary experience in these years. For such reasons, academic qualifications about the form and stability of the relationships between money and nominal incomes were put on one side in the generalised move by the monetary authorities in most major developed countries, in the mid-and latter parts of the 1970s, towards the adoption of intermediate monetary targets as a financial anchor and public commitment in the struggle against inflation. Furthermore, in retrospect, the years 1976–8 were, for that decade, comparatively calm with relatively few external shocks or policy regime changes, during which standard demand-for-money functions began to recover their previous econometric poise.

All that changed again in 1979 and subsequently. A second oil shock was followed by a change in the US monetary control regime, introduced by Paul Volcker, Chairman of the Federal Reserve Board, on 6 October 1979 (see further Chapter 15), while in the UK the newly elected Conservative government committed itself to a much firmer policy of declining monetary targets for £M3, at the same time as it allowed the price level to be influenced by factors, such as an increase in VAT and a post-incomes-policy jump in public sector wages, that were bound to impart a major upwards kick to price levels. Under these kinds of pressures, the fragility in the statistical relationships between money and nominal incomes, which had surfaced before in 1973–6, became even more pronounced in the early 1980s; this was most apparent in the Anglo-Saxon countries (USA, Canada, UK, Australia, New Zealand), if not in some continental European countries (West Germany, Switzerland, Austria), where neither inflation nor policy regime changes had been so marked. Furthermore, it became increasingly noticeable that the most extreme examples of breakdown in previously regular money stock–nominal income relationships oc-

---

(1986), Cuthbertson and Taylor (1987). Particularly in view of the prevalence of a degree of price – wage stickiness, reviewed in Chapter 1, the validity of treating the general price level as the variable adjusting to shocks, even in a quarterly model in which output and interest rates are treated as predetermined, seems dubious.

---

[1] See Davidson, 'Disequilibrium Money: Some Further Results with a Monetary Model of the UK', Chapter 5 in Goodhart, Currie and Llewellyn (1987).

curred in the case of those aggregates which had been chosen as *the* intermediate monetary target.[1]

This breakdown increasingly focussed attention on the question of whether the causal relationships between money and nominal incomes, etc. should not be regarded as dependent upon the institutional context and policy regime of the day. If these factors changed then one might also expect the macro-economic calculated equations to alter.[2] When the policy regime changed, not only the statistically estimated coefficients, but even the appropriate meaning and form of equation to fit could change also.

This argument was adopted by Gordon.[3] He argued, (pp. 404–5), that given the multiple interactions within the economy between the nominal money supply, real output, the price level and interest rates, 'the short-run money demand functions estimated heretofore may be better viewed as interesting reduced forms than as structural equations that provide estimates of coefficients corresponding to structural parameters derived from the theory of portfolio choice.' So shifts in the estimated coefficients in such so-called demand-for-money functions might reflect, in addition to changes in portfolio behaviour, regime changes or instability in coefficients in related equations – e.g., in the Phillips curve.

Gordon illustrated this point later (1984, pp. 417–19), by showing that a reduced-formed equation with real money balances as the dependent variable will exhibit major changes – e.g., to the signs of the coefficients of certain key arguments – when the authorities change over from a monetary control rule targetting the level of interest rates to one in which the monetary base is targetted – e.g., on the basis of a feedback control rule relating the desired base to real output and inflation. Gordon notes that some investigators have estimated demand-for-money functions over varying sample periods with the stated intention of studying changes in the calculated income and interest rate elasticities of the demand for money: 'Yet such coefficient shifts may tell us more about changes in policy rules than about the characteristics of the underlying money demand function'.

A clear example of the changing reduced-form connections between variables, as policy regimes alter, is to be found in the nature of the short-term relationship between monetary growth and nominal interest rates. In the earlier literature, both Keynesian and monetarist, it was expected that in the short run faster monetary growth would be associated with lower nominal interest rates, as the first effect would be to shift the *LM* curve to the right, with price levels and expectations given. Studies of the response of interest rates to unanticipated *announcements* of monetary growth prior to the adoption of more determined monetary targetting in 1979 generally showed an insignificant reaction. Once committed monetary targetry was adopted in the US and UK in 1979, both casual observation and econometric studies[4] reported a strong, significant *positive* relationship between nominal interest rates and the

---

[1] An illustration of Goodhart's Law, 'that any observed statistical regularity will tend to collapse once pressure is placed upon it for control purposes' (1984, p. 96).

[2] Thus, it was argued that the comparative stability for the demand-for-money functions over the period 1870–1970, for example as estimated by Friedman and Schwartz (1982) owed a great deal to the underlying stability both of the form of the banking system and of the authorities' policy regime in that century; see, for example, Hall (1982), pp. 1552–6).

[3] (1984) Part 1, pp. 403–24.

[4] The large literature includes the following: Smith and Goodhart (1985) Goodhart and Smith (1985) Part 1; Cornell (1983); Grier (1986); Hardouvelis (1985).

unanticipated element in the monetary announcement. There remains, however, dispute whether this relationship represents a policy anticipation effect (i.e., the authorities will have to tighten and raise interest rates because monetary growth is higher than desired), or results from a shift in expectations about future inflation, output and demand for money. My own view on the balance of the evidence, notably the concomitant movement in exchange rates, is that the former explanation is more important. Certainly, once the degree of the authorities' own commitment to monetary targets began to wane – e.g., in the late summer of 1982 in the USA – the strength of the market's response to the announcement also declined.

There are, therefore, a number of explanations (*not* mutually exclusive) to explain the recent fragility in the statistical relationships between monetary movements and those in nominal incomes. I have concentrated so far primarily on two such explanations. The first is that supply shocks can cause monetary holdings to diverge (temporarily) from an underlying (stable) demand for money function, the buffer-stock hypothesis. The second is that changes in policy regime can change the short-term interrelationships between money, interest rates, output and prices. Yet both these explanations concentrate primarily on short-term deviations and disturbances to the relationships. Gordon (1984) suggests that we could, perhaps should, jettison the whole concept of a short-run demand-for-money function, but states (p. 406) that:

> The concept of the long-run demand for money plays such a central role in macroeconomic theory that it is difficult to imagine living without it.

Yet the changes in the apparent trend rates of growth in certain monetary aggregates, and in velocity, notably of £M3 in the UK, in recent years have been too marked to explain convincingly in terms of short-term disturbances or regime changes. The path of the velocity of £M3, shown in Figure 4.1 shows a major disturbance in 1972–3 which returns to trend in 1976 after an acceleration in inflation. From 1979 onwards, however, the slope of the trend appears to have decisively altered. Inflation and

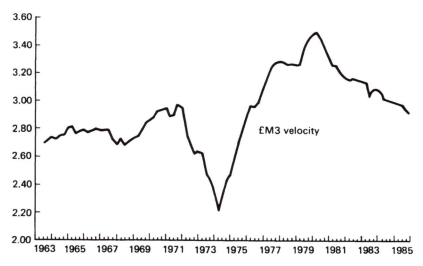

FIG. 4.1

nominal incomes fell, but monetary growth did not. It has become hard, if not completely impossible, to attribute this entirely to a cumulatively worsening supply-side overhang, though fears that some such situation may exist continue to worry the authorities. Nor do regime changes provide a straightforward explanation, since it is hard to see why a policy shift intended to lead to a more determined reduction in the pace of monetary growth should have had a diametrically opposite result.

In the main, the explanation for such recent longer-term phenomena is attributed to financial innovations. In some cases, both the nature and effect of such innovation is obvious and quantifiable. Thus, in the case of M1 in the UK, it is abundantly clear that there has been a remarkable surge in holdings of interest-bearing sight deposits in response to the recent innovation of paying market-related interest rates on such deposits, with some of that increase being switched from non-interest-bearing M1, currency holdings and deposits, and part from other assets. Such cases, where innovations take the form of paying interest on deposits on a more generous basis than formerly, will lead to changes in apparent growth rates that can be appropriately recognised and adjusted by the use of divisia indices, as already noted in Chapter 3, Section 3. The complexity of such indices has, however, hindered their introduction and use for public and policy purposes.

In other cases, however, the nature of the financial innovation affecting monetary growth cannot be adequately measured solely in terms of the changes to the own-interest payable on deposits. The cost of intermediation can be measured by the *spread* between the rate offered by banks on deposits and asked by them on their loans. If the rate of interest on deposits is no lower than the rate obtained by banks on their assets (a zero spread), and there is any net benefit in obtaining intermediary services, (e.g., liquidity), then it would be sensible for all agents to sell assets to, and borrow from, the bank up to an infinite amount, increasing their bank deposits without limit at the same time.[1] In other words, the demand for intermediary services is a function of the price – cost of intermediation itself – i.e., the spread. Perhaps the best of a rather unsatisfactory set of explanations of the remarkably rapid growth of bank and building society lending to the private sector and, simultaneously, of the build-up of private sector liquidity with these intermediaries in the UK in recent years, is that competition and innovation, in credit markets as well as in the form of deposit liabilities, has led to a significant cheapening of the effective spread, or cost of intermediation, and this change in relative price has resulted in a structural increase in the use of such intermediation.

This analysis indicates that one should not look at longer-term trends in the comparative quantities of various financial assets held without a rather wider consideration of such institutional – structural changes. Such structural changes will not, however, necessarily all point in the same direction. At the same time as competition in domestic markets for the business of the smaller, retail customer is leading to an upsurge in mortgage lending and personal sector deposits, various factors are causing the banks to become more cautious and less competitive in the wholesale markets for their operations with sovereign borrowers and large multi-national companies. This latter factor is leading to such wholesale business passing directly through securities' markets (i.e., securitization), with the banks' involvement shifting from their balance sheet (i.e., loans and deposits) to off-balance sheet involvement (e.g., contingent facilities, brokerage fees, arranging swaps, etc.)[2]

[1] See Miller and Sprenkle (1980).

[2] On all this, see the Cross Report, *Recent Innovations in International Banking* and the (1986) issue on Financial Innovations in the *Oxford Review of Policy Issues*. (November) 1986.

The last two decades have been a period of rapid structural change involving a breakdown in the functional divisions between the various classes of intermediaries – e.g., banks, building societies and security market institutions – in a milieu of greater competition. In such circumstances, definitions that depend on such functional divisions lose their clarity. Perhaps the closest historical analogy to the present ferment of structural change in the financial system occurred in the UK in the middle of the nineteenth century, notably with the growth of the deposit-based joint stock banks. That occasion led to a long-running dispute over the definition of money; for example, considerable debate occurred concerning whether the definition included deposits as well as notes. The present breakdown of structural barriers is also likely to confuse the question of the appropriate definition of money. Not only is a wider range of financial institutions able to provide payments' services on deposits – e.g., building societies following the passage of the 1986 Building Societies Act – but also a futher range of institutions – e.g., securities houses and mutual collective investment trusts – may provide payments' services to customers whose assets with them are *not* in nominally-fixed-value deposits but vary in line with the intermediaries' own portfolio asset values. If this latter trend should develop on any large scale,[1] then the whole question of the definition, quantification and interpretation of monetary quantities would become much more problematical and uncertain, as further considered in Chapter 8.

---

[1] As I have argued that it might, see 'Why do Banks need a Central Bank? (1987a).

V
The Principles of Intermediation

Summary

Intermediaries perform several functions. The traditional view of such functions is addressed in Section 1. First, they alleviate market imperfections caused by economies of scale in transactions in financial markets and in information gathering and portfolio management. Among intermediaries, whose main rationale is to be found in this role, are the various investment trusts, unit trusts, pension funds, etc. If it was not for such imperfections, everyone could in theory manage his own financial assets as well as a trust manager. Secondly, intermediaries provide insurance services: people dislike the prospect of accidents such as fire, injury, burglary, and are quite prepared to accept lower mean expected incomes (after payment of insurance premia) in order to insure against the risk of a severe reduction in living standards. These forms of financial intermediation need not involve much risk-taking by the intermediary: the unit trust, whose existence depends on economies of scale, can perform its functions at a profit while matching its assets with its liabilities, while the insurance company can match its assets to the actuarial expectation of its contingent liabilities.

The third, and archetypal type of financial intermediation, involves issuing liabilities of a kind preferred by lenders (at relatively low yields) and investing a proportion of the funds in higher-yielding earning assets of a form which borrowers prefer to issue. The intermediary attracts funds from the public by offering varying combinations of redemption terms – e.g., the date of its maturity, concomitant services and interest payments. If the intermediary offers very liquid liabilities, it will in general have to maintain a larger proportion of low-yielding reserves in its portfolio in order to honour its redemption obligations; so there will normally be an inverse relationship between the liquidity of the intermediary's liability and the rate of interest offered in it, an extreme example being the low yields offered on sight deposits.

In some part, the preference of savers for liquid assets and of borrowers for loans of longer-term maturities can be regarded as a form of insurance against the timing and magnitude of future uncertain cash flows. The desire of depositors for such insurance cannot, however, be provided by a standard insurance contract, since the desire to spend early is privately, not publicly, observable. The role of information asymmetries in determining the need for, and form of, financial intermediaries provides the main theme of Section 2, which sets out the newly emerging theory of financial intermediation.

One of the crucial information asymmetries is that the executives of most businesses know considerably more about their current and future prospects than anyone else. This hinders the development of public markets in the assets of such private-sector firms. There are means of overcoming this asymmetry, via signalling methods and the use of information gathering and disseminating agencies, e.g., auditors, credit rating agencies, etc., but there are limits to their usefulness. Given the absence of well-functioning markets in primary securities issuable by smaller companies and persons, the bank acts as a substitute for such incomplete markets by specialising in assessing credit risk and monitoring loan projects. Such asymmetries of information imply that the optimal loan contract will be of a fixed interest form, supported by collateral and/or bankruptcy penalties and, analogously, the optimal bank liability will also be a fixed interest deposit supported by a buffer of bank capital.

Having discussed the various functions undertaken by financial intermediaries, we then turn in Section 3 to the question of whether there is anything special about banks, as compared with other financial intermediaries (OFIs), in the determination of their respective equilibria, or in the adjustment process to that equilibrium. In both cases the *equilibrium* conditions have to be assessed within a portfolio adjustment framework in which there is *no* fundamental, or significant, difference between the economic context facing banks as compared with OFIs. On the other hand, the impact and dynamic adjustment path resulting from a supply-side shock within the banking system may differ from that arising from a supply-side shock elsewhere, in so far as the counterpart to bank asset expansion is more commonly absorbed in buffer-stock monetary adjustment.

1. The Role of the Intermediary – 1

Because of risk aversion, reinforced by the wish to avoid bankruptcy, there will be a tendency for private-sector borrowers to issue financial liabilities with a life till maturity related to the expected life of the investment to be financed, and in a form (e.g., equity or debt) which reflects to some extent the degree of uncertainty of the proposed investment project. The preferences of such borrowers may not match closely the 'preferred habitats' of personal-sector lenders. Because of their need to keep a sizeable proportion of their assets in liquid form for transaction and precautionary purposes, personal-sector lenders may exhibit a greater preference for shorter-dated assets in capital-certain form than private-sector borrowers would wish to provide, *ceteris paribus*. An excess supply of long-dated, relatively risky, private securities and an excess demand for short-dated, capital-certain, private-sector securities could, therefore, develop. This would lead, naturally, to a rise in yields on long-dated securities and a fall in yields on short-dated securities in order to tempt both lenders and borrowers out of their preferred habitats,[1] in order to restore

---

[1] It is for some reason more common to think of variations in yield tempting *lenders* to depart from their preferred habitat, to take up a riskier portfolio, than it is to consider the possibility of *borrowers* also shifting from their preferred habitat. For example, Leijonhufvud, *On Keynesian Economics and The Economics of Keynes, passim,* (1986) e.g., pp. 202–3, 282–314, 354–85, 401–16) argues that Keynes believes that speculators with regressive expectations might prevent falls in short-term interest rates being translated to the long end of the bond market. But this (if true at all) would be a serious barrier to the successful contra-cyclical use of monetary policy only if borrowers for investment projects were also deterred by risk aversion, or by the same speculative (expectational) considerations, from financing their projects with shorter-dated liabilities.

equilibrium.[1] Certainly the yield curve has had an upward slope more often than not.

This disparity between the preferred habitats of private-sector lenders and borrowers need not, however, extend to the economy as a whole. The private-sector borrower wishes to tailor the time pattern of his liabilities to the expected profile of his returns from investment, in order largely to avoid the dangers of illiquidity and possible bankruptcy. But the government cannot go bankrupt, at least in a closed economy, nor need it worry about liquidity. It can pay off its maturing liabilities by issuing more legal-tender currency. In those cases when the currency is in some part a commodity money (e.g., with gold or silver content), the government can raise the required commodities by taxation, or expropriation, in order to pay its liabilities. The limits to a government's domestic credit are political rather than economic; it can be overthrown but not bankrupted (see Chapter 2).

So the public sector can issue short-dated liabilities, based on its power to levy taxes, with an insouciance which cannot be matched by commercial firms. The public sector is thus in a position to restore the balance between the demand and supply of assets of differing characteristics, either by issuing relatively more short, capital-certain assets to finance its own long-term capital expenditure, or even by acting directly as an intermediary, buying up long-dated private-sector securities with the proceeds obtained from issuing short-dated liabilities to the public.[2] Even in countries where the role of the public sector is most narrowly limited, it still usually provides important intermediary services, in the sense that the issues of public-sector debt tend to alter the overall balance of debt outstanding more nearly in line with public preferences for assets to hold.

Such intermediation should reduce the margin between yields at the long and short end. However, as noted in Chapter 2, the government will be deterred from issuing large quantities of currency, which as legal tender will be accepted at zero interest by the public, for the purpose of reducing longer rates by fears of the likely inflationary consequences which could, *inter alia*, have perverse effects both on the level of nominal interest rates and even on the demand for official currency (if endemic inflation leads the public to seek currency substitutes). Nor have governments on the whole been very adventurous in tailoring the characteristics of their liabilities to suit the varying preferences of the public for differing combinations of return and risk, sticking in the main to standard kinds of fixed-interest debt. An exception to this latter dictum is provided by the UK government's initiative in providing indexed debt in the early 1980s. The topic of indexation is examined at greater length in the Appendix to Chapter 13.

Although in principle the public sector should be capable of providing full financial intermediary services within the economy, in practice it has not done so very

---

[1] *Per contra*, the empirical studies on the term structure of interest rates, reported in Chapter 11, reveal very little evidence of such segmentation in markets and, instead, show that the term structure can be reasonably well explained by one or other version of the expectations theory. Nevertheless, the general arguments for believing in some degree of segmentation in financial markets are so compelling that I feel disinclined to accept that empirical evidence at face value.

[2] During the early 1980s, the monetary authorities in the UK pursued an opposite tack, in order to slow down monetary growth in the face of a surge in bank lending. Long-term debt was sold to the private sector and the funds in excess of the PSBR were used to redeem and/or purchase short-dated assets from the banking sector. Although it could be argued that the growth of institutional savings, via insurance companies and pension funds, had shifted the preferred habitat for savings, nevertheless the process of 'overfunding' the PSBR appeared unnatural to most observers.

extensively, and the provision of such services has been largely left to the private sector. The interplay of the preferences of lenders and borrowers, in the context of information and transaction costs which they face, has led to the development of various distinguishable kinds of intermediary service by the private sector.

The first function of intermediation is to alleviate the market imperfections caused by economies of scale in transactions in financial markets and also in information gathering and portfolio management. Included among intermediaries, whose main rationale is to be found in this role, are the various investment trusts, unit trust and also, perhaps, pension funds.[1] If it were not for the above imperfections, everyone could in theory manage his own accrued assets as well as a trust manager. In those cases when the main function of intermediaries is of this kind, overcoming market imperfections, it is not necessary for them, in order to show a profit, to adopt a risky position with the maturities of their assets not matched to, and usually longer than, the maturities of their liabilities. The existence of transactions costs, and imperfect markets, makes some kinds of matching intermediation profitable. Economies of scale in both brokerage and management make it cheaper for the small investor in equities to acquire an adequately diversified holding by buying shares or units in investment funds than he can do by himself. The manager of such a fund runs the risk of having the inflow to his business decline, and his judgement questioned, if his portfolio does not perform comparatively well, and faces risk common to all unit-trust managers of shifts in the public's demand for equities, but subject to observing proper, non-fraudulent business conduct he runs no risk of either illiquidity or insolvency.

Similarly, there will generally be considerable economies of scale in arranging loans to, or new issues for, businesses in large single units, rather than in many smaller portions. The size of such loans, or new issues, may well be beyond the ability of any one person, or even institution, to finance, at least without devoting an excessively large proportion of their portfolio to that one security, so that it may be desirable to divide the provision of the required finance among many investors. Intermediaries of varying kinds have the expertise, information and market advantages to specialise in 'splitting bulk' (as wholesalers and retailers do for commodities) in this way. The intermediary may, perhaps, do no more than introduce the lenders and borrowers to each other, a pure brokerage service. Or it might go further and hold the liability of the borrower on its books as an asset, or as a contingent asset (e.g., an acceptance), matched by a liability of an exactly equivalent form. In this case, however, the

---

[1] The conditions under which pension funds operate also, in practice, provide a way of forcing most income recipients to save more than they otherwise would voluntarily do. The justification for imposing such forced saving, other than for the purposes of allowing a higher level of investment expenditure at full employment, is that people may suffer from a form of myopia, in which they discount future consumption and value current material gratification to a greater extent than the actuarial uncertainties of life and death really warrant. It is possible that many people recognise their excessive susceptibility to current temptations and will actually be grateful for some compulsion in this respect. For example, many sign on for regular savings programmes (i.e., in Christmas clubs or with insurance schemes) in part as a method of self-control over the use of income. In an analogous vein I would go to the dentist only on crisis occasions if I had to book the day ahead, since the prospect of immediate discomfort would outweigh the known greater longer-term benefits. Therefore, I arrange a booking some weeks ahead so that both the discomfort and the benefits of the visit are reasonably distant. Having booked the visit, inertia and shame force me to keep it. This line of analysis reappears in Chapter 15, with a discussion of precommiting rules vs discretion, and time inconsistency.

intermediary, despite maintaining a balanced portfolio, does run the danger of debtors defaulting. It is, however, the specialised knowledge of borrowers' credit-worthiness that makes such intermediation profitable. Beyond that, of course, the intermediary may take advantage of yield differentials, caused in part by divergences in preferred habitats, to obtain a profit by raising money from lenders on cheaper terms than it on-lends to borrowers, but that takes us into consideration of another function of intermediation.

The second main type of services provided by intermediaries covers insurance. The natural hazards facing people often seem to have a probability distribution exhibiting considerable negative skewness. Thus the chances of early death, or fire, or burglary, or accident, etc. are quite remote, but when such accidents do occur they leave the unfortunate victim(s) much worse off. So the probability distribution of expected incomes in the face of such natural hazards may look rather like that shown in Figure 5.1, where the tail on the left represents those suffering the occasional serious accidents of life. It is a recognised fact that most dislike negative skewness, and are prepared to receive a lower mean expected income in order to offset the skewed distribution. This can, of course, be achieved by buying an insurance claim which will pay out in the event of one of these accidents occurring. The premium that will have to be paid for such coverage will depend on the actuarial probability of such accidents, and also the extent to which the probabilities of occurrence can be actuarially established, the yield which the insurance company can obtain on the assets which it holds, the profit margins in the insurance business, etc. Even when the expected income distribution is not skewed, people may want to insure against falling into the lower tail of the income distribution. People will often accept a lower mean income, if by doing so they can reduce the variance (riskiness) of prospective outcomes.

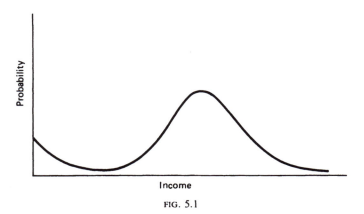

FIG. 5.1

Intermediaries providing insurance services can also do so perfectly well while continuing to maintain a matching portfolio, relating the form and maturity of their assets closely to the actuarial expectation of their liabilities. The expected variance of the calculated actuarial outcomes will, however, lead them to maintain certain additional precautionary balances among their assets. It should be, however, possible in principle to distinguish between the service of providing insurance and holding a matching portfolio against such contingent liabilities, and the services of intermediation between borrowers and lenders with differing preferred habitats, taking advantage of the resulting yield differentials. Insurance companies may undertake certain intermediary services of the latter kind, through the management of their asset portfolio, in addition to their main function.

Not only do people dislike negative skewness, but there are also some signs that they would prefer to be in a situation where they face a positively skewed income probability distribution. A small chance of a large gain is worth having even if the purchase of this chance reduces the mean expected income very slightly. A gamble of this kind adds to the spice of life, whereas a gamble in the face of a negatively-skewed distribution raises fears because people are apt to exaggerate in their own minds the probabilities of dramatic events.[1] There is evidence, for example, that the demand for premium bonds is a function of the size of its largest prize rather than of its mean expected yield.[2] The football-pool organisations felt it necessary to vary their method of scoring drawn matches in order to lower the probability and thus raise the much publicised top-prize for selecting a given number of (score) drawn matches. In this respect several kinds of gambling which offer a very small chance of a large prize against a relatively small entry fee, represent a form of financial intermediation (state lotteries and premium bonds do so explicitly); this is the obverse of insurance, which for a relatively small entry fee will offset the material results of low-probability disasters.

Although intermediation of these kinds, based on specialised information or the provision of insurance, is important, the archetypal financial intermediary is one which makes its profits by issuing liabilities of a kind preferred by lenders, accordingly at relatively low yields, and invests a proportion of the funds obtained in higher-yielding assets of the form which borrowers prefer to issue. This is possible, in particular, because the intermediary services carried out by the public sector have not resulted in a closure of the margin between the yields on very short, sight liabilities and longer-dated liabilities. The gap between the zero nominal yield on legal tender (it makes no difference for this purpose whether such currency is full commodity money, e.g., gold-based coinage, or fiat money with a zero production cost), and the positive yield on longer-dated assets thus makes it profitable for intermediaries to bid for cash until the marginal cost of attracting another unit equals the marginal return obtained from buying some other longer-dated asset.

So the third, and main, form of intermediation involves taking advantage of these differing preferences of borrowers and lenders by issuing liabilities of a kind attractive to lenders at relatively low yields. The intermediaries offer liabilities, often in a fixed value, capital-certain form, which possess certain advantages of security, yield and ancillary services such as bookkeeping, financial advice, favoured access to loans, etc. which may suffice to attract lenders, leading them to substitute the liabilities of these intermediaries among the assets in their portfolio in place of other assets – e.g., public-sector debt, including currency, or other private-sector debt.

The purchaser of any asset, real or financial, must proffer, and the seller will anyhow demand, final settlement for the deal at some stage in a means of payment,

---

[1] The work of Professor G. L. S. Shackle is particularly interesting and stimulating on this whole subject; see his seminal book on *Expectations in Economics* (1949) and his response to the debate which that book caused in his subsequent book on *Uncertainty in Economics* (1955, Part 1).

[2] See Rayner (1969).

money. If a financial intermediary makes its own liabilities more attractive to wealth holders – say, by offering a higher rate of interest – so that wealth holders are induced to shift out of asset i into holding more of the intermediary's liabilities, the transition must take two stages, first a sale of asset i for money and then the deposit of such money with the preferred intermediary. A financial intermediary, even if it is a bank (some of) whose own liabilities serve as money, can always attract more monetary (cash) reserves to support its own liabilities, by bidding for them. An individual bank which makes its deposits more attractive will obtain a positive balance with other banks in the clearing house. This will not raise the cash reserves in the banking system as a whole, but the resulting increase in bank, and other private-sector, interest rates (when the reserve base is squeezed) relative to the yields on public sector, and foreign, assets will lead people to shift out of these latter assets. If they then sell such assets back to the public sector, they will obtain monetary claims on the government (currency or deposits at the Central Bank – high-powered money), which will mainly end up deposited with the banks.

The banks' (the intermediaries') capacity to attract cash – by bidding for it – is not limited by their ability to get the public to substitute directly between bank deposits (financial-intermediary liabilities) and the currency (money) which they, the public, already hold. If the banks (the intermediaries) can induce the public, by offering better terms, to sell other assets for legal tender (for money) and subsequently place such currency (money) with themselves, then their reserves will rise just as much as if they had induced the public to switch directly out of currency (money). Of course, the banks' ability to obtain cash is conditioned on the authorities' willingness to accommodate the public's desire to switch out of the other assets via currency into bank deposits at a price which makes the transfer still desirable. But under several common circumstances, for example when the government has fixed the exchange rate or is seeking to stabilise or peg interest rates, this will be the case for a range of assets such as foreign assets or public-sector debt, particularly those forms of public-sector debt such as national savings which have a fixed capital value or are shortly due to mature. Naturally, the corollary also holds that the authorities can act in such a way as to limit the access of the public to additional cash, except at unfavourable prices; even in the case of national savings, which can be redeemed at fixed values, in some cases virtually on demand, the authorities can respond – if they so desire – to any increase in the rates offered by intermediaries to depositors by raising the rate offered on national savings.

Just as sellers of an asset will insist on being paid in money, so equally purchasers of any asset will be concerned to establish the terms upon which they can subsequently realise that assey for money, that is whether the asset is marketable or not, whether the issuer has specified the terms on which he will be prepared to redeem the asset e.g., at call, at short notice, after some specific maturity, and whether the issuer will be ready (albeit applying some penalty) to redeem on request before the due maturity. In order to attract lenders to deposit money with themselves, financial intermediaries have to compete for funds by offering attractive redemption terms, as one dimension of the set of incentives (including interest payments), which they offer to depositors.

In so far as they stand ready to redeem their own liabilities, the intermediaries will require monetary reserves to honour these obligations. Even the banks, (some of) whose own liabilities count as a means of payment, will require cash reserves against their monetary liabilities to meet outflows of cash. This will be in some small part to meet the possibility of an increased desire by the public for currency, but to a much greater extent to meet potential cash drains resulting from imbalances in inter-bank clearings or from net payments by the private sector to the public sector or to foreigners. Both of these latter sectors may have a limited willingness to build up and to hold claims on the domestic banking sector and will usually require their net claims on the banking sector to be settled in a manner involving a transfer of high-powered money (the monetary liabilities of the public sector).

The general public's use of currency forces the banks to hold additional till cash, but otherwise is not a crucial element in determining the needs by banks for cash reserves. Indeed, the arrival of a cash-less society would leave the banks' requirement for reserves (other than in the form of till cash) relatively unaffected, since these are determined to a much greater extent (ignoring predictable seasonal and holiday variations in the public's currency demand) by the need to settle irregularities in inter-bank clearing and also net payments flows between the private sector on the one hand and the public and overseas sector on the other.

If *everyone*, including the public sector and foreigners, was prepared to accept the liability of any intermediary, whether it be bank, building society, or insurance company, as final settlement for any debt, then the deposits of that intermediary would become equivalent to legal tender for all practical purposes. Then such intermediaries could issue paper without having to offer any interest or other costly service, and with a virtually zero production cost they could expand their deposits indefinitely,[1] using the proceeds to buy up all other assets until inflation became so rampant that the public was induced to switch to other assets as a means of payment, or until their power to act in this way was restrained by political forces. The necessary constraint on the banking system (*a fortiori* on the financial intermediaries) is that some payments, which could perfectly well be settlements between the banking system and the authorities – in which the public plays no direct part – have to be made in cash, legal tender.[2]

Thus all intermediaries, including banks, will have to maintain sufficient monetary reserves to honour their redemption obligations. These obligations depend on the specific redemption terms offered by the intermediary on its liabilities. In general, the longer the maturity and/or the higher the penalty cost of early redemption, the less likely is an early drain of reserves from the intermediary, so the smaller reserve ratio need be held.[3] With deposits of a form that allow a larger proportion of the

[1] This subject was explored in a provocative but, in my view, confused way by Pesek and Saving (1967); certainly readers of this book should also refer to some of the critical reviews, for example by Johnson (1969, pp. 30–45, especially pp. 31–7) and Marty (1969, pp. 101–11). At this stage in the analysis we are concerned with the determination of the volume of deposits; questions of wealth effects arising from the actions of banks and intermediaries, which were also raised by Pesek and Saving and discussed in these reviews, are considered later on in Chapter 12.

[2] One might ask what would happen if there was no dominant base money extant into which financial intermediaries had to make their liabilities convertible. While this remains a purely hypothetical scenario, it would still be possible in such a system to prevent intermediaries from exploiting their opportunity to extort seignorage (by imposing an inflation tax) with the requirement that intermediaries purchase licences in the open market that allow them to issue (legal tender) notes and sight deposits. Variations on this theme have been played by Fama (1980) and Duck and Sheppard (1978).

[3] Over medium-length periods, say of six months to one year, however, the need of the public to maintain an adequate holding of a means of payment to carry on normal expenditures and the relatively low interest elasticity of such means of payments may well make the longer-term stability of aggregate holdings of demand deposits greater than that of time deposits, so that the overall portfolio of assets held against current accounts can, perhaps, be more 'unbalanced'

counterpart proceeds to be invested in earning assets, a profit can still be made even though a higher yield will have to be offered to offset the attractions of deposits with shorter maturities and easier reconversion arrangements. So there can be a spectrum of capital-certain assets issued by intermediaries, with those offering deposits of longer maturities and with tougher penalty clauses having, in general, to proffer higher interest yields, and with those providing assets with more favourable redemption terms (which forces them to keep additional low-yielding monetary reserves to honour these obligations) giving lower interest payments.

At the limit, financial intermediaries can offer sight deposits, which can be redeemed in legal tender on demand without penalty. When a payee in some deal is satisfied with the reputations of both the payer and the intermediary to be ready and able to honour their commitment to pay legal tender, if required, the payee will very often be prepared to accept payment by the transfer of a sight claim on the intermediary rather than in cash. The transmission of cash involves certain costs of transport and safekeeping avoided by cheque transfer, and the latter also puts some of the book-keeping costs on the intermediary.

So, once their reputation (their 'name' in financial parlance) became established, there was a natural tendency for intermediaries offering sight deposits (essentially banks) to become involved in operating a payments transmission system. This process was cumulative, since the transmission services offered to holders of demand deposits increased the attraction of such assets. Something of a division has, therefore, developed between sight deposits with accompanying payments transmission services, and all other time and notice deposits offered by intermediaries, on which transmission services are only offered grudgingly, if at all. The willingness to offer sight deposits, and associated payments transmission services, which makes such deposits an acceptable means of payment, is one possible distinguishing mark between banks and other financial intermediaries. It is, however, not a very clear dividing line, since many well-established financial intermediaries (e.g., merchant banks) may consciously discourage their clients from using their services for effecting regular payment transactions and yet would regard themselves as proper banks. Conversely, certain savings institutions, such as the Trustee Savings Banks in the United Kingdom, which have not traditionally formed part of the banking sector are now offering depositors limited facilities for making cheque payments.

If the yield on longer-dated time deposits has, in general, to be higher than that on short-dated deposits, how must the yield on demand deposits compare with the fixed zero yield on currency? On the whole holding demand deposits is safer, easier and more convenient than holding cash, and a payment by cheque rather than through

---

than the portfolio held against time deposits. Moreover in many countries, including the United States and the United Kingdom, banks generally refrained, until the end of the 1970s at least, whether by convention or by regulation, from offering any interest on current accounts. So, not only was the aggregate demand for such deposits relatively insensitive to variations in yields on other assets, but the demand for deposits with each individual bank not greatly affected by inter-bank competition. That state of affairs has, however, now been fundamentally altered by the innovation of paying (market-related) interest on *chequeable* deposits. The implications of this are considered further in Chapter 15. In contrast, the aggregate demand for time deposits is likely to be more strongly affected by variations in relative yields, and the demand for such deposits with any one bank will probably respond sensitively to inter-bank competition. So from a prudential point of view, one could make out a good case for applying a higher reserve ratio to time deposits, especially to large deposits obtained through the money market, than to demand deposits.

cash brings with it certain recording and book-keeping services, which is one reason why any slightly dubious transaction, which transactors like to keep 'off the record', is normally settled in currency. For most purposes, therefore, demand deposits, at the same yield, are superior to cash in convenience. People would prefer to hold demand deposits even at some small negative rate of interest; that is, indeed, what they pay in bank charges. Bank charges, which represent in part a fee for the use of transmission services and in part a payment to the banks for safekeeping and other services, allow the banks some leeway to discriminate between customers, depending on the size and activity of their respective balances.

To conclude, the first priority for any intermediary must be to attract money from the public, by providing liabilities with a combination of yield, conditions of payment, etc. that prove attractive to the public and yet allow the intermediary the prospect of a reasonable profit. Unless it can obtain money from the public in the first place, it can hardly take advantage of any specialised opportunities in lending.

2. The Role of the Intermediary – 2

One of the fields within monetary economics where theoretical and analytical advances have been most successful in extending our understanding in recent years has been the reassessment of the fundamental principles of the role and functions of intermediation itself. In Section 1 of this chapter, which recounts the theory of intermediation as it was broadly understood circa 1973, intermediation was attributed to three main functions:

1. overcoming imperfections owing to economies of scale and information in transactions;
2. insurance;
3. differing holding period preferences for savers and lenders; information costs and problems were regarded as important, but in a rather vague and general manner.

Currently, the role of transactions costs, while still relevant and in certain circumstances crucial (e.g., in explaining mutual collective investment funds such as unit trusts), is regarded as less central to the analysis of intermediaries, while greater importance is attached to the associated problems of incomplete financial markets and informational asymmetries. Thus Leland and Pyle (1977) write (p. 382):

> Traditional models of financial markets have difficulty explaining the existence of financial intermediaries, firms which hold one class of securities and sell securities of other types. If transactions costs are not present, ultimate lenders might just as well purchase the primary securities directly and avoid the costs which intermediation must involve. Transactions costs could explain intermediation, but their magnitude does not in many cases appear sufficient to be the sole cause. We suggest that informational asymmetries may be a primary reason that intermediaries exist.

Again, Bernanke (1983) writes (p. 263) that:

> We shall clearly not be interested in economies of the sort described by Eugene Fama (1980), in which financial markets are complete and information/transactions costs can be neglected. In such a world, banks and other intermediaries are merely passive holders of portfolios. Banks' choice of portfolios or the scale of the banking system can never make any difference in this case, since depositors can offset any action taken by banks through private portfolio decisions.

Before we proceed to examine the nature and form of the key informational asymmetries, and how they help to explain why financial markets are incomplete, we turn to the latter two functions of intermediation noted in Section 1 – i.e., insurance and the reconciliation of differing preferred habitats between savers and lenders. It has been appreciated recently that these two functions are closely related, in the sense that the differences in the preferred habitats between ultimate lenders and borrowers can be analysed in terms of their search for insurance against untoward contingencies. Ultimate lenders – savers – thus prefer, on the whole, a more liquid asset as protection against the contingency that they will need to undertake higher (than currently foreseen with certainty) expenditures in the near future. Because production processes are quite lengthy, and capital equipment is long lived and often has a poor second-hand market (see discussion in Chapter 1), borrowers will often only be able to pay back lenders after some lengthy time lag. In the meantime they will be illiquid, and will wish to protect themselves against the contingency of having to repay their borrowing at an early date – e.g., by undergoing the uncertain process of trying to raise replacement funds from some other lenders on possibly much worse terms. Indeed, as Lewis shows in his paper of this title (1986), one can treat 'Banking as Insurance'.

This approach has been rigorously formalised and analysed by Diamond and Dybvig.[1] They construct a model where consumers – savers – face a risk of needing to consume in the first period of a two period model and where producers – borrowers – have access only to an illiquid technology which provides a positive return in period 2.

The first question that this approach should induce is that, if the basic function is one of insurance (of early need for funds among savers; against premature requirement for funds among borrowers), why then is the need not met through an ordinary insurance contract? It should be possible for an agent to lend directly to the ultimate borrowers and simultaneously take out an insurance contract to be activated in the case of early need for liquidity.

The problem with such use of insurance is that the subjective, perceived need for early expenditure on consumption is privately observable only by the person involved.

Diamond and Dybvig thus consider two types of consumer,

> Type 1 agents care only about consumption in period 1 and type 2 agents care only about consumption in period 2... Each faces a privately observed, uninsureable risk of being of type 1 or of type 2... By comparison, if types were *publicly* observable as of period 1, it would be possible to write optimal insurance contracts that give the *ex ante* (as of period 0) optimal sharing of output between type 1 and type 2 agents.

In this context of privately observed, and thus asymmetric, information, 'banks can be viewed as providing insurance that allows agents to consume when they need to most' (quotations from pp. 405–6).

In the Diamond and Dybvig model, consumers can invest their endowments in the basic technologies themselves (i.e., lend directly to ultimate borrowers), using the two available instruments: a liquid, but unproductive storage technology, and an illiquid, but productive technology. Because agents 'can write only unconditional contracts as there is no public information on which to condition', those who have the misfortune to be type 1 agents will find that prices will be such that they will be able only to

---

[1] Diamond and Dybvig (1983).

obtain consumer goods as if they had put all their endowment in the unproductive storage technology. Direct investment would thus not provide any insurance in this model against early liquidity needs. Instead, the bank can provide a degree of insurance by paying a yield greater than zero to early withdrawers and a yield less than that available on the more productive investments to the later withdrawers, thus providing a degree of insurance against the risks of being an early, rather than late, withdrawer.

In order to make such interest payments, the bank has to invest a proportion of its assets in the illiquid, but productive technology, which by definition yields nothing if realised early. Accordingly, if the bank underestimates the number of depositors who do withdraw early, it may not have assets available to make its promised pay-off to the later prospective type 2 withdrawers. Consequently, given that the deposit contract involves 'a sequential service contract which specifies that a bank's pay-off to any agent can depend only on the agent's place in line', Diamond and Dybvig can show how bank runs are generated, with type 2 agents seeking their money back before they really need it; their analysis therefore also provides an explanation for the role of deposit insurance.

While the general concept of banking as insurance and the particular approach of Diamond and Dybvig are helpful and illuminating, they do not on their own provide a complete explanation for the particular *form* of banking that exists. The liquidity insurance argument suggests why investors will put their funds with an intermediary, but does not suggest why the intermediary will primarily make fixed interest loans, nor why the returns on bank liabilities should not be contingent (as is equity) on the earnings of its assets.[1]

It may be argued that the provision of liquidity involves immediate access to payments' services, and that this requirement means that liquid deposits must be almost immediately convertible *at par* into cash (the dominant base money). I believe, however, that this is not so, either in theory or practice (see Goodhart, 'Why Do Banks Need a Central Bank?' (1987). It is already the case that money market mutual funds in the USA, Merrill Lynch Investors Account holders, and certain other collective investment funds will provide certain limited payments services on the basis of claims upon them which are *not* fixed in nominal value terms, but vary in value according to the fluctuations in the market value of the fund. While it is certainly true that the varying market value of collective investment funds would make the fund holder uncertain of how large a cheque she could draw at any time before exhausting the value of her funds, similarly a depositor at a bank that offers overdrafts is often uncertain both as to the exact current state of his account (since monitoring is costly, see Chapter 3), and how much overdraft the bank manager will give before refusing to honour the cheque. Payment facilities are thus quite normally in that sense probabilistic, whether offered by a bank or collective investment fund. There may be inhibitions about making payments out of assets (intermediary liabilities) that vary in nominal value over time, but I believe that such inhibition is probably due to familiarity with the existing traditional payments' system. Instead the main reason, in my view, why the payments' system has remained based on the banking system's deposit, or giro payment, has been the massive economies of scale historically

---

[1] See Bernanke and Gertler (1985) especially note 7, where they refer to Jacklin (1985) to support their claim that, 'In the Diamond-Dybvig model, for example, there is nothing to prevent banks from offering equity contracts which perform the insurance function', (Jacklin, 1985).

established in the supply of payments' services (e.g., the branch network, clearing house and other fixed costs). Technological changes – e.g., electronic transfers and automated teller machines (ATMs) – may radically change the production possibilities for providing such services, allowing a possibly far wider range of intermediaries to offer payments' services on the basis of a much more diverse set of assets–liabilities.

So, at least in theory, the archetypal financial intermediary *could* be one that took a direct *equity* stake in a diverse portfolio of companies and offered investors a claim which was liquid in the sense of being instantaneously cashable but whose value varied in line with the value of the assets in the intermediary's portfolio; in other words, a unit trust offering payments' services. Yet this is exactly what we do *not* observe. Unit trusts do not generally offer payments' services and banks largely hold fixed interest loans, a large proportion of which are not even marketable, and issue debt, fixed interest deposits, of differing maturities against themselves. Why should this be the prevailing state of affairs?

In order to explain this I believe that we have to turn to another informational asymmetry. A major asymmetry exists because entrepreneurs and company executives know far more about the conditions and prospects for their own company, private inside information, than anyone else. We have already seen the importance of this in our earlier discussion of market structure in Chapter 1. This same asymmetry is again of crucial importance in influencing the structure and nature of financial markets and intermediaries.

As a general matter, borrowers will have much better inside information on their prospects, notably for making future payments on equity or debts contracts, than anyone else. As we saw in Chapter 1, the higher the ratio of insider trading and information to general liquidity trading, the larger the market maker's spreads, and the costs of transaction, would have to be, and the less the likelihood of establishing a well-functioning open market in such securities. Indeed, efficient, broad, liquid asset markets in private company securities (as compared with public sector debt) are a relatively recent historical phenomenon.

There are several ways of trying to overcome this informational asymmetry and to enhance the public availability of information on the 'true' value and worth of companies. It is, of course, to the benefit of successful companies to have such information revealed, since such knowledge will increase their marketable net worth. The problem is that other, actually less successful, companies will want to make outsiders think that they too are successful by dissimulating their true position.

One response to this latter problem is for the more successful companies to try to signal their better results in a fashion whereby the inherent incentives would deter less successful companies from mimicking the more successful. One such signal is for the owner and company executives to buy an increasing proportion of their own equity, see Leland and Pyle (1977), and the references to the literature on signalling equilibria in markets therein. The disincentive to an executive in a truly *unsuccessful* company buying more of his own equity is obvious. Indeed, company analysts do watch and analyse directors' and executives' purchases of shares in their own companies; the danger of manipulation of this signalling tactic is of such magnitude, however, that company law prevents any such inside purchases/sales during periods of special sensitivity (e.g., just before announcements of annual results). It is often argued that dividend payments represent another form of signalling. Given the comparative tax disadvantages to dividend payments, relative to sales of equity by shareholders, whose value should rise with the availability of retentions, it is difficult to explain the continuation of the custom of dividend payment unless such payments provide other benefits – services – such as signalling continued confidence in the company. However, exactly how such signalling really works has not been rigorously analysed and there remains no satisfactory explanation yet of the dividend puzzle.

Another approach to the information asymmetry problem is to pay somebody, or some institution, to spend resources and time in providing independent, publicly available, information on the company. The archetypal institution of this kind is the accountant who audits the company's books and professes himself satisfied that they provide a 'true and fair' account. Several other information producing entities also exist, such as credit rating agencies, financial newspapers, various consultants, etc. The role of such information producers was nicely analysed by Ramakrishnan and Thakor in their paper on 'Information Reliability and a Theory of Financial Intermediation' (1984). They were primarily worried about the problem of how to organise the incentive structure to encourage the information producer to exert the optimum amount of effort to produce correct information, and they argued that information producers will tend to merge together to form intermediaries partly in order to take advantage of easier internal monitoring of effort. In my view, the quality of information production is more generally sustained by the possibility of repeat purchases over time in a context where 'reputation' is crucial (also see the discussion in Chapter 1).

A more serious problem for independent information production relates to the method of payment. If the firm pays the information producer, there must arise some concern that the firm will pay more, hire the agency more often, etc. if the reports are favourable, than otherwise. If the firm hires the independent information producer, is its independence compromised? For example, in the case of accountants faced with a client company which wants to window-dress its published accounts, there will be a tension between desire to maintain reputation on the one hand and desire to keep business on the other.

There is, therefore, an inherent difficulty in having the companies themselves financing the independent information production. There is also a problem in getting the using public to finance it, since such information, once obtained, becomes a public good. It, therefore, becomes difficult for the information producer to recoup the cost of the exercise from users by normal pricing methods.[1] It has been suggested that, in conditions where the public good attributes make collection of such information for publication unrewarding, the value of that information can be internalised by having the intermediary buy the assets for its own portfolio. The fact that published accounts will *subsequently* reveal such purchases, so that any systematic information available to information-collecting company X will be publicly revealed by observing its actions, is not a serious hindrance to its portfolio transactions since the intermediaries' activities cannot be instantaneously and continuously monitored. Thus, if others in the market revise upwards their estimate of company Y because they observe that company X has bought its shares, the time lags in the process will allow company X a capital gain from the difference between its purchase price and the subsequent revaluation as others follow the leader. If markets worked so perfectly that there were

---

[1] The whole question of how information is produced, collected and disseminated, and the cost structure and methods of remuneration of information producers, is both important and yet insufficiently researched and analysed. Again, this may be a legacy of the neoclassical assumption of perfectly clearing markets in which all such informational problems are assumed away.

no such lags, there could be no return from collecting information, and we would be back with the paradox outlined by Grossman and Stiglitz (1980).

Although signalling devices and information producing intermediaries can help to overcome some of the problems caused by information asymmetries, the difficulty and costs of establishing open markets in primary debt – equity – instruments remain formidable. There are sizeable set-up costs involved as part of the process of obtaining a new listing. Moreover, if the company is relatively small and unknown, and trading volume small, the size of spread will be so large that the market will be relatively imperfect. So, for small, even perhaps medium-sized companies, *pro tanto* for persons, the option of raising funds from issues of marketable securities simply does not exist. At the time when banking was first developed, asset markets only existed for government debt and for a handful of private-sector chartered companies.

In this sense financial markets have been, and remain, incomplete. When banks moved outside their original function of providing safe-keeping for the deposit of specie and valuables (cloakroom banking), the particular skill that they had to learn was to choose among borrowers and lending projects which did *not* provide marketable securities for them to buy. This leads on to the question of what is the optimal form of contract for a banker to provide to a borrower who has private inside information about his own project which the lender cannot observe publicly. This question has now been rigorously studied, notably by Diamond (1984) and Gale and Hellwig (1985). The conclusion of these studies is that the optimal contract will be in the form of debt supported by non-pecuniary bankruptcy penalties (and or collateral), which will be imposed in the case of short-fall in repayments of interest and principal. Thus, when it is costly, or impossible, to monitor the true outcome of a project, for which money has been borrowed, the best solution is to offer debt contracts of the kind which banks and building societies actually provide. Such contracts are a method of bypassing incomplete markets.

Just as borrowers from banks have private information on their own condition not publicly available to banks, so banks have private information on their own condition not publicly available to their depositors. By analogy to the preceding analysis the optimal contract which lenders should make with banks is also a fixed-interest debt contract. Moreover, with the majority of both assets and loans denominated in broadly similar terms, fluctuations in interest rates, for example, will have a broadly offsetting effect on bank liabilities and assets. Consider what would happen to a financial intermediary whose assets were primarily in equity or indexed form, but whose liabilities were mainly in fixed-interest nominal debt form, or vice versa. In so far as the value of its assets was subject to different sources of variation from those of its liabilities, then the intermediary would be extremely, unsafely unbalanced, and its net worth would fluctuate sharply.

The latest 'new view' of financial intermediation sees the key function of banking as residing in its role of making fixed-interest loans, in conditions of information asymmetry, thereby overcoming the inefficiencies due to incomplete financial markets. The same conditions determine that the liability structure of such intermediaries will also be primarily in fixed-interest debt form. The provision of payments services, by contrast, is inessential to the function of banking,[1] and might be just as well, or

---

[1] Although the provision of payments services is not essential to the function of banking, the information obtained by bankers from observing the payments' flows of their customers may provide useful information about their comparative credit-worthiness as potential borrowers, see Section 3.

perhaps better, carried out by other kinds of financial intermediary (see Goodhart, 'Why Do Banks Need a Central Bank?' (1987a)).

This reassessment implying that the crucial feature of banking lies in the particular nature of its *asset* portfolio, consisting largely of non-marketable and non-marketed loans, is recent. Until the last few years much of the analysis of banking proceeded, explicitly or implicitly, upon the assumption that bank loans were no different from other marketable securities. See for example the surveys by Santomero (1984) and Baltensperger (1980).

The new approach closely follows the line of argument pursued by Bernanke and Gertler (1985), as the following quotations (pp. 1–5) make clear:

> The basic premise is that, in the absence of intermediary institutions, financial markets are incomplete. This incompleteness arises primarily because of certain informational problems. By specializing in gathering information about loan projects, financial intermediaries help reduce market imperfections and thus facilitate lending and borrowing. Accordingly, changes in the level of financial intermediation due to either monetary policy, legal restrictions, or other factors, may have significant real effects on the economy... When embedded in a broader general equilibrium setting, this model implies that banks play an important role in real allocation and are not merely financial veils. Critical to this result is the premise that both banks and depositors have private information about certain aspects of their respective opportunities and needs. With no private information financial intermediation would be irrelevant to economic activity, as in the Miller–Modigliani analysis.
>
> There are three distinguishing characteristics of banks that are particularly important for our purposes. First, banks specialize in the provision of credit for projects which, because of high evaluation and monitoring costs, cannot easily be funded by the issuance of securities on the open market. The information intensity of bank investments, in turn, makes it difficult for outsiders to ascertain the value of bank assets at any given moment. Second, banks finance their lending by the issuance of liabilities which are, for the most part, non-contingent claims, and which are typically more liquid than bank assets. Finally, bank capital (although small relative to bank assets) plays a vital role as a 'buffer' – i.e., the existence of capital allows banks to meet fixed interest obligations despite variations in deposits or asset returns... We begin our simplified analysis of the banking sector with the assumption that there exists a pool of potential investment projects which are costly both to evaluate and to audit if undertaken. We assume that banks are able to perform two intermediary functions, at a cost: First, they determine which projects in the pool are viable and worthy of investment. Second, they monitor the projects in which they invest depositor funds in order to determine their true *ex post* returns. We hypothesize that there exists an informational economy of scope in *ex ante* and *ex post* project evaluation to motivate why a single institution performs both of these functions. Further, it is assumed that the banks' evaluation and auditing technology requires a fixed set-up cost, which discourages individuals from independently evaluating projects.
>
> The information that a bank obtains, about both *ex ante* project viability and actual *ex post* project returns, is taken to be the private knowledge of the banker. This assumption is admittedly overstated, but it reflects what many argue is a crucial aspect of banking; the intimacy and privateness of the relationship between banks and their loan customers (especially long-term customers with complex or non-standard credit needs). For example, Diamond (1984) gives an excellent exposition of how banks typically establish a close relationship with loan customers, which is maintained through the application process and throughout the life of the loan; this extended relationship is necessary to monitor whether loan covenants are being satisfied. As

Diamond argues, because information about the current status of outstanding loans is costly to obtain and highly idiosyncratic, it is not easily observed by bank depositors or other outsiders. For our purposes, the assumption that banks' information is private is a convenient way to introduce agency costs in banking in a manner that makes the general equilibrium analysis tractable. One can view our postulated information structure and its implications as a stand-in for a more complex agency model.

Although simple, the above framework allows us to motivate the three features of banking given above. First, the fixed cost of the evaluation and auditing technology explains the need for specialisation (by banks) in the provision of credit for certain projects. Second, the premise that the information a bank acquires about its loan projects is not publicly observable rationalises in a simple way, and in a way consonant with the agency-cost approach, the heavy reliance of banks on debt finance. Since bank creditors cannot directly observe the return on the bank's portfolio, they will not accept claims with returns contingent on this information, because of the potential for dissembling on the bank's part (the moral hazard problem). It follows that equity contracts are inadmissible, and that banks must issue debt to finance investment. Finally, the privateness of the bank's portfolio and the associated reliance of the bank on debt finance implies that banks must hold a 'buffer stock' of capital, in order to guarantee the returns on their liabilities. Depositors will accept non-contingent claims only from banks which can meet their obligations under all possible outcomes of their respective portfolios. Hence, banks must have net assets in order to self-insure, in the absence of comprehensive federal deposit insurance. It follows, as will be seen, that the degree of financial intermediation by banks depends critically on the availability of capital in the banking sector... Once we have developed the model of banking described above, we will embed it in a stylised general equilibrium framework. using this framework, we will argue that banks matter to real activity mainly because they provide the only available conduit between savers and projects which require intensive evaluation and auditing. Factors which affect the ability of the banking system to provide intermediation, or which affect the cost of intermediation, will therefore have an impact on the real allocation. Among the factors affecting intermediation, we will show, are adequacy of bank capital, the riskiness of bank investments, and the costs of bank monitoring. We will show also that our model is potentially useful for understanding the macroeconomic effects of phenomena such as financial crises, disintermediation, banking regulation, and certain types of monetary policy.

I shall consider some of these implications – e.g., for credit rationing, for the transmission mechanism of monetary policy, for the role and functions of Central Banks, etc. – in subsequent chapters. The one remaining issue examined here is the question whether innovations may be removing capital market imperfections, increasing the completeness of coverage of financial markets, and hence removing the need for the existence of banks. This thought is prompted by the growth of techniques to allow the development of securitisation, and of secondary markets in assets such as mortgages which previously had been non-marketable. Thus in the US, and prospectively in the UK, individual mortgage loans originated by one financial intermediary can be packaged together and resold as a *marketable* security to other purchasers, financial intermediaries or even ultimate lenders. There are some suggestions, perhaps even plans now, to try to transform other kinds of traditional non-marketed bank loans into marketable securities, for example loans made to purchase cars for which the car bought can act as collateral.

Where the borrower is, however, a sovereign country, a public body or a large company, borrowing through the open market has for decades been an alternative to bank borrowing. The choice between the two for this kind of borrower depends on relative cost and convenience. Following a decade (the 1970s) in which the trend was for an increasing proportion of lending to be undertaken via bank intermediation (e.g., bank syndicated lending), in the 1980s the trend has been for the 'securitisation' of such lending, with bank involvements in brokerage, providing contingent facilities, consultancy, etc. being conducted on an 'off-balance-sheet' basis.[1]

The costs and difficulties of establishing a successfully working market in primary securities provide a limit to the extensibility of securitisation. Market expansion was possible with housing loans primarily because the form of the collateral was such that the risks of significant losses were extremely low. Personal confidential knowledge of the particular prospects of the borrower, or indeed of the particularities of the individual dwelling collateralised, thus becomes less important. Indeed, if one can structure loans so that they are collateralised against assets whose marketable resale value will generally, at least when subject to the law of large numbers, exceed the value of the loan, then one can certainly visualise transforming that loan also into a marketable security. More frequently, however, the absence of available collateral, poor second-hand markets for the specific assets owned by borrowers, or the risk that general uninsureable risks (e.g., of economic depression) will depress simultaneously the value of all the collateral offered, will prevent this development. Bernanke and Gertler (1985), who discuss this same question (p. 38) thus note that:

> From the point of view of the purchasers of these securities [mortgage backed bonds], this high rate of collateralisation performs a buffer role and thus substitutes for bank capital. However, since most loans by intermediaries are not so highly collateralised, at least during the period following issuance, the potential for decoupling loan issuance and ownership is necessarily limited.

3. Banks and OFIs: Differences and Similarities

In the previous sections, the various functions which financial intermediaries perform were recounted, and the reasons why intermediaries issue liabilities, and hold assets, with a range of characteristics were explained. But the question remains why, even with a range of preferred liabilities and assets, there need be more than one institutional type of intermediary offering all these intermediation services. Why should there be such a varied assortment of intermediaries, including distinct institutions such as banks, building societies (Savings and Loan Associations (SLAs) in the United States), finance houses, insurance companies, etc.?

In particular, the very act of carrying on business with a customer, whether as lender or borrower, increases the extent of information which both sides have of each other. This is especially true in the case of banks. Since the greater proportion of all the payments of their customers pass through their books, they ought to be in an excellent position to know whether it will be good business to extend loans to a particular customer. Similarly, even if to a lesser extent, the experience of a building society in taking deposits and offering mortgages to their clients should facilitate their ability to make a wide range of other personal loans and to undertake a wide range of additional customer services. One reason why an intermediary is likely to find any external constraint on the nature of its portfolio or business to be irksome is that the experience and information obtained in providing one kind of intermediation service

---

[1] For reasons described in Goodhart (1986c).

can be used to develop another kind of service more cheaply. If there are indeed informational economies of this kind (i.e., that each contact lessens the cost of the information required to arrange some further financial transaction), why then are there so many different kinds of financial intermediary in existence? Since their role in operating the payment mechanism gives the banks especially favourable access to information, why do the banks not provide the complete gamut of financial services for their clients?

A partial answer is that there are limits to such informational economies, with differing kinds of intermediation requiring specialised forms of information. Insurance business requires specialised actuarial assistance and a judgement of risks of quite a differing nature from those familiar to bankers. Lending on the collateral of real property, especially in the case of mortgages, requires some specialised knowledge of the property in question, and of the likely market for that property. The information required to decide whether it will be good business to provide a short-term advance to a company can be in some respects rather different from that needed if an institution is considering buying equity in a company.

So a bank diversifying into the insurance business, or home mortgages, or leasing, might have to set up a specialised subsidiary to do such business. The economies still to be obtained (e.g., a more centralised control of the asset portfolio) could be rather sparse, and there could be disadvantages as the growing range of business covered either attenuated the specialised information of top management on each aspect of that business, or else led to an unwieldy expansion of the managment structure, involving co-ordinating committees and such like.

Furthermore, the inherent market power of the banks, especially arising from their direct access to detailed information on their customers, has led on occasions to political demands to curb their strength and functions,[1] a political pressure which in some countries, for example the United States, has been reflected in legislation strictly limiting banking activities.[2] There is often concern whether information obtained in the provision of one form of intermediary service might not lead to a conflict of interest, or alternatively to an 'unfair' advantage, in the provision of some other financial service. The existence of 'economies of information' also raises the possibility that these could be exploited against the best interest of clients or of the economy to establish a monopoly position. This is one reason why there may be institutional barriers to the unbridled expansion of financial conglomerates. In recent years, technological development has led to increasing competition world-wide in the provision of financial services and this has also been associated with a strong tendency towards deregulation. These forces have resulted in the partial breakdown of the artificial barriers between financial intermediaries – e.g., between commercial banks and capital-market institutions such as investment banks, stock-brokers, etc. – and in the establishment of universal banks. These more recent structural changes and financial innovations are further discussed in Chapter 8.

Anyhow, banks, whose current accounts, demand deposits, provide a medium of

---

[1] A good example is provided by the *Investigation of the Financial and Monetary Conditions in the United States*, before the House of Representatives' Subcommittee on Banking and Currency, under House Resolutions Nos 429 and 504, otherwise known as the *Money Trust Investigation* or *Pujo Investigation*, in 1912/13.

[2] For example, the Bank Holding Company Act 1956, as amended by the Bank Holding Company Act 1970, specifies the restricted conditions upon which a bank holding company may acquire interests in non-banking activities in the USA.

exchange (and a means of payment) for their customers, must by definition be holding a portfolio of assets which must all, except for cash reserves, have a longer maturity than their sight-deposit liabilities. They face on this account, perhaps, a greater risk of illiquidity than other financial institutions, the form of whose liabilities gives them more time to prepare their defences. Even though in ordinary times banks can rely on a quite stable (and relatively interest inelastic) volume base of current accounts, once a story circulates that a bank's liquidity could be imperilled, the resulting run could easily force the temporary closure of the bank even if it has been prudently and well managed.[1] Moreover, banks hold a large proportion of their customers' money balances, required for current transactions uses. A bank closure (failure), therefore, not only entails some possible loss of wealth, the extent of loss depending on the possibility of reorganisation and on the realisable value of the counterpart assets, but more immediately forces that bank's customers to realise other assets in order to replace the immediate loss of liquidity if ordinary day-to-day household and business expenditures are to be carried on.

This secondary response, the subsequent round of forced asset sales and/or borrowing under pressure arising from a banking failure may be contrasted with the result of a failure of intermediaries with longer-dated liabilities, whose failure will generally derive from insolvency rather than illiquidity, since by definition they should have had time to realise marketable assets. In the latter instance, claimants on the failed company will have suffered some loss of wealth, and will lose the specific services provided (e.g., insurance), but there will be less immediate pressure to sell other assets in a scramble to restore liquidity. Certainly the most infamous general financial crises and panics have been prominently associated with banking failures, for example Overend Gurney & Co. (1866), the City of Glasgow Bank (1878), even the averted failure of Barings (1891) in the United Kingdom, the Credit-Anstalt in Austria (1931), the Knickerbocker Trust Co. in New York (1907) and the waves of banking failures in the United States from 1931 to 1933. In contrast it is harder to think of a general financial crisis resulting from a failure of a non-bank financial intermediary.[2]

The failures of cut-price insurance companies, of unsavoury investment funds, etc., may lead to severe losses of wealth and inconvenience to those unwary enough to be sucked in, but they do not – it seems from experience – spark off a cumulative process of asset realisation, withdrawal of funds from other intermediaries and deflation.

---

[1] For example, the banking crisis of 1907 in the United States was detonated by a run on the Knickerbocker Trust Co., which was in fact well managed and solvent, see Chapter 4 on 'The 1907 Crisis' in Goodhart (1969). More recently, a collapse of confidence in some of the fringe banks in the United Kingdom in 1973, following the suspension of Cedar Holding and London and County Securities, led to a large-scale withdrawal of market funds from all banks of a similar class, irrespective of their probity, solvency or management qualities. At one point this contagion even led to some concern about the condition of one of the large British clearing banks.

[2] The failure of the Atlantic Acceptance Corporation in Canada in June 1965 caused widespread repercussions. In the next year, there were fears for the viability of Savings and Loan Associations in the United States during the credit crunch of 1966. Moreover, by the 1980s, building societies (S & Ls in the USA) had largely taken on the attributes of banks with much the same exposure to runs, and with such runs having similar potential consequences. Financial crises originating outside the banking sector are certainly possible, but experience does seem to suggest that they are less serious. It is possible that the crash of October 1987, almost, provided a counter example.

For this reason, the authorities are likely to impose more stringent prudential requirements on the composition of bank-asset portfolios than on other intermediaries, since with banks the social, external costs of failure may well be much greater than the private costs of failure, whereas the gap between the social and private costs of failure is less marked for OFIs. Since the regulation of banking activities thus tends to be more strict, in the frequency and extent of inspection, in constraints on the permissible asset portfolio, in capital requirements, than is the case with other forms of intermediation, there is bound to be some tendency to form separate subsidiaries for banking and other forms of intermediation even when a holding company is able to control both. Furthermore, legal and tax advantages may be given preferentially to certain kinds of intermediaries (e.g., mutually-owned institutions), or to businesses specialising in certain defined fields (e.g., building societies), and these distinctions also are likely to maintain a diversity among financial intermediaries.

So, besides the natural factors that may limit economies of scale and information as the coverage of a financial intermediary increases and so allow more scope for any advantages from specialisation to come into play, the authorities may also erect regulatory barriers to prevent banks from expanding into certain other lines of business and impose additional prudential requirements on them in order to lessen the danger of liquidity crises. The authorities' interventions have generally acted to increase the diversity of financial intermediaries, by limiting competition from those institutions with the greatest opportunity for exploiting economies of information and by granting certain extra advantages to intermediary services to the poor, in the provision of housing mortgages, etc.

The argument so far has not only suggested reasons for the continued existence of a diverse group of financial intermediaries, specialising in the provision of differing services, but has also pointed up some of the ways in which banks differ from other financial intermediaries. The banks operate the main payments transmission services in many countries. Their sight deposits are generally treated as a means of payment. Their position gives them great market strength in command over funds and in access to information, though it also leaves them liable to special risks. Because of the wider social consequences of such risks, the authorities have generally imposed more intensive regulations and controls on banks than on other intermediaries. Banks issue liabilities with particular properties (e.g., sight deposits) and offer their own special kinds of financial services, e.g., transmitting payments. In a valid sense, banks can, therefore, be said to create bank deposits. But it is equally true to state that insurance companies create insurance contracts, that property unit trusts create property bonds, that building societies create their own shares and deposits. If you should devise a new liability with characteristics of a kind attractive to the public, then you could be also said to have created that.

The real issue, in the debate whether a bank is or is not similar in kind to OFIs, is not over the question of whether a financial intermediary creates its own liability, since they all clearly do so, but over the limits upon such creation. There are those who argue that the expansion of bank deposits, because of the role of demand deposits as a means of payment, is not subject to the same constraints as the expansion of other intermediaries. This assertion, however, runs counter to the arguments set out earlier in Section 1, which may be restated as follows.

The amount of any asset which the private sector wishes to hold, given its wealth and the various characteristics of that asset, depends on the relative yields on that and on other assets. This will be as true for bank deposits as for any other asset. The volume of bank deposits which the public will hold will depend on the relative return on bank deposits *vis-à-vis* all other assets. Meanwhile the return, in the form of specific interest payments or services, which banks can offer to depositors will depend on the yields that the banks can obtain on their earning assets and their desire for liquidity. An expansion by the banks of their deposit liabilities, through the offer of higher interest payments or more services, will entail rising costs, while the counterpart increase in their assets may bring about a lesser rate of increase, or fall, in revenues, as the banks offer lower rates on advances or offer loans to less creditworthy borrowers, in order to expand their earning assets. Given the exogenous and policy parameters of the system, there will be a stable equilibrium determinate volume of bank deposits. Exactly the same analysis holds true for all OFIs. In this sense, the determination of bank deposits and of other intermediary liabilities is exactly similar.

What qualifications have to be made to this general proposition, if any, to take account of the special characteristics of bank deposits, and what are these crucial characteristics? The first critical issue is whether banks do need to offer a higher relative yield on deposits in order to get people to hold a larger proportion of their assets with the banking system. It may be a useful clarification to present a viewpoint on this matter contrary to the one above, set out in a quotation taken from Moore's *Introduction to the Theory of Finance*.[1]

He writes as follows:

> Section one considers the market supply and demand forces that in the absence of government regulation determine the volume of financial intermediation. Non-monetary intermediaries are considered first. The expansion of total assets and liabilities of different intermediary groups are shown to be constrained by the asset and debt preference of surplus – and deficit – spending wealthowners. In competitive equilibrium the rate that an intermediary group charges borrowers exceeds the rate it pays to lenders by a premium just sufficient to cover the average costs of intermediation plus a normal rate of profit.

So far so good; however he continues:

> The situation is formally similar for monetary intermediaries. But because their liabilities are readily acceptable as a means of payment, and so impose no constraint on the exercise of purchasing power, bank intermediaries unlike nonbanks need not increase the return paid on notes and deposits to induce wealthowners to increase their nominal lending to the banking system. . . Depending on the prevailing marginal return earned on tangible assets and the degree of price flexibility, this market-determined [that is without explicit government regulation] volume of monetary intermediation will not in general be consistent with general price level stability.[2]

In order to dissect the above quoted passage, it is necessary to distinguish between a means of payment which is legal tender and an asset which can be used as a means of payment but is not legal tender. Any intermediary, institution or individual, not only banks, whose liabilities were granted the status of legal tender could issue them without limit, until inflationary pressures caused the collapse of the political or monetary system, possibly of both together. If insurance-company paper became legal tender, it would instantly issue claims at zero interest rate, or cost, to an extent which would 'not in general be consistent with general price level stability'.

---

[1] Moore (1968) Chapter 7, pp. 185–6
[2] Pesek and Saving present a similar analysis in their book on *Money, Wealth and Economic Theory* (1967).

But, without legal-tender status for their liabilities, banks are forced to attract additional reserve assets to maintain a sufficient reserve base to support their own expansion. In order to obtain those extra reserve assets the banks will have to bid for them, which takes us back to our previous analysis. In this respect they are no different from other intermediaries. If the authorities set the rates at which they will exchange various assets, generally foreign-exchange or public-sector debt of one kind or another, for cash reserves, then the banks can obtain additional cash reserves by raising their deposit rate or offering improved services, causing people to switch out of public-sector debt, or foreign assets, into bank deposits. This process is limited by rising marginal costs and falling marginal revenues.

If the authorities try to limit the volume of cash reserves accruing to the banks, they will have to let rates on public-sector debt and foreign exchange adjust to prevent any inducement for the public to shift out of public-sector debt – or for there to be any currency flow across the exchanges – as the banks bid for funds.[1] The extent that banks will be prepared to push their bidding for funds will be mainly influenced by the strength of demand from the private sector for bank loans, as the rate on such loans rises in line with other market rates (with the banks at each stage trying to maintain an optimal portfolio distribution).

The banks are, therefore, competing with the public sector to attract the funds of the private sector; the size and rate of expansion of the banking system depends on the outcome of that competition. In turn, the impetus for the banks to compete comes in large part from the opportunities to use those funds profitably – i.e., from the private-sector demand for loans. So long as bank deposits are not legal tender, and banks therefore need to attract reserve assets to support their deposit holdings, the banks are subject to the same general principles in the determination of the volume of their deposits as any other intermediary.

But even if this general principle be granted, that bank expansion will be limited in the same way as that of OFIs, by the rising cost (relative to the extra revenues generated) of attracting additional deposits, another distinction between the actual process of the determination of the volume of bank deposits on the one hand and of the liabilities of OFIs on the other is sometimes made. This is that banks can often pay for purchases of private-sector assets (though less so of public-sector assets) by writing up their own liabilities, whereas OFIs have to run down their reserves (usually of bank deposits rather than of cash). The ability of banks to pay in this manner will not, of course, be advantageous if the public then immediately withdraws cash reserves from the banks, by using the cheque payment to add to their currency holdings, or to make payments to the public sector for taxes, to buy foreign exchange from the public sector's reserves, or to buy other public-sector debt. What matters to the banks, when they purchase earning assets is the redeposit ratio, the proportion of their payment which will be redeposited with them. Equally, the loss of reserves suffered by the non-bank financial intermediaries, as they expand their earning assets, depends on the proportion of such payments that will be redeposited with them.

The volume of the banking sector's cash reserves will be affected only by flows of funds between the public sector and the private sector, as the members of the private sector pay taxes, receive payments from the government, buy or sell public-sector debt or foreign exchange and add to, or run down, their cash holdings. Flows of funds within the private sector involving payments between two members of that

---

[1] And to offset those flows from personal-currency holdings to bank deposits which the authorities cannot prevent people from undertaking.

sector, which do not involve any transactions with the public sector, will not alter the cash base of the banking system. Thus any purchase by the banks of earning assets from the private sector (e.g., by making loans) will lead to a redeposit of the means of payment, whether this was originally made in the form of cash or a cheque on the bank itself, except to the extent that the subsequent adjustment of portfolios leads to an outflow of funds from the private to the public sector, say as the public wishes to hold more currency itself or to buy more foreign exchange from the public sector's reserves, in order to buy foreign assets.

On the other hand the purchase of earning assets by non-bank financial intermediaries must be matched by an equivalent initial reduction in their reserve assets. Funds, money, will be redeposited with non-bank financial intermediaries only so long as these latter offer relatively attractive terms. So their ability to obtain and to hold reserves depends on their ability to make their liabilities competitively attractive in relation to all other assets whether public-sector or private-sector debt.

Banks' cash reserves are, therefore, immune from the effect of competition for funds within the private sector, so long as this does not affect the flow of funds between the public and the private sectors, whereas non-bank intermediaries' reserves will be directly affected by such competition. It might, therefore, be thought that the redeposit rate,[1] following on from an expansion of earnings assets, of the banks would be much higher than that of the non-bank financial intermediaries. Or to put the point in another way, the marginal cost curve of a bank might be much more elastic than for a non-bank financial intermediary, since any initial attraction of cash reserves by the banks (e.g., by offering a higher yield) will allow a multiple expansion of deposits as the bank payments – to add to their earning assets – lead to redeposits of these payments with the banking system, whereas the non-bank financial intermediary will have a lower redeposit rate and, therefore, a steeper marginal cost curve.

This essentially brings us back to the question of the validity of the concept of 'buffer stock' money. If the money stock in existence *at any time* has to be that specifically demanded by the public at existing levels of incomes, wealth, interest rates, etc. then the size of the money stock, just like the size of outstanding OFI liabilities, will be determined by those same arguments. If, however, supply-side shocks (e.g., to bank credit demand) can lead the money stock to diverge from the 'underlying' demand for money at least in the short run (while it is not possible for *non-bank* liabilities to diverge from the specific demand for them through a similar mechanism), then this functional role of money balances as a buffer stock may indeed cause the impact effect of bank expansions to be rather different from that arising from supply-side shocks elsewhere in the financial system.

Of course, in full equilibrium the public will hold only that volume of deposits, whether of banks or of any other financial intermediary, consistent with its asset preferences, dependent on its overall wealth and relative interest rates. But, if the buffer stock notion is correct, then both the impact effect, the dynamic adjustment and the final equilibrium may be qualitatively different following a supply shock in the banking system than one originating elsewhere within the financial sector. If this is indeed correct, then much of the particular importance attached to the monetary aggregates, largely composed of bank deposits (e.g., as perceived by monetarist

---

[1] For an analysis of the different positions of the banks and the non-bank financial intermediaries in terms of their relative redeposit ratios, see Sheppard and Barrett (1965 pp. 198–214).

economists) as contrasted with wider financial aggregates, must depend on this role of money as a buffer stock.

Be that as it may, the process of adjustment to demand and supply-side shocks within the financial system is, in my view, best modelled within a portfolio adjustment framework. So, in the first edition of this book, the process whereby the volume of deposit liabilities of financial intermediaries was determined was illustrated by a simulated portfolio adjustment model with numerical examples. In the second part of this simulation, the above arguments concerning the equilibrium and adjustment process of banks and OFIs were illustrated. Although an appreciation of portfolio adjustment models and processes is, indeed, important for a proper understanding of how financial intermediaries work, the actual examples provided were quite long and the numerical simulations were no more than illustrative. Accordingly, in this edition, the models and their numerical simulations have not been included.

VI

Controlling the Supply of Money: A Problem for the Authorities?

Summary

It is true, by accounting identity, that changes in the money stock can be expressed in terms of changes in the high-powered money base in an algebraic formula that depends also on two ratios, the public's currency – deposit and the banks' reserve – deposit ratios. Moreover, movements in these two ratios are generally quite stable and predictable; so a knowledge of movements in the high-powered money base should allow one to predict the movements in the money stock with some accuracy. This is so whether or not the authorities are concerned to control the rate of growth of the monetary base or the money stock. Furthermore, the high-powered money base, in most countries, more or less corresponds to the monetary liabilities of the Central Bank, consisting of notes and coin outstanding and deposits of the banks with the Central Bank. It would seem, on the face of it, as if any Central Bank should be in a position to control its own liabilities, and thus the money stock. But even if the monetary authorities are pursuing some other objective, such as pegging rates on public-sector debt or on foreign exchange, which commits them to exchange cash for the asset whose rate is pegged and thus loosens their control over the monetary base, the ensuing growth in the volume of high-powered money will be related to the growth in the money stock.

For such reasons it is common, indeed customary, in monetary models to take the high-powered money base as exogenously given, determined off-stage, and then to relate the money stock to this base by a multiplier relationship, incorporating the behavioural responses affecting the two ratios involved. The derivation and nature of such multiplier relationships are discussed in Section 1. This approach, however, abstracts from all the main operational problems facing the authorities. It reveals nothing about the difficulties possibly confronting the authorities in achieving any desired level for the monetary base. It suggests by itself nothing of the implications for interest rates, markets and financial institutions of the authorities' choice of targets and market procedures. It gives no idea of the underlying forces with which the authorities may have to contend in controlling the money stock. Indeed, in making the initial assumption that the monetary base is under their control, all their operational problems are implicitly assumed to have been resolved.

We examine some of these problems in Section 2. For example, when the public sector runs a deficit, say as a result of an expansionary budget, it has to find the requisite finance; this can be obtained either by non-monetary borrowing, domestically or externally, or by money creation. Although the monetary implications of fiscal actions may be taken into consideration, many other factors also enter the budget decision; from the point of view of the monetary authorities, the size of the deficit to be financed is, therefore, an external parameter which they have to accept. Moreover, several of the financing flows are outside the control of the monetary authorities; debt maturities are ineluctable, and in so far as rates and terms on the non-marketable savings instruments issued by the government are sticky, flows into and out of such instruments tend to vary perversely with the intended direction of monetary policy. Finally, and more important, open-market operations to control monetary expansion will cause interest-rate movements which under a fixed exchange-rate system can induce large-scale international capital flows; these flows will to some extent offset and frustrate the domestic monetary actions and, under a flexible exchange rate system, may lead to (substantial) fluctuations in exchange rates, see Chapter 18.

The burden of controlling the pace of monetary expansion falls mainly on the authorities' open-market operations. In some circumstances this burden can seem insupportable. In particular, the authorities can rarely foretell with any confidence how the market will respond to their operations. Investors' demand for bonds is not just a simple function of current bond prices but also depends on the expectations generated in an uncertain world. The existence of short-dated bonds, whose certain yield to redemption rises as interest rates rise, should provide, however, a fairly stable anchorage for the market, even when most investors work to short planning periods. Even so, uncertainty about the market's response and fear of large, erratic and unpredictable variations in interest rates may make the authorities tentative in such operations.

Market response to the authorities' operations will depend in part on the strength of competition for money from the private sector, as described in Section 3. If borrowers from the banks are not deterred by higher rates, the banks will bid up lender rates in competition with the authorities in an upward spiral. Faced with this situation, the authorities in the United Kingdom have often reacted by imposing direct controls on the banks. But it is extremely difficult to tell thereafter what proportion of the underlying demand for credit – the basic cause of the upwards pressure in rates – has been diverted to other channels and what proportion has been choked off. Even when the authorities are prepared to rely on general market instruments, rather than on direct controls, their ability to monitor developments and to bring about smooth adjustments is hindered by various lags in the system.

Most economic models take the money stock, or the high-powered money base, as given. This is not the way it appears to the authorities. To them the control of the pace of monetary expansion often involves a difficult struggle: four main factors determine how difficult this struggle will be:

1. the interest elasticity of the demand for advances;
2. the size of the public-sector deficit;
3. the elasticity of substitution between foreign and domestic assets in an open economy, when exchange rates are fixed, or the extent of resulting fluctuation in exchange rates when these are flexible; and
4. market reactions to the authorities' open-market operations

1. Multiplier Analysis?

In Chapter 5, the determination of the volume of liabilities (and of assets) of both banks and OFIs was examined and explained in terms of the interplay of the portfolio preferences of both the general public and of the intermediaries. Given the values of the exogenous variables, and those directly controlled by the authorities, the process involves continuous portfolio readjustment in the face of changing relative yields. This approach seems very different, at least superficially, from the multiplier analysis, the manner in which the determination of the liabilities of financial intermediaries, especially of banks, is usually described.

There is, however, no real contradiction between the two. The (bank) multiplier analysis simply concentrates on a rather narrower set of behavioural responses, and treats the remaining aspects of the adjustment process as given, determined off-stage. Indeed, at the limit, the multiplier analysis can be treated purely as an identity without any behavioural content at all. The liquid financial assets held by the general public (L) can be defined as comprising two components, being respectively their holdings of the monetary liabilities of the government (C) and of the liabilities of the financial intermediaries (F). It is, therefore, possible to set down the identity.

$$L = F + C$$

which must hold exactly by definition.

Similarly, it is possible to give a name, a description, to the sum of the monetary liabilities of the government sector held on the one hand by the general public (C) and on the other by the financial intermediaries as reserves (R). The title now commonly applied to this latter set of assets is 'high-powered money' (H). If the currency in the hands of the public was transferred by them to financial intermediaries in exchange for deposits, the intermediaries' cash reserves would rise equivalently, allowing and encouraging them (at the prevailing set of relative yields) to expand their lending – presumably, assuming a previous condition of equilibrium, by making loans more attractive to borrowers, say, by cutting the rates charged – and thus cause an increase in both their assets and their liabilities. The term 'high-powered' reflects the fact that financial intermediary deposits are some mutliple of their reserve holdings, so that – assuming that the financial sector maintains fairly stable cash–reserves ratios – one would see a multiple increase in deposits accompanying an increase in cash reserves. The additional identity

$$H = R + C$$

can thus also be set down, which again must hold by definition.

By algebraic manipulation of these two identities, (i.e., dividing both by F), it is possible to arrive at a third identity

$$L = H\frac{1 + C/F}{(R/F + C/F)}$$

describing the total holding of liquid financial assets in terms of the level of high-powered money and two ratios, R/F the financial intermediaries' cash reserve – deposit ratio, and C/F the general public's currency – deposit ratio. Since this relationship is also an identity, it always holds true by definition; changes in the public's holding of liquid financial assets can, therefore, be expressed in terms of these three variables alone.

One of the several features distinguishing banks from other financial intermediaries, which has already been noted, is that other financial intermediaries hold their reserves mainly in the form of bank deposits, while banks hold their reserves in the form of the monetary liabilities of the government sector. A shift in the public's preferences between bank deposits and the liabilities of other financial intermediaries (OFI) could, therefore, alter the R/F ratio. One way of dealing with this potential cause of variation in the R/F ratio is to partition the financial sector into two parts – banks and OFIs – and construct a multiplier for each separately.

Defining the money supply, M, as equal to deposits (D) plus currency in the hands of the public (including the OFI),[1] we can write:

$$M = D + C$$

which together with the identity

$$H = R_b + C$$

where H is high-powered money, as before, R_b now represents bank reserves of high-powered money and C is currency holdings elsewhere in the private sector (including OFI), enables us to arrive at a third identity:

$$M = \frac{H\left(1 + \dfrac{C}{D}\right)}{\left(\dfrac{R_b}{D} + \dfrac{C}{D}\right)}$$

describing the money stock in terms of the level of high-powered money and two ratios, R_b/D the banks' reserve – deposit ratio, and C/D the general public's currency – deposit ratio.[2] By an exactly similar process, one can define the money stock M as consisting of two parts: M_p, that held by private sector (exclusive of OFIs) and M_F, that held by the OFIs as reserves; and also define the general public's liquid financial assets (L) as equal to M_p, plus their holdings of the liabilities (OFI) of the non-bank financial intermediaries. Then from the two identities:

$$M = M_p + M_F$$

and

$$L = M_P + \text{OFI}$$

we can construct the identity

$$L = M \frac{(1 + M_p/\text{OFI})}{(M_p/\text{OFI} + M_F/\text{OFI})}$$

Indeed, one can go on constructing further, bigger and more complex multiplier identities to take account of various distinctions between intermediaries and between liabilities.[3] These more complicated formulations, however, sacrifice the one great

---

[1] For a detailed note on various possible alternative definitions of the stock of money in the United Kingdom, see the *Bank of England Quarterly Bulletin*, Vol. 10, No. 3 (September 1970) pp. 320–6, and subsequent Bank of England papers reporting on statistical changes in the definitions of the monetary aggregates are to be found in the *Bank of England Quarterly Bulletin* (1982b and 1987a).

[2] An array of slightly differing identities can be obtained from algebraic manipulation of the two basic identities. The differences between them have no analytical significance. See Friedman and Schwartz (1963) especially Appendix B; and Cagan (1965) especially Chapters 1 and 2.

[3] For example, see McLeod (1962) pp. 611–40; Brunner and Meltzer (1964) pp. 240–83, especially pp. 242–56; Fand (1967) pp. 380–400.

virtue of the multiplier approach – its simplicity – without obtaining equivalent benefits in the area of their greatest deficiency, their lack of behavioural content, for such multipliers generally do not illuminate the behavioural process whereby people and institutions adjust their overall portfolio to arrive at some general equilibrium. Yet to be able to express changes in the money stock, or in the total holdings of liquid financial assets, in terms of only three variables has considerable advantages of brevity and simplicity, though even these advantages may be lost in those circumstances where there is a plethora of differing kinds of banks or intemediaries, and of deposits, each involving separate reserve ratios.

None the less, the lack of any innate theoretical, or behavioural, content in the multiplier approach, *per se*,[1] may be realised more easily by noting that multiplier identities can be constructed over a virtually limitless range of cases. Take any aggregate, X, which can be decomposed into two parts, Y and Z, so that

$$X = Y + Z$$

then if the provision of Z is constrained by the identity

$$U = W + Z$$

one can construct the identity

$$X = U \cdot \frac{(1 + Z/Y)}{(W/Y + Z/Y)}$$

and various other mathematically-equivalent identities. Consider, for example, the potato multiplier of total personal expenditure, E. Personal expenditure is used for the purchase of potatoes (P_p), and of other goods and services (O), so that

$$E = P_p + O$$

The total production of potatoes (P) either is sold to persons (P_p) or goes to other uses (P_o), so that

$$P = P_p + P_o$$

then

$$E = P \cdot \frac{(1 + P_p/O)}{(P_o/O + P_p/O)}$$

In short, total personal expenditure is a multiple of the value of the production of potatoes, with the size of the multiplier depending on only two ratios, the ratio of expenditure on potatoes to expenditure on other goods and the ratio of sales of potatoes for uses other than personal consumption to other personal expenditure.

One can spread one's wings in the construction of exotic multipliers. Take, for example, the academic multiplier of total wealth. Let W represent total wealth, which is defined as comprised of human and non-human wealth, so that

$$W = W_N + W_H$$

---

[1] It is possible, of course, to add behavioural content by analysing the derivation of the elements in the identity in terms of the underlying behavioural relationships. But that leads back towards specifying the full structure of the system, as we did in Chapter 5. If it is necessary to specify the structure of the system in order to understand why the multiplier works as it does, it is difficult to see what advantage is to be gained from using it as an analytical tool in the first place.

Let $W_H/W = d$; let the value of human wealth be related to educational input (E); assume, for simplicity only, a linear relationship, so that

$$W_H = a + bE$$

Let the ratio of expenditure on academic lectures (A) to total education expenditures be g – i.e., $A/E = g$ – then it follows that

$$W = \frac{a}{d} + \frac{b}{gd}A$$

Total wealth is thus some multiple of expenditure on academic lectures, plus a term, a/d, which may in the short run be taken as constant. Moreover, both g and d are between 0 and 1, since they relate a component of an aggregate to an aggregate, while we may presume that b is greater than unity, since education is widely regarded as a worthwhile investment for society. Total wealth is therefore related to expenditure on academic lectures by some very large multiplier. Apart from the simplifying assumption of the linear relationship between education expenditures and human wealth, and of the approximate short-term constancy of the a/d ratio, it is all true by definition.

These examples are intended to persuade readers either that it will be of enormous benefit to the nation to increase the salaries of academic lectures multifold or, alternatively, that the multiplier approach needs cautious handling if it is to be used as a basis for explaining something large (say, national income, or the money stock) from movements in a much smaller component of that aggregate, say autonomous investment, or high-powered money, grossed up by some function which involves ratios connecting the small total to the large.[1] In order to use such an approach to 'explain' variations in the larger total – as contrasted with describing such movements, which definitional multipliers, however ridiculous, can always do – some further conditions are necessary.

The primary condition is that the ratios linking the two variables should be predictable, say a stable function of other variables which will also be predictable, under all prospective circumstances. Clearly, if the ratios vary unpredictably, then information on the value of the small variable will not allow one to forecast how the large variable will change. But even if the ratios seem stable under one set of circumstances, they may not be so generally. Consider again the previous example of the academic multiplier of total wealth. It may be that the ratios in that example (b, g and d) have remained fairly stable over time, reflecting the preferences and structure of the system. If the authorities, however, should alter that system by doubling (or halving) expenditure on academic lecturers at a stroke, the values of the ratios would alter quite sharply, so that the previous stability would be shattered. Obviously, in this case, the authorities cannot rely on the continued stability of this multiplier to vary total wealth by adjusting expenditure on academic lecturers.

If the ratios remain stable and predictable under *all* feasible states of the world, then if you know the value of the small variable you will be able to predict with a high degree of confidence what the value of the large variable will be. In this sense, and this sense only, it is possible to say that variations in the small variable (say, the high-

---

[1] The multiplier approach is, alas, used indiscriminately by all schools of macro-economic analysis. The Keynesian multiplier, relating changes in incomes to changes in autonomous expenditures, is of this genre. The theory of distribution developed by N. Kaldor (1955) pp. 83–100 is essentially based on a definitional multiplier of this kind.

powered money base) explain the variations in the large variable (say, the money stock). It should be noted that this usage of the term 'explanation' does not depend on whether the small variable is being determined exogenously (say, as a control variable by the authorities) or endogenously, when these are alternative possible states of the world. All that is necessary is that the relationship should be predictable and stable in all possible states; indeed the bank multiplier will in some respects, perhaps, be most useful if the relationship remains unaltered *whatever* the state of the world, in our previous example whether the high-powered money base is, or is not, being fixed consciously by the authorities.

On the whole, the bank multiplier relating the money stock to the high-powered money base has been quite useful in the above manner.[1] As long as the probability distribution of deposit inflows and withdrawals, and the penalties resulting from a cash shortage, remain fairly constant,[2] the banks' reserve ratio is likely to remain a stable function of relative yields on alternative assets. Similarly, the public's desired currency – deposit ratio usually remains fairly constant over time, changing gradually in response to slow-moving institutional factors, and also perhaps to the relative yield attractions of holding deposits. It is possible, however, that if the authorities should suddenly change their system of monetary control, say by moving from a system in which they fixed interest rates in the market as their prime target to one in which they concentrated upon determining the monetary base, the subjective uncertainties – and penalties – facing the banks might change, resulting in possibly unforeseeable changes in their desired reserve ratios.[3] And if developments in the banking system should make the public revise their views of the safety of their deposits, the public's desired currency – deposit ratio could change very sharply, as in the United States in the 1930s. Nevertheless, as Friedman and Schwartz, and Cagan, have shown in the case of the United States, the relationships involved in the bank multiplier have remained fairly stable over a long run of years and during several different monetary regimes – e.g., gold standard with no Central Bank, Federal Reserve System in its differing phases of operation. So if you know what the change in the monetary base has been over some period, it is likely that you will be able to forecast what the change in the money stock will have been over the same period with reasonable accuracy, irrespective of the nature of the monetary regime or of changes in that regime. In this respect, the bank multiplier has some useful explanatory content, as compared with the other examples of the potato multiplier or the academic multiplier, which have none.

Moreover, this ability to forecast the larger aggregate (e.g., the money stock) from movements in the smaller variable (e.g., the high-powered money base) requires that only a few ratios be predictable. If one instead looks at the wider canvas, at the complete portfolio adjustment of the sectors concerned, involving the interplay of all the asset preferences, the number of behavioural functions which have to be included

---

[1] See, in particular, the work of Cagan (1965).

[2] On this subject, see Morrison (1966).

[3] Changes in official reserve requirements will naturally alter the desired reserve ratio; but the response should be fairly predictable.

The difficulty of predicting how the banks, and indeed how the remainder of the financial system, might respond to the introduction of monetary base control (MBC), and thus the problems of operating such a system in the transitional period, were arguments deployed against a move to MBC in the UK in the early 1980s, see HM Treasury, *Monetary Control* (1980) and Bank for International Settlements, Monetary and Economic Department, *The Monetary Base Approach to Monetary Control* (1980).

in the analysis mounts up at giddy speed. The multiplier approach, on the other hand, concentrates on the determination of one aggregate and eliminates analysis of a great proportion of the accompanying behaviour. Yet it achieves this extra simplicity, as compared with the more general approach, at a considerable cost in terms of information about the process at hand. Indeed, the informational content of the mutliplier approach is remarkably slight.

Consider what the bank multiplier does not tell you. In the first place, it provides no information on the factors which affect the determination of the high-powered monetary base. There is no *a priori* reason to believe that the authorities' intention is generally to control this variable; it may be endogenously determined. Indeed, historical experience would suggest that in the main the system has been such (e.g., the authorities' chief concern has been for the level of interest rates) that the monetary base has been determined endogenously.[1] During such periods, it does not take analysis much further forward to say that the money stock varied by x per cent because the high-powered money base altered by y per cent. This only raises the question why the base changed.

Moreover, even when the authorities are giving priority to controlling monetary aggregates, the problems and operations involved in achieving such control are not indicated, or illustrated, by the bank multiplier. In particular, to start by assuming that the high-powered money base is given is to ignore virtually all the really interesting matters of concern to the monetary authorities. These issues are taken up at more length in Sections 2 and 3 below.

Even more important from an analytical viewpoint, the multiplier approach gives little or no indication of the behavioural process involved in the quantitative adjustments. The bank multiplier shows only that if you can observe the change in the monetary base between two occasions, and can predict the two relevant ratios, then you will be able to predict the change in the money stock with a high degree of confidence. This allows very little to be deduced about the *process* of adjustment. Indeed, most of the accounts of the dynamic process of adjustment which are derived from the multiplier approach are at best misleading and often wrong.

For example, the impression is still occasionally given that once some additional high-powered money is introduced into the system it cannot be expelled, and the system will have to adjust until all such extra reserves are held either as currency by the private sector or in bank reserves. This is wrong: every time the general public or the banks make a payment, by cheque or currency, to the government sector, the level of high-powered money falls.[2]

Moreover, even when the process of monetary expansion involves the purchase of private-sector assets, financial or real, the transaction will involve certain shifts in relative yields, incomes and wealth that are likely to have some subsequent effect

---

[1] 'Whereas everyone agrees that the monetary authority is capable of determining the money stock, we must nevertheless recognise that we live in the real world where there are lags and where the monetary authority apparently has never sought to control the absolute level of the nominal stock of money, opting instead to affect "credit conditions"', Klein, Discussion of Fand's paper on 'A Monetarist Model of the Monetary Process.'

'However, concern over market interest-rate movements has been a major factor influencing Federal Reserve acquisition of Government debt over the last two decades.' Stewart (1972) p. 8.

Also see Thygesen (1971), especially chapter 5.

[2] Unless the government sector keeps the proceeds with the domestic banks; even when this occurs, it is usually only temporary.

upon payments to the government sector. For example, increased expenditure on real assets is likely to cause – though admittedly after a rather long time lag – higher tax payments and – rather sooner – more imports; the purchase of equities, driving up the price–earnings ratio, apart from its effects on capital gains tax receipts, will alter relative yields in favour of public-sector debt and foreign assets. Of course the authorities, having undertaken an initial injection of additional reserves, say by an open-market operation, can try to offset subsequent portfolio adjustments whereby the initial injection would be cut back. They can lower taxes, lower yields offered on public-sector debt and/or lower the exchange rate. With a dynamic process of portfolio adjustment, requiring continual adjustments of yields and rates by the authorities in order to maintain any given level, or rate of growth, of the monetary aggregates, it is hard to see any virtue in treating the high-powered money base as given, even for expository purposes.

Furthermore, the usual description of the multiplier process suggests that an injection (or withdrawal) of cash reserves from the banks forces, in response, a quantitative change in the volume of their earning assets, irrespective of relative yields and rates. Except in so far as such rate movements affect the banks' demand for cash reserves, they appear to have to respond mechanically. The unstated implication of this analysis is that the banks are not trying to achieve any desired portfolio equilibrium. This is wrong; banks do not respond to a cash shortage by calling in loans on a large scale; it would not be good business to do so. Supporters of the base multiplier approach might respond that there is no inherent requirement for the banks to call in *loans*; it merely requires them to dispose of non-cash assets – e.g., marketable (government) bonds. But why should a bank sell a bond, possibly at a loss, if it can meet the cash shortage at an overall lower cost by bidding for cash, by raising the rates it offers on deposits? Frequently the banks' response is to change the rates offered, to raise rates on deposits and loans, rather than to make any large quantitative changes in their existing asset portfolio. The reduction in bank advances that follows a restrictive monetary policy – ignoring direct ceiling controls – will generally be due to a decline in demand for advances from the private sector as the banks are induced, by declining liquidity and rising bond rates, to raise rates on advances, rather than from a calling-in of existing advances by the banks.

The main conceptual criticism of the bank-multiplier approach, as indeed of multipliers generally, is that it obscures the behavioural process whereby people and institutions choose to apportion their wealth or income, presumably in some reasonably rational fashion, in the light of perceived circumstances. Multipliers may reveal the result of rational choice, but they do not illuminate that process. It was for this reason that in Chapter 5 the analysis of the determination of the supply of financial liabilities (and/or of money) was described instead in terms of the interplay of the preference functions of the public and of the intermediaries.

2. Government Finance and Open-market Operations

Just as the algebra of the banking mutiplier effectively obscures the underlying behavioural process of portfolio adjustment in response to relative prices, so the assumption of an exogenously-given monetary base effectively obscures consideration of the real problems facing the monetary authorities and their responses to such problems. So a first step is to abandon the assumption that the high-powered money base (H) is given. Instead, we may start by examining the factors determining the outstanding totals of all the various forms of government debt extant, including the cash liabilities of the public sector. In order to do this, it is helpful to turn to yet another accounting identity, taken from the accounts of the flow of funds,[1] which describes how the financial deficit (or surplus) of each sector is financed by flows of funds through the various financial markets. In order that this accounting identity may be satisfied, it is necessary that a public-sector deficit, after taking account of certain financial transfers (e.g., receipts from privatisation sales, local authority loans for house-building, etc.) must be financed by borrowing from other sectors, by issuing additional debt to them or by running down claims upon them (e.g., foreign-exchange reserves which represent claims on the overseas sector).

The provision of finance to the public sector occurs in a variety of ways.[2] For the purpose of this analysis, such borrowing may be grouped into three components: finance which directly brings about an increase in high-powered money, ΔH, finance raised by other domestic borrowing and finance raised by receiving the domestic monetary counterpart of accommodating an external currency outflow, when the Central Bank intervenes in the foreign-exchange market to support sterling. It may be useful to sub-divide this second item, the finance obtained by other domestic borrowing, into three separate components:

1. the use of funds to repay maturing debt,
2. transactions (borrowing or repaying) in non-marketable debt – e.g., in the United Kingdom premium savings bonds, national savings certificates, etc, and
3. operations in marketable debt.

This accounting identify can then be set out as follows

$$PSD = OMO + NMD - MAT + ECF + \Delta H$$

where PSD is the public-sector deficit after taking account of various financial transfers such as sales of council houses and privatisation receipts, OMO represents the outcome of the authorities' operations in marketable debt, NMD represents the outcome of transactions in non-marketable debt, MAT shows the required use of funds to pay off maturing debt, ECF gives the total finance obtained from, or required by, accommodating external currency flows and ΔH represents the increases in the public sector's monetary liabilities, high powered money.[3] This identity represents what Hansen terms the European type of public-sector budget constraint. In the US form of this constraint, the government finances itself entirely by selling debt in the market, and the Central Bank then decides how much of this debt to buy.[4] As Hansen notes,

> What can be done under one of these budget constraints can also be done under the other one[5]

---

[1] Consult, for example, the regular 'Analysis of Financial Statistics' in each issue of the *Bank of England Quarterly Bulletin*.

[2] See, for example, 'Funding the public sector borrowing requirement, 1952–83,' *Bank of England Quarterly Bulletin* (1984c).

[3] Including for this purpose the increase in bankers' balances with the Bank of England Banking Department (counterbalanced by holdings of public-sector debt by the Department).

[4] Several countries, beside the USA, such as West Germany, have systems of Government finance which incorporate a US, rather than a European, budget constraint. The reason for concentrating here on the European form of the constraint is simply that it is the one appropriate for the UK, not that it is more generally applicable.

[5] B. Hansen, 'On the Effects of Fiscal and Monetary Policy: A Taxonomic Discussion' (1973)

but the '*automatic* responses are different under the two systems'. Rather than jump backwards and forwards between these alternative systems, we shall fix in the remainder of the chapter on the European-type budget constraint. Nevertheless, such differences can cause confusion, which can perhaps best be dispelled by reference to Hansen's paper on the subject.

This ('European-type') accounting identity can equally well be reversed to show the various financial flows accompanying any change in high-powered money as follow:

$$\Delta H = PSD - OMO - NMD + MAT - ECF$$

This identity at least points the analysis towards explicit consideration of those elements in the financial system which have traditionally been the main concern of the authorities (at least within 'European-type' systems) i.e., the size of the public-sector deficit, operations in public-sector marketable debt, the weight of maturities to be financed, the impact on the foreign-exchange market – and on the reserve position – of a balance-of-payments deficit (or surplus).[1]

Certain of these financial flows are, largely or entirely, outside the control of the monetary authorities. For example, the volume of maturities to be refinanced in any one year is ineluctably determined by prior contractual arrangements. The problem of refinancing maturities can be exaggerated, however, since holders (such as financial institutions) who are attempting to maintain a balanced portfolio can usually be tempted to switch regularly towards slightly longer-dated debt in order to maintain the desired balance of their portfolios. Even so, the occasion of a maturity reduces the transaction cost to holders of moving out of public-sector debt, and causes such holders, of necessity, to reconsider their investment plans. For such reasons, maturities of debt issues of a kind brought previously in large quantities by less active portfolio managers, especially in the personal sector, can be expected to cause more serious refinancing problems to the authorities.

Although the monetary implications of any proposed fiscal change may be given some weight in the determination of fiscal policy, many other considerations of very different kinds also enter, and may well sway the judgement about the proper balance between expenditures and revenue of the public sector. To this extent, variations in the size of the fiscal deficit must also be regarded as outside the control of the monetary authorities. Indeed, variations in the size of the public-sector deficit may on occasions even hinder the intended thrust of monetary policy.[2]

---

pp. 546–71. The importance of giving explicit recognition to the existence of the public-sector budget constraint was earlier noted by Christ, for example in his papers on 'A Short-run Aggregate-Demand Model of the Interdependence and Effects of Monetary and Fiscal Policies with Keynesian and Classical Interest Elasticities' (1976) pp. 434–43; and 'A Simple Macroeconomic Model with a Government Budget Restraint' (1968) pp. 53–67.

[1] The impact, and relative importance of this latter, *ECF*, clearly depends crucially on whether the exchange rate is fixed, or pegged, so that the authorities are committed to intervene to offset any (net) pressure forcing the exchange rate to the boundaries within which it is to be held, or whether the exchange rate is allowed to float, in which case the authorities can choose whether, or not, to intervene to offset pressures driving the rate in one direction, or the other.

[2] Tew, in his article on 'The Implications of Milton Friedman for Britain' (1969) pp. 757–71, has termed the financing requirement which arises from the public-sector deficit and debt maturities 'the flood'. In order to check the growth of the monetary aggregates, the authorities have to undertake the often extremely difficult task of damming this flood.

Moreover, it is difficult to devise fiscal measures that can be frequently altered without involving considerable disturbance of one kind or another. It is, therefore, usual to alter tax rates and forward expenditure plans only once a year in the annual Budget. Even then, lags intervene between the policy change and the resulting effect on monetary flows, so that the public sector deficit in any given year may be conditioned as much by previous Budgets as by current fiscal changes. For all these reasons, the monetary authorities cannot hope to vary the size of the public-sector deficit in the short run as a flexible instrument for the purpose of achieving some desired rate of growth in the monetary aggregates. This problem is seen in even more extreme forms in other countries where the executive faces difficulties on occasions in obtaining legislative agreement to their fiscal proposals.

In principle, it would be possible to envisage the authorities frequently varying the rates of interest offered on non-marketable debt for the purpose of inducing some desired level of flows into these instruments. In practice, however, in the United Kingdom rates on some of these instruments have been notable rather for their constancy.[1] In periods of monetary squeeze, rates offered on non-marketable securities have thus generally tended to become less competitive. The result was that flows of funds into national savings tended to move inversely with fluctuations in market interest rates.[2] The adoption of the policy of monetary targetry in the late 1970s and early 1980s led the UK authorities to vary the yields offered on such non-marketable securities considerably more quickly and flexibly, which mitigated, but did not entirely reverse, the tendency for flows into such assets to be the reverse of that desired for monetary policy purposes.

The likelihood of capital inflows from abroad as domestic interest rates rise, thus altering the external currency flow to be financed (ECF), when the exchange rates are pegged, can form a further obstacle to the successful achievement of market operations intended to squeeze domestic liquidity. If such capital flows respond very sensitively, and in relatively large volume, to variations in financial conditions in any country, then under a regime of fixed exchange rates the autonomy of that country to undertake an independent financial policy is limited. On the other hand, in such conditions it becomes easier to achieve a desired level of international reserves by inducing large-scale capital movements.

Two of the monetary flows affecting the level of H (PSD and MAT) are thus to some considerable extent outside the control of the authorities, while another two (NMD and ECF) tend to respond perversely to interest-rate changes, in that an

---

[1] For example, the rate of interest on Post Office Savings Bank ordinary accounts, retitled National Savings Bank ordinary accounts in 1969, remained constant at $2\frac{1}{2}$ per cent from the foundation of POSB in 1861 by Gladstone until 1970, when Jenkins took steps to raise the rate offered.

[2] Earlier evidence of this was obtained from some simple regressions:

$$NMD_t = 18.98 - 47.98dC_{t-1} - 31.54dC_{t-3} + 0.594NMD_{t-1}$$
$$\quad\quad\quad (18.70)\quad\quad (22.54)\quad\quad (0.14)$$
$$R^2 = 0.56$$

$$NMD_t = 18.58 - 65.09dBS_t - 34.63dBS_{t-1} + 0.594NMD_{t-1}$$
$$\quad\quad\quad (22.19)\quad\quad (23.74)\quad\quad (0.12)$$
$$R^2 = 0.61$$

where NMD represents the inflow into non-marketable debt in £million (seasonally adjusted), dC is the change in consol rates and dBS the change in building society deposit rates, observed quarterly over the period 1963 Q3 to 1970 Q4.

increase in domestic interest rates will tend to lead to cash flows from these sources causing increases in the high-powered money base. In addition, there could be some decline in the banks' desired reserve ratios as interest rates on earning assets rise relative to rates on reserves.

In order to achieve a desired level of H, or more usefully of M, the authorities have, therefore, to try to offset movements, which may on occasions be very large, in all these other flows[1] by inducing people to purchase – or if need to be, to sell – marketable government debt. If these flows should require a very large amount of financing, then any attempt to restrict the rates of growth of the monetary aggregates imposes a severe pressure upon a Central Bank's operations in marketable debt.

Previously, in our assessment of the adjustment process within the financial system, it was assumed that the authorities could regulate the rate of return on public-sector debt, in particular the yield on marketable bonds. Under conditions of uncertainty, however, an investor can be sure only of the nominal yield on a marketable fixed-interest bond when he plans to hold that bond till maturity,[2] and even then he will face uncertainty over the prospective real yield and whether his income – expenditure plans will develop as intended. Investors have to allocate their funds on the basis of their expectations of the real yield obtainable on the various available investments. Uncertainty about future developments usually deepens the further ahead in time one peers; for example, the dispersion of our subjective probability distribution for future rates of inflation[3] is likely to be an increasing function of time. Apart from opportunities afforded to match assets against liabilities,[4] the uncertainty about the likely yield on an asset holding will tend to increase the longer the horizon to which the investor looks.

These considerations suggest that most investors would plan to review their asset holdings quite frequently, even though they may at each review compare the expected uncertain return over each relatively short planning period – i.e., the period between reviews – against the relatively safe *nominal* yield to be obtained on an asset with a maturity life equal to that of the contingent requirement for funds. So the return which investors are calculating, when deciding how to apportion their portfolio, will

---

[1] There is, however, some tendency towards negative covariation in these flows in the short run – i.e., they interact in a way that produces some partial compensation, which alleviates certain of the difficulties facing the authorities. A large foreign-exchange inflow usually encourages sales of gilts and also reduces company demand for bank credit. A big public-sector borrowing requirement implies a large private-sector surplus, which may induce large private-sector purchases of public-sector debt and, perhaps, lead to some reduction in the demand for advances. Moreover, a large public-sector borrowing requirement is more likely to coincide with an exchange outflow than with an inflow.

[2] Even this will only strictly be true for a pure discount bond – i.e., a bond whose whole return is represented by the current discount from the final redemption value. All other bonds that offer regular coupon payments before redemption will leave the holder uncertain as to the future interest rate at which he can re-invest such payments.

[3] It was partly to provide investors with a hedge against such uncertainties that the authorities issued indexed gilt-edged bonds in the UK in the 1980s. An account of this development is given in the Appendix to Chapter 13.

[4] These opportunities are greater for financial institutions, which can match assets against liabilities with both expressed in nominal-value terms, than for persons whose contingent liabilities, future expenditures greater than incomes, are in real terms and who were offered no asset offering a dated certain real yield before the UK government issued indexed bonds in the early 1980s (see the Appendix to Chapter 13).

frequently be the expected return over quite a short planning peiod. The expected return on a marketable bond, with a life till maturity longer than this short planning period, includes the known nominal interest payment plus the uncertain capital gain or loss on the realisation of that bond at the end of the period. With a short planning period, a change in the running yield resulting from a change in the price of purchasing the known interest payment(s) over that period will have a relatively small effect on the overall expected yield in comparison with any changes from expected gains or losses. So, under these circumstances, the market demand for an asset, following a change in its price, is likely to be strongly influenced by the effect of that change on expectations of the short-term future level of its price.

If a shift in the present price of an asset causes no revision to previous expectations of future price levels, then a decline in present prices will increase expected future capital gains from holding that asset. However, it is perfectly possible that expectations of future price levels might be lowered in line with a current price reduction, leaving the expected capital gain on the asset unaffected, or even lowered by more than the current change – i.e., when expectations are extrapolative.

Those reviewing their portfolios after such a change in the price of an asset, who have regressive expectations, expecting the price change to be reversed, will be tempted to buy that asset; those with extrapolative expectations will tend to sell, subject to inertia, transactions costs, etc. In a market with no transactions or information costs, so that reallocation of portfolios would occur continuously and instantaneously, equilibrium in the market for any asset would be obtained only when the sales of those expecting price falls in the next period were exactly balanced by the purchase of those expecting price rises. Even in a real-world approximation to such a perfect market, in financial markets where information is made available fairly cheaply and transactions costs are relatively low, the mean expectation of the price of each asset in the next short-term period must be that it will be at nearly the same level as now, at least over short periods. Over longer periods, there will be expected capital gains on, say, redeemable bonds selling at a discount, which expected capital gains will form part of their normal equilibrium prospective yield. In the very short run, however, any expected rise in the price of an asset would represent a very large yield at an annual rate, and would therefore induce portfolio switching into that asset. So if investors should think that the price of some asset in the next period will fall, they will sell that asset now, thus lowering its price.[1] Furthermore, if they expect its price to

---

[1] If, in addition to behaving rationally by selling when there is an expectation of a further fall in price and buying when prices are expected to rise, the market is also efficient in its use of information, then there should be no significant correlation between past and current price changes – i.e., in a regression of the form

$$Ep_{t+1} - p_t = b(p_{t-n} - p_{t-n-1})$$

b should be insignificantly different from zero. Otherwise the market should use the available information to buy (sell) the asset now, changing p_t, until $Ep_{t+1} - p_t = 0$. This does appear to be the case in some financial markets (e.g., the stock market); see the various contributions to the book on *The Random Character of Stock Market Prices* (Cootner (ed.) 1967). The position in the gilts market is less clear; Sargent (1972) concluded (p. 94) that 'The predictions of the random-walk version of the model are fairly decisively rejected by the data'. Continuing empirical studies of the workings of financial markets have resulted in conflicting empirical results in tests whether they accord with the Rational Efficient Market (REM) hypothesis. There do appear to be some findings inconsistent with that hypothesis but the deviations are sufficiently minor (in duration or extent) to leave the REM hypothesis as the dominant paradigm. See Summers and Poterba (1987), Kleidon (1986) pp. 953–1001 and Marsh and Merton (1986) pp. 483–96.

change in any future short period, say to fall between $t + n$ and $t + n + 1$, and there is a futures market, operators could sell the asset forward at time $t + n$ and repurchase at time $t + n + 1$, thus hoping to enjoy a capital gain.[1]

If asset markets are to show stability, they cannot be dominated by investors with extrapolative expectations, since equilibrium will only occur when there is a balance between the pessimists and the optimists. But is there any theoretical reason why any, or all, asset markets need be stable? Apart from the empirical observation that asset markets do generally achieve equilibrium, usually without very large price fluctuations, why should expectations not be generally extrapolative? One reason which may be advanced to expect stability, is that certain aspects of the future can be foreseen with reasonable assurance, and this limits the potential instability of the system.

Consider, for example, a situation in the market for fixed-interest debt in which everyone had a planning period of one day, whereas the shortest available security (say, a Treasury bill) had a longer life to maturity (say, twenty days). If extrapolative expectations dominate and there is an initial fall in price, the expected return over the one-day planning period will continuously induce further sales, but the expected return from such transactions will be subject to *uncertainty* whether prices tomorrow will fall, or not. As prices fall, the *certain* yield on holding a Treasury bill for twenty days will rise continuously. Assuming risk aversion, the every-increasing certain yield on Treasury bills must outweigh at some point the uncertain subjective prospect of further falls in price. Moreover, people will realise that other people will be tempted by the rising certain yield on short-dated securities. So the very uncertainty of price expectations implies that prices of short-dated assets must be given a fairly stable anchorage by their certain redemption yields. Furthermore, if prices of short-dated assets are relatively stable for this reason now they can, presumably, be expected to be relatively stable in future. If then future expected short rates are viewed as likely to stay relatively stable, arbitrage should ensure that prices of longer-dated assets will also exhibit a measure of stability.

The prospect of a fall in bond prices, particularly if the fall is at the short end of the market, leading to a limitless collapse of the market thus, in my view, chimerical. Nevertheless, this claim that the market will not exhibit complete instability, whatever the process by which expectations are generated, still allows considerable room for large-scale price fluctuations under certain circumstances, especially when there is a sudden change in conditions which scares and unnerves the market.

It is, therefore, not entirely reassuring to the authorities to believe that there will be some finite reduction in prices on fixed-interest debt which will increase the demand for debt, to the extent necessary to achieve some given change in the monetary base, if they do not know what that required price change might be. In circumstances which seem to require additional debt sales, say because policy calls for some reduction in the rate of monetary expansion, uncertainty about the appetite of the market for debt

---

[1] Taken to an extreme, this might appear to suggest that no asset market would be in full equilibrium unless prices are expected to remain unchanged on balance for ever thereafter, which simple observation will show to be untrue. Rather, the expectation of capital gain (loss) on any asset over any future period, after taking account of transactions and information costs and also of the expected flow of dividend and interest payments, must not be such as to lead operators to borrow (lend) money over the same time period in order to buy (sell) that asset. This qualified statement is, of course, much weaker, and implies only that in a rational market intelligent operators will not allow fairly sure opportunities for profit to slip away, not that markets expect the price of IBM shares, or consols, or the dollar exchange rate to remain constant for ever. A helpful analysis of exactly what are (and what are not) the implications of the hypothesis that rational investors are operating in an efficient market is provided by Sargent (1972) Section II, pp. 76–85.

might suggest that the authorities would be well advised to make their main efforts at the shorter end of the market where price and demand are supported by the certain short-term yields to maturity.

In any case, it is the *uncertainty* about the response of the public to changes in the authorities' operations, rather than the possible sharp effect upon bond prices (and interest rates), that is often most disturbing. Even if their attempts to make small additional purchases (sales) should result in very large falls (rises) in yields on bonds, the authorities would be happier in undertaking open-market operations[1] so long as they *knew* what the market response was likely to be. The question whether erratic variations in interest rates[2] are as damaging to the economy as erratic variations in monetary quantities is deferred until Chapters 12 and 15. It remains, however, the case that the greater the instability of interest rates, in response to open-market operations designed to control the growth of the money stock, the greater the trepidation of the authorities in using this technique for that purpose.

If the market's response to changing conditions were determinate, totally predictble, it would not matter how the authorities' market operations were institutionally organised, that is to say whether they operated primarily on quantities or on prices. thus, if the demand function for debt instrument i was of the form

$$D_i = f(P_{it}, P_{it-1}, \ldots, P_{it-n})$$

where this functional relationship was known, fixed and exact, it would make no difference whatsoever whether the authorities fixed a certain level of sales (S^*) and allowed the current price P^*_{it} to be determined on the market, or fixed the price level at time t at P^*_i and accommodated the demand for debt that would occur at that price by sales of S^* of debt. The result is identical.

On the other hand, when the response of the market to changed conditions is unpredictable, it will make a considerable difference whether the authorities' operations are couched in terms of offers to buy or sell certain quantities of assets at prices to be determined in the market, or in terms of offers to buy or sell assets at certain prices with quantities to be determined in the market. In the first case, asset prices will take the brunt of unforeseen fluctuations in preference functions; in the second case asset quantities, stocks, will be subject to greater uncertainty. The question of how to decide whether one would prefer a bit more price instability and less quantity instability, or vice versa, is a subject discussed further in Chapters 10, 13, 14 and 15.

One of the factors influencing the trade-off between price and quantity instability is the structure of the debt market itself. One of the reasons why the UK monetary authorities tended to operate in such a way as to lessen price instability – e.g., by issuing new public sector debt, gilts, through a tap rather than a tender system – was that they were concerned that the structure of the market, prior to the 'Big Bang' in 1986, was too under-capitalised and fragile to cope with the strains of greater price

---

[1] If the objective of policy was to reduce the rate of monetary expansion (assuming a closed economy), an increase in bond rates might do so by pushing up advances rates, and thus lowering the demand for bank loans, or more directly by cutting back the demand for real assets, and thus incomes and the demand for money, rather than by inducing any initial switch from private-sector debt into public-sector bonds.

[2] It is sometimes argued that private speculators could, and would, take over the job of stabilising bond rates if the authorities should withdraw from this function. There is some slight truth in this, but on my reading the record of the private speculator as a 'stabilising influence' has not been impressive. See further comment on this issue in Chapter 18 in the context of freely-floating exchange rates.

volatility. The increase in the number and capitalisation of market makers in the gilts market in the course of the 'Big Bang' has allowed the Bank of England to experiment with the introduction of tender issues for ordinary gilts (indexed gilts having previously been introduced by tender) from 1987 onwards.

In practice, the debt operations of the authorities in most countries usually represent something of a compromise between those who argue the case for less rate instability and those who call for less quantity instability. A system in which the central government finances its deficit itself by tender sales of marketable debt at whatever price it can get, and the Central Bank then, independently, chooses what total of debt to buy on the market to achieve the preferred money – bond asset quantity mix (i.e., with a US-type public-sector budget constraint), would seem to be in the best position to minimise quantity instability. In reality, the possibility of severe price instability forces an erosion of the Central Bank's putative independence from concern with the prices obtained on bond sales. Bond sales, in countries where the institutional arrangements are of this kind – for example, in the United States and Canada – are not made in a simple take-it-or-leave-it fashion. Instead, the markets will usually be carefully prepared in advance for the quantitative offer. Tenders will be underwritten, prices discussed with key people in the market, repurchase clauses arranged, 'even-keeling' undertaken, etc. One should not disregard the circumscribed nature of the authorities' quantitative operations, constraints which have the effect of reducing price instability at the cost of some increase in quantity instability.

On the other hand, countries such as the United Kingdom, where operations are carried out by fixing prices at which the authorities will sell (buy) certain fixed-interest securities on the market, would seem to minimise price instability at the expense of greater quantity instability. But in practice, concern with avoiding price instability is likely to be tempered by worries about quantity instability. So the authorities are likely to vary their quoted prices more rapidly in response to undesired quantity responses from the market, and even to limit their willingness necessarily to quote prices at which they would unconditionally buy in stock from the public.[1] So, by the end of the story, whatever the initial institutional arrangements for market operations may have appeared, they are likely to be run in such a way as to achieve the desired compromise (trade-off) between rate and quantity instability, a compromise largely reflecting the received economic wisdom of the day and, therefore, likely to be held at much the same point in different countries irrespective of their initial institutional framework.

3. Competition with the Private Sector

One of the reasons why it is difficult to foretell the initial response of the private sector to open-market operations undertaken by the authorities is that it depends on the strength of competition for money from the rest of the economy. If there is a strong demand for bank loans from the private sector, when banks' cash reserves are

---

[1] When the monetary authorities in the United Kingdom shifted the emphasis of policy towards paying greater attention to controlling the rate of growth of the monetary aggregates, one of the concomitant steps was to reduce the extent of intervention in the gilts market, and no longer necessarily to provide outright support for that market. See the various articles on 'Competition and Credit Control' in the *Bank of England Quarterly Bulletin* (1971) which have been brought together into a special offprint under that title.

squeezed by open-market operations, the banks are not going tamely to cut back on potential good business. They will be under pressure to raise the rate which they charge on advances, to restore portfolio equilibrium as rates on alternative assets (e.g., bonds) rise, and they will, then, bid for the funds necessary to provide the cash reserves to support creditworthy borrowers at this new higher rate by raising the yields which they offer to depositors. The competition from the banks for funds will diminish the yield differential in favour of public-sector debt, and therefore force the government to push rates on public-sector debt higher yet in order to restrain monetary expansion.[1]

The authorities sometimes react to such prospects of competition for funds between public-sector and private-sector borrowers via the banks by directly controlling the banks' ability to compete, either by quantitative ceilings on their loans to the private sector, by ceilings on the rates they can offer to depositors, or by ceilings on rates they can charge borrowers.[2] Such credit rationing is further discussed in Chapter 7.

In all these cases, however, the limitation on the ability of the banks to compete leaves untouched the basic cause of the upwards pressure on rates, which is the competition for funds by the *ultimate* borrowers in the private and public sectors. In so far as the banks cannot avoid the controls, and their efforts to do so will of themselves involve cost and frictions, the demand by ultimate borrowers will be diverted to other intermediaries and through other routes – e.g., inter-company borrowing – avoiding intermediation altogether. The imposition of direct controls on banks forces the private sector away from achieving its preferred configuration of holdings of private-sector assets and liabilities. This may allow a given volume of public-sector debt to be sold on slightly more favourable terms (i.e., lower yields), as well as keeping down bank interest rates. On the other hand, other interest rates, in markets to which the excess demand has been diverted, will be higher. In addition, the rationing of bank loans by forcing excluded borrowers to look elsewhere to unfamiliar and generally higher-cost lenders, raising information and transactions costs, will lead to some cut back in the demand for borrowed funds from private-sector borrowers.[3]

The extent to which direct controls on banks lead to a diversion, as compared with a net reduction, in ultimate borrowing is, however, not known. The authorities have little idea of the overall effect of their actions when they introduce credit rationing, and the selection of this or that figure for, say, the maximum expansion in loans to the private sector is an arbitrary process involving little or no economic justification.

The maintenance of ceiling controls, particularly when these are set in terms of some quantitative limit to the total volume of loans, cumulatively distorts the allocation of funds. It also becomes that much harder to use the rate of growth of the

---

[1] 'The most probable outcome, in fact, is a tendency to a competitive spiralling of Treasury bill and temporary money interest rates as the markets compete for an inadequate supply of funds,' p. 31 of Cramp's, 'The Control of Bank Deposits' *Lloyds Bank Review, No. 86 October* (1967) pp. 16–35. In view of the subsequent problems of the UK authorities in controlling the pace of monetary expansion after the removal of ceilings on bank advances in 1971, Cramp's analysis appears not only correct but almost prophetic.

[2] These latter restrictions induce banks to cut back on such loans as other rates rise, in order to maintain overall portfolio equilibrium.

[3] 'A diffused difficulty of borrowing,' to use the term coined by Harrod and adopted in the Radcliffe Report, *The Committee on the Working of the Monetary System: Report*, para. 460.

affected aggregates as an indicator, or monitoring device, of economic developments, particularly on occasions when the controls are introduced or relaxed. For example, after decades during which rates payable on bank time deposits had been fixed by the London clearing bankers in relation to Bank Rate, and years during which bank loans to the private sector had been restrained by quantitative ceilings, in the autumn of 1971 the banks became free, and encouraged, to compete for business. To what extent did this change in the system account for the much more rapid expansion of bank deposits, relative to the growth of incomes, in 1972 and in 1973 than in former years? Even with hindsight it is difficult to answer that question, and it was not possible to make an accurate guess in forecasting.

The extent that banks and other intermediaries will push up rates in competition with the public sector for funds depends largely on the interest elasticity of the demand for loans in the private sector. If borrowers are prepared to pay a higher rate, it will be worthwhile for intermediaries to bid more aggressively for funds to meet their requirements. With the growth of advances in the United Kingdom hedged around by ceiling controls for decades before 1971 (and subsequently in the 1970s by the 'corset' control, first introduced in 1973–4, interspersed with easier periods when the authorities contented themselves with the lighter touch of 'moral suasion'), the time path of advances has been so disturbed by these extraneous factors that an accurate estimation of the ordinary economic determinants of bank lending to the private sector in this country has been made extremely difficult. This has made it harder for the authorities to reckon how far they might have to push up interest rates in order to bring about some given reduction in the demand by the private sector for borrowing. Various empirical estimates of the demand for bank advances have been made in the United Kingdom[1] but the range of uncertainty remains extensive.

The situation may be further complicated by lags in the response of demand for bank loans to changes in the rates charged. Arranging the financing of a project, even a simple exercise such as consumer-borrowing for the purchase of a car, requires a certain amount of time. The money will usually not be drawn till the negotiations, plans, etc. are almost completed. By this time, a project will have developed a momentum of its own and last-minute cancellation will be a step unpopular to both sides. So a rise in advances rates is, perhaps, more likely to have an effect in causing withdrawals and reconsiderations of plans, the financial arrangements for which are at a somewhat earlier stage of negotiation.

If the demand for advances is a *lagged* function of the rates charged, and there is some empirical evidence that such lagged responses are usual in monetary affairs,[2] then it becomes much more difficult to adjust financial conditions smoothly from one equilibrium situation to another without setting up cyclical eddies and instabilities. Consider, for example, a situation in which the demand for advances only responds very slightly to changes in interest rates in period 1, and then reacts much more strongly in period 2. Then if the authorities want to cut back advances steadily, they have to raise rates very sharply in period 1 (weak effect), since advances are mostly a function of the unchanged interest rates in the previous period. Then advances will go down so much in period 2, as people react to the higher rates in period 1, that in order to maintain a steady decline in advances, the authorities may have to cut rates below

[1] For example, by Norton (1969) pp. 486–90 and subsequently by Goodhart in (1984a) Chapter IV.

[2] See, for example, Pierce and Thomson (1973) pp. 115–32, especially pp. 128–31.

the initial starting level in period 2. In period 3 rates will have to rise even more to counteract the low rates in period 2, etc.

This kind of model can clearly be given a formal algebraic representation, in which it appears in a difference, or differential, equation format, whose stability (or instability) depends on the coefficients and structure of the system. The sort of model discussed above could be representated as a simplified, linearised two-equation model, as follows:

$$L_t = a_1 r_{Lt} + a_2 r_{Lt-1} + ,\ldots, a_i r_{Lt-i}$$

The demand for loans is a function of current and previous rates charged on loans:

$$r_{Lt} = b_o + b_1 r_{bt}$$

The banks set the rate for loans in line with the current market rates on government debt.

The signs of all the 'a' coefficients are presumably negative, while $b_1 > 0$, so that if the authorities raise market rates with a single jump to a new level, which is then held, advances will decline in all periods towards a new lower equilibrium level. However, the rate of decline in each period may be very variable, depending on the values of the 'a' coefficients. If the authorities should wish to bring about a steady rate of change in the level of advances, they might not find themselves able to do this, even assuming full information on the coefficients, without imparting some variation, even possibly instability, into the time path of the instrument, in this example market rates (r_b). For example, assume that the demand for advances takes the following linear forms:

(i) $L_t = 10,000 - 700 r_{Lt} - 200 r_{Lt-1} - 100 r_{Lt-2}$
(ii) $L_t = 10,000 - 200 r_{Lt} - 600 r_{Lt-1} - 200 r_{Lt-2}$

and that the rate on bank loans is set by the banks at a constant mark-up over bond rate, so that $r_L = b_o + r_b$. Then a once-for-all change in r_b, say an increase of 1 per cent, would lead to a similar reduction, after three periods, in bank advances of 100 in both cases. But if the authorities desired a *steady* decrease in advances of 100 per period, the requisite time paths of r_b in cases (i) and (ii) would be as shown in Table 6.1.

TABLE 6.1

Change in r_b	1	2	3	4	5	6	7	8	9
Case (i)	+0.14	+0.10	+0.09	+0.10	+0.10	+0.10	+0.10	+0.10	+0.10
Case (ii)	+0.50	-1.0	+3.0	-7.5	+20.0	-52.0	+136	-356	+934

Given lagged responses, the pursuit of steady adjustment in some objective variable(s) may bring with it, then, a danger of inducing instrument instability.[1] The likelihood of inducing unstable conditions in financial markets by holding to a policy of maintaining a stable rate of growth of the money stock might be increased if market operators became able to anticipate how the authorities were likely to react in

[1] See, for example, Holbrook (1972) pp. 57–65. A paper in this field, of particular relevance to the issue of controlling the money supply, by Hester and Britto on 'Stability and Control of the Money Supply', was presented by Hester at a meeting of the Money Study Group at the London School of Economics (1973).

each situation. Whenever dealers saw any weakening in the rate of growth of $M1$ below the supposed target of the authorities they might seek to buy Treasury bills and other short-term fixed-interest debt in the expectation that the Federal Reserve would have to drive market rates down further in order to restore the rate of growth of the money stock. The onset of sluggishness in $M1$ would thus cause a general strengthening in the demand for market debt, in anticipation of the Fed's reaction, and vice versa, when the expansion of the money stock was seen as pushing the Fed into a more restrictive posture. This kind of response, which commentators[1] have seen as likely to recur whenever the authorities *aimed* to achieve some constant rate of growth of the monetary aggregates in principle, could exaggerate yet further the resulting fluctuations in market rates and make it even more difficult to maintain a steady pace of monetary expansion in practice.

Institutional arrangements may further exacerbate such problems. Banks tend to relate the rates which they charge individual borrowers, depending on their various categories, to some notional prime rate, or base rate. This rate is a highly visible administered one, and much public comment is evoked when it changes. This induces banks to delay altering such rates until financial conditions have clearly shifted significantly. So, when the authorities act to undertake open-market sales and to raise interest rates, rates on bank loans will lag behind somewhat. The resulting continued, or even enhanced, demand for bank loans will place further pressure on bank reserves, so that banks will be forced to bid even higher for certificates of deposit (CDs) and large time deposits in order to attract funds.

As a result, CD rates would rise relative to base rates. Indeed, there were several occasions in the United Kingdom, in 1972 and 1973, when for several months at a time there was small potential turn to be made by a customer whose credit standing enabled him to borrow at the finest, blue-chip rate in borrowing money from his own bank to reinvest with another, in CDs! In this case, the initial effect on the monetary aggregates of a restrictive policy can actually be perverse.[2]

The most serious, and extreme, example of this syndrome occurred later, after Chairman Volcker of the Federal Reserve Board introduced a modified version of monetary base control in October 1979. In this new approach, the authorities attempted to maintain a steady rate of growth of non-borrowed bank reserves. Although the resulting pressures on the monetary system were eased by the ability of banks to increase or repay *borrowed* reserves, as market interest rates varied relative to the Fed's administered discount rate, nevertheless the attempt to operate the system in this fashion not only caused the volatility of interest rates to increase drastically, by a factor of about three or four,[2] but also led to enhanced short-term

---

[1] For example, A Wojnilower, in his talk on 'A New Monetary Environment' to the New York State Bankers Association, 16 November 1973 in the section on 'The Consequences or a Money Supply Policy'; and Pepper (1973).

[2] Difficulties of this sort with the working of the new organisational form of the banking system in the United Kingdom, which had been unveiled in 1971 with the publication of the consultative document on 'Competition and Credit Control,' *Bank of England Quarterly Bulletin*, Vol. 11, No. 2 (June 1971) pp. 189–93, were largely responsible for the adoption of the supplementary technique, involving calls for non-interest-bearing deposits to be placed with the Bank of England in relation to the growth of interest-bearing deposits above some allowable rate of expansion, which was introduced in December 1973, which became known as the 'corset'; for a post-mortem account of the working of this control instrument, see *Bank of England Quarterly Bulletin* Vol. 22, No. 1. (March 1982)) pp. 36–44.

[2] Dickens (1987).

volatility – i.e., from quarter to quarter – in the growth rate of the aggregates themselves. While the monetary aggregates were broadly controlled in accordance with their targets over the longer one-year target periods, and the resulting shock to inflationary expectations was no doubt salutary at the time, nevertheless the operational problems of this approach were so serious that it was effectively abandoned in the latter half of 1982.

4. Complications and Conclusions

Interpretation and analysis of monetary developments is never easy, but it is, at least, facilitated by the frequency and promptness with which monetary data are available in the United States.[1] In most European countries, including the United Kingdom, data are available only once a month, reporting the position as at the close of business on a single day. The monetary position on any one day is subject to a whole range of random factors, strikes, proximity to a movable holiday – e.g., Easter – large new issues on the Stock Exchange, foreign-exchange crises, etc. whose effects can be only roughly estimated. In addition, the data are not entirely accurate: for example, banks may not always be in a position to tell whether they are dealing with another bank as agent for another party or as a principal. The total of reported interbank claims on other banks thus differs from the total of reported interbank liabilities to other banks. The attribution of 'float' between deposits and overdrafts, and between sectors, represents an informed guess rather than a known statistic. The estimation of seasonal factors in the course of seasonal adjustment is subject to uncertainty and is often revised. There are other examples of weak points in the data, and there always remains residual human error. With observations occurring once a month, the expected size of the random variation can often be quite large relative to the systematic component.

The random fluctuations in these occasional data make it all the more difficult to observe what the trends in the system really are at any time.[2] If action is taken early on the basis of one or two months' figures there will be a danger of taking an unnecessary step, while if action is delayed until the need for it can be more firmly established there will be an opposite danger of the system diverging even further from its desired path (the more so since there will have been an additional lapse of time in compiling the statistics, a period requiring several weeks in the United Kingdom).

The authorities are uncertain what is really happening; they are uncertain of the precise effects on the system of the steps they may take to adjust it; they are uncertain of the timing of these effects. In this world, a generous modicum of instability is inevitable. As already noted in Section 2, and discussed further in Chapter 14, there is some choice over the form in which one may prefer to suffer such instability. If the authorities try to maintain some given rate of change in each period in the quantities,

---

[1] 'The daily average money supply series published by the Board is a constructed series based on member bank deposit data, weekly condition reports of large commercial banks. Federal Reserve Bank balance sheets, ... [etc.]. This series is published weekly with an eight-day lag; that is, the first estimate published for a statement week ending Wednesday comes out a week from the subsequent Thursday. These estimates are usually revised to a degree over the weeks immediately following publication, as new or revised figures dribble in', from Axilrod and Beck (1973) p. 95.

[2] Mills (1981).

the monetary aggregates, by open-market operations irrespective of market conditions or of lagged reactions, they may be able to do so only at the expense of considerable price instability in such markets. Equally, the more price stability is maintained, the more severe may be the quantity instability.

To recapitulate, it is neither very helpful nor very informative, at least from the standpoint of the responsible authorities, to be told that, given stable – predictable ratios for banks' cash reserves and the public's currency – deposit holdings, the total money stock will – indeed must – vary in line with the high-powered money base. What matters are the problems that the authorities face in trying to alter the monetary base and the money stock, and the effect that actions to this end may have on other variables – e.g., interest rates. In this chapter, we have tried to outline some of the main critical factors which do determine whether the authorities would have a simple – or, at the other end of the scale, a virtually impossible – task in trying to control monetary expansion.

There would seem to be four such main factors, which are:

1. the interest elasticity of the demand for advances;
2. the size of the public-sector deficit;
3. the elasticity of substitution between foreign and domestic assets in an open economy with fixed exchange rates, or the extent of resulting fluctuations in exchange rates when these are flexible; and
4. market reactions to the authorities open-market operations.

Consequently the most useful statistical approach to the presentation of monetary data, for purposes of interpretation and analysis, is that which highlights these critical factors. Accordingly official monetary statistics in the United Kingdom, in the *Bank of England Quarterly Bulletin* and the CSO's *Financial Statistics*, contain tables of that accounting identity in which changes in the money stock are expressed in terms of the following components: the public-sector deficit, sales of public-sector debt to the non-bank public, bank advances to the private sector and external financing of the public sector.[1] This has become generally known as the 'counterparts' approach to the analysis and assessment of monetary developments.

An example is given in Table 6.2, taken from the *Bank of England Quarterly Bulletin* Vol. 28, No. 3 (August 1988) Table 12.1 in the Statistical Annex.

---

[1] You may note that changes in the banks' cash reserve base are not separately distinguished in this presentation. The elements that are included show the volume of additional bank lending, in aggregate, to the central government, but not how this is split up among cash reserves, special deposits, Treasury bills, bonds, etc. Does this latter not matter? The banks generally do have a good deal of freedom in deciding the form in which they prefer to take-up, or to sell, government debt, to finance the authorities' residual borrowing requirement (i.e., that total not financed by the non-bank public or from overseas). Nevertheless, the authorities can seek to induce the banks to hold their public-sector debt in one or other ways by varying the rates offered, or can force the banks by direct control to hold more of some particular asset (e.g., by varying reserve requirements or calling for special deposits). As these measures force the banks to wish to readjust their portfolios, they will change the rates they offer on deposits and advances and this step will alter, for example, the non-bank public's take-up of government debt and the demand for advances. A call for special deposits by itself need have no effect whatsoever on the total money stock, if it simply leads to a rearrangement of the banks' holdings of public-sector debt with no subsequent effect on relative interest rates (or on the non-price conditions that banks, particularly when operating under external constraints, may vary in order to influence the total of advances). The extent of the effect will depend on the adjustments in relative yields that ensue throughout the system.

TABLE 6.2 (£m)

| | Public sector borrowing requirement (surplus −) | | | Purchases (−) of public sector net debt by UK private sector (other than banks) | | | External and foreign currency finance of public sector (increase −) | | Banks sterling lending to UK private sector[a] | | External and foreign currency transactions of UK banks | Net non-deposit sterling liabilities (increase −) | Change in M3 (columns 3 to 9 + 11 + 12) | |
	Central government borrowing requirement	Other public sector contribution	Total	Other public sector net debt	Central government debt — British government stocks	Other	Purchases of British government stocks by overseas sector	Other	Unadjusted	Seasonally adjusted			Unadjusted	Seasonally adjusted
	1	2	3	4	5	6	7	8	9	10	11	12	13	14
Unadjusted														
Financial years														
1984/85	+10,164	− 64	+10,100	+ 453	−9,362	−3,727	−1,339	− 682	+18,585		+ 337	−2,658	+11,707	
1985/86	+10,962	−5,308	+ 5,654	+1,592	−2,800	−2,267	−2,276	+ 427	+21,389		− 721	−1,991	+19,007	
1986/87	+10,497	−7,059	+ 3,438	+2,681	−1,734	−2,528	−2,613	+1,116	+30,427		− 615	−4,586	+25,586	
1987/88	+ 734	−4,206	− 3,472	+1,204	−3,797	−2,150	−3,604	+11,934	+44,728		−6,838	−4,582	+33,423	
Quarters														
1985 3rd qtr	+ 4,465	−1,626	+ 2,839	+ 494	− 730	− 618	− 377	− 46	+ 4,309		− 32	− 916	+ 4,923	
4th	+ 4,450	−2,465	+ 1,985	+ 821	−1,018	− 737	− 550	+ 377	+ 5,154		−1,747	+ 489	+ 4,020	
1986 1st qtr	− 826	−1,056	− 1,882	+ 104	− 92	− 68	− 72	+ 374	+ 7,520		+ 812	− 571	+ 6,125	
2nd	+ 6,377	−3,946	+ 2,431	+1,669	− 820	−1,158	− 767	+ 388	+ 5,650		+1,221	−1,661	+ 6,953	
3rd	+ 3,960	− 418	+ 3,542	+ 107	− 782	− 810	− 540	+ 443	+ 6,733		− 874	+ 574	+ 6,359	
4th	− 1,050	− 620	− 1,670	+ 337	−1,640	− 420	− 725	+ 162	+10,542		−1,607	+ 943	+ 3,712	
1987 1st qtr	+ 1,210	−2,075	− 865	+ 568	+1,508	− 140	− 581	+1,333	+ 7,502		+ 645	−1,408	+ 8,562	
2nd	+ 4,044	−2,593	+ 1,451	+ 835	−1,814	−1,115	− 983	+4,048	+ 8,176		− 634	−1,507	+ 8,457	
3rd	+ 356	+ 118	+ 474	+ 498	−1,029	− 437	−2,183	+ 263	+11,252		−2,026	− 797	+ 8,073	
4th	− 1,599	− 869	− 2,468	− 20	−2,173	− 496	− 340	+5,956	+11,738		−1,673	− 938	+ 9,586	
1988 1st qtr	− 2,067	− 862	− 2,929	+ 109	− 839	− 102	− 98	+1,667	+13,562		−2,505	−1,340	+ 7,307	
2nd	+ 140	−1,790	− 1,650	+ 672	+ 365	− 135	− 457	+ 568	+14,731		−3,958	−1,054	+ 9,082	
Months														
1987 Jan	− 3,298	− 369	− 3,667	+ 34	+ 508	+ 351	+ 169	+ 248	+ 1,492	+ 1,697	− 516	+ 304	− 1,077	+ 1,997

Feb.	+ 195	− 547	− 352	+ 175	+ 326	− 209	− 103	+ 142	+ 2,577	+ 2,676	+ 193	+ 134	+ 2,883	+ 2,842
Mar.	+ 4,313	− 1,159	+ 3,154	+ 359	+ 674	− 282	− 647	+ 943	+ 3,433	+ 2,529	+ 968	− 1,846	+ 6,756	+ 4,260
Apr.	+ 2,459	− 1,785	+ 2,014	+ 265	− 558	− 63	− 234	+ 1,789	+ 1,118	+ 2,190	+ 1,114	+ 12	+ 3,229	+ 3,491
May	+ 1,623	+ 363	− 162	+ 481	− 1,017	+ 454	+ 191	+ 2,855	+ 2,346	+ 2,560	− 363	− 592	+ 3,285	+ 2,377
June	− 38	− 117	− 401	+ 89	− 239	− 598	− 940	− 596	+ 4,712	+ 4,009	+ 843	− 927	+ 1,943	+ 2,372
July	− 299	− 217	+ 416	+ 266	+ 645	+ 121	− 1,215	+ 401	+ 4,599	+ 4,486	− 1,531	+ 1,640	+ 4,268	+ 3,668
Aug.	+ 845	+ 452	+ 628	+ 428	+ 285	+ 233	− 539	+ 323	+ 1,134	+ 2,633	+ 796	− 29	+ 2,147	+ 2,255
Sept.	+ 190	− 345	+ 262	+ 196	+ 99	− 83	− 429	+ 185	+ 5,519	+ 4,329	− 1,291	− 2,408	+ 1,658	+ 2,475
Oct.	− 660	− 1,145	− 1,005	+ 11	+ 54	− 69	− 911	+ 3,788	+ 2,965	+ 2,924	+ 629	+ 357	+ 5,797	+ 6,506
Nov.	+ 477	+ 621	− 1,622	+ 326	− 1,541	+ 247	+ 619	+ 150	+ 3,305	+ 3,278	+ 168	+ 348	+ 1,206	+ 119
Dec.	− 462		+ 159	− 335	− 686	− 180	− 48	− 2,318	+ 5,468	+ 5,000	− 2,470	− 1,643	+ 2,583	+ 2,522
1988 Jan.	− 5,870	+ 409	+ 6,279	− 106	− 471	+ 223	− 258	+ 373	+ 5,100	+ 5,597	− 1,676	+ 1,069	− 2,025	+ 1,050
Feb.	+ 154	+ 621	+ 467	+ 137	+ 784	+ 87	− 241	+ 40	+ 2,458	+ 2,553	+ 457	+ 174	+ 693	+ 890
Mar.	+ 3,649	+ 168	+ 3,817	+ 140	+ 416	− 238	− 401	+ 1,334	+ 6,004	+ 4,889	+ 372	− 2,583	+ 8,639	+ 5,589
Apr.	− 673	+ 455	− 1,128	+ 429	+ 813	− 98	− 273	+ 302	+ 4,366	+ 6,075	− 1,673	+ 299	+ 1,411	+ 3,079
May	− 214	+ 346	+ 560	+ 68	+ 465	+ 42	+ 56	+ 186	+ 3,111	+ 3,128	+ 225	+ 460	+ 2,547	+ 1,189
June	+ 1,027	+ 989	+ 38	+ 311	+ 713	− 79	− 240	+ 80	+ 7,254	+ 6,174	− 2,060	+ 893	+ 5,124	+ 4,770

Seasonally adjusted (financial year constrained)

Quarters

1985 3rd qtr	+ 3,771	− 1,946	+ 1,825	+ 513	− 730	− 575	− 377	− 52	+ 4,585	− 51	+ 581	+ 4,557
4th	+ 3,522	− 2,093	+ 1,429	+ 489	− 1,018	− 548	− 550	− 424	+ 5,079	− 1,587	+ 53	+ 2,923
1986 1st qtr	+ 2,747	− 1,624	+ 1,123	+ 554	− 92	− 350	− 72	+ 390	+ 6,508	+ 538	− 410	+ 8,189
2nd	+ 5,643	− 3,391	+ 2,252	+ 1,729	− 820	− 1,078	− 767	+ 429	+ 6,475	+ 819	− 1,772	+ 7,267
3rd	+ 2,851	− 762	+ 2,089	+ 205	− 782	− 481	− 540	+ 449	+ 6,879	+ 299	− 225	+ 5,987
4th	− 842	− 464	− 1,306	+ 242	− 1,640	− 649	− 725	+ 214	+ 10,419	− 1,417	− 1,306	+ 3,404
1987 1st qtr	+ 2,845	− 2,442	+ 403	+ 915	+ 1,508	− 320	− 581	+ 1,350	+ 6,902	+ 282	− 1,360	+ 9,099
2nd	+ 2,395	− 1,953	+ 442	+ 932	− 1,814	− 1,097	− 983	+ 4,091	+ 8,758	+ 544	− 1,545	+ 8,240
3rd	+ 297	− 288	+ 9	+ 170	+ 1,029	− 69	− 2,183	+ 258	+ 11,448	− 1,936	+ 328	+ 8,398
4th	− 1,600	− 735	− 2,335	+ 146	− 2,173	− 345	− 340	+ 5,900	+ 11,202	− 1,428	− 1,426	+ 8,909
1988 1st qrt	− 358	− 1,230	− 1,588	+ 248	− 839	− 639	− 98	+ 1,685	+ 13,039	− 2,930	− 1,349	+ 7,529
2nd	− 1,206	− 1,122	− 2,328	+ 777	+ 365	− 114	− 457	+ 610	+ 15,377	− 4,065	− 1,127	+ 9,038

TABLE 6.2 (£m)

	1	2	3	4	5	6	7	8	9	10	11	12	13	14
	Public sector borrowing requirement (surplus −)			Purchases (−) of public sector net debt by UK private sector (other than banks)			External and foreign currency finance of public sector (increase −)		Banks sterling lending to UK private sector[a]		External and foreign currency transactions of UK banks	Net non-deposit sterling liabilities (increase −)	Change in M3 (columns 9 + 11 + 12)	
	Central government borrowing requirement	Other public sector contribution	Total	Other public sector net debt	Central government debt British government stocks	Other	Purchases of British government stocks by overseas sector	Other	Unadjusted	Seasonally adjusted			Unadjusted	Seasonally adjusted
Seasonally adjusted (calendar year constrained)														
Quarters														
1985 3rd qtr	+ 3,983	− 1,999	+ 1,984	+ 494	− 730	− 577	− 377	− 51		+ 4,524	− 115	− 610		+ 4,541
4th	+ 3,155	− 2,097	+ 1,058	+ 501	− 1,018	− 558	− 550	− 422		+ 5,327	− 1,367	+ 71		+ 3,042
1986 1st qtr	+ 2,153	− 1,611	+ 542	+ 599	− 92	− 248	− 72	− 449		+ 6,490	+ 515	− 413		+ 7,712
2nd	+ 5,462	− 3,326	+ 2,136	+ 1,644	− 820	− 1,077	− 767	+ 391		+ 6,415	+ 730	− 1,770		+ 6,918
3rd	+ 2,593	− 751	+ 1,842	+ 283	− 782	− 468	− 540	+ 427		+ 6,859	− 462	− 277		+ 5,440
4th	− 1,746	− 352	− 2,098	+ 257	− 1,640	− 663	− 725	− 213		+ 10,681	− 1,231	− 1,297		+ 3,071
1987 1st qtr	+ 2,708	− 2,488	+ 220	+ 1,053	+ 1,508	− 381	− 581	+ 1,351		+ 6,637	+ 257	− 1,351		+ 8,713
2nd	+ 2,699	− 1,931	+ 768	+ 825	− 1,814	− 1,203	− 983	+ 4,091		+ 8,765	− 626	− 1,535		+ 8,288
3rd	+ 644	− 304	+ 340	+ 105	+ 1,029	− 172	− 2,183	+ 258		+ 11,398	− 2,061	+ 365		+ 8,349
4th	− 2,040	− 696	− 2,736	+ 102	− 2,173	− 432	− 340	+ 5,900		+ 11,561	− 1,258	− 1,412		+ 9,008
1988 1st qtr	− 392	− 1,273	− 1,665	+ 357	− 839	− 631	− 98	+ 1,686		+ 12,758	− 2,918	− 1,333		+ 7,317
2nd	− 954	− 1,087	− 2,041	+ 691	+ 365	− 124	− 457	+ 609		+ 15,383	− 4,149	− 1,118		+ 9,159

[a] Including net purchases by the issue Department of private sector commercial bills and of promissory notes relating to shipbuilding paper guaranteed by the Department of Trade and Industry

It is, of course, the case that no accounting identity by itself provides any theoretical explanation of the process of the determination of the money stock. But a well-chosen identity should lead the user of the statistics to go further to enquire the reasons for the fluctuations in debt sales, in international capital flows, etc. One cannot display the complete working of the monetary system in a single table, but one can, at least, encourage users to ask the right kind of questions about the more important behavioural relationships by one's choice of accounting identities.

VII
Credit Rationing

Summary

In this chapter, we examine the determinants and extent of credit rationing. The most common form of credit rationing is actually that imposed by the authorities' own credit controls. This is explored in Section 1. Such controls are common in developed countries, and have also been pervasive in less developed countries, LDCs. They have been introduced both for macro-policy purposes, to reduce credit extension, monetary growth and aggregate expenditures without having to raise interest rates as high as would otherwise have been required, and for micro-policy reasons, to 'improve' the allocation of scarce credit. Both justifications are, at best, dubious. Disintermediation and adverse structural effects hinder the use of credit controls for macro-policy purposes, while such arguments as can be put forward to suggest that official guidance can result in better credit allocation than the free market seem strained and unlikely to be important enough in reality to justify the practice.

Turning in Section 2 to credit rationing that arises from the internal working of credit markets, we follow Jaffee and Modigliani in distinguishing between 'disequilibrium' and 'equilibrium' rationing. 'Disequilibrium' rationing occurs when lenders are slow to adjust the interest rates that they charge on loans as external conditions change. Two examples of such behaviour are given. First, in those cases when interest rates are administratively set by a cartel or by a prominent market leader, various considerations, some 'political', will slow the speed of adjustment to equilibrium. This can be quantitatively highly significant, as in the case of UK building societies. Second, in many markets, lenders (market makers) set limits on their exposure to counter-parties. A common reaction to information on the changing credit-worthiness of such counter-parties, at least initially, is to change such limits rather than the rate charged.

Finally, in Section 3, we explore the possibility of the existence of 'equilibrium' rationing – i.e., rationing that would still occur after full adjustment to a static equilibrium. Although the actual empirical extent of such rationing is unclear, it has been the subject of greater theoretical interest. Because of the increasing risk of default as interest rates and loan size increase, a bank's offer curve for loans will tend to be backward bending. Faced with such a curve, borrowers will choose their best *available* option, which will often involve them in borrowing a lesser sum than they would want at that interest rate in an unconstrained condition. Whether that should or should not be described as 'rationing' is a semantic question. When bankers cannot distinguish between borrowers with more or less risky positions, they may then be forced to ration borrowers in circumstances when, with fuller information, both they and the prospective borrower would have preferred to arrange a larger loan at the same interest rates. We end by enquiring whether such information asymmetries can be relaxed or eliminated by varying the collateral requirements, as well as the interest rates, negotiated in the loan agreement. This latter issue seems, as yet, to be undecided.

1. Credit Control

There has been continuing interest and some analytical advance in recent years on the subject of credit rationing by banks. The main focus of the recent analytical interest has been to explore whether forms of rationing might be inherent (endogenous) within the ordinary workings of the credit and labour markets, for example as a consequence of innate information asymmetries.[1] Whatever the current state of the theoretical debate on the likelihood of such 'equilibrium' rationing, it has not yet proved possible to provide virtually *any* empirical estimation of the scale of such effects. There is, therefore, a curious feature in this field that the intensity of *theoretical* interest on the subject of the various forms and causes of rationing is, if anything, inversely related to their known, empirically demonstrable, frequency of occurrence.

In practice, then, the most common form of rationing is that imposed on the banking system *exogenously* by the authorities. Such external constraints may take several forms. In less developed countries, these frequently take the form of ceilings on interest rates on both deposits and bank loans. With the demand for bank loans often – indeed, generally – higher than the available supply at the pegged set of rates, there will frequently be subsidiary qualitative guidance about the distribution of rationed bank loans to preferred classes of borrowers. Such constraints on the free working of the price mechanism in credit markets have been widespread – indeed, the rule rather than the exception in LDCs.[2]

Credit rationing in this genus – i.e., imposed by the authorities – has not, however, been limited to LDCs. Most industrialised countries outside of North America imposed direct controls over the volume of bank lending for some, often most, of the time from 1945 till the 1980s. Examples of such controls are 'window guidance' in Japan, the pre-1971 credit ceilings and the 'corset' in the UK, the latter taking the form of an incremental control on the rate of expansion,[3] the *encadrement du credit* in France, and the various forms of lending controls in countries such as Italy, Sweden, Holland, South Africa and New Zealand that flourished in the 1960s and 1970s and have been largely dismantled during the course of the 1980s.

Unlike the LDCs, where a major, if not the main, component in the system of rationing (or 'repression' as it has now come to be called) takes the form of limits on the interest rates that banks may offer or charge,[4] most of the control mechanisms imposed in developed countries took the form of quota systems, either with the level of, or rate of change in, the allowable volume of lending set by the authorities. This was generally accompanied by a modicum of qualitative guidance, given varying degrees of support by official monitoring and penalties for disobedience (ranging from low in the UK to quite high in certain other countries), in the form of preference

---

[1] See the many works of Stiglitz on this subject referenced in 'Information and Economic Analysis – A Perspective' (1985b) pp. 21–41.

[2] See, for example, Fry (1982a) pp. 731–50.

[3] See the article on 'The supplementary special deposits scheme', *Bank of England Quarterly Bulletin* March 1982a).

[4] See Fry (1982a) and (1982b) pp. 1049–57.

for exporters and manufacturing industry and deterrence on lending to importers, service industry and, above all, to personal consumers; the constraints involved in such lending quotas were consciously qualified and relaxed, most notably in France and Holland, by allowing the banks to lend additional funds beyond their quota allotment when such extra funds were raised by banks from 'non-monetary' liabilities – e.g., long-term savings deposits, bonds and other forms of capital issue.

Such quotas (lending ceilings) in the industrialised countries were rarely reinforced by direct controls on bank lending rates. Nor, despite the urgings of economists, were quota allowances as a rule ever auctioned off by the authorities, nor were units of quota rights made transferable in officially blessed markets. Instead, the quota rights become absorbed into the value of the property of those to whom they were initially allocated – e.g., into the value of farms in the EEC allocated milk quotas under the Common Agricultural Policy – and the quota rights could be transferred *en bloc* by buying – selling the property to which they are attached. These institutional practices continue to the present day.

The existence of such ceiling controls clearly restricts the supply of bank loans, making the supply curve vertical, as shown by line AB in Figure 7.1. This need not, however, induce credit *rationing*, since profit-maximisation would seem to suggest that banks, subject to such controls, should raise their lending rates from r_0 to r_1, thereby achieving the greatest possible return from the constrained volume of lending. In general, and over a wide range of examples, this did *not* happen. Much more frequently, banks maintained their lending rates at a customary, or cartel determined, or administratively set margin over deposit rates, and then allocated the scarce funds through various forms of non-price rationing – e.g., the authorities' qualitative guidance, established banker–customer relationships, political influence and other forms of corruption, queuing and persistence, etc. Possibly the banks felt

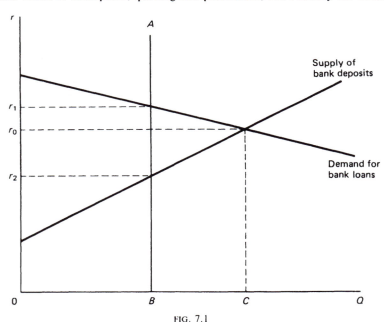

FIG. 7.1

that any steps which they took to benefit themselves by raising the margins over their cost of funds in such cases would have been so widely unpopular that it would have caused the authorities rapidly to expropriate such gains by higher taxes or to prevent them by also setting limits on lending rates.

Although it was uncommon for banks to alter their margins (spreads) over the cost of deposits in response to short-run changes in the tightness of imposition of lending ceilings, in the longer term these had an adverse effect on competition and efficiency and, thus, led on average to higher margins than would otherwise have occurred. Many of the banking systems outside the US were operated by a cartel; in such cases, lending ceilings were easier to introduce and in some ways the ceilings tended to reinforce official acceptance and support for the cartels. Again, within a system of lending ceilings, a bank manager's only real decision is which credit-worthy applicant to refuse; this naturally prevents bankers from even considering ways to improve, to extend and to cheapen their role as providers of credit. For example, the retail deposit clearing banks in the UK moved to enter the personal mortgage market only in the early 1980s – thus drastically lowering the cost of borrowing to persons with available unused collateral in the form of their home equity, when they began to believe that such credit controls had been finally abandoned.

Nevertheless, the combination of credit rationing, higher margins and loss of incentives for greater efficiency brought about by the imposition of credit controls on an already cartelised system led inevitably to pressures for financial flows to be diverted to other uncontrolled channels. This process has become known as 'disinter-mediation' and has taken a variety of forms in various countries, for example, the growth of inter-company trade credit or commercial paper, the development of fringe banks and other uncontrolled finance houses, the continuation and even expansion of 'traditional' money-lenders, etc.

More recently, with the growth of multi-national companies and of multi-national banks serving them, together with the fall in the transaction and information costs of undertaking financial transactions abroad, the ability of the authorities to constrain total lending, rather than simply to divert financial intermediation abroad, has increasingly depended on the maintenance of a comprehensive set of exchange controls. In recent years, the growth of competition facing the cartelised national banking systems both from indigenous non-banks (fringe banks) and from internat-ional cross-border intermediation, together with a shift in public views and ideology towards relatively uncontrolled free markets, has led many countries to dismantle their systems of direct credit controls.

This raises an important issue concerning the objectives that were originally thought to be attained by the imposition of such credit controls. There was generally a macro-policy objective to control the level of aggregate demand, by influencing the growth of credit and of money, and a micro-policy objective to 'improve' the allocation of resources by diverting cheap capital to favoured users, and to limit or prevent access to capital by less-favoured borrowers (e.g., persons).

The argument for credit controls as a macro-policy instrument is that they could work quickly and effectively, especially in crisis, and would allow a given degree of restraint to be applied at considerably lower levels of interest rates than would otherwise be necessary, especially if borrowers were generally interest inelastic; this proposition was said by some[1] to be true in the USA, but was more commonly applied to other countries. Moreover, if there were 'political' or other constraints on

---

[1] Wojnilower (1980) pp. 277–339.

raising interest rates to restrain aggregate demand, because of the sensitivity of certain borrowers – e.g., those with housing mortgages – or because of the fragility of financial intermediaries who borrowed short and lent long, then credit controls might be seen as the only way to achieve the desired degree of monetary and financial constraint. Particularly when interest-rate changes were seen as occasioned by a political decision, rather than by the outcome of market forces, administered increases in such rates were often more immediately *politically* unpopular than tightening credit ceilings, where the adverse effect of loan refusals would not be so *immediately* obvious and where the odium would be shared with the bank manager to whom the rationing decision would be delegated.

There were, however, numerous and serious disadvantages. It was impossible ever to tell with any clarity what overall effect such controls were having; the equilibrium level of bank lending in the absence of such controls, the proportion of funds shifting into other channels through disintermediation, and the credit quantities actually being restrained were all unknown. Admittedly, knowledge of functional relationships within the financial system has been so slight that one cannot predict with much greater confidence the effect of an increase in interest rates. While the inability to make these latter predictions acted as an argument for introducing direct credit controls, the *ex post* effects of general changes in market rates were not so obscured by shifts of financing flows towards less easily measurable channels that the exercise was fruitless.

Furthermore, experience demonstrated that, once imposed, it was difficult to get rid of ceiling controls. Because it was impossible to estimate the dammed up volume of rationed credit demand, it was always felt to be risky, an 'unripe time', to open the sluice gates. Moreover, the removal of direct controls would, it was often argued, be seen as a political signal to the banks in particular, and to the private sector in general, of encouragement for expansion; the number of occasions in recent decades when governments have wanted to appear to support unbridled expansion have been few. Although the introduction of any novel form of credit rationing was almost always accompanied by pious assertions that it was strictly temporary, once in place they tended to take root. Moreoever, even when some relaxation or even temporary removal was achieved, as in the case of the 'corset' during the 1970s, bank behaviour was conditioned by expectations of its potential reimposition, which in itself led to various distortions.[1]

This tendency for credit controls, once imposed, to persist led to worsening structural problems. On the one hand, experience and familiarity with the system led to more ingenious methods of avoidance and evasion being discovered, so that the authorities feared that its macro-policy efficiency was being undermined, though they were unable to test that hypothesis without actually taking the risky step of removing the controls. On the other hand, the persistence of rationing led to an enervating loss of competitiveness and incentives for efficiency in the central core of main banks, and to an artificial stimulus to the fringe of uncontrolled institutions and markets. The structural effects on the financial system were undeniably adverse, though their availability as a 'quick fix' has led, and will again lead, myopic governments to overlook their longer-term debilitating effect.

The micro-agrument for credit rationing, that the resulting allocation of credit – e.g., under the influence of qualitative guidance – will in consequence be improved, is difficult, if not impossible, to countenance. In the first place, such credit rationing,

---

[1] As noted in the *Bank of England Quarterly Bulletin* article on the 'corset'.

and limits on bank interest rates, will tend to reduce the available return and attractiveness on banks' deposits; in Figure 7.1, the equilibrium rate of return on banks' deposits will fall from r_0 to r_2 and the volume of deposits from OC to OB. The resulting lower level of bank deposits is not a sign of financial rectitude but rather an indication of the lower perceived quality of, and return on, such deposits. In LDCs, bank deposit holdings represent a major outlet for personal savings, an outlet that can be particularly valuable – e.g., in accumulating a sufficiently large *masse de manoeuvre* to allow the financing of projects with increasing returns to scale. So, reducing the attractions of bank deposit holding can both reduce total savings and shift savings into channels – e.g., retained profits, jewellery, or inter-family lending – that might provide a less efficient allocation.

Moreover, the normal assumption of economists is that the allocation of credit via the price mechanism will allow the projects with the highest expected present values and internal rates of return to obtain the funds, eliminating projects with lower expected rates of return. Any other method for allocating credit *must* thus lead to a *less* efficient allocation. This loss of efficiency will be especially marked if the process of allocation is based on political power-broking and other forms of personal – political influence and corrupt practices. The latter state of affairs is, alas, quite common.

There are a number of defences of credit rationing that may be offered. First, as will be described at greater length in Section 3 on 'equilibrium' credit rationing, the nature of the loan contract[1] is such that the downside risk to the borrower is generally more limited than the upside potential. Under these circumstances, a higher rate of interest may induce a shift towards projects with a higher risk (variance of outcome) but lower mean expected rate of return. Oliver Hart[2] offers an example of a firm that has two projects with the following return probability (p. 137):

	Return in £	Probability
Project 1	0	1/3
	15	1/3
	30	1/3
Project 2	0	4/5
	40	1/5

The bank cannot observe the choice of project and has to set an interest rate on the fixed debt loan made to finance either project. Call the firm's return R and the payment back to the bank (principal plus interest) by the borrower, D.

Then (p. 138):

> the only feasible contract now is one that specifies a noncontingent amount D that the firm must repay to the bank. Of course, this payment is only going to be feasible for the firm in states where the ex post return $R \geq D$. If $R < D$, we follow the SW [Stiglitz–Weiss] assumption that the firm goes *bankrupt* and pays the banks what it can, i.e. R.
>
> At what level should the bank set D? The problem is that, as D changes, so may the firm's choice of project and this imposes a kind of externality on the bank. In

---

[1] A fixed debt contract, under conditions where the outcome of the project is uncertain (stochastic) and both monitoring and bankruptcy are costly.

[2] In his comment on the paper by Stiglitz and Weiss, 'Credit Rationing and Collateral', in Edwards *et al.* (eds) (1986) pp. 136–43.

particular, given that the firm receives $R-D$ if $R \geqslant D$ and 0 if $R < D$, we see that, if $D < 15$, the firm will choose project 1 since:

$$(1/3)(0) + (1/3)(15 - D) + (1/3)(30 - D) > (4/5)(0) + (1/5)(40 - D)$$

On the other hand, if $35 \geqslant D > 15$, it is easy to see that the firm will choose project 2 (note that if $D > 35$, the firm's profit falls short of the manager's effort cost and so the firm won't borrow at all). Finally, if $D = 15$, the firm is just indifferent between the two projects.

This theme – that higher interest rates may lead to riskier projects being preferred by borrowers in conditions where the bank cannot easily monitor the assumption of risk by borrowers – is central to the 'equilibrium' credit rationing literature; how important is it, however, in practice? If interest rates were allowed to rise to their equilibrium levels in LDCs, would banks find *ex post* that their lending was being used for much riskier purposes, with a lower expected mean return, *and* that they had no means of observing and restraining this shift *ex ante* (e.g., by covenants, collateral, etc.)? And even if there was some such shift to riskier projects with a lower mean expected return when returning to a free market system, would this justify the maintenance of a rationing system with constrained interest rates, given the inefficiencies and the incentives for improper methods of credit allocation that this latter entails?

Further arguments for credit rationing at the micro-level are:

1. That the time rate of discount among personal borrowers (e.g., for borrowing to finance ceremonies, etc.,) is much greater than the social rate, so that scarce credit will be absorbed for conspicuous consumption instead of productive investment unless persons are rationed. The actual extent of this syndrome can be exaggerated and it is not clear that the problems involved would be ameliorated by forcing desperate personal borrowers away from banks to the higher-charging unregulated money-lending market.
2. That such rationing helps to provide a source of revenue to the government, by inducing banks to take up government debt at a lower interest rate than would otherwise be necessary, that government expenditures have a higher expected social rate of return than the rationed private expenditures, and that alternative sources of government finance are either not available or would have even more distortionary effects on the economy. A problem with this line of argument is that government's desire to tax the banks, which can be argued on its own merits, does not *have* to involve restrictions on the interest rates that banks can set or on the volume of loans that they may choose to make.
3. That imperfections, rigidities, controls, etc. elsewhere in the system have caused important prices, notably exchange rates, to deviate from their true 'equilibrium' value. The true value of foreign currency may thus be much above its pegged official rate. Accordingly, estimated private returns may differ from social returns, with the social returns on production of tradeables greater relative to non-tradeables, and especially greater relative to imports not essential for the production of tradeables. In order to offset this difference between calculable social and private returns, it is desirable, so it may be argued, to direct credit towards more socially desirable uses. There are several problems with this line of argument. If the unwanted difference in private returns remains (i.e., if providers of services expected a higher rate of return than do manufacturers) the channeling of credit to

lower-return manufacturers may induce these agents simply to pass on the funds to the higher-return service producers (e.g., via an inter-company market or via trade credit) thus obtaining a turn in the process. Perhaps more fundamentally, it is questionable whether the authorities actually have the ability to estimate differences between social returns and private returns with any accuracy, and whether they are likely to be influenced by 'political' rather than by 'economic' considerations in reaching their judgements. Moreover, if certain features in the economy clearly do cause a divergence between social and private returns, it is perhaps better to try to eliminate that divergence at its source (e.g., by devaluing an over-valued exchange rate) rather than introduce yet further distortions, (e.g., credit rationing) as an insufficient offset.

This latter set of arguments, however, is beginning to lead this discussion out of the field of monetary economics into the area of development economics, where, indeed, such issues are more fully discussed.[1] My own judgement is that there is little justification to be found either at the macro- or micro-level for the imposition of constraints on banks' portfolio choice which lead to credit rationing. Nevertheless, such credit rationing schemes have been frequently adopted, even in industrialised countries, and are pervasive in LDCs.

2. Disequilibrium Rationing

We move on next, having considered those frequent circumstances in which credit controls are *exogenously* imposed by the authorities onto the banking system, to an analysis of situations in which the workings of the wider financial system itself lead to conditions in which credit is rationed – i.e., in which borrowers would be willing to pay a higher rate of interest to obtain additional credit and yet are not offered the opportunity to do so. In the literature,[2] a distinction has been made between 'disequilibrium' and 'equilibrium' rationing. Disequilibrium rationing is that which occurs because lenders are slow to adjust certain parameters in the provision of loans to changing conditions (e.g., the interest rate or customer limits) and/or because borrowers may be concerned about the public signal that a shift in their cost of credit, relative to their peer group, may entail for wider perceptions of their credit-worthiness. In this sense, 'disequilibrium' rationing takes place since market prices and terms do not adjust perfectly and instantaneously to changes in external conditions. 'Equilibrium' rationing, on the other hand, is rationing that would still persist even when complete adjustment to a given set of external conditions had been completed.

In this Section, we consider 'disquilibrium' rationing. The main cause of such rationing is market imperfections of one kind or another. The main form of such imperfections that causes rationing in practice is the fixing of 'administered' interest rates, either by cartels or by prominent market leaders. Since the rationing is caused by an imperfection, analysts find such 'disequilibrium' credit rationing less interesting to study than 'equilibrium' credit rationing; it is, however, much easier to estimate and measure, and in certain cases (e.g., the UK personal mortgage market from 1945 till about 1983) of considerable quantitative importance.

---

[1] See Fry (1982a and 1982b) and Fry (1981) pp. 261–70.

[2] Following Jaffee and Modigliani (1969) pp. 850–72.

When an interest rate is fixed administratively, it will take administrators time to react. When variations in that rate are 'politically' sensitive – e.g., the Building Societies' Association advised mortgage rate or the 'prime' rate in the USA, those responsible want protection from outside criticism of moving rates upwards too far, too soon, and are likely to delay upwards changes until justification is demonstrable. The effect on balance sheets (i.e., the squeeze on liquidity when administered interest rates are slow to follow market rates upwards) may be offset in part by a similar delay in lowering administered rates relative to market rates on the reverse tack. Again, changes in interest rates may involve transactions costs; in the case of UK building societies it can involve renegotiations with existing mortgagors to determine whether and to what degree their monthly payments will change as the variable rate on mortgages shifts.[1] Next, the adoption of publicly announced and infrequently changed interest rates may reduce borrowers' search and information costs; the need for bankers to publish such rates, and to be prepared to justify changes in them publicly, may help to reassure less-well-informed borrowers that better-informed bankers are not taking advantage of their comparative ignorance. These latter arguments were set out in more detail in Chapter 1, Section 3 which discussed the determinants of the speed with which market makers, in this instance, banks or building societies, adjusted prices.[2]

The speed of adjustment may also be slowed if the financial institutions involved are not seeking to maximise short-run profits, either because they believe that their interest-setting behaviour may cause a public or political reaction that could affect their long-run profit opportunities, or because they are, by their deeds of foundation, not profit-maximising institutions (e.g., certain mutual funds, such as the UK building societies). In either case, however, the option to ignore short-run profit-maximising opportunities is facilitated by the existence of a cartelised, oligopolistic market structure. For example, Anderson and Hendry[3] present a model in which building societies choose the rate on deposits, the rate on mortgages and the stock of mortgages to minimise a cost function. This calculus reflects the costs associated with divergencies from building society objectives which are assumed to be:

1. To maintain advances as a given proportion of deposits.
2. To satisfy mortgage demand.
3. To avoid large changes in the stock of mortgages and in the rates on deposits and mortgages.
4. To maintain a constant reserve ratio.
5. To maintain a 'reasonable' rate of interest on mortgages.

Clearly objectives 3 and 5 may conflict with objective 2 and lead to occasions when the mortgage interest rate was held too low to satisfy all demand.

There are various econometric methods available for estimating the 'underlying' demand in cases where demand is not limited by price but by some form of rationing device, such as queuing in the case of building societies or refusing new customers and

---

[1] The monthly payment consists partly of interest and partly of repayment of principal. The mortgagor has some flexibility in choosing whether to respond to an increase in the variable interest rate by raising the monthly payment or by extending the duration of the mortgage, thereby lowering the proportion of principal being repaid and raising the proportion of interest payment in the given monthly payment.

[2] Similar arguments, particularly applied to credit markets, have been presented by Milde (1974) pp. 489–507.

[3] Anderson and Hendry (1984) pp. 185–21.

limiting funds to established customers in the case of banks. Jaffee and Modigliani (1969, pp. 866–72) took the proportion of loans granted to risk-free prime customers as their proxy for 'disequilibrium' credit rationing and examined the determinants of such rationing. The extent of such estimated excess demand has often been found to be large and variable (notably again in the case of UK building societies, at least up till 1982, after which the provision of mortgages in the UK became subject to much fiercer competition between banks and building societies, and the building societies' cartel was abandoned).[1]

There can be no reasonable doubt that such rationing exists and is quantitatively important. There is, however, greater doubt whether other kinds of transitional effects may lead to 'disequilibrium' rationing. Consider a number of cases. First, banks will generally establish loan limits for individual counter-parties. Because they cannot observe *changes* in the credit-worthiness of counter-parties easily or cost-lessly, they usually establish a rule of thumb whereby counter-parties can borrow at a rate appropriate to their average risk-class up to a limit. If a borrower's condition changes, say due to a wish to borrow more funds at a higher rate in order to take on riskier projects, it will take time and effort (and therefore cost) to renegotiate larger limits; in the meantime, the borrower will be rationed.

Again, a new borrower will normally impose additional and higher monitoring, informational and set-up costs on a bank than an existing customer. This fact may be known to both sides and yet a *new* borrower of risk-class B, say, may prefer to borrow a lesser sum at the same interest rate as an *established* borrower of risk-class B, rather than pay a higher rate to cover the extra costs, because that higher rate might be mistaken by others to indicate that the bank had graded the new borrower as really being in risk-class C. This latter phenomenon may be quite widespread. The estimation of credit-worthiness is difficult and expensive in terms of time and effort; because of this, the relative interest rate charged against a borrower by a bank can frequently be used as a signal for other potential lenders or other trading partners. In consequence, if a borrower is faced with a known offer curve (supply schedule) of loans from a bank willing to offer more at a higher rate of interest, the borrower may rationally prefer to borrow less at a lower rate in order to preserve the borrower's reputation.

Indeed, a common feature of markets, in cases where adverse news affects one of the participants – say, a borrower on the inter-bank market – is that the borrower's allowable limits are cut back severely, since the borrower is unwilling to publicise his worsened position and the lenders can, at the same time, privately reduce their exposure. The response of markets is, therefore, often discontinuous in the face of adverse reports on a participant. The participant will find his access increasingly rationed at the going interest rate for someone of his initial risk-class; if matters get worse, he may find himself with no access to the market at all, and then, unless there is a satisfactory resolution, this exclusion is likely to force a public restructuring, after which the participant may be reassessed and graded as being in a quite different risk-class. Some typical examples of this would be the way financial markets reacted to the worsening problems of Continental Illinois Bank in 1984 or Latin American LDC sovereign borrowers in 1982. Grunewald and Pollock,[2] (pp. 565–6) put the same point more forcefully:

> There is much current discussion of letting money markets discipline bank behavior.

[1] See Wilcox (1985) especially Table 3, p. 180.
[2] Grunewald and Pollock (1985) pp. 563–75.

The assumption is that funds providers, like stockholders, will carefully monitor the financial soundness of their banks and pressure risky banks to take remedial measures. Short-term funds managers, however, do not wish to spend the time and effort to closely monitor banks, an activity whose effectiveness they doubt in any case. They prefer to have no worry, either buy bank paper they do not have to worry about, or simply do not buy – why take a chance? In particular, why take a chance of your own analysis being wrong? In either case, little monitoring is required.

The stock market is a pricing system and prices describe a continuum. A stable supply of the shares of a company is given a price which reflects its assets, cash flow and risk relative to other companies. At any perceived risk level, there is some clearing price for the shares. The money market, in contrast, is a rationing device. All bank paper has more or less the same yield (or price), but the supply of funds may shrink drastically when perceived risk crosses a certain threshold. Past some level of perceived risk, there is no price at which funds are available. Either a bank is sound and can borrow funds, or the bank is perceived as too risky and can borrow but little. Short-term money managers will not risk illiquidity or loss or principal *at any price* once past the risk perception threshhold.

The most notable aspect of this contrast is the money managers' perception of minimal risk over a broad range of bank characteristics, followed by a great sensitivity (perhaps overreaction) past the critical threshold point of perceived unacceptable risk, and discontinuous rationing out of the bank.

Monitoring and information costs can thus make markets react to adverse news about credit-worthiness by adjusting limits, rather than price, because *both* borrowers and lenders prefer that course. This will cause quantity adjustments, rather than price adjustments, up to a point where the market ceases to provide the participant with the capacity to sustain the business. At that juncture, there will be a crisis and a major discontinuous shift in market prices, frequently following a period in which the market is effectively closed. Even in broad and liquid markets, a sufficiently sharp change in perceived conditions may make market makers unwilling to quote prices in any large quantities to participants, and the market may, officially (e.g., after a limit up or limit down shift) or unofficially, temporarily grind to a halt while the changed circumstances are reviewed and reassessed. In many markets, market makers offer terms which include both ask–bid prices *and* the amounts that they will deal in at such prices. Increased uncertainty will lead to a reduction in the amounts offered, as well as to a widening in the bid–ask spread. If there are any constraints on adjustments in prices (e.g., because the borrower does not want the firm's worsening creditworthiness publicly revealed), then the adjustment will be primarily via quantities, at least initially.

Does this kind of quantity adjustment count as credit rationing, particularly in those cases when the borrower *prefers* the adjustment to take place in that way? That is a matter, in part, of semantics. Undoubtedly, the borrower would, if unconstrained, want to borrow more than was available at the given price. Once reputation – and hence future trading opportunities – become determined by present price behaviour and determination, it clearly becomes more difficult to use standard static demand and supply analysis.

Perhaps the best approach, which provides some of the flavour of the above discussion, is that adopted by Jaffee and Russell.[1] In their Figure 5, (p. 661) reproduced here as Figure 7.2, they show how the borrower's demand curve *DD'*,

---

[1] Jaffee and Russell (1976) pp. 651–66.

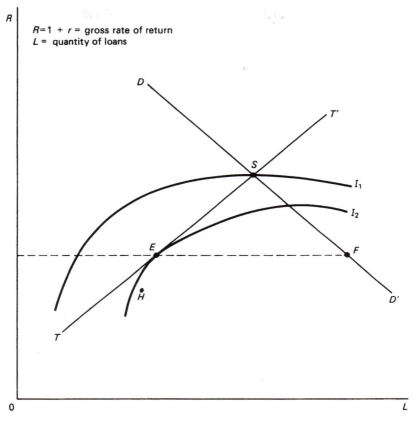

FIG. 7.2

passes through the highest point of each iso-utility curve, I_1, I_2, I_3, etc. with utility becoming greater as the curves decline towards the horizontal axis. If the borrower is then faced with an offer curve TT', a supply schedule of alternative amounts that the lender would provide at each rate, (i.e., with lender acting as market leader and the borrower as follower), the borrower will not prefer the point of intersection of his demand curve and the lender's offer curve, point S, but will instead choose a point such as E on the lender's offer curve where a better (because lower) iso-utility curve is obtained.[1] It is ambiguous whether such a result counts as credit rationing.

---

[1] Jaffee and Russell explore another problem. Suppose that some borrowers are more likely to repay than others but that the bank cannot tell the two kinds apart. By offering a contract at point H, a bank can attract the better (more honest) borrowers since they can move to a lower (i.e., better) utility curve; the worse borrowers will prefer E to H because they would rather have a larger volume of loans since they expect to default and face the given bankruptcy costs anyhow. The bank making the new contract will benefit from this offer by attracting only the good customers. However, when sufficient good customers have been attracted away from E by banks offering H, the existing E contract ceases to be viable since the bank is faced with proportionately more dishonest borrowers applying for the E contract. If everyone then tries to

3. Equilibrium Rationing

Undoubtedly, the greatest analytical interest concerns the question of whether it is possible for credit rationing to exist as a feasible equilibrium state in a static system which has fully adjusted to all publicly available information. This is so despite the lack of *empirical* evidence concerning whether any such rationing occurs – and, if it does, whether it is of any quantitative significance. The analytical fascination presumably derives instead from a more general theoretical interest with the way that markets work. While we know that market imperfections and rigidities occur, causing unemployment and other distortions, it is an open question whether these are the result of transitional frictions, which will pass in time, or whether they stem from an inherent feature of the innate working of markets.

Concern with such 'equilibrium' rationing goes back to the initial contribution of Hodgman (1960, pp. 258–78). Shortly, thereafter, it became established[1] that, for a loan attached to a project of a given size with a *known* probability distribution of outcomes, the likelihood of the borrower defaulting (i.e., being unable to pay back the initial principal plus the interest rate charged) increased as the rate of interest increased. With a finite distribution of outturns, the probability of default at some point become unity.

If there are no *monitoring* costs, because the given project and its prior probability distribution are known and its outcome is always reported truthfully, and no *bankruptcy* costs are imposed on either borrower or lender arising from the default itself, then few problems would arise from this increasing probability of default. In the absence of monitoring costs (particularly if bankruptcy costs existed), or if such monitoring becomes costless and perfect on the payment of a fixed sum,[2] both sides would settle for an equity contract rather than a debt contract. In the absence of bankruptcy costs, assuming that monitoring costs exist and that the lender is able to monitor more effectively after bankruptcy (e.g., by putting in a receiver) there would be no reason why the lender should not raise the rate of interest *until* default becomes inevitable, thus enabling him to observe the outcome at the cost of paying the entrepreneur a fee for his pains. In this sense, forcing a firm into bankruptcy (receivership) becomes an information-enhancing strategy. The reason why it is not adopted, except under duress, is that it imposes costs for borrowers in the form of lost collateral – and often more important, in the form of lost reputation; while for lenders, the costs appear in the form of the time and effort of having to put the situation right or alternatively of having to sell off existing assets, often into weak second-hand asset markets. Given the costs of monitoring *and* of bankruptcy to the lender, the optimal contract for the lender will be a fixed debt contract, reinforced and supported by bankruptcy costs and collateral requirements on the borrower.[3]

---

obtain contract *H*, including the worse quality borrowers, it will be dominated again, from the viewpoint of the lender, by contract *E*. This kind of indeterminacy problem was described and discussed by Hirshleifer and Riley in their excellent review paper, 'The Analytics of Uncertainty and Information – An Expository Survey' (1979) pp. 1375–1421, on pp. 1406–8, and crops up from time to time in financial literature – e.g., Smith (1984) pp. 293–317. While the analysis is complex and intellectually demanding, it is not clear that it has much practical relevance.

---

[1] Most notably by Freimer and Gordon (1965) pp. 397–410.

[2] See Diamond (1984).

[3] See Diamond (1984), Bernanke and Gertler (1985) and Gale and Hellwig (1985) pp. 647–64, and also the discussion in chapter 5 (pp. 118–21).

Given, then, such monitoring and bankruptcy costs, bank lenders will choose to provide fixed-interest debt contracts and default will have adverse consequences. So, following Jaffee and Russell (1976, Figure III, p. 657), we can chart the probability λ of the borrower being able to pay back[1] the fixed principal (L), and interest rate (r) of a loan of a given size, as r rises in Figure 7.3 below. Since we have assumed a finite distribution of outcomes from the project for which the fixed loan was made, then the probability of pay back falls to 0 as r rises to infinity.[2] Since default is costly, this outcome is less profitable to the bank than some interior point of maximum return. Accordingly, at some point, for a loan of a given size, the offer (supply) curve of the lender becomes backward bending, as in Figure 7.4 below, derived from Jaffee and Russell's Figure IV (p. 659).

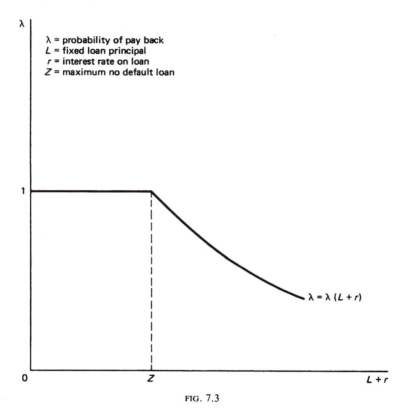

FIG. 7.3

So far, we have been examining examples where the size of the loan is taken as fixed and indivisible. If, however, as is the case in reality, the loan size could be continuously varied, then Freimer and Gordon (1965) show that, *if* the probability distribution of outcomes for the financial project (per unit of finance) was not itself a

---

[1] Note that $1 - \lambda$ is the probability of default.

[2] Point Z is the maximum size of loan repayment for which $\lambda = 1$. Repayments greater than Z are accompanied by a non-zero probability of default.

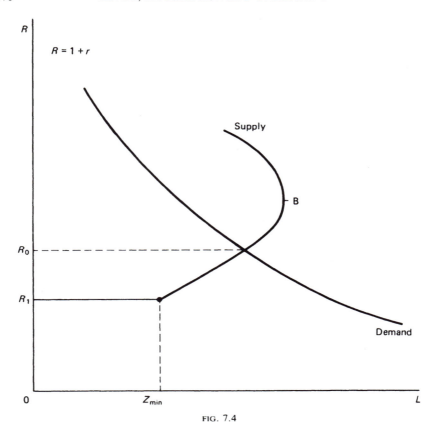

FIG. 7.4

function of the size of the loan, and *if* the riskiness of the bank's own portfolio was not a function of the size of its individual exposures, then the banker's preferred size of loan would actually increase indefinitely with r. Of course, both qualifications fail in reality. Gale and Hellwig thus make diminishing returns to investment the central feature of their credit-rationing model (1985, p. 650). The borrower will undertake his most profitable opportunities first, so additional finance will be used to complete projects with lower expected mean returns. Again, no banks are large enough that they can expand any individual exposure indefinitely without assuming greater risk. The limitation of large exposures plays an important part in the Bank of England's supervisory requirements.

So, for a given rate of interest, the size of loan which a bank will be prepared to offer to a borrower will also have an interior maximum, and Figure 7.4 holds not only for loans of a given size but also for cases where loans can be divisible.[1] Given a backward-bending supply curve, any point on that curve above B is inefficient, in the sense that the borrower would reject it, because the borrower can obtain a point on a lower (i.e., better) iso-utility curve by choosing the point on the offer curve tangential

---

[1] Borrowers are assumed never to default on a loan of size less than Z_{min}. Since all such smaller loans are perfectly safe, by assumption, they all bear the same riskless rate of interest, R_1.

to the best (lowest) iso-utility curve, as has already been demonstrated in Section 2. Thus, a borrower with the demand, offer and iso-utility curves shown in Figure 7.2 will choose point E rather than point S. Again, the borrower would like to borrow OF at that interest rate but, given the available schedule of interest rates and quantities on the lender's offer curve, settles for OE.

At least in the case of divisible loans,[1] given the supply schedule of the banks actually on offer, the borrowers actually prefer to choose the lower loan volume – lower interest option rather than the inefficient contract at point S. In what sense does this involve true rationing?

So far, however, we have been working with the maintained assumption that the probability *distribution* of the uncertain outcomes of the projects was known perfectly to both borrower and lender. Stiglitz and Weiss[2] drop that artificial assumption. Instead, they assume that the bankers cannot tell for sure what kind of

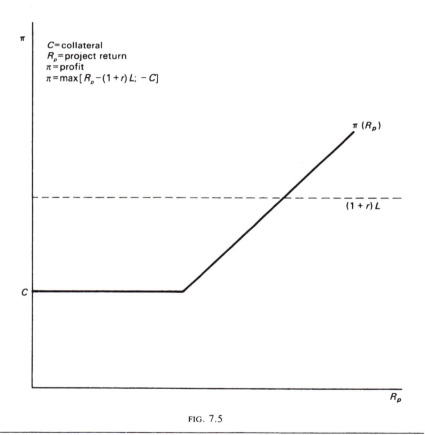

FIG. 7.5

---

[1] Where loans are not divisible, some of the set of identical borrowers with similar projects will find themselves rationed. Whether they will have more luck applying to other banks will presumably depend on the cost of funds, credit assessment, etc. of these other banks.

[2] Stiglitz and Weiss (1981).

project a potential borrower will undertake and cannot either obtain such information or constrain the borrower to a given project *ex ante* without considerable cost. The borrower has private information on his intentions that is not available to the lender, a situation of asymmetric information. Moreover (Stiglitz and Weiss, 1981, p. 343) they demonstrate that:

> the interest rate a bank charges may itself affect the riskiness of the pool of loans by either:
>
> (1) sorting potential borrowers (the adverse selection effect); or
> (2) affecting the actions of borrowers (the incentive effect).

In Section 1, we gave a numerical example of the effect of interest-rate changes on the actions of borrowers. More generally, the limited downside risk to a borrower, entailing lost collateral and reputation, combined with the upside potential where the borrowing firm obtains all the profit on successful outcomes above the interest charge, make the profits of a borrowing firm a convex function of the return on the project (see Figure 7.5) rather akin to taking out a call option on the project. Accordingly, for projects with similar *mean* expected returns, the riskier projects, with a *larger* expected *variance* of return, will provide at any level of interest rates, a *greater* return to the borrower and a smaller return to the bank. So, as interest rates

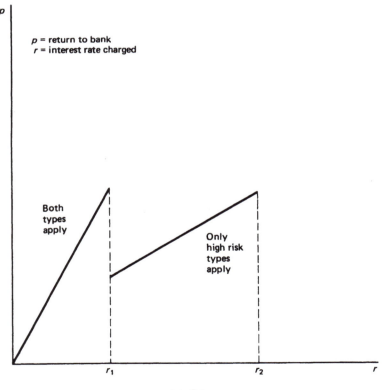

FIG. 7.6

begin to rise, both safer (lower variance) and riskier borrowers apply for loans. Then, as rates rise further, only riskier type borrowers will apply (Figure 7.6 below, taken from Figure 3, p. 347 in Stiglitz and Weiss, 1981).

This tendency for riskiness of default to worsen as interest rates rise leads to an interior maximum, with a backward-bending supply curve and credit rationing in exactly the manner already described. The difference in this case is that the bank cannot establish its offer curve for loans in full knowledge of the borrowers probability distribution of outcomes. If the bank knew that probability distribution, it could set different terms to the differing borrowers, accepting all the low risk borrowers at lower interest rates, and accepting the higher risk borrowers only on different terms (e.g., higher collateral). Since the bank cannot tell the borrowers apart, because it will be in the interests of all borrowers to misrepresent the claim that they are low-risk types, and since higher interest rates lead to adverse selection and adverse incentive effects, a bank will often choose a rate of interest at which it will refuse some borrowers altogether or offer them a smaller size loan; while under conditions of fuller information on their project outcomes, the bank would have willingly offered a larger loan at a given interest rate which would have been willingly accepted. In that sense, the bank and some borrowers are forced under asymmetrical information conditions to accept a worse contract, involving a smaller (perhaps nil) loan, than they would have preferred if full information had been available. Neither the borrower nor the bank is at a full information equilibrium, prompting Stiglitz and Weiss to claim (1981, p. 394) that they provide 'the first theoretical justification of true credit rationing'.

The analysis so far has proceeded on the maintained assumption that the bank could control two parameters in its loan decision – the rate of interest and the volume of loans offered at that rate. There is, however, yet another parameter which a bank can vary – i.e., the collateral or covenants required.[1] As has been noted earlier, the larger the collateral which the borrower places with the bank, the greater the cost of default to the borrower, and the less the cost of default to the bank. Indeed, at the limit, if the borrower puts up collateral C equal to the amount that must be repaid, $L(1 + r)$, there is no default risk whatsoever for the lender.[2] This raises the question whether it would be possible to improve on rationing equilibria (with zero or fixed collateral) by varying the amount of collateral.

This latter possibility was raised earlier by Azzi and Cox,[3] who argued that the possibility of varying collateral would eliminate 'equilibrium' rationing of the form posited by Jaffee and Modigliani (1969). In their reply in the *AER*, Jaffee and Modigliani accepted the formal analysis but argued that collateral was scarce; its use to support funding therefore involves costs.

More recently, Bester[4] has returned to the same point, but now in the context of the form of 'equilibrium' rationing posited by Stiglitz and Weiss (1981). The problem in

---

[1] There is, in fact, yet another parameter that can be varied, ie the duration of the loan. The shorter the life of the loan, the greater the incentive on the borrower to perform, or risk non-renewal, and the greater the chance of the bank to enforce repayment before an adverse outcome proceeds too far. On the other hand, the administrative costs, etc., are greatly increased. So, as uncertainty about the condition of some class of borrowers increases (e.g., LDC countries in the period 1979–82) the average maturity of their (new) loans is likely to fall.

[2] And equally no reason why the borrower should want then to borrow from the bank rather than using the firm's own free funds to finance the project.

[3] Azzi and Cox (1976) pp. 911–17.

[4] 'Screening vs Rationing in Credit Markets with Imperfect Information' (1985) pp. 850–5.

this latter case is that the banker cannot distinguish between riskier and less risky lending projects and may, therefore, be forced to ration both. Bester argues that the banker could use alternative combinations (contracts) of collateral and interest to persuade borrowers in the course of choosing between the alternative contracts to reveal truly whether they are undertaking riskier or less risk projects. Assuming borrowers are equally risky averse, those with safer projects in mind will have a different subjective trade-off (indifference curve) between collateral requirements and interest rates than those with riskier projects; the choice of a particular loan contract by the borrower therefore reveals information to the banker about the true risk of the borrower's projects.

Following Bester's diagram (1985, p. 853) we can then draw the indifference curves, aa' and bb', of those with safer and riskier projects respectively, in Figure 7.7. Bester argues that the bank should be able to offer contracts such as X and Y, which provide it with equal expected returns, so that all 'safe' borrowers are induced to take contract X with a lower interest rate and higher collateral and all risky borrowers to accept contract Y with a much higher interest rate but no collateral. Stiglitz and

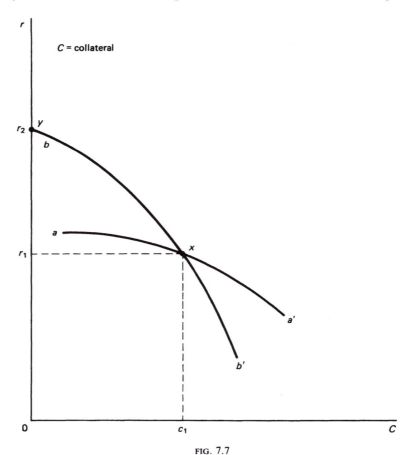

FIG. 7.7

Weiss, in their further paper on 'Credit Rationing and Collateral'[1] (1986), responded to this challenge by arguing that potential borrowers would not just be differentiated by the riskiness of their projects, as in Bester, but also by their wealth. The authors then argue that the bank cannot distinguish between wealthier and less wealthy borrowers (1986, p. 103) and that wealthier borrowers, for any given contract of a particular collateral–interest rate pair, will undertake riskier borrowing (1986, p. 112); this result occurs because of decreasing absolute risk aversion (1981, p. 404) and because wealthy borrowers 'may be those who, in the past, have succeeded at risky endeavours. In that case they are likely to be less risk averse than the more conservative individuals who have in the past invested in relatively safe securities, and are consequently less able to furnish large amounts of collateral' (1981, p. 402). In these circumstances, they show that:

> there exist complete pooling equilibria (in which only one type of bank contract is offered) and separating equilibria (in which there exists at least two contracts; the mix of borrowers accepting each differs). Each of these equilibria may be characterised by credit rationing.

While Stiglitz and Weiss have shown that there exist some conditions in which the possibility of simultaneously varying both collateral requirements and the interest rates will not eliminate credit rationing, the particular assumptions adopted in their paper seem odd. Whereas the likely use, and hence riskiness, of borrowed funds is indeed private information, there are plenty of relatively reliable methods of establishing a firm's net worth or even the wealth of an individual. Moreover, the idea that wealthier individuals will choose riskier projects and will have an incentive to signal that they are poor, and hence will undertake safe projects, hardly sounds true to life. It probably would be true, if indeed we lived in a one-period world and the true cost of default was strictly limited to the loss of collateral. In reality, the greater cost of default is often the loss of reputation, which is likely to be a more pressing concern for the rich, than the poor. Be that as it may, it would be an unusual bank manager in the real world who was seen to seek out poorer clients and refuse loans to wealthier clients.

Such comments suggest that this subject, the inter-relationship between banks' collateral requirements, interest rates on loans and credit rationing, will remain on the agenda for further theoretical analysis. What can surely be stated is that the availability of satisfactory collateral is strictly limited for large groups of potential borrowers (e.g., persons). In that case, whether or not the availability of collateral might in *theory* eliminate credit rationing, in *practice* it exists. The greater problem, however, is measuring its extent.

One possible handle on this empirical issue is to examine situations in which the availability of collateral to a group of borrowers increases markedly, and then measure the extent of the resulting rise in lending to borrowers in this class. Such a change occurred in the UK in the mid-1980s, when a wider class of home-owners became able to use this ownership as collateral for mortgage finance for general purposes, whereas previously mortgage borrowing had been strictly rationed to those buying new houses. The dramatic rise in personal sector borrowing between 1980–8, largely based on such mortgage borrowing, suggests that the extent of such rationing and the imperfection and incompleteness of credit markets may be large.

---

[1] (1986, p. 102).

VIII
Why Do Banks Need a Central Bank?

Summary

A Central Bank has two main functions. Its first (*macro-economic*) function, the operation of discretionary monetary policy, has already been touched on in Chapter 6, and will be further discussed in Chapter 10 and Chapters 13, 14 and 15. In this chapter, by contrast, we consider a Central Bank's second (*micro-economic*) function, of providing support (e.g., via Lender of Last Resort assistance), and regulatory and supervisory services to maintain the health of the banking system.[1]

One of the reasons why many markets work imperfectly is that there are differences in the information available to the various participants in the market – i.e., information asymmetries. As noted in Section 1, this feature is particularly marked in the case of the provision of professional services, including investment and financial advice, but extending far further, encompassing doctors, lawyers, etc. Since what is being sold in such cases is, in some large part, specialised knowledge, information asymmetry is inherent. Furthermore, an individual's requirement for such assistance is usually infrequent, but the potential impact on their utility if the professional gets it wrong can be devastating. So, the usual guarantor of quality, which is the need to protect reputation to ensure repeat buying, may be insufficient. In such cases, the professionals involved may come together to form a 'club', to provide entry controls and guarantee quality, though often also to restrict competition and raise minimum charges, etc. Some facets of a Central Bank's micro-function may be seen in its adoption of the role of manager of the 'club' of banks.

But the role of a Central Bank, in its support for the banking system, goes much further than that of a typical central professional body – e.g., in regulations on, and lender-of-last-resort support for, domestic commercial banks. It is often argued that the need for a Central Bank to carry out such functions arises from the joint role of banks in providing both portfolio management and payment services. Thus, if the portfolio management turns out badly, and losses are made, the public good of the provision of payments services throughout the banking system may be put at risk. This claim is analysed in Section 2 and it is argued that it is not generally valid. It depends on the particular characteristics of the typical asset portfolio held by banks. A number of suggestions have been put forward to restrict the range of assets banks could hold. If banks, or other intermediaries offering payments services, were restricted to holding absolutely safe assets, or were restricted to holding only *marketable* assets, and were closed as soon as a fall in the value of such assets reduced the positive capital value (solvency) of the banks to some preordained limit, then the

---

[1] Much of the material in this chapter has been derived from my earlier papers – e.g., *The Evolution of Central Banks* (1985), 'Why do we need a Central Bank?' (1986a), and 'Why do Banks Need a Central Bank?' (1987a).

support role of the Central Bank could be much reduced. In Section 2, I offer yet another alternative suggestion, that financial intermediaries might offer payment services on the basis of liabilities whose value might vary in line with the value of its marketable assets. Once again, such an institution should be safe, and protected against runs, so Central Bank support would be otiose. Whether such a development is likely to take place is considered.

But if banks were restricted to holding only marketable assets, who would provide the non-marketable loans which now provide the staple of bank assets? In Section 3, I describe how banks have a comparative advantage in the information, monitoring and enforcement arrangements inherent in the exercise of making loans, when the alternative of borrowing through primary markets is too expensive, primarily because of the information costs necessary before primary markets can work efficiently, together with other causes of economies of scale therein. The nature of the involvement between bank and borrower has led banks to make such (non-marketable) loans on a fixed-nominal-value basis; similarly, the nature of the relationship between depositor and bank has caused bank deposit liabilities to be on a fixed-nominal-value basis.

But this condition, in which banks make non-marketable loans, of an unknown 'true value', on a fixed-nominal-value basis backed by liabilities also convertible into cash at a fixed-nominal-value, brings with it possibilities for abuse by bankers and for contagious panics. Even if banks did not offer any payments services – i.e., if they funded themselves only with time deposits or CDs – these circumstances would still involve the need for bank regulation, and for Central Bank support to prevent crises affecting sizeable parts of the banking sector – i.e., systemic crises.

1. The Central Bank as Organiser of the 'Club' of Commercial Banks

The purpose of this chapter is to consider the analytical case for having a (publicly-owned) Central Bank. One aspect of this issue has already been discussed at great length in the literature and will be further addressed in Chapter 15 below: this is the question of 'rules versus discretion' in the conduct of monetary policy. If it is right for the government to run a discretionary monetary policy, then it needs an institution to carry out that job, and that institution would effectively be a Central Bank. Although few would now be willing to give up discretionary monetary policy, and that in itself will sustain the existence of such an institution, let me try to put that argument firmly on one side for the moment, until it is tackled again in Chapter 15, and go on to ask a second question. Within the context of *whatever* kind of monetary policy that may exist, whether discretionary, or based on rules, gold standard or whatever, is there a necessary micro-function for a Central Bank to undertake, this being primarily to supervise, regulate, and carry out Lender of Last Resort functions? Note that these latter functions are not carried out generally in other industries. The issue can be put concretely. Why should Johnson Matthey Bankers or Continental Illinois be saved when the governments of both the UK and the US have allowed companies to fail in other industries and uneconomic coalmines to close down?

Let me begin with the general observation that the inadequacy and insufficiency of information may make the working of markets imperfect (see Chapter 1) and may require the intervention of certain outside bodies to improve efficiency. Indeed, if one should start from a neo-classical, Walrasian, position wherein all markets clear perfectly and there is a unique stable equilibrium, it becomes extremely difficult to see any necessary role for a Central Bank. Many economists who believe that the economic system in general, and commercial banks in particular, would be naturally stable if left on their own, thus argue that the foundation of Central Banks has been primarily as a means of raising additional revenue for the government, for example, via the inflation tax, seignorage from monopoly note issue, forcing commercial banks to hold public sector debt at below market rate via reserve requirements, etc. They view such actions by the (public monopoly) Central Bank as representing a burden – an imperfection on an otherwise well functioning commercial banking system.[1]

Several reasons why markets do *not* clear perfectly were set out in Chapter 1. In particular, for our present analysis, in those cases where it is difficult or costly for a buyer of a product, a good or a service, to obtain sufficient information on the quality of that good or service that he is buying, there is a tendency for individual sellers to try to raise their profit margin and their share of the market by cutting the costs of production and by lowering the quality of the product provided.[2] Seen from the other side, that is from the producer's standpoint, the problem presents itself as one of 'free riding': producers of cheaper quality products benefit from the better reputation of higher quality producers and, in the process of producing cheaper quality products, also damage every other producer's reputation.

One response to this, of course, is that both buyers and sellers may find it profitable to increase the information available in the market-place by paying for it to be provided. The role of advertising is obvious, as are its limitations from the view-point of a buyer wishing to obtain accurate and unbiased information about product quality. Buyers may be willing to pay for additional information from an independent testing agency. In addition to such producers as *Which?* and the *Good Food Guide*, there are credit rating agencies and agencies that do provide specialist information on banks. The demand for the services of one such agency, Bruyette–Keefe, rose so much in the United States after the Continental Illinois debacle that the agency had to double its staff. Even so, when it is costly and difficult for anyone, even a specialist, to obtain such information, when the criteria for judging quality are

---

[1] This school of thought played a part in the monetary discussions in England during the debates on the subject prior to the 1844 Bank Charter Act, though it was ultimately unsuccessful, see White, *Free Banking in Britain: Theory, Experience and Debate, 1800–45* (1984). Although W. Bagehot was a supporter, *en principe*, of this school, see *Lombard Street* (1873, reprinted 1962) Chapter II, pp. 32–3 and Chapter IV, pp. 52–3, the case for 'free banking' and for the abolition of Central Banks was thereafter rarely put forward, either by academics or practitioners, until recently. In the last few decades, academics who are suspicious of the motives or the skill and wisdom of government intervention, following Hayek, have joined with neo-classicists who argue that the system would be innately stable in the absence of public sector (Central Bank) support. There is a growing volume of literature on this, for example the various papers by White, such as 'Competitive Money, Inside and Out' (1983) pp. 281–99, the papers by Dowd, for example, 'Automatic Stabilising Mechanisms Under Free Banking' (1987) and the papers by Glasner, for example, 'Economic Evolution and Monetary Reform' (1983). Also see Rhymes, 'Further Thoughts on the Banking Imputation in the National Accounts (1986) pp. 425–41, especially pp. 435–40. I have tried to put the counter-argument, why banks do need a Central Bank, in a number of papers from which this chapter is largely drawn; these include *The Evolution of Central Banks* (1985), 'Why do we need a Central Bank? (1986a) and 'Why Do Banks Need a Central Bank?' (1987a) pp. 75–89.

[2] Both Milton Friedman, in his *Programme for Monetary Stability* (1959b) and Klein, in his paper on 'The Competitive Supply of Money' (1974) have applied this general analysis to the production of money.

subjective and uncertain, and when the form of the service crucially involves the nature of the personal relationships established, so that repeated searching is effectively ruled out (think of your doctor or lawyer), then the option of leaving the provision of information to the market-place cannot be fully satisfactory.

This latter claim is challenged by some. Hayek stresses reputation as a stabilising factor, as do several other economists of that view; reputation, however, also has a public good element, externalities relating to the reputation of others in the same field, that can easily be misused by free riders. Also, it is only too easy to appeal to the gullible by promising to offer a higher yield. Particularly when it is difficult to check directly and quickly the quality of the service, it is all too easy to persuade people that you have discovered a miracle cure. By the time that it is patently obvious that this is not so, the fake doctor may have obtained a large sum of money and moved on. In the field of banking, for example, it is extremely difficult to distinguish between a relatively high rate of return that is offered because of greater efficiency or one that is offered because the institution is also undertaking a much riskier strategy, for example by investing in assets with a higher return but of lower general quality such as 'junk bonds'. Because high return often is associated with high risk, it is notable that the rate of profitability in banking has *not* proved to be among the useful forward indicators of the likelihood of failures, for example in Z score exercises.[1] If people had infinite lives, and/or if memory did not decay, and if relationships between buyer and potential seller were capable of being repeated and repeated continuously, then reputation might, indeed, suffice to maintain the stability of the system. In practice, however, these conditions do not occur.

Moreover, in their infrequent dealings with professional advisers – e.g., doctors, lawyers, bankers, accountants, estate agents, stockbrokers, etc. – clients are usually seeking advice and assistance about a matter which may have a major impact on their well-being and/or where a sizeable proportion of their wealth is involved. It is much easier to rely on the doctrine of *caveat emptor* when the customer is almost as well informed as the supplier, when there are reasonable prospects of repeated purchases so that reputation is important, and when the single transaction is not such that an inadvertent (or fraudulent or negligent) outcome would seriously affect the client's welfare. In contacts with professionals, clients seeking their services are naturally at an informational disadvantage, since professionals provide essentially specialist information, will often have only an occasional, or once-off, relationship, and may frequently have their well-being greatly affected by the advice and actions of the professional.

What then generally happens is that the producers of such a service join together to form a club. The club has qualifications for entry and rules of conduct. It benefits buyers by representing a guarantee of a certain quality or proficiency and it benefits sellers by dealing with the free rider problem. The club may, of course, also operate as a cartel, which is its main economic drawback. In addition, the club may provide certain compensation funds, or insurance, both to its own members and to clients who have due cause for grievance because of the misdoing of one of the club members. Think of almost any professional service, and one will see how it works. So far, however, both theoretical analysis of the provision of information to the market and the theory of clubs have hardly been applied at all to the provision of financial services, nor indeed to professional services more generally. Indeed, insofar as it has

---

[1] See Marais (1979).

been developed, the theory of clubs has been analysed at such a high level of abstraction, particularly in the form of mathematical theory, as to be hardly relevant at all to practical economic developments.[1]

In some large part, therefore, informational asymmetries (e.g., in the provision of professional services) will call forth a natural private-sector market response in the form of self-regulatory, practitioner-run clubs. There are, however, several inherent problems in relying on such private clubs to maintain quality control. First, they may simultaneously indulge in anti-competitive, cartel agreements, exaggerating restrictions on entry beyond what is desirable, and fix prices, commissions, interest rates, etc. in an oligopolistic fashion. Second, customer protection is often best provided by some insurance scheme. This may be difficult both to establish and to police within the private sector since assessment of riskiness is often arbitrary, as in the case of financial intermediation, and the need to keep a close check on members' behaviour might need to involve powers to acquire information and to force changes in operating behaviour that would most easily be undertaken by the state. Third, any such insurance scheme will be generally accompanied by an enhanced tendency for those covered to assume the risks insured against since the downside risk will be met, in part at least, by the insurance agency while the upside return goes entirely to the insured entity; this is an obvious case of moral hazard. For this reason, it is all the more important for the insurance agency to be able to monitor and to control the actions of the insured which, once again, may require the coercive powers of the state if it is to be adequately done. This general subject, concerning the desirability, or otherwise, and form of regulation, especially in the provision of financial services, is, however, considered at greater length in Chapter 9.

There are thus several problems to be faced in running clubs. Another of these is that the task of obtaining compliance with the rules of the club, and in awarding any benefits or insurance pay-outs under club rules, requires detailed information on the activities of club members, as Lloyds Insurance has discovered. If a club manager is also one of the competing members, he may be in a good position to obtain inside information on the activity of competitors. This may not, however, always be a problem, witness the set-up of the Stock Exchange Council, but this may be possible only where rules are relatively simple and the entry qualifications are clear. In many other cases, the club manager needs, in order to avoid conflicts of interest, to be an outsider, an independent, non-competitive entity. Indeed, the whole question of the purpose and organisation of clubs, notably in the provision of financial services, is topical and important. Thus, in the reorganisation of the London capital markets during the 'Big Bang' process, the nature and form of the clubs involved have been totally shaken up and rearranged.

So, one could regard the Central Bank as a manager of the club of banks. This perspective can explain a lot about a Central Bank's role and functions, in particular its relationships with other commercial banks. But it does not provide a full explanation, particularly not of the lender-of-last-resort function of Central Banks. Other club managers do not have the ability to rescue ailing members in the way that a Central Bank can and does rescue banks. So once again, one may well ask what is so special about banks that they need to have a Central Bank in support?

---

[1] See for example the survey article on the 'Theory of Clubs' by Sandler and Tschirhart (1980).

2. Banks' Twin Functions in Providing Both Payments and Portfolio Management Services

Because of informational asymmetries, many professional services will need some modicum of regulation, whether self-regulation or statutory regulation. Particularly if there is a desirable role for client insurance schemes, the regulator must be able to monitor and to control certain aspects of the activities of the purveyor of the service – e.g., the adequacy of the capital maintained by the business. But the role and functions of a Central Bank in seeking to sustain the health of the banking system generally go well beyond those of regulators of other services, or of regulators acting in other parts of the financial system, such as the Securities and Investments Board (SIB) in the UK.

It is often argued that such extra attention is due to the twin functions of the banking system in providing both payments and portfolio management services. Fama[1] thus describes banks as having two functions, the first being to provide transactions and accounting services and the second being portfolio management. Yet, transactions services are carried out by other institutions (e.g., Giro, Post Office, non-bank credit card companies, etc.) without much need for special supervision by a Central Bank.[2] More important, I shall argue that it would be perfectly possible (and generally safer) for transactions services to be provided by an altogether different set of financial intermediaries – i.e., intermediaries providing mutual collective investment in (primarily) marketable securities. If this was to occur, would it make such mutual investment intermediaries (e.g., unit trusts, open-end investment trusts) into banks? Would such intermediaries then become subject to the same risks as banks and need to be subject to the same kind of supervision/regulation?

I believe that there is no necessary reason why banks alone among financial intermediaries should provide transactions services; as well, in their role as portfolio managers, banks have much in common with other intermediaries acting in this capacity (although, as I shall argue later, in Section 3 certain crucial distinctions remain between the characteristic form of portfolios held by banks as compared with those held by non-bank financial intermediaries). Nevertheless, it is this joint role that is often held to give a special character to banking and to require special treatment for banks through the establishment of a Central Bank (e.g., to provide lender-of-last-resort (LOLR) and other support services for banks in difficulties). Such support goes beyond the assistance envisaged for other financial intermediaries that get into trouble.

Tobin states (1985, p. 20) that:

> The basic dilemma is this: Our monetary and banking institutions have evolved in a way that entangles competition among financial intermediary firms with the provision of transactions media.[3]

But what actually are the problems caused by this entanglement? The problem is often seen, and so appears to Tobin, as arising from the propensity of banks, acting as competing financial intermediaries, to run risks of default which, through a process

---

[1] In his paper on 'Banking in the Theory of Finance' (1980).

[2] Except insofar as the Central Bank has a direct concern for the smooth and trouble-free operation of the payment system itself (e.g., the working of the clearing houses and the settlement systems, as contrasted with the institutions providing the transactions services).

[3] 'Financial Innovation and Deregulation in Perspective' (1985) p. 200.

aggravated by contagion, puts the monetary system, whose successful functioning is an essential public good, at risk.

Tobin (1985) thus states:

> Even if bank managers act with normal perspicuity in the interests of the stockholders, even if all temptations of personal gain are resisted, sheer chance will bring some failures – insolvency because of borrowers defaults or other capital losses on assets, or inability to meet withdrawals of deposits even though the bank would be solvent if assets' present values could be immediately realised. The probability is multiplied by the essential instability of depositor confidence. News of withdrawals triggers more withdrawals, *sauve qui peut*, at the same bank, or by contagion at others. For these reasons the banking business has not been left to free market competition but has been significantly regulated.

Tobin's suggestion is that:

> This problem could be avoided by segregation and earmarking assets corresponding to particular classes of liabilities permitting a depositor in effect to purchase a fund which could not be impaired by difficulties elsewhere in the institution's balance sheet. In this way, a bank would become more like a company offering a variety of mutual funds, just as these companies – which are not insured – are becoming more like banks.

In particular, Tobin, following an earlier suggestion made by Friedman, advocated 100% reserve-backed funds for checkable deposits.[1] Tobin thus continues:

> The 100%-reserve deposit proposed, . . ., would be one such (mutual) fund, but there could be others. For example, many households of modest means and little financial sophistication want savings accounts that are safe stores of value in the unit of account. *They can be provided in various maturities without risk by a fund invested in Treasury securities. They can be provided as demand obligations either by letting their redemption value fluctuate with net asset value* or by crediting a floating interest rate to a fixed value [my emphasis].

With such illustrious and wide support from economists, why has this idea not had more practical success? The concept of a 100% segregated reserve against checkable deposits would, however, reverse the evolution of banking. Initially, goldsmiths received deposits of gold coin from customers and acted purely as safety vaults. It was the realisation that it would be profitable, and under most circumstances relatively safe, to loan out some proportion of these reserves to prospective borrowers, in addition to the loans made on the basis of their own capital, that transformed such entrepreneurs into bankers. Naturally, when such early bankers did run into difficulties, by over-trading, proposals were made to force such commercial bankers back to stricter segregation. The forerunner of the Swedish Riksbank, founded by John Palmstruch in 1656, was thus organised on the basis of two supposedly separate departments: the loan department, financing loans on the basis of longer-term deposits and capital, and the issue department supplying credit notes on the receipt of gold and specie. But even when Palmstruch's Private bank had been taken over by Parliament,

> A secret instruction, however, authorised the advance by the exchange department to

---

[1] As has Henry Wallich in his paper, 'A Broad View of Deregulation' (1984b) in addition to several other US economists.

the lending department of the funds at its disposal, though on reasonably moderate terms.[1]

The reason why such segregation and hypothecation of certain safe assets to checkable deposits will not work in the case of commercial banks is that it largely removes the profitability of banking, along with its risks. The regulatory constraint on the banks' preferred portfolio allocation, under such circumstances, would be seen – as historical experience indicates – as burdensome; attempts would be made to avoid or to evade such constraints – e.g., by the provision of substitute transactions media at unconstrained intermediaries which, being free of such constraints, could offer higher returns on such media. Only in the case of non-profit-maximising banks, such as the Bank of England, divided into two Departments on much the same theoretical basis by the 1844 Bank Charter Act, would such segregation be acceptable and not subject to avoidance and evasion. Of course, if the public sector were prepared to subsidise the provision of payment services either by operating them directly itself or

by paying some interest on the 100%–reserves

held in private sector intermediaries, then it could be done; however, in the light of Congress' recent response to suggestions for paying interest on required reserves in the USA, it seems difficult to envisage the public being prepared to vote tax funds for this purpose.

Anyhow, there is a simpler and less expensive alternative which Tobin almost reaches when he comments that the public's savings accounts could be:

provided as demand obligations, . . ., by letting their redemption value fluctuate with net asset value.

People are so used to having payment services provided against checkable *fixed nominal value* liabilities, with 100 per cent convertibility of demand deposits, that many have not realised that payment services could be just as easily provided by a mutual collective investment financial intermediary, where the liabilities are units representing a proportional claim on a set of marketable assets. The value of the units fluctuates, of course, with the underlying value of the assets in the portfolio. Because the market value of the portfolio is known, the value of the unit can be published each morning and each depositor then knows how much his or her units are worth. Because there will be a period of float, between writing a cheque in payment for a purchase and the cheque being presented for payment at the financial intermediary on which the cheque is drawn, during which underlying asset values will change and, because the attempt by the mutual funds to meet net outflows by net sales of assets could itself influence prices, one could expect a mutual fund to limit payment services and convertibility.[2] The concept of required minimum balance has been adopted often enough by commercial banks and the public is familiar with it. The cheques would, of course, have to be drawn in terms of the numeraire; otherwise, they would not be useful in clearing debts. The value of the drawer's units would change between

---

[1] See Flux, 'The Swedish Banking System' (1911) p. 17, and Goodhart (1985) pp. 109–16 and 159–62.

[2] This could be done by requiring some minimum balance in units to be held normally, with a progressive penalty in terms of yield foregone for dropping below this balance, plus some emergency arrangements for occasional overdrafts, say from an associated bank.

the date of writing and presenting the cheque,[1] and, therefore, in a period of falling asset prices, there would be a danger of the drawer being overdrawn at the latter date while having had funds to spare at the earlier date; this problem would seem also to be generally soluble by only providing guaranteed payment services up to a minimum credit balance in units, plus an emergency overdraft arrangement, perhaps with an associated bank.

I see no insuperable technical problem to the provision of payments' services by mutual collective investment intermediaries in this manner. They would need to hold some liquid reserves, vault cash to pay depositors' demanding currency, and liquid assets to meet net outflows at times when the fund manager judged that it would be inopportune to realise investments; note that these latter funds are needed neither for liquidity nor for solvency purposes. Liquidity is always available from the ability to sell marketable assets and solvency is assured because the value of liabilities falls with the value of assets. Instead, the desire for liquid assets would arise from a wish to maximise the net asset value of units under varying market conditions, and thus improve reputation, service fees and managerial earnings.[2] Nevertheless, the need to hold at least some vault cash might lower the expected return on the intermediaries' assets; the effect of this on the demand for units should be more than counterbalanced by the improved liquidity to the unit holder of his investments and the associated advantages of being able to use them for transactions purposes.

Be that as it may, the current trend already is for limited transaction services to be provided by investment-managing non-bank financial intermediaries on the basis of depositors' funds, the value of which varies with the market value of the underlying assets. Merrill Lynch cash management service is one example. Certain other unit trusts and mutual funds, such as money market mutual funds, are also providing limited payment services. Similarly, certain building societies and certain mortgage businesses in other countries are already allowing borrowers to draw additional top-up mortgages to a stated maximum proportion of the market value of their house.[3]

A common response to this idea is that, whereas it would be perfectly possible as a technical matter to provide payment services against liabilities with a varying market value, the public would not happily accept it and it would not succeed in practice. It is argued, for example, that there is a large psychological gulf between being absolutely certain that one has the funds to meet a payment and being 99 per cent certain of that. Is such 100 per cent certainty a general feature of our existing payment system? Unless one monitors one's bank account, outstanding float, etc. continuously and knows exactly what overdraft limits, if any, the bank manager may have set, the willingness of the bank to honour certain cheque payments will have a probabilistic element.

---

[1] It would, of course, be just as simple to keep the value of each unit constant but alter the number of units owned by each depositor as asset values change. I cannot see why that shift in presentation should affect people's behaviour in any way.

[2] This analysis stems from Tobin (1958) pp. 65–86.

[3] Building societies are entering more actively into the provision of payment services now that the Building Societies Act 1986 has been passed into law. Payments will normally be on the basis of their nominally fix-value convertible liabilities. The example above, however, envisages building societies, in certain circumstances, also being prepared to monetise assets with a varying market value.

Lawrence White[1] put the general case against basing payment services on liabilities with a varying market value most persuasively:

> Demand deposits, being ready debt claims, are potentially superior to mutual fund shares, which are equity claims, in at least one respect. The value of a deposit may be contractually guaranteed to increase over time at a preannounced rate of interest. Its unit-of-account value at a future date is certain so long as the bank continues to honour its obligation to redeem its deposits on demand. No such contractual guarantee may be made with respect to an equity claim. A mutual fund is obligated to pay out after the fact its actual earnings, so that the yield on fund shares cannot be predetermined. In the absence of deposit rate ceiling regulation, the range of antici- pated possible returns from holding fund shares need not lie entirely above the deposit interest rate. Risk-diversifying portfolio owners might therefore not divest themselves entirely of demand deposits even given a higher mean yield on mutual funds. It is true that the characteristic pledge of money market mutual funds to maintain a fixed share price, or rather the policy of investing exclusively in short-term highly reputable securities so that the pledge can be kept makes fund shares akin to demand deposits in having near-zero risk of negative nominal yield over any period. The difference between predetermined and post determined yields – between debt and equity – nonetheless remains. The historical fact is that deposit banking did not naturally grow up on an equity basis.

Because the provision of payment services by mutual funds, whose liabilities have a market-varying value, would not only be a somewhat novel concept but would also worry those unused to any probabilistic element in payments, I would expect its introduction to be gradual and probably to start with richer customers better able to cope with such probabilistic concerns. Moreover, such a limited introduction could prevent the mutual funds making use of economies of scale in the provision of payment services. There are, therefore, some observers who believe that this possible development will fail the practical test of success in the free and open market.

On the other hand, there seems no technical reason why the trend towards the provision of payments' services against the value of units in a collective investment fund (up to a minimum balance) should not proceed much further, especially now that technological innovations in the provision of such services (e.g., shared auto- mated teller machines (ATMs), electronic fund transfer (EFT) and home-banking), are transforming the production function of payments' services, especially in reduc- ing the economies of scale to a network of manned branch buildings. White's arguments (1984a, pp. 707–8) that the provision of payments' services by non-bank (mutual fund) intermediaries has been more expensive could be reduced in force, or even reversed, by the new technologies in this field.

Moreover, there would seem considerable cause to welcome such a development, not only for the extra competition that this would inject in this area but also because the characteristics of mutual, collective investment funds should serve to make them naturally more suitable purveyors of payment services than banks. In particular, both the likelihood of a run on an individual bank and of systemic dangers to the monetary system arising from a contagion of fear, would be greatly reduced if payments' services were provided by mutual collective-investment intermediaries, rather than by banks. For example, the announcement of bad news reducing the market value of such an intermediary's assets, assuming an efficient market exists, would immediately reduce the value of depositors' units. There would be no risk of insolvency for the intermediary, and no advantage, again assuming an efficient market, for any

---

[1] 'Competitive Payments Systems and the Unit of Account (1984a), p. 707.

depositor to withdraw his funds from that intermediary.[1] Again, since the asset portfolios of such intermediaries are publicly reported and their value at any time is exactly ascertainable, there would seem little scope for rumour or fear to take hold. Certainly, if a particular fund manager did significantly worse (better) than average, depositors would find it difficult to distinguish bad (good) luck from bad (good) management and would probably switch funds in sizeable amounts to the *ex post* more successful fund; such switching of money between funds would hardly damage the payments' system, rather the reverse.

There would still be a possibility of a sharp general fall in market values leading depositors to shift *en masse* out of market valued unit holdings into the fixed nominal value numeraire, thereby forcing the collective investment funds to sell further assets and deepen the asset price depression. Unlike the case of a run on the banks, which raises the subjective probability of failure elsewhere and thus reduces the expected return on holding deposits, at least the falling market values on the assets in the portfolio of the mutual fund should tend to increase the expected running yield on such units and thus act as an offset to the inducement to hold cash. Moreover, it would still be possible for the authorities, perhaps the Central Bank, to undertake open-market operations to offset the shift of unit holders into cash, possibly by buying the assets, say equities, that the funds were selling. There are precedents for such actions: at one time, the Japanese Central Bank intervened to support Stock Exchange values.

A monetary system in which transaction services were provided to unit holders of collective investment mutual funds would thus seem inherently safer and more stable than the present system in which such services are provided to a sub-set of bank depositors. Indeed, the nature of bank portfolios, largely filled with non-marketable assets of uncertain true value held on the basis of nominally fixed-value liabilities, would seem remarkably unsuited to form the basis of our payment systems. Why did it develop this way? The answer is, I think, to be found in the accidents of historical evolution. Broad, well-functioning and efficient asset markets are a reasonably recent phenomenon. Because of people's need both to borrow and to find a secure home for savings, banks developed well before mutual collective investment funds. The historical form of bank development led them inevitably into the payment business. Thereafter, the economies of scale involved in the existing structure of the payment system, the clearing houses, branch networks and the intangibles of public familiarity and legal and institutional framework, left the banks largely – indeed, in some Anglo-Saxon countries absolutely – unrivalled in the provision of payments' services.

Owing to the various innovations noted earlier, such bank monopoly of the payment system may now be coming to an end. The authorities should welcome the opportunity to encourage the development of a safer payment system. They should

---

[1] Mutual funds seeking to attract depositors, in part on the grounds of an offer to provide payments' services, face a trade-off in this respect. Because of depositors' familiarity with fixed-nominal-value convertible deposits as a basis for the payment system, some mutual funds, to attract such depositors, have given commitments to hold the value of their liabilities (normally) at such fixed nominal value. But this opens them up to runs as soon as the publicly observable value of their assets falls towards or below the (temporarily) fixed value of their liabilities. This happened with the UK Provident Institute in April 1986. White (1984a p. 707) and Professor Mervyn Lewis, in personal discussion, have reported such behaviour among mutual funds in the United States and Australia, respectively. It has been reported that there have been runs on money market mutual funds in the USA, which have stopped only when sponsoring institutions have guaranteed $1 nominal face value.

certainly not put obstacles in the way of properly-run collective investment funds offering payment services. Indeed, there is a question about what concerns the authorities, and/or the Central Bank, need to feel about the amount of monetary units thereby created and with the state of the intermediaries creating them.[1] So long as such intermediaries abided by their deeds of establishment and restricted their investments to marketable securities of a certain class, with the value of the units adjusted continuously in line, solvency should never be in doubt and would not be affected by the additional offer of payment services. Similarly, liquidity would be assured by marketability. So, it is not clear why a Central Bank should need to impose any additional regulation/supervision over mutual funds offering payment services.

Moreover, in a world where payment services were predominantly provided by monetary units of collective investment funds rather than by banks,[2] why should the authorities pay any particular attention to the quantity of money itself, especially since its nominal value would shift automatically with asset market prices? In such circumstances, how would the quantity of money be measured? Indeed, the intuition of this section is that the monetisation of assets is not necessarily limited to a restricted set of financial intermediaries (i.e., banks). A much wider range of financial intermediaries could, in principle, monetise a much wider set of assets than is currently done. Under these circumstances, the definition of money would either have to contract to become synonymous with the dominant, 'outside' base money, assuming that such money still continues to exist,[3] or become an amorphous concept almost devoid of meaning.

A further proposal, advocated by several American economists,[4] is that banks be

---

[1] There would still have to be protection against fraud, but that is a common requirement, not particularly related to the provision of transactions services.

[2] Something of a halfway house between a monetary unit and a bank demand deposit would be an indexed demand deposit provided either by a bank or another intermediary. It might actually be slightly more difficult technically to organise payment services on the basis of these, rather than on mutual funds invested in marketable assets, since the latter are continuously revalued while the former have partly unanticipated jumps on discrete occasions with the publication of the (RPI–CPI) price index to which the deposit was related. Again, payment might be guaranteed only up to some minimum real or nominal balance. Some way would also have to be found to allow continuous revaluing of the deposits through the month in line with the anticipated change in the forthcoming RPI. Still, these technical problems should be surmountable. Given that there are fiscal advantages to most tax-brackets of depositors in holding indexed rather than nominal deposits (i.e., no Capital Gains Tax on the inflation element in the indexed deposit, whereas income tax on the whole nominal interest on ordinary deposits is charged, less the allowance given against bank charges) and that, in the UK, riskless short-term assets for such an intermediary to hold exist in the form of government indexed bonds (see Chapter 13, Appendix), it is surprising that no intermediary has yet started to offer indexed banking with both liabilities and assets in indexed form. Perhaps the most likely reason, besides inertia and set-up costs, is that intermediaries basically require a combination of riskier and higher yielding assets, together with safe assets, to hold against liabilities, all denominated in the same form. The disincentive for intermediaries in the UK from setting up as indexed bankers is an apparent absence of borrowers prepared to take loans in indexed form. Why that should be so is beyond the scope of this Section (but see, however, Chapter 13, Appendix).

[3] For surveys of this latter issue, see White (1984a) and McCallum (1985).

[4] See, in particular, Kaufman (1987) and the references therein, notably Benston et al., (1986) especially Chapter 8; Kane (1985) especially Chapter 4; and Federal Reserve Bank of Chicago, *Proceedings of a Conference on Bank Structure and Competition* (1986).

forced to revalue their assets at the close of business each day at current market prices ('mark to market'), and that banks be forcibly and immediately closed, taken over by the regulatory authorities, or merged with another bank, as soon as their net capital value (solvency) fell close to zero. Since banks would be closed *before* they became insolvent, depositors could receive, and the regulatory/insurance agency could safely provide, 100 per cent insurance cover. There could, of course, still be problems arising from fraud, and the inconvenience of having deposits unuseable in a closed bank, even if remaining of guaranteed nominal value, could still lead depositors to seek timely withdrawals from a bank facing difficulties.

If there *was* a known, objective value for all the assets which commercial banks held, so that banks *could* 'mark to market' every evening at the market's close, then they would, on current arrangements, be offering fixed nominal value deposit liabilities against market-value-varying assets. This would seem to represent a somewhat risky position for bankers, normally risk averse individuals, to adopt. I would, therefore, expect that any tendency for banks to restrict, voluntarily or not, their assets to those that had an objective, verifiable market value would be accompanied by a desire to have their liabilities also adjust in line with such changing market values. Proposals to require banks to restrict their asset holdings to such assets as could be given an instantaneous objective market value would, I would expect, thus lead to a shift towards 'mutual fund banking'. The familiarity and current preference of depositors for fixed-nominal-value deposits would support the status quo, but risk aversion among bankers would provide a driving force for changing to 'mutual fund banking'.

Note that all three of the proposals outlined here for eliminating the possibility of systemic risk and contagion – i.e., the Tobin–Friedman proposal of requiring that banks hold only 'safe' assets against means-of-payments deposits, the Kaufman proposal of mark to market accounting and rapid closure and my own[1] of 'mutual-fund banking', all have at their core the requirement that financial intermediaries providing payments services should only hold *marketable* assets. This would seem to indicate that it is the fact that banks' portfolios largely consist of *non-marketable*, or at least non-marketed, assets that is quite largely responsible for the particular problems of ensuring stability within the banking system, a subject to which we turn next in Section 3.

3. Bank Portfolios and Central Bank Support

It would appear, therefore, that the provision of payment (monetary) services on units offered by collective investment intermediaries, or perhaps by banks whose assets are restricted to a subset of *marketable* securities, would not, *ipso facto*, require the involvement of the authorities to monitor and regulate the provision of such services. An associated question is whether the withdrawal of commercial banks from the provision of payment services, so that demand deposits, NOW accounts, and the like were no longer offered, would absolve the Central Bank from its basic concern with the well-being of the banking system. If banks offered only time deposits, CDs, etc., leaving payment and transaction services to others, would there be any need for special support for the banking system?

---

[1] My own proposal in the sense that I regard it as a desirable development; not that I was the first to envisage the concept of 'mutual-fund' banking. Others have had the same idea in broad outline.

The answer to this, I believe, is that cessation of payment services would make little difference to banks' riskiness or to the real basis of Central Bank concern with the banking system. There is little or no evidence that demand deposits provide a less stable source of funds than short-dated time deposits, CDs or borrowing in the inter-bank market; rather, the reverse appears to be the case.[1] Recent occasions of runs on banks have *not* involved an attempt by the public to move out of bank deposits into cash but have merely produced a flight of depositors from banks seen as too excessively dangerous to some alternative placement (not cash). The Fringe Bank crisis in 1973–4 in the UK and Contintental-Illinois are instances of this.[2] Earlier, it was suggested that flows of funds from one collective investment fund to another would not have damaging repercussions for the payment system if such funds offered monetised units and provided the bulk of such services. Yet I shall argue that, even were banking to be entirely divorced from the provision of payment services, such flows between *banks* could be extremely damaging for the economy and would require a continuing support role for a Central Bank to prevent – and, if necessary, to recycle – such flows.

The reasons why this is so are to be found in the fundamental *raison d'être* of banking itself. In particular, consider the need for banks to act as intermediaries in the first place. Why cannot people simply purchase the same diversified collection of assets that the bank does? There are, of course, advantages arising from economies of scale and the provision of safekeeping services, but these could be obtained by investing in a collective investment fund. The key difference between a collective investment fund and a bank is that the former invests entirely, or primarily, in marketable assets, while the latter invests quite largely in non-marketable or, at least, non-marketed assets.

Why do borrowers prefer to obtain loans from banks rather than issue marketable securities? The set-up costs required to allow a proper market to exist have represented, in practice, formidable obstacles to the establishment of markets in the debt and equity obligations of persons and small businesses. Underlying these are the costs of providing sufficient public information to enable an equilibrium fundamental value to be established (e.g., the costs of issuing a credible prospectus) and the size of the expected regular volume of transactions necessary to induce a market maker to establish a market in such an asset. In this sense, the particular role of banks is to specialise in choosing borrowers and monitoring their behaviour.[3] Recall the analysis

---

[1] Of course, the risk of a run still depends in part on a maturity transformation by the bank, with the duration of liabilities being generally shorter than that of assets. But even if there was no maturity transformation, a fall of asset values relatives to the nominally fixed value of liabilities would make depositors unwilling to roll-over or extend further funds to the bank, except on terms which made such depositors preferred creditors relative to depositors with later maturities, a course which would be subject to legal constraint. So, the absence of maturity transformation would delay the development of a run but would not stop depositors from running when, and as, they could.

[2] Earlier US historical experience examined by Aharony and Swary (1983) pp. 305–22 points in the same direction.

[3] An interesting question, suggested to me by Professor Mervyn Lewis, is to what extent banks obtain useful information about borrowers' conditions from their complementary function of operating the present payment system. In so far as banks do obtain information that is useful for credit assessment from the handling of payment flows, this would provide a strong economic rationale for the present combination of banking functions. Research into, and analysis of, the customarily private and confidential question of information

in Chapter 5, Section 2. Public information on the economic condition and prospect of such borrowers is so limited and expensive that the alternative of issuing marketable securities is either non-existent or unattractive.[1]

Even though banks have such an advantage, *vis-à-vis* ordinary savers, in choosing and monitoring prospective borrowers, they too will be at a comparative disadvantage, compared with the borrower, in assessing the latter's conditions, intentions and prospects.[2] Even though there would be advantages in risk sharing resulting from extending loans whose return was conditional on the contingent outcome of the project for which the loan was raised, it would reduce the incentive on the borrower to succeed and the bank would have difficulties in monitoring the *ex post* outcome. Businessmen, at least in some countries, are sometimes said to have three sets of books, one for the tax inspector, one for their shareholders, and one for themselves. Would the banks see one of these or would there be yet another set of books?[3]

In order, therefore, to reduce their own information needs and monitoring costs while increasing borrowers' incentives to succeed, banks have been led to extend loans on a fixed nominal value basis, irrespective of contingent outcome, with the loan further supported in many cases by collateral and with a duration often less than the intended life of the project to enable periodic reassessment; in addition a defaulting borrower may face various bankruptcy costs. Even so, both the initial and subsequent valuations of the loan by a bank do depend on information that is generally private between the bank and its borrowers or, perhaps, known only to the borrower.[4] Recall again the analysis in Chapters 5, Section 2, and Chapter 7, Section 3. The true asset value of the bank's (non-marketed) loans is always subject to uncertainty though their nominal value is fixed, subject to accounting rules about provisions, write-offs, etc. Under these conditions, it will benefit both bank and depositor to denominate deposit liabilities also in fixed nominal terms. The banks will benefit because the common denomination will reduce the risk that would arise from reduced covariance between the value of its assets and of its liabilities, as would occur, for example, if its liabilities were indexed, say to the RPI, and its assets were fixed in nominal value, or alternatively if its assets fluctuated in line with borrowers' profits while its liabilities were fixed in nominal value. The depositor would seek fixed

---

relationships between banks and their borrowers needs to be developed further; we cannot say with any confidence now how far banks benefit in seeking to assess credit worthiness from their provision of payment services.

[1] This argument has been advanced by economists such as Leland and Pyle (1977) pp. 371–87; Baron (1982) pp. 955–76; and Diamond (1984) pp. 393–414.

[2] At least this will be so until and unless a large borrower runs into prospective problems in meeting contractual repayment obligations. To a casual observer, banks seem to try to limit the informational costs of making the initial loans (e.g., by resorting to standardised grading procedures); once a sizeable borrower runs into difficulties, the bank responds by greatly increasing its monitoring activities, becoming often very closely involved with that borrower's future actions.

[3] This is not, as it happens, a purely hypothetical question. The Muslim prohibition on interest payments is causing Islamic countries to require their banks to issue Mushariqi loans, which do represent a form of equity share in the project being financed. Students of banking theory and practice might find it informative to give closer study to Islamic banking.

[4] Much recent literature on banking and credit has assumed that the borrower's selection and management of projects may not be observed by any outside party, even the banker himself. See, for example, Stiglitz and Weiss (1981) pp. 393–410, and (1983) pp. 912–27.

nominal deposits from the bank for the same reason that the bank sought fixed nominal value terms from borrowers: depositors cannot easily monitor the actual condition, intentions and prospects of their bank, so that information needs and monitoring costs are lessened and the incentives on the bank to perform satisfactorily are increased by denominating deposits in fixed nominal terms.

John Chant[1] has similarly identified the non-marketable nature of bank loans as providing a rationale both for the fixed-nominal-value form of bank deposits and as providing a rationale for external Central Bank regulation. Thus:

> The distinction between marketable and non-marketable securities appears to correspond with the degree to which information required to verify and monitor the value of the investment is publicly supplied by the borrower. While the matter is one of relative emphasis, marketable securities are identified with those for which the borrower supplies the bulk of the information required by investors, whereas with non-marketable securities the lender gathers more of the information (pp. 27–8).

> The fact that deposit-taking intermediaries are identified with the holding of non-marketable securities suggests that these intermediaries participate in the monitoring and enforcement function to a greater degree than other intermediaries. Moreover, the fixed money value of deposit liabilities appears to be consistent with the need to create appropriate incentives for agents to carry out effective monitoring and enforcement (p. 29).

> The deposit-taking institution appears to provide a more efficient solution to monitoring and enforcement problems. The agent, who is delegated with the responsibility for monitoring and enforcement, becomes the residual claimant to income. Thus his returns are directly dependent upon his performance. By this interpretation the deposit-taking institution serves as a device to overcome the problems present in any delegation of monitoring and enforcement to agents (p. 25).

> Deposit taking institutions have been identified as monitors and enforcers of loan contracts on behalf of the ultimate lenders. This function of managing risk is performed by acquiring non-marketable securities for which the institution takes the responsibility for screening information about the borrower. The value of these assets is specific to the deposit-taking institution who has verified the expected returns from the project, who has gained the information required to monitor the projects and who understands the problems with respect to enforcement. These dimensions of the customer relationship have to be built up with experience over time. The value of these claims would be less for an outside party who has not gained the knowledge embodied in the customer relationship. In addition to the specific nature of the capital used in intermediation, another aspect of intermediation also appears to favour the use of preventive regulation. Intermediaries typically have many customers, each with rather small amounts on deposit relative to the total. Under these conditions, the transactions costs in co-ordinating recourse for customers appear to be substantial and the incentive for any one depositor to commit resources to increase the probability of a remedy is also slight (pp. 51–52).

The combination of the nominal convertibility guarantee, together with the uncertainty about the true value of bank assets, also leads, however, to the possibility of runs on individual banks and systemic crises. Since no one actually knows the 'true' value of such non-marketable loans, the fact that the value of a sub-set of such loans has been found to be impaired at a bank or banks is bound to throw doubt on the

---

[1] In his paper on the 'Regulation of Financial Institutions – A Functional Analysis' (1987).

position and solvency of other banks who are believed to have made similar kinds of loan. Moreover, once the nominal convertibility guarantee is established, the effect of better public information on banks' true asset values is uncertain. For example, 'hidden reserves' were once justified by practical bankers as likely to reduce the likelihood of runs and to maintain confidence. Again, Central Bankers have been, at most, lukewarm about allowing a market to develop in large syndicated loans to sovereign countries, whose ability to service and repay on schedule was subject to doubt, because the concrete exhibition of the fall in the value of such loans could impair the banks' recorded capital value and potentially cause failures. An economist might ask who was being fooled? Yet, on a number of occasions, financial institutions have been effectively insolvent, but, so long as everyone steadfastly averted their gaze, a way through and back to solvency was achieved.

Be that as it may, under these conditions of private and expensive information and fixed nominal value loans, any major flow of funds between banks is liable to have deleterious effects on *borrowers*, as well as on those depositors who lose both wealth and liquidity by having been left too late in the queue to withdraw when the bank(s) suspended payment. Even if the prospects of the borrower of the failed bank are at least as good as on the occasion when the borrower first arranged the loan, the borrower will have to undergo expensive search costs to obtain replacement funds. Assuming the borrower searched beforehand and found the 'best' deal, the post-suspension likelihood is that the borrower will obtain less beneficial arrangements.

Bank runs, however, tend to happen when conditions for many borrowers have turned adverse. The suspicion, or indeed the knowledge, of that is what prompted the run in the first place. Accordingly, the expected value of the loans of many borrowers will have fallen. If they are forced by the receiver to repay the failing bank to meet the creditors' demands,[1] they would not be able to replace the funds required on the same terms, if at all, from other banks. One of the features of a banking crisis is the tendency for banks to recoil from making further loans to the sector(s) whose difficulties caused the initial solvency problems, whether these be LDCs in the post-1982 period or railroads in some of the nineteenth-century banking panics. At such times of contagious fear, banks often try to upgrade the quality of their assets by shifting from riskier non-marketable loans to government bonds. At such times, there will be a reassessment of relative riskiness and many classes of borrowers will find credit harder to obtain, not only because certain banks have failed but also because, after such reassessment, borrowers may find continuing banks increasingly unreceptive to their needs. Bank failures will thus place the economic well-being, indeed survival, of many borrowers at risk, as well as impairing depositors' wealth.[2] Consequently, flows of funds from suspect banks to supposedly stronger banks can have a severely adverse effect on the economy, even when there is no flight into cash at all. A Central Bank will aim to prevent and, if that fails, to recycle such flows,

---

[1] Insofar as constraints, either external or self-imposed, exist which stop the receiver from calling in loans outstanding at failed banks, this source of potential loss to society would be lessened. Even so, at a minimum, the borrower would lose the ability to obtain additional loans from the failing bank and that ability could be crucial to survival in a cyclical depression.

[2] This feature of banking, whereby calling of loans by failed banks causes economic disruption, has been recently noted and modelled by Diamond and Dybvig (1983) pp. 401–19 and by Bernanke (1983) pp. 257–76.

subject to such safeguards as it can achieve to limit moral hazard and to penalise inadequate or improper managerial behaviour.[1]

To summarise and conclude, it is often claimed that banking is special and particular, requiring additional regulation and supervision by a Central Bank, because banks are unique among financial intermediaries in combining payments' services and portfolio management. I hope to have demonstrated that this is false. Monetary payment services not only could be provided, and are increasingly being provided, by other collective-investment funds but could also be provided more safely than by banks. Moreover, the characteristics of such funds are such that their entry into the market for the provision of monetary services need not cause the authorities any extra concern; they could be left to operate under their current regulations. Similarly, if banks were to abandon the provision of payment services and restrict their deposit liabilities to non-checkable form, it would not much reduce bank riskiness. They would still require the assistance of a Central Bank.

All this follows because the really important distinction between banks and other financial intermediaries resides in the characteristics of their asset portfolio which, in turn, largely determines what kind of liability they can offer: fixed value in the case of banks and market-value-related for collective investment funds. It is these latter differences, rather than the special monetary nature of certain bank deposits, that will maintain in future years the distinction between bank and non-bank financial intermediaries.

---

[1] Even in the absence of a Central Bank, there will be some incentives for commercial banks to act, either independently or collusively, in the same way (i.e., to recycle deposit flows to banks facing liquidity problems and to support or take over potentially insolvent banks). The public good aspect of such actions will, however, be less compelling to competing commercial banks (e.g., why help a competitor that got into trouble through its own fault?) and the risk to their own profit positions of such action more worrying to them than to a Central Bank. Moreover, the usual circumstances of a rescue, at very short notice under conditions of severely limited information, makes it more difficult for commercial banks to act conclusively, than for an independent Central Bank to act swiftly and decisively.

IX
Financial Regulation

Summary

The provision of financial services in general, and banking in particular, is closely regulated and supervised in most countries. In the UK, in the years 1986–7, three new Acts were passed involving major changes in the regulatory framework for the financial system; the Building Societies Act 1986, the Financial Services Act 1986 – establishing an entirely new regulatory authority, the Securities and Investments Board (SIB), and an accompanying extended regulatory system – and the Banking Act 1987.

Yet the analytical basis justifying this panoply of financial regulations is not that secure, and indeed has been under strong challenge by economists and lawyers in the USA. We examine their critique of regulations in Section 1. The older concept of regulation being introduced as a public service to correct market failure is denounced as a travesty of reality, with no firm theoretical basis in (utility)-maximising behaviour. Instead, Stigler and Peltzman have argued that regulation should be viewed as a form of wealth transfer brought about by an essentially political process of maximising effective support for such measures. In such cases, a well-organised, cohesive lobby is likely to be most effective. The approach emphasising the import-ance of lobbying on each issue is, naturally, better fitted to US political circumstances than to those in the UK, where individual MPs are more subject to the Party Whip, and the decision of the Executive is generally 'rubber-stamped' by the Legislature. Even so, it would hardly be feasible for any supervisory authority to operate effectively without a modicum of voluntary co-operation from the supervised. In that sense, regulation always has to be designed to be acceptable to the regulated; a degree of 'capture' by the regulated industry is inevitable and all regulatory systems, whether statutory or 'voluntary self-regulation' in form, must be practitioner-based to some large extent.

Having considered this general critique of regulation, we then move on, in Section 2, to examine the arguments that *can* be advanced to justify regulation, specifically within the financial sphere. There are three conditions that have been identified as requiring governmental intervention. The first concerns the existence of natural monopolies, a situation which is not applicable to financial services. The second relates to externalities. The main argument here is that bank (and certain other financial market) failures can cause externalities, additional losses, on the economic system which justify support for the system in the form of lender-of-last-resort functions by a Central Bank and/or deposit insurance. Such support, however, induces banks to take up riskier positions, a problem of moral hazard, and that, in turn, justifies monitoring financial intermediaries to constrain excessive risk-taking.

The third condition involves information asymmetries. These are likely to be especially severe in the case of professional services since the service itself is based on the much greater specialised knowledge of the professional. Transactions costs often make it expensive to separate the functions of principal and agent, so conflicts of interest can frequently occur. The involvement of the customer with the professional is generally infrequent, so that quality control through the option of repeat purchases is limited, whereas such control is of major importance to the customer who has little capacity personally to check on the qualifications or to monitor the performance of the intermediary. Under these circumstances, a variety of additional regulatory controls, including insurance against fraud and negligence, minimum entry standards, etc, have been advocated. Even so, it would remain desirable to try to estimate both the benefits and the costs of regulation in order to achieve the optimal balance.

1. The General Theoretical Critique of Regulation

In the course of the last two decades, the thinking of the economics profession and of a sizeable proportion of the legal profession in the USA has grown distinctly critical, if not downright hostile, to government regulation of, and intervention in, US industries, including service industries. The older concept that such regulation is introduced as a public service in order to correct market failure is now broadly scorned. It is difficult to find papers (e.g., in the *Journal of Law and Economics*) supportive of this case for regulation in almost any form or circumstance, whereas the contrary position – that regulation distorts, misallocates, and restricts competition and raises prices to the consumer as a generality – is widely represented.

Indeed, as long ago as the early 1960s, a session at the December 1963 American Economic Association on 'The Regulated Industries' resulted in a conclusion strongly adverse to regulation in general. One of the two main discussants, Ronald Coase (1964) commented:[1]

> The views expressed in the papers presented in this session seem, where they overlap, to be broadly in agreement. What the regulatory commissions are trying to do is difficult to discover; what effect these commissions actually have is, to a large extent, unknown; when it can be discovered, it is often absurd.

Many such similar quotations, criticising the impact and effect of government regulation, can be easily found from a myriad of primarily American economic (and legal) academic papers. It is true, however, that most of these papers were concentrating on the regulation of US industries, such as public utilities, airlines, taxicabs, etc. and on professional services (e.g., doctors, lawyers, beauticians, barbers, etc.), rather than referring specifically to the regulation of financial services. Indeed, in their valuable bibliography, *The Economics of the Professions*, by Foley, Shaked and Sutton,[2] there is no single reference directly concerned with the regulation of financial services. However, when American economists have turned their analysis to the subject of the regulation of financial services, the criticisms of the design and conduct of such regulation generally remain and the conclusion, that there is a *prima facie* case for less, rather than more, regulation remains unchanged. Benston (pp. 2–3 writes that:[3]

---

[1] Coase (1964 p. 194.
[2] Foley *et al.* (1981).
[3] Benston (ed.) (1983).

with the exception of deposit insurance, most regulations [on financial services] are not useful except for those who benefit from constraints on competition.

This current theme, that regulation is probably best avoided since it is distortionary, restrictive and anti-competitive, therefore does carry over in US economists' writings to the specific area of financial services. It does, however, appear that British economists have been more tolerant and supportive of regulation, at least in the financial field. Indeed, many of their recent studies have been undertaken in the aftermath of occasions of failure by the authorities, notably the Bank of England, to prevent certain failures (e.g., the fringe bank crisis of 1973–5 and Johnson Matthey Bank in 1984). These studies often point to gaps in the supervisory – regulatory net, with the implications that more, rather than less, regulation may be desirable.[1]

Nevertheless, it is difficult nowadays to deny that both the mainstream and the leading edge of economic analysis is to be found in the US literature. This literature is strongly critical of government regulation, direct or through an agency, in virtually every field of economic activity, including financial services. Although such criticism has not been strongly echoed in the UK (perhaps even the reverse holds), the weight of such US criticism would indicate that there is a *prima facie* case *against* all further regulatory steps in the UK and in favour of further deregulation. Yet, of the three measures concerned with financial regulation enacted by Parliament in 1986–7, only one (the Act to allow Building Societies to undertake a wider range of activities) could plausibly be described as broadly deregulatory since it reduces the constraint of prior regulations. The other two major Acts (the Financial Services Act and the Act to revise the 1979 Banking Act) either impose new regulations where none existed before, as in several areas in the Financial Services Act, or seek to tighten up existing regulations. Given the weight of US economists' and lawyers' criticisms, how can that be justified? I shall turn to a discussion of possible arguments for such additional UK regulation in Section 2.

First, however, I want to consider another main feature of the US economic literature on government regulation, its analysis of the *political* calculus. Early empirical studies of the effect of regulation[2] generally concluded that regulation failed so miserably and blatantly to achieve the results that a public interest theory of regulation would have indicated, (i.e., to offset market imperfections so as to simulate the welfare-maximising, Pareto-optimal, conditions of perfect competition – thereby also protecting the consumer), that the most likely explanation was that the true, underlying (and often covert) objectives of regulations were different from the professed ones.

A number of early US studies of the apparent failure of regulation to protect consumers, and to provide a simulation of the working of perfect competition, led to the hypothesis that the regulatory process was subject to a process of 'capture' by the industry or interest group which it was initially designed to control; the initial 'public interest' incentive for regulation was subverted (e.g., by the desire of regulator and regulated, who naturally were in much closer contact with each other than with the general public, for compromise and a quiet, comfortable life).

Stigler,[3] has denied that, in general, there ever was an initial pristine state of 'public

---

[1] Examples of such British work would include Reid (1982), Moran (1984), Gardener (ed.) (1986), Hall (1986) and (1987).

[1] Notably Stigler and Friedland (1962); see also Jordan (1972).

[2] In his famous article (Stigler 1971), as subsequently extended and developed by Peltzman (1976).

interest' which became subsequently open to 'capture'. He and Peltzman query the 'political' process through which 'public interest' regulation is supposed to be achieved. Peltzman (1976, p. 212) thus states that:

> Stigler seems to have realized that the earlier 'consumer protection' model comes perilously close to treating regulation as a free good. In that model the existence of market failure is sufficient to generate a demand for regulation, though there is no mention of the mechanism that makes the demand effective.

Instead, in Stigler's model,

> there is essentially a political auction in which the high bidder receives the right to tax the wealth of everyone else, and the theory seeks to discover why the successful bidder is a numerically compact group.

Stigler and Peltzman regard that

> what is basically at stake in regulatory processes is a transfer of wealth

(Peltzman 1976, p. 213); and that the choice of agents contributing taxes and receiving benefits depends on a *political* calculus. Peltzman seeks to express this calculus formally. He assumed that politicians seek to maximise majority support, M, which is a function of the number benefited by regulation, n, and the probability that they will subsequently support the politician, f, less the number who are harmed by the regulation, $N-n$, times the probability that this will influence them to vote against the politician, h; in algebraic notation,

$$M = n.f - (N - n).h. \tag{9.1}$$

In turn, f is a function of the value of *per capita* net benefit, g, which depends on the amount of benefit transferred to the gaining group, T, *less* the amount spent by the beneficiaries in lobbying support, replying to opposition, etc., K, and the cost, C, of organising a cohesive group of beneficiaries, which rises with the size of the group n; again:

$$g = \frac{T - K - C(n)}{n} \tag{9.2}$$

The probability of opposition, h, depends in turn on the tax rate required to make the transfer, t, and the *per capita* expenditure to limit opposition, K, so:

$$h = (t, K/(N - n) \tag{9.3}$$

Peltzman then maximises (9.1), finding the optimal levels of n, T, and K by using a standard Lagrangian multiplier. The maximum is, as may be expected, one of balance where:

> the marginal political product of a dollar of profits [the return from a transfer] . . . must equal the marginal political product of a price cut [cost of the associated tax] (Peltzman 1976, p. 223).

A number of empirical implications follow from this analysis; for example, that:

> Regulation will tend to be more heavily weighted toward 'producer protection' in depressions and toward 'consumer protection' in expansions (p. 227).

There are many regulatory instances that certainly seem to lend themselves to analysis within such a framework. The political bargaining over CAP, indeed much, if not most of the decision-making process within the EEC, seems to be capable of analysis within this framework.[1] Furthermore, Parliamentary bills which cover issues where the potency of the Party Whips diminishes (e.g., the 1986 Sunday Trading Bill) would seem to be capable of analysis within the Stigler – Peltzman framework. But, even though the 1986-7 financial Acts passed by Parliament (e.g., the Financial Services Act 1986 and the Banking Act, 1987) would meet *some* of the Stigler–Peltzman expectations (i.e., consumer protection is more likely during expansionary periods (1976, p. 227) and regulation of any kind more likely in a growing industry, since there are more profits to redistribute (1976, p. 225)), it is somewhat difficult to describe the political processes that led up to the Financial Services Act within the Stigler–Peltzman analytical context.

Perhaps the failure of the UK financial regulatory process to fit neatly into the Stigler–Peltzman model[2] owes something to the greater strength of Party control over MPs in the UK than over Congressmen in the US. In cases where every vote depends on obtaining a fluid majority of relatively independent Congressmen whose own tenure depends, in part, on how their individual voting record appears to various powerful interest groups in their separate districts,[3] one can see the potential force of the Stigler–Peltzman model; as earlier noted, the structure of European political institutions would suggest its frequent application there as well.

On the other hand, such a political calculus seems less applicable to the UK context of firmly Whipped parties. Unless the benefits or losses from the wealth transfer involved in regulation seem to loom very large to his (her) own constituents, (e.g., West Cornish MPs are *bound* to advocate subsidies to tin mining irrespective of economic considerations), an MP will usually be required (and feel obliged) to follow the Party line. So, normally, the passage of a Bill will be quasi-automatic, once the governing executive has decided upon it, and, unless the key Ministers are *persuaded* that the measure – say, to tax some group or activity – is not in their wider interest, the organisation of pressure group lobbying will have lesser effectiveness than in the USA. Under such conditions, with the passage of most bills effectively guaranteed once the executive has decided on them, and with a wide range of parliamentary Acts having been passed during the life of a Parliament before the voters have their own say at the election, it would seem relatively more difficult to mobilise interest group effectiveness in the UK.

And yet there must still be *a* political calculus at work, even if the Stigler–Peltzman model does not seem to fit the facts for the 1986-7 financial Acts passed by Parliament (though, perhaps, it can be applied to the Building Societies Act, since it could be claimed that this benefits a cohesive interest group, namely the Building Societies themselves). The Cabinet has to choose what bills to present to Parliament, and time is short and limited. The political decision is one of choice subject to constraints, as is the economic decision. What political pressures, therefore, induced the government to put forward these bills? What were the considerations that caused these bills to have priority? What were the constituencies that supported the bills?

Consider the various players. First, there are the financial intermediaries to be regulated. As will be discussed next, the exercise of regulation, whether statutory or practitioner-based (and the distinction is becoming blurred) is hardly possible

---

[1] For an example from the financial field, see Sargent (1986).

[2] The 'political phases model' of Weingast (1980) is a stage more realistic than the Stigler–Peltzman model, but even that does not easily fit the facts in this instance.

[3] It may be noted that Peltzman (1984) has written on this subject.

without the willing acceptance of the regulated. Given some of the compliance costs that would seem to be involved in the operation of the Financial Services Act, what has been the *quid pro quo* that encouraged the financial intermediaries, if not to support the passage of the Act, at least not to lobby strenuously against its adoption?

As for the general (or at least the investing) public, the benefit would seem to lie primarily in the provision of greater protection for the individual investor. But why not rely on transparency of information, the due process of law, and *caveat emptor*? I shall review the economic arguments that *can* be made for the regulation of financial services in Section 2, but at this juncture I want to raise one worrying possibility. It appears often to be the case that there is a psychological tendency to give excessive, undue weight in decision-making to extreme, atypical examples of loss and disaster. They are newsworthy and stick in the memory. The Gower Report[1] was commissioned in the aftermath of several quite dramatic and fully reported cases of financial impropriety causing severe investor loss. The connection of the Banking Act 1987 to Johnson Matthey is obvious.

In fact, the actual amount of loss in each case was comparatively small, though concentrated in its impact. The public may then support a regulatory proposal that actually harms them on balance because the restraints on competition and the deadweight costs of compliance and administration may considerably outweigh the extra likely losses in an unregulated state. Yet, because they attach a greater weight – than would be actuarially correct – to avoiding the risk of severe loss, they may still support the measure. If this was so, one can easily see on Stiglerian grounds why the government would give the measure its support. The resulting tax on the majority of investors would be too low for them to notice. The financial intermediaries would have to be bought off with enough concessions to make them willing to help make the system work. The danger that the government faces is the (admittedly low) probability of a failure, severely affecting some, even if only a few, voters and thus being newsworthy, of a kind which could have been prevented by regulation and whose possible occurrence was previously known. Where the potential disadvantages of regulation are widely spread and difficult to pin-point (e.g., restriction of competition) whereas the benefits are clear (i.e., in helping to prevent embarrassing failure or even simply to be seen to be taking 'remedial' action in the aftermath of a newsworthy failure), the likelihood of such regulation passing into law, whatever the true balance of costs and benefits, becomes consequently greater.

As Stigler, has noted,[2]

> A law is enforced, not by 'society', but by an agency instructed to that task. That agency must be given more than a mandate (an elegant admonition) to endorse the statute with vigor and wisdom: It must have incentives to enforce the law efficiently. There are at least two deficiencies in the methods by which most agencies are induced to enforce the laws properly.
>
> The first deficiency is that the enforcement agency does not take into account, at least explicitly and fully, the costs that it imposes upon the activity or persons regulated ... In the area of economic regulation, guilt is often an inappropriate notion, and when it is inappropriate all costs of compliance must be reckoned into the social costs of enforcement ... The second deficiency in the design of enforcement is the use of inappropriate methods of determining the extent of enforcement. The annual report of an enforcement agency is in effect the justification of its previous expenditures and the

---

[1] *Review of Investor Protection* (1984).

[2] (1970).

plea for enlarged appropriations ... The agency may recite scandals corrected or others still unrepressed, but it neither offers nor possesses a criterion by which to determine the correct scale of its activities (pp. 531–2).

Stigler goes on to argue for a cost–benefit study, leading up to a cost-minimising decision whereby an enforcement agency expands its activities until the expected marginal reduction in costs to society from the undesirable activity being controlled is equated with the marginal costs of administration, compliance and other costs (e.g., restriction of competition), arising from the operations of the enforcement agency.

Moreover, the incentives facing the staff of a supervisory–enforcement agency are clearly on the side of trying to reduce the probability and/or the extent of failures, without worrying greatly about the costs of such regulation, particularly where these fall in a widespread manner (e.g., compliance costs and reduced efficiency, innovation and dynamism) on others in the economy. If one was the responsible supervisor when bank X or financial intermediary Y failed with consequential public concern and blame, the resulting obloquy is likely to have a notably adverse effect on one's subsequent career. On the other hand, the costs of a rigid constraint by the regulators on risk-taking and competition, in order to limit the risk of failure and loss, are likely to be distributed much more widely; the individual member of the supervisory agency can also plead, in the perhaps unlikely case of being attacked for being overly restrictive, that he or she was merely vigorously carrying out the statutory requirements.

Because of the fear that this incentive structure will encourage supervisors to be excessively zealous in imposing regulations, several American economists have applauded the possibility of a multiplicity of alternative, overlapping competitive regulators so that 'competition in laxity' could offset the incentive to undue zeal, even though the spectacle of 'competition in laxity' among overlapping supervisory agencies would seem at first glance a bureaucratic nightmare! Thus, Hirshleifer wrote that[1]

he does not allow for possible *competition among different regulatory agencies*. This can be an important feature of a number of political situations. One case of particular interest has free entry into the regulation business, combined with freedom on the part of the targets of regulation to 'vote with their feet' for the regulatory jurisdiction of their choice. So an appropriate constitutional arrangement can lead to a kind of long-run zero-profit equilibrium in the regulation industry, in which 'do-nothing regulation' is the final outcome! (Some good news, at last).

In particular, Kane, who has done much specialised work in this area, has advocated more competition among regulators and in the provision of deposit insurance.[2]

Although there are generally sanctions for non-compliance, non-co-operation or misdirection of the regulators, it is generally impossible for a supervisory enforcement agency to operate effectively without a considerable extent of willing support among the regulated (e.g., in the provision of an information base, in being prepared to discuss foreseen problems in a spirit of trust and mutual acceptance, and in discussing the practical application of regulations in a spirit of some compromise). Whether the emphasis of regulation is more towards *statutory* regulation or 'voluntary' *practitioner-based self-regulation*, the exercise can probably hardly work with-

---

[1] Hirshleifer (1976).
[2] See Kane (1985) and (1972), also see Bloch (1984).

out a considerable modicum of practitioner support for the exercise. In that sense, the sharp dividing line between these two forms of regulation has probably been exaggerated; all regulation will need to be largely practitioner-based. The differences, such as they are, will probably lie more in the style, staffing and operational format of the supervisory agency rather than in the ultimate need for a modicum of practitioner involvement and acceptance. To that extent, the earlier concept of the 'capture' of supervisory agencies by the industry to be regulated, suborning an earlier public interest goal, was always naive. Unless the supervisory agency is 'captured' from the outset, in the sense that the regulators can discuss regulatory issues in an amicable fashion with the regulated, and agree on compromises to deal with points of friction, the whole exercise is probably infeasible.

The serious question, therefore, is *not* whether the form of regulation needs to be made broadly acceptable to the great proportion of the regulated, since the answer is 'yes', but rather how such regulation can *best* be made acceptable. The common, general answer is that regulation is most frequently made acceptable to the regulated by including certain elements of restriction of unfettered competition, generally in the form of restrictions over entry (e.g., licensing) but extending into restrictions on the operation of business (e.g., advertising), limitations on ways of drumming-up business, such as 'cold-calling',[1] and in many cases extending further into constraints over pricing, though this final step was *not* incorporated into the Acts extending financial regulation passed by Parliament in 1986–7.

Why is such restriction in the interest of most members of the regulated sector? There are two sources of benefit: one socially beneficial, the other not. First, as will be discussed at greater length in Section 2, the public may have difficulty in discerning, either in advance or after the event, the quality of the service that it has been receiving. The limitation on entry, for example to those who pass a test of being fit and proper persons (e.g., to run a bank) and have sufficient assets (e.g., capital adequacy) for that function, will serve as a quality control guarantee to the possibly ill-informed public, and therefore may encourage greater demand for the product[2]

---

[1] 'cold-calling' is the practice of making unsolicited approaches to people, whether by telephone or in person, for the purpose of generating additional business.

[2] The tougher the entry control, i.e., the higher the qualifications demanded, the higher becomes the quality guaranteed, and thus the higher the charges that those involved could demand. This led Shaked and Sutton to note in their paper 'Imperfect Information, Perceived Quality, and the Formation of Professional Groups' (1982) that there is a problem:

> For members of such professional groups, characterized by their common attainment of some minimal entry requirements, are in the eyes of the imperfectly informed consumers to whom they provide services, 'equally well qualified', and command a common fee. But insofar as this implies that the less able earn a quasi-rent which reflects in part the superior abilities of their more able colleagues, it would seem intuitively obvious that the more able would find it preferable to separate themselves from their fellows, forming a smaller and more profitable coalition. Thus professional groups would vanish, and 'certification' drive out 'licensing'. In practice, however, the 'co-operative' solution, involving the formation of a professional group, is typical.

In my view, however, it is more common to find private practitioner-based certification (e.g., belonging to a higher quality specialisation such as a surgeon or an Accepting House) co-existing with an externally required minimum entry level. One reason for such mutually-satisfactory coalitions is that much of the demand for the specialists' high-cost service may be directed there by the more general practitioner. The demand for high quality services may thus be an increasing function, up to a point, of the size of the profession as a whole, which is a slight gloss on Shaked and Sutton's conclusions.

Given economies of scale in the provision of information, the supervisory agency releases the public from the choice of having to undertake sizeable search costs or risk receiving sub-standard services. It may be asked whether such quality guarantee could not be better provided by private-sector credit rating agencies. In certain areas, the provision of information might be sub-optimal unless undertaken by a public agency since the state is in a much stronger position to require the harmonised provision of certain, possibly sensitive, information than a private agency would be; in addition, information generally becomes a public good once it is released and this implies that the government has a further justification for market intervention.

Whereas the enforcement of a minimum level of competence, together with some form of insurance (user-protection) for those instances when a consumer finds that the actual services provided do *not* actually achieve the quality level implicitly guaranteed, may be defensible on account of information problems, it is harder to justify further constraints, either on the conduct of business or on pricing policies, on such grounds. While it is perfectly reasonable to try to prevent misleading advertisements, there seems no case, on informational grounds, for preventing advertising as such, at least by those who possess the licensed minimum qualifications. Indeed, further restraints on the conduct or pricing of business usually do little except protect the market position of those within the regulated industry. Naturally, most of the regulated will be in favour of such constraints since they raise industry incomes and profits. Before turning next to an analysis of the arguments in *favour* of such regulation, in Section 2, it may be well to repeat that the Chicago School of economic analysis has entered a powerful *prima facie* case *against* regulation, whether of financial services or elsewhere. The case for regulation is *not* self-sufficient and requires more careful construction than it is sometimes given.

2.   The Economic Arguments for Regulation

In much of the preceding discussion of the Chicago School's *prima facie* case against regulation, an industry subject to regulation has been implicitly compared with an industry constrained by perfect competition. In reality, of course, relatively few industries operate under perfectly competitive conditions. Even so, there remains a *prima facie* case against regulations that would drive such industries further from the competitive ideal and a presumption that anti-trust, free-trading, deregulatory measures would be desirable in such cases.

The case *for* regulation should not rest then on denial of the existence of perfect competition as a benchmark against which the effects of regulation should be measured, but rather on identification of specific conditions within markets which may call for government intervention. Three such conditions have been identified in the literature.[1]

The first such condition, which relates to the existence of possible *natural* monopolies (e.g., in a range of public utilities, gas pipelines, etc.), need be of relatively little concern to a study of regulation in financial services since there are only a few instances of such natural monopoly, or of the need for regulation in that respect, in the financial field. One example of a potential monopoly may be provided by the role of a clearing-house within the payments system. It is naturally efficient to operate only one such, within a given area. But the owners of the clearing-house may exclude

---

[1] See Elzinga (1980) pp. 108–9; Arrow (1973) and (1963); and Horowitz (1980).

competitors, or allow them access only on disadvantageous terms. There is, therefore, a case in these circumstances for external (e.g., governmental) intervention to ensure fair access to the clearing-house. There are, perhaps, other aspects of the payments system – (e.g., the general acceptance of certain plastic credit (or debit) cards, where the economies of scale are such as to provide potential monopolistic abuse – which may need to be checked by external intervention.

It is also arguable that the provision of information is akin to a public good, which might best be provided by the public sector, since providing information to one recipient does not restrict – indeed, facilitates – its enjoyment by other potential recipients. See the discussion of the provision of, and payment for, financial information in Chapter 5, Section 2. Whether information is best assembled and transmitted onwards by public or private sector bodies is an important, but under-researched, question. Be that as it may, the provision of information may have *some* of the characteristics of a 'natural monopoly'.

The second such condition relates to the possible existence of externalities, with pollution being the standard example. There *are* some examples of possible externalities in the financial field. The failure of one bank may throw doubt on the viability of others, and a contagion of panic withdrawals may result. This possibility is not common to *all* financial intermediaries, however. Where the institution is a mutual collective fund whose liabilities are valued in terms of a *pro rata* share of the assets, there will be less incentive to withdraw funds in the face of a supposed, or actual, fall in the asset value of the funds' portfolio.[1] As I have analysed in greater length in my paper, 'Why do Banks Need a Central Bank?' (1987), the combination of a convertibility guarantee in nominal terms on bank liabilities together with an asset portfolio whose nominal value is subject to uncertainty leads to the possibility of bank runs.[2] If bank A fails, this may cast doubt on the solvency of bank B if there are reasons to believe – as there well may be – that there is a positive correlation between fluctuations in the value of their respective portfolios. See also the preceding discussion in Chapter 8.

Even so, one may ask, where lies the externality? If bank B is solvent, it will be able to meet such a run and continue. If not, the run may concentrate losses on those left behind in the queue to withdraw, but the losses had been suffered anyhow. The answer to this is twofold. First, the need to realize assets to raise cash to honour the convertibility guarantee would drive down asset prices, and raise real interest rates, above the 'non-run' equilibrium. There could be two equilibria, a 'run' equilibrium in which real interest rates were temporarily high and real losses suffered by bank depositors – shareholders, and a more desirable 'non-run' equilibrium avoiding such real losses.

The second reason why externalities may exist in the face of such instances of contagious panic concerns the fixed nature of capital, the weakness of second-hand markets[3] (e.g., for capital equipment), and the time required for production. Because of such factors, borrowers are often in no position to repay loans by selling their existing business. If a bank, facing a run or having failed, should call in its loans, the borrowers' only hope in many cases is to find new funds from elsewhere. Not only is

---

[1] Though if the fund tries to peg the price of its liabilities at a level which some believe may be above the value of the supporting assets, then it is inviting a run, as apparently happened to the UK Provident Institute in April 1986.

[2] Also see Diamond and Dybvig (1983).

[3] Largely because of the problem identified by Akerlof (1970).

that search expensive in itself but the very conditions (e.g., adverse economic developments) that caused concern about the value of the bank's portfolio will make it hard for the borrower to obtain additional funds from elsewhere. In particular, economic history is replete with occasions when the failure of a bank (or banks) which had become over-extended to a certain class of borrower[1] is then followed by a refusal of banks, and other intermediaries, to extend further credit to members of that class, and indeed by an attempt to reduce the existing exposure. This immediately jeopardises the continued existence of other members of that (rationed) class and, because of the fixed nature and weak second-hand markets for existing capital assets, leads to potentially avoidable waste. As Bernanke's work, 'Nonmonetary Effects of the Financial Crisis in the Propagation of the Great Depression', suggests,[2] it may have been the failure of banks, and the withdrawal of their ability to grant credit, rather than the contraction of the money stock, as such, that was primarily responsible for the depth of the American depression in 1931–33.

Although there continue to be arguments over the precise source and cause of externalities arising from bank runs, the existence of such externalities has been generally accepted by most economists. Two main lines of defence have been adopted. The first is lender-of-last-resort actions by the Central Bank, whereby the Central Bank lends to the bank in difficulties facing net withdrawals to obviate the need for that bank to dump assets in a depressed market and/or call in loans. The second step has been to introduce various forms of deposit insurance. Unless such insurance is priced so as accurately to reflect the *ex ante* risk of bank failure, the existence of such insurance – whether explicit in the case of the FDIC or implicit in the case of banks expecting the Central Bank to arrange, *ex post facto*, a rescue package for its depositors – is likely to lead some banks in some circumstances, especially where adverse conditions have already impaired shareholder equity, consciously to choose a riskier strategy on the grounds that in the event of failure the insurer, or Central Bank, or taxpayer, picks up most of the tab, while in the event of success, the rewards go to the risk taker. Because of such moral hazard conditions, together with the complexities of trying to price insurance premia accurately to reflect risk, there is a recognised case for regulation, notably to enforce capital adequacy requirements.[3]

All this is standard. What is, perhaps, more interesting is the question whether, and where, similar externalities exist elsewhere within the financial system. One such case *may* be found in the form of market structure. The problem faced, for example, in the London tin market in 1985–6 suggested that losses faced by a large player in a market, where deals are made between dealers without the interposition of a clearing house as the counter-party in each case, may lead to a chain of potential failure that can threaten the very existence of the market itself. In order to maintain the smooth functioning of markets, with or without the involvement of a central Clearing House to provide insurance against credit risk, the authorities may feel that intervention is necessary to prevent the operators in the market taking up riskier positions than are consistent with the continued smooth running of such markets. Another example of the kind of market disturbance which could be described as involving externalities is

---

[1] E.g., railroads in the nineteenth century; farmers in the US Mid-West and sovereign borrowers from less developed countries in the twentieth century.

[2] (1983).

[3] See, for example, Chase (1978).

the collapse of the Singapore Stock Exchange in 1986, and the threatened collapse of financial markets in several centres in October 1987.

The role of the Bank of England in regulating financial markets and the concern of the Securities and Investments Board (SIB) with the form, operations and control of Registered Investment Exchanges (RIEs) can thus be defended under this general heading of externality. The loss arising from the excessively risky strategy of a market operator may well fall on others, such as the clearing house and/or users of the market, so that regulations may be required to limit the assumption of risk by such operators.

In those cases when the assumption of risk or the use of fraudulent practices leads to losses falling on a wider range of agents besides those choosing the strategy, there is a case both for insuring against the adverse effect of failure and for directly limiting the risk exposure of those involved. Limits on large exposures, foreign-currency positions, and connected lendings are examples from the banking sector of direct limits on risk exposure. Insurance in banking is provided, either explicitly in the case of the FDIC or implicitly (at least to some extent) by Central Bank-arranged rescue packages. Similar externalities may perhaps exist in other financial markets and may likewise be contained through some combination of insurance and direct constraints over risk.

Kareken and Wallace have, however, claimed,[1] that in the special case where all potential depositors had full information on bank strategies and the potential outcome of such strategies, banks would be led to choose strategies with zero bankruptcy risk in the *absence* of deposit insurance and/or regulation. If depositors get a fixed return under good outcome conditions and a lower, possibly zero, return under bad outcomes, they would – if they had the information – place funds only with institutions which eliminated the possibility of bad outcomes. Unless deposit insurance can be priced accurately in relation to risk, so as to make bankers continue to prefer the no-bankruptcy choices of strategy, the introduction of deposit insurance, by transferring the risks of loss from depositor to the insuring agency, *encourages* banks (or other financial intermediaries) to assume additional risk, especially in those circumstances where the equity-holders and managers have already suffered such losses that they have little or nothing more to lose themselves by 'going for broke'.[2]

The assumption that potential investors have full, even much, information on the actual and potential strategy choices open to financial intermediaries and/or on the probable risk – return implications of these portfolio strategies is, however, implausible. Accordingly, there remains a case for some direct limitation on risk in those cases where externalities appear to exist, whether or not deposit insurance is also in operation. Where economists, such as Kareken,[3] have made their case is that the further provision of various forms of insurance is likely to *enhance* the need for direct controls over risk exposure.

---

[1] Kareken and Wallace (1978).

[2] There is a large literature available on these latter points, including Kane (1985).

[3] See also his further papers, 'Deregulating Commercial Banks: The Watchword Should Be Caution' (1981) pp. 1–5; 'Deposit Insurance Reform or Deregulation Is the Cart, Not the Horse' (1987) pp. 1–9; 'Bank Regulation and the Effectiveness of Open Market Operations' (1984).

Such an interaction between the provision of mispriced insurance[1] and the need for additional risk controls to inhibit the resulting moral hazard distorts the allocation of resources in several ways. This has led to some pressure (e.g., from economists and from the larger, safer units), for pricing of insurance more closely in relation to perceived risk; so far, however, practical problems of measuring risk appear to have stymied this latter approach.

In any case, the existence of externalities at certain points within the financial system would appear to justify some combinations of direct risk control and insurance. It is sometimes argued that yet further controls are necessary or desirable as a protection against externalities (e.g., entry control and controls over pricing, such as Regulation Q, and the prohibition of interest payments on demand deposits in the USA). So long as the insurance programmes and the direct controls on risk did constrain the financial intermediaries' choice set in order adequately to reflect the extra social costs of the externalities involved, it is hard to see the justification for any further constraint on competition on this account. Thus, if the insurance premium and/or the constraints on portfolio strategy *were* appropriately related to risk, it is hard to see why *any* new entrant with any size of capital or background experience should be barred from entry.[2]

Although regulation to limit adverse externalities such as contagious panic in banking and financial markets is important, the larger part of the regulations involved in the Financial Services Act are intended to meet the third main market imperfection that is taken as a justification for regulation: information problems. An essential part of the provision of professional services involves the application of specialised information to dealing with the customer's problems, whether accounting, legal, medical or financial. Thus, Arrow in 'Uncertainty and the Welfare Economics of Medical Care' (1963) noted that:

> information, in the form of skilled care, is precisely what is being bought from most physicians, and, indeed, from most professions.

The first requirement that most people need when they apply to professionals is diagnosis of how best to meet their needs. This is not exclusive to professional services, however, since sellers generally will have specialised knowledge of their product range, whether goods or services, and will often be able to diagnose how best to meet a customer's needs. Generally, therefore, there will be an information asymmetry where the seller has more information than the buyer; this is likely to be especially so in the provision of professional services, most of which consist of the application of specialised information.[3]

Diagnosis can be difficult and expensive. So, except in vital issues such as major medical cases, it can be rare for purchasers of services to ask for second opinions. That has two implications. First, customers will want reassurance that, given their

---

[1] Usually in the form of being related to size of balance sheet, rather than to any estimate of risk, thereby subsidising the small and risky units at the expense of the large diversified units. In his book, *The Regulation and Reform of the American Banking System 1900–1929* (1983) E. N. White argues that the characteristics of deposit insurance, as adopted in the US (i.e., with premia related to volume of deposits rather than to risk) were not inadvertent, nor due to an inability to identify risk, but rather to a 'political' desire to sustain the US unit banking system.

[2] If a previously convicted confidence trickster with virtually no capital wanted to become a futures broker, the insurance premium required in advance would no doubt be effectively prohibitive.

[3] On this see Weingast (1980).

own inability to evaluate the standard of diagnosis – advice that they are receiving, the level of expertise of all those whom they approach for such advice achieves at any rate a minimum of competence. Second, given the extra cost of a second opinion and the economies of dealing with only one professional, it is normal for those requiring professional services not only to ask for diagnosis but also to execute the suggested remedial action through the same professional. One does not normally go to one doctor solely for a diagnosis, and then a second doctor for treatment unless the first doctor recommended it; in any case, the second doctor would usually insist on confirming the diagnosis for himself. Similarly, one does not often ask one stock-broker for investment advice and then execute the suggested order through a second.

In consequence, professionals generally act both as agent for the customer, in diagnosing the problem and considering the best remedial action, and as a principal in executing with the customer the prescribed action. This inherent dual capacity, common to most professional services, naturally gives rise to conflicts of interest in cases where the professional acting as agent prescribes action which he knows is to his own benefit as principal rather than to the customer's. There is *nothing* special about financial services in this respect. For example, shop assistants who suggest higher-priced items in order to obtain a higher commission on sales are subject to the same principal – agent conflict. Benham and Benham[1] offer a humorous parable, 'The Informers' Tale', about a society which tries to limit such principal – agent conflicts of interest by requiring that all consumers of goods and services use the office of an 'Informer' to select the goods and services best suited to that consumer. The fatal flaw in this fictitious suggestion is that consumers are *required* to go to an 'Informer' and to accept the 'Informers'' advice before a purchase can be made. Naturally, this leads to an excessive allocation of resources to this function and to the consumers' own real preferences being over-ruled by the preferences of the 'Informers'.

Darby and Karni, in their paper with the intriguing title, 'Free Competition and the Optimal Amount of Fraud',[2]

> distinguish then three kinds of qualities associated with a particular purchase: – search qualities which are known before purchase, experience qualities which are known costlessly only after purchase, and credence qualities which are expensive to judge even after purchase.

Since the provision of professional services inherently involves information asymme-tries, whereby the professional knows far more than the customer, there are likely to be particular problems connected with the first and third of these qualities in the purchase of professional services.

As already noted, customers will often not be in a position to make an informed estimate (at any rate initially) of the calibre of the advice and services of the professional. Even though the resulting experience of using such services may be clear cut (e.g., the patient got better or died, the Inland Revenue did or did not accept the accountant's claim, the barrister won or lost, the investment manager did or did not beat the FTSE index) it is difficult to differentiate skill from luck, at least without a large number of repeated trials and under controlled conditions. It follows from this fact that customers searching for professional advice have to rely on publicly-known qualifications and reputation based on personal contact. This underlies the import-ance of publicly-available qualifications and the need for some minimum standards.

---

[1] Benham and Benham (1980).
[2] (1973).

Even though the experience qualities associated with a past purchase are acquired without additional cost after purchase (e.g., one knows whether one recovered after taking a drug and whether the car was fault free or not), the purchase may represent such an important step for the individual that the individual may again want some insurance against a faulty product. Legal protection against fraud or product liability may be sufficient in some cases, but again it can be difficult with professional services to distinguish low skill from bad luck. Rather than suffer from inadequately tested drugs, unskilled drivers, dirty kitchens, or unskilled professionals, there will be a demand for controls over entry. Normally, the existence of small purchases – small in relation to total wealth and small in relation to post-experience effect utility – and possible repetition of purchase helps to ensure quality control. When conditions connected with the purchase make its effect large, particularly when the prior search quality information is difficult to obtain, there will be a demand for entry controls and various forms of insurance, such as repair guarantees on consumer durables, to limit the risk of post-experience disasters; this will occur even when it is possible to apply to the courts for protection against fraud or product liability.

By their nature (i.e., dealing with the use of money) financial services are probably more prone to fraud than other professional services. Since transaction costs lead to economies of scale in handling money, most people, other than the very wealthy, generally use only a few financial intermediaries. Consequently, the loss of funds as a result of frauds by such an intermediary can frequently wipe out much of the wealth of the customer. There is, therefore, likely to be considerable public demand both for preventive measures against fraud (e.g., entry control, capital adequacy requirements and supervisory monitoring) and for insurance to limit the *ex post* exposure to such personal disaster. There was, admittedly, not much public clamour in the UK for extra protection against fraud in the provision of financial services prior to the passage of the Financial Services Act 1986, but that may have been because adequate public protection against fraudulent loss had previously been achieved by restricting the provision of most financial services to closely controlled cartels (e.g., the Building Societies Association). There had previously been relatively little loss through fraud in the UK financial system, but the move towards a more competitive, open financial system, though beneficial in many other ways, did, however, raise the issue of customer protection against fraud in a more acute form, which has now been met by the establishment of the Securities and Investments Board (SIB).

It is, however, in the third area defined by Darby and Karni, of credence qualities, that professional services generally lead to the worst information problems.[1] When I take my car back from the repair shop, I can observe clearly enough whether it is

---

[1] Darby and Karni (1973) consider the conditions that affect the likelihood of excessive services being charged up to the ignorant customer. These include the likelihood of the action affecting the future flow of orders, e.g.,

> tourists and casual customers are likely to be defrauded to a greater extent than regular and steady customers,

and the availability of unused resources in the firm (e.g., a fully occupied garage is less likely to undertake inessential repairs than an underutilised one; on the other hand, a fully occupied garage may be less worried about adverse reputational effects).

They go on to consider the case for government intervention in markets for credence goods. They consider official evaluation of the quality of credence goods but argue that the job could be done better by private rating firms. They also consider the imposition of minimum quality standards but claim (p. 84) that this would not allow:

working properly. What I do not have is the information to check whether all the repairs listed were needed, completed and even done accurately and properly costed. It would take me a great deal of time and effort to check that. Similarly, as an ordinary investor, it is difficult to discern whether the investments that I was advised to make by my professional adviser were actually optimal or benefited him in his role as principal because they led to extra commission income on unnecessary turnover ('churning'); they also may not have been done at the best available price or may have benefited the financial operator in his joint role as principal in some other way. A large proportion of the regulations being imposed by the SIB[1] involve intervention in order to deal with credence problems.

Where credence qualities are involved, the relationship between customer and professional must involve considerable trust, as Arrow emphasizes in the two papers quoted earlier. One defence for the consumer is the transmission from person to person of suspicions when that trust is abused. Another protection, also emphasised by Arrow, is the development of professional ethics. The two defences may, however, sometimes conflict. Since it is difficult to distinguish poor skill from bad luck, the abuse of trust (e.g., in the calculated promotion of unnecessary expenditures) may be

> producers to choose the degree to which they will guarantee their diagnosis, say, by choice and posting of quality class, A, B or C, or the like.

They suggest (p. 85) that:

> A form of government intervention which combines both methods is for the government to prescribe standards for self-rated classes A, B, and C which are then enforced by private individuals filing remunerative malpractice suits if the claimed standards are not met.

They continue (p. 85) by stating that:

> There seem to be two arguments which might justify these forms of governmental intervention. The first is that it is cheaper to communicate the fact that one is subject to uniform government standards than individual rules, but this is a fairly weak argument since uniform private standards are established wherever the cost is worth the trouble. The second argument is of more interest. If a reward is offered to anyone discovering the shop violating uniform private standard A, the reward and probability of loss must be such that their expectation just covers the cost of an investigation. If instead governmental enforcement is utilized, then a small probability of loss and a high fine could be established. As a result, less resources could be devoted to production of costly evaluations of the quality of services provided. This follows from the fact that production of information about any shop by costly tests is a natural monopoly.

On the subject of the detection and punishment of quality failure, also see Blair and Kaserman (1980). It is interesting that the case for government intervention in this particular field may relate to its comparative advantage either in detecting quality failure (e.g., by being able to enforce the provision of more data) and/or in imposing coercive penalties.

Darby and Karni go on, however, to argue that public-sector supervisory agencies will be more subject to bribery than would private market schemes for upholding quality (pp. 85–6) so that they do not find it:

> clear that the proposed scheme of governmental intervention can improve on market methods of monitoring the provision of credence goods.

But we can, perhaps, leave this latter thought on one side.

---

[1] E.g., the 'Conduct of Business Rules', Chapter 3 in Securities and Investments Board, *Drafts Relating to Rules, Regulations. Orders and Directions to be Made by the Securities and Investments Board as Designated Agency under the Financial Services Bill* (1986).

observable with any clarity only by a peer group; professional ethics may, however, prevent such investigation from taking place at all.

Although relationships must involve trust, there is still potential for abuse. There is, therefore, a case for regulation to deal with the various problems that arise from asymmetric information, particularly perhaps the need to prevent fraud and to improve credence qualities. I shall next consider three forms of such controls: entry controls and licensing, depositor protection, and issues related to credence problems, notably conflicts of interest.

Although it is dubious whether it is possible to justify entry controls in order to limit externalities, such measures may be justified on informational grounds under several headings. First, the fact that professional services involve the application of specialised information virtually ensures that the ordinary consumer cannot distinguish the quality of his purchase in advance; in addition, the fact that diagnosis is generally expensive means that the consumer wants to be assured of a known minimum level of quality. Second, in cases when the failure of certain purchased services – goods – advice may have a devastating effect on that person's post-experience welfare, customers are going to seek minimum quality guarantees or some other form of insurance, in addition to such options of restitution through the courts as may be open to them. Third, the existence of credence problems implies the need for trust between the informationally-disadvantaged purchaser and the more strongly-placed professional. That, too, would be assisted by quality guarantees and the adoption of professional ethics.

The issues here are not so much whether measures to assure minimum quality are desirable but why they need the force of government statutory support and why the quality control need necessarily be in the form of a licence, without which no one can offer the service, rather than through certification, implying that the certified have attained some prescribed level of competence. Since banking in the UK moved away from a certification system (e.g., Section 123 bank, Section 127 bank, authorised bank, etc.) to its present licensing system, it is of interest to inquire whether the defects of the previous system were due to the bad alignment of supervisory control over the various rungs or whether the certification process itself was faulted.

Most professions will tend to set up their own schemes of certification if the private market rewards seem to justify the time and effort. Presumably private groups would find it harder to prevent those without the requisite qualifications either operating or misrepresenting to others that they had the necessary qualifications. So, it may be the additional *coercive* powers of the state that makes quality controls more easily enforceable at lower overall costs which provides the rationale for state action. Moreover it can be argued that one monitoring agency (the government) may be able to monitor, and enforce compliance, at a very much lower overall cost than a multitude of private agents. If such monitoring, and enforcement, was to be delegated to a single private agent, say, would this not provide that private agent with more (monopoly) power than would be consistent with a democratic system?

This, however, leaves open the issue of whether quality control should be through licence or certification. Most economists prefer certification.[1] The line at which licensing is drawn, in principle, is likely to be sufficiently high to enable the customer to be reasonably certain of getting a fully professional service. One argument for certification is that some customers may not need a fully-professional service and would prefer a cheaper but more limited option. Moreover, since failure to obtain a

---

[1] See, for example Beales (1980).

licence will have a major adverse effect on income, the borderline cases will go to greater lengths than under certification, including legal redress, to reverse the decision. There will be strong pressures, at least in certain cases, on those administering licences to soften the rules for borderline cases. So, in practice, the quality level actually achieved by the licence may be lower than expected in principle. Furthermore, the gentler gradation available through certification not only avoids the all-or-nothing licensing step but also gives more room for learning by doing, a virtue that was recognised at the time of the ladder of banking recognition that was operated in the UK before 1979, whereby banking-type institutions were granted increasingly higher official status as they gained experience and reputation.

The arguments in favour of licensing are, presumably, information transparency, simplicity and administrative convenience. It is argued that the public will not be well enough informed to distinguish between the different levels of certification and will tend to believe that *any* level of certification, if carried out by the authorities, provides, for example, a guarantee of quality. Moreover, it could be difficult to restrain those with lower-level certificates from doing the more complex parts of the professional function while still unqualified. If the rationale of state entry into the field of quality control rests on its unique coercive power, then the exercise of that power should be undertaken in a clear-cut, transparent and simple context. Perhaps for these administrative reasons, *statutory* quality control tends to involve single minimum-level licences, whereas private professionals often establish a wider range of self-certification.

Since the problems facing the customer arise from asymmetrical information, there would seem no case for *any* limitation on advertisements, other than to ensure that they do not misrepresent.

The second main area of regulation that one may consider under this general heading covers customer protection; in the case of financial services, this applies primarily to depositor protection. It rather strains semantic purity, however, to describe this as an *information* problem. The consumer will be able to tell, all too well, whether the financial intermediary has failed through fraud, inadvertence, excess risk, etc. just as he can tell whether his car or TV failed. Why then should not the customer rely solely on full information – with misrepresentation being made illegal – and due process of law, with caveat emptor ruling otherwise?

As an example of customer protection, the deposit insurance schemes now ruling for banking and building societies in the UK, with their high level of co-responsibility,[1] are patently and recognisedly not meant as insurance against bank runs and crises;[2] they are *not* intended to meet externalities. Instead, their purpose is to give some protection to the customer, above and beyond that available through the law, which may be unable to bring about restitution and is anyhow slow-acting. It is here that the informational arguments primarily enter. It is argued that the poor will not have the competence to assess risk. Moreover, they are more likely to be undiversified than the rich. There is a distributional argument for providing some minimum, proportional extra insurance safeguard for them. Furthermore, such depositor

---

[1] Only 75 per cent of principal is guaranteed up to a relatively low (compared with the FDIC) maximum.

[2] The Federal Deposit Insurance schemes, for banks and S&Ls, in the USA *are* designed primarily for this latter systematic purpose. The point of this section is to show how the function of deposit insurance schemes for the provision of investor protection can be assessed *separately* from the function of deposit insurance in the provision of systemic support.

protection has the added advantage for the regulatory agency that it can allow financial intermediaries to fail without the agency being accused of presiding over a system which brings total ruin to widows – orphans, etc.

If there had been an effective demand for such protection, one might have expected the private market to provide it. After all, the collapse of one's house or car can also be devastating. In many other cases, insurance in one form or another (e.g., guarantees, warrants, or straight insurance) is made privately available. This leads on to a much larger subject concerning the public or private provision of insurance. In those fields, such as unemployment and financial intermediation, where the risks involved are closely tied up with government policy and where there is a low probability of a disaster of such a magnitude that ordinary private insurance can not cope, as, for example, in the failure of the insurance coverage of S & Ls in Ohio and Maryland in 1985, then there is a tendency to turn to the public sector for such protection.[1]

The UK case is somewhat unusual in this respect. There was little evidence of much public demand for depositor protection through insurance at banks and building societies. There was no tendency for the private sector to provide it voluntarily. Instead, the authorities put considerable pressure on the banks – building societies not only to provide such protection but also to pay for it, see Moran (1984). On the other hand, the terms of the insurance are so constrained, with large co-responsibility, low maxima and limits on maximum contributions, that the cost to the participants of the scheme would also seem to be strictly limited. Indeed, overall, it would seem to be a scheme with limited objectives, limited cost and, perhaps, limited justification.

The final informational problem considered here, concerning credence qualities, raise some of the most difficult issues. The difficulties do not occur so much in assessing the case for regulation but in designing how regulation can meet the cost-benefit criterion, so that the marginal costs of regulation do not exceed the marginal returns to be obtained. As earlier described, the combined principal – agent role of professionals as diagnosticians amd executants of remedial action leads to potential conflicts of interest in many guises and forms. It is well to remember, however, that similar conflicts of interests and general credence problems arise in most professional activities. One might ask whether the provision of data, constraints, requirements and penalties applied in the regulation of the relationship between financial intermediary and ordinary client should also be repeated with lawyers, accountants, doctors, etc. – and if not, why not?

One way to try to limit conflict of interest is to seek to endorse single capacity (separation of the agent–principal functions). In so far as that separation involves additional costs, there will tend to be pressures to evade such a limitation; in particular, international competition with markets not subject to such high-cost regulation will lead to pressure for deregulation, as in the case of the Stock-Exchange. It would be interesting to discover what the cost implications for Lloyds Insurance market of the adoption of single capacity might be.

If the economies of scale and scope are such that the option of single capacity operation is too expensive or otherwise unattractive, see Benham and Benham (1980), there remain the options of trying to limit conflicts of interest (e.g., by 'Chinese Walls', prosecution of the use of insider information, etc.) or of monitoring the quality of service provided in such cases. To undertake monitoring on a continuous

---

[1] See Diamond and Dybvig (1983).

basis by checking and requiring the provision of all data on services where there were credence problems would seem an extremely expensive option, though the availability of computers, and filtering software programmes to catch outlying observations, should help to make some forms of misbehaviour easier to monitor and catch. It is, perhaps, the computer frauds that delete pennies from a vast number of deals that will remain harder to catch. On the other hand, sufficient information would need to be stored, even if not necessarily monitored, in order to allow audit trails to be established.

In so far as economists have turned their minds to dealing with such credence (conflict of interest) problems, their general preference, on grounds of cheapness, has been for occasional, random checks, going into considerable depth and detail with subsequent full publicity, rather than attempting to monitor all players on a continuous basis.[1]

---

[1] See Beales (1980, p. 134) who claims that:

Thus entry restricting through licensing apparently does not reduce the incentives or the incidence of unnecessary services. In the jurisdiction with output monitoring, however, the incidence of unnecessary repairs was substantially lower. In short, output monitoring is an effective way to reduce the incidence of unnecessary services, and input monitoring is not.

X
The Determination of Interest Rates

Summary

Monetary economics is a subject wherein academic theories and practitioner market experience often seem widely divorced; the determination of the stock of money (Chapter 6) and the operation of foreign exchange markets (Chapter 18) are but two examples. Analysis of the determination of the level of money market interest rates is, alas, another. Accordingly, in this chapter, we try to weave together both practical market experience and more abstract theoretical considerations.

We start in Section 1 with a factual restatement of Central Bank operations. On a day-to-day basis, the determination of the level of market interest rates is a relatively simple affair; the level is set by Central Bank intervention in money markets to balance the market's desire for cash (high-powered money). The authorities could, in principle, choose to control the quantity of high-powered money instead, but, because of the short-run inelasticity of the market's demand for cash, they have *not* generally chosen to do so. Even in those examples (e.g., Switzerland and the American Federal Reserve Board between 1979 and 1982) when there have been some forms of operation tending in this latter direction, these operations have incorporated safety valves to prevent excess instability in interest rates. An account of how these systems worked in practice is given in the Appendix at the end of this chapter.

Nevertheless, any attempt to hold market interest rates *constant* over any sustained period of time would soon cause more general economic instability; over such long periods of time, the Central Bank sees its ability to influence interest rates constrained by a set of more important political, expectational and real factors to which it has to react continuously. In this context, the adoption of pragmatic monetary targets has allowed such reactions to become more flexible. The inter-relationship between the level of money market rates, set in the short term by the authorities, and rates on longer maturities is discussed in Chapter 11.

Whereas the authorities actually set interest rates in the short run so that the money stock becomes an endogenous variable, most academic analysis of the determination of the rate of interest assumes that the authorities fix the level of the money stock. In Section 2, the theoretical determination of interest rates and the market demand and supply equilibrium of money are discussed. We start with the Neo-classical Theory in which all markets clear perfectly and instantaneously and claim that, in these conditions, monetary disequilibrium is reflected in and adjusted away by general changes in prices; the real interest rate is a function of real variables (e.g., productivity and thrift) and nominal interest rates incorporate an expectation of future inflation (the Fisher effect) plus the real interest rate.

If markets are imperfect, however, with labour and goods markets adjusting slower than financial asset markets, then there will be an initial 'liquidity preference' effect on both nominal and real interest rates. Keynes exaggerated the importance of the 'liquidity preference' effect, relative to the longer-term 'loanable funds' theory of interest, in order to differentiate his approach from the Classical. This led to an invalid concentration upon a small set of financial interest rates as providing the sole means of short-term equilibration of the demand and supply of money and, similarly, the sole transmission channel for monetary policy.

Nevertheless, the process of determination of interest rates *does* depend on the degree of market imperfection in the time horizon under consideration. As already noted, in the short run, the market rate of interest is determined by the balance between demand and supply of high-powered money. This determines both the market interest rates payable on bank deposits and charged for bank loans. The demand for money is *not* the same as the demand for bank credit, as will become clear in Section 3 which discusses the banks' balance sheet. I argue that the general acceptability of money means that some sub-sets of bank deposits are used as buffer stocks, adjusting passively in the short run to fluctuations in the demand for bank credit; fluctuations in bank credit demand, therefore, rule the monetary roost.

This turns out to cause problems for monetary controllers, since such credit demand has proved unpredictable and unresponsive to interest-rate fluctuations. Rather than vary interest rates drastically to influence bank credit demand, the monetary authorities in the UK have sometimes sought to compress bank lending to the *public* sector. The resulting practical problems of 'overfunding' and the 'bill mountain' in 1980–5 are recorded.

1. Practical Issues

The determination of the level of interest rates in UK money markets, and indeed in the money markets of most industrialised countries, is, in practice, a relatively simple issue. For reasons which will be discussed at greater length in Section 3, the banking system and money market in London will normally face the prospect of a cash deficit on any day. The prospective flows of cash from the banking system to the public sector will, therefore, exceed the prospective flows in the other direction, draining banks and the money market of the stock of high-powered base money reserves that they need in order to preserve convertibility between deposit liabilities and currency.[1] The financial system's demand function for base money is extremely inelastic: since base money, cash and bankers' balances at the Bank of England, is non-interest-bearing, bankers will not want to hold any large surplus in excess of minimum requirements; on the other hand, they have to maintain such minimum balances to honour their convertibility pledge and thus remain in business.

Given, then, the prospective short-fall in the stock of available cash, and the banking system's inelastic demand for cash, the Central Bank[2] is faced with the

---

[1] See 'The Management of Money Day by Day' (p. 107), 'Monetary Control' (p. 137) and 'The Role of the Bank of England in the Money Market' (p. 156), in Bank of England, *The Development and Operations of Monetary Policy: 1960–1983* (1984).

[2] I am *assuming* here the existence of the standard structure of a modern financial system with a Central Bank issuing liabilities, notes and deposits, which are 'high-powered' in the sense that commercial banks denominate their own deposits as convertible into such 'high-powered money', and hence keep cash reserves in the form of such high-powered money. T. Congdon has noted, in private correspondence that, in order to provide a more general theory, it would be necessary to examine how this structure evolved. He has explored this question himself in his paper, 'Is the provision of a sound currency a necessary function of the State?' (1981), and I

opportunity of choosing the rate of interest (i.e., the price) at which it will buy assets in the market in order to relieve the cash shortage. Naturally, it will buy the cheapest (lowest price – highest interest rate) paper that is offered to it first; the crucial decision is, however, the 'stop rate' (the highest price – lowest interest rate) at which it will buy paper. Assume for the moment that the Central Bank correctly forecasts the prospective cash deficiency. If the market thinks that the Bank's chosen 'stop rate' is too high (the price of paper is too low), and refuses to sell paper to the authorities at that rate, then the cash shortage is not fully relieved; the pressure to obtain the requisite reserves will force banks and other money market operators to raise the rates that they bid for money (and to lower the price at which they will sell paper), until interest rates get driven up to the level at which the authorities are prepared to relieve the shortage. *Per contra*, if the market is concerned about future increases in interest rates, and seeks greater liquidity by selling more paper (e.g., Treasury or commercial bills) than is necessary to meet the cash shortage, then the resulting excess of non-interest-bearing cash reserves seeking some positive nominal return will drive down interest rates to a level consistent with the authorities' aims.

Similarly, if there is a prospective cash surplus in the market, interest rates will tend to be declining. The authorities can prevent this from continuing by entering the market and setting a maximum interest rate – minimum price at which they would be prepared to buy all bills offered to it. Given the banking system's highly inelastic demand for reserves, the authorities are forced to take day-to-day decision, on the level of interest rates at which they will relieve a cash shortage or 'mop up' a cash surplus. Only if the market is approximately in balance, with the stock of cash equal to that required, is the Central Bank in a position to *avoid* choosing the rate at which it will restore equilibrium between the demand and supply of cash.[1] An attempt was made in the UK, in setting up arrangements for a new mode of operation in the London money market in September 1981, to try to organise the system so that such a rough balance would normally pertain, with the conscious aim of encouraging the determination of interest rates to shift more towards 'market forces' and away from the discretionary choice of the authorities.[2] In the event, as will be reported in Section 3, that intention was rapidly overtaken by developments which forced the system back towards the previous norm in which the market was consistently short of cash on a day-by-day basis, prior to the authorities' operations to relieve such shortages. Moreover, if the Central Bank is keen to reinforce (rather than to relinquish) its powers to control market interest rates, as has been more frequently the historical case, it has various means – e.g., of selling paper to the private sector or by refusing to renew loans to the banks – which leave the banking system in a cash short position. This leaves the Central Bank with great power to set and to vary money market rates on a day-to-day basis. If you ask why the level of market rates today is x per cent in New York, or y per cent in London, or z per cent in Frankfurt, the answer is that the Central Bank chooses that it should be so.

Does the short-term determination of interest rates have to be this way, by the discretionary choice of the authorities? As we shall see, many economists argue that it

---

have also considered it in my monograph, *The Evolution of Central Banks: A Natural Development?* (1985). It would, however, take us too far away from our main topic here to explore this (fascinating) subject.

---

[1] There is a good paper on this issue, 'Why does the Reserve Bank set the Interest Rate', by Whittaker and Theunissen (1986).

[2] See 'Money Market Operations Since 1981' (p. 50), in Bank of England (1984a).

is a misconceived system. Yet, given the extremely inelastic demand for reserves, any attempt by the authorities to determine the short-run level of the quantity of reserves, rather than of the level of interest rates, will provoke drastic short-term variations in interest rates. Figure 10.1 demonstrates such variations as the demand function for base money fluctuates.

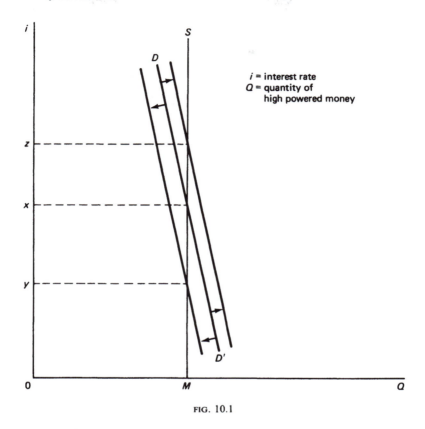

FIG. 10.1

Those who advocate tighter monetary base control (MBC) claim, firstly, that short-term fluctuations in interest rates might be less damaging in their effects on the economy than the loss of control of the monetary aggregates that arises from present practices and, secondly, that a structural shift to MBC would induce behavioural responses that would lessen such inelasticity. In particular, if greater fluctuation in interest rates was to be expected, it would pay banks to hold some excess reserves as precautionary balances. Furthermore, some examples of countries, which are supposed to have adopted MBC, are adduced as showing that it is consistent with tight monetary control *without* undesirable volatility in short-term interest rates.

The case studies for Switzerland and the American Federal Reserve Board (1979–82) are examined in the Appendix to this chapter.

An examination of the operational methods of the Swiss National Bank reveals that these are closer in reality to the normal practices of other Central Banks, and less akin to strict MBC, than advocates of MBC generally realise. As for the US experience between 1979 and 1982, despite the incorporation of safety valves to dampen 'excessive' interest-rate volatility, the extent of such volatility both in interest rates and in (short-term) monetary growth increased dramatically.

What, however, are the limits on Central Bank power to set interest rates? We shall consider several issues. First, there is the question of the ability of the Central Bank to control the *term structure* of rates; second, the ability of Central Banks to control interest rates over *time*.

A third issue has been raised by N. Wallace, notably in his paper[1] on 'A Legal Restrictions Theory of the Demand for "Money" and the Role of Monetary Policy', in which he claims that the ability of the Central Bank to control interest rates depends on the (legal) prohibition on the private issue of commercial bank notes; also see Kareken (1984) and Jao (1984). I believe that Wallace's analysis is incorrect, and have expressed my reasons for this in an earlier paper, 'How Can Non-Interest Bearing Assets Co-exist with Safe Interest-Bearing Assets' (1986b); also see L. H. White, 'Accounting for Non-Interest-Bearing Currency: A Critique of the "Legal Restrictions" Theory of Money' (1986). Accordingly I shall not consider this latter topic further here.

Let us now take the first issue: the authorities' ability to control the term structure, as well as the level, of money market interest rates. Earlier, the authorities were described as intervening in the money market to buy or sell paper, thereby fixing the interest rate at which the demand and supply of high-powered money would be equated, without being specific about the tenor (the maturity) of the paper in which they were dealing. The authorities could, however, theoretically deal in any kind of paper or asset in order to equate the demand and supply of high-powered money. In practice, they have usually chosen to operate in money markets in assets of relatively short maturity (e.g., one week and one month paper in the UK). There are various advantages to dealing in very short-term money markets. Such markets tend to be very broad, liquid and professional and the short tenor involved reduces the extent of capital gain – loss directly attendant on the authorities' operations. Thus, their operations can be diffused most widely throughout the system while having the minimum necessary *direct* impact on market participants, which latter might constrain the authorities' freedom to vary interest rates. Moreover, short maturities are easier to deal in, since investors are less affected by expectations of capital gains or losses.

This procedure, as earlier described, allows the authorities to determine nominal interest rates on a day-to-day basis in the markets in which they operate; how then are interest rates in other markets (the term structure) determined? Suppose, for example, that there was a cash shortage of £x and that the authorities wanted long rates to fall below short rates. Could they then *buy* £2x of long paper and go on *selling* short paper until the level of interest rates at that short maturity was driven into equality with the authorities' desired level? In practice, the authorities' tend to concentrate their market operations, for determining the general level of interest rates, in their preferred short-term market and rarely try to influence the term structure.[2] Whether the authorities can influence the term structure, as well as the level, of interest rates depends on the comparative influence of market expectations of future short-term

---

[1] (1983).

[2] Though Operation Twist in the USA in 1961–2 is a well-known, but only partially successful, counter-example. See Malkiel (1966) especially pp. 219–21.

rates, as compared with current flow supplies of, and demand for, instruments of different maturities. This question will be taken up again in Chapter 11. For the moment, we need note only that most studies of this subject suggest that expectational influences are relatively powerful relative to structural shifts in flows in different segments of the market. If this describes the real state of affairs, the authorities would find it relatively difficult to influence the term structure as well as the general level of interest rates,[1] except in so far as they can manipulate the markets' future expectations – which is a difficult exercise, and often counter-productive.

So far, we have reviewed how the authorities control the level of market interest rates, in that part of the market in which they operate, in the course of a working day. If they can, as has been explained, effectively control the level of short-term interest rates on a day-by-day basis, does that mean that the authorities can equally be considered to be in control of interest rates on a longer-term, lower frequency basis (i.e., month by month or year by year)? The answer to this question is *no*: the longer the relevant time horizon, the less can the authorities be regarded as in control. This is an absolutely crucial fact and it is important to understand why this is so.

The essential point is that the authorities control, on a short-term basis, the level of *nominal* interest rates. What is important for expenditure decisions (e.g., on investment and consumption) is the level of real interest rates – i.e., the level of nominal interest rates (i) deflated by the expected rate of inflation, $E\dot{p}$. We can thus express real expenditures (y) as a function of real interest rates:

$$Y_t = f\,(i_t - E\dot{p}_t) \tag{10.1}$$

We can also hypothesise that expectations of future inflation may either be a function of anticipated monetary growth, ($\dot{M}$) a monetarist hypothesis, or a function of inflation in past periods, probably with a coefficient of unity, plus a term reflecting the pressure of demand represented by the gap between actual and 'equilibrium' output (y^*), an augmented Phillips curve – Keynesian approach; thus:

$$E\dot{p} = a\,\dot{M} \tag{10.2a}$$

or

$$E\dot{p} = \dot{p}_{t-1} + b\,(y_t - y^*) \tag{10.2b}$$

Finally, there is a demand for money function:

$$M = f\,(p,y,i) \tag{10.3}$$

---

[1] The authorities normally operate at the short end of the money market, leaving longer-term interest rates to reflect expectations of future short-term interest rates. What, however, determines rates at even shorter maturities than that chosen by the authorities for their operations (e.g., overnight rates when the authorities are acting at one week)? In such circumstances, as Flemming's paper, provisionally entitled, 'Three Points on the Yield Curve', in *The Monetary Economics of John Hicks*, (1989) forthcoming, records, ultra short rates tend to move in the opposite direction to longer term rates. When the market expects interest rates to rise, it will put a premium on liquidity and the authorities will have to tend to overdo 'assistance' to the market in order to prevent the general level of market rates from rising. On both counts, overnight rates will tend to soften, when longer-term rates are hardening, around the pivot of the authorities' chosen discretionary level of rates. This apparently perverse behaviour of the overnight rate may cause some embarrassment to the authorities in their conduct of policy (e.g., if the upwards pressure on interest rates is associated with downwards pressure on the £ exchange rate), and represents a further reason why market operations are concentrated at the very short end of the maturity spectrum.

Assume that the system is initially in balance with $y = y^*$, $\dot{p} = E\dot{p} = 0$ and $\dot{M} = 0$. Then, let there be a stochastic random upward (downward) shift in y in equation (10.1). With the authorities fixing i, this will cause an increase (decrease) in M and in $y - y^*$, so $E\dot{p}$ must rise (fall). With $E\dot{p}$ rising (falling), y increases (decreases) further and the system moves further away from equilibrium. Given normal values for the coefficients, the system becomes unstable, with both real and nominal values moving ever outwards (to their limits) should the authorities try to peg the level of interest rates indefinitely. This is, of course, merely Wicksell's cumulative process in modern guise, see Wicksell (1898).

It is this inherent instability of interest-rate pegging that makes monetarist economists so concerned with the preference of the authorities to fix the level of interest rates rather than a monetary quantity. The authorities in Central Banks and Ministries of Finance are, however, perfectly aware of their inability to hold the rate of interest at some arbitrary nominal level, inconsistent with more fundamental equilibrium in the economy. What would happen, for example, if the Bank arbitrarily sought to enforce, as it technically could, an obviously inappropriate nominal interest rate, say 2 (or 20) per cent. First, a combination of the shifts in relative international interest differentials, together with concern about the authorities' policy objectives, would cause the exchange rate to weaken (appreciate) sharply. Despite a strong relative rise (fall) in longer-term rates, as the market showed its doubts both about the continuity of those extreme present policies and concern with the effects on future levels and rates of change of prices, the low (high) level of nominal interest rates would require the authorities to take ever more expansionary (restrictive) open market operations and would lead to some secondary monetary expansion (contraction), though the extent of that would depend *inter alia*, on the length of time such policies were expected to persist. Soon these policies would impact on prices – both directly via asset markets (including the exchange rate) and indirectly via the pressure of demand, and on output and expenditures. Sooner rather than later, the economic consequences of trying to hold interest rates pegged at a grossly inappropriate rate would overwhelm that policy.

Whereas the authorities have virtually complete technical control over the level of interest rates in the very short run, in a longer-term context they have much less influence. What can they achieve in such a longer-term context? At the extreme, there are those who believe that all markets adjust relatively rapidly and efficiently to restore full-employment equilibrium. One of these markets will be that for loanable funds, determined by investment demand, driven in part by improved technological productivity, and the flow of savings, influenced by the thriftiness of the community. In such a model, the level of real interest rates will be driven solely by real forces – i.e., by productivity and thrift. In so far as these forces remain relatively stable over time, then real interest rates will also remain stable.[1] In this model, the authorities' only influence is over nominal variables. Any attempt to use monetary expansion to lower interest rates will, almost immediately, backfire as the results become visible to the market, since higher monetary growth would then be translated into expectations of worsening inflation, and hence *higher* nominal interest rates.[2]

---

[1] At one stage, it seemed that the evidence for the post-war world was consistent with real rates remaining roughly constant and nominal interest rates varying closely in line with expectations of inflation. See Fama (1975) pp. 269–82. Subsequent experience of clearly negative real interest rates in many Western countries in the 1970s, followed by historically high real interest rates in the 1980s, proved different.

[2] See Friedman and Schwartz (1982) especially Chapter 10.

This 'rational expectations – perfect clearing market' hypothesis is extreme, not so much because expectations may not always be rational (the empirical evidence on that remains mixed), but because markets do not clear quickly or perfectly.[1] Market structures are such that the initial response to shocks occur through adjustments to quantities, instead of prices; in certain markets (e.g., the labour and goods markets) price movements are relatively sluggish and sticky.

Accordingly, the authorities' operations in financial markets, even though these do adjust to 'news' relatively quickly, can influence real as well as nominal interest rates. In the very short run, in which all labour and goods prices can be taken as fixed, the authorities' technical operational control over nominal interest rates is similarly a control over the level of real interest rates. As time passes, and all market prices adjust, the level of 'real' interest rates becomes increasingly determined by the interplay of real variables, productivity and thrift. In this long-term context, all that the authorities can influence is the level of nominal variables – i.e., the level and rate of change of the money stock and of prices and the nominal level of interest rates.

Given the slow nature of price adjustments and the persistence of quantity adjustments, the 'long term' mentioned above in the abstract may represent an uncomfortably long period of years in reality. During this intervening period, the authorities will have some varying influence also over the real rate of interest.

Let us recapitulate. At any point of time the authorities determine the nominal level of interest rates in the money market. The system is, however, unstable in the sense that any attempt to hold nominal interest rates constant indefinitely will lead the system to explode. In the short run, however, the authorities can control both nominal and real interest rates. As the time period extends, the level of real interest rates will be increasingly controlled by real forces – i.e., productivity and thrift – which determine what the equilibrium real rate must be. In this longer run, the authorities can control only nominal variables.

Monetarist economists appear to believe that the authorities are unaware of the potential instability in the economy were they to peg interest rates *indefinitely*. This is not so. Given the structure of financial markets, in particular the interest inelasticity of the financial system's demand for cash reserves, Central Bankers feel that they really have no option but to provide the needed reserves on a day-to-day basis, at a rate of interest that they *have* to choose. They do not, however, choose that level arbitrarily nor, once a level has been selected, do they feel it incumbent on them to hold that level fixed.[2]

Instead, the authorities normally vary interest rates in response to movements in other indicators which provide information to them whether rates need to be raised or lowered. When the authorities have a target for the exchange rate of the domestic currency with some outside store of value (e.g., gold, dollars, or Deutschmarks, the

---

[1] For reasons surveyed at length in Chapter 1 and reinforced by our study of rationing in Chapter 7.

[2] Since the choice of interest rate is, in practice, both economically important and administratively chosen, any change in it is politically charged and carries important market signals. For such reasons, there have often been political pressures on Central Banks to defer and to reduce unpopular upwards *increases* in interest rates; in response, Central Bankers themselves tended to become reluctant to *lower* interest rates. In consequence, the politically determined incentive structure *was* such as to make nominal interest rates undesirably sticky and rigid, leading to worsened instability. It was this appreciation that in some large part led Central Bankers to adopt 'pragmatic monetarism' as a means to free interest rates from 'political' control, by shifting interest rates more aggressively towards the achievement of some intermediate target monetary aggregate.

fluctuations in that exchange rate normally dominate the authorities' reaction function. When the authorities do not have an exchange rate target, they may replace that with an objective for some internal *nominal* variable, such as the rate of growth of some monetary aggregate or the current and prospective rate of growth of inflation itself (see Chapters 14 and 15).

Such a process involves lags. These will include the lag before recognising the need to change the monetary instrument (i.e., the recognition lag), the lag between recognising the need for change and putting it into effect (i.e., the policy lag); and the lag between changing the instrument and that having an effect upon the goal variables (i.e., the operational lag). I have noted elsewhere, particularly in the discussion of the working of monetary targetry, how such lags may cause instrument instability, whereby the desire to hold some goal function constant may lead to increasingly unstable and exaggerated fluctuation in the instrument. This can, similarly, happen if interest rates are used to try to fix the growth rate of some nominal variable (especially if undertaken in mindless pursuit of some half-baked 'rule').

We noted earlier that, in the long run, when markets had fully adjusted, the monetary authorities could not influence real variables since these were influenced purely by real forces. Thus, in this context, such variables as the long-run equilibrium level of unemployment or rate of growth of output are determined by more fundamental factors reflecting the institutions and nature of our society. The authorities cannot, through purely monetary means, reduce this long-run equilibrium level of unemployment or raise the growth rate. The attempt to do so can only increase nominal variables (e.g., the level and rate of change of prices). Indeed, since worsening inflation tends, in reality, to lessen the efficiency of the working of the market system, the result is likely to be counter-productive.

This consideration leads those who believe that market adjustments occur efficiently and rapidly to restore equilibrium to advocate that the authorities should ignore the current level of real variables (e.g., unemployment) in choosing the indicators and intermediate nominal targets that the authorities should use as a guide to interest rate adjustment. Others on the Keynesian wing, who are more pessimistic about the equilibrium properties of free markets, will argue in response that the authorities must have regard for the current level of, and prospects for, such real variables when choosing the setting of their policy instruments. As so often, the argument reduces to a more fundamental view about the efficiency with which micro-markets adjust to achieve macro-equilibrium.

2. Theory

Theoretical analysis of the determination of interest rates has not been helped by economists' frequently resolute refusal to look at the way markets function in reality and to impose invalid abstractions of their own in theoretical models. In this instance, the assumption that the authorities determine the nominal size of the aggregate money supply, leaving the interest rate to be determined by market forces, rather than vice versa as is almost always the practical reality, has been a potent cause of confusion. Similarly, attempts to analyse the determination of interest rates in a static and timeless context is not helpful when, as we have seen, the relative weights of the forces influencing interest rates vary depending on the period of time under consideration – e.g., short- or long-term, one day or one decade.

Nevertheless, most theoretical analysis has proceeded on the assumption that the money supply *is* fixed by the authorities, and has then examined the factors that adjust to bring the demand and supply of money into equilibrium and determine the rate of interest. We have already, in Section 1, outlined the gist of the main theoretical approaches. The Classical and Neo-classical formulation is thus based on an assumption of perfect, instantaneously clearing markets. In this context, with the demand for money being written as

$$M_D = f\,(Y, P, Ep + r)$$

where r is the real interest rate, Y and r are determined by real factors. The supply of money is, therefore, driven into equality with the demand for money by changes in prices (in all markets and for all goods and assets) *and* by changes in expectations of future inflation (now usually assumed to be rational). Changes in Ep affect nominal interest rates which, since money is usually assumed to be non-interest bearing, influence the relative return and, hence, the demand for money.

There are a number of difficulties with this formulation of the determination of the nominal rate of interest, (as a real rate, determined by real factors – e.g., productivity and thrift, plus the expected rate of inflation). First, given the availability of zero-yielding cash as an alternative asset to hold, the nominal rate of interest cannot be forced below zero.[1] Accordingly, expectations of significant future falls in prices *must* raise the real rate of interest. The authorities *can* impose real deflationary effects on real interest rates and real output, even if they cannot, in some contexts, reduce real interest rates below, and raise real output above, some equilibrium level.

Second, this theoretical approach has the real rate of interest adjust to equate the desired flow of new lending (savings) and of new borrowing (investment) at the equilibrium level of output (a loanable funds approach). The argument then raised is that the demand and supply of such financial instruments (bonds) will also depend on whether the rate of interest is also such as to make holders of the existing *stock* of bonds, often very large relative to the current flow supply of new bonds, content to go on holding them. The net demand–supply for bonds of existing wealth holders will depend on their expectations of the relative returns of holding various assets. What happens if the plans – expectations of existing wealth holders are such as to lead them to try to readjust existing assets in such a way as to drive the real rate of interest away from the level that would equilibrate the flow demand for bonds (savings) and flow supply of bonds (investment) at the equilibrium level of output?

In that case, the economy would not be in full equilibrium. *If* markets adjusted perfectly and instantaneously, prices would then *immediately* move to a level that would alter the wealth of existing holders of currency (and, more important, of bonds if the Ricardian equivalence effect, discussed in Chapter 13, did not hold exactly), to a point where the incentive to save would be sufficiently shifted to restore full employment at a real interest rate that equated both the stock demand and supply of existing wealth holders and the flow demand of savers and investors. The fact that the Pigou effect, whereby a given nominal stock of assets becomes more valuable in real terms as prices fall, can rescue the Classical loanable funds approach from the accusation that it ignores the more important stock demand for bonds, does not serve to lessen ones disbelief in the likelihood of markets ever working in practice in this stylised fashion.

---

[1] I can require my income or sales to be paid in legal tender, and I can always insist on holding that, rather than buying an asset which will depreciate in nominal terms over time.

The essential weakness of the Classical loanable funds theory is thus not that it ignores the stock demand for assets, but that is is insecurely based on an assumption of perfect and instantaneously clearing markets. Keynesian theory is, instead, based on the more plausible hypothesis that prices in labour and goods markets are relatively sticky, in contrast to financial markets where prices adjust rapidly. This can be seen in an extreme form in the standard IS/LM formulation, in which prices in goods markets are constant, at least until there is a resultant change via a subsidiary Phillips curve equation, whereas interest rates change instantaneously. In such a context, the authorities can obviously bring about a change in real, as well as in nominal interest rates by monetary measures.[1]

Keynes was, however, so keen to make a break with previous Classical analysis that he pushed his new Liquidity Preference theory, and his accompanying analysis of the process by which the demand and supply of money could be equilibrated, further than was justifiable. First, as Tsiang has consistently pointed out:[2]

> the transactions demand for money is primarily a function of planned expenditures rather than a function of income[3] ... Indeed, it was partially admitted by Keynes himself in his reply to Prof. Ohlin (*EJ*, Dec. 1937). His recognition in that article of the demand for finance for planned investment clearly implies that the transactions balance for investment expenditures is primarily a function of the investment expenditures planned. He was also on the point of saying that the same is true in the case of the demand for finance for consumption expenditures, but his adamant position in denying savings any role in determining the interest rate apparently caused him to hold back, (Keynes, Dec. 1937, pp 667–8). Yet if this line of reasoning is carried to its logical conclusion, it would lead us to the conclusion that Keynes's denial of any direct influence of savings on the rate of interest and his consequent deposition of savings as a social virtue can all be traced back to his own self-confessed overlooking of the 'finance demand for money' for consumption as well as for investment expenditures.

Besides the refusal to countenance any influence of the flow demand for bonds from savings on the rate of interest, Keynes's approach led to a misleading analysis of the process whereby the demand and supply of money became equated. An increase in the money supply brought about by the authorities was thus supposed *initially* to have its effect transmitted fully, and solely, via adjustments in interest rates in financial markets. If there was a change in M/YP occasioned by a change in M, then the interest rate i would change sufficiently to satisfy the demand-for-money function.

Now, if one assumes that the authorities raise the supply of money by distributing bank-notes, throwing them down from a helicopter perhaps, the implausibility of this hypothesis becomes clear. If you receive an extra £50 in cash out of the blue, would you then redistribute your increased wealth among a small sub-set of financial assets? The answer is surely no. An increase in the money stock would be used to increase expenditures in *all* markets, not just the money or bond market, to a point where the marginal utility of expenditures in each market was equated. The attempt to

---

[1] For an earlier work that clearly analysed the dependence of the Classical and Keynesian theories of interest rate determination on their differing assumptions about the relative speeds of price adjustments in markets, see Hicks, 'The Classics Again' (1967).

[2] His latest paper on this subject, provisionally entitled, 'Sir John Hicks's Contributions to Monetary Theory and What We Would Like to Expect of Him'; is in *The Monetary Economics of John Hicks* (1989) (forthcoming).

[3] For an explicitly forward-looking demand for money function see Cuthbertson and Taylor (1987) p. 103.

constrain interest rates to be a mainly monetary phenomenon led Keynes to force the transmission mechanism of monetary policy through an interest rate strait-jacket.

There is, perhaps, more excuse for this error if one drops the somewhat fanciful example of 'helicopter money'. Under normal circumstances, the authorities increase the money supply by buying financial assets – though, in fact, government purchase of any good or service will do as well. Clearly, the seller of the financial instrument to the authorities must be prepared to exchange that instrument for money. Has the demand for money now been brought into equality with the increased supply by this initial change in interest rates, so that subsequent effects on the economy will depend on the consequential impact of such interest rate changes on expenditure decisions? The answer to this is 'no'. The change in the price offered by the authorities for the financial instrument in which they were dealing did lead to a willing decision by its holder to sell that asset, but that did not mean that the erstwhile asset-owner actually wanted to *hold* the money offered instead. While the person had no choice but to accept money initially, she or he could easily be intending to spend it subsequently in other markets.

Chick puts this issue[1] nicely in her paper, 'On the Place of *Value and Capital* in Monetary Theory' (1989):

> The money one has on hand at any one time, therefore, may be demanded or may merely have been accepted. One could say that the hallmark of general acceptability is the divorce of money balances held at a particular point of time, especially the end of the period, from demand for them.
>
> But how do we describe this situation? At one level only demand counts as volition; acceptance in the course of trade is more or less out of one's control. At another level one accepts money in the course of trade willingly, though in the language of Hick's later work this acceptance does not constitute volition.
>
> Both aspects of the transactions demand are true even though they appear to be contradictory. One must accept them both ... The descriptive difference – demand vs acquisition by trading – is appropriate to the method in which each is embedded. In a one-period model, willingness to accept without intention to hold has no place, as discussed above. However, as soon as the period is seen as one amongst a series of periods in the stream of time, it becomes rational to acquire money without really intending to hold it: that is, money, even a non-commodity money, can become 'generally acceptable'.

As Chick notes, Keynes never seemed to move beyond the 'voluntaristic' Cambridge approach to transactions balances. Accordingly, the sale of bonds to the authorities by the asset holder *had* to be at the same time an increased demand for money, rather than just an acceptance of money on the way to purchasing other things. It was the insistence on forcing money holding at all times into a portfolio-theoretic explicit demand theory that led to the manifest faults of Keynesian liquidity preference and monetary theory.

In a sense, both the Classical loanable funds approach and the Keynesian liquidity preference approach were flawed because they attempted to impose equilibrium conditions (full market clearing equilibrium in the first case and money market

---

[1] This idea, of a temporary equilibrium in which people accept money that they do not wish to hold for long, is not, of course, new. It has, for example, frequently featured in M. Friedman's analysis, see for example his 1965 paper on 'Money and Business Cycles' (1969a). But the central theoretical importance of this distinction (e.g., for the analysis of the determination of interest rates) has not often been perceived.

equilibrium in the second), in conditions when they were inappropriate. Instead, one should accept that market disequilibrium conditions and 'buffer-stocks' of money exist for sufficiently long periods of time to make it essential to model the determination of interest rates in that context.

Indeed, in a full equilibrium with all markets clearing, equilibrium between the demand and supply of money *is* matched by an equilibrium between the demand and supply of all other goods and assets. In these circumstances, as Hicks demonstrated in *Value and Capital*, Walras's law indicates that the demand and supply of bonds, *or of any other asset*, is the counterpart of the supply and demand for money, so that the liquidity preference theory of interest rates (or of any other asset price, or of peanut prices), is equivalent to the loanable funds theory.[1]

One cannot, therefore, usefully discuss the determination of the rate of interest without some prior assumptions about the market context within which the analysis is to be made. Moreover, as already described in Section 1, the nature of the appropriate market context changes with the time frame involved. If, for example, one was to ask why the interest rate had changed from yesterday to today, one would concentrate on the authorities' market operations and on shifts in the money market's needs for cash, augmented in longer-term markets by expectational changes, on the implicit assumption that both real factors and prices in markets for labour and goods would be constant. If one was asking why the average interest rate differed between the seventeenth and twentieth centuries one would concentrate on an entirely different set of explanatory factors – e.g., inflationary expectations and real variables such as productivity, entrepreneurship and attitudes to risk, thrift and wealth accumulation.

Meanwhile, an assessment of why interest rates vary over intermediate time periods, say from one year to the next or from one decade to the next,[2] would involve a combination of real and purely monetary variables. In so far as one can estimate expectations of future possible inflation, so that one can identify and calculate 'real' interest rates, the determination of the latter will be almost solely a monetary phenomenon in the short run, in which markets did not clear, and almost solely a real phenomenon in the long run, in which markets can be assumed to clear perfectly. In between, real interest rates will be determined by a combination of real and monetary forces.

The shorter the time horizon, the less the assumption of perfect market clearing is acceptable and, thus, the less appropriate is the Classical loanable funds approach. At least the Keynesian Liquidity Preference theory implicitly assumed imperfect markets and sticky goods – labour prices. However, in Section 1, I claimed that the main factor influencing interest rates on a day-by-day basis is not the general balance between the supply of, and demand for, money as represented by, and defined as, one of the broader monetary aggregates, but rather the balance between the demand by the banks and central financial intermediaries in the money market for cash (high-powered money), and the supply of cash by the authorities, a rather special, restricted form of liquidity preference.

If, then, market interest rates are set in the short run by the demand and supply for high-powered base money (cash and balances at the Central Bank), what then brings about equilibrium between the demand and supply of money more broadly defined? This question will be examined in Section 3.

---

[1] See Chick (1989).
[2] As in Blanchard and Summers (1984) pp. 273–324.

3. The Demand for Money and the Demand for Credit

Because of banks' convertibility commitment, any bank can always turn the liability of another bank into high-powered money. So, although day-to-day pressure in the money market depends on the overall net balance between the demand and supply for high-powered money, the individual bank is indifferent, to a close approximation, about whether it obtains cash, a cheque drawn on the Central Bank or a cheque drawn on any other bank; they are all equally good for meeting its individual cash reserve deficiency. What appears in the money market as a whole as a shortage of 'high powered' cash reserves thus appears to the individual commercial bank Treasurer as an undifferentiated need for money to meet the various requirements of the bank: to provide loans, to purchase financial assets and to hold cash reserves.

So, the market rate of interest, determined by the balance of demand and supply for cash, also determines the rate of interest that banks are prepared to pay when they bid for funds, for deposits, in wholesale markets (e.g., for large overnight or short-term deposits or for longer-term CDs), and when they set administered rates for time deposits. In the past, banks, either by law as in the USA or by cartelised convention as in the UK, offered no interest on demand deposits (current accounts). When inflation and nominal interest rates were low, the costs to the banks of handling the paper work involved in cheque transfers largely offset the returns to be made from investing the interest-free deposits. Since any interest payments would be taxable, while bank charges for clearing transactions could not be deductible from pre-tax incomes, there was a net advantage to both banks and customers of a cross-subsidisation, with the banks' interest earnings from such demand deposits used to depress bank charges below their true economic cost (see also Chapters 2 and 4). While the incentive for, and practice of, such cross-subsidisation still exists, the experience of higher nominal interest rates in a competitive milieu is forcing banks to begin offering specific interest on certain categories of demand deposits. The same market forces now affect the determination of interest rates on demand deposits as well as on other kinds of deposit.

Back in the eighteenth and early nineteenth centuries, banks obtained funds, cash and balances with other banks, primarily by issuing their own notes. There are technical difficulties that make it harder to pay interest on notes, so such notes were also usually non-interest-bearing.[1] Subsequently, for various reasons primarily concerned with establishing the Central Bank's ability to control both the high powered money base and the concurrent level of market interest rates, the note issue became centralised in the Central Bank and commercial banks were legally prohibited from issuing notes. Recently, certain economists have raised questions of how interest rates would be determined if that prohibition was relaxed. I addressed that question in my earlier paper, 'How Can Non-Interest-Bearing Assets Co-Exist with Safe Interest-Bearing Assets' (1986).

Let us now examine the process whereby the demand and supply of money become equilibrated in conditions as they currently exist. We start with money market rates, set in the short run by the authorities in accord with some reaction function. This determines the interest rates that banks will bid for various sub-sets of deposits (e.g., wholesale overnight deposits, CDs, time deposits, etc.). With the interest rates offered by the banks thus determined, the volume of deposits forthcoming at these interest

---

[1] But not always, (see Goodhart 1985) pp. 44, 53.

rates depends on the demand-for-money functions. This is all very simple; instead of writing:

$M_D = f(y, p, i)$
M_S set by authorities
$M_S = M_D$

we write instead:

$i = f$ (authorities' reaction function)
$M_D = f(Y, P, i, i^*)$

where i^* represents the returns on other non-monetary assets.

Unfortunately, it is all just a bit too simple. The problem is that deposits are the liabilities of banks and banks have a balance sheet which must balance. How do we know that the interest rate set in the money market will allow the banks' balance sheets to balance? We can write down the commercial banks' balance sheet in simplified form, as

Assets		Liabilities
Cash Reserves (R)		Deposits (D)
Loans	(L)	Capital (K)

$$R + L = D + K$$

We assume, for expositional purposes, that the banks' capital stock is fixed; that there is a minimum required reserve–deposit ratio; that the authorities set market rates on a daily basis as described; and that the banks' demand function for non-interest-bearing cash is extremely interest inelastic. Now, the demand for credit is not the same as the demand for money, as Brunner and Meltzer[1] frequently noted. If the volume of deposits is determined by the demand function for money, at the policy determined level of market interest rates, what forces ensure that $R + L = D + K$ at every single moment? Let us rehearse some possibilities. We have not yet established what determines the rate of interest charged by banks on loans, r_L. In theory what might happen is that the volume $D + K$ is given at the policy determined market rate of interest payable for money, r_D; this then determines the possible volume of loans and, given the demand function for credit, r_L varies relative to r_D to equilibrate the volume of bank credit with the predetermined volume of deposits. In reality, this theoretical possibility does not hold. The margin between r_L and r_D, the spread, determines the profitability of intermediation, and, while it may vary somewhat in relation to the relative strength of loan demand, in practice competition in banking tends to keep the spread quite low and stable. Thus:

$$r_L = a + b(1 + R/D) r_D$$

where a and b depend on the pressure of competition.

Nor, subject to the special cases discussed in Chapter 7, can we rely on credit rationing to bring the demand for credit into line with a predetermined volume of bank deposits.

With the demand for credit *not* being the same as the demand for money, and

---

[1] For example, Brunner and Meltzer (1972) pp. 951–77.

interest rates being determined in the manner explained, then one of the two aggregates, either bank deposits or bank loans *must* vary to some extent passively as a residual in order to maintain the banks' balance sheet always in balance. In practice, people are not generally willing or able to allow their borrowing to adjust passively on a regular, continuous basis[1] but they *are* always willing to accept money temporarily, even if they do not intend to hold it for more than a short space of time. Such general acceptability is the key feature of money. Money does thus act as a 'buffer-stock' *par excellence*. Therefore, at any point of time, some sub-sets of bank deposits are *not* determined by a demand-for-money function at a given level of interest rates, but instead are simply a reflection of the demand for *credit* at the given level of interest rates. Put another way, at any point of time, the demand for credit at given interest rates determines the stock of money – in theory the reverse *might* have been true, with the demand for money at given interest rates determining the volume of bank credit. In markets as they actually exist, it is the former, not the latter, that happens to be more generally true.

Depending on which set of deposits in practice acts as the main buffer stock, which may vary depending on institutional circumstances, there may well be other subsets which are determined to a close approximation at the given level of interest rates by a demand-for-money function. Nevertheless, if one is concerned with a broad monetary aggregate, comprising the bulk of bank deposits, it is the demand for credit that, to use Keynes's phrase, 'rules the roost'. When the demand for credit rises at a given level of interest rates, the overall volume of broad money will rise in line.

Accordingly, if the authorities should be primarily concerned, as they have been in the UK from the late 1960s until 1985, with the path over time of a broad monetary aggregate, in this case $M3$ or $£M3$, then the crucial concern for controlling that aggregate is the predictability and interest elasticity of the demand for credit (bank loans). As it happens, this demand function has turned out to be both unpredictable and extremely interest inelastic. This caused serious problems for those responsible at the Bank of England and the Treasury for monetary control. In a simple banking system, such as outlined in the above simplified balance sheet, it is not possible to reduce aggregate deposits without reducing aggregate bank loans by almost as much. Banks will always lend to credit-worthy borrowers if the borrowers are willing to pay the going rate for money. Given the unpredictability and inelasticity of the demand for credit function, the level of interest rates necessary to hold down broad monetary growth to some target level – e.g., as given by the Medium Term Financial Strategy (MTFS) in the UK in recent years – was generally unknown and, in its implications for the real exchange rate, output, etc., often unacceptable.

In the period 1973–80, the above problem was mitigated by a direct control mechanism, the 'corset', which directly penalised banks' bidding for funds beyond a certain rate of growth and indirectly prevented them from competing more aggressively for loans; indeed, the 'corset' held them back from the exploitation of whole areas of potential new lending business (e.g., mortgage lending). When the 'corset'

---

[1] Wealthy agents, notably companies, can allow their overdraft position to vary passively between quite large limits. In their case, spreads may be low enough at times to encourage them to hold simultaneously large gross deposit and gross overdraft positions, see Chapter 3. So, the gross position on both deposits and advances may depend sensitively on the spread; their true buffer may be the net liquid asset position and either overdrafts or deposits may respond passively to stochastic cash flows.

was lifted in 1980, the problems of monetary control in these conditions became acute.

It is time now to add an additional level of complexity into our stylised model of the banking system in order to explain the actions and operations of the UK monetary authorities over the last few years. Besides loans to the private sector, banks buy and hold government bonds, usually on a short-term basis. We can thus revise our simplified model of the banking sector as follows:

Assets	*Liabilities*
Cash	Deposits
Bonds	Capital
Loans	

Both bonds and cash are claims on (lending to) the government, so it is possible to rewrite the above balance sheet as follows:

Assets	*Liabilities*
Banks lending to: Government	Deposits
Banks lending to: Private Sector	Capital

So, assuming bank capital is constant, the following identity also holds:

Δ Bank lending to Government + Δ Bank lending to private sector = Δ Bank Deposits

The government in a closed economy borrows either from the banking or the non-bank private sector (NBPS), so a further identity holds:

Public Sector Borrowing Requirement (PSBR) = Δ Bank lending to Government + Δ Government borrowing from NBPS

Government borrowing from NBPS may occur because the NBPS are holding more monetary claims on the government (i.e., currency), or because they have bought more non-monetary government debt (e.g., Treasury bills, government bonds (gilts) or various other forms of public sector debt – e.g., National Savings Securities). Thus:

Δ Government borrowing from NBPS = Δ Currency holding of NBPS + Δ Government debt holdings of NBPS

Remembering that Δ Money supply = Δ Currency holding of NBPS + Δ Bank deposits, we can collect terms and rearrange as:

Δ Ms = PSBR − Δ Government debt holdings of NBPS + Δ Bank lending to private sector

The purpose of this manipulation of accounting identities is to establish that there is an alternative route, besides raising interest rates sufficiently to choke off bank lending to the private sector, to reduce the rate of growth of the money stock. The alternative is to induce the non-bank private sector to purchase enough government debt, relative to the PSBR to cut bank lending to the public sector, as an offset to (usually faster-growing) bank lending to the private sector.

How did the process work? Assume that the PSBR in any period was 100 while net government debt sales to the NBPS were 120. The NBPS would owe 20 to the public sector, which they would pay by writing cheques to the government drawn on their banks. This would initially cause a reduction in bankers' balances. In turn, the reduction of such balances would cause banks both to bid for funds by raising interest rates, since the demand for bank loans is interest inelastic, and to sell liquid assets or allow them to run off on maturity. Most liquid assets held by banks were short-dated government securities. The authorities, following an interest rate reaction function, would buy back such liquid assets from the banks, thus restoring depleted cash reserves and completing the exercise.

Apart from direct credit controls, the scenario described above has been the standard method for reducing monetary growth in the UK, since bank lending to the private sector has proved so unresponsive to interest-rate variations (at least within the limits that have been attempted). This process was facilitated for a long time by the disequilibrium in bank portfolios at the end of the Second World War. Lending to the private sector had been tightly restricted at a time when total bank deposits had grown rapidly, so the banks found themselves with an unbalanced portfolio consisting mainly of government debt. Thus, even by 1951, the shape of the London Clearing banks' asset portfolio was as follows:

Asset Portfolio, £, %, end December 1951

Cash	8
Treasury bills	12
Other short-term liquid assets	12
Government bonds	31
Loans to private sector	30
Other	7
	100

Source: Bank of England, *Statistical Abstract*

Despite restraints from the direct credit controls over bank lending to the private sector which were in force most of the time from 1950 to 1980, the impetus for extra private sector borrowing from banks was such that this grew considerably faster than total bank assets – liabilities. In order to reduce the upward pressure on aggregate monetary expansion, the authorities tried to squeeze banks' holdings of public-sector debt by lowering the PSBR and/or increasing debt sales to the NBPS.

Starting in 1980, and continuing for the next four years, this latter process was subjected to extreme pressures. On the one hand, the objective of achieving a particular targeted rate of growth of the broad money supply, £M3, was given special, indeed over-riding, political priority. On the other hand, the increase in short-term interest rates in 1980 and 1981, while only having limited direct influence on lending, was among the influences, along with North Sea oil and market belief in the economic policies of the Conservative government, driving the exchange rate to extraordinarily high levels, at which the production of tradeable goods in the UK became unprofitable (see Chapter 18).

Accordingly, the monetary authorities set out, more positively and consciously than in former years, to over-fund the PSBR by selling more debt to the NBPS than necessary to finance the PSBR. This soon, however, ran into a technical problem: by

1980, the combination of fast growth of bank lending to the private sector and intermittent 'over-funding' to offset it had denuded the banks of a sufficient stock of public-sector debt to transfer back to the authorities in exchange for cash, to replace cash balances depleted by over-funding. Thus, the banks' asset portfolio proportions looked very different by 1980:

Asset Portfolio, All Banks, £, %, end December 1980

Cash	2
Treasury bills	2
Other bills	4
Government bonds	4
Loans to private sector	41
Other*	47
	100

*Of which interbank balances amounted to about half.
Source: Bank of England Quarterly Bulletin

The banks became unwilling, indeed virtually unable, to run down their holdings of government securities any further. Indeed, the regular weekly auction of Treasury bills, which had been so central to money market operations in the 1950s, 1960s and 1970s, became reduced to a residual token amount, retained largely to keep members of the market aware and informed of the *modus operandi*, against the possibility of a change in circumstances leading to its revival being necessary. Instead, bank liquidity and money market operations became based, as had been the case before 1914, on banks' holdings of *commercial* bills. When banks needed more liquid assets, they would bid a finer rate for commercial bills than for ordinary loans to the private sector, thereby inducing those borrowers with first-class names to switch from loan finance to bill finance.

Within its own framework of reference, the over-funding exercise was remarkably successful. Although bank lending to the private sector surged ahead over the years 1980–4, at an annual average rate of no less than 19.6 per cent per annum, and the PSBR regularly exceeded its budgetary target, nevertheless public-sector debt sales to the NBPS were sufficiently expanded to hold the rate of growth of £M3 to the much lower average annual rate (1980–4) of 12.5 per cent, though even this involved sizeable overshoots of the set targets in 1980 and 1981.[1]

This success was achieved at a cost. First, the exhaustion of commercial bank holdings of public-sector debt (e.g., Treasury bills) meant that the authorities had to relieve over-funding pressures on banks' cash reserves, by buying, discounting or undertaking repos in commercial bills from the market. As these matured, the drawers had to pay the holder of the bill (i.e., the Bank of England), thus leaving the private sector short of cash again and in need of further bill purchases. The over-funding exercise led the authorities to accumulate a 'bill mountain', much of which, being short-dated, was always maturing; this situation forced the market into a

---

[1] From Goodhart (1986c) p. 83.

regular, start-of-the-day, *huge* prospective cash shortage with the authorities, which had to be relieved, on terms which the authorities *had* to choose. The bill mountain, which on occasion included forms of assistance other than bills, began in late 1981 and rose to a peak of £18bn in mid-1985, causing the prospective start-of-the-day market cash shortage in the mid 1980s to average about £3/4bn.

As already noted in Section 1, the authorities had reviewed their money market procedures in 1981 with the hopes of operating the system in such a way that the market would normally find itself at the start of each market day in overall cash balance. This would allow the Bank of England to refrain from market intervention, leaving interest rates to the free play of demand and supply in the money market, with the fluctuations in such market-determined interest rates to be limited only by the famous unpublished bands, the limits at which the Bank would have intervened. The purpose of the exercise was to give more room for market forces to influence interest rates. In the event, the system never had a chance to operate as intended. The use of over-funding to control monetary growth rapidly pushed up the bill mountain and this led to massive, endemic, daily cash shortages which the authorities had to relieve at a stop rate which they had to choose.

Second, the need to purchase bills was often so pressing, owing to the inter-action of over-funding and large-scale bank lending, that interest rates on commercial bills were driven down, in large part by the Bank's own actions, relative to other market interest rates. Such distortions in relative interest rate patterns were held to give rise to certain forms of market arbitrage, some of which (hard abitrage) may have led to additional bank lending, thus actually exacerbating the initial control problems. There was considerable anecdotal reporting of such 'hard arbitrage' but little solid evidence has emerged.

Third, the exercise whereby the Bank sold long-dated bonds to the NBPS and then bought back commercial bills from the banking system in order to keep the money market's cash position in balance, was hard to understand and at times seemed anomalous. Apart from the question of cost, if yields on long-dated debt were above those on bills, (though for much of this period the yield curve was downward-sloping), the exercise had a somewhat 'cosmetic' appearance and gave rise to questioning whether it really was £M3 that the authorities should be controlling, or whether the focus of attention should not be better directed to some other monetary or financial indicators.

So long as £M3 remained the cynosure of attention, and bank lending not responsive to interest rates, the authorities felt that they really had no alternative except to continue along the over-funding, bill-mountain, treadmill. Once the relationship between £M3 and nominal incomes was recognised to be tenuous and unpredictable (see Chapter 15), so that less weight became placed on achieving a target path for it, the first step that the Chancellor took, even before £M3 became officially and publicly down-graded as a monetary target in his speech on 17 October 1985, was to abandon the policy of over-funding in the summer of 1985. Instead, the aim became to achieve a full funding of the PSBR (i.e., to sell just sufficient debt to the NBPS to finance the PSBR). While this latter objective has a certain superficial plausibility there is, in fact, no strong analytical case for it and debt management in the UK after 1985 entered a period in which there were no clear analytical guidelines.

Appendix: Monetary Base Control: The Examples of Switzerland, and of the USA in 1979–82

The main example of monetary base control that is usually quoted pertains to Switzerland.[1] There are a number of features about the operation of this policy in that country that are worth noting. First, this policy option has worked[2] in some part because the institutional and market structure in Switzerland encouraged a more elastic demand for commercial bank reserve balances at the Swiss National Bank than exists in other money market centres. Thus, Kohli and Rich note[3] (pp. 916–7) that:

> the central bank cannot operate a system of monetary base control unless commercial banks hold excess reserves, that is reserves in excess of the legally required level. In order to prove this proposition, suppose that the SNB [Swiss National Bank] – for some reason – decides to reduce the monetary base. If commercial banks did not hold any excess reserves, the restrictive measure of the SNB, in the short run, would result in a reserve deficiency since bank deposits could hardly react instantaneously to a fall in the monetary base. Unless the SNB were prepared to tolerate a reserve deficiency, it could not help providing assistance in the form of discount and Lombard loans to commercial banks in order to make up the deficiency. Thus, if commercial banks did not maintain excess reserves, the SNB could not reduce the monetary base, at least not in the very short run.

An interesting question is what conditions existed in Switzerland that may have made its commercial banks more willing to hold excess reserves (i.e., to have a more elastic demand function for reserves) than in other countries. Three such conditions may be identified:

1. The unwillingness of the Central Bank to provide additional cash freely at some administratively chosen interest rate.

---

[1] Thus Kohli and Rich, in their paper on 'Monetary Control: The Swiss Experience' (1986) state that, 'It is interesting to note that the SNB [Swiss National Bank] seems to be the only central bank in the industrialized world to rely on the monetary base as a target variable even though Karl Brunner and other leading monetarists have consistently argued in favour of such an approach'.

[2] P. Bridel, in private correspondence with me, has commented that, 'As from January 1st, 1988, the whole Swiss system of reserve requirements has been completely altered, making the money market transmission mechanism more akin to other countries'. Accordingly he warned that I should put this account of SNB operations in the past tense.

[3] Kohli and Rich (1986).

2. The relatively under-developed nature of the domestic Swiss money market.
3. The low nominal interest rates that have generally prevailed in Switzerland.

The question of whether the Swiss approach could be translated successfully elsewhere depends in part on the relative weighting that should be applied to these three factors.

Moreover, the SNB has run its MBC technique in an extremely relaxed fashion. There has been *no* attempt to use a required reserve ratio as a fulcrum to enforce a multiple change in the money stock in response to a given change in base money. Thus, Rich and Beguelin,[1] state (p. 94) that:

> Despite the existence of a cash reserve requirement, the banks enjoy considerable discretion in determining the size of their base money holdings. The reason for this lies in two rather peculiar features of the legislation concerning reserve requirements.
>
> First, the Swiss Bank Act obliges the commercial banks to hold a specified amount of cash, but does not stipulate that cash must necessarily consist of base money ... Claims on foreign banks, in particular, are an attractive reserve asset since, unlike base money, they yield interest ... Second, although the Swiss commercial banks are expected to comply with the cash reserve requirement at all times, data on their assets and liabilities are available only for the last working day of each month. For this reason, the state of their cash reserves is checked only at month-ends. Indirect evidence suggests that, within the month, their cash holdings frequently fall short of the required level. This rather relaxed approach to enforcing the cash reserve requirement is one of several reasons for the marked seasonal fluctuations in bank demand for base money. As indicated earlier, the SNB accommodates to some extent the seasonal fluctuations in demand by expanding the monetary base at month-ends. Thus, it is reasonable to assume that, within the month in particular, the banks have considerable leeway in managing their holdings of base money.

SNB operations to inject (withdraw) base money did *not* bite against a firm required reserve ratio in order to force a multiple expansion (contraction) of the money stock. How then did they work? Kohli and Rich (1986, p. 917) explain that:

> If the SNB wishes to decrease the monetary base, the initial effect is to reduce excess reserves of commercial banks. In the very short run, a decision to diminish the monetary base through, say, a reduction in the SNB's foreign exchange swaps leads to an increase in short-term interest rates, prompting commercial banks to substitute interest-earning assets for excess reserves. Since the policy shift does not instantaneously affect domestic output and prices, the drop in the monetary base, at first, is merely offset by an interest-induced rise in the base velocity. However, as time wears on, higher (real) interest rates will lower output and eventually prices, causing the nominal demand for base money to decline. Thus, the initial rise in interest rates and base velocity is reversed.

This approach and explanation of the transmission mechanism is, however, essentially similar to those offered by virtually all other Central Banks. They, too, observe indicators, perhaps the growth of some monetary aggregate or the level of the exchange rate, that suggest that monetary policy is too easy (or tight). They then take steps to vary interest rates in a countervailing manner. This impinges on output and prices and, hence, on the demand for money and credit. In reality, the Swiss approach is not so different from standard Central Bank operating policy.

A second and more interesting example of an alternative operating procedure is

---

[1] Rich and Beguelin (1985)

that adopted in the US by the Fed between 6 October 1979 and the Fall of 1982. Before 1979, the Fed had set the Federal Funds rate in the manner described earlier. Then, in October 1979, the Fed switched, for reasons that will be discussed at greater length in Chapter 15, to trying to control *non-borrowed* reserves as the main instrument for seeking to achieve better control over its intermediate monetary target, M1. Given the predicted level of reserves required for other (non-M1) deposits (e.g., time deposits) and the prospective level of *borrowed* reserves, the Fed could estimate the requisite level of non-borrowed reserves necessary just to satisfy desired reserves at the targeted level of M1.[1] If M1 should actually rise faster (slower) than this, then the level of non-borrowed reserves provided would be insufficient (excessive) and this would put sharp upward (downward) pressure on interest rates, which should serve to influence prices, output and relative interest rates in such a way as to drive actual M1 back into line with desired M1.

However, given the extremely inelastic short-term bank demand for reserves, would this procedure not lead to 'excessive' interest rate volatility? Two safeguards designed to moderate such a tendency were built into the scheme. First, the operating instrument chosen was non-borrowed reserves. As the use of this instrument drove market interest rates up (down), a gap opened between market rates and the Fed's discount rate, the pegged rate at which banks could borrow from the discount window. Shifts in the size of this gap provided strong incentives for banks to borrow more (less), which offset the initial shortfall (surplus) in non-borrowed reserves.

Second, the Fed introduced relatively wide and unpublished bands for permissible interest rate fluctuations. If interest rates fell to the bottom band level or hit the upper band, the Fed would over-ride its own objective for non-borrowed reserves in order to limit interest rate fluctuations. In practice, the Fed stated that this safeguard was rarely required to be used, perhaps in part because the bands were rather wide and often adjusted, or alternatively because, when interest rates moved outside the band, a FOMC phone conference was always held to decide what action to take, and the action almost always was to move the band; I am indebted to Professor B. Tew for this final suggested reason.

Nevertheless, this new system was accompanied by a dramatic rise in the volatility of short and long interest rates in the USA, by a factor of about 4.[2] Moreover, for reasons discussed in Chapter 15, the *short-term* variability of monetary (M1)[3] growth also increased. In the face of various pressures to revert to a more flexible and discretionary policy (e.g., with the onset of the LDC debt crisis) the Fed abandoned its experiment with a modified MBC in the summer of 1982 and reverted to procedures (i.e., targeting the level of *borrowed* reserves), that amounted *in practice* to a return to the earlier procedure of accommodating short-term shifts in the banking system's demand for reserves at an interest rate chosen by Central Bank discretion.

In *principle*, there are some differences between the pre-1979 and post-1982 approach. In earlier periods, shifts in the demand for reserves were automatically accommodated at a known, pegged, Fed Funds rate. Now the accommodation is more discretionary, and the Fed Funds rate can vary somewhat around the underlying level desired by the Fed, so that the Fed's position and objectives are not

---

[1] See Federal Reserve Staff Study, *New Monetary Control Procedures* (1981) and also Axilrod (1983).

[2] See Dickens (1987).

[3] See Wallich (1984).

so patently apparent as in the earlier period. Even so, the main thrust of the current operating practice, involving the accommodation of shifts in the demand for reserves at an interest rate chosen at the Fed's discretion, has much more in common with the pre-1979 procedures than with the 1979–82 experiment with MBC.

So attempts to move away from market arrangements whereby market interest rates are set by the Central Bank, both in the USA and in the UK, as examined in Section 3, have had limited success. There are relatively few qualifications that we need to make to the claim that the Central Bank sets the level of market interest rates on a *day-by-day* basis.

XI

The Term Structure of Interest Rates

Summary

In order to simplify the analysis, whether of the determination of *the* rate of interest, as in Chapter 10, or of the demand for assets within the context of a portfolio adjustment model, it is necessary to reduce the size of the model to manageable proportions. This is often achieved by aggregation over assets which are close substitutes, where relative variations in supply will have little impact on prices. It is exactly such issues, whether long-dated bonds are close substitutes for short bonds or whether variations in the relative supply of bonds will affect the pattern of bond prices, that lie at the heart of arguments about the determination of the term structure of interest rates. It is, perhaps, unfortunate that analysis of the term structure often begins in a certainty context since then all assets are virtually perfect substitutes by definition, though the mechanics of the relationship between present bond rates, implicit forward rates, and present and forward bond prices can be set out more easily in such circumstances.

If investors were risk-neutral and held similar expectations, then the introduction of uncertainty would not alter the term structure greatly. Both assumptions are, however, implausible. It is, therefore, necessary to take account of risk aversion among investors with differing holding periods and expectations. The attempt to do so by adding a constant liquidity premium into an equation otherwise based on risk-neutral behaviour (i.e., assuming that the sole objective is to maximise the mean expected return) is unsatisfactory. The risk involved in adding a bond of differing maturity to the portfolio is not theoretically a constant but depends on several factors, such as the expected variance and covariances of the bond, the investor's holding period, etc. The analytical considerations are reviewed in Section 1.

If investors exhibit risk aversion, short bonds should not be very close substitutes for long bonds; some economists, in particular Culbertson, have gone so far as to argue on such grounds that the market will be segmented. On the other hand, bonds of adjacent maturities are likely to be very close substitutes, though less so at the short end of the market. The interesting question then is how quickly, if at all, does the degree of substitution fade as the distance along the maturity spectrum increases.

Such a question can be answered only by examining the data. In Section 2, a number of the earlier empirical studies, undertaken in the 1960s and the first half of the 1970s, are first surveyed. Much of the increased interest in this subject then can be traced to Meiselman's reformulation of the expectations hypothesis, in terms of systematic revisions to expected future short-term rates in the light of errors in forecasting the current short rate. Such studies usually relied on obtaining observations of implicit forward rates from calculated yield curves and the tests of their hypotheses could have been affected by the method used to construct such curves. The studies undertaken by Modigliani, with Sutch and Shiller, got away from the use of constructed yield curves by regressing actual long rates on past and present short rates. Almost all these early empirical exercises produced quite good statistical fits. There seemed at that time, circa 1975, no doubt that expectations played a major role in determining the term structure, though exactly how these expectations were formed and revised remained uncertain. More surprising, in view of the prevalence of risk aversion, was the general failure of such empirical studies to reveal any clear signs of supply factors influencing the pattern of rates, though a number of reasons can be adduced in partial explanation for this.

In the course of the 1970s, the rational expectations theory was applied to the analysis of asset price determination. This theory posited that, in an efficient market, prices should incorporate all available public knowledge. This approach occasioned some more rigorous tests than had the earlier studies of the role of expectations in determining the term structure; as is discussed subsequently in Section 3, research undertaken in the late 1970s and early 1980s revealed two major features of the term structure that appeared *inconsistent* with the rational expectations, efficient market hypothesis. First, given the auto-correlative, time series properties of short rates, long rates appeared to *under-react* to changes in short rates. Second, given the historical time path of short rates (and company dividends), long rates (and share prices) seemed excessively volatile. These two findings, which appear at first glance contradictory, can be explained either if long rates (and share prices) are also influenced by other long-lasting factors (e.g., changes in the preferences and attitudes to risk of investors), or if there was good reason at times for investors to believe that the future time path of short rates (and dividends) would diverge markedly from those that *did* historically occur. Both these latter hypotheses may have some explanatory power. Even so, this research leaves the expectations theory with relatively little role in the determination of long term rates. We seem to know less now than we had believed that we knew in the early 1970s.

1. The Theory of the Term Structure

There are in any developed economy very many different assets, real and financial. The question when, and under what circumstances, it is appropriate to aggregate certain of these assets into sets forms a link between the subject matter of previous chapters and the theory of the term structure of interest rates. In order to study the process of the determination of the general level of interest rates or of portfolio adjustment, as described in previous chapters, it is necessary to limit the size of the exercise to manageable proportions by aggregating the numerous assets into a smaller number of groups.

How does one choose which assets to group together into larger aggregates? The process of aggregation should reduce the system into a model of more manageable proportions, but has the result of obscuring some of the inter-relationships one wishes to examine. The objective is to aggregate in such a way as to minimise the loss in explanatory power obtained in exchange for greater simplicity.

In particular, the process of aggregation prevents any explicit consideration of the effect of variations in the relative supplies of the aggregated elements which leaves the aggregate supply unaffected. Aggregation will thus not be appropriate when variations in the relative supplies of the individual elements have any significant effect on the variables or problem under consideration. This, of course, implies that the appropriate degree of aggregation depends on the problem at hand. If your interest is planning the production schedule for the future issue of bank-notes, the analysis of the problem would hardly be advanced by aggregating over all denominations of notes. If, however, your concern was the growth of the national economy, the substitution of more £10 notes for £5 notes, leaving the overall note issue unchanged in value terms, is unlikely to affect any crucial variable in the system.

In general, the greater the degree of substitutability between any two items, the less information will be lost by treating them as an aggregate. If two small items are very close substitutes, then a shift in relative supplies will only require a very small shift in relative prices to restore equilibrium. If relative prices are virtually unchanged, the effect on the rest of the economy of the shifts in relative supplies within the aggregate is likely to be minimal. In such circumstances, aggregation over these items would normally be appropriate.

In many ways, the nub of the major issues in dispute in the analysis of the term structure of interest rates has resided in the question whether it is appropriate to aggregate over all central government (or public-sector) bonds. The questions whether investors regard bonds of differing maturities as close substitutes; whether the bond market is segmented, with separate demand (and supply) schedules for bonds of different maturities; whether shifts in the relative supply of bonds of different maturities alter the term structure, are all essentially raising the issue whether it is appropriate to aggregate short and long bonds[1] (with otherwise similar characteristics).

Government bonds are, in normal circumstances, free of default risk. They do bear different coupons and sometimes have unusual call provisions, but their main characteristics are basically similar, except that the various outstanding bonds differ in their term till maturity. Is this difference of sufficient importance that one should treat short-dated and long-dated bonds separately in any analysis of financial adjustment within the economy, or would a sale by the authorities of short bonds balanced by a purchase of longs (to the same value, say) with no net effect on the money stock, leave the economy relatively unaffected?

At first sight, it may look entirely implausible to regard long-dated bonds, or perpetuities, as close substitutes for short-dated bonds. But it is always possible for an investor to hold a series of short bonds rather than a long bond over some long holding period, or to hold a long bond for a short time and then sell it rather than hold a short bond (to maturity). If people should have very firm expectations about the future returns available on short bonds, and the future prices at which they can sell long bonds, then investors will choose that sequence of bond holding that will maximise their expected holding-period return. If all investors have similar expectations, their portfolio adjustment will drive bond prices to levels at which the total return (interest plus expected capital gain or loss) for each sequence of bond holdings will be expected to be the same over any given period. If, then, more of bond i is supplied, and less of bond j, in these circumstances where all investors have uniform, very sure expectations, it will take only a minimal increase in the current market yield of bond i and fall in that of bond j to make investors switch from bond j to bond i. In such circumstances, shifts in the relative supplies of the various bonds will have hardly any effect on relative prices, and aggregation in, for example, a study of general portfolio adjustment would be appropriate.

Indeed, in an economy without any uncertainty, one can aggregate over all assets.

---

[1]See Leijonhufvud (1968), especially Section III.

All assets must have the same certain return over a given period[1] irrespective of their superficial characteristics. All assets would be perfect substitutes; there would be only one kind of financial asset. With a certain future, the return to be obtained on holding bonds (or any other asset) over an n-year period would have to be identical whether a bond with a life of n years was held to maturity, or whether a sequence of shorter bonds was held with the proceeds being reinvested, or whether a longer bond was held to be sold after n years. If they were not identical, a sure arbitrage profit could be made by simultaneously purchasing the asset with a higher yield and selling the asset with the lower yield. Assume that the sequence of buying two one-year bonds is known to give a higher return than holding a two-year bond. Then all holders of two-year bonds should sell them and reinvest in one-year bonds – in the sure knowledge of the coming yield on next year's one-year bond – until the returns over the two-year holding period are driven into equality. In this circumstance, a visitor from Mars could deduce from the present term structure of rates *exactly* what everyone foresaw with certainty for future short rates of interest and for future asset prices on all existing bonds at future dates. The expected future short rates would thus be those making the return on a sequence of short holdings exactly equal to the return on long holdings. Abstracting from the complication of periodic coupon payments, which require reinvestment at the future expected rates – i.e., treating all bonds as pure discount bonds (the return from which arises entirely from the discount from their final maturity value at which they are sold) – the expected yields will be equal when:

$$(1 + R_k)^k (1 + {}_{t+k}r_n)^n = (1 + R_{k+n})^{k+n}$$

where R is the rate offered currently (spot), the subscript R_{k+n} meaning that this rate is offered over a period of length $k + n$; r is the expected future rate, r_n is a future rate over n periods, and ${}_{t+k}r_n$ is a future n-period rate which is expected to occur $t + k$ periods from now.

By means of this equation, in a world of certainty, one could deduce all future expected short rates from the current structure of spot rates, e.g.:

$$(1 + {}_{t+1}r_1) = \frac{(1 + R_2)^2}{(1 + R_1)}$$

The one-year rate expected to rule next year can thus be deduced from the current two-year and one-year spot rates. Equally, the expected n-year forward rate on a bond of maturity $n + 1$ can be obtained by a similar calculation, e.g.:

$$(1 + {}_{t+1}r^n)_n = \frac{(1 + R_{n+1})^{n+1}}{(1 + R_1)}$$

---

[1] This certain return could, however, vary as the length of the holding period varies, depending on foreseen variations in real economic conditions such as thrift, investment opportunities, harvests, etc. An investor with a short holding period cannot take advantage of, say, higher certain future short-term rates beyond that period, since he would have to borrow funds at these future higher rates to finance his investment. In this certain economy, the certain return (on all assets, long or short) over n years may differ from the return obtainable over q years ($n \neq q$) but the investor in each case will be indifferent whether he holds sequences of short or long assets to obtain the certain return.

and it follows, of course, that certainty of future forward rates also implies certainty of future asset prices.[1]

If investors were subject to uncertainty but ignored such uncertainty – i.e., they were risk-neutral – they would still take any arbitrage opportunities that seemed to offer an expected positive return, irrespective of the risk involved. If one abstracts from such imperfections and practical problems as transactions costs, brokerage margins between borrowing and lending rates, restrictions on short sales, differential tax considerations, etc. any such investor would attempt to eliminate any differential between expected returns on alternative sequences of bond holdings over any period by borrowing (making short sales of) that sequence of assets with the lower expected rate to invest in the asset sequence with the higher expected return without limit.

This follows irrespective of the holding period of the investor.[2] If the return over n years from holding a long bond is greater than that from holding a sequence of short bonds, the investor with a holding period of k years $(n > k)$ can still buy the n-year bond and arrange to borrow on short bonds from k till n to finance his holding if that course promises an arbitrage profit.[3]

The characteristics of a market consisting of, or dominated by, risk-neutral investors with identical expectations would be very similar to those that would hold under conditions of certainty. The implicit forward rates that can be calculated, using the previous formula, from the current spot rates would represent the mean expected future rates, rather than the future certain rates. The assumption that all, or a dominating proportion, of investors have identical expectations is, of course, extreme. There are, moreover, some difficulties inherent in envisaging a system dominated by risk-neutral investors with differing expectations. What would happen if there were inconsistent expectations, for example with A seeing an arbitrage opportunity over an n-year horizon in selling longs to buy a sequence of shorts, while B believes that a return can be made from arbitrage in the opposite direction. This difference of opinion must be a reflection of disparate views about some future short rate. If there was a market in future short-term loans,[4] risk-neutral A would be

[1] For a thorough analysis of the relationship between models based on expectations of future rates and those based on expectations of future asset prices, see Luckett (1967) pp. 321–9 and Malkiel (1966), especially Chapter 3.

[2] This implies that the holding periods of each investor are exogenously given, say by their prospective income and expenditure plans. In principle, of course, such plans – and therefore intended holding periods – would be influenced by the available yields on assets. As is discussed further in Chapter 12, the propensity to save out of incomes does not, in practice, respond sensitively to changes in yields. We shall, therefore, disregard the point that holding periods and interest rates are jointly determined, as a complication of secondary importance in fact, and treat these holding periods as predetermined.

[3] But even if arbitrage did equalise the expected returns for each investor on all sequences of holdings over any given period, the equilibrium expected holding-period returns could still differ between investors depending on the length of their respective holding periods.

[4] This is a market where one could contract to borrow, or to lend, money at some negotiated rate for some specified time period to be taken up at some future date. Some future markets of this kind do exist, for example the futures market in certificates of deposit in London. Such markets should not be seen only as vehicles for speculation; they can also be used for hedging. For instance, a banker's customer may arrange to draw upon his facility in three months' time (to finance, say, an investment project) and the existence of a futures CD market will allow the banker to hedge his position in advance. During the 1970s and 1980s, the range and scale of financial markets increased greatly, encompassing not only additional and broader financial futures markets, but option and swap markets as well (see Chapter 15, Section 3).

prepared, say, to contract to borrow an infinite volume of future short-term loans at the going rate, expecting to be able to re-lend them at a higher rate, while risk-neutral *B* would be prepared to make future contracts to provide an infinite volume, expecting to be able to borrow then to finance the loans at a lower rate. Both would be prepared to extend their future obligations without limit, so long as they were not prevented by some external constraints.

The problem of accommodating inconsistent expectations among risk-neutral investors can be overcome by making the pragmatic assumption that there are certain costs of dealing or certain other limitations on an investor's operations (e.g., restrictions on short sales) so that investors may see prospective arbitrage opportunities but not be in a position to take full advantage of them. In this case, each investor, depending on the limitations on his own operations, will have to concentrate his own holdings in that asset (and liability) sequence which offers the highest expected return over his own holding period. Because of the spread of expectations, risk-neutral investors with limited access to resources would concentrate their holdings in those bonds offering the highest subjectively-expected returns; the issue of additional bonds of maturity length *M* would require some additional investors to switch their individual funds into that bond and this can only be done if more investors come to believe that holding bond *M* offers the highest expected return.

If the spot rate on bond *M* (i.e., R_m) rises relative to the spot rate on other bonds, R_i, then, *ceteris paribus*,[1] holding bond *M* will offer a relatively higher return in investors' opinions, compared with other alternative sequences of bond holdings. To obtain holders for a larger issue of bond *M*, its price must thus fall relative to the market in a series of steps whose length depends on the wealth (and access to borrowed funds) of each additional risk-neutral investor attracted into holding this bond, as illustrated in Figure 11.1.

The range of investors' expectations has been empirically studied through surveys and questionnaires by Malkiel and White.[2] These studies show the range to be quite wide. Nevertheless, there were not very strong *a priori* reasons to dismiss the *possibility* of closely similar expectations among investors in the market. Indeed, professional investors largely receive the same information and communicate frequently with each other. One could, perhaps, reasonably expect that the relative rate adjustments needed on this account to restore equilibrium, as the supply of bonds of

---

[1] The main *ceteris paribus* condition is, of course, that the change in current spot rates should not affect future expected short rates (and also future expected asset prices). With risk-neutral investors, the equilibrium condition between spot rates, given expectations of future rates, r_i, is given by the relationship

$$(1 + {}_{i,k}r_n)^n = \frac{(1 + R_m)^m}{(1 + R_k)^k}; \; m = k + n$$

If r_i remain constant, a rise in R_m relative to R_k must induce purchases of bond *M*. However, if the change in R_m should cause some revision of expected r_i, it would be possible for r_i to change in such a way that a rise in spot notes, R_m, could have no effect, or even a perverse effect, on the demand for bond *M*. The question of the relationship between changes in current spot rates and expected future short rates is taken up further in this chapter. For the moment, however, let us accept that variations in relative spot rates would be needed, and would suffice, to restore equilibrium after a shift in the proportions of different stocks outstanding in a market dominated by risk-neutral investors with limited access to borrowed funds (at the default free-lending rate) and with a spread of differing expectations.

[2] See White (1971) pp. 293–314, and Malkiel and Kane (1967) pp. 343–55.

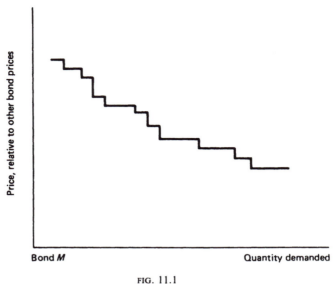

FIG. 11.1

different maturities varied, might be very slight – i.e., that the demand schedule in Figure 11.1 might be virtually horizontal. In this case, the assumption that all investors were alike could possibly be regarded as a useful, simplifying approximation, except that the assumption is apparently belied by the empirical evidence.

On the other hand, the proposition that there are a sufficient number of risk-neutral investors to dominate the determination of market prices does seem contrary to 'common sense' – i.e., that potent mixture of intuition and casual empiricism. As noted previously, the idea that many investors would accept *unlimited* additional uncertainty to raise the mean expected return by a minute amount appears psychologically absurd. Nor does one commonly observe – indeed, never does one observe with institutional investors, who often dominate financial markets – individual portfolio behaviour that would be consistent with risk-neutrality, such as concentration of funds in that asset, or group of assets, offering the highest mean expected return, plus maximum possible borrowing (up to the point where the cost of borrowing equals the mean expected return on the preferred asset(s)) in order to add further to such holdings.

If, on such grounds, pure risk neutrality is dismissed as implausible, it simply will not do to seek to capture risk aversion by adding some constant premium (a 'liquidity premium') to otherwise risk-neutral behaviour. This has been a common practice in the literature; for example, in Hicks's analysis, 'forward short-term rates are biased estimates of expected future spot rates ..., the bias being a risk premium ... It is commonly assumed that risk premia increase monotonically at a decreasing rate with term to maturity.'[1] But if the *raison d'être* of the risk premium is risk aversion, then the premium cannot theoretically be a constant. It must itself be a function of such factors as the expected variance and covariance with other assets of each bond, of the relationship between the supply of the various bonds and the number of investors

---

[1] Consult Masera (1972a) Chapter 1, Section 1.6.

with holding periods of a similar duration – i.e., of factors which influence the perceived risks of holding the differing bonds. In particular, the risk premia should, in theory, be a function of the relative supplies of the differing bonds.

The additional risk involved in any switch in the maturity distribution of an investor's bond portfolio will be a function of his own particular intended holding period(s) and cannot be ascertained without some indication of that. If an investor with a long holding period holds a long bond, he can be sure of its nominal value on maturity and the income risk that he suffers from uncertainty about the rate at which he can re-invest any intermediary dividends – if the bond is not a pure discount bond – will be less than if he held short bonds and was re-investing both the capital and interest. On the other hand, possible variations in expectations[1] of price inflation will lead to an increase in the risk (to the investor with a long holding period) of holding long bonds because he could not retain the flexibility of switching between bonds and, say, real assets without considering premature sales, and thus run a capital risk on his long bonds. So a switch in the portfolio from shorter to longer bonds may, or may not, represent a reduction in risk for investors with long holding periods. For investors with short holding periods, the avoidance of risk, whether of varying nominal or real return, will be achieved by holding short rather than long bonds.

In any case, given risk aversion, investors would have to be tempted out of holding 'quasi-safe' assets, of a length approximately coincident to their holding period, by an offer of higher rates to offset the assumption of additional risk. Depending on the degree of risk aversion, one would expect that relative rates on a given supply of stocks of differing maturities would be influenced by the distribution of holding periods among investors. At any time, if the supply of long-dated bonds was proportionately large relative to the frequency of investors with long holding periods, then the rate on long bonds would have to be higher relative to short rates to tempt risk-averse investors out of their safe shorter bonds. Indeed, the basis for the introduction of liquidity premia was largely a belief in the existence of some such constitutional or congenital weakness of this kind in the long end of the market.[2] Nevertheless, this 'premium' cannot be treated as a constant, nor is it necessarily positive. Its size should depend on the ratio of the proportionate supply, from a given total supply of bonds, of bonds of a particular maturity to the proportion of investors with roughly that holding period.

How large would these risk premia have to be to tempt investors to switch? The margin between the yield on the 'safe' or 'quasi-safe' asset and on a riskier asset should depend on the risk premium (a function of the investor's risk aversion) multiplied by a factor measuring the extra risk incurred by adding that particular asset to the overall portfolio. If most market operators are characterised by a considerable degree of risk aversion, the premium required for them to shift from a roughly matching portfolio, with assets approximately equal in maturity[3] to liabilities

---

[1] Note that 'in principle there ought to be different rates of expected inflation, according to the period of time over which the expectation is entered', Masera (1972b) pp. 127–36.

[2] See Masera (1972a) Appendix to Chapter 1 and pp. 18–19.

[3] The concept of maturity is not entirely straightforward for bonds which provide regular interest payments. When such coupon payments occur, each bond can be thought of as providing a whole set of separate payments at different maturities. In such cases, the 'duration' of the bond, which represents a weighted average of the maturities of the individual payments, with the weights normally being taken as the present value of the future payments, is a more appropriate statistic than its date of maturity. A bond with a larger coupon but a similar final maturity to another will have a shorter duration. See Macaulay (1938) Chapter 2 and Masera (1972a) Chapter 1, pp. 4–5.

or to expected contingent requirements, would have to be large. Nor is there much to be gained in the way of risk avoidance by diversifying the bond portfolio; in practice, spot rates (and prices) of bonds tend to move quite closely together. With a high covariance between movements in spot rates (and prices) of bonds, the risk in holding differing bonds mainly depends on their own individual expected variance of return over the planned holding period.

So, assuming that the distribution of holding periods among all investors (weighted by funds available for investment) remains relatively constant in the short run,[1] variations in the proportions of bonds of different maturities supplied ought to cause fluctuations in relative yields in order to restore equilibrium. There are, therefore, two good reasons – differences in expectations and risk aversion among investors with differing holding periods – why one should expect relative rates to be sensitive to changes in the balance between the supply of bonds of various maturities. In so far as these factors operate, the pure expectational theories of the term structure, relating the implicit forward rates (or implicit forward prices) that can be calculated from current spot rates entirely and directly to expectations about mean future expected rates (and/or future expected asset prices), with or without the addition of a constant term, should be deficient. When there is strong risk aversion, bonds of widely differing maturities will not be close substitutes.

Aggregation in portfolio studies, over all such bonds irrespective of maturity, would then be inappropriate. Instead, investors should be regarded as having separate demand functions, possibly containing quite different arguments, for bonds of different maturities.

Some economists, for example Culbertson, have emphasised the extent of segmentation within the bond market that may occur from risk aversion among investors with disparate holding periods. Complete segmentation, however, implies extreme risk aversion – i.e., that investors would not be prepared to accept even a small additional risk in exchange for a large improvement in the mean expected rate of return. This sounds as, or more, implausible -- and just as contrary to casual observation of normal behaviour – as the view that investors are completely indifferent to risk.

Moreover, the additional risk assumed when an investor with an n-year holding period shifts from holding a bond with a maturity of n years to one of $n+1$ or $n-1$ is not very large, especially when n is already quite large. Adjacent bonds within the maturity spectrum should be relatively close substitutes and the prices on such bonds should move closely in concert. The degree, however, to which the prices on bonds move together, in response to a *similar* rate change on all maturities, depends on the maturities of the bonds. For a given change in rates, the potential price fluctuations for long-term bonds are roughly similar over a wide range of maturities but the price fluctuations in short-term bonds will depend sensitively on the exact length of life.

---

[1] This assumption can be challenged. Cyclical variations in incomes and savings may cause considerable fluctuations in the relative flow of funds into differing savings media, particularly as between discretionary and contractual savings forms (e.g., insurance and pension funds). Funds deposited with life insurance companies are *more* likely to be re-invested in longer-dated assets by the intermediary than funds deposited with savings banks. Thus, variations in relative interest rates over the cycle *could* reflect cyclical fluctuations in the strength of supply and demand of funds by risk-averse borrowers and lenders with very strong preferences for borrowing (lending) in each particular maturity segment. For arguments along these lines, see the work of Culbertson (1957) and (1965) Chapter 10.

'Hence, bonds of longer maturities, which are mathematically almost equivalent securities in terms of price responsiveness to changes in the level of interest rates, may plausibly be expected to be close substitutes whose yields would consequently be very similar. Conversely, in the short and intermediate range of the maturity spectrum, the extension of maturity even for a few years implies considerably different price risks and opportunities for capital gains'.[1]

Those factors causing a reassessment of current spot-bond rates and, by the same token, of forward implicit rates and forward implicit asset prices, factors such as changes in the pace of inflation, in political stability, in investment opportunities, in the state of the balance of payments, and in monetary policy, would mostly seem likely to persist over a period of time, sometimes undergoing a permanent step change, and sometimes a cyclical swing. The likelihood of a situation developing in which variations in expected forward short rates would be uncorrelated must therefore be extremely low. The more variations in forward expected rates are positively correlated, the greater will be the covariance in spot-asset price movements.

Unless there is a quite extraordinary degree of risk aversion in the bond market, asset prices especially at the longer end of the market and redemption yields on bonds of adjacent maturities are thus virtually bound to move closely together. This degree of substitution over any short range within the maturity spectrum implies that there should be continuous price adjustment throughout overlapping small segments over the whole spectrum, except perhaps at the very short end of the market, and that there would be little loss in aggregation over any narrow range; it does not imply that it is possible to aggregate over the whole spectrum. Given risk aversion, a shift in the supply of long–, relative to short–, dated assets may have little effect on price relativities between two adjacent bonds but could, in principle, cause a large swing in relative rates at the extremes of the spectrum.

Most empirical analysis in the 1960s and early 1970s, following Meiselman[2] or Modigliani and Sutch,[3] tended to concentrate on the relationship between rate movements at the very short end of the market, e.g. in Treasury bill rates, and changes in rates throughout the rest of the market, with the presumed line of causation running uni-directionally from changes in short rates through to changes in longer rates. There were several reasons for this. First, several of the studies, implicitly or explicitly, treated the holding period as equal in length to the maturity of the short asset. The yield on this asset then fixes the certain yield on the 'safe' asset against which prospective combinations of risk and return on the other bonds must be compared. Second, the rate on this short bond, or bill, is treated as determined largely by the actions of the monetary authorities but, in any case, by economic factors – e.g., the rate of growth of the money stock relative to the rate of growth of prices and incomes. Given that this one rate is thus exogenously fixed and that all other rates are linked to it via the pattern of expectations, the whole term structure then becomes a function of monetary policy in the broad sense, as described in Chapter 10.

The implication is that other factors which might be expected to influence the pattern of rates directly (e.g., changes in rates on other assets such as real capital,

---

[1] Malkiel (1966) p. 59, but see all of Chapter 3.

[2] Meiselman (1962).

[3] Modigliani and Sutch (1966) pp. 178–97, and (1967) pp. 569–89, and Modigliani and Shiller (1973) pp. 12–42.

which might be thought to be fairly close substitutes for bonds of similar maturities[1] or open-market operations by the authorities in longer-dated bonds) do not do so, except to the extent that they have some direct effect on the pattern of expectations. Rather, such factors are held to affect the term structure indirectly by altering the rates of growth of money incomes or of the money stock and, thus, the bill rate. On such grounds, expectation theorists have often advocated a monetary policy of 'Bills Only'[2] as more direct and effective than operations in longer bonds, where the market in the United States is anyhow less broad (so that the market's response to large-scale operations by the authorities would be less stable and less predictable).

To be sure, this is challenged by those who believe that risk aversion among investors with differing holding periods and differences in expectations are factors capable, in principle at least, of limiting the extent of substitution between bonds with far-apart maturities. On this latter view, systematic disturbances to the pattern of relative rates and prices can be introduced at any point in the spectrum – not just at the short end – by a number of other factors (e.g., variations in rates on a range of other assets which might be substitutes for bonds of different maturities, such as real capital and equities at the long end and capital-certain assets, foreign Treasury bills, etc. at the short end). Adjustment to disturbances in rates can then travel in both directions, from long to short as well as vice versa, through substitution. between bonds of adjacent maturities.

Since there is not much doubt that bonds of adjacent maturities will be close substitutes[3] in portfolios except, perhaps, at the very short end of the market, movements in spot rates over any narrow range of maturities are likely to accord reasonably well with the expectations hypothesis. The interesting question is how rapidly, if at all, does the degree of substitution fade as one moves further along the spectrum. The association between movements in four-year and six-year rates may be close but is there also a close link between movements in four-year rates and twenty-year rates? Can one find other variables which also systematically affect this latter relationship,[4] such as changes in rates on other assets or shifts in the relative supplies

---

[1] On this point see, in particular, A. Leijonhufvud (1968) Section III, pp. 111–87; here he states that 'In the Liquidity Preference theory, physical stores of value with a low rate of turnover are not good substitutes for those with a high rate of turnover, nor are long bonds good substitutes for short bonds. Obviously, then, short bonds cannot be close substitutes for long-lived capital goods', and 'Keynes' assumption of a high elasticity of substitution between bonds and capital goods must consist of streams of approximately the same duration' (quotations from p. 171).

[2] A short summary of the arguments involved in this issue and references to the extensive literature on the subject can be found in Masera (1972a) Chapter 7, pp. 195–204.

[3] Unless institutional intervention by the authorities prevents this. In the United Kingdom, for example, the authorities used to designate certain short-term assets as reserve or liquid assets which the banks had to maintain against their liabilities, while other, fairly comparable, short-term assets were not so designated. The result then was that any pressure by the authorities on the reserve-asset base of the banks caused a marked divergence between the rates on reserve assets which fell (or rose less) relative to the rates on non-reserve assets. Differing tax provisions can also lower the elasticity of substitution between bonds of similar maturities.

[4] The existence of other significant variables affecting the relationship between short rates and long rates is not, however, necessarily a refutation of the expectations hypothesis, since any variable which systematically affects the pattern of future expectations could shift the yield curve (in this theory) without involving any current adjustment in short rates. Nevertheless, if a range of other variables were shown to affect the shape of the term structure, the explanatory power of the pure expectations hypothesis and the ability to discriminate between it and other explanations of the term structure, involving some segmentation, would be reduced.

of bonds? Are there any signs of breaks in the links of substitution along the spectrum, dividing the bond market into discernible segments?

On such questions there is little alternative but to appeal to the facts. It is not the intention here to reproduce the empirical findings in any great detail; nevertheless, the form and specification of the various econometric studies, most of them based on some version of the expectations theory, are of interest and a short resume of a number of the earlier key studies follows at the start of Section 2. We later examine the direction and findings of some of the subsequent empirical work in this field. When there are a number of empirical studies, each specified in different ways using data from different countries over various time periods, it becomes difficult to assess the results. Nevertheless, given the possible strength of factors that might be expected to weaken the links of substitution between the short and long ends of the bond market, the extent to which expectational theories, mainly along the lines pioneered by Meiselman and Modigliani, explained movements in the rate structure was initially impressive and even surprising.

Subsequent work, however, raised more doubts. Even so, on the basis of these early results, it became extremely difficult to deny that expectational factors played a major role in determining the term structure of interest rates. It remains, however, much harder to establish beyond doubt that such expectations of future mean rates (and/or of future prices) of bonds are the *only* factors determining the shape of the yield curve.

Almost more surprising than the earlier relative success of the pure expectational theories in explaining the term structure of rates has been the difficulty experienced by research workers in this field in finding evidence that shifts in the relative supply of different kinds of bonds, or rates on other assets that might be substitutes for bonds of different maturities, or the degree of risk (as measured by the variance) on particular bonds, have had much effect on relative rates in the market.[1] One suggestion that has sometimes been advanced, in partial explanation of this negative finding, is that changes in relative rates between long and short bonds might cause compensating changes in the supply of bonds in the market, tending to restore the previous balance. 'The monetary authorities and private issuers are influenced by the structure of interest rates in determining what maturity of security to issue. Since the direction of causation works both ways, it is not appropriate to posit that changes in the relative supply of debt instruments cause changes in the relationship between short- and long-term interest rates . . . Since the supplies of debt instruments depend on a fairly complicated set of relationships . . . it is not surprising that the specification of an identifiable supply equation has thus far proved elusive'.[2]

In the United States, where most of these empirical studies have been made, the volume of private-sector debt in a form closely similar to public-sector debt is relatively large and the available data on such debt are 'extremely crude'.[3] It is thus possible that observed variations in the outstanding maturities of public-sector debt in the United States have been a most inadequate proxy for variations in total supplies of differing maturities of relatively default-free debt. Indeed, if companies were risk-neutral (and all had similar expectations), any variation in relative yields away from the pattern determined by their expectations of future mean rates would cause a readjustment from the supply side sufficient to force market prices into line

---

[1] See, for example, Malkiel (1966) Chapter 8; Modigliani and Sutch (1966) especially p. 191; White (1974); Nordhaus and Wallich (1973) especially Table 2.

[2] Malkiel (1966) p. 225.

[3] Malkiel (1966) p. 222.

with expectations, irrespective of the behaviour of possibly more risk-averse investors.

In practice, however, one would expect companies to be just as risk averse as individuals, or more so. If so, it would require an even larger incentive in terms of relative expected returns to get companies to shift their preferred pattern of financing. Moreover, the transaction costs of new debenture issues are relatively large, so that it is often cheaper for companies to stick to established channels of finance.[1]

Furthermore, in the United Kingdom as contrasted with the United States, the size of the market for public-sector debt overshadows the market in company debentures. The difference in size became even more marked from 1973 onwards when the onset of virulent inflation caused nominal interest rates on debentures to rise to a level that company treasurers were not prepared to accept, whereas the authorities pressed ahead with government debt sales as a means of restricting monetary growth, as noted in Chapters 6 and 10, Section 3. Operations by the authorities in public-sector debt here therefore largely determine variations in the maturity structure of the whole outstanding debt. Of course, one of the authorities' concerns is to minimise the cost of the National Debt to the Exchequer, so that the issue of new stock in the various maturity ranges will not be *entirely* independent of the ruling rate structure. The authorities have, however, usually maintained tap stocks on offer regularly at the relatively short and relatively long end of the market (the market for medium-term issues in the range five to fifteen years being regarded as constitutionally weaker), and the keenness of the authorities to make sales of such virtually continuous taps has, in the main, been influenced by more pressing factors than a desire to minimise expected interest costs over time to the Treasury. Conditions for examining the effect of changes in the supply of debt of various maturities upon the shape of the yield curve thus seem more propitious in the United Kingdom than in the United States. Nevertheless, there is little evidence of any more obvious effect of changes in supply conditions upon the pattern of relative rates in the United Kingdom than in the United States. Indeed, in an extensive search for possible supply-side effects from the authorities' debt management operations on UK long-dated gilt yields (given short-dated yields), David Gowland and I reported completely negative results.[2] Thus, 'We tried exhaustively to find evidence of debt management operations affecting (relative) yields – and we believe that they should so affect relative yields – but all our results were negative'. Instead, the generality of empirical work has found so little evidence of supply-side effects and segmentation within the government bond market that the conventional wisdom is that such conditions do not exist.

All told, the evidence to date in favour of close substitution between bonds, irrespective of differences in maturity, and against segmentation, owing to the existence of risk-averse investors with differing holding periods and diverse expectations, seems surprisingly strong.

---

[1] For example, in 1970–2 in the United Kingdom, there seemed to be a considerable rate advantage for companies offering debentures with a ten-year life in place of the customary twenty-five to thirty-year debenture. In the event, few companies took advantage of this apparent opportunity since there was not such a broad market in medium-term company debentures; the extra transaction costs nullified the rate advantages.

[2] See 'The Relationship between Long-dated Gilt Yields and Other Variables' (1978) pp. 59–70.

2. Empirical Studies of the Term Structure of Interest Rates

The first studies of the expectations hypothesis compared the implicit forward rates, which can be calculated from the pattern of current spot rates, with the actual rates that later occurred in the market (i.e., they compared $_{t+k}r_{n,t}$ with $R_{n,t+k}$). These studies generally showed that the predictive power of implicit forward rates was quite weak.[1] This was not, however, a conclusive test of the expectations theory since it remained possible for the current structure of rates and asset prices to be determined entirely by current expectations, even if these expectations should subsequently be proved erroneous.[2]

In his study on *The Term Structure of Interest Rates*,[3] Meiselman brilliantly developed the expectations hypothesis, side-stepping the complications inherent in comparing inferred expectations with future outcomes, by reformulating it in terms of a systematic process of revising expectations. He put forward the hypothesis that expected future short-term rates would be systematically revised on the basis of errors made in forecasting the current short-term rate: '*changes* in, rather than *levels* of interest rates can be related to factors which systematically cause *revisions of expectations*.'[4] On this basis, he constructed an error-learning model of the form (using the notation already introduced on p. 241):

$$_{t+n}r_{1,t} - {}_{t+n}r_{1,t-1} = f_n(R_{1,t} - {}_{}r_{1,t-1}) \qquad n = 1,2, \ldots$$

where $R_{1,t} - {}_{}r_{1,t-1}$ is the error (E) between last period's forecast of the current one-year rate and its actual value, and $_{t+n}r_{1,t} - {}_{t+n}r_{1,t-1}$ is the revision to the one-year implicit forward rate expected to occur at $t+n$ between last period and now.

One contentious point is worth noting, that revisions to all forward rates are the result of errors only in forecasting the shortest rate and not in any errors of prediction elsewhere in the market.

He tested a linear version of this relationship against the data, of the form

$$_{t+n}r_{1,t} - {}_{t+n}r_{1,t-1} = a + bE_t + u$$

where u is a stochastic error term.

If 'a' was non-zero it would imply that forward implicit rates changed over time, even if there was no 'error' in forecasting current short rates, and this might be taken as evidence for the existence of liquidity premia.[5] However, the converse, that 'a' = 0 would show that there were no such premia, did not hold, as was shown by Kessel and Wood.[6] Since the one-year forward implicit short rate $_{}r_{1,t-1}$ could itself incorporate a liquidity premium, the calculated 'error' could be partially a true 'error' and partially represent the unwinding of a liquidity premium. In practice, most

---

[1] See the studies quoted by Masera (1972a) p. 16, footnote 21.

[2] If the errors could, however, be shown to be systematic and not just random, it would throw doubt on the expectations hypothesis since rational investors should use past experience to eliminate systematic errors from forward predictions; the market expectation of any relevant variable should represent the best forecast that could be made of that variable on the basis of all the information available at the time of the forecast. See Muth (1961) pp. 315–35.

[3] (1962).

[4] Meiselman (1962) p. 18.

[5] Predictable, systematic changes in forward rates would not, however, be consistent with a rational, efficient market. See Sargent (1972) pp. 74–97, especially p. 77.

[6] Kessel (1965) pp. 16ff. and Wood (1963).

empirical studies using Meiselman's approach have found that 'a' is not significantly different from zero. These studies have also shown that the value of 'b' usually varies between 1 and 0, dropping towards 0 (as does also the value of the correlation coefficient) as n rises.

One may next ask whether revising expectations in the manner hypothesised by Meiselman is an optimal method of forecasting, whether 'investors' expectations are equivalent with the optimal forecasts of statistical theory for a certain specified class of statistical models'.[1] If the expectations theory is to hold, and all available information is to be used efficiently, it must not be possible to predict that an implicit forward rate will itself be changing in a systematic manner over time.[2] Sargent showed that 'Meiselman's equations are implied when things are restricted a bit more than they need to be [to satisfy the above condition]'.[3] However, his empirical tests suggested that the values of b actually found are too low to be fully consistent with the expectations hypothesis in an efficient market.[4] And his conclusion on the basis of his several tests is that, 'The evidence ... implies that it is difficult to maintain both that only expectations determine the yield curve and that expectations are rational in the sense of efficiently incorporating available information'.[5]

Since implicit forward rates are all derived from present spot rates, the error-learning model can be restated in terms of a difference of a function of spot rates at time t and a function of spot rates at time $t - 1$.[6] There might, therefore, be a danger

---

[1] Sargent (1972) p. 74.

[2] This implies that forward rates must follow a martingale; a sequence

$$(X_t, X_{t+1}, X_{t+2}, \ldots)$$

is said to follow a martingale if

$$E(X_{t+1}/X_t, X_{t-1}, X_{t-2}, \ldots) = X_t;$$

the above requirement thus implies that

$$(_{t+1}f_{t,t} + _tf_{t+1}, \ldots _{t+1}f_{t+j-1}, R_{t+j})$$

follows a martingale. See Sargent (1972) pp. 75–6.

[3] Sargent (1972) p. 75 and Section II, pp. 76–85.

[4] Sargent (1972) p. 93, 'It has also been noted that Durand's one-year spot rates seem to be adequately approximated by a first-order autoregressive process. Thus, for the period 1905–54, the following regression was obtained by the method of least squares:

$$R_t = 0.2073 + 0.9278 R_{t-1}$$
$$\quad\quad (0.1995)\ (0.0544)$$
$$R_A^2 = 0.8554$$

Including additional lagged Rs resulted in a drop in the adjusted R^2:

> If the above equation is accepted as an adequate description of spot rates, then under the hypothesis of rational expectations B_1 ought to have an expected value of about 0.93. Meiselman's estimate is only 0.703 ... The difference between them should be taken seriously.

[5] Sargent (1972) p. 94.

[6] From the relationship:

$$(1 + _{t+n}r_{1,t}) = \frac{(1 + R_{n+1,t})^{n+1}}{(1 + R_{n,t})^n}$$

the error-learning model can be arranged as:

$$\left[\left\{ \frac{(1 + R_{n+1,t})^{n+1}}{(1 + R_{n,t})^n} - 1 \right\} - \left\{ \frac{(1 + R_{n+2,t-1})^{n+2}}{(1 + R_{n+1,t-1})^{n+1}} - 1 \right\} \right] = f_n \left[R_{1,t} - \left\{ \frac{(1 + R_{2,t-1})^2}{(1 + R_{1,t-1})} - 1 \right\} \right]$$

See Masera (1972a) p. 133.

that the positive correlations observed from Meiselman's model could simply be a function of the tendency of spot rates to move in concert rather than a confirmation of his specific hypothesis about the formation of expectations. This possibility may be tested by comparing Meiselman's model with a simpler model of the form

$$\Delta_{t+n} r_{1,t} = f(\Delta_t R_{1,t})$$

i.e., that the current change in the calculated implicit one-year rate, expected to rule in $t+n$ years, is a function of the actual change in current one-year rates.

The contrast with Meiselman's model can be seen by noting that

$$\Delta_t R_{1,t} \neq R_{1,t} - {}_t r_{1,t-1}$$

that is, the actual change from year to year in the one-year rate is not equal to the 'forecasting error' (E_t).

This latter model is usually described as an 'inertia' model: it implies simply that all rates tend to move together. When the two alternative models are directly compared (e.g., by Masera)[1] Meiselman's model usually gives a better fit; this suggests that his particular expectational hypothesis has some real predictive power in comparison with the null hypothesis that all rates tend, for whatever reasons, to move together.

A serious complication in testing any model which seeks to examine the relationship between implicit forward rates and actual market developments is that, in practice, implicit forward rates can only rarely be deduced directly from actual spot market rates and prices. There are often gaps in the maturity spectrum between adjacent bonds. Some bonds have peculiar call provisions. More important still, bonds generally bear differing coupon rates. This would in any case complicate rate and price comparisons, but these difficulties are often exacerbated by tax conditions, whose impost may vary both between interest income and realised capital gain and between different kinds of investor in the market.

The result has been that empirical studies using this kind of approach have tended to have two parts: first, a continuous yield curve is estimated from the scatter of actual market rates, and second, the test of the hypothesis is carried out on the estimated yield curve. As illustration, Figure 11.2 shows the actual scatter of yields to redemption of government bonds and the yield curve calculated[2] by the Bank of England on 29 December 1972. Unfortunately the results of this second test are not independent of the methods employed to obtain the yield curve.[3] In general, construction of yield curves by freehand or by fitting some low-order polynomial curve imposes a continuous. smooth curve upon the scatter of rate observations. But the imposition of such a smooth curve of itself implies a continuous regular process of adjustment and substitution along the spectrum. Thus, any test of the expectations

---

[1] Masera (1972a) pp. 131–5.

[2] This curve shows the yield that would have to be offered on a new stock at each maturity which was to be sold at par. When interest rates have been rising the par yield curve will lie above the yields on existing redeemable stocks, since their yield to maturity includes a sizeable capital appreciation which is taxed on more favourable terms than interest income.

For an account of the method used to fit this curve, see the paper by Burman and White (1972) pp. 467–86; and Burman (1973) pp. 315–26.

[3] For example, economists found very different results when applying Meiselman's models to UK data, depending on the method employed to fit yield curves. The more angular interpolations used by Grant gave worse fitting results than the technique (of multiple regression) used by Fisher or the freehand curves adopted by Buse; see their various articles on this subject in *Economica*, as follows: Grant (1964) pp. 51–71; Fisher (1964); Grant (1964) pp. 412–22; Fisher (1966) pp. 319–29; Buse (1967); Fisher (1967) pp. 298–313.

Par yield curve for British government securities 29/12/72

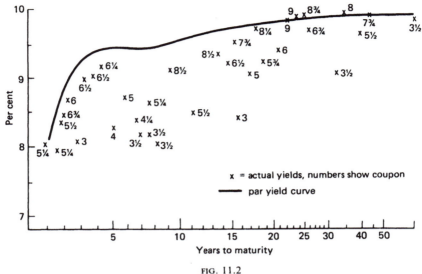

FIG. 11.2

hypothesis, however subtle in formulation, based on an artificially constructed yield curve rather than the raw data, must be suspect of serious favourable bias.

Indeed, this whole approach of constructing an *ad hoc* smoothed yield curve from the raw data and then applying a complex hypothesis to it is dubious. The need, instead, is to devise a term-structure model that will incorporate, *inter alia*, coupon and tax effects in order to explain the raw data. Then, having tested the whole model against the raw data, a yield curve could be derived that predicts the differences in yield between maturities required to take account of expectations and risk, but abstracts from coupon and tax effects. This can be done: a yield curve obtained in this manner was published for many years by the Bank of England,[1] showing the yield that would need to be offered on a newly issued bond priced at par, if it was to be in line with the market.

Unfortunately, this approach, though theoretically attractive, had some practical deficiencies. It was not possible, in practice, to distinguish between expectations of higher future interest rates and additional risk aversion with respect to longer-dated bonds. More seriously, the approach implied that the yield curve *should* be monotonic beyond the point at which expectations were taken to be constant, which appeared to conflict with the facts. Moreover, there were difficulties in splicing the two segments of the curve (i.e., the short end) where expectations for future short-term interest rates were assumed to be made for each year independently, and the long end, where expectations for future short-term interest rates, beyond a (five-year) horizon, were assumed to be all identical. Despite some practical adjustments to the basic model, it was thought not to track market developments adequately, and from 1987 the Bank reverted to a yield curve fitted to the individual observations, after

---

[1] See Burman and White (1972) pp. 467–86.

adjustment for coupon effect, with no attempt to constrain the form of the equation on theoretical grounds.

Despite the probably favourable bias imparted by testing the expectations hypothesis against an artificially smoothed yield curve, in some studies Meiselman's model did not provide a very good fit, with the values of 'b' and of the correlation coefficients declining rapidly as n increased.[1] Even so, the general conclusion drawn from the earlier studies,[2] up till 1975, was that expectations played a major part in determining the term structure – and supply factors a surprisingly minor role. But how these expectations were formed, over what future period they apply, and how they are revised remained uncertain. This subject, the term structure, then became a fertile field for the application and testing of the rational expectations hypothesis which the economics profession adopted enthusiastically in the course of the 1970s.

3. Rational Expectations and the Term Structure

In this final section, we shall primarily examine the application of the rational expectations, efficient market theorem to the analysis of the term structure. This theorem states that in an efficient market all available public knowledge should have been utilised in fixing current prices, so that it should prove impossible to use existing information to obtain systematic excess returns from investments in future periods. At first it appeared that this hypothesis was strongly supported, but we shall go on to adduce more recent evidence (e.g., of under-reaction of longer rates to changes in short rates) that have subjected the rational expectations hypothesis to severe challenge.

A further challenge to the rational expectations hypothesis has appeared in the literature that examines the extent of variance in share–bond prices and discusses whether such variance is too large to be consistent with rational expectations (i.e., the variance bound studies). The question whether such variance is excessive or not is closely tied up with the issue of whether the time path of interest rates (dividends) is mean-reverting and, in a statistical sense, stationary or not. Unfortunately, it has proved extremely difficult to discriminate statistically between efficient systems and those involving certain long-term persistent errors (i.e., with 'fads and fashions').

Unlike labour markets and many goods markets, the markets for financial assets do appear to operate efficiently. It was natural, therefore, that the rational expectations theory[3] would be applied to the analysis of the determination of the term structure of interest rates.

Although the standard model of the determination of long rates, developed by Modigliani and Shiller in 1973 continued to predict well out of sample until about 1981,[4] there were doubts whether its structure, involving a relationship between the long rate and a long distributed lag of previous short rates and inflation, was

---

[1] For example, in Masera (1972a) pp. 131–5.

[2] A wider set of these pre-1975 empirical studies was reviewed in the first (1975) edition of this book.

[3] That investors would make optimal use of all publicly available information in determining asset prices, developed by Muth (1961) and by Samuelson (1965).

[4] When it began to underestimate long rates substantially, see Shiller et al. (1983) pp. 173–223.

consistent with rational expectations. In particular, did it imply that one could make predictions about *future* changes in implied forward rates from existing historical data?[1]

Beginning with Sargent's excellent paper, 'Rational Expectations and the Term Structure of Interest Rates' (1972), economists began to apply this (rational expectations) theory to the analysis of asset price determination, including the determination of the term structure. As emphasised by Merton,[2] the rational expectations hypothesis has held up extremely well under repeated testing. It has been extremely difficult to find evidence of publicly available historical data that could enable an investor to predict future asset price changes and to achieve systematic above-average returns. It has been equally difficult to find evidence of any systematic serial correlation in asset returns.[3]

From the outset, however, Sargent (1972) found one important discrepancy. In the decades since 1945, short rates have exhibited extremely high first-order autocorrelation; thus, when one regresses a short-rate, say a three-month Treasury bill, on its first lag:

$$R_t = a + bR_{t-1}$$

one generally finds a value of b above 0.9, and often insignificantly different from unity, implying that short rates follow a time path approximate to a random walk. According to the rational expectations theory, investors should have made use of this historical fact to revise their expectations of future short rates in response to any

---

[1] If we write:

$$R_t = f(r_t, r_{t-1}, r_{t-2}, r_{t-3}, \ldots)$$

where R_t is a long rate and r_t is a short rate

can we then write:

$$_{t+1}R_{t,t} - {}_{t+1}ER_{t,t-1} = f(r_{t-1} - r_{t-2}, r_{t-2} - r_{t-3}, \ldots)$$

i.e., that one can predict changes in longer-term forward rates from changes in *past* spot rates? This would be inconsistent with the martingale properties of forward rates, as already noted in Section 2, p. 252, footnote 2.

[2] 'On the Current State of the Stock Market Rationality Hypothesis' (1986).

[3] Summers, 'Do We Really Know that Financial Markets Are Efficient?' (1986b) writes:

One statement of the hypothesis of market efficiency holds that . . .

$$E(R_t) = E\left(\frac{P_{t+1}}{P_t} - 1 + \frac{(1+r)_t}{P_t}\right) = r \qquad (3)$$

where the information set in . . . (3) is taken to be Ω_t.

Equation (3) also implies that:

$$R_t = r + e_t \qquad (4)$$

where e_t is serially uncorrelated and orthogonal to any element of Ω_t.

Market efficiency is normally tested by adding regressors drawn from Ω_t to (4) and testing the hypothesis that their coefficients equal zero, and/or by testing the hypothesis that e_t follows a white noise process. The former represent tests of 'semi-strong' efficiency while the latter are tests of 'weak' efficiency. A vast literature, summarized in Fama (1976) has with few exceptions been unable to reject the hypothesis of market efficiency at least for common stocks. This has led to its widespread acceptance as a scientific fact.

change in current short rates. Instead, as Sargent noted in 1972 for the US, and as Goodhart and Gowland,[1] showed for the UK, investors appear to revise their expectations of future short rates by less than the historical auto-regressive properties of short rates would indicate was appropriate. In short, long rates under-react to changes in short rates.[2]

This trait was then found to have an even more serious associated consequence for the rational expectations theory. With long rates under-reacting to changes in short rates, any major downward (upward) move in short rates would lead to a marked upward (downward) slope to the yield curve. With short rates moving down (up) and tending to remain so in an auto-regressive manner, the long rate on balance has tended to fall when the yield curve is upwards sloping, and vice versa. This means that there *are* excess returns to be made by investing long when the yield curve is upwards sloping; a higher running yield is augmented by capital gains. It also flatly contradicts the implication that long rates should *rise* over time when the yield curve is upwards sloping, since implicit future short-term rates are by definition higher than spot short rates. This finding[3] has recently been resurrected by several economists who have noted that these results are seriously at odds with the rational expectations hypothesis.[4] Indeed, the question by the mid-1980s appeared rather whether the expectations theory has any role to play in the determination of the term structure.[5]

The failure of the term structure to predict the *direction* of change of long-term rates has been matched by a complete failure of the term structure to predict the future short-term path of interest rates. Thus, Mankiw and Summers (1984) regress the difference between the three-month Treasury bill yield ruling in three-months time, r_{t+1}, and the six-month Treasury bill rate, ruling at time t, R_t, on the six-month–three-month Treasury bill yield spread at time t (i.e., $(R_t - r_t)$).

---

[1] (1977).

[2] This finding has since been reconfirmed in a number of further tests, e.g. Shiller *et al.* (1983), and Mankiw and Summers (1984) pp. 223–42.

[3] Which has been subjectively known since Macaulay's study (1938).

[4] See Mankiw and Summers (1984) Shiller *et al.* (1983) and Shiller (1985). Shiller *et al.* (1983) 'show here that changes in interest rates do not bear a positive relation to the predicted change and that, as Macaulay first noted, long-term rates tend to move in the opposite direction from the predicted change' (p. 188). So, 'The simple theory that the slope of the term structure can be used to forecast the direction of future changes in the interest rate seems worthless' (p. 215).

[5] Thus Shiller (1985, pp. 30–1) comments that:

> The tendency of long rates to rely too heavily on the past rather than current short rates accounts partly for the dramatic failure of the slope of the term structure to predict changes in long-term interest rates. Thus, for example, the term structure tends to be upward sloping when the short rate has dropped below its average value for the past five or so years. Since the short rate does not revert quickly above its average value over the last five or so years, the result is that the long rate will be subsequently lower, not higher as the expectations theory would predict.
>
> The dramatic failure in U.S. data of the slope of the term structure to predict the direction of future interest term rates is not due only to the underreaction noted above. The failure is also due to a component of the long-term interest rate (one might suppose it a 'fads' or 'fashion' component or alternatively a time-varying risk premium component) that is mean-reverting and unrelated to the history of short rates. This component also contributes to the high volatility of short-term holding yields on long-term bonds.
>
> The expectations theory, however, is not completely without value. The reaction of long-term interest rates to short term interest rates appears to show *some* relation to the stochastic properties of short rates.

On this equation, of the form:

$$(r_{t+1} - R_t) = a + b(R_t - r_t),$$

the coefficient b ought to be unity.[1] Instead they obtain values of b that are negative and significantly different from unity.

Mankiw and Summers then continue by modifying the expectations theory to include a time-varying risk premium, thus:

$$R_t = \theta_t + \frac{1}{2}r_t + \frac{1}{2}E_t r_{t+1},$$

where θ_t can be interpreted as a time-varying liquidity premium.

They note, however, that (p. 16):

> once it is extended to include a time-varying liquidity premium, the expectations theory becomes almost vacuous. The liquidity premium is a deus ex machina. Without an explicit theory of why there is such a premium and why it varies, it has no function but tautologically to save the theory. If fluctuations in the liquidity premium are needed to account for a large fraction of the variance in the slope of the yield curve, then the expectations theory fails to provide a strong basis for understanding these fluctuations. Estimating the extent of variations in the liquidity premium thus provides a way of evaluating the power of the expectations theory as a vehicle for understanding the term structure of interest rates.

When they decompose the variance of the spread between six- and three-month rates into the variance in expected changes in short rates and in the time-varying liquidity premium, they find that (p. 18):

> This decomposition implies that expected changes in the short rate account for only 23 percent of the variance in the spread ... We can reject the null hypothesis that var $\theta_t = 0$, while we cannot reject the null hypothesis that expected changes in the short rate account for none of the spread between three-months and six-month bills.

Accordingly, if the expectations hypothesis plays *any* role, it must be accompanied by other (uncorrelated) factors that cause the major part of the variability of longer-term bills and bonds and of share prices. Indeed, as Shiller and others have demonstrated, the volatility of bond (and share) prices has been considerably greater than would seem consistent with the actual historical time path of short-term interest rates (and dividends), *if* investors had any reasonable foresight of that path.

The price volatility (variance bounds) literature begins with an assumption of *perfect foresight* of future short-term rates (or dividends). One could then construct a perfect foresight estimate of relevant current long-term rates, thus:

$$R_t^* = (1 - y)\sum_{k=0}^{\infty} y^k r_{t+k}$$

where y is a weighting variable in a linearised expectation model since, in a coupon bond:

---

[1] Note that if $b = 1$ and $a = 0$, then:

$$R_t = \frac{r_{t+1} + r_t}{2}$$

The long rate is an equally weighted average of the current and subsequent short rates.

expected short-term interest rates in the near future carry more weight in determining the long yield than do expected short-term interest rates in the more distant future[1]

Similarly, one could construct a perfect foresight share price,[2] as

$$p^* = \sum_{\tau=1}^{\infty} \frac{d_\tau + k}{(1 + r)^\tau}$$

where d is the dividend paid.

Such perfect foresight estimates can then be compared with prices of bonds (or shares) which depend on *expectations* of future short-term interest rates (or dividends) given the information set Φ. In algebraic notation:

$$R_t = E(R_t^* / \Phi_t)$$

and

$$P_t = E(P_t^* / \Phi_t)$$

So that,

$$R_t^* = R_t + \varepsilon_t$$
$$P_t^* = P_t + \xi_t$$

where

$$E(\xi_t / P_t) = E(\varepsilon_t / R_t) = 0 \text{ by rational expectations}$$

and

$$\text{Var}(\xi_t / P_t) > 0$$
$$\text{Var}(\varepsilon_t / R_t) > 0$$

This forms the basis for the variance bound

$$\text{var}(P_t) \leqslant \text{var}(P_t^*)$$
$$\text{var}(R_t) \leqslant \text{var}(R_t^*)$$

Kleidon (1986, p. 955) notes that, 'The logic behind the bound is the simple and general notion that the variance of the conditional mean of a distribution is less than that of the distribution itself. Since the price P_t is a forecast of P_t^*, the variance of the forecast P_t should be less than that of the variable being forecast'. If one then estimates P_t^* or R_t^* from the historical time series of dividends or of short-term interest rates, it follows a notably smooth and stable time path,[3] whereas the actual time path of share prices or long rates is far more variable, indeed massively so. Accordingly, so long as investors had any reasonable appreciation of the historical time path that these dividends – short rates *would* follow, then the volatility of share prices – long rates seems grossly excessive.[4]

The critical question then actually becomes how much 'real', effective information investors have at any time of the future of short-term interest rates (dividends). If they really can use information on present and past events to provide a reasonable prediction of actual future short-term interest rates (dividends), then there is no

[1] Shiller (1979) p. 1194.
[2] Kleidon (1986) pp. 953–1001.
[3] See Shiller (1979) Figure 3, p. 1200, or Kleidon (1986) Figure 1, p. 955.
[4] Kleidon, in his study of stock market prices, notes that the variance bounds methodology

question that long-term bond (share) prices have been too volatile. This question is addressed in the rapidly expanding literature on this subject in terms of whether the short-term interest rate (dividend) time series is stationary or not. If in the short-term interest rate series:

$$r_t = a + br_{t-1} + e_t,$$

the coefficient b is less than unity, then the value of r ultimately reverts towards a constant mean and is stationary. If the value of b is 1, however, the series is a random walk and, as with values greater than 1, does not revert to a mean; it is non-stationary. As we have already noted, since 1945 at any rate, the value b in the equation above for short-term rates has often appeared insignificantly different from unity and the path of share prices, earnings and, to a slightly lesser degree, dividends also[1] appears to approximate a random walk, see Kleidon (1986, p. 995).

As Kleidon notes (p. 972):

> To see whether the degree of correspondence between P_t^* [perfect foresight prices] and price [actual prices] in Figure 1 is consistent with the valuation equation (1),
>
> $$\left[P_t = \sum_{\tau=1}^{\infty} \frac{E(d_{t+\tau}/\Phi_t)}{(1+r)^\tau} \right]$$
>
> we need a model that specifies the information [Φ_t] available to the market about future cash flows. One possibility – favoured by Grossman and Shiller[2] – is to assume that shareholders have a large amount of information about future dividends. Then the only way prices could be rational is if discount rates vary greatly because of changes in aggregate consumption, which is their solution. Unfortunately, as discussed [later in the paper], this solution fails when applied to other data.

should represent a test of a cross-sectional relationship across different possible outcomes (economies) at a point in time. Hence, the result that must occur is

$$\text{var}(P_{t+1}/\Phi_t) < \text{var}(P_{t+1}^*/\Phi_t) \tag{1}$$

since P_{t+1} represents one possible outcome, the actual one that takes place, while P_{t+1}^* incorporates many potential outcomes according to differences in possible dividend innovations. Remembering that:

$$P_t^* = \frac{P_{t+1}^* + d_{t+1}}{1+r} \tag{2}$$

it can be immediately seen that the variance bounds tests performed in practice,

$$\text{var}(P_{t+1}/\Phi_t) \lessgtr \text{var}(P_{t+1}^*/\Phi_t^*) \tag{3}$$

where Φ_t^* incorporates information on past and present values of P^*, is biased due to the inclusion of future information (d_{t+1} and the implicit future value of d_{t+i} incorporated in P_{t+1}^* in equation (2) above) in the P_t^* element of Φ^*. The smoothness of P^* relative to the actual P series is therefore unrelated to agents' expectations (and issues of market efficiency) and is only a function of the autocorrelation process in dividends.

Kleidon makes a further criticism of the variance bounds approach by stating that a finite set of *ex post* dividend values is not necessarily indicative of the information used to determine market prices. The full information used for market valuation includes all factors that impinge on the path of future *ex ante* expected dividends. In addition, the calculation of correct present valuations requires the use of a time-varying discount factor (r_t) in place of the constant (r) used in most empirical work.

---

[1] Kleidon suggests that this may occur because companies try to smooth the time path of the dividends that they pay out.

[2] (1981) pp. 222–7.

An alternative explanation is much more consistent with the data. Using the (geometric) random walk for prices traditionally used in finance and assuming that the only information available at time t is the past history of dividends, we see ... that there is sufficient uncertainty about future cash flows to imply the large divergence between prices and p^* seen in Standard and Poor's [share price index] data.

Merton (1986) put the same point very nicely (pp. 39–40):

> If, in fact, the levels of expected real corporate economic earnings, dividends and discount rates in the future are, ex-ante, well-approximated by a long average of the past levels [plus perhaps a largely-deterministic trend], then it is difficult to believe that observed volatilities of stock prices in both the long and not-so-long runs, are based primarily on economic fundamentals ...
>
> Thus, if the well-informed view among economists and investors in the 1930–1934 period was that corporate profits and dividends for *existing* stockholders would return in the reasonably near future to their historical average levels [plus say a six percent trend], then market prices in that period were not based upon fundamentals. If this were the view, then it is surely difficult to explain on a rational basis why the average standard deviation of stock returns during this period was almost three times the corresponding average for the forty-eight other years between 1926–1978. If once again in the 1962–1966 period, the informed view was that required expected returns and the levels and growth rates of real profits in the future would be the same as in the long past, then stock prices were (*ex ante*) too high.
>
> If, as is the standard assumption in finance, the facts are that the future levels of expected real corporate economic earnings, dividends, and discount rates are better approximated by nonstationary stochastic processes, then even the seemingly extreme observations from these periods do not violate the rational market hypothesis.

We thus currently seem to have two contending views. The first is that short-term rates, dividends and earnings broadly follow a non-stationary random-walk path, so that any new information causes a marked shift in share (long bond) prices; the comparison of actual prices with 'perfect foresight' prices related to the chance pattern that these short-term rates, dividends, etc. did actually follow is thereby essentially meaningless. The second view is that there are, or investors believe there are, mean-reverting tendencies in (stationary) short-term interest rates, dividends, etc. so that the extent of volatility in share (long bond) prices has to be explained by other factors.

This difference of opinion has led to further reconsiderations of whether the relevant financial series are stationary or exhibit random-walk properties. More important, in my view, than the actual historical statistical properties, is how investors appear to react to news (e.g., of changes in interest rates or dividends). As noted earlier, there is much accumulating evidence that investors in bond markets under-react to changes in short-term interest rates. So, even if the latter *have* approximated to a random walk, investors seem to have treated them as stationary. Accordingly, the volatility in long bond prices *cannot* be due to a rational response to changes in a non-stationary series of short rates.[1]

If so, what causes such excess volatility? The suggestion by Shiller that these may be due to 'fads and fashions' is not particularly helpful, to say the least. I would hope that some room will eventually be found again for changes in supply-side factors – e.g., shifts in flows of funds between different groups of risk-averse investors with

---

[1] Similarly, the question of whether the volatility of share prices is due to a rational response to a non-stationary earnings–dividends series or to other factors might be best tackled by examining how share prices react to dividend announcements.

differing and possibly changing preferred habitats, effects from changing tax regimes, etc. to play a larger role alongside (rational) expectations.

Finally, one may ask, if the rational expectations theory now seems to have such limited power in explaining the term structure of interest rates, how is it that we used to give it such credence? Summers, 'Do We Really Know that Financial Markets Are Efficient?', argues that this occurred because the normal tests of 'semi-strong' and 'weak' efficiency, described earlier, have little power to discriminate between market efficiency and a system where

$$P_t = P_t^* + u_t$$

with P^* being the rational expectation price level, and

$$u_t = au_{t-1} + v_t,$$

so long as a is close to unity. Thus, he argues (pp. 20–1):

> The preceding analysis suggests that certain types of inefficiency in market valuations are not likely to be detected using standard methods. This means the evidence found in many studies that the hypothesis of efficiency cannot be rejected should not lead us to conclude that market prices represent rational valuations. Rather, we must face the fact that our tests have relatively little power against certain types of market inefficiency. In particular, the hypothesis that market valuations include large persistent errors is as consistent with the available empirical evidence as is the hypothesis of market efficiency. These are exactly the sort of errors in valuation one would expect to see if market valuations involved inflation illusion or were moved by fads as some have suggested . . .
>
> The standard theoretical argument is that unless securities are priced efficiently, there will be opportunities to earn excess returns. Speculators will take advantage of these opportunities arbitraging away any inefficiencies in the pricing of securities. This argument does not explain how speculators became aware of profit opportunities. The same problems of identification described here, which confront financial economists also plague 'would be' speculators. If the large persistent valuation errors considered here leave no statistically discernible trace in the historical patterns of returns, it is hard to see how speculators could become aware of them. Moreover, cautious speculators may be persuaded by the same arguments used by economists to suggest that apparent inefficiencies are not present. There is another logically separate point to be made here as well. Even if inefficiencies of the type considered here could be conclusively identified, the excess returns to trying to exploit them would be small and uncertain.

Clearly, this will remain an area of much continuing debate and research.

XII

The Transmission Mechanism of Monetary Policy

Summary

This chapter examines the various channels whereby monetary policy may influence expenditure decisions. We begin with the standard Keynesian *IS/LM* paradigm in which shifts in the money stock cause changes in interest rates in a widening circle of financial markets starting with short-term money markets and extending to long-term bond and foreign-exchange markets. In turn, such changes in financial conditions then affect expenditures. Most large-scale (Keynesian) macro-economic models retain this basic transmission mechanism.

Having briefly recapitulated the *IS/LM* framework in Section 1(i), we then examine (in Section 1(ii)) how it can be related to the wider and more general portfolio adjustment models of the form used as an analytical aid in earlier chapters. Not only is the *IS/LM* model highly simplified, with an extreme degree of aggregation over both sectors and assets, but also the model constrains and limits the range of relationships that are treated. The paths along which substitution between assets is allowed to occur are thus unduly limited, being restricted to a single route from money to bonds and from bonds to real assets. Second, wealth effects are ignored; yet, the positions of the *IS/LM* curves depend on the level of wealth and changes in the variables in the model will alter wealth.

Within the framework of the *IS/LM* model, the potency of monetary policy depends on the relative magnitude of the interest elasticity of the demand for money, already reviewed in Chapters 3 and 4, as compared with the interest elasticity of the demand for goods. Estimates of the latter are examined in Section 1(iii) using two recent surveys emanating from the Bank of England and the Federal Reserve Bank of New York for the UK and USA respectively. Apart from the transmission route via the exchange rate, the calculated interest elasticities appear to be quite low, especially in the short run.

Such findings of low interest elasticities of expenditures (i.e., a steep *IS* curve) formed the centrepiece of Keynesian scepticism of the power of monetary policy. So, we next turn to examine the monetarist counter-offensive in Section 2. Although monetarists did confront Keynesians (initially successfully) over the subject of the stability of the demand for money function, they did not directly challenge the findings of low interest elasticities in expenditure functions. Instead, they argued – I believe correctly – that Keynesians had artificially and wrongly limited the width of the channels whereby monetary shocks might work through to the economy as a whole. A monetary disturbance, monetarists claim, would not just initially affect prices and yields in money markets but would have a much more generalised effect on assets and expenditures. This more general relationship was evidenced and supported by the (econometric) relationship between monetary stimuli and changes in nominal incomes. Such reduced-form studies led to a lengthy discussion and literature on the nature of statistical causality, reverse causation, etc. which has more recently died down, partly with the worsening instability of demand for money functions, partly with the shift in theoretical interest to the rational expectations – perfect clearing market neo-classical paradigm.

A problem with the monetarist approach is that the finding of long lags in the demand for money function, which should cause the arguments in that function to *overshoot* initially in response to a money supply shock, appeared to conflict with the empirical finding of lengthy lags between monetary stimuli and changes in prices and output. Neo-classicists provided one possible resolution with their distinction between anticipated monetary shocks (implying immediate price adjustment) and unanticipated shocks (slower output and price responses). This explanation, however, presupposes perfectly flexible markets. In the absence of such perfect markets, an alternative explanation of the findings about the dynamic adjustment of the system is that, in the short-run, agents allow their money holdings to respond passively, within some limits, to monetary shocks, a 'buffer stock' mechanism. This is discussed in Section 3. We indicate how such buffer-stock adjustment mechanisms can be modelled. A problem with this approach is that some large well-known agents – e.g., the public sector and large companies – can always borrow additional funds on very fine terms. In their case, money balances will not necessarily serve as a buffer and some other set of assets (e.g., *net* liquid assets) may be more appropriate. This leads on to the conclusion that it is market *imperfections* that give 'money' its strategic importance within the economic system.

We take this insight, that it is the existence of market imperfections that gives certain assets, which form a part of total wealth, their particular importance over into Section 4, where we consider wealth effects. A change in the real value of the National Debt (e.g., caused by a fall in the price level) thus does not really represent a change in wealth since we owe the debt to ourselves, and will have to repay it in future taxation, the Ricardian Equivalence Theorem. On the other hand, the change may allow for a relaxation of certain constraints on agents' choice and behaviour (e.g., non-negativity of bequests and capital market imperfections). The issue of whether an increase in the real value of *outside* money balances represents an enhancement of wealth is more difficult since there are no interest payments to make. Even so, in a perfect information – perfect market context, any shock to real balances would become immediately exhausted in price adjustments, so once again any real changes deriving from nominal monetary shocks find their origins in some kind of market imperfection.

1. The Keynesian (*IS/LM*) Framework

(i) Introduction

The *IS/LM* model, initially constructed by Hicks[1] to provide a simplified exposition of the central ideas in Keynes's *General Theory*, remains the central paradigm of macro-economics even after forty years. As shown in Figure 12.1 below, the *IS* curve traces out those combinations of interest rates (on government bonds) and incomes at which the *ex ante* demand for autonomous expenditures, primarily domestic private investment but also government expenditures and exports, will be in equilibrium with

---

[1] (1937) pp. 147–59.

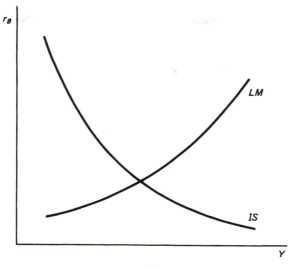

FIG. 12.1

the *ex ante* absorptions from the circular income stream, primarily domestic private savings but also government tax revenues and imports. The *IS* curve, therefore, traces out those combinations of *r* and *Y* at which the goods market will be in equilibrium. Since *I* is believed to expand more in response to a fall in *r* than *S*, and *S* is believed to be more responsive to a higher *level* of *Y* than *I*, the *IS* curve normally slopes down and to the right.

In this formulation of Keynesian macro-economics, the money stock, *Ms*, is supposed to be fixed by the authorities, though, as we have already described in Chapter 10, the authorities in practice generally set the level of interest rates, readjusting these latter in response to changing economic conditions. With *Ms* given and with the interest rate on money assumed to be zero, the *LM* curve traces out those combinations of *Y* and interest rates on government bonds at which the demand and (given) supply of money are in equilibrium. With the own rate of interest on money fixed at zero (by assumption), a higher rate available on alternative financial assets (i.e., government bonds) causes a substitution out for money while higher incomes lead to a higher transaction demand for money; recall the analysis in Chapters 3 and 4. Accordingly, the *LM* curve traditionally slopes up and to the right.

Not only is *Ms* given but, in the short run, the level of prices is also taken as given by existing contracts, expectations, etc. No distinction need thus be made, at least at the simplest level of exposition, between nominal and real variables. A change in interest rates (or incomes), say brought about by a shift in the marginal efficiency of investment, would represent a real change as well as a nominal change. By assumption, the level of real incomes can be increased (i.e., the economy is working below its absolute full-employment capacity level) unless the contrary is explicitly specified.

This does not mean that prices are believed to be independent of the level of demand (i.e., the extent to which capacity is being utilised in the economy). There is, in most Keynesian models, a subsidiary Phillips curve equation, further discussed in

Chapter 13, whereby prices adjust in response to deviations of actual output from some equilibrium, 'full-employment' level of output (e.g., $P_t - P_{t-1} = f(y_t - \bar{y})$), where P is the price level, $\bar{y}$ the equilibrium level of real incomes and y_t is the current level of real incomes).

This model does actually represent the theoretical core of most large-scale models of the economy now in use. Changes in monetary conditions are perceived as having their main effect on the economy via causing shifts in interest rates at the short and long end of the market for fixed interest government debt which then affect an array of other financial asset yields on mortgages, equities, bank loans, etc. This then affects expenditures, depending on the respective interest elasticity of demand for each disaggregated category – e.g., corporate fixed investment on construction, housing, inventories, etc. In addition, such effects may be reinforced by credit rationing, as already described in Chapter 7, and by 'wealth' effects, which will be discussed further later in this chapter. An increasingly important channel of influence for monetary effects in a regime of floating exchange rates has been their impact on the exchange rate and, thus, both on exports and imports and also, directly, on import prices. The Phillips curve equation is often amended to incorporate changes in import prices, thus:

$$P_t - P_{t-1} = f(y_t - \bar{y}, \Delta P_m)$$

where ΔP_m is the change in import prices.

Since the authorities have, in practice, generally set interest rates directly as a policy instrument and since the demand for money functions have become less stable in recent years, as described in Chapter 4, Section 2, most macro-economic models now in use in the UK short-circuit any modelling of the *LM* curve and enter the level of short-term interest rates directly as a policy determined variable. If the resulting level of the money stock and corresponding credit counterparts are then specifically modelled, these became endogenous, residual (memorandum) variables with no direct impact on the economy. Thus, the general structure of most Keynesian macro-economic models is of the form:

$$E_j = f(y, i - \dot{p}, e, X) \tag{12.1}$$

$$e = f(y, i, X) \tag{12.2}$$

$$\dot{p} = f(y - \bar{y}, \dot{e}, X) \tag{12.3}$$

$$y = \Sigma E \tag{12.4}$$

where E_j is real expenditure on the J_{th} category of expenditure, y is real output, i is the policy determined rate of interest, $\dot{p}$ is the current rate of inflation (so that $i - \dot{p}$ is a proxy for the real rate of interest), e is the exchange rate and X is a vector of other exogenous, policy determined and predetermined variables, including lagged values of the endogenous variables.

Clearly, the real interest elasticity of expenditure is a crucial feature in determining the efficacy of monetary policy within this system. We examine empirical studies of this in Part (iii) of this Section. First, however, it might be helpful to examine how the simplified *IS/LM* model may be reconciled with the more general portfolio adjustment framework that we have used as our more general paradigm heretofore.

(ii) Fitting the IS/LM *model into a portfolio adjustment framework*

The proportionate amount of any asset which people will wish to hold in their portfolios depends on their total wealth and the relative yields (including prospective capital gains – losses) which they perceive on all the various available assets. This applies to the whole range of assets, both tangible and financial. Seen in this light, monetary policy affects expenditure decisions by causing changes in these relative yields and also by causing variations in people's wealth through altering the market value of outstanding assets. Such effects on real expenditure can notionally be divided into two parts. First, there is the effect on the savings decision of the personal sector to refrain from current expenditures on goods and services in order to add to holdings of financial assets. Second, there is the effect on the investment decision of the productive sector to expand their real assets in order to increase the current-flow output of goods and services.

Taking the investment decision first, a reduction in yields on financial securities, including money (where the yield may be largely in the form of providing services of convenience), will open a gap between the yields available to investors on purchases of real assets and the reduced yield on financial securities and, therefore, make it profitable for the members of the productive sector to run down their own holdings of financial assets or issue new financial liabilities upon themselves in order to obtain funds to purchase additional real assets. A fall in yields available on financial assets, relative to those on tangible assets, should therefore lead to an increased demand for real assets. Asset prices will be bid up. The increase in the price of real assets relative to their cost of construction will encourage an expanded output of new assets, increasing production in the investment-goods industry. This concept has been formalised and quantified in the guise of Tobin's q.[1] As demand and production in the investment goods industry rises, the price of new capital equipment will rise. The rise in prices of new tangible assets will be tempered by the elasticity of supply of the industry producing that good and by the existence of any pool of unutilised or under-utilised assets which can be drawn back into full operation.

Second, changes in financial conditions may cause revisions to plans for adding to existing asset holdings by saving out of current incomes. A fall in yields will lessen the volume of consumption goods in future periods which can be obtained by giving up a unit of present consumption. The substitution effect will deter those members of the personal sector who are intending to add to their financial assets by saving and would encourage those who want to run down accumulated financial assets or to borrow (i.e., to dissave). On the other hand, the reduction in interest rates will lessen future incomes from current savings and thus reduce the available options for consumption over time – the budget constraint – to a prospective saver. In order to maintain consumption levels in future periods in the face of lower expected incomes, people may feel impelled to save more as interest rates fall. For net savers, therefore, the substitution and income effects of a change in interest rates pull in different directions.

The position of a prospective saver, with incomes preceding consumption, can be depicted as in Figure 12.2, with all income (Y) obtained in period 1, requiring saving to occur for consumption in period 2. With a given income $Y = OA$ in period 1, and interest rate r, this individual faces the budget constraint curve AB, where $OB = Y(1 + r)$. A fall in interest rates to r' will shift the budget constraint curve to AC, where $OC = Y(1 + r')$. The new equilibrium point, X', may either be to the left (less consumption in period 1) or to the right of the initial equilibrium point (X) depending on the shape of the individual's indifference curves, drawn here to show a situation in which consumption/saving in period 1 is unchanged by the fall in interest rates.

---

[1] See Hayashi (1982) pp. 213–24 and Chirinko (1986) pp. 137–55.

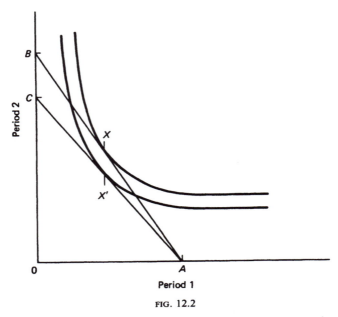

FIG. 12.2

A borrower, though, who wishes to consume initially in excess of his income and to pay off his debts subsequently, will find the income effect reinforcing the substitution effect, as interest rates vary. In practice, the standard life-cycle pattern of employment followed by retirement will lead those obtaining income from labour services to be, on balance, net savers. On the other hand, the productive investing sector is by nature a net borrower since it has to issue financial liabilities (including equities) on itself to purchase the real assets which will subsequently provide the returns to meet the debt obligations. On these grounds, one might expect the effect of reductions in interest rates to have a more expansive effect on the demand for real assets by the productive sector, plus the demand for consumer durables and housing, than in stimulating a greater demand by persons for additional current consumption of goods and services. Indeed, even the sign of the response (more or less) of personal savings to changes in interest rates is uncertain.

Although a fall in interest rates raises the cost to a saver of obtaining a present command over a future stream of earnings, it equally raises the market value (wealth) of those assets already held. This increase in wealth of existing asset holders should also counter the depressing impact of the income effect – of lower interest rates – on the propensity to consume of the personal sector. Indeed, casual behavioural observation, for example that prices of assets, such as houses, which the young will want to buy in the earlier part of their life cycle hardly ever enter into 'cost of living' indices,[1] whereas people are extremely conscious of changes in the prices of assets which they already own, suggests that the 'wealth' effect may outweigh the 'income' effect for the personal sector. This asymmetry is plausible in a world of uncertainty and information costs. The assets currently held are there for sure; the prospect of buying assets in the future is hypothetical and uncertain. When share prices rise, the share owner feels better off; in contrast, the young person who will probably soon

---

[1] See, on this subject, Alchian and Klein (1973) pp. 173–910.

start to purchase shares is usually left completely unmoved. On such grounds, there is further reason for expecting financial expansion to stimulate real expenditures.

The general forms of portfolio adjustment, excluding credit rationing, in response to changes in financial conditions are conceptually relatively simple.[1] The difficulty has been rather to identify and to estimate the workings of these effects empirically, through observation of the real world. This task is made harder because the complete structure of the economic system, in which these transmission mechanisms are deemed to work, is extremely complex. As already noted, this leads analysts to try to reduce the scale of the problem by aggregating, both over different kinds of assets and over different members of the economic community. Such aggregation both simplifies the exercise and focuses attention upon a chosen few critical relationships between the selected aggregates, but it does obscure differences in form and behaviour among the elements within each combined set, a drawback which may be serious if disparate elements are aggregated together. The initial selection of aggregates in any study can, indeed, exert a pervasive, and unrealised, influence upon the way in which the analysis develops.[2]

Within the basic Keynesian model, as simplified by Hicks, the economy is aggregated into two groups, the private sector and the public sector (or government), with three forms of assets: real assets, public-sector bonds and money, also a liability of the public sector. Attention is concentrated upon the adjustment process of the private sector. The government is generally assumed to hold no private-sector debt and this allows all private-sector debt to be eliminated from consideration by a process of consolidation. Firms, financial intermediaries and persons are not separately distinguished.

The portfolio-adjustment matrix can, therefore, be collapsed into a smaller size, as shown below:

	rK	rB	rM	X	W_{t-1}	S
K	$a1$	$a2$	$a3$	$a4$	$a5$	$a6$
B	$b1$	$b2$	$b3$	$b4$	$b5$	$b6$
M	$c1$	$c1$	$c3$	$c4$	$c5$	$c6$

where K represents real assets, B government bonds, M government monetary liabilities, rK, rB, rM the yields on each asset, X a vector of other variables, such as incomes, the expected rate of change of prices, etc., W_{t-1} the value of wealth at the start of the period, and S represents additions to wealth during the period.[3]

Moreover, the implicit assumption is usually made that $rM = 0$ at all times (and/or that $a3 = 0$) and that $c1 = 0$. Thus, with X initially given, an increase in the monetary liabilities of the government (M) will have two effects on the demand for real assets by the private sector, a wealth effect and a substitution effect.[4] The substitution effects

---

[1] The inter-relationship between such general forms of portfolio adjustment and the simpler, Keynesian, IS/LM models has been extensively examined by Tobin, for example in his paper, 'A general equilibrium approach to monetary theory' and in a number of subsequent writings.

[2] Consult Leijonhufvud (1968) Section III.

[3] Note that the changes in wealth can occur either through revaluations, as market yields on existing assets change, or by new savings flows. The implications and effects on the economy of these two channels are different and should be modelled separately.

[4] This example of an increase in governmental monetary liabilities with other things being equal is, however, extremely artificial. Normally, a change in the public sector's monetary liabilities will be the counterpart of a change in government expenditures, or taxes, which will

will then, by assumption, work entirely via the rate of interest on government bonds. If the impact of the wealth effect on the demand for real assets and on the propensity to save is thought to be relatively small, the effect of monetary changes upon the economy then depends only on the relative sizes of the elasticity of demand for money in response to changes in bond rates ($c2$) in comparison with the elasticity of demand for goods in response to changes in the bond rate (a combination of $a2$ together with the elasticity of response, if any, of the propensity to consume to interest-rate changes).

On the assumption that rK, rM and B, the value of outstanding bonds,[1] are given, it is then possible to describe this system in a further reduced set of equations, as follows:

$$I = f(Y,rB)$$
$$S = f(Y,rB)$$
$$I = S$$
$$Md = f(Y,rB)$$
$$Md = Ms$$

where Md is the demand and Ms the exogenously-determined supply of government monetary liabilities and Y is the level of money incomes.

From this set of equations, the standard diagram (Figure 12.1) already set out, directly follows, where the IS curve traces out those combinations of rB and Y which satisfy $I = S$, and the LM curve shows those combinations allowing $Md = Ms$.

The yield on public-sector bonds (rB) thus enters as an argument into the IS/LM model but the process of achieving equilibrium in the market for bonds does not overtly appear. This often confuses people. However, we know that the coefficients in the portfolio matrix have to satisfy certain constraints in order to maintain balance-sheet identities. Thus, the coefficients in columns 5 and 6 must add to unity since all wealth must be held in one of the existing assets. Similarly, the sum of the coefficients in columns 1 to 4 must add to zero: since wealth, the balance sheet constraint, accounts for all asset holding, a rise in rB, say, causing a shift into bonds must be balanced by a shift out of all other assets taken together, (note that this is after taking appropriate note of the effect of the change in rB in revaluing the existing stock of bonds). Because of these constraints, knowledge of the values of the coefficients in all the rows (or individual asset-demand equations) except for one row (or equation) allows one to deduce the coefficients in this omitted row (or equation). The equilibrium conditions for any one market, from a set of markets, can be derived from the equilibrium condition in all other markets plus the various balance-sheet constraints. If these constraints are satisfied and all the markets, less one, are in equilibrium, then the final one must also be so. In this sense, Walras's Law allows one to eliminate one of the markets (here, bonds) from specific attention in the model. As will be seen, however, this does not imply that the value of bond holdings should be

change private-sector incomes, etc. (i.e., X not constant), or the counterpart of an open-market operation, which will change B and rB. It is possible to imagine a government distributing additional money as a gift out of the blue to its citizens; indeed, this has even formed part of the programme of a political party – the Social Credit party in Canada. Even so, it is probably best to regard such an example as an attempt to isolate the purely monetary effects of some transaction, in which the counterpart may also have some conceptually separable impacts upon economic activity.

[1] In practice, a change in rB *will* change the value of B and, hence, the value of the financial assets of the private sector. Unless the private sector's demand for goods is unaffected by such revaluations (see Section 4 below) there will be further 'wealth' effects on the system.

treated as irrelevant to the determination of incomes or of interest rates.

(iii) An appeal to the facts

So, within the *IS/LM* model, the impact of monetary and financial developments upon expenditure decisions in the economy depends on the *relative* sizes of the interest elasticity of demand for money ($c2$ in the matrix) and of demand for goods ($a2$ in the matrix plus any effect of changes in bond rates on the propensity to save). Consider, for example, the effect of an open-market operation undertaken by the authorities in the bond market. The impact on the real economy will depend not so much on the *absolute* values of either the interest elasticity of the demand for money, reflecting the extent of substitution between money and bonds, or of the interest elasticity of the demand for goods, but on the *relative* values of these two elasticities. The higher the interest elasticity of demand for money *relative* to the interest elasticity of demand for goods, the less the impact of open-market operations on the demand for goods. It is the relativity between the two elasticities that determines the response, not the absolute level of either elasticity.

Although the *relative* values of these interest elasticities (reflecting the relative degree of substitution between these assets) would appear to be the main factor in determining the extent of monetary influence, apart from credit rationing, nevertheless a world in which there was in all cases a lesser absolute degree of substitution would be different in certain important respects from a world characterised by generally high elasticities. Changes in the quantities of assets would be accompanied by much larger changes in asset prices in systems where elasticities were generally low. Under such conditions, wealth effects, such as they may be, would become rather more important in comparison with inter-temporal substitution effects.

If the question of the relative values of these two interest elasticities, of the demand for money and the demand for goods – or, if you prefer, of the relative slopes of the *IS/LM* curves – lies at the centre of dissension about the potency of monetary policy, then it would seem that the easiest way of resolving the issue would be to survey the empirical evidence obtained in reported research studies on the estimated values of these elasticities; one might then weigh up the evidence and announce a result, hedged about with a thicket of qualifications. Surveys of the empirical evidence have been made. Some of the recent studies of demand-for-money functions were mentioned in Chapter 4, Section 2. Recent innovations, notably the increasing availability of interest-bearing forms of demand deposits, have, however, served to make it somewhat harder to observe the interest elasticity of the demand for money. Meanwhile, surveys of the effects of monetary policy, notably of interest rate changes, on the economy continue to be made. Earlier, Fisher and Sheppard brought together a useful collection of empirical studies on the effects of financial factors on expenditures in the United States.[1] More recently, there have been studies by Easton, 'The importance of interest rates in five macroeconomic models', for the UK[2] and by Akhtar and Harris, 'Monetary Policy Influence on the Economy – An Empirical Analysis', for the USA.[3]

Easton's objective was to assess the role of interest rates in the five main macroeconomic models of the UK, those constructed respectively by the Treasury, the Bank of England, the National Institute, the London Business School and Liverpool University. The Bank, National Institute and Treasury models are fairly similar,

---

[1] (1972).
[2] (1985).
[3] (1987).

standard Keynesian models of the kind already discussed, with a key short-term rate being policy determined. In these three models (p. 49).

> The components of aggregate demand are modelled in some detail and interest rates affect various of them. Interest rates also affect the exchange rate and hence the trade balance. Financial aggregates are influenced by interest rates but they do not themselves have a strong direct impact on activity.
> The activity side of the *LBS* model is also similar, but the distinguishing characteristic of this model is the integrated financial sector. Within this sector, certain asset returns are modelled as jump variables which immediately move to the market clearing level in response to news.
> The Liverpool model is based on a fundamentally different new classical or equilibrium approach, with markets always clearing [which will be discussed in Chapter 13]. This means that the properties of individual equations are dominated by the overall model properties which force the economy to the equilibrium path even in response to discretionary policy.

Easton then runs two main exercises. First, he provides a detailed analysis of the interest-rate effects within the five models on a single equation or single sector basis. As well as identifying where such effects are present, he attempts to illustrate the relative magnitude of these effects in a single equation context by isolating individual equations from the rest of the model. Second, he reports the results of simulations run on the models of a 2 per cent cut in domestic nominal interest rates in two versions, that is with exchange rates either fixed or floating.

When Easton came to study the simulations of the models as a whole, he noted (p. 84) that:

> One of the major differences between the models is in the response of the exchange rate but this undoubtedly reflects the difficulties of estimating satisfactory equations in this area. In an open economy such as the United Kingdom, the exchange rate is particularly important and so the differences in the exchange rate path account for many of the differences between the overall simulation properties. However, there are also important differences in other areas, notably consumption. Whilst such differences may to an extent reflect alternative views on how the economy works, they also reflect the intermediate stage of much of the underlying work in this area.

It would appear, from this and similar studies elsewhere, that probably the main effect of monetary policy, at least for a small, open economy, works through its influence on the exchange rate; this effect has not so far been clearly isolated or measured, however (see further Chapter 18). For the rest, the results of the simulations with exchange rates fixed suggested relatively small increases in GNP with some considerable differences between models in the overall effects on the differing components of expenditure.

Turning next to the study of the USA, Akhtar and Harris examine the effect of changes in interest rates and of the exchange rate upon expenditures, though they do not attempt the even more difficult exercise of trying to measure the impact of monetary policy measures on the exchange rate itself. They examine the effect of various interest rates (e.g., real, nominal and constructed cost of capital) on three categories of expenditure which are generally regarded as the most sensitive to such effects, these being residential construction, consumer durable goods and producers' durable equipment. They report that:

> Expenditures in all three sectors show a significant long-run response to interest rate

movements over the full sample period, 1960–86 . . . Interest rate effects are particularly large in the housing sector, indicating that a 10 percent decrease (increase) in the mortgage rate – e.g., from 10 to 9 percent – would gradually lead to about an 8 percent rise (decline) in expenditures on residential construction. The interest sensitivity of expenditures in the other two sectors is also substantial but well below that for the housing sector. Together, the results for the three sectors imply that a 10 percent decline in the general level of interest rates would augment expenditures in the long run by 3.2 percent.

Again

These findings suggest that monetary policy continues to have powerful long-run effects on the economy. The declining impact of credit rationing seems to have been offset by the increasing sensitivity to interest rates and the greater role of exchange rates.

But

The implications of the results in this study are considerably less favourable for monetary policy over the short- to medium-term. The channels of policy influence are complex and operate with long and variable lags. The increased importance of exchange rates and the external sector has added further complexity and uncertainty to the workings of the policy channels. Our results suggest that the extent and timing of the lagged interest and exchange rate effects are uncertain, making it difficult to assess the short- to medium-term influence of monetary policy on economic activity.

While it is always hazardous to generalise, current conventional wisdom suggests that the most powerful channel whereby monetary policy affects the economy (i.e., via causing changes in exchange rates) is difficult for the authorities to predict and to control in the course of their operations. They have a greater ability to influence nominal interest rates but changes in such rates – with exchange rates fixed – have a less powerful effect on the economy, especially perhaps in the short run.

This suggests that the interest elasticity of demand for expenditures has been rather low and, given the actual historical experience of interest-rate fluctuations in recent decades, would seem to imply that monetary policy measures cannot have been of primary importance for the determination of money incomes. Particularly during the earlier period of pegged exchange rates under the Bretton Woods system up till 1973 (see Chapter 17), the interest elasticities of expenditure were just too low. Thereafter, analysis of the effect of monetary policy on the economy has been complicated by the need to take account of how such policy may have affected the course of exchange rates, not an easy exercise nor one with clear-cut answers.

During the course of the 1950s and 1960s, during which Keynesian theories reached the apogee of their influence on macro-economic policy decisions, the econometric evidence of relatively low interest elasticities of expenditures, a steep *IS* curve, was sometimes supported by *a priori* arguments to support the case that the interest elasticity of demand for money might be high, a flattish *LM* curve, and the demand for money unstable. These are, of course, the conditions – within the context of the *IS/LM* Keynesian paradigm – in which monetary policy would be quite unimportant. The Radcliffe Report was thus in effect a detailed and brilliant exposition of the institutional basis for believing money, however defined, and other liquid financial assets to be close substitutes, culminating in that well-known sentence, 'There are many highly liquid assets which are close substitutes for money,

as good to hold and only inferior when the actual moment for a payment arrives'
(para. 392).[1]

2. The Monetarist Counter-offensive

While Keynesian analysis of the relatively weak effect of interest-rate changes on
expenditures combined formal econometric studies with direct anecdotal evidence
(e.g., surveys of businessmen), the assertions in the Radcliffe Report about the
potential instability and high interest elasticity of the demand for money were largely
based on institutional argumentation and a priori theorising; this was not entirely the
fault of the authors of this Report since adequate monetary data to run econometric
studies of this latter functional relationship had not been available in the UK
beforehand – and the Report was instrumental in repairing this deficiency.

As has already been described in Chapter 4, the first major step in the monetarist
counter-offensive was to demonstrate, using econometric studies, that the demand for
money function was not unstable, nor exhibited a high interest elasticity. Instead, by
the early 1970s, the studies seemed to have concluded that the demand for money was
a predictable function of a small number of variables, notably incomes and interest
rates. At one point, Milton Friedman believed that he had shown that the demand for
money was *entirely* insensitive to interest rates,[1] but it was soon generally accepted
that the demand for money exhibited a significant, quite stable, and relatively low
interest elasticity.

These findings exploded the earlier, more extreme suggestions that control over
monetary growth could not exert much influence over interest rates or incomes.
Clearly this was not so. Given a stable demand for money function, a policy
determined change in the money supply would have to lead to a sizeable shift in some
or all of the arguments in the demand for money function in order to restore
equilibrium between the supply and the demand for money.

While Keynesians accepted this latter argument, they still asserted that the
transmission channel was primarily via interest rates – i.e., that it was interest rates
that adjusted to equilibrate money demand and supply – and, moreover, they claimed
that this channel should be quite narrowly specified, via short-term rates on fixed
interest government debt to long-term rates along the yield curve, and thence to
equity yields, etc. In addition to weaknesses at each linkage, there was the final
finding of a low interest elasticity of demand for expenditures.

At this particular point, there was a crucial difference between the basic paradigms
maintained by Keynesians on the one hand and by monetarists on the other.
Keynesians, implicitly or explicitly, believed – and so constrained their models – that
there was no direct substitution between real assets and money; the chain of
substitution worked just between money and 'bonds' and then between 'bonds' and
real assets. Monetarists believed that there was direct substitution between money
and virtually *all* other assets.

In the monetarist view, money is not regarded as a close substitute for a small range
of paper financial assets. Instead, money is regarded as an asset with certain unique
characteristics which cause it to be a substitute not for any one small class of assets
but more generally for all assets alike, real or financial.

---

[1] It is, however, a justifiable complaint that the Radcliffe Committee never studied in any
depth the question of how serious this final qualification might be.

[1] Friedman (1959a) pp. 327–51.

The crucial issue that corresponds to the distinction between the 'credit' [Keynesian] and 'monetary' [monetarist] effects of monetary policy is not whether changes in the stock of money operate through interest rates but rather the range of interest rates considered. On the 'credit' view, monetary policy impinges on a narrow and well-defined range of capital assets and a correspondingly narrow range of associated expenditures . . . On the 'monetary' view, monetary policy impinges on a much broader range of capital assets and correspondingly broader range of associated expenditures.[1]

In simple terms, this means that if someone feels himself to be short of money balances, he is just as likely to adjust to his equilibrium position by foregoing some planned expenditures on goods or services, as by selling some financial asset. In this case, the interest-elasticity of demand for money with respect to any one asset or particular groups of assets is likely to be low, because money is no more, nor less, a substitute for that asset – real or financial – than for any other. More formally, all goods and other assets which are not immediately consumed may be thought of as yielding future services. The relationship between the value of these future services and the present cost of the asset can be regarded as a yield or rate of return which is termed the 'own-rate of interest' on the asset concerned. Keynesians and monetarists agree that asset holders will strive to reach an equilibrium where the services yielded by a stock of money (convenience, liquidity, etc.) are at the margin equal to the own-rate of interest on other assets. Keynesians by and large believe that the relevant own-rate is that on some financial asset, monetarists that it is the generality of own-rates on *all* other assets. Keynesians, therefore, expect people to buy financial assets when they feel that they have larger money balances than they strictly require (given the pattern, present or prospective, of interest rates), whereas monetarists expect the adjustment to take place through 'direct' purchases of a wider range of assets, including physical assets such as consumer durables.

According to a monetarist's view, the impact of monetary policy will be to cause a small but pervasive change on all planned expenditures, whether on goods or financial assets. The impact of changes in the quantity of money will be widely spread, rather than working through changes in particular interest rates. A rise in interest rates, say on national savings or on local authority temporary money, would not cause a significant reduction in the demand for money – because these assets are not seen as specially close substitutes for money balances. Such changes in interest rates would, rather, affect the relative demand for other marketable assets, including real assets. Expenditure on assets, real and financial, is viewed as responding quite sensitively to variations in relative own-rates of interest; indeed, monetarists generally regard most expenditure decisions as responding more sensitively to variations in interest rates than Keynesians are prone to believe. The generalised effect of monetary policy in influencing all own-rates of interest will, however, tend to be outweighed in each individual case by factors special to that asset (changes in tastes, supply–demand factors particular to that market, etc.), so that no single interest rate can be taken as representing adequately the overall effect of monetary policy. As monetary changes have a pervasive effect, and as their effect is on relative 'real' rates, it is a fruitless quest to look for *the* rate of interest – particularly the rate on any financial asset – to represent the effect of monetary policy.

The crucial distinction between the monetarists and the Keynesians resides in their widely differing view of the degree to which certain alternative financial assets may be

---

[1] Friedman and Meiselman (1964) p. 217. This section provides an excellent statement of the theoretical basis of the monetarist viewpoint.

close substitutes for money balances; in particular, the difference concerns whether there is a significantly greater degree of substitution between money balances and such financial assets than between money balances and real assets. An example may help to illustrate the importance of this difference of view. Assume that the authorities undertake open-market sales of public sector debt (effectively to the non-bank private sector). The Keynesian would argue that interest rates would be forced upwards by the open-market sales (and by the resulting shortage of cash in relation to the volume of transactions to be financed). Interest rates would not rise by much, however, because an increase in rates on financial assets, such as finance house deposits, which were close substitutes for money, would make people prepared to organise their affairs with smaller money balances. The authorities would therefore have reduced the money supply without much effect on financial markets. Because expenditure decisions would be affected only by the second-round effect of changes in conditions in financial markets, and not directly by the fall in the quantity of money, there would be little reason to expect much reduction in expenditures as a result – both because the interest-rate changes would be small and because of the apparent insensitivity of many forms of expenditure to such small changes in interest rates.

The monetarist would agree that interest rates on financial assets would be forced upwards by the initial open-market sales. This increase in rates would not, however, tend to restore equilibrium by making people satisfied to maintain a lower ratio of money balance to total incomes or to wealth. The initial sales of financial assets (as part of the open-market operation), resulting in higher interest rates, would only bring about a short-run partial equilibrium in financial markets. In other words, because of the fall in their price, people would wish to hold more of these financial assets and this would be achieved through the open-market sales. The counterpart to the desire to hold more of the cheaper financial assets would not, probably, be to hold smaller money balances but rather to hold less of other goods. It, therefore, follows that such open-market sales enable people to make the desired changes in their portfolio of non-monetary financial assets but leave them holding too little money. Full equilibrium, including the market for goods, would be re-established only when the desired ratio of money balances to incomes was restored. This would be achieved (and could only be achieved) by a reduction in real expenditures. Which expenditures would be cut back would depend on the response to the changing pattern, overall, of prices (yields) on the full range of assets, set in motion by the initial monetary disturbance. In sum, monetary policy, by causing a reduction in the quantity of money, would bring about a nearly proportionate fall in expenditures elsewhere in the economy. In the meantime, interest rates, initially forced upwards by the authorities' activities in undertaking open-market sales, would have drifted back down as the deflationary effect of the restrictive monetary policy spread over the economy, affecting both the demand for capital (borrowing) in the markets and the rate of price inflation.

I have little doubt that, once again, the monetarists had the best of this argument. If one receives a windfall gift of money, the normal response is not to place the funds in some interest-bearing financial asset but to purchase a range of assets, real and financial. If so, then tests for the efficacy of monetary policy that assume that such effects work through a limited set of channels are simply incorrectly designed. Monetarists never challenged the findings of low interest elasticities of expenditure in the individual 'structural' expenditure functions. Instead, they claimed that these were irrelevant for an examination of the direct connections between money and nominal incomes.

At an earlier stage in this debate, there was some confusion whether Milton Friedman, and the monetarists more generally, were content to work within the IS/LM paradigm[1] and were actually arguing that the interest elasticity of expenditure was, in reality, high – but that the estimates derived from the individual structural equations were, for one reason or another, biased – or whether they were actually denying the basic paradigm. There were, indeed, occasions when Friedman appeared to be prepared to set his own analysis within the *IS-LM* framework. In my view, this was a temporary aberration and, in the main, the monetarists adopted the more radical approach of rejecting key elements – notably the absence of any direct substitution between money and goods – in the Keynesian paradigm.

In order to study these more direct links, the monetarists examined the relationship between changes in nominal incomes (or in real output) in aggregate and current and past changes in the money stock (or in real balances). Indeed, it is doubtful whether the results of the empirical estimates of expenditure functions, showing relatively little impact of financial variables upon expenditures, would have been so questioned and challenged if it had not been for such further, and quite different, sets of empirical results showing for the United States a close relationship between changes in money incomes and current and prior movements in the money stock. The following equation fitted well:

$$\Delta Y_t = b1 \Delta M_t + b2 \Delta M_{t-1}, \ldots, bn \Delta M_{t-n} + cX$$

where X is a vector of other included explanatory variables and c is the associated vector of coefficients.

It may, however, be noted that relationships of this kind were not equally good in all countries; in particular, in the United Kingdom, such relationships in general fitted quite poorly in the early tests of such relationships.[2] Nevertheless, a statistically strong relationship was then found in the United States and in some other countries.[3]

The crucial point was that this finding appeared to be inconsistent with the conclusion that financial variables did not strongly affect expenditures. To be sure, it does not follow that, even where there are only weak monetary effects, monetary changes would never be associated with changes in money incomes. If the changes in the money stock were associated with increases in budget deficits, with current-account surpluses, or with an increased demand to borrow for investment purposes from entrepreneurs, then both the rise in money incomes and in the money stock would be associated with additional income-creating expenditures. If, on the other hand, the rise in the money stock was the counterpart of some financial transaction – say, an open-market operation – then a Keynesian would argue that, with an interest

---

[1] See his articles 'A Theoretical Framework for Monetary Analysis' (1970) pp. 193–238, and 'A Monetary Theory of Nominal Income' (1971a) pp. 232–7. Also note the resulting symposium commenting on Friedman's position in the *Journal of Political Economy* (1972) in the special issue on Monetary Theory, with contributions by Brunner and Meltzer, Tobin, Davidson, and Patinkin with a response by Friedman (pp. 837–950).

[2] See among others, Artis and Nobay (1969) pp. 37–42, and Goodhart and Crockett (1970) Appendix II, pp. 197–8.

[3] Much of this work was undertaken by the economists at the Federal Reserve Bank of St Louis and published in their *Review*. The most influential of these papers was the study by Andersen and Jordan (1968) pp. 11–23. Further papers extending this approach to a wider selection of countries were presented by Keran (1970a) pp. 8–19 and (1970b) pp. 16–28.

elasticity of demand for money relatively greater than of demand for goods, the resulting effect on relative yields should exhaust itself mainly in causing readjustments in financial markets with little impact on real expenditure. Given that view of the relative elasticities, the relationship between changes in the money stock and in money incomes should be variable as the economic developments associated with the changes in the money stock alter. In particular, the relationship between changes in the endogenous element of expenditures, mainly consumption, and in the 'exogenous' expenditures (e.g., government expenditure, exports, etc.) should be expected to be closer than the relationship of these same endogenous expenditures with changes in the money supply.

Friedman and Meiselman tested this relationship for the United States and found the opposite to be true, that the money multiplier was more stable then the 'Keynesian' multiplier.[1] Considerable further empirical digging[2] suggested that it was a moot point whether or not the one statistical relationship fitted better than the other. In a sense, such fine comparisons were somewhat beside the point: even if the Keynesian multiplier fitted very well also, it was undeniable that in the United States – though not in the United Kingdom – there was at times in the 1970s a very good statistical fit between monetary changes and subsequent changes in money incomes.

Such studies of the 'direct' relationships between monetary changes and movements in prices and output became entangled with a number of primarily econometric issues, such as the nature of 'causality' in economic systems and methods for structuring a set of equations to test for such causality, issues that are not central to our current concerns and will not be discussed here.[3] A further development that occurred in the context of the widespread application of rational expectations at the end of the 1970s and the 1980s involved the prediction that the effect of monetary changes upon the economy might differ depending on whether these were anticipated or unanticipated. This latter issue will be taken up in detail in Chapter 13; however, in order to recall the developing chronology of the macro-economic debates in recent decades, it is perhaps better to review the state of the discussion prior to the onset of the latest neo-classical, rational expectations analytical approach.

Tests for the importance of variable A (B,C,D) in influencing variable X most usually came to take the form of vector auto-regressions, in which variable X was regressed on its own past values and on prior values of other variables, which were thought likely to affect it:

$$X_t = f(X_t - 1, X_t - 2, \ldots X_t - n, A_t - 1, A_t - 2, \ldots A_t - n)$$

If the prior values of variable A helped to explain changes in variable X, having taken into account X's own past history, then there was some possibility that A might be influencing X. This was only a possibility, however, since variable A could just be acting as a proxy for certain other incorrectly omitted variables.

A wide range of studies were conducted along these lines for the USA, the UK and a variety of other countries. In general, during the 1970s, it was possible to find at least some definitions of the money stock whose prior movements appeared to influence the development of prices and output (nominal incomes) in this particular

[1] (1963).

[2] See the paper by Poole and Kornblith, 'The Friedman–Meiselman CMC Paper: New Evidence on an old Controversy' (1973) pp. 908–17.

[3] Those wishing to pursue this subject further might like to consult Sims (1971) pp. 540–52; and Granger (1969) pp. 424–38. See also Leamer (1985) and Pierce and Haugh (1977) pp. 265–93.

sense.[1] There were, however, some studies that suggested that when a wider range of other variables, including interest rates, were also entered into such a vector auto-regression, the significance of prior monetary changes diminished.

Much energy was devoted to such studies in the 1970s, but it petered out in the 1980s. Attention switched to the distinction between anticipated and unanticipated monetary changes but the results often seemed inconclusive; in the course of the 1980s, moreover, the stability of demand for money functions eroded, as described earlier in Chapter 4, so that velocity became less stable and all linkages between money and nominal incomes became subject to greater uncertainty. In this latter context, it was no longer clear whether the direct relationships between money and nominal incomes were closer and more stable than could be satisfactorily explained within the Keynesian paradigm.

Nevertheless, prior to this later breakdown of monetary stability, there had been a long period during the late 1960s and 1970s during which the direct relationship between monetary aggregates and nominal incomes appeared to be closer than seemed consistent with the Keynesian model. Keynesians frequently sought to explain this as resulting from 'reverse causation'. As noted in Chapter 10, the authorities in practice usually set interest rates, rather than trying to control the monetary base directly. Keynesians generally accepted the econometric findings of the stability of the demand for money.[2] Accordingly, if there was a stable function:

$$Md = f(Y,i)$$

and i was set by the authorities, then M would fluctuate in line with movements in Y. Indeed, Keynesians have noted that, once the authorities really determined to control the growth of the money stock (e.g., in the USA and UK in 1979 and the subsequent few years) this coincided with the weakening of the predictability of velocity.

One obvious problem with this response is that the vector auto-regressions often showed *prior* changes in M influencing present changes in Y; indeed, it was accepted that contemporaneous correlation was entirely ambiguous about the direction of 'causality'. The reverse causality argument suggested, however, that prior changes in Y should influence current changes in M and *not* the other way around. The lead of changes in money balances over money incomes could thus hardly be explained on the grounds that money holders were seeking to adjust these in anticipation of changing future expected transaction requirements.[3] It would involve an opportunity cost in forgone interest receipts to build up money balances significantly in advance of anticipated requirements. Moreover, is it to be believed that households, who hold the bulk of the money stock, are likely to be good predictors of future changes in their incomes and expenditures?

A more interesting question, however, is whether the authorities might be able to predict future developments. Assume that the authorities want to achieve some desired level for an economic variable, say national income Y. The level of national income will be affected by a number of disturbances (e.g., foreign developments and population trends) which they cannot control, described by a vector Q. The authorities can command, more or less, a number of policy instruments (control tools) which they can influence, say $X1, \ldots, Xn$. Let $X1$ be a policy instrument which is known to have a positive but lagged effect on incomes, so that

---

[1] See Litterman and Weiss (1985) pp. 129–56 and Williams *et al.* (1976) pp. 417–23.

[2] Though see Hardy and Ericsson (1983).

[3] This argument was, however, put forward by Davidson and Weintraub (1973) pp. 1117–32, especially pp. 1117–19.

$$\frac{dY_t}{dX_1} \simeq 0 \text{ but } \frac{dY_{t+n}}{dX_1} > 0$$

Expressing the deviation of actual from desired incomes as a function of current disturbances, Q and from the lagged policy instrument, we can write:

$$Y_t - Y^* = b_1 X_{1,t-n} + b_2 Q_t$$

Clearly, if the authorities are using that instrument X_1 for stabilisation purposes, then they will aim to set

$$X_{1,t-n} = \frac{-b_2}{b_1} Q_t$$

In reality, of course, the authorities are uncertain of the lags in the system, the values of b_2 and b_1, and at times $t - n$ when they have to set the value of X, they are uncertain about the future values of Q. Under such circumstances, they will be lucky to fix X just right to offset all other disturbances and they will likely over or under adjust.

If the authorities were accurate forecasters of future movements in Q, the sign of the correlation between X_{t-n} and $Y - Y^*$ would depend only on whether they were able exactly to offset movements in Q – which would bring about a zero correlation ($r = 0$) – or whether they over-adjusted ($r > 0$), or under-adjusted ($r < 0$) their actions.[1] Thus, if the authorities can forecast with some accuracy future exogenous disturbances, the correlations between money incomes and various alternative forms of control tool, say the growth in the money stock and/or the fiscal deficit, cannot be simply interpreted as measuring their net effects on the economy. Instead, the results represent a combination of their direct economic impact plus their systematic covariation with other economic factors not included in this equation. One might thus even wonder whether the much stronger correlation in the United States between the money stock and money incomes than between fiscal variables and money incomes implied a more effective use of fiscal policy than of monetary policy as a contra-cyclical stabilising device, rather than providing evidence of their direct economic effects. It should be repeated, however, that this does depend on the possibility of accurate forecasting because, otherwise, there is unlikely to be any systematic covariation with excluded exogenous disturbances.

Although it is possible on these and other grounds[2] to argue that the timing relationship between movements in the money stock and in money incomes, observed in past decades in the United States, need not prove the existence of a causal chain running from monetary changes to variations in money incomes, it does constitute a powerful presumption for this hypothesis. The onus really came on those who did not believe in the implied causal link to provide evidence of an alternative explanation of the relationship. A number of hypotheses were put forward to suggest possible explanations but there was no hard evidence produced to support these hypotheses.

A further argument advanced by Friedman to support the claim that the direct relationship was 'caused' was that the authorities' handling of, and approach to, monetary policy and control has varied at different times (i.e., in differing monetary

---

[1] On this subject, see Peston (1972) pp. 427–31; Goldfeld and Blinder (1972) pp. 585–640, with comments and discussion, pp. 641–4; Kochin (1972).

[2] See, for example, Tobin (1970) pp. 801–17, and the subsequent 'Comment on Tobin' by Friedman (1970) and 'Rejoinder' by Tobin (1970) pp. 318–29.

regimes such as the gold standard, periods of pegged interest rates and periods of relatively successful (1960s) and unsuccessful discretionary policy (interwar period and 1970s). Yet, over such long periods, despite the changing regimes, the broad nature of the relationships remained unchanged. A sceptic might respond that, until 1979, in *all* the prior regimes the authorities had given the main emphasis to managing the level and structure of interest rates. Moreover, the basic institutional framework had also remained relatively constant. Both these conditions were to be upset in the early 1980s.

A supporting argument to the above, outlined in Section 3 of Chapter 10, is that the level of interest rates established by the authorities may encourage credit expansion that will cause a change in the money supply, and force it out of line with the demand for money that would accord with the levels of incomes and the (policy determined) levels of interest rates then occurring. Since the credit market is distinct from the money market – but the interest rates ruling in the two markets are closely linked – the fact that the authorities are determining interest rates in the short-run does *not* mean that the money supply naturally moves into immediate equilibrium with the demand for money. There can still be autonomous money supply shocks and certainly in the UK such shocks have affected the time path of M3 (earlier £M3), though not so clearly having any affect on the narrower aggregates.

3. Buffer-stock Money

In several respects, then, the monetarists had the better of the arguments with the Keynesians. At least until the mid-1970s, the demand for money did appear to be a predictable function of a few variables and exhibited relatively low interest elasticity. The Keynesian claim that monetary policy affected the economy only through certain narrowly defined financial channels appeared hard to sustain – though it remained tenaciously defended by many mainstream Keynesians, and informs the structure of most Keynesian models. The monetarist claim that there are forces and factors affecting the money *supply* independently of the variables in the demand for money function, *even* when the authorities are pegging interest rates, appears justified when the monetary aggregate is broadly defined (M3, though generally less so when it is narrowly defined (M1). The evidence from the reduced form (e.g., VAR) studies of the direct relationships between money and incomes – at least prior to the 1980s – while inconclusive, nevertheless seemed somewhat more consistent with monetarist than with Keynesian prior expectations.

On the other hand, some of the internal dynamics of the monetarist system have seemed implausible and even inconsistent. The Keynesian *IS/LM* paradigm is based on the reasonable assumption that financial markets (e.g., bond prices and interest rates) adjust relatively quickly, whereas prices in goods markets respond slowly (indeed in the *IS/LM* model they are fixed in the short run). It is thus perfectly consistent for equilibrium in the money market to be achieved initially by a rapid adjustment of financial prices and yields which then lead first to output changes, with the relatively long lags built into expenditure functions, and thence to price changes, depending on the lags inherent in the Phillips curve. The monetarists perceive, indeed have emphasised, the same lags in the adjustment of output, and thence of prices, to monetary stimuli, while at the same time insisting that money demand and money supply are always equilibrated (e.g., following money supply shocks); moreover, such equilibration in their model is not achieved at the outset entirely by changes in prices and yields in financial markets. Friedman has thus, claimed[1] that output changes respond to innovations in monetary growth with a lag of about nine months, and that such monetary stimuli are then largely exhausted in price adjustments after about two years.

However, if the money stock (Ms) is partly exogenously determined, if the demand for money function (Md) includes long lags, and if the instantaneous equilibration of Ms and Md does *not* come about entirely, or primarily, through changes in interest rates, then the other variables in the demand for money function, real incomes and prices, *must* exhibit initial overshooting (not inertia and slow adjustment) in order to equilibrate the demand and supply for money. So, the relatively slow adjustment of output and even slower adjustment of prices to monetary stimuli seem inconsistent with the instantaneous equilibration of money demand and money supply in money markets. There are several possible answers to this conundrum. As reported above, Keynesians claim that such equilibration (of Ms and Md) *does* occur initially entirely via changes in interest rates – and that Ms is rarely exogenously determined. As will be described in Chapter 13, neo-classicists, assuming a combination of rational expectations and perfectly clearing markets, argue that prices will adjust instantaneously to *anticipated* changes in the money stock whereas the adjustments in real output occur in response only to changes in unanticipated monetary growth. While expectations are probably best modelled as being 'rational' (whatever that may mean exactly in a complex world where information gathering, storage and manipulation are costly, for reasons set out in Chapter 1), I am disinclined to believe that most market prices exhibit complete flexibility.

There is, however, a further potential explanation of this conundrum, which is that agents do not have a single-valued demand function for money, but treat it as a buffer stock. This concept of buffer stock money was explored earlier in Chapter 4, Section 3, where some of the arguments, such as whether the existence of individual monetary buffer stocks could plausibly be extended to account for a significant aggregate buffering effect,[2] were examined. Most of the studies of buffer-stock money, both empirical and theoretical,[3] have concluded that the analytical approach is better suited to a broad money concept (e.g., M3). In this case, variations in the credit counterparts may drive the actual stock of money away from the 'underlying' demand for money – as represented by the aggregate sum of return points for money balances which agents would re-establish after hitting a limit in their individual buffers, see the earlier discussions in Chapters 4, Section 3, and Chapter 10, Section 3. The immediate effect of the money supply shock, such as a surge in bank lending to the private sector, say caused by a removal of government controls, is thus partly met by a change in financial conditions (e.g., interest rate changes) but largely initially balanced by a passive build-up of broadly defined monetary balances (M3). Since this build-up would be taking a larger proportion of agents up towards, or over, their limits, assuming occasional and costly monitoring for the latter case, the excess of the actual money stock (M3), determined by supply-side conditions in credit markets,

---

[1] See Friedman and Schwartz (1982) p. 407, and Brillenbourg and Khan (1979).

[2] As Milbourne demonstrates (1987) when monitoring of monetary balances is instantaneous and costless, individual buffering behaviour does not translate into significant aggregate buffering, since the large jumps to the return point of those hitting a limit will offset the internal moves within the limits. If monetary monitoring is only occasional and/or costly, buffering behaviour can have much greater aggregate effect.

[3] See Milbourne (1987) pp. 130–42 and Laidler (1984) pp. 17–34.

over the 'underlying' demand for money should then be an additional factor influencing expenditures.

This formulation has a number of attractive features, especially perhaps for monetarists of the more traditional school (i.e., *not* rational expectation – perfect clearing market neo-classicists).[1] It shows exactly how monetary shocks can drive expenditures,[2] apart from the well-known interest rate route: it allows an 'underlying' demand for money function with long lags to coexist with relatively long lags between monetary stimuli and subsequent effects on output and, thence, on prices, and it emphasizes the separate existence and nature of the markets for credit and for money, and treats interactions between these as having a crucial impact on the dynamics of the macro-economic system as a whole, a point forcibly made in several papers by Brunner and Meltzer.[3] Keynesians should also find the concept of financial buffers in a world of uncertainty with slow-adjusting goods and labour markets inherently appealing. Its adoption would allow them to avoid both the problem that overshooting appears an inherent feature of a system with long lags in the demand for money function and the implausibility of the assumption that all initial adjustments to monetary shocks occur through associated changes in prices in a narrow set of financial markets. Indeed, I had hoped earlier that some general acceptance of this approach might provide the basis for a reconciliation between monetarists and Keynesians.[4]

Yet, acceptance of the buffer-stock notion has been somewhat patchy and limited, especially in North America. This is partly due to remaining doubts whether the buffering concept (e.g., as devised by Miller and Orr at the micro-level) can be properly translated to the aggregate economy. It is partly because the vanguard of theoretical macro-economists, notably in the USA, have espoused the neo-classical model – in which prices *do* adjust instantaneously to anticipated monetary changes – in recent years, which provides an alternative set of answers to the internal conundrums inherent in traditional monetarist dynamics.

More generally, the buffer-stock money approach has proved quite difficult to model empirically and has not shown sufficiently improved empirical results to induce existing model builders, whether Keynesian or otherwise, to incorporate this additional feature into their own models. Probably the best recent example of an attempt to incorporate buffer-stock money into a small macro-economic model of the UK is that constructed by Davidson.[5] in this model, the broad money stock (M3) is determined in the short run by the credit counterparts (through the balance sheet identity whereby bank liabilities must equal bank assets, see Chapter 10, Section 3 and Chapter 6). Then,

> The scheme used to model money and related variables is an *error correction system*. Briefly, a relation of the general form:

$$\frac{M}{PY} = F(Y, r_1, r_s, p)$$

[where r_1 is a long-term rate of interest, r_s a short rate] is assumed to represent a target,

---

[1] As Bordo, for example, has recognised in some of his recent papers, referred to in Bordo (1986) pp. 339–415.

[2] In effect it refutes the old Keynesian taunt that the direct links between money and incomes operated through a hidden 'black box'.

[3] See Meltzer (1986) pp. 161–94.

[4] Goodhart (1984a) Chapter X, pp. 272–3 especially.

[5] 'Disequilibrium Money: Some Further Results with a Monetary Model of the UK' (1987).

towards which (the inverse velocity of) money would tend in a steady state. The deviation of the right-hand from the left-hand side of [the equation above, with M on the left-hand side given by the credit counterparts], denoted V, is embedded in a system of dynamic adjustment equations describing the evolution of money-stock components [credit counterparts], income and commodity and security prices (Davidson, 1987, p. 130).

Thus, the deviation from the underlying demand function (V) enters again as a potential explanatory variable in the individual structural equations modelling the dynamic adjustments of all the other structural variables, including the credit counterparts themselves – e.g., bank lending to the private sector, real expenditures, goods prices, exchange rate, etc. Econometrically, this involved the use of cross-equation restrictions, since deviations from one equation are being entered as arguments in other equations in the system. 'The (incomplete) system is estimated by a variant of non-linear Three Stage Least Squares.' Thus, like the earlier model of the Australian economy (RBA 76) by Jonson, Moses and Wymer,[1] based on a similar buffer-stock approach, the econometric methods applied were somewhat complex.

Empirical problems with this approach extend well beyond mere complexity. This approach to modelling is, in practice, at least as reliant as any monetarist model, or perhaps more so, on there being stability in the underlying demand for money. Buffer-stock models attempt to separate out transient money supply shocks from the underlying demand function. However, if the latter function is itself behaving in an unpredictable fashion, then this exercise becomes extremely difficult. On the other hand, if the world is, indeed, characterised both by transient money supply shocks, which are largely passively buffered, and by occasional shifts in money demand functions, then there is no alternative to this difficult exercise.

There is, however, an even more fundamental complication which goes right to the heart of the question of why the money stock, in one of its many definitions may, or may not, be a crucial strategic variable within the economic system. Certain earlier critics of the buffer stock approach, notably Kaldor[2] and White,[3] argued that another major route whereby any excess holding of money would be extinguished without affecting real expenditures would be via repayment of outstanding bank borrowing. A transient supply shock, say in the form of unusually large public sector payments not funded by debt sales, might then be largely offset by a reduction in private-sector bank borrowing, with no increase in the money stock, rather than by a commensurate increase in the monetary balances of the private sector. Some such offset will, of course, occur. Note that this is specifically modelled in Davidson's paper, where the monetary deviation (V) enters as a significant variable, albeit with a lag, reducing bank lending.

More important, the crucial, strategic importance of money must rest on capital market imperfections of the kind described in Chapters 1 and 2. If markets were perfect, individual agents could always remedy any monetary shortage by borrowing against their expected human wealth at the interest rate appropriate to their correctly estimated risk class. Lack of information, lack of trust, etc. drive a wedge between the rates at which agents can lend and those at which they can borrow. So, many agents

---

[1] Jonson, Moses and Wymer, 'The RBA76 model of the Australian economy' (1977).
[2] (1980).
[3] (1981).

face effective capital markets constraints which prevent them from borrowing to adjust their liquid assets. Accordingly, the need for liquidity (e.g., to meet the cash-in-advance constraint, see Chapter 2) which is also essentially due to the same market imperfections, represents for many agents a strategic constraint. Where borrowing opportunities are limited or restricted by high cost, and where repayment schedules on existing debt are frequently fixed, money balances represent the key financial buffer. Thus, for individuals and smaller firms, the role of money as a key financial variable and buffer stock seems justified.

As reviewed earlier in Chapters 3 and 5, however, capital market imperfections are less prominent for larger firms and public bodies. The spread between borrowing and lending rates narrows in their case. When this spread or margin narrows sufficiently, such agents may choose, and indeed regularly do so, to hold simultaneously both deposit liabilities and have outstanding borrowings, and to vary the gross amounts of both up or down as the spread narrows or widens. In the absence of market imperfections, the volume of monetary balances is chosen as part of a wider portfolio adjustment exercise depending on relative interest rates; and the wider importance of variations in this one asset would be limited. Put another way, the economic behaviour of governments and other public-sector bodies, who can borrow under central government guarantee, is *not* significantly constrained by their monetary holdings. As large corporations find that their credit ratings come to approximate those of governments, their actions also will not be constrained by their monetary holdings. In the case of many corporations, market imperfections involved in raising long-term finance, notably the relatively heavy costs and long time delays, may make the *net* liquid asset–liability position *the* key financial buffer for them.[1]

The importance of monetary holdings, and the question of which assets may act as the main financial buffer, are thus not necessarily homogeneous across all agents and sectors of the economy, but may differ depending on the precise financial market conditions that each agent–sector faces. This naturally makes both economic and econometric analysis rather difficult, especially at times when financial market conditions and the extent of market imperfections are changing rapidly. Indeed, as such imperfections disappear, the question whether money either matters or has any clear identification may well become more pressing. At the limit, economic behaviour will be constrained by total (human and non-human) wealth, given relative prices, and the importance attached to certain sub-sets of liquid assets by Keynesians and Monetarists alike may diminish. Even if this were to occur, there would still be a demand for high-powered base money, assuming that convertibility of bank deposits into government-issued fiat base money remains in place, as seems most probable. The authorities can then still operate via their control over the issue of such base money, and hence over nominal interest rates, to affect nominal variables and inflation, see Chapter 10. But fluctuations in the various monetary aggregates may cease to serve as accurate indicators of how to shift policy.

4. Wealth Effects

In perfect markets expenditures would thus depend only on total (human and non-human) wealth and relative prices, including interest rates of course, and not on

---

[1] See the study on 'An empirical model of company short-term financial decisions', by Chowdhury, Green and Miles (1986).

holdings of particular sub-sets of assets. Where imperfections exist, however, shocks to the amount of certain strategic variables, such as money balances, can influence economic behaviour independently of their overall effect on wealth and relative prices by relaxing certain constraints on behaviour caused by these imperfections.

In the previous three sections, we have been considering the effect of changes in nominal monetary balances caused by supply-side shocks, whether induced by authorities or otherwise. In this section, we consider changes in real monetary balances caused by price changes. The greater bulk of the money supply consists of bank deposits which are matched through the balance sheet identity with bank assets. Most of these assets now represent claims on the private sector. Thus, at 30 June 1987, £ deposit liabilities of the UK banking sector to the non-bank private sector amounted to 170.2bn, while £ claims of the UK banking sector on the non-bank private sector amounted to £ 183.2bn.

When there is a nominal increase in both bank lending to, and bank deposits of, the UK private sector, there is no net change in wealth; however, the increase in lending will have been generally voluntarily chosen in order to provide funds for some kind of expenditures. As these expenditures are undertaken, the process will not only involve an increase in incomes and wealth, but may also relax liquidity constraints. The process is thus unambiguously expansionary. The same cannot be said when there is a change in real money balances offset by an exactly similar change in real bank lending to the private sector occasioned by an (unanticipated) change in prices. Net wealth will not have changed. The outcome may depend on differing reactions among the gainers and losers. In a world characterised by market imperfections and bankruptcy costs, any serious unforseen change is quite likely to force losers to react more abruptly and forcefully than gainers. Thus, at times of unanticipated inflation, personal-sector depositors may well reduce their consumption – to rebuild their depleted liquid assets – by more than companies, benefiting from a fall in the real value of their borrowing, expand investment. Indeed, there was evidence in the 1970s and 1980s that the propensity to consume in the UK was a negative function of unanticipated inflation.[1] *Per contra*, at times of unanticipated deflation the reduction of company expenditures may well exceed any stimulus from higher consumption, given matching changes in real assets and liability values. In the face of such imperfections, a major unanticipated change, despite having a symmetric effect on the real value of assets and liabilities, may still exert a strong deflationary effect on total expenditures. There may also, of course, be further distributional effects, but we shall not pursue this issue.

Cases where unanticipated inflation *may* have asymmetric effects on the value of the private sector's financial wealth are, perhaps, of more interest. The simple schema of the banking system's balance sheet may be written down once again, as

Liabilities	Assets
Deposits of public sector	Cash
Deposits of private sector	Other financial claims on public sector
Capital	Financial claims on private sector
	Real assets

---

[1] As discussed by Hendry and von Ungern Sternberg 'Liquidity and inflation effects on consumers' expenditure (1981).

First, even assuming for the moment that public-sector deposits exactly balance the claims of banks on the public sector, private-sector bank deposits will rarely exactly equal bank claims on the private sector. In order to ensure solvency and to provide a buffer against adverse contingencies, a bank will generally have a capital base, of equity and various forms of longer-dated bonds – whose claims are subordinate to those of deposits – in excess of the value of real assets (e.g., bank buildings, computers, etc.). An unanticipated change in price levels will, therefore, also change the real value of bank capital. The actual *market* value of bank capital will also respond, however, to expectations of bad debts and to expectations of possible changes in the net interest income of banks as prices change. Since traditionally, until the 1980s, most demand (sight) deposits offered zero nominal interest payments, some inflation might benefit bank profits by easing the bad debt position of borrowers and by raising expected nominal interest rates and hence the spread over sight deposits. On the other hand, with the amount of nominal bank asset claims greater than the nominal amount of bank deposit liabilities, it would erode the existing real value of bank capital. One reason for noting that (unanticipated) price changes will affect the real market value of bank capital, as well as of bank deposits, is that some earlier authors claimed that the ability to issue means of payment at zero interest provided a source of wealth to the issuer, so that an increase in the real volume of such deposits, whether matched by banks' claims on the private sector or not, would represent an increase in wealth.[1] This analysis by Pesek and Saving[2] always struck me as unnecessarily complex and convoluted. The kernel of reality in it was that institutional (e.g., regulatory) and other structural considerations would influence the capital base and profitability of banking. When considering the effect of changes in the real value of bank assets and liabilities, it would be quite common, but mistaken, to overlook the associated effect on the real market value of bank capital.

The key distinction in this literature, however, is between those private-sector money balances that are matched by (can be netted off against) bank claims on the private sector, which are usually described as *inside money*, and those money balances, which are matched by net claims on the public sector or foreign assets, *outside money*. Unquestionably, if the real value of our claims on foreigners increases, then we are better off. The more interesting question has been whether it is possible to say that the private sector is better off if the value of its claims on the public sector has increased, whether these are held directly or intermediated via the banking system.

If such public-sector debts have been incurred to purchase real assets, then, of course, the profits, if any, from such assets can be used to pay off the interest and principal on the government bonds, and the analysis is no different from that in which the private sector raises funds by selling bonds or equities to finance the acquisition of real assets. But how should one address those cases when government bonds are part of the National Debt (i.e., not backed by real assets), perhaps because the debt was earlier incurred to finance defence expenditures or transfer payments to others (i.e., expenditures that did not lead to the acquisition of real assets providing some positive future cash flows)? I shall abstract from analysis of the case when the real value of government debt is increased by a current public-sector deficit since that depends in some large part on whether the economy was, or was not, initially at an equilibrium full employment level, and whether therefore the bond issue might be associated with

---

[1] On this see Pesek and Saving (1967).

[2] It evoked much interest at the time with reviews and commentaries by a number of economists, notably Friedman and Schwartz (1969).

a temporary, or permanent, increase in the country's real output and, therefore, in its tax base.

Instead, let us concentrate on the case in which there has been an unanticipated price change leading to a change in the present real value of the promised nominal flow of coupon and redemption payments on government bonds. Has the wealth of the private sector changed? The first answer is that it has *not* since, ignoring net claims of non-residents, we owe the National Debt to ourselves. We may either expect that debt to be repudiated or inflated away (a form of repudiation), in which case its present value will be less, or to be financed in future periods by tax finance. Let us concentrate on the final option, that coupons and redemptions will be financed by future taxes. Then, if we can use the same discount rate to discount both future payments to bond holders and tax receipts, then the present value of the tax payments will equal the present value of public-sector bond debt. An unanticipated fall in prices raising the present value of bond indebtedness will raise the present value of taxation by the same amount. Wealth has not changed. This is known as the Ricardian Equivalence Theorem.[1] Moreover, if the higher real value of taxes is not levied in lump sum form, it may have adverse incentive effects, reducing future equilibrium real output.

The counter-argument was then raised that the increased real value of government bonds, following an unanticipated fall in prices, was a tangible, immediate, observable phenomenon. *Per contra*, the countervailing increase in taxation would occur only in future; its incidence would be uncertain, and it would largely fall on future generations. In his brilliant paper, 'Are Government Bonds Net Wealth?'[2] Barro argued that so long as each generation cares about the consumption prospects of the next generation (i.e., the consumption of generation 2 enters the utility function of generation 1), then the system can effectively be analysed as if people had infinite lives.

If generation 1 had achieved the optimal balance between their own consumption and the consumption of generation 2, involving a non-negative bequest of funds to generation 2, then an increase in the present value of bonds matched by an increase in future taxation reducing generation 2's consumption[3] possibilities would simply be undone by raising the level of bequest in order to return to the initial equilibrium. Moreover, if individuals are risk averse, the uncertainty about the future incidence of taxes may even induce them to save *more* in order to protect generation 2's consumption against the risk that taxation might fall unduly upon ones own children. In a world of continuing generations, each so concerned with the next generation's consumption as to have a non-negative bequest motive, there is thus a theoretical case that government bonds should not be treated as net wealth.

In Section 3, we eventually came to the conclusion that concern with the strategic importance of certain sub-sets of financial assets (e.g., with the monetary aggregates) lay primarily in the existence of certain market imperfections, constraints and rigidities, without which expenditures would depend solely on total wealth and

---

[1] See Chapter III in Tobin (1980) for an extended discussion of the implications of the Theorem.

[2] (1974).

[3] The analysis goes through even if some of the taxation is expected to fall on generation 3 or beyond; since generation 2 is concerned with generation's 3 consumption, a prospective fall in the latter will raise the size of bequests generation 2 wish to make and reduce their planned consumption at the same time.

relative prices. One such constraint is that one cannot easily force future generations to make transfers back to the present (i.e., to require negative bequests). Yet, as shown diagrammatically in Figure 12.3, the unconstrained optimum position might well be at point X with a negative bequest rather than at point Z with a positive bequest. This could occur because some of generation 1 were childless, or because generation 1 might reasonably appreciate that economic growth might lead their children to have a higher standard of living than their own. Because of the difficulty of forcing future generations to contribute to the present generation's consumption, most people are probably at corner solution Y.[1] The rise in the present value of government bonds may then allow the present generation to circumvent the non-negative bequest constraint and raise present consumption.

In our earlier assessment of the factors imparting strategic importance to money, the imperfection to which particular attention was paid was the wedge between the

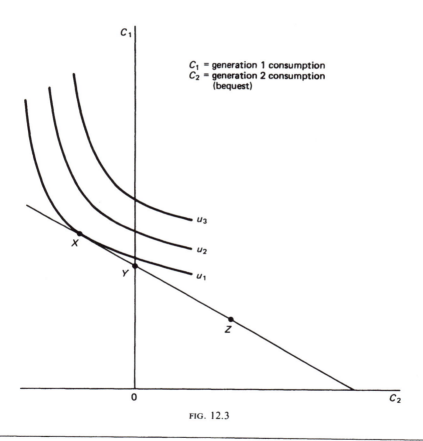

FIG. 12.3

returns on saving and the cost of borrowing for individuals and less-well-known companies. The increased value of their holding of public-sector debt would make it less necessary for such agents to borrow – at rates well above the risk-less rate available to government – or would provide them with sufficient collateral to borrow at lower rates, thus relaxing a liquidity constraint on their inter-temporal life-cycle choice of consumption patterns. More generally, a one-time switch from tax finance to bond finance will allow those whose effective rates of time discount is higher then average, but could not borrow because of imperfections and contraints, to spend more, whereas those with relatively low rates of time discount will buy the bonds, partly to offset the future, uncertain, heavier incidence tax. If output was already constrained by full employment supply limitations, there would be a rise in consumption balanced by an increase in real interest rates and a fall in investment; otherwise, output would rise. In any case, the switch would have real effects.[2]

The question of whether a change in the real value of government bonds represents a change in net wealth is not semantically well phrased. Since in a perfectly valid sense the National Debt is owed to ourselves, a change in its value cannot really be properly classified as a change in wealth. Nevertheless, a change in the value of government bonds may well relax certain market imperfections and constraints and thus have significant effects on the real economy.

The denial that government bonds represent net wealth rests on the fact that as a country we owe such debt to ourselves and have eventually to pay off the interest and principal via higher taxes. How about the case of government currency issue where no interest need ever be paid? If the currency is convertible into a commodity (e.g., gold) or into some foreign currency (e.g., as the Hong Kong dollar is directly convertible into US dollars), then the authorities' reserves of such commodities[2] or foreign currency clearly count as national wealth. Fiat currency, however, is an asset in the hands of its holder, bears no interest and is not redeemable in terms of any other good.

Consider, however, a currency reform in which, say, 1000 old francs or lira were to be exchanged for 1 new franc or lira. Apart from rounding problems, as fractions became rounded up or down, and money illusion, nothing real should change. Next, consider a fully anticipated doubling of the money stock. Again, unless there were certain price rigidities (e.g., owing to existing contracts, etc.) or money illusion, nothing real should change. With perfectly clearing markets, any initial anticipated change in real balances, whether caused by a nominal monetary change or by some price shock, ought to lead to a subsequent adjustment in prices to restore equilibrium. If the change in prices was associated with some real change in productivity, etc, then that would obviously involve real effects; in the absence of such an effect and assuming full information, perfectly clearing markets, etc. any effect of price changes on real monetary balances should be immediately dissipated in a recovery in the general level of prices.

Any effect of monetary changes on real activity is again therefore due to market imperfections (e.g., a failure to anticipate or to observe such developments), constraints on price flexibility due to contracts and other factors causing sluggish

---

[1] All this has been well analysed in Tobin and Buiter 'Fiscal and Monetary Policies, Capital Formation, and Economic Activity' (1982).

[2] Even so, there will be some element of circularity since the market value of such a commodity will be enhanced by its monetary use in the economy.

adjustment in prices (see Chapter 1 again) and the kinds of market imperfection previously discussed in this Section. While it is possible, therefore, to describe the effect of a rise in M/p as representing a wealth effect with an impact on real economic activity, that effect would not be present in a full information perfect market clearing system. As in the case of bond finance, it is the imperfections and rigidities in the economy that give monetary policy shocks their influence over the real economy.

XIII
The Effects of Nominal Monetary Changes on Output, Employment and Inflation

Summary

In Chapter 12, the subject of the division of monetary induced expenditure changes into price, output and employment effects was largely ducked. This topic is addressed in the present chapter. A general theme, throughout the chapter, is the consideration of the imperfections that may allow a deviation of actual from potential (equilibrium) output to occur, leading to unused capacity and involuntary unemployment. In a world of certainty, there would be no undesired unemployment or disequilibria arising from incorrect and inconsistent decisions. In the real world, there is neither the information nor the marketing mechanisms (e.g., a Walrasian auctioneer) available to allow equilibrium to be achieved. In a complex, decentralised economy, in which individual decision-makers can only conjecture about the likely actions of others in the economy, there is much scope for inconsistent decision-making (e.g., by investors and savers) to lead to disequilibria. The institution of money provides the information network which enables a complex, decentralised economy to function at all. Since money is a necessary adjunct to such an economy, the disequilibria are sometimes regarded as monetary phenomena; it is, however, the inconsistency of decisions within the system, not the existence of the monetary framework, which is the proximate cause of disequilibria.

As already argued, price adjustments are not likely to be perfectly flexible and the resulting stickiness of prices will cause monetary policy changes, even when anticipated, to have real effects. Even if prices and wages did fall flexibly in response to excess capacity, this might not, however, stimulate a depressed economy if it generated expectations of further price falls. The process of sequential decision-making in modern economies tends to produce autocorrelated price movements. It may be more realistic to expect the rate of change (rather than the level) of prices to remain constant. The simple relationship between price inflation and the extent of spare capacity has thus to be adjusted to take the anticipated rate of inflation ($E\dot{P}$) into account, as expressed in the following relationship:

$$\dot{P}_t = b_0 + b_1 \frac{1}{UE_t} + b_2 E\dot{P}$$

where UE = unemployment level

In theory, b_2 should equal unity. If $E\dot{P} = \dot{P}_{t-1}$, then the *rate* of inflation will accelerate, stabilise or decline as the sum of

$$b_0 + b_1 \frac{1}{UE_t}$$

is greater, equal or less than zero. This formulation suggests that only in the short run can an advantage in higher real output and real incomes be obtained from running the economy at an inflationary pressure of demand. In the longer run, inflation would accelerate without limit, the long-run Phillips curve being vertical, and no advantage in higher real output would remain to offset the worsened rate of inflation. Earlier experience had, however, suggested that wage – price adjustments, even in the longer run, were rather less volatile than this analysis would suggest; the value of b_2 calculated in empirical studies using data from the 1950s and 1960s was usually well below unity, often in the region of 0.5. In the 1970s, however, inflation accelerated throughout the Western world, in spite of a higher average level of unemployment in many countries. This partly reflected the evaporation of the last vestiges of money illusion, a growing consciousness of inflation. The calculated value of b_2 in empirical studies then rose to unity, or sometimes even higher.

We next turn in Section 2 to consider both recent historical experience and theoretical developments with the Phillips curve inter-relationships between nominal demand, output and inflation. The main practical problem has been that the estimated position of the vertical Phillips curve, or Non-Accelerating-Inflation Rate of Unemployment (NAIRU), has tended to shift rightward – i.e., to involve a higher level of unemployment over time; in fact, the estimated rightward shifts of the NAIRU have quite closely tracked the movements of actual unemployment. We examine various suggestions to explain why this might have happened – i.e., that those with existing jobs (the insiders) adjust their wage claims in response to potential *changes* in unemployment, not to its *level*, and that the experience of unemployment may impair the human capital of the unemployed (i.e., a hysteresis effect). Whatever the explanation may be, such variability in the NAIRU further undermines any case for seeking to run the economy at some pre-selected pressure of demand or level of unemployment and it also raises questions about the usefulness of the concept itself.

The main *theoretical* interest has been the application of rational–forward looking expectations to this analysis. So long as $E\dot{P}$ was based on backward-looking-adaptive expectations, then current monetary policy would affect real output, even if only temporarily. But if expectations are forward-looking, agents will adjust their price expectations to take account of anticipated monetary policy effects, leading to the Sargent–Wallace policy impotence theorem. This suggests that unanticipated monetary changes should affect output, whereas anticipated monetary changes should not do so; empirical tests of this hypothesis, begun by Barro, have had mixed effects.

Superimposing forward looking rational expectations onto the augmented Phillips curve leads on, however, to a Lucas-type functional relationship between deviations of actual from equilibrium output on the one hand and errors (surprises) between current inflation and the rate of inflation expected for the period on the other. In its simplest form, the theory suggests that such deviations should be serially uncorrelated; this is implausible, however, because most real variables exhibit persistence in their cyclical fluctuations around their trends. Various amendments and supplements to the neo-classical model have been proposed to account for such persistence.

According to one neo-classical model, deviations from equilibrium are caused by imperfections in the transmission of information on certain key variables (e.g., national price trends or monetary growth). This seems implausible in a society where such information is rapidly and widely available at little cost to agents. In another version of the neo-classical model, the 'real' business cycle model, fluctuations are caused by stochastic technological shocks impacting on a system that remains in equilibrium: this view is not easy to square with observed unemployment. A much more likely source of market imperfection is to be found in price stickiness; such price stickiness would provide an alternative, and on this view more sensible, explanation of real-world macro-economic phenomena.

Finally, in the Appendix, we examine a case study of indexation, the UK experiment with the provision of indexed gilts from 1981. We start by considering the costs of unanticipated inflation and how indexation can theoretically reduce such costs. Against that background, we ask why practical politicians and Central Bankers have been so averse to the introduction of indexation. Then, in the second part of this Appendix, we record the various arguments that were deployed in the discussions leading up to the introduction of indexed gilts and briefly recount the resulting experience with the instrument.

1. Uncertainty, Unemployment and Price Expectations

Even if we knew the exact relationship between changes in the money stock and subsequent changes in expenditures and money incomes, there would still remain the question of the division of that change into price and output movements. It is not much help, for policy purposes, to be able to predict with reasonable accuracy that a 5 per cent increase in the money stock would lead, say, to a 4 per cent increase in money incomes, if it is not possible to forecast what proportion of that 4 per cent increase will reflect price inflation and what proportion a rise in the volume or output.

In Chapter 12, this subject of the division of expenditure changes into price and output responses was largely ducked, apart from occasional *obiter dicta*. The standard Keynesian analysis of this subject has been simple. The greater the margin of spare capacity in any industry or economy, the more the response to demand changes, expressed in nominal terms, is liable to be reflected in output changes; the nearer to full capacity, the more the response is likely to be reflected in price changes. Continuing stimulation of the economy is, therefore, likely to lead to a diminishing expansion of real output and growing inflation as spare capacity is drawn back into use. Measuring the extent of spare capacity by the level of unemployment, this implies that the short-run[1] relationships between unemployment and inflation will be non-linear, probably tracing out a hyperbola as shown in Figure 13.1, where $\dot{P}$ represents the rate of price inflation and UE the level of unemployment.

This account presupposes the possible existence of spare capacity and essentially describes the form of the commonly-observed relationships rather than explaining the reasons for them. In particular, how can unemployed resources coexist with unfulfilled wants so long as there is an efficient price mechanism? In a world of certainty, such maladjustments would not occur. Everyone would know from the outset the underlying distribution of wants on the one hand and skills and resources on the other. Each individual would be able to elect an optimal life plan of activity and expenditures consistent with equilibrium, which would entail working so long as the marginal utility, in the form of wage and work satisfaction, was greater than or equal to the marginal costs in leisure opportunities forgone. People might be 'resting' but they would be doing so by preference.

---

[1] The short run is defined here as the period during which expectations about the future, particularly about the prospective rate of inflation, are taken as given. The implications of allowing for revisions in such expectations over time are considered later in Section 2.

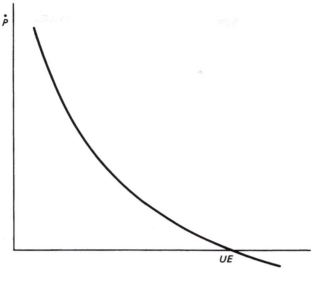

FIG. 13.1

In a world of uncertainty, there is neither the information nor the equilibrating mechanisms available to allow equilibrium to be achieved. Decision-makers have to respond as best as they can to very limited information. If sales should fall, producers have to guess whether it would be better for them to lower their offered prices or to cut back on output. Workers, combined into trade unions, have to decide whether to aim for a higher wage-low employment industry or seek to keep the industry more labour intensive by accepting lower wages.

In an atomistic free-enterprise economy, the results of the decisions of one group will often depend on the conjectured reactions of another group.[1] If I cut my price, will my competitors follow my example? If we accept a lower wage settlement, what effect will that have on other union bargains? For this and other reasons, the

---

[1] The consequences of this atomistic, sequential process of decision making are far-reaching. Consider this quotation from Clower, 'The Keynesian Counterrevolution: A Theoretical Appraisal' (1985) pp. 117–18:

> Established preference analysis tacitly presupposes that selling, buying and saving plans are all carried out simultaneously ... The notion that all household decisions are accomplished at a single stroke seems to be an analytically convenient and intuitively plausible procedure as long as we consider each household to be an isolated performer of conceptual experiments. When households are considered to be part of a connected market system, however, ... what is then presupposed about planned sales and purchases cannot possibly be true of realised sales and purchases, unless the system as a whole is always in a state of equilibrium ... If we entertain the notion of developing market models that will have practical application to situations of chronic disequilibrium, however, we must surely question the universal relevance of the 'unified decision' hypothesis and, by the same token, question whether the usual household supply and demand functions provide relevant market signals.

elasticities of response to a wage–price decision are a matter of pure conjecture. How much larger a volume of sales will be achieved by a price reduction or how many jobs will be saved by accepting lower wages are virtually impossible to forecast. Moreover, in the short run, habit and custom tend to keep price elasticities well below their long-run level. It is difficult, therefore, to point with clarity to obvious, *immediate* beneficial results of price reductions, even if the longer-run effects of certain relative price trends may be painfully clear. The disadvantageous effects of price–wage reductions are immediately obvious and certain: if the union leader accepts a lower wage, then this fact is immediately reflected in everyone's pay-packets; if he holds out for a higher wage, then employment in the industry may be lower than would otherwise be the case and each worker faces a higher probability that his own job might be terminated; but these represent only hypothetical outcomes, in some cases with low subjective probabilities. Also, when the level of employment is cut back, there is often some other more immediate cause acting as trigger to the decision which can play the role of scapegoat.

If an individual worker cannot retain or obtain some particular job which would provide him with greater prospective rewards than in other alternative jobs, why does he not offer his labour at a lower rate, so long as that still leaves him better off than in any alternative occupation? Clearly, unions will strive to prevent this happening since the possibility of competitive bidding down of wage rates by aspiring entrants would limit their own ability to select that combination of relative wage and size of industry that they prefer. But even in a non-unionised industry, the transaction costs of dealing with each worker separately, and the information costs of assembling sufficient knowledge to bargain efficiently, suggest that wages will tend to be held at standardised, common, fixed levels with occasional quantum-jump readjustments, rather than being perfectly flexible. In such cases, workers may well not be able to find jobs, even in non-unionised occupations, despite being prepared to accept wages below the going rate. Because of the learning process involved in becoming part of a productive team, the value to an employer of a long-standing, trained employee is considerably greater than is the case with a new entrant. A job seeker will therefore be unlikely to replace an existing worker by offering to accept a somewhat lower wage.

The rapid growth of unemployment in most industrialised countries during the 1980s led to considerable interest in, and development of, theories which suggested reasons why involuntary unemployment might not be resolved by appropriate shifts in relative prices. Because of training costs, costs arising from higher turnover, and a desire to get a better standard of workers in a system where information on worker quality was limited, worker efficiency might be thought to be positively related to wage levels. If this was the case, employers would not necessarily see any advantage in reducing wages, even when they could easily hire new labour at lower wage levels. Such training and hiring costs provide the existing worker (the insiders) with a partial monopoly which they can exploit quite largely at the expense of the unemployed (the outsiders), who find that they are unable to gain an insider's job by offering to replace the insider at a somewhat lower level of wages. There is a burgeoning literature on these issues and references to some examples of such work are given in the footnote below.[1]

---

[1] Yellen provides a survey of efficiency wage papers in 'Efficiency wage models of unemployment' (1984) pp. 200–5 and an example and references to insider–outsider wage determination models are found in Carruth and Oswald, 'On Union Preferences and Labour Market Models: Insiders and Outsiders', (1987) pp. 431–45.

So, in an uncertain world with market imperfections, training costs, information costs, etc. people will often be unable to obtain the work of their choice,[1] even though they would be prepared to take that job at less than the going rate. This social problem is considerably accentuated by the specific nature of human capacity. A worker is usually trained in some specific skill, with a considerable investment outlay in terms of time and money. The difference between the wage that a skilled worker would get if only he could obtain a job requiring that skill and his alternative prospects in the pool of unskilled workers may be very considerable. Again, a worker will have developed specific attachments to his place of work, housing, schools, friends, etc. Even if a reasonable job can be found in some new area at a distance, an unemployed worker may prefer to risk his chances of finding one nearer home.

A distinction is often drawn between voluntary and involuntary unemployment. This is a dangerous use of words. As long as there are any job vacancies open, in the army, domestic service, etc. even if these are at a distance from home, the unemployed man is voluntarily deciding to refuse them and to wait for a better opportunity. In that sense, virtually all unemployment is voluntary since there are almost always some vacancies for jobs which the unemployed could accept. At the other extreme, there would be some jobs in the economy (e.g., managing director) which virtually any unemployed worker would take if offered. In that sense, all unemployment is involuntary since the unemployed would prefer the nice but unavailable job to their present position.[2] The question of whether it is possible to attach any rigorous or practical and operational meaning to the terms 'voluntary' and 'involuntary' unemployment continues to be debated. A rigorous definition can be given to these terms only in an artificial world where either the nature of jobs or the qualities of the labour force were homogeneous.

---

[1] What would happen if everyone wanted to be Prime Minister? In a certain world without information costs, the results of having Jones rather than Smith in that position would be known. The selection of Prime Minister would not go to the man offering to accept the lowest salary but to the man who could provide the greatest additional value to the community in that job – i.e., productive output less factor cost. So, the individual's choice of jobs in a certain world would be largely swayed by his comparative advantages in the skill required.

In an uncertain world, employers (or selectors of a candidate for any job) have to rely on partial and inaccurate information about the abilities of aspiring candidates for the position. In this condition, people look for information signals – e.g., qualifications, examination results and appearance at an interview. Such sorting processes have their distasteful aspects but the correct inference could well be to improve the process, not to abandon it. In logic, those who object to a system of grading through examinations, etc. should also advocate choosing Prime Ministers by random selection (or perhaps we should all get a five-minute turn at the job).

[2] In addition to the question whether an unemployed man remains in that state 'voluntarily' or 'involuntarily', one can also ask whether an unemployed man became unemployed voluntarily by quitting his work or was laid off involuntarily on his part by his employer. *Pace* much American analysis, which appears to treat unemployment as arising voluntarily through quits, in the United Kingdom, the greater bulk of cyclical and structural unemployment appears to arise involuntarily through lay-offs. Indeed, it would be surprising if it were not so, for, as Tobin noted in his presidential address to the American Economic Association (1972) pp. 1–18, workers can probably better search for new jobs from the standpoint of holding an existing job than from an unemployed position. In part, this is a problem of information costs and the problem for prospective employers of spotting 'lemons' (bad workers); see Akerlof (1970) pp. 488–500. The fact that the candidate for a job already has another one is some evidence that his current employer finds his work satisfactory. If the candidate is unemployed, it raises the possibility that he was let go because he was a relatively poor worker.

In place of this dubious dichotomy between voluntary and involuntary unemployment, Professor Phelps[1] has likened the choice facing the unemployed man to an investment decision. By remaining unemployed and continuing to search for better jobs, the unemployed man forgoes current income from the job vacancies currently available in the hopes of enjoying a larger income in future from the job that he may secure by searching and waiting. He should continue to hold out so long as the present value of the returns to waiting, adjusted for risk, is greater than or equal to the costs involved. In this sense, unemployment is a chosen state and the choice is subject to the process of rational decision-making. Yet the analogy with investment provides too comfortable a connotation since the term 'investment' is generally connected with growth and expansion. For the unemployed worker, it will usually be a choice between two evils: to accept a worse job now, perhaps in a distant community, or to wait in unpleasant straits for the uncertain possibility of getting a better job in due course. Both the economy and the unemployed worker may well be better off if he does not immediately accept the first job offered but assesses as well as possible the prospects of obtaining better jobs.

In an economy with perfect certainty, foreseen changes in the pattern of wants would call forth smooth adjustments in the movements of factors of production between different uses. There would be no wastage of unemployed resources in the midst of want. In the absence of these conditions, uncertainty will lead to error, particularly in the extent of *specific* capital investment in infrastructure, equipment and human skills which remain dependent for full utilisation on the continued, uncertain prosperity of some particular activity.

In the real world, there are therefore a variety of reasons why wages and many prices exhibit a degree of stickiness (inertia) (see also Chapter 1). In due course, however, such stickiness should dissipate and wages and prices should adjust downwards in response to excess supply. Given a fixed nominal money supply, that would lead to higher real nominal balances (the Pigou effect) and lower interest rates which should, in due course, help to bring the economy back to full equilibrium.

Whereas a lower *level* of prices should lead to a restoration of full employment, the continuing decline in prices, the negative *rate of change* of prices, may hinder that process, especially through its effects on future price expectations. A deflationary process is thus quite likely to lead to expectations of further falls in prices which, for any given level of nominal interest rates, will raise the anticipated level of real interest rates and so prove a further deflationary force.[2]

So far in our analysis, it has been implicitly assumed that at all times the best expectation of the price level in a future period would be that it would remain at the same level as now, that all changes in prices were believed to represent once-for-all changes, with no greater probability of a continuation of such price movements in future periods than of a reversal back to some previous level. It might be possible to envisage economies in which successive price movements were not correlated (i.e.,

---

[1] In his book on *Inflation Policy and Unemployment Theory: The Cost–Benefit Approach to Monetary Planning* (1972) especially Part 1. See also Phelps (ed.) (1970), especially the paper by Alchian, 'Information Costs, Pricing, and Resource Unemployment' (pp. 27–52).

[2] A further reason, set out in Section 4 of Chapter 12, for doubting whether a general deflation of wages and prices would have a beneficial effect in restoring a depressed economy is that distributional 'wealth' effects within the private sector, as the debt–deflation process attacks the company sector, could overwhelm any expansionary wealth effect from private-sector holdings of financial assets.

when a fast rate of inflation in period t would give no indication of the probable rate of inflation in subsequent periods, $t + n$). In fact, cyclical fluctuations in real demand and the atomistic nature of the economy, in which my price and wage decision will be influenced by your previous decision – without any mechanism to allow a simultaneous adjustment or even perhaps a quasi-equilibrium to be achieved – tend to lead to to positive autocorrelation in price movements, so that if prices have fallen in the last period, the best estimate of future price movements may be that they will fall again in the next. Indeed, a better forecast based on historical experience is that the *rate of change*, rather than the level, of prices will remain constant (i.e., that the rate of inflation is as likely to increase as to decline in the future).

So a decline in prices may well give rise to expectations of future falls. Such prospective price movements will affect the expected relative yield on holding real capital as compared with fixed-interest financial debt. The expected rate of decline of prices would involve an equivalent expected advantage in holding fixed-interest financial debt rather than real assets whose market value is expected to fall over time. So relative yields have to be revised to take into account such expectations of future price movements. The prospective yield on an asset, after adjustment for these expectations of future price movements, is often described as the 'real' rate of interest; this 'real' rate is, however, a very impalpable construct depending on fleeting expectations.

Expectations of declining prices are, therefore, likely to cause a shift in demand from real to financial assets. *Ceteris paribus*, there would be a fall in the demand for real assets and investment demand would decline. Furthermore, the propensity to save might rise, as the return on delaying expenditures until the expected future fall in prices had occurred became increasingly apparent. Expectations of future price falls, by raising 'real' interest rates given the level of nominal rates, could therefore depress real activity in the economy even further.

Similarly, expectations of future inflation might have been supposed to stimulate further expansion in demand. In practice, however, it has been remarkably hard to observe any strong response in investment demand, at least in the United Kingdom, to fluctuations in the rate of inflation while, as already noted in Chapter 12, Section 4, recent econometric studies[1] have shown that the propensity to consume is adversely affected by inflation. Indeed, at times businessmen have actually alleged that inflationary worries were the cause of *reductions* in investment plans. It may be, however, that uncertainties about the future response of the authorities to a worsening inflation raise the risks of proceeding with an investment and associated financing plan. In so far as accelerating inflation makes planning more difficult, so caution becomes the watchword.

Moreover, until about 1970, nominal interest rates appeared to vary quite closely with changing expectations of price inflation, presumably as both lenders and borrowers took the prospective rate of inflation into account in their calculations; the real rate of interest in the economy was not then significantly reduced by inflation.

Indeed, the rapidity of the response of nominal interest rates to changes in the pace of inflation during the 1950s and 1960s was remarkable. A well known paper by Fama,[2] using data from these earlier years, tested the joint hypothesis that the real rate of interest was constant and that variations in the nominal rate represented efficient predictions of future inflation. The theory of the interaction of expected

---

[1] See Deaton (1981) and Hendry and von Ungern Sternberg (1981).
[2] Fama (1975) pp. 269–82.

inflation and nominal rates of interest, derived from Irving Fisher,[1] usually included a hypothesis of adaptive expectations, whereby expectations of inflation depend on some distributed lag of past inflationary experience. In general, this formulation ensures that during periods of accelerating inflation, expectations and, therefore, nominal interest rates would lag behind actual inflationary experience. Furthermore, the higher nominal interest rates should reduce the demand for money and (private-sector wealth); with a given stock of nominal money balances and bond holdings, there would then be some fall in real rates of interest. An acceleration in inflation would, on this account, therefore, be reflected partly in higher nominal rates of interest but also partly in lower real rates and greater output.[2]

But if people formulate their expectations rationally, these should not *systematically* diverge from actual experience. Indeed, their expectations should not be continuously worse than the predictions of economic models, the results of which are in any case often published. Furthermore, if one assumes an economic system without money illusion, where economic plans are all made in real terms, then foreseen changes in the rate of price inflation should become very quickly embodied in nominal interest terms, as Sargent (1973) has argued.

In addition, it became increasingly obvious to people during the 1960s and 1970s that each time the rate of inflation went up another notch, whether owing to expansionary demand management, wage push or imported inflation, the government of the day had little stomach for imposing sufficient prolonged deflation and unemployment to reverse the previous jump in the rate of inflation. Whatever the going rate of inflation was, the authorities would validate it. Indeed, in these circumstances, the surprising feature was, perhaps, the relatively slow rate of acceleration of inflation.

Moreover, the actual sharp acceleration of inflation during the 1970s and subsequent deceleration during the 1980s were associated with a marked fall and then rise in real rates of interest, whether these were calculated by deflating nominal rates by current rates of inflation or by survey data on inflation expectations. Such a time path is consistent with rather slowly adjusting adaptive expectations. It has proven quite difficult to find alternative convincing explanations for the marked apparent fluctuations in real interest rates, especially for the continuing high levels of real rates during the years of slow growth, high unemployment and declining inflation in the early 1980s.[3]

At the same time as evidence from the time path of interest rates was, it would seem, giving some cause for doubting whether expectations did take full account of all publicly available information but might adjust instead more slowly, the theoretical concept that expectations *would* be rationally formed was taking the economics profession by storm. It is a very lucid concept, obviously appropriate within a framework of self-interested maximisation processes.

If the pressure of demand is sufficiently high in any period to generate an increase in the rate of inflation from some previous steady level – given that the best estimate of the future had been for no change in the current *rate* of inflation – then the resulting real wage rate will be less than will have been expected and less than the bargaining strength of labour under conditions of high demand should provide. Other decision-makers, besides labour union leaders, taken unawares by the accelera-

---

[1] One statement of his theory can be found in his book, *Theory of Interest* (1930) pp. 399–451.
[2] On this subject, see Sargent (1973) pp. 429–80.
[3] Blanchard and Summers (1984) pp. 273–334.

tion in the rate of inflation will incorporate this new information into their pricing decisions in the next period. Earlier, a simple relationship between the rate of inflation (price changes) and the pressure of demand (the extent of spare capacity) was posited. Now, this relationship needs to be adjusted to take the *anticipated* rate of inflation into account. This may be expressed in an equation of the form:

$$\dot{P}_t = b_0 + b_1 \frac{1}{UE_t} + b_2 E\dot{P}$$

where b_0 is a negative constant representing, *inter alia*, the trend growth in productivity, UE represents the level of unemployment and enters the equation in this way in order to capture the non-linearity of the relationship, $\dot{P}$ represents the rate of price inflation and $E\dot{P}$ the anticipated rate of price inflation. In the absence of money illusion, one would expect decision-makers to attempt to achieve some desired real outcome for wages, profits, etc. and this implies that the coefficient b_2 on $E\dot{P}$ should be 1. Of course, we cannot observe exactly how expectations are formed but people are likely to make efficient use of existing historical information on the time path of inflation. If in previous years changes in the rate of inflation have not exhibited auto-correlation, then the best expectation of the forthcoming rate of inflation would be that it would not change from its recent pace, except in so far as other current developments, whether political or economic (e.g., elections of a new government or devaluation) give grounds for revising forecasts. Under these circumstances, the best expectation of current inflation should be for a continuation of the previous rate, so that:

$$E\dot{P} = \dot{P}_{t-1}$$

Given the values of b_0 and b_1, there should be some value of UE such that:

$$b_0 + b_1 \frac{1}{UE_t} = 0$$

In this case, from the previous argument, $\dot{P}_t = \dot{P}_{t-1}$, so that if the level of unemployment is at this 'equilibrium' level, then the current rate of inflation, whatever it may be, will persist. If:

$$b_0 + b_1 \frac{1}{UE_t} \lessgtr 0$$

over time, then the rate of inflation must continually accelerate (> 0) or decelerate (< 0) as the faster (slower) inflation from each period becomes built into anticipations. In any short period, the existence of a given set of expectations, and indeed of a given set of contractual arrangements, will, however, act as a check to price flexibility and so a change in the pressure of monetary demand will bring about a temporary change in the utilisation of factors of production and in the rate of growth of output (and not just a readjustment in price levels). Decision-makers will then presumably learn from their past errors in predicting the rate of inflation and adjust their expectations on the basis of unfolding historical experience. In the longer period, it will thus become increasingly hard to maintain a very high level of capacity utilisation – at a pressure of demand greater than that consistent with a constant rate of inflation – without incurring ever-accelerating inflation. In the short run, therefore, the relationship between capacity utilisation and inflation may allow a considerable gain in output to be had for a limited increase in inflationary pressures; in the longer term, it will be neither attainable nor desirable for the pressure of demand in

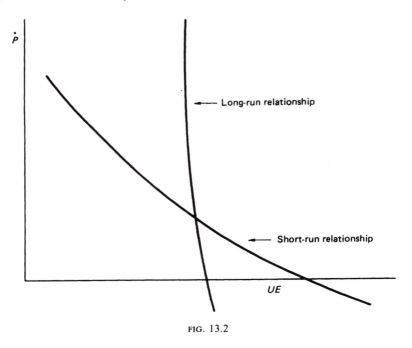

FIG. 13.2

the economy to diverge far from that level which will stabilise the rate of inflation.

The short-run relationship between capacity utilisation and inflation, frequently termed the Phillips curve, is thus likely to look quite different from the long-run relationship, as shown in Figure 13.2.

In practice, however, earlier experience suggested that wage–price adjustments were rather less flexible – or perhaps less volatile – than the preceding analysis would suggest. For example, most early econometric studies of a Phillips curve relationship of the form:

$$\dot{P}_t = b_0 + b_1 \frac{1}{UE_t} + b_2 E\dot{P}$$

(where $E\dot{P}$ in turn is derived from a distributed lag on previous prices), in industrialised countries during the 1950s and 1960s, found values of b_2 well below unity, often in the region of 0.5.[1] A number of reasons were advanced to account for this, for example that so long as inflation remained below some threshold, it was easier and simpler – and approximately as good – to assume a zero rate of inflation as laboriously to incorporate some small and uncertain expectation into all calculations.

In any case, during the 1970s, conditions changed abruptly in most countries. The

---

[1] The sum of the coefficients on lagged price changes in the Phillips curve (wage equation) incorporated in the SSRC–MIT–Penn (SMP) model of the US economy, at least in its 1971 form, was 0.57. Solow undertook special studies of this relationship in both the United States and the United Kingdom and also obtained values for b_2 of about 0.5; see *Price Expectations and the Behaviour of the Price Level* (1969) and Rousseas (ed.) (1968) pp. 1–16.

previous, relatively stable relationship with $b_2 < 1$ seemed to break down and inflation in several countries accelerated despite high levels of unemployment. Indeed, in the United Kingdom, assuming that the value of b_1 remained constant at its pre-1969 level, it would have required values of b_2 in excess of 1 in order to explain, in terms of this very simple relationship, the acceleration in wages and prices between 1969 and 1975. Perhaps that experience reflected the evaporation of the last vestiges of money illusion, as inflationary pressures intensified during the latter years of the 1960s for a number of reasons, (e.g., Vietnam, devaluations in the United Kingdom, etc.).

2. Rational Expectations and Policy Impotence

So long as workers and businessmen are concerned about *real* wages, *real* profitability, etc. in their bargains over wages and pricing decisions (as they should be in the absence of money illusion), then the coefficient b_2 *should* equal unity – except, perhaps, when inflation is so low that information–calculation costs lead to some threshold effects. The question about how such expectations might be formed has remained more debatable. Most of the earlier literature used the implicit assumption that expectations were based on past experience, a backward-looking 'adaptive expectations' approach. This, however, implies that agents would take no account of current policy actions and announcements, which seems at the same time irrational and improbable.

Instead, following earlier contributions by Muth,[1] it has become generally posited that agents' expectations would be 'rational', that is that they would use all publicly available information, including both information on current and future policy and on models of how the economic system works, to generate optimal forecasts. While this latter method is clearly the correct general approach, its actual application is less clear-cut in a world in which the collection and interpretation of information can be extremely costly – notably in the use of time – and in which there remains great uncertainty about how the economy really works and can best be modelled. All too often, economists have tended to assume both that information is costless and that their own preferred model of the economy is unanimously accepted by all other agents.

Be that as it may, we shall defer consideration of the implications of shifting from adaptive to rational expectations until later in this section. For the time being, we shall simply note that so long as $b_2 = 1$ in equilibrium with actual inflation equal to expected inflation, the Phillips curve will be vertical. Any level of unemployment lower than the level at which

$$b_0 + b_1 \frac{1}{UE} = 0$$

would cause ever accelerating inflation; any higher unemployment level would cause the rate of inflation to decelerate without limit. This critical level of unemployment is known as the Non-Accelerating-Inflation Rate of Unemployment or NAIRU.

The actual level of NAIRU is thought to be determined by real factors. Let us assume that the share of wages in national income is approximately constant (as happens to be the case). Then, in a closed economy, real wages can grow only at a rate

---

[1] Muth (1961) pp. 315–35.

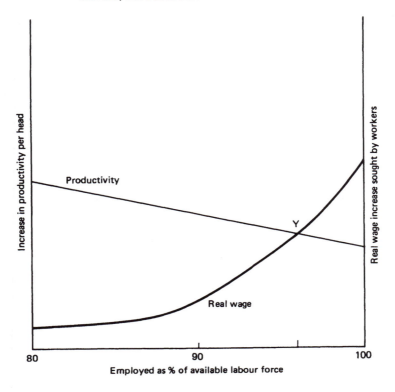

FIG. 13.3

depending on the growth of real output per head. So the level of unemployment has to be such as to make workers prepared to settle for the growth of real output that their own productive efforts in aggregate make available[1] (Figure 13.3). The less are the discomforts of unemployment, the more unionised and/or aggressive the work force and the more the labour force prefers high wages for existing workers to generating more employment, the higher will the level of unemployment have to be in order to induce the work force to accept the increase in real incomes that their own productivity makes feasible. Equally, the higher the growth of productivity, the lower will be the NAIRU consistent with any given degree of labour aggression on wages.

Of course, there are qualifications. Real wages per head can grow faster than productivity if the share of wages in national incomes is growing or if the terms of trade are improving, but neither of the above can occur for long without causing serious imbalances in the economy. Moreover, the rate of growth of productivity is

---

[1] In Figure 13.3 the slope of the relationship between productivity increases and employment is shown here as downwards. This is probably the case in a longer-term context, since the most efficient will be employed first and fewer workers would have more capital per head. In a shorter-term context, however, productivity fluctuations may be pro-cyclical for the reasons outlined above.

not a constant, independent of what is happening to the economy either cyclically or structurally. Productivity per head thus normally increases during the boom, as labour hoarding is unwound, and falls during depressions. This tends to exacerbate cycles since it takes longer for tightening labour markets to reveal their underlying inflationary proclivity during period of expansion, and vice versa during depressions.

Longer-term structural issues are even more contentious. It is widely believed that there is a degree of pressure for higher real wages in the UK which is generally in excess of the increase in output per head that the relatively sluggish British economy can generate. This simultaneously exerts both inflationary pressure on prices and wages and deflationary pressure on output as governments and businessmen try to cope with the consequence of high *nominal* wage bargains. Economists from Cambridge[1] have proposed the solution that the rate of growth of productivity per head be raised by an expansionary policy, with fiscal encouragement for investment. In the transitional period, until the higher investment should lead to more rapid output growth and thus meet the workers' aspirations, inflation would be kept under control by some combination of exchange controls over international capital flows and foreign trade (improving the terms of trade), by policies shifting the distribution of incomes towards wages, and by incomes policies.

There are numerous objections to such a go-for-growth policy. For example, is a shortage of new investment really the main constraint on an otherwise attainable faster rate of growth of output? Can various exchange controls, fiscal measures and incomes policies really succeed in keeping a lid on inflation until the expansionary policy successfully delivers higher growth? The experience of periods of expansion in earlier decades in the UK suggested that the answers to both these questions would be 'no'.

The alternative, right-wing view was that little could be done to encourage real growth by *demand* management. There were longer-term *supply*-side measures that could be taken to encourage risk-taking and entrepreneurship, to improve incentives, to improve education, etc. but the best that the authorities could do in the short run would be to try to weaken union power and to reduce workers' aspirations, and to provide a stable context in which entrepreneurs could run their businesses with the minimum of interference from outside distractions in the form of taxation, inflation and union opposition – all of which require time and effort to forecast and to avoid their adverse effects. In this latter view, the key constraint on growth is managerial and entrepreneurial capacity. Over the years 1982–7, the rate of growth of output per head in the UK did increase but that followed a severe slump in 1980–2, so that, so far, the record over the first two electoral periods of the Conservative government returned in 1979 has been relatively similar – in terms of growth of output per head – to that experienced in earlier decades.

If the level of the NAIRU at any time was exactly predictable, then the authorities would presumably still choose the desired level of unemployment relative to the NAIRU, depending on the concurrent rate of inflation, either to maintain the existing inflation rate (at the NAIRU) or to reduce inflation by a slightly higher level of unemployment. The fact that the medium-term Phillips curve is vertical, not downward-sloping, does not of itself destroy the case for demand management to seek to achieve a given level of pressure in the economy; it does, however, restrict the range of feasible and sensible options. What does, instead, limit the perceived usefulness of demand management is the combination of the view that there is only

---

[1] Dixon (1982–3) pp. 289–94.

one level of unemployment which is sustainable in the economy in equilibrium (and to which the economy will tend to revert if the authorities maintain a stable nominal policy rule – e.g., constant monetary growth) *and* that the authorities do not know what this level is. Without perfect knowledge, they would be bound to aim at an incorrect level of unemployment. Assuming the NAIRU to be fixed, this would just engender extra price instability without much offsetting benefit. In the absence of rational expectations, to be discussed subsequently, the *short-run* Phillips curve is not, however, vertical and this can allow somewhat complex calculations of the relative effects on utility of more short-run employment prospects balanced against a higher permanent rate of inflation.[1] This consideration may be seen as particularly important when some shock has driven the actual level of unemployment temporarily well above the estimated natural rate.

As has already been noted, various suggestions have been put forward by economists from differing ideological camps for lowering the NAIRU, either by raising the rate of growth of productivity or by relaxing underlying pressures and tensions in the labour market. What, however, has been unfortunately the case is that over the 1970s and 1980s, far from the NAIRU having been reduced, it has appeared to shift quite sharply upwards in most industrialised countries. The combinations of inflation and unemployment for the UK for the years 1970–85 (annual averages) are plotted out in Figure 13.4 below.

This figure indicates that one might have estimated the NAIRU to have been around 3 per cent at the beginning of the 1970s: Paish earlier had estimated it at about 2 per cent.[2] Subsequently, however, there appeared to be a series of lurches in the

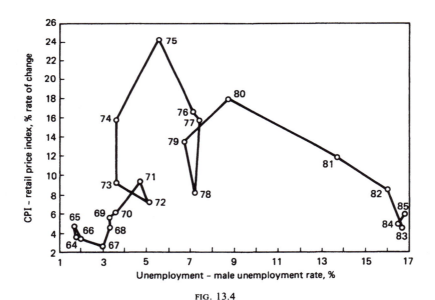

FIG. 13.4

---

[1] For an example, see Tobin (1972) pp. 1–18.
[2] Paish (1968) pp. 1–30.

economy, each taking the Phillips curve to a more adverse position, upwards and to the right. By the mid-1980s, it would appear that inflation stabilises (i.e., at the NAIRU) when unemployment remains over 10 per cent.

This has been, to put it mildly, a disastrous occurrence. Why has it happened? No one really knows but the following may have contributed. First, the rate of growth of output per head in all industrialised countries slowed sharply in the 1970s and early 1980s, partly as a consequence of the oil shocks. Next, the higher levels of inflation may have themselves disturbed the effective workings of the price mechanisms of the economy and have contributed to slower growth. At the end of the 1960s, moreover, expectations about future improvements in real living standards had been raised by previous success, thereby raising workers' aspirations and intransigence over wage demands. Some, notably Minford,[1] have ascribed some part of the rightward shifting of the NAIRU to improved unemployment benefits and to a more aggressive labour force but it is difficult to give such explanations much credence during the 1980s, a time when union strength and workers' aspirations appeared to weaken.

Over these last two decades, it has been notable that whatever the current level of unemployment has been, the best estimate of the NAIRU has been quite close to it, usually a couple of percentage points below. There are again various partial explanations for this. First, the monopoly position of the insiders *vis à vis* the outsiders in the labour market, discussed in Section 1, may be sufficiently strong that they do not feel threatened by the existence of potential alternative entrants, in the shape of the reserve army of the unemployed, but only by imminent lay-offs to themselves. In that case, the Phillips curve would rather take the form:

$$\dot{P} = b_0 + b_1 d\, UE + b_2 E\dot{P},$$

i.e., it is the change, not the level, of unemployment that influences wage demands. If this were to be so, and this hypothesis fits recent data in the UK quite well, the implications would be extremely unpalatable. Inflation could only be reduced further by yet another *increase* in the level of unemployment. Alternatively, unemployment could be reduced back to more acceptable levels, say 4–5 per cent, only by giving up all the achievements obtained in reducing inflation in recent years.

Another line of explanation emphasises the deleterious effect of unemployment itself on the willingness and ability to work of the unemployed. Human skills depreciate faster with disuse. It ceases to be worth retraining the relatively old among the unemployed, who may come to treat unemployment as premature retirement. School leavers who do not find jobs may develop a sub-culture that makes it harder for them to return to the work-force. The long-term unemployed become self-doubting and apathetic. In other words, the event of unemployment may itself change the characteristics of the unemployed labour force and reduce their human skills and potential. This effect is described by the term 'hysteresis', where the time path of some variable (e.g., employment) helps to determine what the *equilibrium* of the system may be. Layard has argued that the rise in unemployment in the 1980s in the UK was concentrated among long-term, over-one-year, unemployed.[2] For the reasons already adduced, these may no longer either be employable or seriously seeking employment. If the long-term unemployed are, for such reasons, no longer considered to be part of the potential work force, then the standard Phillips curve

---

[1] Minford (1983) pp. 207–44 and Minford *et al.* (1983).
[2] Layard and Nickell (1986).

relationship, relating inflation to expected inflation and unemployment (*exclusive of long-term unemployed*) shows much more stability and explanatory power.

If an important aspect of the adverse shift of the Phillips curve is an associated loss of skill by the unemployed, then it does at least point in the direction of certain potential remedies, such as support for retraining schemes and preferential treatment for those hiring the long-term unemployed.[1] It does not, alas, suggest that expansionary demand management by itself would lead the NAIRU to follow the actual level of unemployment downwards as closely as it has appeared to track actual unemployment on the upwards tack. Anyhow, the fact that nominal earnings in the UK continued to rise at about $7\frac{1}{2}$–8 per cent in 1986–7, giving approximate constancy of inflation at about 4–5 per cent with output per head growing at some 3–$3\frac{1}{2}$ per cent, despite unemployment of approximately 11 per cent, is disconcerting. For whatever reason, a high level of unemployment has done relatively little to reduce nominal wage demands. Although we do, as economists, have certain hypotheses to explain why this might have been so with the benefit of hindsight, this adverse development was not predicted in advance; the proposed explanations, therefore, remain tentative, partial suggestions rather than having been tested in successful predictive experiments. In the meantime, the NAIRU appears to remain an unpredictable, unstable variable. While this reinforces earlier doubts about the wisdom of trying to manage the level of demand in the economy by seeking to achieve some chosen level of unemployment, it does also raise the question whether this whole intellectual construct is actually helpful in the analysis of macro-economic developments.

While the most serious practical problems have been caused by the outwards shifts in the apparent position of the NAIRU, the main theoretical interest has attached to the implications of replacing adaptive, backward-looking expectations by rational, forward-looking expectations. When expectations were backward-looking – e.g., $E\dot{P}_t = f(\dot{P}_{t-1}, \ldots \dot{P}_{t-n}, X_{t-1} \ldots X_{t-n})$ – where X is a vector of other historical variables affecting current expectations, $E\dot{P}_t$ is then effectively given independently of current policy decisions. With $E\dot{P}_t$ given, current policy can affect $\dot{P}_t$ only via changes in output and unemployment, *not* directly and immediately by changing current expectations (e.g., of inflation). Accordingly, in the short run at least, the Phillips curve can *not* be vertical and management of the nominal level of demand must be able to influence output, at least temporarily.

Assume next that people believe that the level of real output in longer-term equilibrium is determined by real factors, such as endowments, technology, etc. and, with velocity assumed to be stable, the level of prices adjusts proportionality with the money stock; given the identity $MV \equiv PY$, if Y and V are fixed at Y^* and V^*, $P = bM$, where $b = Y^*/V^*$. Then, if expectations are forward-looking, people will expect that an announced (anticipated) expansion in the money stock will increase prices commensurately; given expectations about the future level of (equilibrium) output, $E\dot{P} = E\dot{M}$ – i.e., the currently expected rate of inflation will be determined by the currently anticipated rate of monetary expansion. In this case, an announced monetary expansion would lead to an exactly equivalent percentage increase in current price expectations and, with $b_2 = 1$, in actual prices. The announced monetary expansion would thus be dissipated immediately and instantaneously in additional inflation.

This analysis formed the basis of the famous claim by Sargent and Wallace[2] that,

---

[1] Layard (1986).
[2] (1975) pp. 241–54.

with rational expectations, nominal demand management – monetary policy – was impotent. Any *anticipated* monetary change would be immediately reflected in changes in inflationary expectations, and hence in prices themselves with no effect, even in the short run, on output. Of course, if agents did not realise that the authorities were expanding the money stock and nominal demand, they would not adjust their expectations accordingly – each agent would, mistakenly, regard part of the general rise in nominal demand as a real shift in relative tastes towards his own product and increase output in response. The authorities could thus still affect output and real variables in the short run by surprising the private sector. If, however, the authorities acted in any systematic manner (e.g., trying to surprise the public with temporary surges in monetary growth in advance of elections, see Chapter 15) then the public would, in due course, come to anticipate that too, and the effect would simply be dissipated in higher (expected and actual) inflation, with no beneficial effect on output.

There is a straightforward and potentially testable implication of this. Anticipated monetary growth should affect price inflation but have no effect on current output. *Unanticipated* monetary growth should affect both output and inflation. Barro was the first to examine this empirically in his two papers in the late 1970s.[1] This initial work provoked a minor cottage industry of broadly similar studies using differing data sets for various countries and differing techniques (e.g., for estimating the anticipated rate of monetary expansion). Unfortunately, as indicated in Table 13.1,[2] the results are not clear-cut.

Of the 63 separate published time series tests mentioned, covering seven developed countries, 33 indicate significant effects on output of *both* unanticipated and *anticipated* monetary policy, 17 indicate that only unanticipated monetary policy had significant effects on output and 13 suggested neither unanticipated nor anticipated monetary policy affected output.[3]

One of the problems of econometric studies which attempt to assess how expectations affect behaviour is that the tests generally involve *joint* hypotheses of how expectations are generated (or that expectations' surveys are accurate representations of expectations more broadly) and of how such expectations influence decisions. If the results do not support prior hypotheses, it is hard to know whether the estimate of anticipations was erroneous or whether the behavioural hypothesis was incorrect, though ingenious efforts have been made to disentangle the sources of failure in hypothesis testing.[4] Anyhow, such tests were, to some large extent, predicated on the assumption of a stable demand-for-money function and, therefore, predictable velocity. If velocity becomes unpredictable, how can agents make a sensible estimate of likely future inflation resulting from anticipated monetary growth? As the stability of demand-for-money functions has diminished, so interest and enthusiasm for the future products of this cottage industry are also likely to wane, leaving this particular issue unresolved for the time being.

Perhaps the most remarkable implication of the rational expectations–efficient markets approach to macro-economics is not the policy impotence theorem but the

---

[1] (1977) and (1978).

[2] Reproduced from an OECD paper by Chouraqui and Driscoll – on 'The Effects of Monetary Policy' (1987).

[3] At least it appears that there have been no reported findings of unanticipated monetary policy being insignificant while anticipated monetary policy had a significant effect.

[4] Mishkin (1982) pp. 22–51.

TABLE 13.1
Time series tests of the role of anticipated and unanticipated monetary policy on output and employment

Country	Both anticipated and un-anticipated policy significant	Anticipated policy not significant unanticipated policy significant	Neither unanticipated nor anticipated policy significant
United States	Small (1979a), Froyen (1979b), Mishkin (1982c, 1982a), Boschen and Grossman (1982), Peseran (1982d), Makin (1982e), Marrick (1983), Cannerella and Garston (1983), Cairns and Lombra (1984j), McGee and Staisiak (1985f), Driscoll *et al.* (1983h), Sheehey (1984f)	Barro (1977a, 1978c), Sheffrin (1979i), Leiderman (1980j), Barro and Rush (1980k), Barro and Hergowitz (1980j), Fitzgerald and Pollio (1983l), Neftci and Sargent (1979), Attfield and Duck (1983j), Lillien (1982c)	Haraf (1983j), Wasserfallen (1984m, 1985a), King and Plosser (1984a), Sims (1980a), Litterman and Weiss (1985)
Japan	Pigott (1987), Seo and Takahashi (1981), Hamada and Hayashi (1985), Taniuche (1980), Gochoco (1986), Fitzgerald and Pollio (1983l)	Parkin (1984)	
Germany	Bailey *et al.* (1986n)	Demery *et al.* (1984d)	Wasserfallen (1984m, 1985a)
France	Fitzgerald and Pollio (1983l)		Bordes *et al.* (1982o), Wasserfallen (1984m)
United Kingdom	Symons (1983p), Garner (1982q), Driscoll *et al.* (1983h), Fitzgerald and Pollio (1983l), Bean (1984l), Alogoskoufis and Pissarides (1983d), Bailey *et al.* (1986n)	Attfield *et al.* (1981l, 1981j), Attfield and Duck (1983f)	Wasserfallen (1984a), Demery (1984d)
Italy	Fitzgerald and Pollio (1983l), Bailey *et al.* (1986n)	Smaghi and Tardini (1983r)	Wasserfallen (1984m)
Canada	Jones (1985) Darrat (1986s)	Wogin (1980j)	

a	*American Economic Review*	n	presented at the Third International Conference on Money and Banking, Strasburg
b	*Journal of Economics and Business*		
c	*Journal of Political Economy*	o	document de Travail, Université de Limoges
d	*Economic Journal*		
e	*Review of Economic Studies*	p	*Manchester School Journal*
f	*Journal of Money, Credit and Banking*	q	*Quarterly Review of Economics and Business*
g	*Review of Economics and Statistics*		
h	*Journal of Macroeconomics*	r	*Gironale Degli Economisti Annali de Economia*
i	*Economic Inquiry*		
j	*Journal of Monetary Economics*	s	*Canadian Journal of Economics*
k	Fischer, S. *Rational Expectations and Economic Policy* (1980)		
l	*European Economic Review*		
m	mimeo, *Volkswirtschaftliches Institut*		

claim that fluctuations of actual output around equilibrium output arise not from Keynesian demand management failures but from incorrect estimates of the general level of prices; since price surprises make it difficult for agents to distinguish shifts in relative prices from changes in the general price level. In fact, this follows very simply from the basic expectations-augmented Phillips curve. Since the level of unemployment will vary with the divergence of actual output from equilibrium output, we can rewrite the basic equation as:

$$\dot{P}_t = b_1(y_t - y^*) + b_2 E\dot{P}_t$$

It is generally recognised that b_2 equals unity, and so this can be rewritten as:

$$b_1(y_t - y^*) = \dot{P}_t - E\dot{P}_t$$
$$y_t - y^* = 1/b_1(\dot{P}_t - E\dot{P}_t)$$

The deviation of actual output from its equilibrium is thus a function of the difference between the actual and the expected price rise, the forecasting error. With rational expectations, moreover, the forecasting error should be purely stochastic with a zero mean and no significant auto-correlation. Accordingly, the deviation of actual from equilibrium output should be purely stochastic with a zero mean and no significant auto-correlation.[1]

David Laidler presents the Neo-classical approach in a nice, compact manner in his paper, 'Some Macroeconomic Implications of Price Stickiness'[2] (pp. 40–1):

A log linear version of the . . . simple New-classical system may be written as follows, where: y^* is the permanent component of the logarithm of income; y is its transitory component; m is the logarithm of nominal money; $Em_s\backslash I_{-1}$ is the nominal money supply that agents at the end of period -1 rationally expect to circulate during the current period, given information available up to the end of period -1; p is the logarithm of general price level; $Ep\backslash I_{-1}$ is a rational expectation of p formed at the end of period -1; and Ep/I is that expectation as modified by contemporaneously available information, or, as we have termed it, the currently perceived price level:

$$m_s = m_d = \delta_0 + \delta_1 y^* + p \tag{1}$$
$$y = v(p - Ep\,|\,I) \tag{2}$$
$$Ep\,|\,I_{-1} = Em_s\,|\,I_{-1} - (\delta_0 + \delta_1 y^*) = Em_s\,|\,I_{-1} - m_{s-1} + p_{-1} \tag{3}$$
$$Ep\,|\,I = (1 - \theta)p + \theta Ep\,|\,I_{-1} \tag{4}$$

Substituting (4) into (2) produces a more commonly used form of the New-classical aggregate supply curve.

$$y = d(p - Ep\,|\,I_{-1}) \tag{2a}$$

where

$$d \equiv v\theta$$

This model yields the following reduced forms to describe output and real balances:

$$y = d(m_s - Em_s\,|\,I_{-1}) \tag{5}$$
$$m_s - p = b_0 + b_1 y^* \tag{6}$$

Thus, the New-classical model explains output fluctuations as being caused by unanticipated fluctuations in the money supply, without giving up the assumption of

---

[1] See Lucas's original paper, 'Expectations and the Neutrality of Money' (1972).
[2] (1988).

price flexibility and clearing markets; but it does not, in the absence of further extension, predict any persistence of fluctuations in output, nor does it predict systematic deviations of actual money holdings from their long-run desired level.

Equation (4) above is Lucas's formulation taken from his 1973 paper, 'Some International Evidence of Output-Inflation Tradeoffs'. Basically, Lucas argues that in those circumstances where monetary policy and the general level of inflation have been very unstable, agents will revise their expectations of the *general* level of prices markedly as they see prices around them, their local prices, change – i.e., θ will be very low (note that with full information, θ is zero and equilibrium output and employment always persist). *Per contra*, when monetary policy and inflation rates have been stable, agents will interpret changes in local prices as shifts in relative prices, maintaining their previously formed expectations of the general level of prices.

As we have derived it above, the Lucas surprise function seems to follow directly from a few simple and plausible concepts, the absence of money illusion ($b_2 = 1$) and rational use of information in constructing expectations. Yet the conclusions, particularly that deviations of output from its equilibrium level will be stochastic and serially uncorrelated, seem grossly at odds with common observation. Real variables such as output, real expenditures, productivity, employment and unemployment clearly exhibit cycles around their longer-term trend rates of growth, with periods when they remain persistently above or below their trend growth rates – i.e., the 'transitory' element does exhibit strong positive serial auto-correlation.

Next, it does seem implausible that the serious traumas in the real economy, the high level of unemployment that most developed countries have recently suffered, the sharp reduction in output below potential output and the scrapping of equipment, factories, firms and even whole industries in the UK in 1980–2, could be ascribed to agents' failures to predict the general level of prices and to distinguish accurately between local and relative price shifts and general inflationary trends. Data on national price trends (e.g., retail and wholesale price indices, business selling and buying prices, raw material prices, earnings, wages, productivity and unit labour costs, current monetary trends, etc.) become available every month. There are regular surveys and forecasts of future inflation over the next year or two. Admittedly, the various indices may have their statistical shortcomings and attempts to estimate the 'underlying' general rate of inflation from the mass of detail are subject to error and uncertainty. Even so, any agent who wished to know what the current general rate of inflation was, or what commentators expected it to be over the next year or so, should have no difficulty whatsoever in obtaining plenty of information. Communication of such information is good and relatively costless to the recipient. Moreover, if it really was thought that real economic traumas were caused by insufficient information on prices, it would not seem excessively difficult to obtain and provide – free of charge – even more information on price formation, costs, etc. No one seriously proposes, however, that unemployment, output cycles, etc. can be significantly ameliorated by providing more frequent and comprehensive data on price movements!

The neo-classical economists have accepted that the real economy does exhibit persistence, but they reckon that there are various channels whereby they can make transitory output fluctuations exhibit positive serial auto-correlation without having to change the basic structure of their model. For example, the process of inventory decumulation in period 1, following a surprise shock to prices, could lead to output being higher and, with a given money supply, to prices being lower in period 2. We might thus rewrite the augmented Phillips curve as:

$$\dot{P}_t = b_1(y_t - y^*) + b_2 E\dot{P} - b_3(y_{t-1} - y^*)$$

which, with $b_2 = 1$, leads to:

$$y_t = 1/b_1(\dot{P}_t - E\dot{P}_t) + b_3/b_1 y_{t-1} - (1 - b_3/b_1)y^*$$

If $b_3 > 0$, this equation provides a channel for persistence. There are also various other routes whereby lagged values of y_t, the transitory element of real output, might enter into such an equation and introduce persistence and cycles.

Another explanation is that there may be auto-correlated shocks to potential (equilibrium) supply, periods when the introduction of new technology and techniques are faster or slower. A considerable amount of effort has been expended in recent years by neo-classical economists in attempts to demonstrate that historical US trade cycles *could* have been largely caused by such real, supply-side fluctuations. This reinterpretation of historical cyclical experience as being due to *real* factors, rather than to fluctuations in Keynesian nominal demand, has become another cottage industry in the USA.[1]

Whether or not one finds the evidence presented for the relative importance of real factors convincing in the US case, and many do not (see Summers, 1986), this genre is less popular in the UK. The cycles in the 1950s and 1960s in the UK were clearly associated with policy responses to fluctuating pressures on the pegged exchanged rate, often termed 'stop-go'. While the 1971–6 cyclical episode reflected both supply shocks, (e.g., the 1973 oil shock) and the UK policy response to such shocks, the 1980–2 slump was primarily caused by a misaligned, over-valued exchange rate, which in turn was associated with extremely tight monetary policy.[2] The attempt to ascribe cyclical fluctuations, the persistence of transitory fluctuations in output, to real supply-side factors rather than to nominal demand factors has found, so far, little support in the UK.

There are some aspects of the modern real business cycle literature which are attractive. As noted earlier, the NAIRU does appear to have shifted markedly over recent years and some part of such shifts may well have resulted from 'real' changes in preferences, in the pace of technological innovation, etc. Again, if one wants to compare changes in growth rates, average labour utilisation, hours worked, etc., from decade to decade, the methodology employed by such theorists appears appropriate. The attempt, however, to try to attribute short-run (e.g., year to year or quarter to quarter) cyclical variations in unemployment, output, productivity, etc. primarily to auto-correlated shocks to supply-side (technological) forces seems less compelling, either theoretically or empirically.

The UK consensus anyhow is that fluctuations in output around the equilibrium level (with the latter determined by factor endowments, technology and other supply side factors), must be due to imperfections of some sort in the market system. The question is just what are the key imperfections. For the reasons indicated, the claim that these may be various shortcomings in the availability and interpretation of information on price movements seems, to me, to be implausible. Instead, it seems

---

[1] See the papers by Manuelli (1986), Prescott (1986) and Summers (1986a) on aspects of the real business cycle theories, *Federal Reserve Bank of Minneapolis Quarterly Review*, pp. 3–33; also McCallum (1986) pp. 397–414. A recent working paper by King, Plosser and Rebelo presented at the Money Study Group Conference in September 1987, will no doubt have been published by the time this book is available.

[2] Niehans (1981).

much more likely that the various factors reviewed at length in Chapter 1 cause market makers to adjust prices relatively slowly, at discrete intervals, despite having adequate information on general price trends.[1]

In the paper, 'Some Macroeconomic Implications of Price Stickiness (1988), Laidler explores a model of this kind[2]:

> Consider now an alternative version of the same basic model which introduces an element of price stickiness to *replace* the New-classical postulate that agents do not have contemporaneous access to information about the general price level, so that, in what follows, everyone is permitted to know that variable's value. Suppose that two kinds of sellers operate in the system, producing goods which are imperfect substitutes for one another: 'fix-price' firms who set their prices for the current period at the end of the previous period, basing them on expectations formed using information then available, and who stand ready to sell any amount of output at those prices; and 'flex-price' firms who may vary their prices as well as their output in response to demand during the current period. ... Consider a week following one in which all price expectations were fulfilled and in which the economy was, therefore, in full equilibrium at permanent income; let expectations about this week's prices have been formed, and then let the nominal money supply be unexpectedly increased. With prices initially set at their expected levels, there will exist an excess supply of real balances, giving rise to a planned increase in agents' rate of flow of expenditure. This extra expenditure will be distributed between fix-price and flex-price producers. The former will, by assumption, supply any extra output demanded, but the latter will raise the relative (and hence the money) prices of their output in order to reduce the demand facing them.
>
> This price increase will have two effects. The overall increase in the demand for goods will be damped down as real balances are reduced; and its composition will be switched towards the output of fix-price producers. If there were no fix-price sellers, then the attempts of flex-price firms to raise their relative prices would be frustrated, and with each firm having full knowledge of the current price level, the latter variable would be forced up until the excess supply of money which caused the initial increase in demand for goods was completely eliminated. We would be back in a full Walrasian system just as we would be in the New-classical model if we allowed agents contemporaneous access to correct information about the general price level. So long as there are some fix-price sellers in the system, however, the process will stop short of this point. The price level will increase less than in proportion to the increase in the quantity of nominal money. An excess supply of real balances and its associated rate of flow of expenditure (and hence of output) will therefore persist and be observed.

If some prices are sticky, fixed for a time, then even anticipated monetary growth will change real output, real cash balances and real interest rates, at least temporarily.[3] This suggests that the policy impotence theorem depends on the relative speed with which monetary policy and goods prices adjust. If goods prices are relatively slow to adjust and sticky (e.g., with long-term wage contracts, infrequently changed price tags on large durable goods, etc.) whereas monetary policy changes – leading to

---

[1] Laidler (1988) comments that 'a little price stickiness goes a long way in macroeconomics'. Thus it is 'sufficient to enable us to explain not only why output fluctuates in response to monetary shocks and why such output fluctuations persist over time, but also why real balances vary, with positive serial correlation, around their long-run desired value'.

[2] Also see Fischer (1977a) pp. 191–205 and Fischer (1980).

[3] Indeed, given lags in the demand for money function, overshooting in such variables might occur if it were not for the treatment of monetary balances as 'buffer stocks', see Chapter 12, Section 3.

changes in real interest rates – can be introduced overnight, then in the short run monetary policy, whether anticipated or not, remains effective. This seems to be a reasonable simulacrum of how the system actually works.

In a long enough time period, all contracts will come up for renewal and all prices will be revised. In such a long period, all prices can be regarded as effectively flex prices and accordingly, in such a long-term context, the policy impotence theorem will hold. If one considers, for example, economic developments decade by decade, real output is constrained only by real factors, and shifting rates of growth of the money supply will primarily be reflected in a differing rate of inflation.

How long is the period in Western developed countries during which a sufficiency of price stickiness remains to make anticipated monetary policy have real effects? That is not known for certain, but Friedman's claim that monetary stimuli affect real expenditures after about nine months and then become largely exhausted in price adjustments after about two years may provide a clue.

Neo-classical macro-economics have hitherto been largely based on imperfections in information transmission on monetary and price data. Keynesian and old monetarist macro-economics are both implicitly based on imperfections in the form of price stickiness, a lack of perfectly flexible Walrasian markets. As emphasised from the outset in Chapter 1, the latter seems a much more plausible assumption than the former.

Appendix: UK Indexed Gilts: A Case Study of Financial Indexation

1. Why Academics and Central Bankers Hold Different Views

What change of market practice has a whole series of the world's greatest economists, such as Jevons, Marshall, Irving Fisher, Keynes and Milton Friedman, virtually unanimously recommended; and which practical men in authority, notably Central Bank Governors, have generally firmly resisted as far as they could and have adopted only with the utmost reluctance? The answer is a move to indexed contracts, expecially long-term contracts (e.g., wages, tax brackets and financial contracts).

Economists reckon that there are only very limited costs in a *fully* anticipated inflation, to which all expectations and institutional arrangements (e.g., accounting practices) had fully adjusted. They reduce to the so-called menu costs of having to change prices more frequently (the higher is the known rate of inflation), the informational costs of working out the appropriate price adjustments, and the costs arising from the supposed technical inability to pay interest on currency.[1] The latter cost induces the public to economise on cash holdings, thereby increasing transaction costs (shoe-leather costs), and imposes a tax on their existing currency holding, thus reducing their wealth. Against this, the increase in government revenue from seignorage (i.e., from the inflation tax) may allow some reduction in other distortionary taxes and the substitution out of currency into other assets may marginally reduce real-interest rates, the so-called Tobin effect.[2]

The fact that *fully* anticipated inflation would be relatively painless is, perhaps, less paradoxical than it seems, since if the authorities really could *control* the continuing pace of inflation so exactly, they could also reduce it to a zero rate by a fairly simple currency reform, as Leijonhufvud has pointed out.[3] Accordingly, it is fair to regard any inflation as

---

[1] Both Huston McCulloch in his discussant's note, 'Beyond the Historical Gold Standard' (1986) p. 75 and I, in my paper 'How Can Non-Interest-Bearing Assets Co-exist with Safe Interest-Bearing Assets' (1986b) pp. 1–12, have argued that this technical problem could be overcome by offering lottery prizes, based on random drawings of the serial numbers of outstanding notes, so that the *expected* return on currency holding was the same as on other assets.

[2] See Tobin and Buiter 'Fiscal and Monetary Policies, Capital Formation, and Economic Activity' (1982).

[3] For example, he wrote in 'Inflation and Economic Performance' (1981):

> The quick and painless way to end an anticipated inflation is a currency reform that I call the 'blueback' scheme. Since, under the assumed conditions, 'greenback' dollars depreciate in real purchasing power by 15 per cent a year, one could create a new 'blueback' currency and make it, by law, appreciate relative to greenbacks at 15 percent per year. On the initial date the exchange rate between the two monies is one for one, but from that day onward bluebacks grow constantly in their legal capacity to extinguish debts contracted in greenbacks. One year later, 85 cents blueback will pay off a $1 greenback debt; two years later, it takes about 71 blueback cents; ten years later 19 cents.

occurring because the authorities are *not* fully in control – a key point whose implications will be considered further later. Since inflation is, by assumption, not under full control, equally it cannot be perfectly forecast or anticipated.

In contrast to the limited cost of anticipated inflation, the costs of unanticipated inflation are large. These have been tabulated at some length in the paper by Fischer and Modigliani, 'Toward an Understanding of the Real Effects and Costs of Inflation'.[1] Although in many cases the losses from unanticipated inflation (e.g., to lenders) are matched by unexpected windfalls (e.g., to borrowers), the additional uncertainty is disliked by risk-averse agents. Agents should, however, be able to avoid such additional uncertainty by agreeing to write their contracts in indexed form. After all, rational agents should be concerned with real outcomes. Why then are contracts not written in indexed form, which would allow the bargain to be established in a real form, undisturbed by nominal shocks to the price level?

In practice, we observe relatively few indexed contracts except in countries suffering from extremely high (e.g., treble digit) inflation. Why should this occur when the advantages seem so obvious?

One argument is that the uncertainty about inflation over the next few months, out to say a year ahead, is relatively low in most countries not subject to war, political crisis or ongoing hyperinflation, so that the benefits from indexation would be too low to make it worthwhile drawing up a more complicated contract.[2] Such administrative costs would be greatest where indexation was unfamiliar and the main institutional arrangements, e.g., taxation and accountancy, were all maintained on a nominal basis.[3] But as McCallum

---

If the originally held expectations of constant 15 percent greenback inflation of indefinite duration were indeed rational, then the blueback reform will ensure perfect price-level stability indefinitely. The scheme has two advantages over disinflation. First, employment is entirely unaffected. It is not necessary to suffer through a recession to get back to constant prices. Second, no one is swindled in the process. The real terms of contracts remain to be fulfilled as originally envisaged. The creditor who after 10 years received 19 cent blue, instead of $1 green, is getting exactly what he expected to get in real purchasing power.

Both of these advantages of the currency reform over disinflation stem, of course, from the fact that nothing is really done about the greenback inflation. The rate of greenback inflation is not reduced at all; it is only made subject to an arithmetical conversion. It is a cheap trick, if you will. But it does not 'evade the real issue'. On the contrary, 'really doing something' about the greenback inflation would be an irrational, destructive policy under the conditions assumed. It is assumed that we start from a quite stable monetary standard which happens to have the somewhat peculiar property that the money depreciates in real purchasing power at 15 percent a year. To disinflate is to adopt a policy that is inconsistent with this system of expectations. It breaks the prevailing regime and wreaks havoc, therefore. The Blueback system, in contrast, merely removes the peculiar property of this stable regime.

In the text above, I ignored the inflation tax on real balances and its allocative effects. In the case where greenback money is being taxed at 15 percent per annum, the blueback scheme introduces a new non-taxed money that will, therefore, immediately displace the old currency. Since the demand for real balances will be larger once money is no longer taxed, a larger nominal supply must be provided in order to avoid deflationary pressure on the blueback price-level and the associated, probable consequences for employment.

---

[1] Originally published in *Weltwirtschaftliches Archiv* (1978) pp. 810–32; reproduced in (1986) as Chapter 1.

[2] See McCallum (1986) pp. 409–10.

[3] Thus Fischer (1986) p. 154, suggests that, 'An issue worth further investigation is that of the possible existence of both indexed and nonindexed equilibria. Given that individuals typically want to be hedged, the incentive for an individual to introduce an indexed contract in a

notes 'this argument does not predict that there will be no linkage [of contracts to price indices] or indexation. On the contrary, it suggests that the benefits of linkage would outweigh the costs in the case of large contracts of long duration–mortgages for instance'.

A reason why one might have expected indexation to be most prevalent in long-term financial instruments is that these are the vehicle primarily used by savers to accumulate wealth over the earning period of their life cycle in order to finance their consumption (e.g., out of pensions) in old age. In practice, the wage earner has the power to adjust wages fairly closely to inflation; in addition, tax rates, even when not formally indexed, have been generally adjusted discretionally in reasonable conformity to inflation. But the old have had no such protection. The case in equity for providing the pensioner with a safe asset which protects savings against the ravages of inflation has always been strong.

Yet, prior to the recent issue of indexed instruments by the UK authorities (i.e., National Savings 'Granny bonds' in 1975 and indexed marketable gilts in 1981), the number of examples of such indexed financial instruments, other than in countries suffering extremely high inflation, has been remarkably limited.[1] The most extensive usage of index-linked bonds (other than in countries with hyperinflation) was in Finland from 1947 onwards, comprising some three-quarters of all government bonds and most of the outstanding bonds of financial institutions by the end of the 1960s. In France during the politically and financially disturbed period of the 1950s, there was fairly extensive indexing of public and private fixed interest securities. By 1957, about 55 per cent of outstanding French public bonds were index-linked while index-linked issues accounted for 80 per cent of all private bonds issued there in 1954. In 1958, however, when the New Franc was created under the stabilisation programme introduced after the devaluation of that year, the government banned most forms of indexation.[2] Indeed it has been common for the authorities to draw back from all forms of indexation, including indexation of financial instruments, as a component of a determined, counter-inflationary stabilisation programme. Following their experience of hyperinflation, the German authorities became adamantly opposed to any form of indexation. Even in cases where the inflation rate was so high that some form of indexed protection became unavoidable, the authorities generally looked on its adoption with regret and reluctance.[3]

One reason why the private sector has not introduced index-linking has been the opposition of the authorities to such contracts; on other occasions, the absence of inflation adjustments in the tax system has served as a barrier. Thus, the ability of borrowers in the UK to treat all nominal interest payments as a business expense, chargeable against tax even if much of such interest payments merely offset the effect of

---

nonindexed economy may be small, and since money is used as both unit of account and medium of exchange, there is a bias toward the economy not being indexed. But if indexation is already extensive, the private incentives may be to use indexed contracts. This argument can be seen very clearly in the case of financial intermediaries, who would likely be willing to issue indexed liabilities if they could hold indexed assets. But it applies also to households, who would be more willing to borrow indexed short term if their incomes were indexed.

---

[1] See, for example Fischer (1977b) reproduced in (1986) as Chapter 10.

[2] And the costly experience with the 1973 *Rentes Giscard*, which were indexed to gold, served to reinforce doubts about the wisdom of indexation.

[3] Thus, in the *Evening Standard* City comment of 2 December 1976, it was reported that Professor Simonsen, who had introduced financial indexation to Brazil, had stated that index-linked government stocks should be avoided: 'Professor Simonsen stated unequivocally that he would not recommend any country to embark on indexation if it could possibly avoid it, because it undoubtedly did build inflation more or less permanently into the system. If, however, you had got to the stage where something drastic had to be done, indexation was probably the least harmful choice'.

(anticipated) inflation in eroding the real value of the principal, has served as a disincentive to the issue of standard forms of indexed debt.[1]

This once again serves to draw attention to the question why the authorities have been, in practice, so opposed to indexation, even including indexation of financial instruments (where the equity argument is particularly strong). The argument has rested partly on historical experience. There are, however, a number of more analytical considerations. First, standard models (e.g., Fischer, 'Wage Indexation and Macroeconomic Stability') show that indexation protects output and employment in the face of nominal shocks but destabilises them in the face of real shocks.[2] Academic economists, especially monetarists, tend to perceive and to criticise nominal shocks induced by misguided government policies. Governments naturally tend to believe that their policies are optimal and often see the fluctuations in nominal magnitudes as largely resulting from a (passive) reaction to external (real) shocks. The perceptions of the authorities and of academic economists about the relative incidence of real and nominal shocks on the economy are thus likely to be markedly different.

Second, just as academic economists often accuse the monetary authorities of adopting time inconsistent policies, (see Chapter 15, Section 2), so the authorities may tend to believe that the private sector would pursue time inconsistent preferences. Inflation is thus frequently perceived by the public as a more serious problem than unemployment, but the short-term costs of disinflation deter them from being prepared to accept the necessary medicine. Fischer and Huizinga in their paper 'Inflation, Unemployment and Public Opinion Polls'[3] note 'the apparently inconsistent result that inflation is generally supposed to be the more serious problem, while it is preferred that policy be directed at reducing unemployment'. If the short-run costs of inflation are made less by indexation, the temptation would be enhanced for the private sector and the electorate to vote for, and to support, policies aimed at short-run reductions in unemployment at the expense of a longer-term much worse combination of unemployment and inflation. Central Bankers' fear of indexation may, therefore, be partly due to a belief that the private sector often expresses a myopic and irrational preference for the soft option and that indexation is a recipe for making that soft option seem softer yet.

Third, as noted earlier, the occurrence of inflation does represent some loss of control by the authorities, whether due to a real shock, such as the oil shocks in 1973 and 1979, union power, or to a failure to operate monetary policy effectively. The effect of indexation is to reduce the inertia, owing to wage–price stickiness, whereby shocks become passed onto prices only in partial form, with the remainder of the effect falling on real output. If there are adverse shocks tending to increase inflation, whether nominal or real, the effect of indexation is to exacerbate the purely inflationary effects of such shocks. Without indexation, and in conditions of wage–price stickiness, the inflationary impulse is moderated by declines in real wealth, by falls in real wages, etc. Now, if the government did have *complete control* over events, it could induce deflationary nominal shocks (e.g.,

---

[1] This problem could be partially circumvented by the provision of a bond paying inflation compensated interest (i.e., a real interest rate of x per cent plus an add-on for the actual recent rate of inflation). This is quite close to a variable rate instrument, except that in the latter bond the real rate may vary, while in the former instrument it would be fixed. Such inflation compensating bonds were analysed and considered by both private-sector bodies and by the authorities in the UK in the 1970s and 1980s but were not, in the event, introduced.

[2] Originally published in (1977c) pp. 107–48, reproduced in (1986) as Chapter 5. Thus (1986, p. 164) 'In summary, indexing shields real output from nominal disturbances by permitting constancy of the real wage in the face of such disturbances; indexing does not permit the stabilizing effect on real wages that would otherwise result from price level movements when disturbances are real'.

[3] Originally published in (1982) pp. 1–19, now reproduced in (1986) as Chapter 4.

by reducing the money stock) with a minimal impact on real output; indexation would then enhance the desired effect in reducing inflation.

It was along this line of reasoning that Milton Friedman advocated indexation plus monetary restriction as an appropriate counter-inflationary policy. But the very existence of inflation reveals that conditions, perhaps a series of adverse supply shocks, perhaps political circumstances, have weakened the power of the authorities to control events. In that case, adverse shocks likely to exacerbate inflation must be seen as more probable and the ability of the government to maintain a disinflationary policy more doubtful. If inflation is seen as a symptom of loss of governmental control, then the case for a policy such as indexation, which exacerbates the adverse effects of further such control failures and depends for its beneficial effects on the authorities regaining full and appropriate control, must be called into question. The academic argument for indexation seems to depend in part on the academic's view that the same government could and would simultaneously be able and willing to introduce those demand management policies and/ or rules that the academic believes appropriate. In reality, governments are subject to 'political' pressures that constrain their actions. Central Bankers are painfully aware of this and of the corollary that indexation can be a highly dangerous instrument.

The most extreme example of circumstances when political pressures tend to constrain governments occurs during wartime or civil strife. Lack of power and doubts about the government's future viability may make it harder for the authorities to borrow or to raise taxes. Resort to the printing press may then provide the only, or best, alternative source of finance to them. Indexation reduces the opportunity for governments to benefit from an inflationary tax by reducing the volume of additional real resources the government can attract from the private sector through printing an additional nominal value of currency and by pushing inflation rapidly up to such a level that the flight from currency will offset the inflation tax gains. Some right-wing commentators believe that the common dislike of governments for indexation is due to the fact that it blunts their ability to manipulate such an inflation tax. I believe that this is wrong. Given the public's vociferously expressed dislike of inflation, it would rarely be in any government's interest consciously to choose to inflate – recall Chapter 2, Section 3. Instead, circumstances place weak governments in positions where they cannot avoid inflationary shocks. This may seem a fine distinction but it lies, I believe, at the root of the difference of view between academics advocating indexation and the authorities, notably Central Bankers, resisting it.

The above arguments are directed against indexation in general. The authorities in the UK have usually tended to assess the various benefits of, and the strengths of the arguments against, indexation as differing depending on the particular contract under consideration. As already noted, the argument in equity (i.e., the need for protection from unanticipated inflation) seems strongest in the case of the provision of inflation-hedged financial instruments for pensioners and weakest in the case of wages. Again, concern about indexation serving to reinforce adverse inflationary shocks was greatest in the case of wages and less so in the case of financial instruments, especially since actual nominal interest payments would be lower in the early years of the life of an indexed instrument and so could not be held to have increased input costs or the need for additional borrowing.

This dislike of wage indexation was much enhanced by the disastrous experience with Prime Minister Heath's policy in indexing wages beyond a threshold in 1973. The subsequent oil-price shock triggered the thresholds and so an external, real shock generated an internal wage–price spiral than was worse than in virtually any other country. Finally, the authorities here have tended to prefer those forms of indexation that eased their own financial management problems and disliked those that added to government expenditures.

The authorities in the UK have thus implicitly created a merit ordering for indexation which in the early 1980s could be approximately ranked, going from good to bad:

1. Financial instruments restricted to old-age pensioners.

2. Long-term financial contracts.
3. Taxation.
4. Pensions.
5. Government expenditures.
6. Wages.

The extent of difference between the cases for indexation of these separate contracts was felt to be sufficiently marked that, during the early 1980s, the Conservative government was taking steps to try to *de-index* government expenditures by forcing Departmental programmes to return to a nominal, in place of the previous real, basis and to limit the indexation of public sector pay; at exactly the same time, it was extending the range of indexation on financial instruments and taxation.

This was not illogical; it was simply that the strength of the arguments, pro and con, varied depending on the contract–market under consideration. Nevertheless, a primary concern in each case for any further step to extend indexation to contracts–markets at the top of the merit table was that it should not weaken the case for restricting and withdrawing indexation for contracts–markets at the bottom of the table. This was known as the 'contagion' or 'spreading' argument. If faced with a choice between a fully-indexed system and a completely unindexed system, the authorities throughout the 1970s and 1980s (up to the present, at least) in the UK would have chosen the latter. However, in those cases where 'contagion' was thought to be a remote danger and the benefits of indexation was greatest, the authorities were prepared to consider such cases favourably.

I shall not deal further with the arguments or policy measures relating to indexation of items 3 through 6 of the merit table but in the following section, I shall concentrate on the discussions concerning financial indexation in the UK over the last two decades.

2. The UK Experience, 1970s and 1980s

The possibility of issuing indexed financial instruments was raised on a number of occasions after the Second World War, notably during periods of worsening inflation, which also often coincided with times when it proved difficult for the authorities to sell conventional nominal instruments, both non-marketable National Savings and marketable bonds (gilts). The question arose for example in 1950–1. It is not surprising, therefore, that the issue next arose forcefully in 1974 due to the inflationary climate at the time.

This had several facets. First, the Page Committee to Review National Savings advocated the introduction of indexed national savings and suggested an outline scheme.[1] Largely because of fears of 'contagion', the government did not make such instruments as widely available as Page had advocated, but they did introduce two restricted instruments in 1975. The first of these was an indexed-linked National Savings Certificate which could be purchased only by retired persons (men over 65 or women over 60). This became known as the 'Granny Bond'. The second was an indexed Save As You Earn instrument. Both had ceilings on the amount that could be invested. The sums subsequently invested in such instruments were at times sizeable but only between the fiscal years 1979–80 and 1981–2 represented a really major source of government finance, despite periodic relaxations in the age and ceiling restrictions (see Table 13.2 below).

Besides the particular case for providing an inflation-hedged financial asset for the old age pensioner (OAP), the 1974 upsurge in inflation led to a more general reawakening of interest in indexation. The National Institute of Economic Research devoted much of their November 1974 issue to four papers on various aspects of indexation and discussed the advantages that could be expected from either a voluntary or a statutory programme

---

[1] *Committee to Review National Savings*, Cmnd 5273 (1973), especially pp. 190–8.

TABLE 13.2 (£m)

	1975/76	1976/77	1977/78	1978/79	1979/80	1980/81	1981/82	1982/83	1983/84	1984/85	1985/86	1986/87
Net inflow in financial year												
I-L NS certificates	246	255	234	268	749	1285	2095	– 127	– 221	– 278	– 198	– 406
I-L SAYE	25	89	88	109	128	130	104	– 28	– 12	– 33	– 106	– 86
A Total index-linked	271	344	322	377	877	1415	2199	– 155	– 233	– 311	– 304	– 492
Total net inflow to National Savings												
B (i) as published	500	994	1094	1618	968	2239	4244	3036	3278	3071	2106	3365
B (ii) adjusted for comparability[a]	408	992	1861	1444	1374	2504						
C PSBR	10,253	8304	5373	9235	10,020	12,687	8632	8844	9745	10,195	5751	3447
A as percentage of B (ii)	66.4	34.7	17.3	26.1	63.8	56.5	52.1	– 5.1	– 7.1	– 10.1	– 14.4	– 14.6
A as percentage of C	2.6	4.1	6.0	4.1	8.8	11.2	25.5	– 1.8	– 2.4	– 3.0	– 5.3	– 14.3

[a] The adjusted figure *includes* net inflows to the NSB Investment Account throughout (it was treated as an OFI until December 1980), and also *excludes* net inflows to the TSB Ordinary Accounts, which were part of National Savings up to September 1979.
Source: Table 39, *Financial Statistics* (1987).

of indexation. The arguments for indexation in general, and for encouraging indexed financial instruments to be issued either by the private or public sectors, were taken up and supported in the Press, notably by the influential commentators, Anthony Harris and Samuel Brittan in the *Financial Times*.

Of more immediate relevance to *financial* indexation, the rise in nominal interest rates to over 10 per cent during 1973 had made company treasurers unwilling to float additional conventional debt issues in the UK corporate bond market. This led some innovative characters in the private sector to wonder whether an index-linked issue might be a possible viable alternative source of debt finance and soundings were made for the authorities' reactions.

The reactions were negative. There were a number of strands. The views of most European official colleagues, expressed in various OECD and EEC Committees, were firmly, in some case vehemently, opposed to financial indexation. Current nominal interest rates were then extraordinarily negative in real terms and there were fears that the introduction of an indexed bond with a guaranteed positive real rate, if held to maturity, might (somehow – the discussion was a bit confused) drive up interest rates on conventional nominal bonds. There were concerns that the issue of indexed-linked bonds would require changes in, or put added adverse public pressure on, the non-indexed status of current taxes (e.g., capital gains tax) which the authorities were not ready then to accept. But above all, shortly after the disastrous 1973 experiment with partial wage indexation, the argument that any further steps towards indexation, beyond the tightly restricted National Savings instruments, gave rise to possibilities of contagion won the day.

Whereas the flurry of excitement and discussion about financial indexation in 1974–5 was quite largely concerned with the provision of private-sector indexed bonds, the next bout of interest in this general topic, in autumn 1976, was primarily concerned with the possibility of issuing indexed public-sector gilts. The structure of the London capital market then, with weakly capitalised brokers and (few) jobbers,[1] was such that the authorities felt obliged to maintain a 'tap' system of issues, whereby new issues were made at prices closely in line with market prices on the announcement date. If gilt prices then rose, the new issue might be oversubscribed; if prices fell after the announcement date, there would be few outside buyers and the Bank would take up the bulk of the issue onto its own books and peddle the issue out again, i.e., on 'tap', as and when the market showed signs of strengthening. Whatever the advantages of this method – and they were considerable given the structure of the market – it did mean that the authorities found that their debt sales varied between feast and famine. The latter was particularly likely when fears of worsening inflation led to a weak gilts market. Furthermore, in the mid-1970s much greater attention was being paid to the growth of the monetary aggregates. Since debt sales were then in practice the authorities' main instrument for restricting monetary growth (see Chapter 10, Section 3) a debt sales famine led to faster monetary growth. This could lead, and was so accused of leading in 1976, to the following vicious spiral:

Worsening inflationary fears (from some shock) $\longrightarrow$ debt sales famine $\longrightarrow$ faster monetary growth $\longrightarrow$ worsening inflationary fears $\longrightarrow$ debt sales famine $\longrightarrow$ etc.

The argument for indexation of gilts in 1976 was that they could be sold when conventional debt could not, thereby breaking the spiral. Moreover, the collapse of the exchange rate in 1976 was reviving inflationary fears and commentators were again pressing the merits of indexation. There was now, however, another counter-argument to add to the previous list. If it was the authorities who would be issuing the indexed debt, how would this affect the ability of companies to raise additional funds from capital markets? Companies might be unable or unwilling to follow the authorities' example and raise indexed debt. With the conventional corporate debt market closed, their only other

---

[1] For further details, see Goodhart 'The Structure of the London Capital Market' in Goodhart *et al.* (eds) (1987).

alternative then was new equity issues. But might the issue of indexed debt adversely affect equity prices? Equities had proved a poor inflation hedge; with the availability of a better hedge, might not savers, especially the long-term savings institutions, life insurance and pension funds, pour out of equities into indexed gilts?[1] Might the company sector's financing options be adversely affected then by the introduction of indexed gilts?

The possibility of issuing an indexed bond was not, however, the only innovation under consideration for operational use in the gilts market at that time. Two other ideas were floated, a variable interest bond and a convertible, which allowed investors at some future date to opt for a short maturity if inflation and nominal interest rates rose, or a long maturity if the reverse occurred, on terms set out in the prospectus. Both these provided some partial protection for investors against unanticipated inflation. It was felt that these might be saleable in conditions when pure nominal conventional bonds were not; moreover, they did not involve or carry with them the more radical implications, or 'spreading' dangers, which many feared from the introduction of indexed-linked gilts. Accordingly, the decision was taken to proceed with these two new forms of gilt, leaving an indexed issue on one side to be reconsidered perhaps if inflationary pressures and monetary control problems worsened.

In the event, the UK economy recovered, the exchange rate strengthened and monetary and inflationary fears eased somewhat in 1977. Although there remained an undercurrent of interest in the question of issuing indexed gilts, the next major bout of official discussion and analysis of the topic did not occur until 1980. Once again, the authorities were having difficulty in maintaining monetary control in a regime which now, under the new Conservative government, was placing the utmost emphasis on targeting £M3. Periods of bond sale famine or buyers' strikes were even less welcome. It was widely recognised that unfamiliar instruments, such as indexed gilts, would have to be issued by tender auction: there was no existing established market to enable a 'tap' price to be set. Some saw the introduction of tenders of indexed gilts as a means of getting a firmer quantitative grip over the time path of public sector debt sales.

Moreover, nominal bond yields at all maturities rose in 1979–80 to high levels, though not as high as the year-on-year increase in the RPI which was temporarily inflated by the sharp hike in VAT rates (8 to 15 per cent in the June 1979 Budget), the 1979 oil shock and the collapse of the previous incomes policy restraint on public-sector wages. In any case, ten-year bond rates were running at 13.7 per cent at the end of June 1980 and the RPI was 21 per cent up on a year past. By then the government had unveiled the Medium Term Financial Strategy (MTFS) in March 1980, intending to reduce inflation determinedly by a steady, gradual reduction in £M3. If inflation was to be thus controlled, was not the current high level of medium- and long-term interest rates out of line with the government's firm intentions? Would not such borrowing, on conventional terms, prove excessively expensive, and would the continuation of such borrowing not appear to contradict the government's own professed confidence in the reduction of future inflation?

In fact, calculations of the comparative cost of conventional and indexed borrowing did not show such a large advantage for the latter, on the assumption of at least partial success in combating inflation, as might have been superficially expected. Current conventional rates were negative in real terms again. Moreover, the high nominal interest rate was taxable. For investors paying, say, a rate of 40 per cent tax on interest income, the post-tax real rate on conventionals was again markedly negative. Depending on the average tax rate assumed for investors, the inflation rate had to be expected to fall fairly fast to quite low levels to make the predicted cost to the government of issuing indexed bonds cheaper.

With the comparative cost argument turning out to be less clear-cut than initially expected, much turned on views of how the general public would perceive the step. Would the issue of indexed gilts be received as a sign of contra-inflationary confidence (e.g., by

---

[1] For a theoretical treatment of this issue, see Fischer, 'The Demand for Index Bonds' (1975) pp. 509–34, also reproduced in (1986) as Chapter 9.

reducing the benefits from future unanticipated inflation)[1] or might they be viewed as a measure to ease the stress of living with inflation, a prelude to giving up the battle? While presentational conditions were considered important (e.g., that they should not be issued until the rate of change of the year-on-year figure for the RPI had turned downwards and monetary conditions appeared under better control) the counter-inflationary determination of the government was so patent that the confidence effects could be expected to be beneficial.

Among the authorities' counter-inflationary policy measures were steps aimed to *reduce* the ambit of indexation in other fields (e.g., government expenditures) and possibly public-sector pensions.[2] Moreover, the argument that those worried about contagion had expected to hear, being the claim that if the rentier's (bond holder's) real income is to be hedged against (unanticipated) inflation, then so should be the income streams of other income recipients (e.g., wage earners) was then, and indeed largely remained, hardly raised at all in public commentary and discussion. So, the key counter-argument about contagion was fading.

Finally, there was a minor and largely cosmetic advantage for the presentation of government finances. The shift from conventional to indexed gilts – assuming an *exactly equal ex post* cost – reduced recorded interest payments, especially in the earlier years, and these were included in the CGBR and PSBR. This was achieved at the expense of much larger maturities in the later years but under existing statistical accounting practice, these latter did *not* affect the size of the PSBR. Thus, the switch could cause a quite sizeable cosmetic improvement to the appearance of government finances.

Against these putative benefits, the general argument about contagion, though now weakened, could still be made. Concern about the effect on equity prices and on private sector corporate financing opportunities remained, as it had earlier in 1976. Moreover (in part associated with the question of allowing the private sector to compete on level terms in the issue of indexed bonds), their issue would highlight the embarrassing fact that capital gains tax was being levied on purely inflationary, not real, price rises. There would seem to be some likelihood of indexation spreading into further parts of the tax system. tax system.

The major new objection to indexation in 1980 came, however, from the external side. There were reports that OPEC was pressing both for the indexation of oil prices and for the availability of indexed financial instruments in which to invest. Certain other OECD countries were opposed, often vehemently, to indexation in general and to OPEC's floated ideas in particular. The UK might be seen to be breaking ranks. More important, the availability of this new form of financial instrument, an indexed bond issued by a major country with a broad and liquid capital market, was considered possibly attractive to non-residents. At that juncture, however, the pound exchange rate was already under great upward pressure from a combination of North Sea Oil and tight counter-inflationary policies (see Chapter 18) and the prospects of a further boost to the rate were unpalatable, perhaps the more so in view of the extreme uncertainty about how large such inflows and the resulting appreciation might be.

In the event, these latter two concerns, particularly the external effect but also relating to the tax implications, were side-stepped by restricting the investors eligible to take up the

---

[1] They were even described as 'sleeping policemen' to deter a future more inflationary government.

[2] There was much adverse comment about the favoured (indexed) position of public-sector pensions, *vis à vis* unindexed private-sector pensions, and it was widely thought that the government sympathised with that criticism and wished to curtail such indexation. They appointed the Scott Committee to consider this question, *inter alia*, and its report not only supported the continuation of the indexation of civil servants' pensions but talked of extending it to the private sector. So, in the event, nothing was done.

indexed issue[1] to a limited class of eligible holders (i.e., UK pension funds and life insurance companies undertaking pension business). Since these counted as 'gross funds' not subject to tax on income or capital gains, there were no consequential tax implications. The first issue was for £1bn and the demand at the tender was such that it sold at par with a coupon of 2 per cent. Subsequently, real yields on all gilts, including indexed gilts (IGs), rose. The appetite of these institutional investors for indexed gilts was less than had been expected and there was diminishing enthusiasm at the subsequent two tenders for such restricted IGs, £1,000mn of IG 2006 in July 1981 and £750mn of IG 2011 in January 1982.

So, there was a market reason (i.e., to encourage a wider demand) for relaxing the eligibility restrictions. More important, by the winter of 1981–2, the pound exchange rate was sinking back quite fast from its earlier peaks. Nor had the world at large taken much notice or made much fuss about this experiment. Finally, the Chancellor was preparing to extend indexation in fiscal matters, notably to capital gains tax in his 1982 Budget. So at a stroke, all the arguments for restriction fell away and it was removed in that Budget.

Indexed gilts were then available for all to buy and no limitations were imposed that would prevent private sector borrowers from following suit. Many of those engaged in the debates leading up to this point had felt that it was an important step with potentially large and unknown implications. The somewhat surprising impression, in the subsequent five years, is, instead, how little change this step has made. The demand for IGs, both by residents and – as far as can be ascertained – by non-residents has been patchy and the issue of IGs has raised approx. £12bn, out of total gilt issues of £96bn, March 1980–March 1987.[2] Perhaps this was due to the fact that, at times when inflation is coming down quite sharply, IGs tend to under-perform conventionals. What might happen to the balance between IGs and conventionals if inflation was to rekindle has yet to be seen. Be that as it may, the issue of IGs had less effect on debt management overall than the changing attitudes towards over-funding (see Chapter 10, Section 3) and than the structural changes to the capital market caused by Big Bang in October 1986.[3]

Moreover, the authorities' lead has been resolutely ignored by the private sector. By summer 1987, no company had attempted an indexed issue, though some had given the subject some thought. Moreover, given the availability now of a safe indexed asset to hold, one might have expected financial intermediaries to issue indexed liabilities and that would still seem to have some fiscal advantages. No steps in this direction have, however, yet appeared. Given the government's lead and the removal of barriers, the remaining

---

[1] Announced in the Budget of 1981, with simultaneous publication of prospectus, for tender on March 27th.

[2] Cash receipts from issues of British government stocks by the National Loans Fund (£mn)

	Total	Of which index-linked	Index-linked percentage
1980–1	16,084	346	2
1981–2	10,904	2,564	24
1982–3	10,609	2,234	21
1983–4	15,674	2,222	14
1984–5	15,862	1,623	10
1985–6	11,648	825	7
1986–7	15,028	2,309	15

The first index-linked stock was issued only just before the end of 1980–1, which means that the percentage is inevitably lower in that year.

Source: Table 3.6, Financial Statistics (1987).

[3] See Goodhart (1987b) pp. 6–15.

reservations that the private sector apparently feel about financial indexation (e.g., the difficulty of choice of appropriate price index, legal complexity, etc.) are quite unclear. The potentially explosive charge has turned into a damp squib.

One final word of warning is, perhaps, necessary. The existence of indexed debt is often taken to provide a good estimate of longer-term future inflationary expectations (e.g., by subtracting the calculated real yield on IGs from the yield on conventionals). To start with, the calculation of the real yield on the IG is complicated by the administratively necessary link to a slightly *lagged* RPI change. Next, the structural changes (i.e., the changes in eligibility rules 1981–2) make the calculation particularly fraught in the early years. The patchy nature of demand and occasional tenders led to market price movements in the short run that have had little relationship to underlying inflationary expectations. The tax position of IG holders will differ from short to long maturities and, in general, will *not* be the same as that of holders of conventional gilts, with the discrepancy probably greatest at the long end. Such tax considerations mean that the calculated differential will be sensitive to the coupon on the matched-maturity conventional and, of course, matched maturities will imply differing *durations*. Furthermore, inflationary expectations and risk aversion to (unanticipated) inflation are *not* homogeneous. IGs will attract those who are more fearful. A widening of the dispersion – with a constant mean expectation – could encourage demand for IGs. Similarly, a narrowing of the dispersion (e.g., after an election) could reduce the demand for IGs even without any change in mean expectations. Those attempting to use the IG–conventional yield spread as a proxy for inflation expectations should be aware of its limitations.

XIV
Monetary Policy – 1: The Use of Policy Instruments in an Uncertain World

Summary

In a world of certainty, the authorities know the exact effect of varying their control instruments (e.g., through monetary or fiscal policy actions) upon the various objectives of policy, such as full employment, stable prices, etc. Difficulties will be encountered, however, whenever there are more objectives than instruments. In such cases, not all objectives can be fully met and the most that can be done is to achieve the best possible compromise (or trade-off) between the various objectives. An alternative and apparently more attractive approach is to search for further (independent) instruments. But it is a common experience to find that the employment of another instrument can reveal a threat to some further objective. If demand management seems incapable of maintaining both a reasonable level of employment and price stability, the introduction of a prices and incomes policy to help in containing inflation may thus endanger, *inter alia*, the allocative function of the price mechanism.

The most common conflict is between jam today and jam tomorrow. Policy decisions taken with the intention of affecting the economy now are likely, in many cases, to influence outcomes in future periods because of the dynamic properties of the system. In the short run with given expectations, there can be scope for expanding the level of employment without a large acceleration of inflation. But the acceleration of inflation, small though it may be initially, then gets built into the system, thereby worsening future policy options. Similarly, Mundell's proposals[1] for achieving short-term balance, both internally and externally, under a fixed exchange rate, can in some cases lead to a longer-run worsening state of affairs. Since the objectives of our society outnumber the instruments for their achievement, the most that policy can strive to attain even in a world of certainty is a fair compromise.

In Section 2, uncertainty is introduced, but only in a limited form. The authorities are assumed still to know the exact structure of the system but not to be able to foresee the stochastic shocks that may perturb it. Despite the unreality of the assumption of perfect knowledge of the structure, much of the economic forecasting and policy choices that derive from these forecasts proceed as if the deterministic models used were an accurate representation of the underlying system. The main subject of this section is how to cope with the random shocks that cannot be foreseen, even assuming the structural form of the deterministic model to be correct. Put simply, the answer is to identify where the main source of disturbance is likely to occur and to arrange a policy response, in the intervals between periodic reviews of

---

[1] Discussed later in Section 1 of this chapter.

the economy, which will provide an automatic stabilisation against shocks from this source. In the *IS/LM* context, if the main source of disturbance comes from shocks in the goods market (to the *IS* schedule), then the authorities should maintain a stable rate of monetary growth; if the shocks predominantly come in the money market (to the *LM* schedule), then it would be better to stabilise interest rates. Although theoretical explorations of optimal stabilisation policies along such lines have been much in vogue, their practical significance has probably been overstated. Given the assumption of a structurally correct model, the analysis has relevance only over those periods during which the source and forms of shocks to the economy cannot be identified (and thus exactly offset) while reliable data on both the monetary aggregates and interest rates can be obtained. In fact, in the United Kingdom and in many other countries where monetary data are obtained only once a month, information about the development of the economy as a whole (e.g., industrial production, trade figures, etc.) is available just about as soon and with the same (lack of) reliability as the monetary data. The concept of steering the ship by observing monetary signals while waiting for the fog to clear from the economic landscape is, perhaps, peculiar to the North American scene. In other countries, the monetary signals are also fogged out.

In any case, the real problem for policy, raised in Section 3, is that the forecasting models used are, to be sure, not accurate representations of the underlying world. Many economists ignore this problem because each believes that his own preferred model is correct; the policy-maker faced with a plethora of models and advice cannot, however, make such an assumption. This difficulty is most acute when there is a widespread belief that existing models do not capture some important aspects of reality. This was the situation in the United Kingdom, for example in the early 1970s; policy-makers and commentators generally were persuaded, largely on the basis of reports and work emanating from the United States, that monetary factors had a significant impact on the domestic economy but all the existing (extended Keynesian) forecasting models showed this impact to be negligible. So there was a sharp dichotomy in the United Kingdom between expressions of beliefs about the working of the economy and the estimated structure of the forecasting models. In these circumstances, it was difficult to choose an 'optimal' monetary policy and the tendency, when faced with a policy instrument which is believed to be powerful but whose effects may not have been clearly measured, is to play for safety. This final section ends by reviewing exactly what playing for safety may entail in an inflationary world.

1. Objectives and Instruments

In the simple *IS/LM* model, the level of incomes (*Y*) depends on autonomous factors affecting expenditure decisions (e.g., foreign demand for exports) and on the level of the money stock. If such autonomous factors (*X*) are taken as given, then the model can be easily transformed into a money multiplier of the standard form:

$$\Delta Y = f(\Delta M \mid X)$$

where *Y* represents nominal incomes and *M* the money stock.

Indeed, in the *IS/LM* model, the policy instrument, which is always specifically mentioned, is the money stock while the variable which policy-makers are presumably seeking to control is the level of incomes (by setting the level of the policy instrument (M) at that value which will bring the objective, i.e., incomes (Y), to its desired level (Y^*)). The structural IS/LM model depicts the transmission mechanism whereby this occurs and the parameters of the structural relationships show the size of variation in the control instrument necessary to achieve the desired objective. Of course, it was thought possible that in some circumstances, when a liquidity trap existed, changes in this control instrument might have no effect upon the objective. But this was always regarded as an unlikely, indeed pathological, condition and consideration of net wealth effects, the 'Pigou effect', offered an alternative route whereby monetary stimuli could theoretically affect income levels even when nominal interest rates were held in a liquidity trap, since the real value of M/P would be rising as P fell (see Chapter 12, Section 4), or M rose.

The level of money incomes, Y, the apparent objective in the IS/LM model, is not in practice, however, a true objective of economic management. Instead, policy-makers are concerned with the composition of any change in money incomes, generally applauding any increase in real incomes and output (y) but deploring usually any (upwards) change in the level of prices (p). Two consequences follow. The first is that it becomes necessary to consider how a change in money incomes becomes divided into a change in real incomes and prices respectively. This problem is not tackled in the IS/LM model or by the money multiplier approach, and the assumption that either prices or real output can be treated as autonomously given is obviously invalid. This subject was discussed in Chapter 13. Reverting for the time being from rational to backward-looking adaptive expectations, we may perhaps postulate for the purpose of this chapter that the relationship between changes in real income and prices can be reasonably described by equations[1] of the form:

$$\dot{y}_t = f(\dot{m}_t,...,\dot{m}_{t-n},\dot{p}_t,...,\dot{p}_{t-n},y_{t-1} - y^*_{t-1},...,y_{t-n} - y^*_{t-n}) \qquad (14.1)$$

where y^* is full employment income, and

$$\dot{p}_t = f(\dot{p}_{t-1},...,\dot{p}_{t-n},y_t - y^*_t,...,y_{t-n} - y^*_{t-n}) \qquad (14.2)$$

So there are now two objectives, $\dot{y}$ and $\dot{p}$, and only one instrument, $\dot{m}$. Indeed, we can simplify the structure of the above equations into a reduced form to describe the immediate choice set available of the kind

$$\dot{y} = a_1\dot{m} + a_2\dot{p}$$
$$\dot{p} = b\dot{y}$$

We can obtain instantaneous values for the two objectives only in combinations depending on the coefficients in the structural equations:

$$\dot{y} = \frac{a_1}{(1 - a_2b)}\dot{m}$$

and

$$\dot{p} = \frac{a_1b}{(1 - a_2b)}\dot{m}$$

The values of these coefficients will not, however, be constant over time but will depend at each point of time on current conditions (i.e., they are dependent on the

---

[1] Which, it may be noted, are quite similar in format to those contained in the St Louis model of the economy developed by Andersen and Carlson in their paper on 'A Monetarist Model for Economic Stabilization', (1970) pp. 7–25.

past history of the system, the previous lagged values of the endogenous variables and the current and previous values of omitted exogenous variables, here y^*).

As set down, monetary measures directly affect only output, depending on the rate of price inflation and the level of spare capacity, while the rate of inflation, given previous inflationary experience, depends on the pressure of demand. Monetary developments would influence the rate of inflation directly if they were taken as signals of prospective future inflation and thus entered immediately into the formation of current inflationary expectations, as discussed in Chapter 13, Section 2.

A graphical example of such a relationship is shown in Figure 14.1, with the line MM' showing the combination of $\dot{y}$ and $\dot{p}$ attainable as $\dot{m}$ increases. Although the simple algebraic example above made the relationship between $\dot{y}$ and $\dot{p}$ linear, Figure 14.1 presents the relationship as curvilinear, in view of the full capacity constrain on y, and therefore on $\dot{y}$, given the initial level of real incomes[1], y_{t-1}, and also of the

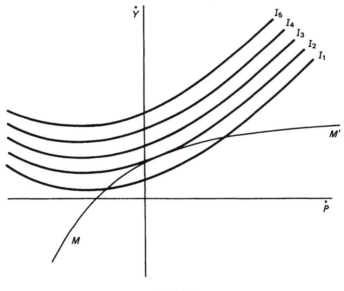

FIG. 14.1

---

[1] Given the initial level of real incomes, y_{t-1}, the higher the current level of incomes, y_t, is pushed, the higher is the current rate of growth of incomes, $y_t - y_{t-1}$. Thus, if we are only concerned with the immediate short-term future, it does not matter greatly whether the real incomes objective is specified in terms of levels or rates of growth (though as noted subsequently the process of change itself may involve tensions). Over the longer term there can, however, be conflict between these two objectives. Running the economy at a persistently lower level of demand might possibly force fiercer competition and thus induce a more efficient economy with a faster rate of growth of productivity and innovation. Alternatively, it might be desired to slow down the rate of growth of the economy (e.g., to conserve scarce resources), but (especially with a continuing growth of productivity) this might make it difficult to sustain a full-employment level of incomes. One should thus distinguish clearly between the two alternative real income objectives, relating to the level on the one hand and the rate of growth on the other, but while dealing only with short-term considerations, as above, the distinction can, perhaps, be left blurred.

downward inflexibility of wages and prices during periods of unemployment and depression. Next, we may imagine the shape of the community's indifference curves derived from their utility function(s); they prefer larger real incomes and less inflation.[1] Given the initial level of real incomes, people may find the attractions of higher real incomes declining and the possible disadvantages of accelerated change mounting as growth becomes faster while, on the other hand, inflation may become an increasing nuisance as it rises to a level where it has to be continually borne in mind in all economic decisions. Thus, the indifference curves must slope upward to the right and will be convex to the origin. The optimal position, where the highest indifference curve is tangential to MM', must always occur before that level of full capacity where all additional monetary stimulus is translated into price inflation.

A more common representation of the same basic relationship is provided by the standard Phillips curve relationship, showing how general demand management can be used to provide various short-run combinations of employment levels and price inflation. Again, one can imagine or even try to estimate[2] the likely shape of the community's indifference curves and show what the hypothetical (short-run) optimum would be (see Figure 14.2).

So, if there are two or more objectives (in this case, current rates of output and inflation) and only one instrument, it is not usually possible to achieve the desired levels of both variables simultaneously. The best that can be done is to reach the preferred available combination of outcomes for the objectives. The natural response to such limitations on our ability to reach our desired targets is to search for another instrument. Thus, if we have two objectives, X and Y, and two instruments, Q and R, so that

$$X = a_1 Q + a_2 R$$
$$Y = b_1 Q + b_2 R,$$

we can achieve any desired values of X and Y simultaneously so long as each of the instruments does have an effect on at least one of the objectives and also that $a_2/a_1 \neq b_2/b_1$ (i.e., that the two instruments are not simple linear transforms of each other, having precisely similar relative impacts on the two objectives, but instead are independent).

It can be more difficult to satisfy these conditions than it may look at first sight. In the present example, we have been considering ways of achieving certain output and price objectives through the use of monetary policy. Well, if monetary policy is not sufficient by itself to achieve the desired outcomes for both objectives simultaneously,

---

[1] Experience of falling prices, if at all pronounced, may also prove to be unwelcome and unpleasant, as depicted in the indifference curves in Figure 14.1, which turn slightly upward in the upper left-hand quadrant.

[2] Chossudovsky, 'Optimal Policy Configurations under Alternative Community Group Preferences' (1972) pp. 754–70, attempted to do this by questionnaire. Goodhart and Bhansali, 'Political Economy' (1970) pp. 43–106, tried to do it by observing the response of political popularity, as measured in the opinion polls, to changes in unemployment and inflation. Both methods have obvious flaws. Nevertheless, the exercise of relating political popularity to (various) socio-economic variables using econometric techniques remained popular and dozens of similar studies were subsequently run. The most interesting feature of such continuing work was that the focus of the electorate's concern seemed to shift over time, notably from primary concern with unemployment levels in the 1950s and 1960s towards concern with inflation and real incomes in the 1970s and 1980s. The dynamic process whereby the public's main concerns shift in relative importance has yet to be modelled or understood fully.

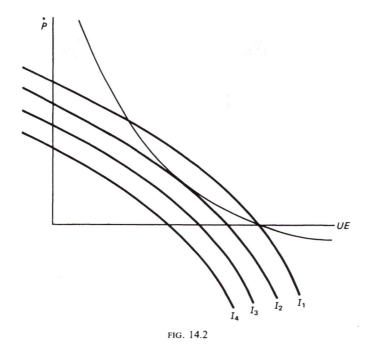

FIG. 14.2

why not appeal to that common alternative standby, fiscal policy? In the first place, some economists argue, and offer supporting evidence from the United States,[1] that given the level of the money stock, variations in the size of the budget deficit financed by bond sales will have little or no impact on the total of real output or on the rate of inflation except in the very short run within the first few quarters. The argument is that the rising interest rates required to sell the additional bonds will 'crowd out',[2] in a relatively short space of time, an equivalent value of other expenditures. Again, however, the supporting evidence in the United States comes from quasi-reduced form equations, money multipliers with additional fiscal variables, and the results, once more, seem inconsistent with the coefficients estimated in structural equations.[3] Moreover, there was no evidence, including replications of quasi-reduced form equations, of strong crowding-out effects in the United Kingdom in the early 1970s.[4]

So, the first question is whether fiscal policy can affect the aggregate level of demand at all or just the allocation of expenditure between different purposes (e.g., between expenditure on public or private goods). The majority of economists believe that fiscal policy can have a significant impact on the level of aggregate demand; indeed, it is the instrument of demand management on which the greatest reliance was placed in many countries, including the United Kingdom, prior to the mid-1970s. This does not, however, necessarily solve our instrument–objective problem because

[1] See, for example, Andersen and Jordan (1968) pp. 11–23.
[2] Spencer and Yohe (1970) pp. 12–24.
[3] Fisher and Sheppard (1972) especially Chapter 4.
[4] See, for example, Artis and Nobay (1969) pp. 33–51, especially pp. 37–42.

the question remains whether fiscal policy affects output and inflation in a significantly different way than does monetary policy. Monetary expansion affects money incomes by stimulating the general level of demand, and so does fiscal policy; they are both instruments of demand management. As such, they can hardly be expected to have significantly differentiated effect on the split of nominal incomes between real incomes and inflation. If so, fiscal policy is not in this context a separate, distinguishable instrument from monetary policy demand management; there would still be two objectives and one basic instrument.

Perhaps fiscal policy can be used in different ways – apart from its aggregate demand-management role – to influence inflation. Certain taxes and subsidies (e.g., indirect taxes) have a direct impact on price levels. Why not, therefore, reduce indirect taxes and raise subsidies to control inflation, and impose other taxes, say on incomes and profits, or raise interest rates and cut back on monetary growth in order to maintain aggregate demand at the desired level? Such policies will, however, affect the allocation of expenditure between the subsidised goods and other output which must be cut back commensurately, and may affect the distribution of incomes and the returns to working, risk taking, etc. If we are also concerned with these outcomes because they affect such objectives as growth, equity, etc. then the use of fiscal policy to affect inflation directly via taxes and subsidies may prevent the achievement of these other objectives. So, it seems that we could find another distinguishable instrument to influence inflation by varying the pattern of taxes, subsidies, etc. via fiscal policy but it would then be necessary to recognise these additional fiscal objectives; so, we would still be left with more objectives than instruments and must continue to accept some compromises in the attainment of economic objectives.

If fiscal policy as a demand-management instrument is too akin to monetary policy in its effects on the economy to have a significantly different impact, clearly prices and incomes policy comes from a very different stable, so there is no question of similar effects.

Once again, however, there are many who doubt whether an incomes policy is an effective instrument. Do attempts to intervene directly in the process of wage negotiation and price fixing, for example, really have any significant effect on the rate of inflation?[1] Moreover, such intervention will tend to prevent relative adjustments of prices and wages from signalling the changing pattern of requirements and scarcities. The imposition of a policy of direct control will, therefore, progressively erode the allocative efficiency of the economic system,[2] with consequential effects upon other objectives such as growth. Moreover, the resulting changes to the institutional structure of decision-making within the economy may trespass upon certain political objectives, for example 'the participatory democracy of collective bargaining'. So, in this case also, the introduction of another instrument to control a recalcitrant objective serves only to draw attention to certain further objectives which will be affected or even endangered by manipulation of the instrument in single-minded

---

[1] See, for example, Lipsey and Parkin (1970) pp. 115–38.

[2] These deleterious effects are usually thought to be relatively slight in the short run but to become increasingly severe as the controls are prolonged. The conclusion is then often drawn that a prices-and-incomes policy is suitable only as a short, sharp crisis measure, after which it would be put aside again. This raises the empirical question whether a temporary policy of this kind would not lead only to an accumulation of repressed price and wage adjustments which would break through with such a surge when the barrier was lifted as to undo any benefit from the previous restraint. Moreover, the expectation that such a policy would only be temporary might further weaken its longer-term efficacy.

pursuit of one objective. For every possible cure, there seem to be two complications; for every possible instrument, more objectives appear in view; compromise is also the art of political economy.

A nice example of this discouraging phenomenon can be provided by reviewing the thesis, attributed to Mundell,[1] for using monetary and fiscal policy for the joint maintenance of internal equilibrium (i.e., some desired level of capacity utilisation) and external equilibrium (i.e., no pressure on reserves) under a regime of fixed exchange rates. Both monetary and fiscal policy affect the domestic economy as demand-management instruments and also influence the balance of payments via changes in the pressure of demand domestically. In addition to this, monetary policy – but not fiscal policy – also affects the balance of payments directly by encouraging capital flows in response to changing international interest-rate differentials.

One can show graphically those combinations of monetary policy and fiscal policy, tightening monetary policy and easing fiscal policy[2] or vice versa, that might achieve the same level of domestic demand, line AA' in Figure 14.3. Since monetary policy has an extra bite, beyond influencing the level of domestic demand, in affecting

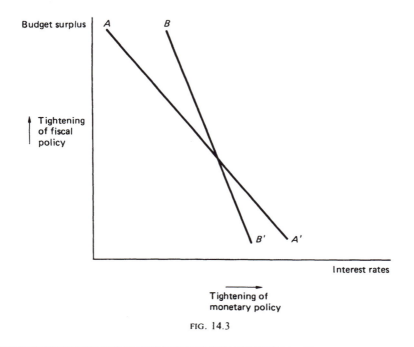

FIG. 14.3

[1] Mundell, 'The Appropriate Use of Monetary and Fiscal Policy for Internal and External Stability' (1962) pp. 70–7, reprinted in Thorn (ed.) (1966) Chapter 26.

[2] This bland phrase, however, can hide an unattractive situation for the monetary authorities, who might have to sell very large quantities of bonds in a fashion that would raise rates sufficiently to choke off excess demand generated by fiscal ease; this would have to be done without causing a financial crisis which would bring the whole pack of cards down and without imposing such severe distributional effects (e.g., a crunch in the housing market) that there would be revulsion from the direction of policy.

external equilibrium, a relatively smaller change in monetary policy, compared to a given change in fiscal policy, would be necessary to achieve the same balance in external equilibrium. Therefore the line BB' in Figure 14.3 showing those combinations of the two instruments giving the same external balance is steeper than line AA'. So, with two instruments, separable and effective, monetary and fiscal policy, it would seem possible to achieve two objectives, internal and external balance.

Indeed, it is generally possible to achieve a desired immediate balance, both internally and externally under these circumstances by an appropriate combination of monetary and fiscal policy, but the result of this policy stance will also have implications for future values of real income, wealth, etc. which are also objectives of policy. The chosen combination of fiscal and monetary policy is likely to influence the allocation of expenditure (e.g., as interest rates rise those forms of expenditure especially sensitive to higher rates will tend to decline). Shifts in the pattern of expenditure, between investment and consumption, are likely to influence the rate of growth of productivity, the time path of consumption, etc. If a balance-of-payments deficit is to be met by raising interest rates, investment and productivity may fall off, leading to worse inflation at any given level of demand and, thus, to a steady worsening in the basic balance-of-payments deficit to be financed.[1]

Furthermore, a rise in interest rates when there is a current-account deficit maintains temporary external balance by sucking in capital inflows which have to be serviced. A current-account deficit financed by attracting additional capital will lead inexorably to a growing deficit on interest and dividends within the current account. Only if the additional capital inflows go to finance domestic investment, the return from which in increased output can service the extra interest payments, as occurred for example during the nineteenth century when British capital helped to finance US and Canadian expansion, is this policy viable in the longer run. Moreover, the long-term continuing flow of capital between any two countries in response to a given interest differential, as wealth increases, is likely to be quite small in comparison with the flow resulting from a portfolio readjustment, as interest differentials alter. Therefore, the financing of any given basic deficit by the attraction of capital is likely to require continuously rising interest rates with cumulative effects on domestic expenditures and the overseas debt burden. So, in the short run, internal and external balance may be achieved by some combination of fiscal and monetary policies; in the longer run, however, this may only be a viable policy under restrictive conditions. Otherwise, it may be a prescription for disaster, meeting current objectives only at the risk of imperilling future ones.

Many of these policy problems arise because of the dynamic nature of the economic system in which the current achieved levels of the objective variables, and also of the control instruments, may affect subsequent values of the objective variables. Incorporating such dynamic relationships into the analysis often raises a whole range of additional problems and difficulties. Thus, in the first example in this

---

[1] Some economists, for example J. Williamson, ascribe some of the blame for the relatively slow growth of the British economy over the last two decades to a policy mix of relaxing fiscal policy, i.e., offering politically-popular tax cuts, to counter periods of high unemployment while jacking up interest rates in face of balance-of-payments crises during time of high employment. This argument would have been more persuasive if it did not seem that inflation had probably kept real rates of interest at such very low levels throughout the whole period. Williamson's theoretical attack on Mundell's theorem is to be found in his paper 'On the Normative Theory of Balance-of-Payments Adjustment' in Clayton, Gilbert and Sedgwick (1971) Chapter VII.

section of the interplay between demand management, real incomes and inflation, there were also such dynamic relationships, as shown for example in equations (14.1) and (14.2) (p. 330); these were ignored and suppressed in the earlier analysis which considered only the immediate, instantaneous choice set available. In particular, as noted in Chapter 13, previous inflationary experience will influence current expectations and thus will affect at any moment of time the possible combinations, or trade-off, between inflation and unemployment. The current choice of available options between growth and output on the one hand and inflation on the other will, therefore, circumscribe the form of future available options. When such dynamic inter-relationships occur, one should not aim for immediate results without paying attention to the future consequences of present decisions. In principle, each objective variable, for example real incomes, could be treated as a vector of dated elements stretching into the distant future, each element weighted by some discount factor, with the decision-maker developing a plan to deploy his policy instruments over time so as to maximise the expected utility attainable from the present values of the discounted future streams of the various objective variables. This represents a highly idealised picture of what might be possible under conditions of certainty; in the real world, where life is uncertain and short, simpler *ad hoc* rule of thumb decision processes are – indeed, have to be – adopted instead. Nevertheless, it is possible to argue the case for, or against, say, having more output and income now, even at the expense of having to accept a higher level of inflation in future (for any given level of demand), on rational grounds, even in actual conditions of real-life uncertainty.[1]

A further example of the kind of problem arising from such dynamic relationships was touched on previously (e.g., in Chapter 6, Section 3), referring to the problem of instrument instability. Even if there is only one objective variable, say incomes, and one instrument, say the money supply, the lagged relationship between incomes and current and prior values of the money stock might be such as to prevent the maintenance of incomes along some desired growth path without forcing movements in the money stock to follow some unstable path.[2]

This instability in the instrument variable may be disliked for its own sake, perhaps involving real operational costs, and might also be such as to make the variations in the instrument required for complete stabilisation of the path of the objective variable in practice incapable of actual achievement.

To summarise, the desires and objectives of man are virtually limitless, while the instruments for achieving those objectives are few. Compromise in the achievement of objectives is inevitable. Moreover, the choice of policy is complicated by the fact that current decisions will affect the system not only now but also in the future, so

---

[1] See, for example, Phelps (1972); and also Tobin (1972) pp. 1–18.

[2] Several earlier papers reported and analysed the problem of instrument instability. In particular, see Holbrook (1972) pp. 57–65, but note also the papers by Poole (1971) pp. 579–614 and Gramlich (1971) Part 2, pp. 506–32, especially pp. 524–30.
If the instrument (X) affects the objective (Y) with a distributed lag so that $Y_t = a_1 X_t + a_2 X_{t-1} + a_3 X_{t-2}, ..., + a_n X_{t-n}$, the values of the a_i coefficients may be such that it will be impossible to bring about a smooth rate of change in Y without causing instability in the time path of X. Thus, if the posited relationship was

$$Y_t = 0.2X_t + 0.6X_{t-1} + 0.2X_{t-2}$$

an increase in Y of one per period would require the following sequence of values of X: $+5$, -5, $+25$, -50, $+150$, -370, $+995$, -2575, $+6775,...$

that consideration has to be paid not only to our present concerns but to the future prospects for the system. This would be a difficult enough task, at least technically, if the authorities had perfect foresight; in a world of uncertainty, high expectations will lead only to disillusionment.

2. Policy Under Uncertainty – I: Random Disturbances

In the discussion in Section 1 on the use of control instruments for the achievement of economic objectives, it was by and large assumed that the authorities knew what they were doing; that they knew exactly how the economic system worked, so that basically their main problem was to compromise between a multiplicity of objectives by the use of a limited number of instruments in a system complicated by inter-temporal relationships. In reality, this is still hopelessly idealised. The authorities do not know the full consequences of their actions; they struggle along in a thick fog of uncertainty.

The simplest form of uncertainty to introduce is to postulate a system in which the authorities are presumed to know the exact form of the structural relationships within that system but that these functional relationships are subject to stochastic, random errors which cannot be predicted. The implications of such an assumption have usually been explored within the context of an IS/LM model, ranging from studies of the simplest basic model to stochastic simulations of full-scale macro-economic extended versions of the IS/LM framework. For heuristic purposes, it is probably easiest to stick to the simplest IS/LM construction.

In this basic model, there are three main behavioural equations which, assuming linearity and no uncertainty, may be written:

$I = a_1 Y + b_1 r$ Investment function
$s = a_2 Y + b_2 r$ Savings function
$Md = a_3 Y + b_3 r$ Demand for money function

Given these relationships and assuming that the authorities have fixed the nominal supply of money, the slopes and positions of both the IS and LM curves are determinate. By varying the quantity of money the authorities can shift the LM curve in order to achieve their desired value of Y.

It may, however, be the case that the authorities know the structure of the system well enough (i.e., the values of the structural coefficients are known with certainty) but that there are unforeseeable random factors, such as strikes, political events, technological discoveries and changes in the weather, which enter to disturb these known relationships. Then, these equations must be rewritten:

$I = a_1 Y + b_1 r + e_1$
$S = a_2 Y + b_2 r + e_2$
$Md = a_3 Y + b_3 r + e_3$

where e_1, e_2, e_3 are each separate random variables with an expected mean value of zero.

So, the authorities still know exactly what the slopes of the two curves are but they cannot now be sure exactly of their position, since both the IS and the LM curve can be shifted from their predicted position in an unforeseeable manner. Thus, as shown in Figure 14.4, the authorities may predict that the IS and LM curves will have

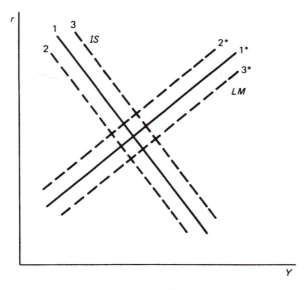

FIG. 14.4

positions 1 and 1* but random forces may shift the curves (though maintaining the slopes) say to 2 or 3, or to 2* or 3* in the case of the *LM* curve.

Why should this matter? As the authorities observe each shift in the behavioural relationships, in response to these random factions, can they not – in the context of this postulated *IS/LM* model – readjust the stock of money in order to offset these stochastic shifts and maintain the level of income at the desired value? One problem is that they may not be able to observe the occurrence of these stochastic forces or at least they may find it difficult to estimate the extent of their effect upon the system, perhaps until some time has passed. The length of time which may have to pass before the authorities can tell whether unforeseen developments have pushed the economy off target will depend on the speed of collection and the reliability of data measuring the course of the economy. If such data are gathered infrequently, far in arrears of current developments, and are inaccurate, then there could be a long delay between a disturbance affecting the economy and the information reaching the authorities to enable them to counter the shock.

When the authorities are deciding on their policy, they will use the latest available information about the economy to try to estimate the positions of the curves. On this basis, in a world adequately described by the *IS/LM* model, they would then set their instrument, the money stock, to achieve that level of interest rates and incomes which they desire. New information is only available at discrete intervals, however, and the process of forecasting and policy review is time consuming. So, revisions to policy occur only at occasional intervals, say once every few months. In the meantime, there will be these disturbances affecting the structural relationships in the system. This leads on to the question of how policy based on forecasts which have to take the expected value of random shocks as zero (the forecasting model being treated as deterministic since the values of all coefficients are assumed to be known) should be handled during periods between policy reviews when the system is responding, in a manner that cannot be clearly observed, to random shocks.

If the money stock is held constant at the level that was initially estimated to give the optimal results, then the interest rate will be forced by these shocks away from the value predicted to be consistent with the desired level of money incomes. If, on the other hand, the interest rate is held constant at this initial level, then the money stock will have to adjust away from the value which seemed optimal at the time of the forecast. In these conditions of uncertainty, owing to limited information, should the authorities choose to maintain the money supply or interest rates nearer to the initial chosen, optimal without disturbance, value?

If the shocks affect only the *IS* curve, assuming normal conditions in which this slopes downward,[1] the economy will fluctuate less in response to such shocks if the authorities stick to their initial money-stock target. This is shown graphically in Figure 14.9. A shift in the *IS* curve, say from *IS*1 to *IS*2 or *IS*3, will change incomes by amounts *OQ* and *OR* respectively if the money stock is held constant, but by the larger amounts *OP* and *OS* if interest rates are held fixed.

If, on the other hand, random disturbances impinge only upon the position of the *LM* curve (that is if these disturbances have their entire effect upon the demand for money function), then the economy (i.e., the level of nominal incomes) would be subject to less disturbance if interest rates were held constant. In this situation, in order to hold interest rates constant, the authorities have to offset shifts in the demand for money by a change in the supply of money. The *LM* curve would not appear to move and the initial *IS/LM* curves and (desired) values of Y and r_b would be unaltered by the random disturbance in the demand for money, compensated

---

[1] There is, however, also the possibility that the *IS* curve could slope upward if a higher *level* of incomes should encourage investment more than savings, perhaps via some form of accelerator-type mechanism. This obviously will cause some difficulties because at any point *off* the *IS* curve the non-equilibrium interest rate, assuming $dI/dr < 0$ and $ds/dr > 0$, will be tending to force the system even further away from equilibrium. This is shown in Figure 14.5, where *A* and *B* are two disequilibrium points and, as normally assumed, the initial response to disequilibria in the goods market is changes in money incomes while the initial response to disequilibria in the money market is changes in interest rates. If, however, the *LM* curve is steeper than the *IS* curve, then a stable equilibrium will still be attained, as shown diagrammatically in Figure 14.6. If the *IS* curve was steeper, equilibrium in the money market would be attained at the expense of continuously exploding incomes, as shown in Figure 14.7. In the first, stable case with *LM* steeper, random fluctuations in the *IS* schedule will necessitate changes in interest rates if an equilibrium is to be restored. Consider a policy of holding interest rates constant in the face of random disturbances, say a fall in the *IS* schedule from *IS*1 to *IS*2. It might seem (see Figure 14.8) as if point *C*, with a higher level of incomes (after a fall in the *IS* schedule!) would be a possible equilibrium, but the economy could never get there: instead, incomes would steadily decline along the line *DD'*. If, on the other hand, the money stock was held constant, equilibrium would be restored at point *E*.

Thus, the same conclusion holds, with respect to the appropriate monetary operations in the face of shifts in the *IS* (or the *LM*) curve, whether the *IS* curve is downward- or upward-sloping, assuming, however, that the structure is basically stable with the *IS* curve cutting the *LM* curve from above.

On the other hand, when the *IS* curve is upward-sloping, monetary policy appears to be more powerful when the interest elasticity of demand for money is high (with a flatter *LM* curve slope – so long as this remains consistent with the stability conditions). This reverses one of the standard results of the traditional model which assumes a downward sloping *IS* curve. See Silber (1971) pp. 1077–82.

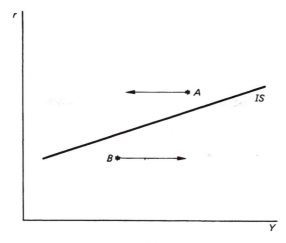

FIG. 14.5

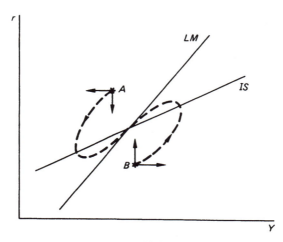

FIG. 14.6

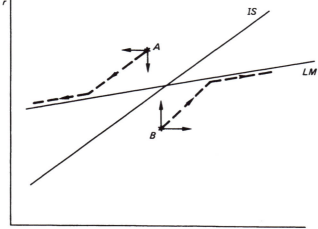

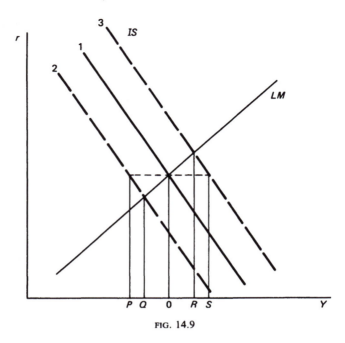

FIG. 14.9

exactly by a change in the money supply. If, however, the authorities maintain the money supply at its initial level, interest rates and thus money incomes must alter in response to this random shift in demand, forcing the economy away from its intended course.

This analysis has had some influence, partly because of the lucidity and elegance

Footnote cont.

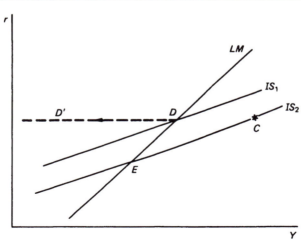

FIG. 14.8

with which it was initially developed by Poole,[1] in providing a theoretical basis and guide for the short-run operations of the monetary authorities in the intervals between forecasting rounds and policy reviews. If the extent of random variation within this interval is much higher in the goods markets (*IS* curve) than in the money market (*LM* curve), the implication is that it would be better for the authorities to stick to the planned rate of monetary growth. If the demand for money, and financial markets generally, exhibit greater instability, then the authorities should stabilise interest rates in these intervals between policy reviews.

On the whole, demand for money functions with quarterly or annual observations – i.e., with the individual periodicity of observation being fairly long – appeared to be relatively stable, at least in the 1950s and 1960s, though that stability was threatened on occasions in the 1970s and, in a number of countries, collapsed in the early 1980s (see Chapter 4, Section 2). Over intervals of this length, of say six months to a year, there are opportunities for considerable, unpredictable shifts in conditions in goods markets, owing to changes in world demand, wars, strikes, political factors, technological changes and shifts in moods, with such initial disturbances exaggerated over time by multiplier–accelerator mechanisms. So, in the medium-term run of say six months, except during periods when (unpredictable) shifts in the demand for money (velocity) appeared to be in process, it might be better to put more emphasis on maintaining the planned rate of growth of the money supply.

In the very short run, however, financial markets can be notably volatile, with prices shifting sharply in response to the wayward play of news and expectations. On the other hand, expenditures and output, abstracting from strikes and natural disasters, roll forward with stolid inertia from day-to-day and week-to-week since revisions to planned expenditure patterns, and *a fortiori* to production programmes, are costly in time and often in money. So, during shorter intervals (e.g., day by day and week by week) the random variance in money markets will probably be large relative to that in goods markets, with the implication that the shorter the time period, the greater the emphasis that the monetary authorities should place on stabilising interest rates in money markets.[2] If the time interval between policy reviews is long enough, this could leave the authorities with a problem of reconciling short-term, day-to-day stabilisation of money markets with the medium-term, quarter-by-quarter objective of obtaining steady monetary growth. For example, if short-term stabilisation of rates allows a faster growth of the money stock over, say, the first few weeks of any quarter than had been intended, would it be desirable to offset that excess by a period of slower growth (than the initially planned rate) and, if so, how soon need, or should, growth be reduced, i.e., over what period is it desirable

---

[1] See, for example, his paper on 'Optimal Choice of Monetary Policy Instruments in a Simple Stochastic Macro Model' (1970) pp. 197–216.

[2] On the other hand, short-period fluctuations in the demand for money function will not matter much, if, in the short run, the *IS* curve is steep. It is only as the *IS* curve becomes shallower in the longer run that monetary instability would be important, and this is the time horizon over which, we have suggested, monetary instability tends to be less marked. I am indebted to David Laidler for pointing this out to me.

How much does greater *short-term* volatility in financial markets, including foreign exchange markets, matter? It is much easier to hedge against short-term fluctuations in financial markets, via instruments such as variable interest rate terms, forward markets and options, than it is to hedge production decisions against longer-term misalignments. Even so, the process of acquiring information about, and using, such hedges can also be costly in time and effort; some smaller consumers and producers will not be able to afford to do so.

to maintain a planned, average rate? Alternatively, should bygones be bygones, and is the best policy to operate in financial markets so as to bring the rate of monetary expansion back to the initial target rate but no further? If bygones are not forgotten, how far back should one look to adjust future policy to offset past diversions from path?

Such issues arising from this analysis on the appropriate conduct of monetary policy stimulated considerable interest among economists and even among practitioners, especially in the United States.[1] But, in my view, the importance of this analysis as a guide to monetary operations was overstated.[2] In the first place, the analytical exposition has usually been based on the simplest possible IS/LM model. It is dangerous to generalise from the conclusions based on a very simple, and as argued in Chapter 12 a seriously misspecified, model to proposals for the conduct of monetary policy in the real world.

Consider, for example, a simple extension of the model to encompass the possibility that there may be lags before the public adjusts its desired money holding to variations, say in interest rates.[3] It may be virtually impossible to control the rate of growth of the money stock in the short run except at the expense of extreme variations in interest rates. Moreover, if the lag from monetary measures to changes in agents' economic decisions is underestimated, and commentators and politicians are inherently impatient for quick results from policy actions, then it may seem to them that not enough has been done and the dose will be repeated. If public expenditures do not rise immediately in response to decisions to spend more, if the money stock does not fall significantly in response to rises in interest rates, the tendency is often to press even harder on the same lever or even to deduce that there is no effect and look for some other instrument of control (e.g., direct limitations on bank advances).[4]

On the other hand, it can be argued that if there are also lags in expenditure–output plans in response to interest-rate changes (and this is generally believed to be the

---

[1] See, in particular, Federal Reserve Board, *Open Market Policies and Operating Procedures – Staff Studies*, including papers by Axilrod, Davis, Andersen, Pierce, Friedman, Poole and Kareken (1971).

[2] Its importance, perhaps, lay more in clarifying the proper analytical approach to policy issues than as a detailed guide to actual policy. Uncertainty is obviously the key to policy but until the late 1960s, economists studied policy almost entirely within the context of certainty models. A need existed to incorporate uncertainty centrally in the formal models so that the real policy issues could be studied analytically; this is what Poole did, purposely setting up the simplest possible model for this exercise.

[3] The most searching early studies of the lag structure of the demand for money function were those undertaken by the staff of the Federal Reserve Board; for example, Thomson and Pierce, 'A Monthly Econometric Model of the Financial Sector' (unpublished).

[4] Many of the actions undertaken by policy-makers which commentators have claimed, with the benefit of hindsight, to have been errors can be attributed to this syndrome. An example in the fiscal field may be the enormous fluctuations in the size of the fiscal deficit/surplus in the United Kingdom during the financial years 1968/9–1973/4. An example in the monetary field might be the fluctuations in interest rates and the money stock in the United States during 1971. During that year, the money stock grew faster than intended during the first half of the year, so interest rates were continuously pushed upwards. Then, when the money stock growth receded from July onwards, partly as a lagged response to previous high interest rates, its growth rate fell below course for the next six or so months despite large reductions in interest rates, which in turn could have been sowing the seeds for a subsequent re-acceleration, and so on. This latter example was also discussed in Chapter 6, Section 3.

case), then it would require extreme variations in interest rates to have much immediate significant impact on nominal incomes. In such circumstances, the lag in the demand for money function could offset the lag in the expenditure function, in the sense that the lag in the demand for money function would initially cause a large change in interest rates; the lag in the expenditure functions would, however, dampen its effect on current demand. As time passed, there could be a fall back in interest rates from the initial peak while the effect on expenditures would contrariwise be building up. So, despite lags, maintenance of steady monetary growth in the face of shifts in the *IS* curve could allow fairly stable growth in money incomes, though at the expense of very large and possibly increasing oscillations in interest rates.[1]

It is thus not necessarily the case that the very large variations in interest rates that would generally be required to stabilise the rate of growth of the money supply in the

---

[1] The formal mathematics of the analysis, nicely developed by Tucker, 'Dynamic Income Adjustment to Money Changes' (1966) pp. 433–49, go as follows:

The basic (Keynesian) model is:

$$I_t = (1 - j)(a_1 + b_1 Y_t + dr_t) + jI_{t-1} \qquad \text{(1) Investment}$$
$$C_t = (1 - j)(a_2 + b_2 Y_t) + jC_{t-1} \qquad \text{(2) Consumption}$$
$$Y_t = C_t + I_t \qquad \text{(3) Income identity}$$
$$Md_t = (1 - m)(e + fY_t + gr_t) + mMd_{t-1} \qquad \text{(4) Demand for money}$$
$$Md_t = Ms_t \qquad \text{(5) Money market identity}$$

where j and m, $0 < j, m < 1$, are the lag parameters b_1, b_2, $f > 0$, $d, g < 0$, and it is assumed (a stability condition) that

$$b_1 + b_2 < 1 + df/g$$

These equations, when solved for Y in terms of M, yield the following first-order linear difference equation:

$$Y_t - A Y_{t-1} = B + D(M_t - mM_{t-1})$$

where

$$A = \frac{j}{1 - (1 - j)[b_1 + b_2 + df/g]}$$

$$D = \frac{Ad(1 - j)}{gj(1 - m)}$$

and B is a constant of no importance.

The shift in the time path of income in response to a unit permanent change in M at $t = 1$ is

$$Y'_t = \frac{D(1 - m)}{(1 - A)} + D\frac{(m - A)}{(1 - A)} A^{t-1}$$

This is the shift in the path that income would follow if there were no disturbances. The second term depends on the difference between A and m (i.e., between a term depending largely on the expenditure lag and the demand for money lag). Tucker notes (p. 440), 'In a general sense, then, it is the *difference* between product-demand lags and money-demand lags, as much as it is the inherent characteristics of the lags themselves, that determines the speed in income adjustment'. In particular, if $m = a$, $Y'_t = D$ and the response of income to a change in the money stock is complete in the first period, whatever the values of m and j.

The analysis of the effects of lags in the system was taken further by several economists, see for example, Tanner, 'Lags in the Effects of Monetary Policy: a Statistical Investigation' (1969) pp. 794–805, and Laidler, 'Expectations, Adjustment, and the Dynamic Response of Income to Policy Changes' (1973) pp. 157–72. For a survey of work in this field see Moore, 'Optimal Monetary Policy' (1972) pp. 116–39.

short run, given lags in the demand for money function, would destabilise the path of money incomes. Nevertheless, the risk of introducing major disturbances in the economy by insisting upon a policy of continuously-fixed monetary growth under such circumstances would increase if, for example, there were discontinuities, caused say by bankruptcies,[1] in the response of the system to variations in interest rates or if the lag patterns were themselves changing and not accurately estimated.[2]

Another reason for scepticism of the practical value of this analysis as a guide to policy action is that it usually abstracts from consideration of the actual availability and adequacy of statistics. The exercise usually proceeds on the implicit assumption that the authorities have sufficient data to monitor the growth of the money stock over very short intervals, say week by week, as well as observing the variations in interest rates, but do not have an accurate or up-to-date estimate of current movements in expenditures and incomes. It needs to be remembered that in this analysis, the structure of the system (e.g., the slopes of the IS/LM curves) is assumed to be known exactly to the authorities, so if they could observe a divergence between actual and desired incomes they could prevent it. In practice, there are, of course, a large number of indicators of varying reliability of the current level of demand in the economy which come out with only a short delay (e.g., unemployment, industrial production, price indices, etc.). It is usually possible to get some inkling fairly quickly of whether the current pace of the economy is above, near or below the target.

On the other hand, in many countries other than the United States, monetary data are only available once a month.[3] Although they are published quite soon after the

---

[1] A good example of this occurred in the United Kingdom in December 1973 when a sharp upward jab in interest rates helped to push a fringe banking institution into failure. This led to an immediate reconsideration of the safety of deposits in all similar institutions and precipitated a general run on these banks. If this had not been staunched by a recycling of deposits, the effects could have been calamitous.

[2] The claim here that sticking to a policy of maintaining some preordained rate of monetary expansion at all times may in certain cases have deleterious consequences should not be taken as implying that it would be better to stick instead to a policy of fixing interest rates. Indeed, a continuous policy of interest-rate stabilisation may well have perverse longer-term effects on interest rates and on the stability of the financial system itself. Persistent efforts by the monetary authorities to cushion interest-rate movements can allow excessive fluctuations in money incomes to develop. The resulting changes in economic activity and in the inflation rate could well produce larger differences between the longer-run peaks and troughs in interest rates than would otherwise occur. The argument is not that the maintenance of stable nominal interest rates is always preferable to the maintenance of a stable rate of monetary expansion (the reverse is probably nearer truth), but rather that a judicious assessment of the complexities of the actual conjuncture should allow a better selection of policy than sticking to any predetermined posture.

[3] W. Poole has reminded me that it is not necessary to assume that the money stock can be continuously observed and controlled if some other monetary variable – e.g., the stock of high-powered money – to which the money supply is closely related can be continuously observed and controlled. The supply of money is then a stochastic function of this monetary base and this equation combined with the stochastic demand for money function would yield the stochastic LM function. The absence of accurate observation (*a fortiori* of precise control) of the money stock in this case increases the variance of the LM function but does not affect the formal analysis in any way.

Unfortunately, this does not help to overcome the actual data problem, at least in the United Kingdom. From September 1981 onwards, banks in the UK did not have to maintain *any* required reserves for operational purposes, though all banks had to hold $\frac{1}{2}$ per cent of eligible

date of collection, the interval now being about four or five weeks in the United Kingdom, each individual observation is subject to a large random fluctuation owing to factors such as the timing of large loans, strikes, the date of large new issues in capital markets, error in the data, etc. These random factors, as noted in Chapter 6, can easily cause changes of $\pm \frac{1}{2}$ per cent in the figures for the monthly aggregates at any one date. Thus, from month to month, unless the money stock is growing very fast, the random variation can easily swamp the systematic element. Imagine that there is an underlying acceleration in the rate of monetary growth during December, with say the first figures to show this collected in January. These will become available in early February.[1] Such data showing a larger than usual jump in the figures between a single date at end-November and a single date at end-December will, however, hardly provide reliable or compelling evidence on the underlying systematic acceleration. It is likely to be early March at the earliest before the authorities accept the evidence of a change in trend that began three months before. By then, they ought to have some indication whether this faster than initially planned monetary growth has, or has not, been accompanied by a divergence of the economy from its intended path.

There are two separable points here. The first is that in circumstances where the monetary series are erratic and infrequently observed, and where the response of the public in adjusting their demand for bank credit and bank deposits to interest-rate variations is lagged,[2] it is simply not possible to obtain a stable rate of monetary

---

liabilities with the Bank of England – on a calculated base re-estimated every six months – in order to provide the latter with financial resources; the clearing banks voluntarily choose to aim at some (small) closing level of operational balances. Even before 1981, without current observations of actual bank deposits, banks could only be required to maintain reserves in relation to their last reported deposit totals. So, in the United Kingdom, the clearing banks then maintained cash reserves related to their last previously reported monthly position, until the last day or so before the new make-up date. Under this system, it was not possible for the Bank of England to estimate, from movements in its own liabilities in the monthly intervals between make-up dates, how the monetary aggregates were growing.

---

[1] The make-up date for reporting banks' deposit (and asset) data changed from a regular mid-month (third Wednesday) to an end-month basis in October 1985 in order to cohere better with fiscal and national income data.

[2] In some circumstances, the initial response can even be perverse. Thus, on occasions in the United Kingdom and also in Canada, the response of the banks to pressures on their reserve base was to raise the rates they bid for additional funds in the CD and inter-bank markets (the wholesale markets), both absolutely and relatively to the rates at which they lent; this occurred because these latter administered rates (base rates or prime rates) were costly to change and politically visible, so banks were unwilling to bear the odium of raising them unless they were convinced of the necessity. The result was that not only might bank advances temporarily become relatively cheaper than other sources of funds but even that in certain circumstances, as pertained in the United Kingdom in June–July 1972 and January–February 1973, a turn might be made by borrowing from a bank to redeposit with the banking system via the CD market. During these occasions when the authorities were trying to restrain monetary expansion, this merry-go-round undoubtedly inflated the totals of both bank lending and bank deposits, at least on a broad definition.

After a further prolonged period during which the pattern of interest rates encouraged such arbitrage, July–December 1973, thereby reinvigorating an unwelcome surge in bank lending and in interest-bearing deposits, the authorities introduced a new special supplementary deposits scheme. This imposed a penalty on banks whose interest-bearing deposits, time

growth, even quarter by quarter let alone month by month, whatever the objective of the monetary authorities may be. Moreover, and more important, the authorities will usually have some information on the nature of the shocks, unforeseen at the time of the previous forecast and policy review, which are currently hitting the economy. They can observe, by and large, how the economy is going just about as well, at least in many countries, as they can observe monetary trends. They can see situations where there is a danger of sizeable shifts in liquidity preference, for example in the aftermath of the Continental Illinois (US) or fringe banks (UK) bankruptcies, and act to alleviate these. Thus, the extent of information available ought to allow the authorities to do better that they could by simple reliance on rules of thumb for the stabilisation of interest rates or of the money stock over some time interval.

The real weakness of this approach in my view is, however, that it emphasises one area of uncertainty, the possibility of random disturbances in the structural relationships, a rather secondary problem for economic management, at the expense of ignoring a far more serious difficulty, our uncertainty about the basic form of the structural relationships themselves within the system. Thus, the standard analysis of this topic usually contains the (implicit) assumptions that the slopes of the IS/LM curves are accurately known and that this system is an accurate representation of the real world. If this was the case, it would be possible at each forecast and policy review to reset the policy instruments in such a way as to obtain with complete certainty the best expected results for the objective variables(s). In practice, in most industrialised countries, forecasts and policy reviews are undertaken several times a year and the use of computers virtually allows any comprehensive, coherent forecast to be updated and revised as each new item of information comes in. Thus, the time interval between policy reviews which allow objectives for both monetary growth rates and interest rates to be reset is now quite short and, if the effort were worthwhile, could be made shorter yet. So, if we really knew how the system worked and if our and if our uncertainties related only to the occurrence of stochastic disturbances to that system, then we could easily reset the controls often enough to make the problem of how to operate in the short intervals between reviews of very minor importance.[1]

---

deposits and CDs were growing too fast (i.e., above an allowed rate of increase). The intention was to force a wedge between rates charged on bank loans and offered on interest-bearing deposits, and thus to ensure that interest-rate relativities did not get out of kilter.

For an *ex post* assessment of how this scheme, which became known as the 'Corset', worked during the period that it was utilised (December 1973–June 1980), see the *Bank of England Quarterly Bulletin*, Vol. 22, No. 1. (March 1982), also reprinted in Bank of England (1984) Chapter 6, pp. 117–28; also, see Spencer (1986) especially Chapters V and VI.

[1] While it seems intuitively plausible that the choice of instruments should make less difference as the frequency of policy decisions increases, it has been formally shown, by Kareken and Wallace, 'The Monetary Instrument Variable Choice: How Important?' (1972) pp. 723–9, that under some conditions the instrument variable choice 'does not of necessity make less difference, or become less important, as the frequency with which the policy is decided increases'. As I understand their analysis, there are some circumstances in which the relative auto-correlations in the error terms in the IS and LM functions are such that the difference in expected outcomes between choosing to fix the rate for monetary growth or nominal interest rates over some long-term period is less than the difference in expected outcomes from the choice in the short run. Kareken and Wallace, however, present no evidence that the economic structure is such as to make such circumstances likely. In any case, the actual expected loss from running either policy will be less if policy decisions are more frequent; in this sense, it will not matter which instrument is chosen. When policy decisions are less frequent, the

3. Policy under Uncertainty – 2: When the Structure of the System is Not Known

The main problem for monetary management has not, however, been our inability to predict the disturbances that will agitate the economic system but in our ignorance of how that system actually works. This latter problem has a number of dimensions. In order to comprehend the working of the real, complex economy, we may try to capture the important features of the system in a simplified model in which the inter-relationships between the variables can be empirically estimated. These econometric calculations not only provide an estimate of the mean (average) coefficient of the value of each specified relationship but also give the standard error of that coefficient; this provides a first and simple measure of the accuracy with which the relationship is defined.[1] These estimates, however, are obtained from models of a particular specification, estimated over a particular data period, during which there was a given institutional and political structure. Models with different specifications, even if estimated over the same data period, often give very different results for economic relationships, well beyond the range of their respective standard errors.

For example, the St Louis reduced-form money multiplier[2] or the Laffer–Ranson model[3] gave quite different implications from one of the extended Keynesian macro-models for the impact over time of changes in, say, the monetary base.[4] Moreover, there may be significant changes in the estimated values of the relationships in similarly specified models over differing data periods.

The policy-maker is then generally faced with a gallimaufry of empirical estimates of any economic relationship. Moreover, he is concerned with a time period, the future, which in certain respects, some predictable some not, will be very different from any past period during which the relationships were estimated. Such uncertain-ties will become even more pronounced should the authorities be considering, perhaps partly on the basis of the (simulation) evidence of existing models, any major change in policy. The so-called 'structural' equations in econometric models are themselves conditional on the institutional framework and policy regimes in place, which influence in turn the expectations and reactions of individual agents. If such background institutions and policy regimes alter significantly, so will the expec-

---

expected loss will be much larger; in some cases, it may be true that the *expected* loss may be much the same whichever instrument is picked but the potential scope for *actual* large losses, if the authorities pick wrong, perhaps by chance, will be much greater.

---

[1] A common, and often justified, complaint of economists providing advice to policy-makers is that the latter turn away from, and find difficult to absorb, forecasts expressed in terms of bands of probability, confidence limits. Instead they want to be given, and work on the basis of, the 'best' mean estimates. Too little attention is paid to available measurements of the errors in estimation. Then, when the point forecasts go wrong – as they must – the quantitative economist is blamed for promising more than he can provide.

[2] Andersen and Jordan (1968).

[3] Laffer and Ranson, 'A Formal Model of the Economy', *Journal of Business* (1971) pp. 247–70.

[4] On this subject see M. J. Hamburger, 'The Lag in the Effect of Monetary Policy: A Survey of Recent Literature' (1971b) pp. 289–98. He concludes that 'estimates of the length of the lag differ considerably'. On the other hand, 'the type of statistical estimating model (structural versus reduced-form equations)' was 'found to be less important' as a factor causing such differences.

tations and reactions of individual agents. Consequently, the 'structural' equations estimated under one regime are quite likely to change in form (i.e., to shift unpredictably) during the transition to another regime. This means that most existing models cannot provide much help in deducing the economic implications of major changes in policy. This is known as the 'Lucas critique' of the use of model simulations to predict the effect of alternative policy choices.[1]

At this point, qualitative considerations (or judgement) have to guide the policy-maker in deciding how much weight to place upon the various alternative quantitative estimates. Indeed, in some cases, the policy-maker may feel extremely suspicious. on *a priori* ground, of *all* the quantitative estimates.

An apposite example can be found in the quantitative estimate of the impact of monetary changes upon expenditures contained in the extended *IS/LM* macro-economic models of the United Kingdom. In these models, for example of the National Institute for Economic and Social Research (NIESR), the direct effect of financial factors, mainly specified as transmitted via changes in a few financial yields, is estimated to be extremely slight. The individual effect that occurs via the influence of financial factors on the exchange rate is believed to be much more important but this latter channel is so uncertain and imprecisely modelled that it is often adjusted by a subjective, *ad hoc*, assumption. Thus, the answer to the question from the policy-maker of what would be the effect of changing the rate of growth of money supply, say by ±5 per cent per annum, or varying interest rates, say by ±3 per cent per annum, obtained from examination of these models is that the impact on domestic expenditures would be extremely slight, with the exception of an uncertain but potentially important influence via exchange rates and a significant but lagged effect on the private housing market.[2]

By the end of the 1960s, however, confidence that these (extended Keynesian) models really gave an accurate representation of the effect of monetary variables on the domestic economy ebbed away, largely as a result of the evolution of economic thinking in the United States rather than from any new developments in domestic circumstances and experience within the United Kingdom. The theoretical works of Friedman and Leijonhufvud gave a basis for belief that changes in financial conditions should affect expenditure decisions, whatever the 'Keynesian' models might show. The empirical results of Friedman and Meiselman, and Andersen and Jordan showed a strong positive correlation between income movements and synchronous and prior changes in the money stock in the United States. Even the 'Keynesian' model developed by the Federal Reserve Board, in association with several universities (the FRB–MIT–Penn model), incorporated a number of channels whereby monetary changes affected the real economy significantly.[3]

This resulted in an unhappy dichotomy between commonly-held beliefs about the importance of monetary policy as a demand-management instrument and the available empirically-estimated models of the economy. The view was widely held by ministers and politicians of both main political parties, by eminent commentators

---

[1] Lucas, 'Econometric Policy Evaluation: A Critique' (1976) pp. 19–46.

For further discussion of this important point, see Currie 'Macroeconomic Policy Design and Control Theory – a Failed Partnership?' (1985) pp. 285–306 and Whiteman 'Analytical Policy Design under Rational Expectations' (1986) pp. 1387–1455.

[2] Consult the study by Easton 'The importance of interest rates in five macroeconomic models' (1985), already referred to in Chapter 12.

[3] De Leeuw and Gramlich, 'The Channels of Monetary Policy' (1969) pp. 472–91.

and by many academics that control over the monetary aggregates is a very important, perhaps the most important, element of demand management. Yet, until the 1980s (e.g., when the Liverpool model of the UK economy was developed) no available model of the UK economy gave any clear indication what effect on the level of aggregate demand a change in the growth of one of the monetary series, say M1, might be expected to have; several forecasting models actually used (e.g., by the National Institute) have implied that the effect would be negligible except for its (unpredictable) effects via changing exchange rates.

Greater emphasis on the development of the monetary aggregates also followed as a result of the increasing inflation, with its implications for financial markets. If one is uncertain what to do, there is a tendency to do as little as possible. Earlier (pre-1970) central bankers often tended to construe a passive policy as one of maintaining nominal interest rates constant. This stance gave no help in stabilising cyclical variations in expenditures in the economy even when prices were and could be expected to remain constant. Allowance for adaptive expectations of price inflation implies further that a policy of stabilising nominal interest rates will be destabilising for the economy (*a fortiori* for rational expectations), since it will tend to cause procyclical variations in real interest rates.[1] Acceptance of this distinction between nominal and real interest rates, arising from expectations of non-zero future rates of change of prices, led to the realisation that the stabilisation of nominal rates in an increasingly inflationary world was not in any conceivable sense 'passive' but produced a positively expansionary policy. So, in a system with varying and possibly volatile expectations of future price inflation – and, indeed, with fluctuating general moods of confidence and depression about the future of the economy – maintenance of nominal rates at some chosen level will not represent a neutral or passive policy,

---

[1] If demand is a function of a vector of exogenous variables, X and real interest rates (nominal interest rates less the expected rate of price inflation), $r - E\dot{p}$, so that:

$$y = f(X, r - E\dot{p})$$

where

$$\frac{dy}{d(r - E\dot{p})} < 0$$

and the rate of change of prices is a function of variations in y around its normal, 'equilibrium', value:

$$\dot{p} = f(y - y^*)$$

where

$$\frac{dp}{d(y - y^*)} > 0$$

with expectations depending on current and recent developments, so that:

$$E\dot{p} = f(\dot{p}_t, \dot{p}_{t-1}, ..., \dot{p}_{t-n})$$

where

$$\frac{dE\dot{p}}{d\dot{p}_{t-i}} > 0$$

then the maintenance of nominal interest rates r at a fixed value will tend to exaggerate a disturbance to the system and may cause it to explode.

nor will it be possible to calibrate the overall effect of monetary policy by measuring variations in nominal interest rates.

Under circumstances of unobservable variations in price expectations and of unforeseen fluctuations in the pressure of demand (shifts in the *IS* curve), the maintenance of the initially-chosen ('optimal') rate of growth of the money stock might appear to be the most 'neutral', stabilising policy; this, indeed, has has been the line advocated by monetarists. There are, however, some complications with this approach. In the first place, as already noted, a policy of holding monetary growth constant will be destabilising in circumstances where there are unforeseen shifts in the demand for money function. Certainly in the short run, volatile swings in expectations can disturb financial markets, so that in week-to-week operations some stabilisation of prices in financial markets may be appropriate and still consistent with steady monetary growth over the medium-term horizon.[1] But the advantages to be obtained from adherence to this latter medium-term target will still depend on the relative stability of the demand for money function over longer intervals, say on a year-to-year basis.

How should policy-makers and advisers respond when there is only limited information available on the underlying workings of the economy? In practice until the mid 1970s, the authorities used the available information to make a judgmental selection of the appropriate policy response. But even if they search diligently for information and use it intelligently when obtained, the existence of uncertainty is bound to lead to error. Professor Friedman queried whether under these circumstances better results might not be obtained by adherence to some rule. He proposed adherence to a constant growth in the money stock.[2] The attractions of this rule, however, depend largely on three postulates – that the demand for money is relatively stable, that there is a unique natural rate of unemployment at which the rate of inflation will stabilise, and that the real economy is basically stable. The first would ensure that shifts in the *LM* curve would not destabilise the economy; the second suggests that discretionary use of demand-management instruments to maintain the economy at any position other than this given natural equilibrium level of demand will ultimately be futile; the third implies that if the authorities do not intervene to disrupt the course of the economy, it will move back to its equilibrium level of demand from any disequilibrium of excess or insufficient demand relatively quickly. We examine the further development of this saga in Chapter 15.

---

[1] See, for example, Davis, 'Short-run Targets for Open Market Operations' (1971) pp. 38–69, and by the same author, 'Implementing Open Market Policy with Monetary Aggregate Objectives' (1973) pp. 170–82.

[2] 'I have favoured increasing the quantity of money at a steady rate designed to keep final product prices constant, a rate that I have estimated to be something like 4 to 5 per cent per year for the U.S...' Friedman (1969a) p. 47.

XV
Monetary Policy – 2: Rules versus Discretion

Summary

The disturbed conjuncture in the early 1970s, with a synchronous boom in many countries in 1972–3 leading on to a surge in raw material prices, the first oil shock and the breakdown in the Bretton Woods pegged exchange rate system, was conducive to the adoption of monetary targets, rather than interest rates, as the intermediate objectives of Central Banks. A brief history of these developments is contained in Section 1. Nevertheless, this step, undertaken in many major industrialised countries in 1975–6, failed to bring about a real break in the inflationary climate. It was widely argued that this was because monetary targetry was operated in too discretionary a manner without sufficient commitment by the authorities.

One of the puzzles of the 1970s was why the authorities had allowed inflation to take such hold when tight monetary policy should have been able to prevent that. The best answer was provided by Kydland and Prescott and elaborated by Barro and Gordon. This is described in a simplified way in Section 2. The argument is that any benevolent authority, sincerely seeking to maximise a social welfare function, which assumed that the private sector's expectations of future inflation were fixed – irrespective of its own actions – would prefer to lower unemployment below the medium-term natural rate at the expense of somewhat higher unanticipated inflation. A rational public would come to expect that action from the authorities, however, thereby raising the base level of expected inflation until it rose to a point where the public's (and the authorities') dislike of any further inflation fully offset any benefit from a temporary reduction in unemployment. The key finding was that this expectational, consistent equilibrium involving discretion was inferior to a condition in which the authorities committed themselves in advance to a rule of holding prices constant and *not* trying to influence the level of output and employment. One limitation of this basic model is that the authorities are clearly themselves acting irrationally in treating the private sector's expectations as fixed. Instead, the authorities will appreciate that they will be penalised by a loss of future credibility if and when they are tempted to renege on their commitment to price stability. This appreciation leads on to a consideration of reputational equilibria and the application of technically sophisticated game-theoretic analysis (*not* pursued here) to this subject.

The claim that more pre-commitment was required to provide credibility and to inspire confidence was sympathetically received by the authorities, notably by the conservative governments coming into power in the USA and UK at the start of the 1980s. Nevertheless, the steps then taken to tighten the operation of targetry were subsequently relaxed and largely abandoned after a few years. This is described in Section 3. This was partly the result of the *success* of these policies in achieving a decisive break in inflation but more important was the increasing erosion of stability in the statistical relationships between monetary aggregates and nominal incomes.

With velocity thus proving increasingly unpredictable, monetary targets were dropped in a widening range of countries. The question then arises how monetary policy should be directed in this new situation. In Section 4, we concentrate on the problem that emerges for major, central currencies which do not, or choose not to, accept the choice of pegging their exchange rate (the latter is considered in Chapters 17 and 18). We consider the relative merits of targeting the monetary base, the aggregate upon whose velocity financial innovations have hitherto had the least apparent disturbing effect, or nominal incomes, and then finally turn to a short discussion of the possible adoption of 'free banking' with the total withdrawal of the authorities from monetary policy actions.

1. The Historical Record, 1973–9[1]

As already outlined at the end of Chapter 14, the majority of which had been drafted in 1973 for the first edition, more attention was already being paid to the growth of the monetary aggregates rather than to the level of nominal interest rates by the early 1970s; in addition, an increasing number of academics and other influential commentators were calling for the adoption of fixed monetary targets. A number of developments subsequently occurred that gave considerable further impetus to this approach.

First, the Bretton Woods system of pegged – but adjustable – exchange rates that had been under increasing strain since 1967–8[2] finally collapsed in March 1973. Until then, the monetary policy of most countries other than the centre country (i.e., the USA) was most usually constrained (anchored) by the objective of maintaining its exchange rate pegged to the dollar. Both intervention – a form of open-market operations – and interest rates were varied in order to defend the exchange rate at the pegged parity. With interest rates thus predetermined, the growth of bank assets and liabilities was endogenous.

Once the international monetary regime shifted from pegged to floating exchange rates, the authorities became free to vary interest rates and/or monetary growth in response to other criteria and to meet other objectives. But what criteria and objectives should the authorities then choose for steering their monetary policy actions?

The second accompanying and associated development in 1972–3 that encouraged monetary targetry was the strong and synchronous boom in many countries, fuelled by a sharp monetary expansion, that led to a major surge in raw material prices generally and sharpened the ability of OPEC to use the weapon of restricting oil supplies in 1973–4. This led to a major inflationary shock. In these conditions, expectations of further inflation were rising, but not easily observable. Policy priorities thus shifted in most countries towards the containment of inflation at the same time as it became harder to tell whether any particular level of nominal interest

---

[1] The essential reading and source material for this Section with respect to the UK is Bank of England, *The Development and Operation of Monetary Policy 1960–1983* (1984). For developments in the USA, see Meek, *US Monetary Policy and Financial Markets* (1982) and also Federal Reserve Staff Study (1981).

[2] 1967 being the date of the British devaluation, 1968 being the date when the US formally abandoned linking the dollar to gold (see Chapter 17).

rates was expansionary or restrictive. With the rate of inflation temporarily reaching levels of 15–20 per cent in the aftermath of the oil shock[1] – and expectations for future years uncertain and widely dispersed, it was difficult to determine whether an interest rate level of 15 per cent, say, was still expansionary or restrictive.

In such conditions of floating exchange rates and high, variable and uncertain inflation, a shift towards the adoption of some form of quantified monetary objective came to seem the obvious course to take, though some Keynesians, notably in the UK, continued to oppose the step as either having an unduly restrictive effect on the authorities' ability to achieve real output and unemployment targets or as being analytically misguided and likely to be ineffective (or even both!). This intellectual trend even triumphantly overcame indications in these years that the stability of the demand for money function was more fragile than had been hoped.

The failure of M1 in the USA, the preferred quantitative indicator there, to rise as fast as predicted – 'The Case of the Missing Money' – has already been discussed in Chapter 4, Section 2. In the UK, the preferred quantitative indicator was M3, a broad monetary aggregate.[2] This measure began to accelerate sharply in 1972 and continued at this pace in 1973 (see Figure 15.1).

This surge in M3 was far greater than could have been predicted from previously estimated demand for money functions, given current and previous values of the arguments in that function.

In response to this monetary acceleration and to the accompanying boom in the economy involving a massive upsurge in housing and property values, the UK authorities raised interest rates, though in the event too little and too late. This had

[1] The following table shows the percentage change in the CPI for the relevant years in the major OECD countries:

	US	Japan	Germany	France	UK	Italy	Canada
1973	6.2	11.7	6.9	7.3	9.2	10.8	7.6
1974	11.0	24.5	7.0	13.7	16.0	19.1	10.9
1975	9.1	11.8	6.0	11.8	24.2	17.0	10.8

[2] There were a number of reasons for this preference. First, such a broad monetary aggregate could be more easily related to the credit counterparts, as already described in Chapter 6. Thus, $\Delta M3 = \Delta$ Bank Lending to Private Sector + PSBR – public sector debt sales to non-bank public + / – net external flows – Δnon-deposit liabilities (e.g., increases in bank capital).

This 'credit counterparts' approach helped to illustrate the relationship between domestic credit expansion (DCE), i.e., the first three elements on the right-hand side above, and net external flows, mainly comprising changes in official reserves and short-term net banking positions: it also allowed a closer co-ordination of the various arms of policy (e.g., fiscal policy, debt management, interest rates and credit controls), within the overall umbrella of monetary policy.

Finally, the statistics for £M3 were slightly more reliable than those for M1, being less subject to measurement error from the inevitably somewhat arbitrary treatment of items in transit ('float' in American parlance). In addition, the econometric performance of the M3 demand for money function had been about as good as that of M1 prior to 1972–3.

In any case, M3 became adopted as the main operational aggregate in the UK as early as 1968–9 and thereafter inertia (and the transitional costs of any change) helped to reinforce its key role.

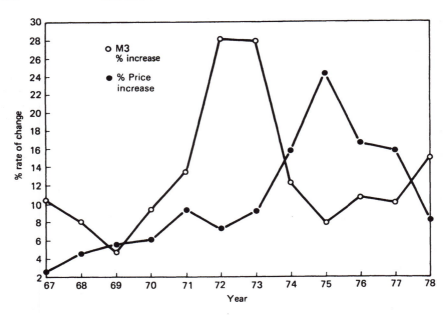

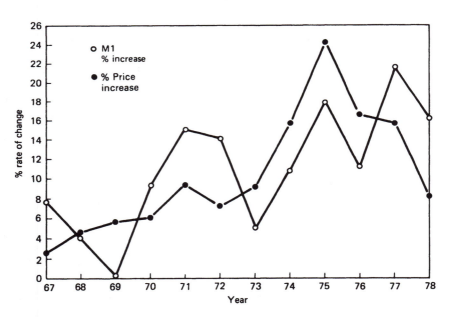

FIG. 15.1

the expected effect of restraining the growth in M1, whose growth fell back markedly during 1973, as can be seen from Figure 15.1.

Despite the fact that the demand for money function for M1 remained relatively stable in this period, whereas that for M3 broke down, and that none of the explanations for the surge then in M3 really carried much conviction,[1] the episode actually served to strengthen the attachment of the UK authorities and markets to M3 as the key monetary aggregate. The reason for this was that the surge in M3 in 1972–3 neatly prefigured the jump in inflation in 1974–5, with a two-year lead, closely in accord with Milton Friedman's estimated mean lag between monetary stimulus and inflationary response. The correspondence between the time path of M1 and inflation was far less close, see Figure 15.1.

Moreover, this association between M3 and subsequent inflation allowed most of the blame for the latter to be placed on the Conservative Government of the time under Prime Minister Heath. This suited both the incoming Labour Government and the newly elected Leader of the Conservative Opposition, Mrs Thatcher, who had managed to depose Heath in 1975, quite largely on the grounds that he had mismanaged the economy badly in 1972–3. Political incentives thus allied with simple economic analysis to reinforce the key role of M3, soon to be redefined as £M3,[2] as *the* key UK monetary aggregate.

Many of those who were doubtful about monetary targetry pointed to the role of the oil shock in causing the inflation of 1974–5 and argued that it was unwise to place so much importance on a single observation of correlation which could well be largely spurious. But even if one abstracted from this particular experience, there was some, albeit rather faint, econometric support for the case that innovations in £M3 provided more information about subsequent innovations in nominal incomes than other monetary aggregates.[3]

Although the Bank of England's ability to respond to the monetary upsurge of 1972–3 by raising interest rates was restricted by political *diktat*, in part because such rate increases would have put greater pressure on the government's fragile prices and incomes policy, the Bank was nonetheless severely criticised, mostly after the event, for allowing it to occur. In the aftermath of this extremely disturbed period which culminated in the property value collapse, fringe bank crisis and equity market sell-off in 1973–4, the Bank sought to adopt and operate unpublished quantified monetary targets for M3. Given the traditional priorities of a Labour Government, with concern for employment and growth much greater than for price stability, and in circumstances when the oil shock was also bringing on a world recession, the government resisted the adoption of monetary targets until the end of 1976. The same conditions and pressures were, however, acting upon the monetary authorities of

---

[1] See Bank of England (1984), especially Chapter 2, p. 44, and the paper by Hacche, 'The demand for money in the United Kingdom: experience since 1971', Econometric Appendix, pp. 172–187 in Bank of England (1984), originally from the *Bank of England Quarterly Bulletin* (1974) pp. 284–305.

[2] £M3 differed from M3 by the exclusion of foreign currency deposits held with UK banks by British residents. There were several reasons for this change of definition. First, with floating exchange rates, foreign currency deposits could not be converted into sterling at a known, fixed rate; in sterling terms, they were more akin to a marketable instrument than to a monetary deposit. Second, the statistic only included a part, perhaps a small part, of total UK residents holdings of foreign currency deposits, much of which were held with banks abroad, for which no data were available.

[3] See, for example, Mills (1983b).

other countries to introduce quantified, published monetary targets. The Bundesbank in West Germany led the way in 1974 and this example was soon followed by many of the other major industrialised countries.[1]

The actual date when the UK first announced quantitative monetary targets is not clear-cut. After the sterling exchange rate had begun to plummet in the Spring of 1976, market and Bank pressures induced the Chancellor to state in a speech announcing restrictive measures in July that the growth of £M3 over the next 12 months 'should' be 13 per cent; it was left deliberately obscure whether the word 'should' implied a forecast or an objective. Following the continuing weakness of sterling in autumn 1976, however, the authorities approached the IMF for a loan; as part of the conditions, the UK authorities had to agree to DCE ceilings. In these circumstances, the government felt that it might as well make a virtue out of necessity and accept an associated £M3 target; this was clearly expressed in the Chancellor's November 1976 speech.

So, by the mid-1970s, most of the major industrialised countries had adopted publicly announced, quantified targets for a key monetary aggregate. The aggregate chosen differed between countries: Central Bank Money in West Germany, M1 in the USA and Canada, M2 in Japan and France, and £M3 in the UK; Switzerland began with M1 and moved to a monetary base target in 1980. The announced target period was generally for one calendar year, though in its initial format in the USA the effective target period was only one quarter at a time, since the target covered the year ending with the calendar quarter following the date of announcement. The target was expressed in a variety of ways: as a single point, which implied that it was certain to be missed, or as a centre-point lying within a range of upper and lower acceptable outcomes. In some cases, the range was expressed in terms of year-on-year change; in most cases, it was expressed in terms of upper and lower percentage rates of growth from the announcement date. This gave rise to the cone shaped targets, for the UK and USA respectively, shown in Figures 15.2 and 15.3.

The early experience (pre-1979) with such targets was somewhat chequered. Certain countries, notably those whose historical record made them especially determined to pursue a firm contracyclical policy, did manage to reduce inflation sharply in the later 1970s, notably Germany and, after a shaky start, Japan. The German authorities in particular felt that the adoption of a monetary target helped to control inflationary expectations and to establish a widely understood nominal framework, enabling inflation to be effectively reduced with less disruption to the real economy.

Although inflation did fall back in the later 1970s from the peaks of 1974–5, the adoption of monetary targets did not herald a decisive break with the inflationary mentality or experiences in the later 1970s in the UK or North America. The critics argued that this was because of several flaws in the conduct of targetry.

First, the authorities were generally continuing to operate by varying interest rates as their control mechanism rather than operating directly to control the growth of the monetary base. Even worse, the UK authorities continued to rely on a direct credit control, the Supplementary Special Deposit scheme or 'corset', whose effect in restraining monetary growth was in some large part cosmetic.[2]

The use of interest rates as the control mechanism meant that in the short run, the rate of growth of the monetary aggregates would respond endogenously to a shift in

---

[1] The US, Canada and Switzerland in 1975 and the UK and France in 1976.
[2] Bank of England (1984) pp. 117–27, and Spencer (1986) Chapters V and VI.

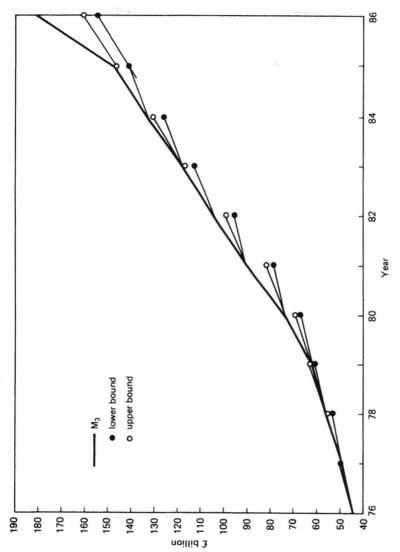

The method of targeting M3 changed in 1985 from the use of cones to the use of tram lines, as shown above.

FIG. 15.2

Source: *Bank of England Quarterly Bulletin* (1986) p. 500.

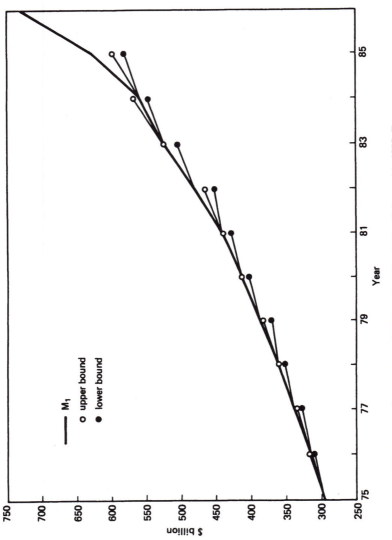

FIG. 15.3

During the 1970s the annual targets were rolled over quarter by quarter. This ceased in 1978. To simplify the chart the Q4–Q4 target ranges for those earlier years are shown.

Source: Federal Reserve Board Bulletin, various issues, e.g. (April 1978, p.267), (April 1985, p. 179).

the demand for money or credit (see Chapter 12, Section 3). Thus, any expansionary impulse would be directly reflected in the short run in faster than desired monetary growth. In order to rein back such inflationary impulses, the authorities should respond to such short-term excess growth by aiming for lower than desired trend growth in the subsequent periods. This was conspicuously not done, however. Instead, the monetary authorities, especially the Fed in the USA, accepted any such overshoot as had occurred in the last period and simply extrapolated the previously chosen growth rates from the new, higher base. This led in these years to the phenomenon of 'base drift', which can be clearly seen in Figure 15.3 for the USA and also appears, though somewhat less obviously, with the UK in Figure 15.2.

Overall, by the end of this first period (1979), critics were arguing that the authorities' adoption of 'pragmatic monetarism' and monetary targets had not represented a real change of heart or of approach – at least in the USA or UK. To be effective, they argued that much more commitment was necessary.

2. Rules versus Discretion

One of the puzzles of the 1970s was to understand why the monetary authorities in general, and the Central Banks in particular, allowed inflation to take such hold. Given that velocity (the demand-for-money-function) was predictable, then the quantity identity ($MV = Py$) indicated that the authorities could control the level of nominal incomes up to a point by exerting their influence to vary the money stock (M).

Given reasonably rational expectations, the analytical case for the existence of a medium-term vertical Phillips curve (the NAIRU) seems overwhelming – though see Chapter 13 for an account of the will-of-the-wisp nature of this latter concept in practice. If the authorities cannot reduce unemployment beyond the NAIRU in the medium–longer term without generating ever accelerating inflation (and equally would neither be able nor want to raise unemployment beyond the NAIRU without imposing ever-deepening deflation), then their only remaining medium-term choice is the rate of inflation. With real output (y) set in the medium term by the same set of real factors that determine the NAIRU, and with velocity (V) being fully predictable, the authorities can, in principle, control the level or growth rate of M to control the level or growth rate of prices (P).

Clearly, it would seem that the optimal choice for the authorities, and of course for the general public, would be for the authorities to select a growth rate for M such that P was zero. Yet increasingly during the 1960s and 1970s, the underlying rate of inflation was accelerating. Why? There were several attempts to explain this paradox. One strand in the literature asserted that there were internal bureaucratic incentives for Central Banks to *prefer* more inflation to less. Some of this work has already been surveyed in Chapter 2, Section 5. My personal experience leads me to discount totally suggestions that Central Banks prefer inflation. While a Central Bank, like any other bureaucratic institution, does have a concern for its own position and power, it is hard to see why these would be enhanced in more inflationary conditions. In any case, Central Bank macro monetary policy is usually largely determined by the head of the Bank whether Governor, Chairman or President, plus a few senior officials; these people are swayed mostly by their concern for public and historic acclaim, what Professor Mayer has described as 'obituary enhancing' results. Since the public has generally seen the main function of the Central Bank as maintaining the value of the currency, a Central Bank governor who fails in that respect is not likely to obtain many plaudits.

If one should dismiss on *a priori* or empirical grounds the notion that the monetary authorities are more stupid or have a greater preference for inflation than, say, the generality of academic economists, how then can one explain the discrepancy between the actual and optimal (zero) rates of inflation in recent years? This problem was brilliantly resolved, first by Kydland and Prescott in 1977,[1] then in two papers by Barro and Gordon,[2] and subsequently (in rather more literary and expositional style) by Barro alone.[3]

Let us start with the implausible assumption that the authorities regard the private sector's current expectations as given independent of the authorities' current actions;[4] we will also assume that the authorities are seeking to maximise a social welfare function over time which exactly and accurately represents the public's preferences. There exists a standard, expectations augmented Phillips curve,

$$U_t = U^* - a(\dot{P}_t - E\dot{P}_t) \tag{5.1}$$

where U^* is the natural rate, as earlier discussed in Chapter 13.

There is also a social welfare function for the authorities and society such that Z, the costs of imperfect policy,

$$Z_t = b_1(\dot{P}_t)^2 - b_2(\dot{P}_t - E\dot{P}_t) \tag{15.2}$$

where b_1, b_2[5] > 0.

---

[1] Kydland and Prescott (1977) pp. 473–91; also see Prescott (1977) pp. 13–38.

[2] Barro and Gordon (1983b), probably the most rewarding single paper in the literature; and (1983a) pp. 101–22.

[3] Barro (1983) pp. 1–16; Barro, 'Rules versus Discretion', in Campbell and Dougan (1986) Chapter 1, pp. 1–30; Barro (1986a) pp. 23–37.

[4] 'Suppose for the moment that the policymaker, when selecting $\dot{P}_t$, treats $E\dot{P}_t$ and all future values of inflationary expectations $E\dot{P}_{t+i}$, as given', Barro and Gordon (1983b) p. 595; also see Barro and Gordon (1983a) p. 106.

[5] This formulation causes Barro and the neo-classicists some problems. If U^* really is a desired real equilibrium, then presumably *reductions* of U_t below U^* as well as increases of U_t above U^* would be undesired and costly. In that case, there would be *no benefit* in surprise price increases and temporary higher employment, and the appropriate cost function would include $+ b_2(U_t - U^*)^2$. Barro answers this by arguing that distortionary taxes (e.g., income taxes that cannot be levied on returns from leisure) and unemployment benefits cause the natural rate to be higher than that which be optimally preferred and would be achieved in the absence of such distortions. Calvo, 'On the Time Consistency of Optimal Policy in the Monetary Economy', *Econometrica* (1978) pp. 1411–28, also emphasises the importance of the existence of tax distortions for inducing the authorities to seek monetary surprises. Leijonhufvud, in his comment on Barro's paper in *Alternative Monetary Regimes*, entitled 'Rules with Some Discretion' (1986) is sceptical. He comments that, 'But why should rational agents dislike anticipated and like unanticipated inflation in a world where the first is basically neutral while the second fools them into behaving inoptimally? The Kydland–Prescott–Calvo–Barro line on this question is that the representative voter has already made the mistake of imposing an income tax on himself, which has induced him to goof off, so that he is actually grateful to be fooled into working more. It is a clever answer – too clever by half, maybe'. This response reinforces my own doubts about what the estimated levels of the NAIRU actually mean and whether, and in what sense, the NAIRU represents an 'equilibrium'.

Barro also notes that unanticipated inflation serves to raise the inflation tax on money holding and serves as a capital levy on existing nominal public sector debt. This may represent a comparatively attractive means of raising additional revenue.

In particular, the policy-maker treats the current inflationary expectation, $E\dot{P}_t$, and all future expectations, $E\dot{P}_{t+i}$, for $i > 0$ as given when choosing the current inflation rate, $\dot{P}_t$. Therefore, $\dot{P}_t$ is chosen to minimize the expected cost for the current period, EZ_t, while treating $E\dot{P}_t$ and all future costs as fixed. Since future costs and expectations are (assumed to be) independent of the policy maker's current actions, the discount factor[1] does not enter the results. The result from minimising 15.2 is $\dot{P} = b_2/2b_1$; unless b_2 is zero, (i.e., no benefit arises from a decline of unemployment below its natural rate, see footnote on p. 362), or $b_1 = \infty$ (i.e., costs of diverging from stable prices are infinite), a policy-maker optimising under the assumption that the private sector's expectations are fixed will choose a positive rate of inflation, depending on the policy-maker's and the public's relative preferences for more employment or more inflation.

However, the assumption that the private sector's expectations about future inflation are fixed independently of the authorities' actions is not consistent with rational expectations. Consider for the moment a starting condition in which the public has initial expectations of zero inflation and the policy-maker proceeds as outlined. Then:

> It may be useful to demonstrate that $\dot{P}_t = 0$ is not an equilibrium for the case where the policy-maker optimizes subject to given expectations in each period. Conjecture that $(E\dot{P}_t = 0)$ holds. In this case the choice of $\dot{P}_t > 0$ would reduce unemployment for period t. A trade-off arises between reduced costs of unemployment and increased costs from inflation. The balancing of these costs determines the chosen inflation rate, ... Under the assumed conditions (marginal cost of inflation is zero at $\dot{P}_t = 0$ and marginal benefit from reduced unemployment is positive when $U_t = U^*$), the selected inflation rate will be positive. However, since people understand this policy choice (rational expectations), the result $\dot{P}_t > 0$ is inconsistent with the conjecture that $E\dot{P}_t = 0$. Zero inflation is not a reasonable expectation for individuals to hold.

> An analogous argument can be used to find the positive rate of inflation that does provide an equilibrium. If a small positive value for $E\dot{P}_t$ had been conjectured, the policy-maker would still have been motivated to select $\dot{P}_t > E\dot{P}_t$, which would be inconsistent with equilibrium. The equilibrium obtains when $E\dot{P}_t$ is sufficiently high, so that $\dot{P}_t = E\dot{P}_t$ is the policy-maker's best choice, given this value of $E\dot{P}_t$. At this point the policy-maker retains the option of choosing $\dot{P}_t > E\dot{P}_t$ or $(\dot{P}_t < E\dot{P}_t)$ so as to accomplish a trade-off between lower unemployment and higher inflation (or vice versa). However, the level of $E\dot{P}_t$ is sufficiently high so that the marginal costs of inflation just balances the marginal gain from reducing unemployment.

(Barro and Gordon, 1983b, pp. 598–9.)

We can illustrate this with a diagram, Figure 15.4 taken from Kydland and Prescott (1977, pp. 478–9), showing a Phillips curve with a slope given by the coefficient a in equation (15.1). Starting off with expectations of zero inflation, an optimising policy-maker would try to reach position B on the highest possible indifference curve. If, however, the private sector was rational, it would expect the policy-maker to act in this way, so that expectations would shift until the consistent equilibrium discretionary position was at point C, where $\dot{P}_t = C = E\dot{P}_t$. In particular, note that (depending on the precise form of the indifference and Phillips curves), the

---

[1] The authorities can take the passage of time into account by choosing P_t, $t = 1 \to \infty$, to minimize (15.3) below, subject to their initial information set, I_0

$$E\left[\sum_{t=1}^{\infty} \frac{Z_t}{(1+r)^t}\right] I_0$$

utility at initial position *A* (zero inflation, natural rate) lies half way between the sought-for but unobtainable position *B* and the expectationally consistent position *C*.[1]

The central result is that utility at *A* is greater than at *C*. If policy-makers would eschew discretion and commit themselves to rules (e.g., a zero inflation rate) then they would achieve a better result.

So far, so good, but there are still loose ends to this analysis. First, the private sector may be behaving rationally in this analysis, with rational expectations, but the policy-makers clearly are *not*. They appear to act on the basis of an assumption that the private sector's expectations are fixed independently of their own actions, which is then clearly and immediately refuted by subsequent developments. Moreover, the authorities have appeared in recent years only partially to accept this case for 'rules'. So, we are left with the opening puzzle, how to explain inflation given that the authorities should be able to control it; are they fools or knaves or is there some further unperceived problem?

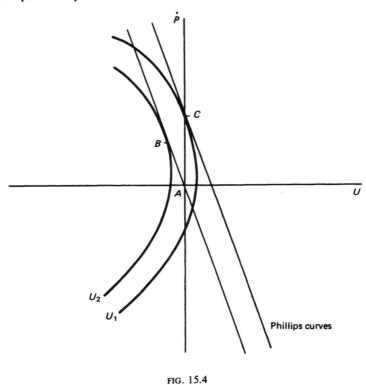

FIG. 15.4

---

[1] See, for example, Table 1, in Taylor, 'Comments' (1983, p. 124) on Barro and Gordon (1983a).
Note also that if the natural rate (U^*) was a true equilibrium in the sense that both downward and upward deviations from it were disliked, then the indifference curves would take on the shape shown in Figure 15.5. The zero inflation, natural rate point *A* would be what is graphically described as a 'bliss point' and both discretion and rules would lead us to that point.

The next stage in the analysis relates to the possibility of the authorities adopting a target but then cheating – i.e., stating at time t_0 that they would behave in a certain fashion but then reneging on that promise at time t_{+i}. This is often described as 'time inconsistency'.[1] Let us assume that the authorities have adopted a zero inflation announced target for all periods but that the world comes to an end in period $t+n$. Then, if inflationary expectations *are* fixed at zero in period $t+n$, the authorities and everyone else would benefit by having unanticipated inflation in that period. But a rational private sector would appreciate that in advance and expect the discretionary level of inflation (B in Figure 15.4) at period $t+n$. If their expectations would be such anyhow in period $t+n$, then the policy-maker and everyone else would certainly benefit from having unanticipated inflation in period $t+n-1$, but a rational private sector would realise that also. So the rule would unravel.

There is generally a short-run benefit from being able to manipulate given expectations, whether the expectations have been influenced by the adoption of a 'rule' or otherwise, offset by a longer-term loss of reputation and credibility. This

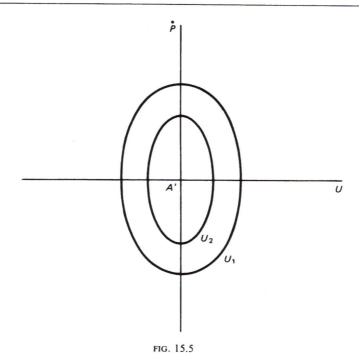

FIG. 15.5

[1] Such time inconsistent actions are quite common whenever an authority has to balance the possibility of short term benefit against longer term loss. Examples given in Kydland and Prescott (1977) include policy towards patents (revoking existing patent rights widens the present availability of existing knowledge but deters future devotion of resources to invention and R & D), capital levies (a non-distortionary method of financing the government now which deters future saving), and flood plain policy (rescuing current squatters on flood plains from present floods encourages future squatters, thereby requiring expensive flood plain protective devices).

approach leads on to analysis of possible reputational equilibria which depend on the extent of benefit from short-term 'cheating', the punishment on the authorities for cheating, in the form of the extent and length of future duration of loss of credibility, and their time discount rate. Clearly, the greater the short-term benefit, the less the future punishment, and the higher the authorities' rate of time discount, the greater the incentive to cheat. The application of such analysis to a possible electoral cycle is straightforward.[1]

Barro and Gordon offer a diagrammatic picture of the relationship between the temptation to renege from a rule and the penalties imposed by future loss of reputation (1983a, p. 112), reproduced in a simplified fashion in Figure 15.6. If expectations were initially fixed at zero, the authorities could obtain a sizeable short-term improvement in utility by reneging. As existing inflation and expectations of future inflation rise, the benefits from cheating fall until the pure discretion solution is reached. Thereafter, if inflation and inflationary expectations are above the pure discretion point, the authorities would benefit by cheating in order to lower inflation below the expected rate. The penalty from loss of future credibility falls as the effect on additional inflation from cheating declines. Given this pattern of temptation and penalties from cheating, the best reputational equilibrium possible would be at X.

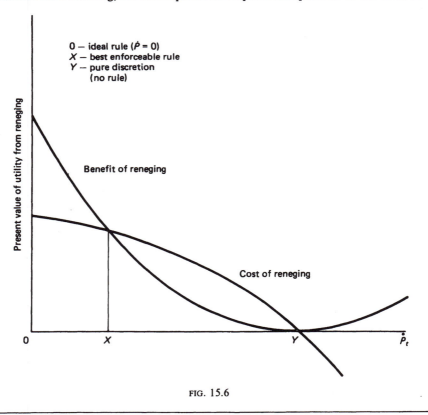

FIG. 15.6

---

[1] See Nordhaus, 'The Political Business Cycle' (1975), pp. 169–190.

This analysis leads on to a number of positive predictions that accord rather well with reality. Inflation will thus tend to rise when the authorities' time rate of discount is high, e.g.:

1. At times of political disturbance – e.g., wars, revolutions, etc.
2. Before elections.

Inflation will rise when the benefit from lower unemployment, higher *unanticipated* inflation is higher, e.g.:

1. When the natural unemployment rate, U^*, is high.
2. During a recession.
3. During a war or other period when government expenditures rise sharply.
4. When the deadweight losses from distortionary conventional taxes are high.
5. When the outstanding real stock of nominally-denominated public sector debt is large.

This view can account for:

(a) A simultaneous rise in the mean inflation rate and in the NAIRU, as has occurred in most developed countries.
(b) The contracyclical response of monetary policy.
(c) A high rate of monetary expansion during wartime.
(d) High rates of monetary growth in some less developed countries.
(e) An inflationary effect from larger real public-sector debt levels.[1]

Subsequently, economists working in this field have extended the analysis of reputational equilibria[2] and have explored the implications of applying this kind of analysis to a multi-country world where the authorities in different countries may or may not co-operate with each other.[3] These latter extensions, mostly involving game-theoretic analysis, have perhaps been more notable for their technical complexity than their practical usefulness and insights.

Be that as it may, this line of analysis has usually indicated the advantage of adopting a precommitted rule, as Kydland and Prescott (1977) put it, even

> When we do have the prerequisite understanding of the business cycle, the implications of our analysis is that policymakers should follow rules rather than have discretion. The reason that they should not have discretion is not that they are stupid or evil but, rather, that discretion implies selection of the decision which is best, given the current situation. Such behaviour either results in consistent but suboptimal planning or in economic instability.

While such a conclusion accords well with the priors of neo-classical–rational-expectation economists, it does depend either on actual unemployment being able to deviate from the natural rate for some persistent period, owing presumably to price stickiness (see Chapter 13, Section 2) or on the NAIRU being somewhat badly distorted so that people would actually much prefer a lower level of unemployment. Otherwise, a discretionary policy-maker would also directly choose the zero inflation objective. This latter consideration hints at analytical developments that could

---

[1] See Barro and Gordon (1983a) p. 114 and (1983b) pp. 600–1.
[2] See the references in Barro (1986b) Sections V and VI.
[3] See Levine and Currie, 'Does International Macroeconomics Policy Coordination Pay and Is It Sustainable? A Two Country Analysis' (1987) pp. 38–74.

assume a more Keynesian flavour or become more consistent with the views of an earlier generation of pre-neo-classical monetarists.[1]

A further constitutional and philosophical question is whether real pre-commitment is ever possible. Any government can rescind the legislation of its predecessor. So, there is no real distinction to be made between a system of rules and one of reputational equilibrium. Even so, the manner in which the rules or constitution are framed will affect the extent of penalty from 'cheating' or breaking the 'rules', and thus the likelihood of the authorities sticking to such rules. As Barro put it (1986b, p. 24):

> The manner of committing future actions varies with the area of public policy. In some cases, such as the duration and scope of patents, the rules are set out in formal law. Then the costs of changing laws (possibly coming under constitutional restrictions against *ex post facto* laws) enforces the government's commitments. However, in the case of the Gold Standard Act in the United States, the existence of a law proved in 1933 to be inadequate protection for those who held gold or made contracts denominated in gold.

Barro's analysis indicates those circumstances in which a monetary or price stability rule is likely to come under most severe threat, notably in wars or other political emergencies, in periods of unaccustomed high unemployment (the observer will rarely be able to distinguish whether a rise is cyclical or a shift in the NAIRU), when the real level of nominal public debt and tax levels are high and, for monetary rules, when velocity becomes unpredictable. The question then arises whether it is better to construct simple, fixed (open-loop) rules which are easy to understand but may get transgressed and repudiated at times,[2] or more elastic rules which adjust for foreseen

---

[1] Cagan, in his (1986) comment 'The conflict between Short-run and Long-run Objectives' on Barro's (1986a) paper, pp. 31–3, puts this well:

In Barro's model, . . . the preferred position of lower inflation and the same unemployment is not reached because the authorities cannot be trusted to foreswear unannounced stimulus to reduce unemployment . . . But that credibility problem is not insuperable. . . . It is the public's insistence, shared and accepted by the authorities, not to subordinate low unemployment to other objectives . . .
Let me substitute for the rational-expectation, market-clearing framework of his model the traditional notions of price inflexibility and long lags in the effect of monetary policy . . . They were an accepted view before Keynes . . .
In this reformulated version of Barro's model, a stable equilibrium appears unlikely. When inflation develops, the authorities can be counted on to slow it down, but they are hesitant to press down too hard and are certainly unwilling to reverse an increase in prices by deflating them. Inflationary pressures from a previous overstimulus may not be eliminated before the next bout of unemployment . . . There is a tendency, therefore, towards escalation of inflation. If the rate of inflation gets high enough, the resolve to bring it down may stiffen, and the objective of low or lower inflation may predominate for a while, as since 1980. . .
Can this process be stopped by nondiscretionary methods of the kind Barro discusses? Yes, of course it can. Will it? I doubt it. I see no evidence that the public is willing to accept nondiscretionary policies and to give up the option to deal not only with severe unemployment but also financial crises. There is today a heightened awareness of the advantages of price stability, and perhaps a new desire to avoid the worst excesses of fine tuning. But no government today would surrender its freedom to deal as it sees fit with macroeconomic problems and would never say that it would.

[2] In his comment, 'Fixed Exchange Rates and the Rate of Inflation', on Cooper's paper, 'A Monetary System Based on Fixed Exchange Rates', Chapter 3 in Campbell and Dougan (1986) Aliber concludes (p. 119):

contingencies in a more complex (closed-loop) manner. The more the authorities seek room to adjust for contingencies, the more the resulting policy tends to mimic pure discretion. Whereas most economists now accept that in *some* contingencies rules would have to be relaxed, there remains a tension between those whose preferences and priors would cause them to advocate simple, tight rules with little adjustment for contingencies[1] and those who would prefer a more elastic response to contingent developments. We shall consider this latter subject further in Section 4.

3. The Historical Record, 1979–87[2]

Much of the general line of argument for pre-commitment to rules, described in Section 2, struck a responsive chord with the authorities, both Central Bankers and politicians. While some of the more technical aspects of game-theoretic analysis were hard to assimilate, the importance of 'reputation', 'credibility', commitment and expectations came as second nature both to financiers and politicians. Moreover, the message even had a seductive addendum. The more determined and confident were the authorities in committing themselves to a contra-inflationary policy, the less would be the costs in additional unemployment, since a credible commitment would lead to a more rapid revision of expectations.

Indeed, there were some economists,[3] translating the theoretical studies of the

---

The review of the experience with fixed exchange rates and their breakdown suggests that one important aspect of any regime designed to achieve monetary stability is the elasticity of monetary rules or arrangements in response to wars and other emergencies. Many monetary arrangements are fair-weather friends; as long as the political environment is stable, these arrangements are likely to provide monetary stability because there is a strong demand for a relatively stable price level. From time to time, however, emergencies may arise; then the issue becomes whether the arrangement may be abandoned (an event like an extended bank holiday) or the monetary rule modified. Counterfactual history suggests that each regime might be tested by its implications for the behavior of the authorities in 1863, 1914, 1933, or 1976. Some analysts might prefer a rigid monetary constitution that would limit the ability of the authorities to inflate; they would then have to consider whether they would risk sacrificing the state to save the constitution.

[1] Thus, Barro (1986b) argues (p. 29):

One difficulty with contingent rules is that they may be difficult to verify. It is easy to confuse contingencies with the type of cheating that I described earlier. Further, the policymaker would be inclined to explain away high inflation as the consequence of some emergency, rather than as a failure to conform with the rules. ... These considerations favour a rule that is relatively simple, such as a constant-growth-rate rule for prices or money. In any case the contingencies should be limited to well-defined events, such as major wars. Although this limitation may miss some gains from contingent action, the greater ease of enforcement makes it less likely that the situation will degenerate into a high-inflation, discretionary equilibrium.

[2] For the UK, Bank of England *The Development and Operation of Monetary Policy 1960–83* (1984) remains the best source for the early years of the period. The papers, primarily on monetary and financial developments, in the *Oxford Review of Economic Policy*, Vol. 2, No. 4 (Winter 1986) are helpful on subsequent developments, together with the Governor of the Bank of England's speeches at Loughborough, 'Financial Change and Broad Money', *Bank of England Quarterly Bulletin*, 26(4) (December 1986) pp. 499–507 and on the occasion of the 1987 Mais Lecture, 'The Instruments of Monetary Policy', *Bank of England Quarterly Bulletin*, 27(3) (August), pp. 365–70.

For the US, see Meek (ed.) (1982) and Lindsey (1986).

[3] Notably Fellner 'The Credibility Effect and Rational Expectations: Implications of the Gramlich Study' (1979) pp. 167–78.

rational expectation neo-classicists into practical policy precepts, who argued that it would be better to jump directly to a monetary rule consistent with zero inflation than to struggle on with the gradualist approach. This latter approach had involved reducing monetary targets, and hence it was hoped nominal incomes, by a small amount, $\frac{1}{2}$ to 1 per cent per annum. If the commitment of the authorities was really credible, so it was argued, expectations of future price inflation would adjust to the rule in either case, so unemployment need not be greater with the more ambitious step. Moreover, the latter would emphasise the commitment and the radical shift of policy of the authorities. Furthermore, by taking the main step to a non-inflationary environment early on, there was less time and chance for adverse shocks, political weariness or public disillusion to set in. One of the favourite analogies of the era was that inflation was like drug addiction; you always needed a higher dose (more unanticipated inflation) to get a 'high' (lower unemployment). A relatively successful way of beating the drug habit was instant and complete removal of the drug, the 'cold turkey' approach, as it was often termed. Analogously, some of the neo-classical advocates of monetary rules advocated a similar approach by the monetary authorities.

In the event, the innate caution of Central Bankers, particularly about the validity of the untried precepts and theories of the neo-classicists, restrained them from attempting any such major policy shift. Projected rates of decline in monetary targets remained gradual. However, the authorities did accept by 1979, after a period of years during which the authorities' commitment to targets – in the USA and UK at least – had seemed to many commentators to be half hearted and contra-inflationary success to be limited, that greater commitment and credibility were required.

First, we shall review the response of the US authorities from 1979–82 and then evaluate the policy adopted in the UK, the Medium Term Financial Strategy (MTFS), during 1979–85. Although the Fed had adopted monetary targets in 1976, the main weakness of the conduct of policy was that the authorities continued to seek to maintain control by small, occasional adjustments in the Federal Funds rate, the main day-to-day money market rate.[1] Although technically the Fed could have made major step changes in the Fed Funds rate, as the Bank of England managed to do, internal political pressures in the US had restrained the Fed from adjusting the Fed Funds rate by more than about 25 basis points ($\frac{1}{4}$ per cent) in any three–four week period. During the turbulent years of the late 1970s, with many shocks and unstable inflationary expectations, this slow, stately process led to adjustments being too little, too late.

This was recognised by all the Board of Governors, whether monetarist in sympathy or not. The main objective of the policy change introduced by Chairman Volcker on 6 October 1979 was to free interest rates so that they would be much more responsive to deviations of actual from desired monetary growth. The central feature

---

[1] Another shortcoming had been that targets were initially rolled over a quarter at a time, too short for meaningful commitment or to demonstrate whether control procedures were being effectively and purposefully applied. The authorities' effective target horizon was extended by House Resolution 50 in 1978, incorporated into the Humphrey–Hawkins 'Full Employment and Balanced Growth Act' of the same year, which required the Chairman of the Fed to testify to Congress every February and July about the Board's proposed monetary objectives. The Fed was required to report on a horizon encompassing the 'calendar year during which the report is transmitted' and also, for the July testimony, to report on 'the calendar year following the year in which the report is submitted'. Full details of the act are found in *United States Statutes at Large* (1978), pp. 1887–1908.

of the new policy was that the Fed's market dealers at the Federal Reserve Bank of New York should conduct their operations to achieve a prescribed path for the banking system's *non-borrowed reserves*, rather than for the Fed Funds rate.

This represented a shift of control methods towards monetary base control and away from interest rate targeting. As already discussed in Chapter 10, with the demand for reserves extremely inelastic to interest rates,[1] such a shift would be liable to cause interest rates in the short term to become extremely volatile. The Fed hoped to limit such volatility through two mechanisms. First, the target was *non-borrowed* reserves. There were various constraints on borrowing from the discount window, but, as market rates (e.g., Fed Funds rate) rose relative to the Fed's administered Discount Rate, banks would be induced to borrow more, thus relieving the immediate cash squeeze. Second, if interest rates still moved too violently despite this safety valve, the Fed maintained wide, unpublished bands which, if breached, would cause a temporary abandonment of the reserve target in order to stabilise interest rates.

As might have been expected, short-term interest rates did become greatly more volatile after this change in policy, see Figure 15.7, with volatility increasing by a factor of about 4 from previous years.[2] Although the extent of such extra volatility had not been closely predictable, the likelihood of such a development had been

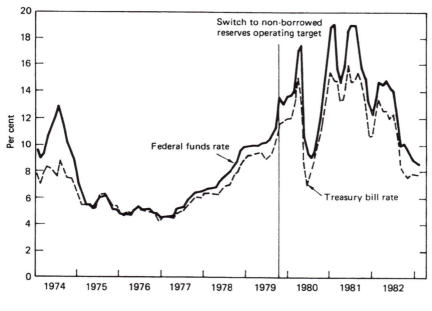

FIG. 15.7

Source: Campbell and Dougan (eds) (1986) p. 184.

---

[1] An inelasticity compounded by the fact that required reserves were still calculated on a lagged accounting basis.

[2] See Dickens (1987).

realised and had been generally regarded as an acceptable cost of the policy switch. At the same time, the average level of short term rates also rose sharply, approaching 20 per cent in nominal terms on several occasions.

During these years, the Fed did achieve reasonable success in meeting its longer-term annual targets and in slowing the trend rate of monetary growth.[1] There were, however, a couple of unexpected and uncomfortable surprises. First, the reasonably successful longer-term record of monetary control was not matched by shorter term (quarter-to-quarter) stability in monetary growth. Instead, as in the case of interest rates, the volatility of short-term (quarterly) monetary growth rates, especially of M1, the main US target aggregate, increased dramatically. Second, a more strongly committed, credible policy of monetary control should have led to greater public confidence in the achievement of lower (and reasonably stable) inflation and interest rates in the further future. Accordingly, one might have expected longer-term bond rates to have responded less (more sluggishly) to the now exaggerated shifts in short-term rates. In the event, the correlation between movements in short and in long rates actually increased.[2] How can we explain these unpredicted developments?

In part, these fluctuations in monetary growth were the consequence of external shocks, notably the imposition by the Carter administration of a direct credit control programme in March 1980 and its removal some months later in July, the introduction of interest-bearing negotiable order of withdrawal (NOW) accounts nationwide at the start of 1981, etc. For the rest, monetarists explained the short-term volatility mainly in terms of a combination of technical shortcomings and lack of conviction on the part of the Fed. The calculation of required reserves on a lagged accounting basis meant that the Fed ultimately had no option but to provide the reserves necessary to accommodate and support whatever nominal money stock the private sector had established at the going level of interest rates. Moreover, the open discount window limited both short-term variations in such interest rates, as actual monetary growth diverged from target, and the Fed's ability to control total reserves or the overall high-powered monetary base. As a result, criticism from monetarists concentrated on the lagged accounting arrangement,[3] the discount window facility and the choice of operating target.

Per contra, the Fed and its supporters emphasised the shocks to the monetary system, the rapid rate of monetary innovation and the growing instability of the demand for money function, see for example Lindsey (1986). My own view is that such volatility was entirely predictable and arose primarily from instrument instability – already discussed in Chapter 6 – resulting from long lags in the demand-for-money function. Given such lags, the more the authorities try vainly for short-term control, the more interest rates will overshoot their equilibrium, leading in due course to monetary overshooting.

---

[1] See, for example, Lindsey, 'The Monetary Regime of the Federal Reserve System,' Chapter 5 in Campbell and Dougan (eds) (1986), Melton (1985) and Wooley (1984).

[2] See Mascaro and Meltzer, 'Long- and short-term interest rates in a risky world' (1983) pp. 485–518.

[3] Laurent of the FRB Chicago advocated the opposite, that reserve requirements should be calculated on a lead basis, i.e., that the maximum amount of M1-type deposits a bank could maintain at a time $t+n$ should be related to its reserve base at time t, see Laurent 'Reserve Requirements: Are They Lagged in the Wrong Direction?' (1979), pp. 301–10. Despite some attractive features, the complexity of the scheme and its predisposition to various forms of avoidance techniques meant that it was never considered seriously.

Turning to the puzzle about bond rates, monetarists claim that the inability of the Fed to control the money stock in the short run and to maintain stable quarter-to-quarter growth rates led to greater uncertainty about the Fed's true intentions. This uncertainty raised the overall risk premium of longer-term bonds. Moreover, the short-term fluctuations in monetary growth were possibly taken as signals of changes in the Fed's longer-term intentions. So, a *temporarily* faster rate of monetary growth may have led to a rise in short-term and long-term interest rates because investors may have feared that it presaged a *permanently* higher monetary growth rate and worsening inflation.[1]

One of the most noticeable features of this period was the way in which US short-term interest rates reacted to the weekly news of unanticipated monetary growth: a large literature explored this phenomenon.[2] There were two main competing hypotheses: the 'policy reaction' and 'monetary expansion' theories. Under the 'policy reaction' hypothesis, the market rationally anticipated that the Fed would react to a monetary overshoot by encouraging interest rates to tighten. In the 'monetary expansion' hypothesis, the news showed that such growth had been, and might remain, faster than had been thought, so that inflation would also worsen; this could be expected to raise present and future nominal interest rates under the Fisher hypothesis. The concurrent price movements in the foreign exchange and commodity markets were more consistent with the 'policy reaction' hypothesis, but concurrent movements in the US bond market seemed more consistent with the 'monetary expansion' hypothesis. Since my personal experience in the Bank of England makes me convinced that the 'policy reaction' hypothesis was the valid one – at least normally – the latter finding remains something of a puzzle.

Despite such short-term instability, the Fed did succeed in slowing the trend rate of monetary growth, halving inflation, and making a major dent in inflationary psychology.

All of this appeared to require unprecedentedly high and volatile interest rates, which in turn helped to induce major financial innovations in the form of new deposit instruments, NOWs and Super NOWs, money market mutual funds (MMFs) and money market deposit accounts (MMDAs). Moreover, restrictive monetary policy did not seem to encourage a general revision of expectations without adverse unemployment effects. Whether it was because monetary targetry was applied inefficiently and without sufficient commitment to be credible, as the monetarists claimed, or whether the rational expectations–rules argument was always more theoretical than plausible, as the Keynesians claimed, the American real economy stagnated and unemployment rose to a post-war record. In addition, in 1982 the combination of falling commodity prices, due to the recession, and sky-high nominal interest rates provoked the Less Developed Country (LDC) debt crises. A combination of comparative success in combating inflation, severe adverse effects on the real economy, the LDC debt crisis which threatened financial stability in the US and, above all, the progressive collapse of the predictability of velocity – in conjunction with a flood of financial and monetary innovations – led Chairman Volcker to call a halt to this experiment in the summer–autumn of 1982. Thereafter, the Fed moved back towards the targeting of borrowed reserves; since the demand for such

---

[1] See on this Mascaro and Meltzer (1983).

[2] For example, see Siegel 'Money Supply Announcements and Interest Rates: Does Monetary Policy Matter?' (1985) pp. 163–76 and Cornell, 'The Money Supply Announcements Puzzle: Review and Interpretation (1983) pp. 644–57.

borrowing was a function of market rates, given the administered level of the discount rate, this was a partially disguised return to using interest rates as the main control instrument. Moreover, the instability of the demand-for-money functions led to such control being increasingly undertaken on a discretionary basis rather than with primary attention being paid to the growth rates of monetary aggregates.

Meanwhile, a Conservative Government was elected in the UK in May 1979 pledged to monetary control – in the form of a target for £M3 – as the centrepiece of its contra-inflationary strategy. This government believed that monetary control would rapidly blunt and then counteract a series of inflationary shocks occurring at the same time; some of the shocks were self-imposed, such as the increase in the general level of the VAT indirect tax from 8 to 15 per cent in the June 1979 budget and the acceptance of the high, catch-up wage awards to public sector workers proposed by the Clegg committee, while others were exogenous (e.g., the second oil crisis). Since inflation was viewed by the government as a purely monetary phenomenon, an edict went out that government officials were not to describe the rise in prices that resulted that autumn following the tax changes, etc., as representing any increase in inflation!

In the event, the rise in prices and nominal incomes caused in large part by such shocks made it harder to restrain the growth of £M3 and interest rates were therefore increased sharply. Meanwhile, the rise in oil prices coincided with the build-up of oil production from the North Sea which rapidly drove the UK current account into large surplus. A combination of the effects of North Sea Oil, high UK interest rates and confidence in the government's contra-inflationary determination led to a sharp rise in the pound's external value.[1] The rise in the value of the pound provided the government with the opportunity, which its free market ideals encouraged, to get rid of exchange controls in the autumn of 1979.

Such exchange controls, in the UK as elsewhere, however also provided the protective barrier behind which direct credit controls and other direct constraints on bank expansion (e.g., high, zero-yielding reserve requirements or interest ceilings, etc.) could be imposed. Without exchange controls, intermediation that is blocked or penalised domestically will simply be re-routed offshore to no real advantage (except a transparently cosmetic distortion of the data) and to the detriment of the domestic banking sector. This implication was quickly realised and accepted and the current local direct control in the form of the 'Corset' was abandoned in July 1980.

Before then, in the Budget of March 1980, the Chancellor unveiled the Medium Term Financial Strategy (MTFS). This was unique both in setting quantified objectives for the target monetary aggregate (£M3) not just for the next year but over the forthcoming four years, and in the extent to which all other macro policies were to be subordinated to the achievement of the £M3 target. Finally, the terms in which the Chancellor described his adherence to the £M3 target implied an unprecedented degree of commitment.[2] It appeared to represent the apotheosis of the school of

---

[1] The rise in the real value of the pound, i.e., adjusted for movements in relative unit costs from 1979:Q1 to 1981:Q2 was remarkable, about 23 per cent, and accounted for much of the deflationary pressures in the years 1980–2. It has, however, been remarkably difficult, even with hindsight, to estimate with any confidence the relative responsibility and contribution of North Sea Oil, tight money and the Thatcher effect for the increase.

[2] 'The Government has announced its firm commitment to a progressive reduction in money supply growth. Public expenditure plans and tax policies and interest rates will be adjusted as necessary in order to achieve the objective' (p. 16), and 'it may be necessary to change policy in ways not reflected

thought advocating precommitment to rules and the defeat of those warning about contingencies and the need for discretion.

From the start, the MTFS ran into technical trouble. The ending of the 'Corset' in July 1980 led to a far larger reintermediation, causing a jump in £M3 of some 5 per cent in the one month alone, than had been predicted. Even in its first year of operation, £M3 was running well above the target range. The standard response would have been to make further open market sales, thereby tightening the monetary base and raising interest rates still further. By the autumn of 1980, however, the value of the pound was reaching levels that were clearly grossly misaligned and this was placing tremendous deflationary pressures on the UK economy. Inflation was beginning to fall rapidly but unemployment was bounding up and whole industries were in a state of imminent collapse.

This placed the government in an unenviable position for which they tended, in part, to blame the Bank. In the event, they neither tried to abide by the letter of their commitment (e.g., by raising interest rates further and trying to claw back the monetary overshoot),[1] nor did they abandon the MTFS; indeed, the Chancellor conspicuously refused to apply Keynesian fiscal restimulation in his March 1981 Budget, despite the onset of the sharpest cyclical downturn in living memory.

The pressure on industry in 1980 and 1981 was so severe that, in many cases, they had to borrow more just to finance their cash outflows. At the same time, the abandonment of credit controls and the incentives on the banks to compete in a deregulated context led to an upsurge in lending to other parts of the private sector, notably to the personal sector on the collateral of mortgages. For such reasons, bank lending to the private sector surged ahead in the years 1979–87 at an average rate of over 20 per cent p.a.[2] Since bank lending to the private sector accounted for almost 70 per cent of the sterling assets of the UK banking system by 1979, it was not easy to hold the growth of sterling bank deposits down to the target levels sought.[3] Of course, interest rates could have been raised further except that the level of the pound remained excessively high and deflationary pressures very strong some years after 1980.

Instead, the authorities turned to the technique of 'overfunding', already described and explained in Chapter 10, Section 3; its objective was to seek to make room for a faster rate of bank lending to the private sector within the target level of bank deposits at unchanged interest rates. This sounds quite a difficult trick to turn but in practice over the years 1982–5 the Bank managed to hold £M3 generally within its target, despite the continuing surge in bank lending. The more serious question was whether the effect of allowing a fast rise in bank credit, while restraining the growth of bank deposits, was actually maintaining a restrictive stance or was largely cosmetic.

In any case, the major overshoots in £M3 in 1980 and 1981 were accompanied by tightening deflationary pressure on nominal incomes. Prior to 1979, with the

---

in the [budget] projections. . . But there would be no question of departing from the money supply policy, which is essential to the success of any anti-inflationary strategy' (p. 19) *Financial Statement and Budget Report 1980–81* (1980).

[1] A growth of 19.4 per cent in 1980–1 compared with a target of 7–11 per cent.

[2] See, among many other sources, Goodhart (1986c), pp. 80–91.

[3] Of around 10 per cent per annum, see Goodhart (1986c) Table 2, p. 83, for details.

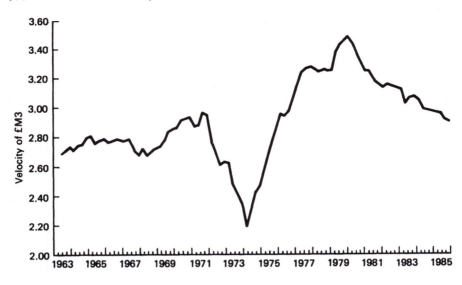

FIG. 15.8

Source: Goodhart (1986c) p. 82.

exception of 1972–3, the velocity of £M3 rose steadily year by year (see Figure 15.8).

Suddenly in 1979, coincident with the switch to the MTFS, the trend in velocity shifted and it began to decline quite rapidly (i.e., £M3 rose faster than nominal incomes). This had not been predicted; for the first few years of the MTFS, the target ranges were set on the basis of the assumption that the prior trend in velocity would soon be re-established. By 1982, it was becoming apparent that such previous statistical connections and regularities as may have existed between £M3 and nominal incomes were no longer in being. This meant that the authorities had little clue any longer what growth rates of £M3 would be consistent with their ultimate objectives for output and inflation. Initially, the authorities reacted by seeking to cross-check their view of the current monetary stance by looking not only at other monetary aggregates (e.g., M1) but also at other nominal variables (e.g., exchange rates, asset prices and inflation itself). Several of the other narrow monetary aggregates then, however, also became distorted by the innovation of the widespread introduction of interest-bearing deposits.

In the event, the links between £M3 and nominal incomes became so tenuous that the government was unwilling to continue with the complex and little understood exercise of overfunding and it was stopped in the summer of 1985.[1] With that abandoned, £M3 began to grow at the much faster concurrent pace of bank lending and the government in the autumn of 1985 effectively abandoned £M3 as a target.

Since then, the Bank and the City have continued to worry about the rapid rate of expansion of lending to the private sector and of the growth of the broader liquidity aggregates, not only £M3 but also the indices of Private Sector Liquidity (PSL).

[1] For a more detailed analysis, see the Governor's Loughborough speech, 'Financial Change and Broad Money' (1986), pp. 499–507.

Meanwhile, the government turned to the monetary base (M0) as its main domestic indicator and target. In the UK, with no required bank reserves, this consists almost completely of currency and notes in the hands of the public and in bank tills. The demand for currency function (its velocity) has remained fairly stable, much more so than for bank deposits; however, few commentators outside government ranks have seen any causal relationship running from the public's holdings of currency (supplied of course absolutely on demand), to nominal incomes – rather the reverse. Meanwhile, while the City and the government may have been bickering on the relative weightings to be placed on M0 and M3, in fact the conduct of monetary policy was primarily determined during the years 1985–7 by using a discretionary judgement of the appropriate external value of the pound *vis à vis* the dollar, its trade-weighted effective index and, increasingly, the Deutschemark.

So, the experiment with the adoption of precommitted rules was seen to have failed and was abandoned in both the UK and the USA. That is not to imply that the experiment was a total disaster. It led in both countries to much tighter policies, high interest rates (US) and a higher exchange rate (UK), than would have been adopted under more discretionary management. This did cause such severe deflation that inflation and inflationary expectations and psychology were tamed, if not broken. Yet, there was no indication whatsoever that the public adoption of rules allowed for an improved unemployment–disinflation trade-off. The resulting depression in the USA and UK was accompanied by as fast a rise in unemployment as the most jaundiced Keynesian had predicted.

What finally caused the exercises to be abandoned was not the rise in unemployment but the increasing instability and unpredictability of the key relationships between money and nominal incomes. Was this an inevitable concomitant of the introduction of such new rules and control methods, or was it just happenstance? In part it was, I believe, such a concomitant, illustrating again the power of the Lucas Critique and Goodhart's Law in this field.[1]

The control methods were bound to cause greater short-term instability in nominal and real interest rates in conditions of high and variable inflation. These fluctuations would cause existing direct regulatory and control measures to place increasing and more variable burdens on those affected, thereby leading to enhanced pressure for deregulation and more competition over a level playing field. Add the recent speed of evolution in information technology to circumstances including extremely variable asset prices, deregulation and enhanced competition and the stage has been set for major institutional innovation.

One way of viewing much of the recent process of innovations is to see this as involving a series of steps, brought about by competition, technological change and de-regulation, that have sharply reduced the cost of intermediation, (i.e., the effective spread between deposit and lending rates). The cost of using the services of a bank or of some other financial intermediary can be measured as the margin (spread) between its deposit (bid) rate for money and its lending (offer) rate. If the use of a bank's intermediation services was costless and free, with a bank offering as large a return on deposits as it charges on loans, then, as Miller and Sprenkle (1980) pointed out, so long as deposits provided liquidity and transactions' services, the optimal volume of both loans taken and deposits placed by individual agents should become infinite. As

---

[1] The Lucas Critique of econometric models has already been described in Chapter 14. Goodhart's Law, 'that any observed statistical regularity will tend to collapse once pressure is placed upon it for control purposes' (1984a) Chapter III, p. 96, is a mixture of the Lucas Critique and Murphy's Law.

the size of the spread has fallen under the influence of greater competition, with innovations improving the wholesale and retail terms offered to depositors, and increasing the range and variety of loan terms available to borrowers, so the volume of intermediation has increased. It becomes sensible for those facing relatively small spreads, such as public bodies, large companies and perhaps now also rich individuals, simultaneously to hold deposits as liquid interest-bearing assets and to have outstanding loans from banks. The greater the spread, the greater the incentive to economise on both borrowing and on holding comparatively expensive deposits; the less the spread, the more willing agents will be to expand their use of the services of financial intermediaries.

Thus, in the demand functions for deposits and for loans, it will be necessary to include as arguments not only the general market level of interest rates, as determined by the authorities, but also the own-rate on deposits and the interest rate on bank loans. Moreover, with the availability of market-related interest rates on deposits and low spreads, the volume of deposits will increasingly prove an elastic function of *relative* interest rates (i.e., the spread between markets rates and deposit rates and the spread between loan and deposit rates). Similarly, the demand for loans will become an increasingly elastic function of spreads between *relative* rates, whereas both loans and deposits will become increasingly inelastic to the *general* level of market rates.

In part, the financial innovations (e.g., better deposit terms and better credit facilities) that led to the expansion of financial intermediation in the 1970s were induced by the more aggressive competition amongst banks and between them and other financial intermediaries. By the same token, the recent innovations supporting securitisation have been induced by the altered preferences of banks and regulators to move away from such high-volume, low-margin business in the pursuit of greater safety and higher capital ratios. This is not to suggest that the innovations have been *entirely* endogenously determined by the industrial dynamics of the banking system. In some part, innovations must derive from an autonomous invention, otherwise they would have been known and available beforehand.[1]

The balance between exogeneity and endogeneity in financial innovation is not easy to determine. It is important, however, to realise the role of the endogenous effect. Some observers, noting the trend in the mid 1980s towards securitisation together with its associated innovations, thus tended to extrapolate that trend and to predict a continuing erosion in the share of bank intermediation in financial flows. The shift towards securitisation has been in some part, however, a consequence of the general feeling that bank margins had fallen too far. Once balance becomes restored between the relative margins involved in channelling financial flows directly through primary markets as compared with indirectly via financial intermediaries, the current trend will slow down. In any case, the trend in the 1970s was all the other way, to channel a greater share of financial flows through bank intermediation; securitisation has only been a short-run phenomenon so far. Moreover, the continuing decline in spreads and in the costs of intermediation facing smaller, retail, domestic customers (e.g., persons and small businesses) means that banks may recoup the volume of business (willingly) lost in lending to sovereign and large multinational companies by increasing their share of business in lending to such smaller, retail customers.

---

[1] Though as Cooper's (1986) paper 'Innovations: New Market Instruments' notes (pp. 1–17), several recent innovations, such as financial futures, employ techniques that were widely known in other areas, such as commodity futures, for decades before they became adopted within the financial system.

It will not, however, be the banks alone that focus on this latter opportunity. One facet of the increased competition in the provision of financial services has been the dismantling of the dividing lines that separated the functions of the different kinds of intermediaries, many of which had been grouped together into protective (and anti-competitive) cartels with the tacit, and sometimes explicit, blessing of the authorities. With the passage of the Building Societies Act 1986, for example, the building societies should be able to provide quite comprehensive banking facilities to their personal customers. Meanwhile, the banks are providing mortgages and, with the advent of the 'Big Bang' in the Stock Exchange, have been establishing their capacity to undertake capital market services, not only in London but worldwide. Moreover, I envisage (Goodhart, 1987a) the likelihood of financial intermediaries such as investment houses, unit trusts, etc. being prepared to make payment services available on the basis of assets other than the standard bank or building society deposit.

Such blurring of functional dividing lines is increasingly making the definitions of aggregates, which depend on such divisions (e.g., the money stock) uncertain and fuzzy. As sight deposits come to offer market-related interest rates, such balances will be held partly as an investment and not just for transaction purposes. Moreover, new payment technologies may induce financial intermediaries to offer such services on the basis of other financial instruments. With banks and building societies liabilities being such close substitutes, and becoming closer, what is the value of an aggregate such as £M3 which includes only bank deposits? In a period of rapid structural change, associated with continuing innovation, the form, pattern and meaning of the financial aggregates becomes fluid and less stable.

The process of competition, deregulation, innovation and structural change has thus broken down the dividing lines between the functions carried out by the various financial intermediaries. Transaction balances will soon be provided by building societies, as well as by banks, and may increasingly become available from other intermediaries on the basis of other kinds of (non-traditional-deposit) assets. An increasing proportion of such sight balances will offer market-related interest rates. Competition between banks, building societies, and perhaps other financial interme-diaries in providing a widening range of liquid assets remains intense. Under these circumstances, the appropriate dividing line or definition of 'money' – once one has gone beyond currency (M0) – is becoming fuzzier.

With such increasing competition, the elasticity of asset holders seeking to shift between one such close substitute asset and another in response to quite minor shifts in relative interest rates and in the costs (i.e., the spreads) involved in differing forms of intermediation, is likely to increase. Since the holding of 'monetary' assets will thus become more sensitive to such fluctuations in *relative* interest rates, the relationship of such holdings to nominal incomes, i.e., its velocity, and to the *general* level of interest rates is likely to become less stable; in that sense, the demand functions for money are likely to become less well explained by standard econometric equations. The monetary authorities will obtain less information from monitoring the growth of the monetary aggregates (e.g., as a guide to future trends in inflation and nominal incomes).

The decline in the extent of information inherent in the time path of the monetary aggregates may, however, serve to reconcile the authorities somewhat to their diminishing ability also to control these. In the first place, the deregulation that has accompanied innovation in part encouraged and in part forced by that process itself, has reduced both the willingness and the ability of the authorities to resort to direct quantitative controls over credit or interest rate ceilings. Secondly, the increasing impact of *relative* interest rates (e.g., the spread between lending and deposit rates) in determining the growth of both lending and deposits is responsible for lessening the authorities' ability to control the growth of the aggregates since the authorities can influence the general level of short-term money-market rates but cannot generally control relativities between money-market interest rates.

4. Whither Now?

During the early years of the 1980s, the previous predictability of financial relationships deteriorated, often alarmingly. Not only did the relationship between monetary aggregates and nominal incomes (velocity) often evaporate but exchange rates became frequently grossly misaligned. The academic prescription of the 1970s, to anchor nominal incomes by an announced, precommitted monetary target and to allow exchange rates to float freely, had been tried and found wanting – though many monetarists claimed that Central Bankers had simply not tried hard enough and that all could have been well with improved control techniques and more determination.

In these circumstances, one relatively attractive option, at least for many smaller and medium-sized countries, was to abandon domestic targets and free floating and to return to a system of pegging the exchange rate to some central, dominant currency. We shall examine the problems that this may entail subsequently, in Chapters 17 and 18. For the moment, we just note that this option is not open to the central country or countries on whom the smaller countries are pegging. For the rest of this section, we shall concentrate on the present problems of managing monetary policy in those countries that cannot, or choose not to, slough off the issue on their larger neighbours by adopting an external peg.

The main innovation discussed at the end of the previous section was the payment of market-related interest rates on deposits which can be used to pay for transactions, though in some cases, such as MMDAs, only with a restricted range of transactions services. In those cases where such interest rates rise towards the average market level, which will be possible only when an economic charge is made to cover the considerable resource costs of facilitating the use of the payment mechanism, agents will increase their holdings of such deposits until, at the margin, their desire for the additional liquidity services is satiated. The payment of market-related interest rates on bank deposits will expand the quantity held towards its micro-level optimum,[1] at which the desire for liquidity is satiated.

While this adds to the efficiency of the financial system, it does mean that, with liquidity demands satiated, the elasticity of substitution between monetary and non-monetary assets will rise sharply. Such increasing elasticity of substitution will rise further if de-regulation and new technologies allow a much wider range of financial intemediaries (e.g., building societies, unit trusts, insurance companies and pension funds) to offer (limited) transactions services to holders of claims on them.[2]

The implication of this is that it was the *constraints* on the banking system (e.g., those that both limited the interest rates which they could offer on deposits and raised the spread between the rates on deposit liabilities and on lending) that caused the

---

[1] See Friedman (1969a) Chapter 1, pp. 1–50.

[2] As I have argued in my paper, 'Why Do Banks Need a Central Bank?' (1987a) pp. 75–89, this is both technically feasible and economically desirable.

demand function for such deposits to be so stable and well defined. As those constraints are eased and market-related interest rates are paid on bank deposits, not only does the previous stability of the demand function erode but the very definition of money becomes fuzzy at the edges.[1]

If so, this implies that the only definitions of money which may continue to be viable to use for purposes of targetry are those wherein interest payments on such liabilities continue to be restricted. Since interest payments are now effectively available on demand deposits, this suggests that the only remaining possible monetary target has now become the monetary base, consisting of currency and non-interest-bearing reserves at the Central Bank. Even here, reserve balances at the Central Bank *could* be interest-bearing and many have advocated that they *should* be.[2]

In any case, the predominant component of the monetary base, in the UK at least, consists of currency outstanding. There are various technical reasons why it is hard to pay interest on currency, though both Huston McCulloch and I have (independently) suggested that this could be relatively easily achieved by running a lottery on the serial numbers of the notes.[3] In any case, the amount of interest obtainable from the currency normally carried would be so low as to make the computational costs hardly worthwhile.[4] So, it is perhaps reasonably safe to assume that currency will continue to be non-interest-bearing.

It is not, therefore, coincidental that following the increasing instability of demand-for-bank-deposit functions, monetarists have generally moved to advocate relating quantitative targets to the monetary base. In the UK for example, the demand function for currency (approximately monetary base) has indeed been more stable than that for wider aggregates in recent years. This is now, perhaps, many monetarists' preferred alternative.

There are, however, many caveats. Developments in information technology (e.g., electronic funds transfers and 'smart cards' with inbuilt memories) may make dramatic changes in payment methods. The authorities' monopoly over note issue could be challenged (e.g., by issuers of travellers cheques offering interest on these). The demand for currency is already influenced by changes in payment methods and it would be a brave economist who confidently predicted such velocity into the further distance. Moreover, much of such demand probably relates to nefarious activities, the 'black economy', gambling, prostitution and drugs, where the anonymity of

---

[1] This is close in spirit to the analysis of Fischer Black (1970) pp. 9–20; see also Hall (1982) pp. 1552–6; and Wallace (1983) pp. 1–7.

[2] Indeed, Hall, 'Optimal Monetary Institutions and Policy', Chapter 5 in Campbell and Dougan (eds) (1986), would make relative variations in such interest rates his main control instrument.

[3] McCulloch, 'Beyond the Historical Gold Standard', Chapter 2 in Campbell and Dougan (eds) (1986); Goodhart (1986b) pp. 1–12.

[4] Thus, White, 'Accounting for Non-Interest-Bearing Currency: A Critique of the "Legal Restrictions" Theory of Money' (1986), comments:

On a note whose initial value equals two hours' wages, held one week while yielding interest at 5 percent per annum, accumulated interest would amount to less than 7 seconds' wages. If the noteholder's wage rate indicates the opportunity cost of his time, then he will not find it worthwhile to compute and collect interest if to do so twice (once at the receiving end and once at the spending end) takes 7 seconds or more, i.e. if it takes 3.5 seconds or more per note-transfer. To indicate the same point less generally, a $20 note held one week at 5 percent interest would yield less than 2 cents. Notes held in cash registers by retailers generally turn over much more rapidly than once a week, of course, so that the threshold denomination may well be extremely high.

currency is prized; indeed, a large proportion of holdings of outstanding notes is never caught in surveys. Would one really want to relate one's target to such a base? Moreover, with deposits being convertible into currency on demand, the volume of currency outstanding is strictly endogenous (demand determined). Alas, those helicopters showering down additional currency notes are only a figment of monetary economists' imagination: there are no supply shocks to currency! Causation runs strictly from nominal incomes and expenditures to currency. Given that the authorities' main objectives are prices and output and that the lead of information on currency outstanding on indicators of output/price changes is short, the case for a monetary base target is hardly compelling.

If the various, earlier perceived, advantages of monetary aggregates as intermediate targets (e.g., stable velocity and prompt and accurate data) have diminished, then there is a growing case for relating the authorities' main control instrument, interest rates, directly to the ultimate objectives of policy, inflation and output (unemployment). The more that one believes that the real economy reverts quickly and automatically to equilibrium, as do the rational expectation neo-classicists, the more one would want the authorities to target the price level alone. The more serious and persistent one believes deviations of actual output from equilibrium output to be (e.g., because of price–wage rigidities), the more that one would want to vary interest rates also in response to the latter.

Barro (1986b) puts all this nicely in his Section VII, pp. 35–6:

> In many theories associated with the 'new classical macroeconomics,' such as Sargent and Wallace (1975), the regular reaction of money to real activity does not smooth out the business cycle. Since people know that recessions inspire monetary accelerations, there are no systematic surprises. Then, if only the surprise movements in money matter for real variables, there would be no implications for the business cycle. It follows that it would be preferable to limit monetary policy to the objective of stabilising the general price level. Any broadening of this objective threatens people's accurate perceptions of prices (which has adverse real effects), but provides no offsetting benefits.
>
> On the other hand, Keynesian theories with sticky prices suggest that regular feedback from output to money can (usefully) smooth out fluctuations in real economic activity. Hence, although it means an increase in the volatility of prices, it is nevertheless worthwhile for money to react systematically to variations in real GNP.
>
> In effect, the proposal to stabilise nominal GNP is an attempt to unite the principal warring factions of macroeconomists. The new classicists are supposed to be happy because monetary policy is governed by a rule, and that rule does entail stabilisation of some nominal magnitude. Then the feedback response of money to real GNP is to be regarded as a minor nuisance, most of which the private sector can hopefully filter out.
>
> Keynesians are supposed to be happy with the scheme because it allows for an active response of money to recessions and booms. Presumably most Keynesians would also accept the feedback from prices to money, although they may not opt for the equal weighting attached to fluctuations in real GNP versus fluctuations in the general price level. Apparently, the main thing that Keynesians have to give up is their 'commitment' to discretionary monetary policy, which seems little to ask.
>
> The choice between the two objectives – stabilising the general price level versus stabilising nominal GNP – corresponds to the weights one attaches to the

validity of the two competing viewpoints about macroeconomics. (Surely one of these views must be correct!) If one attaches little weight to Keynesian theories with sticky prices, then the policymaker's preferred objective would be stabilisation of the general price level.

In fact, as Hall points out (1986), the comparative weights given to output and price deviations by the adoption of a nominal income target are arbitrary. He advocates making a conscious choice of such relative weighting in his *elastic price target*, in which the 'price level target is a constant plus an elasticity times the unemployment rate' (p. 225). Hall notes that 'An elasticity of 2.5 or 3 is a close approximation to nominal GNP targeting' but argues for a larger elasticity, around 8.

There are a number of difficulties still with such proposals, one of them being the slow arrival and inaccuracy of such data. However, this only goes to exacerbate the far more serious problem of lags generally. The combination of data arrival lag, reaction lag and (much longer) lag from policy adjustment to effect on the ultimate variables adds up to some considerable elapse of time: several quarters at least and probably well in excess of one year. This would mean that any simple, automatic relationship of interest rates to output–price deviations is liable to trigger off severe instrument instability.

Hall (1986) sees this problem clearly; thus, he states (p. 286):

> The basic idea of the automatic policy is to [lower interest rates] whenever the economy drops below the elastic target and to [raise them] when the economy is above target. However, some subtleties need to be handled in order to make the policy work smoothly. If policy responds just to the current state of the economy, and there is some lag before a policy change has much effect on either unemployment or the price level, then there is a potential for unstable feedback. Even if the system were not unstable under such a policy rule, a response this month to economic data from last month could be seriously disruptive if it is not self-limiting.
>
> Both the price level and the unemployment rate are measured with a certain amount of unavoidable error. If the price level were high and unemployment low in a particular month, an aggressive policy might call for a [sharp contraction]. ... The immediate impact of this monetary contraction would be high interest rates and financial disruption. If the [contraction were continued] for the whole month, without responding to anything that happened during the month, there would be a month long economic crisis. Even if unemployment and prices responded a bit during the month, the crisis could easily extend into the second month as well. The response in later months could be so strong as to call for a later expansionary move to [very low interest rates].
>
> All of these problems can be avoided by linking [interest rates] not to the most recent data but to future data, say for the forthcoming year. In other words, the elastic target is to be achieved over the average of the forthcoming twelve months, not of the current month alone. The advantage of imposing the target on expectations rather than on historical data is that expectations are instantly responsive to policy.

A problem with this is that forecasting the future is still an art rather than a science and is much influenced by our priors. Keynesian forecasters, such as the National Institute, are thus liable to underestimate inflation and exaggerate the weakness of output while neo-classicists (e.g., those running the Liverpool University model) might have the reverse tendency. Would we be in danger of reverting to 'fine-tuning'? Hall has an ingenious solution, whereby the variations in interest rates are to be related to the expectations of private sector financial institutions rather than to official forecasters.

But that is a detail. The problems remaining to be resolved are:

1. How much relative weight to place on output as compared with price level deviation from target.
2. How to estimate the lag structure involved in order to cope with instrument instability.
3. How best to forecast future deviations of output and price levels.
4. How then to calibrate interest rates in the light of 1, 2 and 3 to achieve the optimal time path.

If these issues could be resolved reasonably, then one might try to reduce the conduct of the exercise to a form of tight rule; even then, however, the authorities should beware the Lucas critique and Goodhart's Law! You cannot simulate in advance how the economy will behave under a new rule unless one can go behind 'structural' equations to predict how each agent will behave in such a new context.

In part out of a belief that the authorities can *never* be trusted because there are incentives on them to 'cheat' and inflate, there is a final school, the 'Free Banking School', which would have the authorities leave the field of providing fiat currency and undertaking monetary policy altogether. Under the leadership of Hayek, with support coming from excellent economists such as Yeager and L. H. White,[1] this school is having an academic revival. In the absence of government fiat money, the basic unit of account into which bank liabilities, both notes and deposits, should be convertible would have to be an object of value.[2] There is room for argument whether there could/should be competing monetary bases or one specified base, and who should choose the base (the authorities?), and what object(s) would make the best base. Assuming that the debate has been satisfactorily concluded, banks would be required to maintain convertibility into the chosen base (or be bankrupt) but would otherwise be unfettered by official regulation (see Chapter 2, Section 5).

The proponents of free banking claim that the various costs of bankruptcy, plus the rewards of good reputation, would suffice to make the banking system conservatively and safely run; both theoretical and historical arguments have been advanced to that end.[3] I am extremely dubious of this case.[4] This question will, no doubt, continue to be debated and discussed.

Be that as it may, it has been recognised from Bagehot[5] onwards that there is no practical possibility of the authorities voluntarily abandoning their controlling position. As Cagan stated (1986, p. 33), 'no government today would surrender its freedom to deal as it sees fit with macroeconomic problems and would never say that it would'.

Free banking will remain an academic mirage. For the rest, small and medium-sized economies have the option of pegging their exchange rate to an external source of value. Central countries can choose between a monetary base target, some version of nominal income target, and discretion, though in practice these are not necessarily mutually exclusive. A country's monetary policy could thus be primarily aimed at nominal incomes, perhaps via some rule, contingent on its exchange rate not moving out of some reference range, all subject to discretionary override.

---

[1] See Hayek (1978a); Greenfield and Yeager (1983) pp. 302–15; White (1984).
[2] See Thompson (1986).
[3] White (1984b); Jonung (1985); Rockoff (1974) pp. 141–67.
[4] See Goodhart (1985) and (1987a).
[5] 1873 (new edn. 1962) Chapter II, pp. 32–3 especially.

XVI
The Regional Adjustment Process

Summary

In previous chapters we were concerned with the process of adjustment over time of various groups in the economy, but these groups were not given a geographical location. In the final three chapters we shall examine how adjustment is achieved spatially, between different areas. For ease of analysis this subject will be divided into two parts. In the first part, in Chapter 16, we shall examine the process of adjustment between regions in a single country where there is a single common currency: then in Chapters 17 and 18 we shall move on to consider the process of adjustment between countries with separate monetary systems and individual monetary policies.

The main emphasis in this study of inter-regional adjustment is that it involves an interlinked process of the achievement of both flow and stock equilibria. A formal model illustrating the nature of the linkages between flow and stock relationships is set out in the Appendix; this model provides much of the analytical basis for the description of the adjustment process in the rest of the chapter. The dichotomy between expenditure-flow relationships and asset-stock adjustments is mirrored in the distinction between the analysis of the determination of the current-account balance and the analysis of how this balance is financed. Reversing the usual procedure, we consider first in Section 1 how regional current-account imbalances are financed.

In general, the existence of an integrated financial system and capital market shared by regions within a country allows regional current-account imbalances to be very easily financed, so much so that there is no analogue at the regional level to the recurring concern at national levels about the adequacy of their foreign-exchange reserves. Given the high degree of substitution between financial claims of similar kinds issued in different regions, a region does not face the same immediate financial pressure to correct a current-account imbalance as does an individual country, with a lower international elasticity of substitution between financial assets. Even so, financial pressures will develop in regions if appropriate adjustment to current-account imbalance is long delayed. If a current-account deficit is not a reflection of local investment opportunities, it will involve a growing burden of debt servicing, rising invisible account deficits, and falling incomes and wealth. Financial pressures to adjust will not appear in the guise of exhausted reserves but of an increasing unwillingness to provide further loans to the borrowers in the indebted area.

Then in Section 2 we turn back to an examination of the determinants of the current-account balance. We start with the simplest case, in which all prices, including factor prices, interest rates, etc., are determined nationally. In this case an external shock, causing say a rise in the region's exports, will cause a multiple increase in incomes and wealth, with the ultimate adjustment required depending on the size of the marginal propensity to import. The time path to that equilibrium, explored in the Appendix, is functionally more complex, and the system may well experience oscillations in the process of adjustment. These changes in incomes and output, with wage levels given, would cause fluctuations in the level of employment or migration. These labour market developments can be painful, and there may alternatively be some flexibility in movements of relative wage rates between regions, though such flexibility is reduced by concern over parity of treatment.

Such flexibility in wage rates would restore employment in depressed regions either through a substitution of labour for capital or by raising the return to capital (and therefore new investment) in the region, even if final prices of goods remained nationally fixed. But this latter is a strong assumption, and we next examine how the current account of a region responds to changes in the prices of its goods relative to the prices of goods produced elsewhere in the country. Given the supply elasticities of production in the regions involved, and the initial trade balance, this depends on the price elasticities of demand in each region for the exports of the other regions. The higher these elasticities, the more favourable the effect on the balance of a relative reduction in prices. This concept of the price elasticity of demand is not, however, an easy one, since changes in relative prices affect incomes and supply conditions, as well as having pure substitution effects. So the increase of sales of exports and fall in imports, following a fall in relative prices, depends on an amalgam of different and even offsetting factors. In particular, if a region (country) is relatively small it ought, by lowering the prices of its products, to be able to displace goods of a similar kind produced by other regions (countries). Thus, whatever the aggregate price elasticity of demand for such goods, the price elasticity of demand facing any one region (country) should be high. In practice, however, the apparent response of trade flows to devaluations has often seemed sluggish, but I attribute this more to slow supply response than to low demand elasticities.

1. Financing Current-account Imbalances: The Capital Account

So far we have been concerned with the process of adjustment over time, in response to changes in the parameters of the system, of various groups in the economy. These groups were not, however, given any location in geographical space; as far as the analysis indicated up till this point, they all lived together at the same spot. In fact, of course, people spread out over regions and countries, and it is therefore also necessary to study how adjustment to shocks and changes is achieved spatially, involving the economic inter-relationships of one area with another.

Sometimes this subject appears even more complicated than it need, because two separable issues are taken together in a complex mixture, rather than distinguished and discussed consecutively. These two issues are, first, the process of regional adjustment between regions who share a single currency (and monetary authority) and, secondly, the question of the effects of alternative possible monetary relationships between individual countries with their own separate distinct currencies. Frequently analysis of the effects of various forms of *inter-national* monetary relationships (e.g., flexible exchange rates, fixed but adjustable rates, the gold standard, etc.) is pressed forward before the process of *intra-national* regional adjustment has been fully explained. Yet if you do not understand how balance between Manchester and London, or Chicago and New York, is maintained, how will it be possible to comprehend clearly economic relationships between London and New York, where the existence of separate currencies introduces a further layer of complexity.

So in this chapter the intention is to discuss adjustment between regions in a single country with one common currency; indeed we shall generally assume that the total money supply in this single country is given. Then having discussed the *intra-national* adjustment process, the analysis is broadened in the next chapter to encompass the additional problems introduced by the existence of several autonomous countries with their separate monetary systems and individual monetary policies.

The first stage, therefore, is to examine the process of adjustment between separate regions within the same country. Many writers dealing with this subject, at least in the post-Keynesian period, focused their attention mainly on the determination of inter-regional trade flows and their inter-relationship with income-expenditure flows: the analysis dealt mostly with the effects of the foreign trade multiplier on the one hand, and of changes in the relative prices of tradable goods on the other.[1] While such flow relationships form a major part of the story, it has more recently been realised that this overlooked the inter-related and equally important question of the achievement of asset-stock balance, with financial assets and money, as well as goods moving from one region to another.[2] In this account we shall try to give a description of the inter-linked process of the achievement of both flow and stock equilibrium, with both expenditure flows and shifts in asset holdings responding to relative prices (and interest rates), as well as to changes in incomes and wealth. The basic framework of our approach is an extended portfolio adjustment model.

A model of this kind is set out in the Appendix. It provides a formalised picture of the structure and workings of one region within a large country which is intended to

---

[1] An early example is to be found in Machlup (1943, reprinted 1950).

[2] There were several strands in this development. The simplest, but nevertheless useful, model which incorporates consideration of asset balance concentrates on the achievement of equilibrium between the demand and supply of money in any region. In this model the demand for money depends, mainly, on domestic incomes, while the supply comes from domestic credit (money) creation and monetary flows via the balance of payments. This analysis was initially developed within the IMF as a guide to policy recommendations in the international sphere, see for example, Polak (1957–8) pp. 1–50 and Argy and Polak (1971) pp. 1–24. This approach was subsequently taken up by certain monetary economists who brought it into the main stream of monetarist analysis, for instance R. A. Mundell, H. G. Johnson and A. K. Swoboda (with their main centre at the International Economics Workshop at the University of Chicago). They emphasised those aspects of the model which reach back to Hume's (1752) classic analysis 'Of the Balance of Trade', from *Essays, Moral, Political and Literary* (1898) pp. 330–41, 343–5, reprinted in Cooper (ed.) (1969) pp. 25–37. Examples of their analysis can be found in Johnson (1972), also reproduced as Chapter 11 in Connolly and Swoboda (1973). The latter also contains contributions on the same subject by Brunner, 'Money Supply Process and Monetary Policy in an Open Economy' (Chapter 8) and by Swoboda and Dornbusch, 'Adjustment, Policy, and Monetary Equilibrium in a Two-Country Model' (Chapter 12). A further paper on 'The Monetary Theory of Balance of Payments Policies' by Johnson was included in Frenkel and Johnson (eds) (1974).

Their analysis concentrated, however, on the achievement of asset balance for only one asset, namely money, and tended to ignore the need to describe and to demonstrate how asset balance is obtained for all assets, in each region, including real capital and non-monetary financial assets. It is, of course, true that in a three-asset world, goods, money and bonds, if the markets for two assets are in equilibrium, the third must also be. This appeal to Walras's law as a justification for omitting specific consideration of the market in non-monetary financial assets fails in those cases when we are interested in the process of adjustment in non-Walrasian systems. In this respect more complete and more satisfactory accounts of the achievement of stock-flow equilibrium for a wider range of assets were developed by Floyd, 'Monetary and Fiscal Policy in a World of Capital Mobility' (1969) pp. 503–17, and Tower (1972) pp. 251–62, with their 'A Reply' from Floyd (1973) pp. 299–303.

be an aid to understanding the process of inter-regional adjustment. The background to the analysis in the remainder of the chapter may become clearer if the Appendix is read first, and there are several references in the text to it. Nevertheless, any formal model can give only a limited and partial representation of the real world, and some may find it indigestible; so it can be skipped, if preferred.

The dichotomy between expenditure-flow relationships and asset-stock adjustments is mirrored in the distinction, in studying the balance of payments, between the analysis of the determination of the current-account balance and the analysis showing how this balance (surplus or deficit) will be financed by flows of financial assets, in the capital account plus reserve movements. Because it seems relatively easier to do so, and accords with our emphasis on asset equilibrium and financial flows, we shall consider these two parts of the balance of payments in reverse order, discussing first the ways in which a (regional) current-account imbalance will be financed.

Nobody doubts that regions do run current-account surpluses (or deficits) in trade with each other; that some regions find it becoming relatively easier or more difficult to sell their goods and services in inter-regional (national) markets; that marked regional disparities in wealth, incomes and unemployment develop between regions and that large net regional migrations take place. Yet despite such signs of balance-of-payments problems, it is often claimed[1] that in inter-regional transactions – as compared and contrasted with international transactions – there are no balance-of-payments problems, or at least that these are of a qualitatively different kind. What this actually means is that the portfolio adjustments required *to finance* a current-account surplus – deficit can be much more smoothly and easily arranged in inter-regional transactions, indeed so simply facilitated that they may pass virtually unnoticed.

To the inhabitants of, say, Manchester a fall in the demand for their goods and services from the rest of the country does not evidence itself in newspaper headlines about exports and imports, but initially in a fall in their monetary balances (see equation (v) of the model in the Appendix) and in the local banks' cash reserves (see equation (vi) of the model). In fact in a branch bank system, in which cash reserves are centralised at Head Office in the main money-market centres, the deficit of the Manchester area (with other areas) at the clearing will not even be settled by reserve flows. Instead the Manchester banks would increase their (book) liabilities at head Office, with an increasingly deficit position (i.e., local loans becoming larger than local deposits). In a branch banking system the initial financial counterpart of a current-account imbalance occurs virtually automatically. In a unit bank system, in which each area bank maintains its own reserves, the initial financing of an imbalance may have a more noticeable impact, since the clearing will provide some areas with surplus reserve funds and lead to pressures on the reserves of deficit areas. Hence the pressures on the area banks to readjust their portfolios in order to restore their desired balance-sheet position may well be more acute and immediate than in a branch bank system.

In any case, whatever the form of the banking system, the inhabitants of Manchester will feel the need to readjust their asset portfolios. Thus an initial fall in exports to, say, London, probably results in a local accretion of stocks of goods. So at the end of the initial period wealth (and incomes) have not yet been changed, but the asset balance has been disturbed with excessive capital (unsold stocks) and insufficient money. In the next period people will want to invest less – to restore their

---

[1] See Ingram, 'Some Implications of Puerto Rican Experience' (1962), reprinted in Cooper (ed.) (1969).

desired holdings of real capital: this will reduce incomes and (the rate of growth of) wealth. This reduction in incomes and wealth will serve to lessen the current-account deficit by holding down imports, but that forms the next part of the story, to come in Section 2. When an undesired reduction in money balances takes place, reinforced by a reduction in wealth, people will attempt to restore their asset balance by running down their holdings of other assets, particularly financial assets which can be relatively easily realised.

Mancunians, at least by the second round of the process,[1] will then be selling financial non-monetary assets and, perhaps, trying to borrow more in order to restore their monetary balances. In some part their attempts to redeem their non-monetary financial assets may put further pressure on financial intermediaries in the area, through a withdrawal of time deposits with local banks, deposits with local building societies, deposits with local Trustee Savings Banks, etc. But a large, very possibly even preponderant, part of their reduction in non-monetary financial assets will take the form of reductions of claims on inhabitants of other regions. This induces a capital flow to finance the current-account deficit; furthermore, in so far as Mancunians borrow outside the region, this also finances the deficit.

Nevertheless, to the extent that Mancunians seek to realise claims on, or to increase liabilities to, local financial intermediaries more pressure will be placed on the latter's balance-sheet position. In round 1 there was a reduction in local money balances (current accounts with banks) balanced (see equation (iv) in the model) by a reduction in the local banks' cash reserves – or by building up a larger deficit position with Head Office. In round 2 the local people are running down their non-monetary financial assets (e.g., time deposits with various financial intermediaries) and seeking to borrow more in the form of loans from them; meanwhile the reduction in imports (via the reduction in incomes) and the sale of non-monetary financial assets abroad may not yet have stemmed the decline in the money stock. So the local financial intermediaries, including of course the banks, are likely to observe a continued (but more broadly spread over different kinds of liability) decrease in their liabilities at the same time as they are faced with a growing demand for credit. To some extent, especially in a unit banking system, this pressure can be met by the intermediaries running down their second line of reserve, their claims on other regions (e.g., by unit banks in deficit areas in the United States running down their balances with correspondents or by selling their holdings, say, of US government debt). Perhaps to an even greater extent, without any apparent commotion at all, such pressures can be absorbed in a branch banking system simply by allowing some areas to become deficit areas (i.e., loans large relative to deposits) financed in effect by other areas (i.e., loans large relative to deposits) financed in effect by other areas becoming, *per contra*, surplus areas.

Furthermore, it may be possible for some financial intermediaries to raise the rates of interest which they offer on their liabilities (or charge on their advances) relative to the general, national rate. Since, we may assume, financial intermediaries in all the regions of this one country are treated as essentially alike in credit standing and attractions (except for the convenience pull of the local banks) a relatively small shift

---

[1] The initial first-round position was one in which the capital stock was £X higher than desired and money balances £X lower. Thus it might be thought that the first-round readjustment would simply be to cut back planned investment by £X, leaving other financial assets untouched. Even at this first round, however, people know that it takes time to restore cash balances by reducing orders for goods, so some liquid financial assets, which are relatively close substitutes for money, will be realised to restore the cash position.

in relative rates should induce a large inter-regional capital flow. Thus intermediaries in, say, the Southern States of the United States, subject to any severe local pressure on their reserves with falling local liabilities and rising loan demands, might be able to deal with this situation fairly easily by raising the rates offered on deposits and charged on loans very slightly above the general national level.

The ease of inter-regional financial adjustment results from the high degree of substitution between financial claims issued in the different regions. This may be contrasted with a significantly lower degree of substitution between financial claims issued in different countries, e.g., because of unfamiliarity with each other's laws and customs, because of the possibility of conflict between autonomous governments, because of concern over exchange rates, etc. At the limit one might assume that there was no substitution at all between the non-monetary financial assets of different countries.[1] In this case a country, suffering a current-account deficit, could not restore its reserves (of internationally accepted cash – e.g., gold, or wampum, or SDRs, or whatever) by selling its non-monetary financial assets to foreigners, or by borrowing from them.

In this international case the inbuilt deflationary effect of a current-account deficit, via the foreign-trade multiplier, is thus further reinforced by financial contraction, taking the guise of sharply rising interest rates and domestic monetary contraction. This contrasts with inter-regional conditions where interest rates do not need to rise much, relatively to other areas, to finance a current-account imbalance and the regional money stock can adjust smoothly to people's preferences. In reality, however, this contrast between international and inter-regional adjustment processes is much too stark, precisely because the assumption that there is little substitution between the financial assets of the different countries (though there is – it will be noted – substitution between their goods) may often be invalid. The higher the degree of substitution between countries' financial assets (e.g., via an integration of capital markets), the greater the ease of financing current-account imbalances without provoking sharp interest-rate fluctuations and monetary disturbances.[2] Still, the degree of substitution between financial assets internationally should generally be lower than inter-regionally, and to this extent the finance of current-account imbalances will require more noticeable increases in interest rates and monetary contraction in deficit countries relative to surplus countries. Unfortunately for quantitatively-minded economists, the degree of substitution between financial assets in different countries does depend on such qualitative factors as people's expectations of future exchange-rate conditions, changes in tax regimes, institutions and laws, the possibility of expropriation, etc.; so the subjective elasticity of substitution may vary quite sharply, even in the short run as 'confidence' fluctuates. A current-account

---

[1] Monetarists, from Hume onwards, have tended to make this assumption in the process of demonstrating how current-account imbalances bring about international monetary flows.

[2] The relatively smooth balance of payments adjustments of countries during the gold-standard period, 1890–1914, is sometimes attributed largely to the flexibility of national price levels in response to monetary movements. An alternative view has been developed which gives much more prominence to the integrated world capital market centred in London. This latter approach notes that the low exchange risk resulting from the assumed permanence of the mint par exchanges allowed adjustments via financial asset substitution to take place with a minimum of monetary disturbances. For examples of this reassessment of the way in which balance of payments adjustments took place during the gold-standard period, see McCloskey and Zecher 'How the Gold Standard Worked, 1880–1913', in Frenkel and Johnson (eds) (1976); Williamson (1964); and Goodhart (1972).

deficit may be easily financed one year and only with considerable difficulty the next.

A region, with high inter-regional elasticity of substitution among financial assets, does not therefore face the same immediate financial pressures to correct a current-account imbalance as does an individual country with a lower elasticity of substitution. Even so, financial pressures will develop if appropriate adjustment to current-account imbalances is long delayed. A current-account imbalance does, however, automatically set in motion changes in incomes, and wealth, and also possibly of relative prices that should serve to improve the position.[1] Moreover, by definition, the local authorities in a single region are not in a position to use *monetary policy* to counter any reductions in incomes, employment and wealth, arising from falling inter-regional competitiveness, that may occur in their locality.

Nevertheless, one can think of situations in which a current-account imbalance would persist. If entrepreneurs see future possible profitable opportunities (profits to be obtained from sales in all regions) from current investment, then a current-account deficit could well develop as a probable accompaniment of the present higher investment. This is not really a situation of imbalance, however, so long as the expectations of future profitable sales provide a reasonable expectation of paying off the presently incurred debts. Essentially a region (or country) running a current-account deficit is getting into debt, and the ultimate creditors of the region have to assess whether expectations of its meeting that debt are good. If a region is running a deficit, not because new profitable investment opportunities are springing up, but because its industries have become uncompetitive, then views of the credit worthiness of the area will be jaundiced. If the shipyards of the north become unprofitable, or its coal mines run down, the region will find it less than easy to meet the cash drain, as sales to other regions fall, by borrowing from the local banks, forcing them into increasing deficit positions within the branch banking system. The financial pressure on a region to adjust its current account will be felt most keenly as the bank manager, under pressure from Head Office, seeks to restrict credit to those industries in the region whose commercial future looks unpromising. Asset sales, perhaps even of real assets at knock-down prices because of their specific nature, and reductions in wealth must follow, reinforcing other factors causing the current account to come back into balance. It is even possible in extreme cases to envisage the collapse of local financial intermediaries, whose fortunes have become too closely linked to the regional industries going through bad times, thus exaggerating the local debt-deflation cycle.

Even though local authorities cannot use *monetary* policy to protect their own people from depression, they can often use *fiscal* policy. They can borrow money in national financial markets to be spent, either directly or via grants and transfers to local inhabitants, in maintaining income and employment levels in their area. But unless their expenditure leads to an improvement in local competitiveness, say by improvements in local transport facilities, the level of income can only be maintained by running up an increasing burden of external debt. This debt has to be serviced; so the maintenance of income levels by borrowing from other regions – after a fall in the competitiveness of local industry – must lead to an increasing net interest outflow, worsening the current account and making the ultimate required adjustment even

---

[1] As financial assets are sold to residents of other regions, or local inhabitants borrow from outsiders, so the net flow of interest payments will become increasingly adverse. If the adjustment of incomes and/or relative prices is slow, the current account could, at least for a time, worsen.

more severe.[1] At some point the external debt burden would become large relative to the capacity of the local population to meet these debt obligations through higher taxes. At this point, unless the central government steps in with guarantees, etc., which represent an actual, or hypothetical, inter-regional aid transfer, the rate of interest which the local government would have to pay to borrow in the national market would rise as its credit standing became impaired. So in this case also financial pressures would eventually mount up, to enforce a return to balance in inter-regional transactions.[2]

Unless supported by a continuing transfer of funds from the central government, a region cannot, therefore, continue to run a chronic imbalance on its current account indefinitely without running up against financial pressures and constraints. Nevertheless, the high elasticity of substitution between financial liabilities of the same class issued in different regions enables regions to finance current-account imbalances with a minimum of difficulty and financial disruption. Clearly the ease with which imbalances between regions can be financed copes with one form in which balance of payments problems are manifest. The concern in each individual country over the adequacy of its stock of international reserves simply has no counterpart in inter-regional transactions.

2. Adjustment to a Current-account Imbalance

Having considered how a current-account imbalance will be financed by flows of financial assets, it is time to revert to an examination of the determination of the current-account position itself. The simplest case to study, with which we shall begin, is one in which all prices of goods, labour, etc., and all interest rates are set on national markets and are fixed independently of conditions in region A, say because A is so small relative to the country as a whole. With all prices constant, by assumption, exports, imports and consumption in A become functions of local incomes, Y_A, local wealth W_A, and incomes in other regions Y_B. While most expenditure *flows* are thus functions of the *levels* of income and wealth, it is the desired *stock* of capital which is a function of local incomes (output) and wealth, and so the *flow* of investment expenditure is a function of the *change* in incomes and wealth. In turn the level of incomes is the sum of expenditure flows on investment, exports and consumption, less imports, while the increase in wealth (prices and interest rates remaining constant) is the sum of net new investment plus the current-account surplus (all this is formally set out in the Appendix). So the current levels of incomes and wealth in A depend in part on the previous path of incomes and wealth in that region.

In this case, ignoring the effect on the invisibles component of the current account of financing trade imbalances (as being too small to matter), the system reduces to a couple of simultaneous difference equations determining Y_{At} and W_{At} in terms of

---

[1] If the rate of time discount is sufficiently high, it may nevertheless appear desirable to take this path.

[2] Ingram (1962) tended to underestimate the inherent limitations on financing continuing deficits, even for regions within an integrated country. This was pointed out by several economists, including Cooper in his editorial introduction to *International Finance* (1969) p. 12. See, for example, Ingram's 'Comment' on P. B. Kenen's paper on 'The Theory of Optimum Currency Areas: An Eclectic View', in Mundell and Swoboda (eds) (1969) p. 99. 'It would seem that capital movements could continue to equilibrate the balance of payments for as long a run as it seems reasonable to be concerned about.'

Y_{At-1} and W_{At-1} with Y_B treated as exogenously given and all prices taken as constant. This is demonstrated in the Appendix, and a numerical example is given. In that example (after an upwards shift in Y_B), the system does converge ultimately to a stable equilibrium, though income oscillates during the process of adjustment around an upwards trend. This oscillation is due to the specification of the investment function, which is in a form akin to the accelerator of standard trade-cycle models. Wealth, however, converges in the example smoothly and monotonically towards the new equilibrium, since the fluctuations in investment are offset by swings in the trade balance – i.e., as investment rises, the trade balance deteriorates and vice versa. The structure of the model is such that it would become dynamically unstable with slightly different, and still plausible, values for the coefficients, but it would in my view be misleading to place much weight on the particular dynamic properties of this extremely simplified model.[1]

Even though a more complex model might be needed to simulate a more realistic time path of adjustment, the ultimate changes in incomes (and wealth) necessary in these circumstances to restore full equilibrium after some external shock can be easily found. When prices are fixed, the demand for imports depends on the level of output. If exports change by £X, and the marginal propensity to import is, say, 0.2, then output must change by 5X to restore the same balance between exports and imports. So when exports rise by 20, incomes have to rise by 100 to restore equilibrium;[2] all the rest of the coefficients in the model merely serve to determine the time path of the economy towards that equilibrium.

The value of the marginal propensity to import is, therefore, critical in determining the size of the multiple change in incomes and wealth in response to an external shock, in conditions where relative prices are assumed to be fixed. In this respect the above value (of 0.2) is probably fairly realistic for middle-sized industrial *countries* (it is lower than this for giant countries such as the United States, Russia or China), but it is almost certainly much higher in relatively small regions such as Manchester in the United Kingdom, or Rhode Island in the United States. In general the smaller the region the higher the marginal propensity to import will be – an unsurprising

---

[1] For instance the investment function incorporated in the model takes, under the assumed conditions, a simple accelerator form, and this undoubtedly exaggerates the degree of instability in the system. Not only are there likely to be practical limitations to prevent negative investment, but also the model implies that expectations (assuming capital to be both specific and long lived) are formed on an incredibly naive basis (i.e., that the current level of output will continue henceforth). It is likely that entrepreneurs will take into consideration both a much longer run of past experience, and rational expectations of future prospective developments, in formulating their views on the probable trends in output to be expected over the lifetime of the capital equipment which they are thinking of installing. There will also, in general, be longer lags in the response of expenditure to changes in incomes than are postulated in this simple model. These lags should serve to dampen the oscillations of the economy as it moves from one (stationary) equilibrium to another after some external shock has hit the system: nevertheless, economies in the real world continue to exhibit some minor cyclical features (e.g., stock cycles) which may be described in terms of dampened models of this kind.

[2] So long as exports ≠ imports, there is a current account imbalance, since we are in this exercise abstracting from the balance on invisible trade. The imbalance will cause a change in wealth in the region, unless it is offset by a contrary movement in the value of domestic real capital (via investment flows); either way, whether the value of wealth or of the capital stock is changing, there will be continuing adjustments in the economy. A full static equilibrium cannot be achieved until the current account is in balance.

proposition. But from this it follows that the smaller the region the easier it will be for that region to adjust to external shocks by relatively acceptable changes in real incomes and wealth, without having to rely on relative price changes: whereas large, self-sufficient regions would have to undertake massive shifts in incomes (wealth) to maintain external equilibrium, in the absence of relative price changes.

To digress for a moment, we have been considering (here and in the example in the Appendix) alternative positions of stationary equilibrium, and whether the time path of the economy would allow a smooth transition from one such equilibrium to another. In practice, of course, there has been in recent centuries continuous growth of both population and technological innovations. Either of these features would prevent the attainment of a stationary equilibrium. With growing knowledge and a growing labour force any equilibrium must be dynamic, with all the various stocks and flows increasing at a fairly steady rate over time. If the stock of capital in a region is growing, and with it the level of money incomes, then the stock of money and other financial assets must also grow, in order to maintain asset equilibrium over time. In order to sustain a growing level of monetary deposits, each region needs a continuing inflow of cash reserves. This inflow of reserves may, possibly, be satisfied by continuing net sales of financial claims on the region to outsiders, with the reserve inflow financed therefore by a capital account surplus. But in order for equilibrium to be maintained, these net sales must not disturb the asset balance in the region between capital, money and other financial assets, nor the current-account balance between exports, imports and net interest payments. A more likely method for a region to satisfy its growing demand for money is for it to run a steady current-account surplus over time.

This, however, raises a more general problem of how to make it possible for all the growing regions, taken in aggregate, to be simultaneously running current-account surpluses in order to satisfy their needs for money.[1] One standard solution for this has been for the monetary reserve to be some real object – e.g., gold or pigs or red feathers – produced in one region but used as a monetary reserve throughout the country. In this case the producing region can treat the monetary object as an export, while the other regions can treat it as an addition to monetary reserves. In this fashion all regions *can* simultaneously run a current-account surplus. Nowadays, with the replacement of real objects serving as money by fiat money, the requirement for cash reserves is probably more largely filled by capital-account transactions, with the monetary authorities undertaking open-market purchases of financial assets offered by those (whether intermediaries or not) in any region wishing to add to their monetary balances. But some part of regional cash requirements may also be met by the governmental centre (e.g., London, Washington, Canberra), with its attendant army of bureaucrats, running a continual current-account deficit with the rest of the country, financed in part by printing money, which the rest of the country is keen to absorb. In this sense the government centre (or centres) may be running, in its geographical dimension, a chronic deficit with other areas.[2]

---

[1] The problem of ensuring an adequate growth of monetary reserves is usually treated as an aspect of *international* monetary relations. Indeed, the problems are more difficult in that context. Analytically, however, there is an analogue in the inter-regional case.

[2] As an exception to our previous comments, there will be no ultimate financial pressure on the government centre to remedy such a chronic deficit because, as explained in Chapters 2 and 6, it always has the power to create legal tender to pay off any debts and cannot become bankrupt economically.

To revert to the main thread of the analysis, when all prices are fixed an imbalance in the current account has to be corrected by a movement of incomes and wealth, the size of which depends on the marginal propensity to import. When the marginal propensity to import is low, the requisite shift in incomes could be very large indeed. With the level of wage rates in the region given (as well as all other prices), the demand for labour will vary with the level of output, resulting in a surplus of labour when demand for the region's output falls off, or a deficiency when there is a surge in the demand for the output of local industries. Such fluctuations in the demand for labour may be met either by variations in employment levels or by inter-regional migration. Both unemployment and migration are painful for those who are forced by circumstances into such a position. These fluctuations in labour markets could be ameliorated by variations in the relative wage rate in each region,[1] whether or not final prices on local goods responded flexibly to shifts in local wage costs.

A reduction in local wage rates *vis-à-vis* the price of capital goods would lead to some substitution of labour for capital, depending on the elasticity of substitution between the factors of production; and, depending on the form of the production function, the return to capital would be affected by the change in wage rates, either encouraging or dampening further investment. The short-term elasticity of substitution of labour for capital is probably quite low, and the fall in wage rates would in these circumstances raise the return on capital employed, given the level of demand, so that a small substitution to labour in existing plants should be reinforced by a significant increase in investment in new plants, in order to increase output for sale both at home and in other regions. Either way, whether by substitution in place of capital or by encouragement of a larger domestic output (or some combination of the two), persistent unemployment in a region should be capable of solution by a reduction in local wage rates relative to wage rates elsewhere.

Why then do we observe continuing higher unemployment in some regions than in others? Why do relative wage levels not adjust to eliminate such maldistribution? In part we need only rehearse the answers which we have already offered to a similar question in Chapter 12. A reduction in wages has a direct, obvious, general, and immediate depressing effect on the income of every worker in that job; its beneficial effect on employment opportunities is hypothetical, tangential, of benefit only to those unknown few who would otherwise have lost their job. Given the decentralised basis of decision-making, and the information available to each worker, it is unlikely that any trade union or group of organised workers would accept a wage cut in some locality because unemployment there was relatively high.

This line of argument, which was used in Chapter 12 to explain the incidence of unemployment, extends even further in this context to incorporate the concept of *parity*. If a worker in a car plant in Coventry is paid £X per week, why should a worker in a car plant in Glasgow be paid any less? People tend to measure their worth, or to feel that they are measured, in terms of their income: is a Scot working in a car plant in Glasgow working any less hard or less intelligently than an Englishman in Coventry? Why should wages for similar kinds of work differ between regions? One answer often is that at the existing wage rates there is relatively high unemployment among Scots, in part because in Scotland, through no fault of the Scots, there may be a historically determined high incidence of declining industries, because transport

---

[1] Migration will still be stimulated by regional wage differentials, but voluntary moves to higher-paid jobs elsewhere are quite different in character from migrations forced by lack of job opportunities at home.

costs are higher, because the land is more rugged and less conducive to economic exploitation. if, then, people insist on parity of pay for Scots in most industries, more Scots will either be thrown into unemployment, or be forced to migrate to more prosperous regions, or find that the only job opportunities open to them are in those industries which offer relatively low wages.

This desire for parity of pay in similar types of jobs, irrespective of different economic conditions in the regions where the jobs are offered, is a curious phenomenon. It often operates with very considerable strength between regions of the same country, especially in unionised industries and where information on regional relativities is easily available to the workers, but seems to dissolve almost entirely in international comparisons. A worker at an engine factory in Peterborough may be prepared to strike for months to get the same wage as a worker in an engine factory in Coventry, but will pay virtually no attention to the pay, or increases in pay, obtained by a worker in an engine factory in Germany, Italy or the United States. It will be interesting to see whether this distinction between the concern for parity within each country and the lack of interest in the same question between countries, will survive the increasing links communication, tourism and, perhaps, even of political ties between countries. Anyhow, inflexibility in adjusting relative (real) wage rates between regions perpetuates differences in regional activity rates and hinders the process of regional balance-of-payments adjustment.

Flexible wage rates should suffice on their own to restore full employment in a depressed region, even where the prices of all traded goods (and services) are assumed to be nationally fixed. This latter assumption is, however, a strong one, and we shall now relax it in order to examine the relationship between price and wage movements and the process of balance-of-payments adjustment more closely. We may start by assuming that the goods of region A (call them A goods) are sold on perfectly competitive national markets. On such markets the aggregate (all-region) demand and supply functions are initially as shown in schedule D_1 and S_1 in Fig. 16.1 with an equilibrium price at P_1 and output at Q_1. To the individual producer, perhaps in region A, the demand schedule will appear horizontal, d_1, and his individual supply function will depend on his marginal cost schedule s_1, as shown in Fig. 16.2, where $p_1 = P_1$.

Now let us assume that there is a fall off (a shift) in the aggregate demand schedule for these goods, perhaps because of a fall in real incomes in other regions or a shift in tastes; demand declines to schedule D_2 (as shown in Fig. 16.1). Unless producers have foreseen this fall in prices their production will have continued at the previous pace, and at the point of time when demand shifts there will be an existing stock of goods (all of which are to be sold on the competitive market) just sufficient to meet prior demand at the old equilibrium price: thus the short-run supply function will be the dashed vertical line S_2, which will now be sold at price P_2.

The individual producer then observes a decline in his horizontal demand curve to d_2 (Fig. 16.2) at prices $p_2 = P_2$, so he now decides to reduce output to q_2. With all producers behaving alike, this would cause a move along the aggregate (medium-run) supply curve S_1 to point Q_2. Clearly this is not an equilibrium either, since at this point there is now an excess demand in the market. Assuming (reasonably enough) that the dynamics of market responses allow convergence to equilibrium, a new quasi-equilibrium will be obtained at price P_3 with output Q_3. The individual producer will then face a steady horizontal demand function d_3 at price $p_3 = P_3$, where he produces q_3 ($\Sigma_1^n q_3 = Q_3$).

We have, however, described this as only a point of quasi-equilibrium. The reason

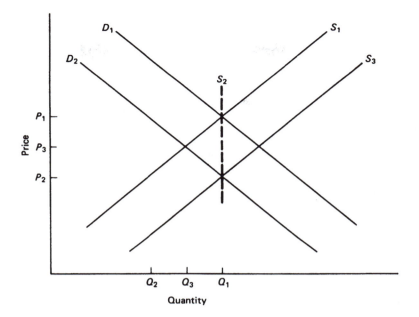

FIG. 16.1

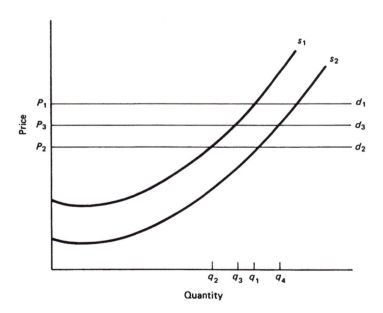

FIG. 16.2

for this is that, at the assumed given level of wages, employment in A production will have declined (and incomes from A production will have gone down). In this case in regions, such as region A, where production of type A goods provides a relatively large proportion of total employment, unemployment will increase. Unless the movement is prevented, for example by nationally-determined wage bargaining, wage rates should fall in jobs in A production, and particularly in areas concentrating in A production, as in region A. If wage rates fall in A production, there will be a shift in the marginal cost schedule to s_2, encouraging the producer to increase his output to q_4.

If all producers of type A goods, irrespective of region, experienced the same reduction in wage rates, aggregate (medium-term) supply would shift to S_3. Whether or not income receipts from sales of A goods would then rise or fall depends on the *aggregate* price elasticity of demand for that good. If it was less than unity, incomes would fall; if greater than unity, they would rise. The assumption, however, that wage rates in A industries fall by a uniform amount is, perhaps, somewhat extreme. In regions such as A, concentrating on the production of A goods, there will be a much larger excess supply of labour than in regions with only a small A production, where labour conditions may be buoyed up by a stronger demand for other goods. So wage rates in region A may fall relative to wage rates elsewhere. Then as A expands production of A goods (after a relative decline in local wage rates) and forces prices down in the competitive market, the supply of A goods from B regions will shrink, as the decline in prices which they face forces them back down along their marginal cost curves. At the limit, when A is a very small producer of A goods, a fall in wage rates in A may allow it to expand its output almost entirely by displacing production from other regions, without requiring any significant fall in prices.

Whereas the concepts of the price elasticity of demand facing individual producers of A goods (here assumed to be infinitely elastic) and in the market for A goods as a whole are straightforward, the concept of the price elasticity of demand for all A goods marketed by producers in region A (or region i for that matter) is more complicated. Their sales, as their offered price changes, do *not* depend just on an independently-determined *demand* curve, but also on the supply response of other producers to changes in price. Their sales, as their prices change, derive from the combined effect of the price elasticity of the aggregate market demand curve and the extent to which their sales displace sales from other regions, where the reductions in prices no longer make it worthwhile producing goods for this market. So the degree of competitiveness between producers in different regions will be a factor determining the price elasticity of demand for the products of any one region. If producers in region i can induce, by a small reduction in prices, producers in all other regions to cut back their market sales, then the price elasticity of demand for goods from region i will be high, even if the price elasticity of demand in the market as a whole is low.

If we consider instead markets where the individual producers are imperfectly competitive, the analysis of the effects of shifts in the demand for certain goods on inter-regional trade flows remains essentially much the same. Under imperfect competition, producers try to fix a price that will – given the expected reactions of their competitors – maximise profits. They maintain that price, in the face of random variations in demand, by allowing stocks of final goods to expand or to contract. If aggregate demand for their goods falls off (e.g., if the demand curve shifts downwards because of a change in tastes or a reduction in real incomes), initially their stocks pile up. A persistent increase in stocks of unsold goods forces them either to cut prices (in the hopes of selling more) or to cut output. If they cut prices, their revenue (per item sold) will fall relative to their costs, so the plants working with the lowest margins will make losses, and will presumably be closed. If they cut output, then the surplus of revenue over cost will be rising as they close their least profitable plants, inducing a greater willingness to shade prices in order to expand business. The path that the adjustment process actually follows will depend on the particular business milieu in which the entrepreneurs find themselves, but it should lead to the establishment of a new quasi-equilibrium in the overall market for these goods, involving some reduction in output and some reduction in price.

Again this will only be a quasi-equilibrium, because employment and incomes in the production of such goods will have declined, and this may induce a secondary effect on wage rates in these industries and in regions heavily dependent on such industries. If labour costs fall in region A relative to other regions, the substitution of production from other regions to region A may be even greater and more rapid (than in the case of perfect competition) as oligopolistic, multi-regional companies reorganise and concentrate production in the more profitable areas. Again this demonstrates the complexity of the concept of the price elasticity of demand for a region's goods. Even though the price elasticity of demand for the individual producer of, say, cars may be less than for, say, sweaters, and the aggregate price elasticity of demand in the market as a whole may be less for cars than for sweaters, nevertheless the response of output, and sales, of cars to shifts in relative costs (and of prices) between regions may be significantly greater than with sweaters. With cars, the major firms may reallocate production between alternative plants in different regions with considerable sensitivity to relative profitability, while each local sweater-maker may strive to his utmost to maintain his own individual sales, and be prepared to absorb reductions in profit margins in the process.[1]

The immediate effect, therefore, of a downwards shift in the demand for the output of a particular region, say region A, will be an initial decline in prices and output (and therefore in incomes) in that region. This, particularly the fall in output and the rise in unemployment, may induce a secondary response of reductions in wage rates and, perhaps, of certain other costs, relative to those in other regions. This would induce a recovery in output in A, and, with a relative fall in costs and a revived output of A goods, prices of A goods would tend to be lowered relative to other goods. If the price elasticity of demand for goods produced in region A, reflecting both the shift of demand to A goods from other goods as relative prices change in the overall market and also the displacement of production of A goods from other regions to A, was low then only few additional sales of A goods could be made without driving prices down to levels at which it was no longer profitable to expand output. Output in A will rise,[2]

---

[1] R. Masera, in correspondence with me, put forward a counter-argument. Oligopolistic multi-regional companies are most common in manufacturing industries subject to economies of scale. Such industries, for example the car industry, are usually fully *unionised*, and concern about *parity* of pay will be strong, quite irrespective of productivity/unemployment conditions. This feature will tend to reverse the conclusions in the main text. Suppose that production in A is heavily dependent on the car industry and is specialised, say, more particularly in big cars. Now the demand for such cars falls. Hence unemployment in A rises, but this need not be accompanied by a general fall in relative wage rates paid in the car industry in region A. In these conditions Masera argues that it is more likely that, in A, production of alternative products, say textiles, will be stepped up, because the excess supply of labour will tend to be absorbed at declining wage rates by those industries where 'parity' with other regions is not directly and immediately called for by trade unions.

[2] Ignoring the possibility that A goods are Giffen goods, the demand for which falls as their prices fall.

following the relative decline in A prices but real incomes may rise or fall depending whether Y_A (output of region A) rose faster than

$$\frac{P_A}{(1-b)P_A + bP_B}$$

(the ratio of the prices of goods produced in A to the cost of living in A)[1] was falling.

The conditions under which a shift in relative prices will improve the current-account balance have been extensively documented in the literature. The conditions most commonly cited[2] require that, on the assumption that the elasticity of supply of both A and B goods is infinite, and that initially $P_A X_A$ (exports) $= P_{B \cdot A} X_B$ (imports), the sum of the price elasticities of demand for imports (into A from B and into B from A, where B is the rest of the country (world) in which A is a region) shall be greater than unity.[3]

From the point of view of the inhabitants of region A, the concept of the price elasticity of B's demands for imports from A as P_A alters seems perfectly straightforward. On the other hand, the concept of the price elasticity of A's demands for imports from B as P_A shifts relative to P_B is more complicated because it incorporates not only the substitution effect, but also some more complex income effects. Via the substitution effect, the propensity to import into A will decline as P_A falls relative to P_B, to an extent depending on the elasticity of substitution. The rise in export volumes (X_A) in A will lead to an increase in incomes there (Y_A) which, *ceteris paribus*, will increase investment (I_A), and via the multiplier consumption (C_A), and thus will serve to buoy up the demand for imports. On the other hand, as P_A falls relative to P_B the real value of incomes derived from A output falls (owing to the worsening in the terms of trade, as

$$\frac{P_A}{(1-b)P_A + bP_B}$$

declines), and this may lead to a cut back in consumption. In short, the effects on the demand for imports (in region A) arising from a change in the relative prices of P_B and P_A are quite complex, and simply wrapping them all up in the single concept of the price elasticity of demand in A for imports from B may possibly serve to obscure the several different effects upon the level of imports. The problem is that price changes do have effects on incomes, etc., but definitions of price elasticities which incorporate income effects are not very satisfactory. One response has been to try notionally to separate the various effects over time. We might envisage an initial impact of price changes on expenditure flows, with real incomes in the various regions being treated as unchanged, followed by subsequent changes in incomes as the foreign-trade multiplier works through, on the basis of the new given set of prices. In practice, however, the adjustments of prices and quantities cannot be simply disentangled in this or any other fashion. Possibly the proper conclusion is that one can only analyse adjustment to a new equilibrium within the context of a general equilibrium model.

---

[1] P_g is the price index of goods imported into region A, and b is the average propensity to import. The notation is taken from the formal model set out in the Appendix. Region B stands for the rest of the country, in which A is a (small) region.

[2] These conditions were first formulated by Marshall (1930) and subsequently by Lerner (1944) Chapter 28. The conditions are, therefore, generally known as the Marshall–Lerner conditions.

[3] For a more general statement of the requisite conditions, and a more elaborate model of trade adjustment, see, *inter alios*, Tsiang, 'The Role of Money in Trade-Balance Stability: Synthesis of the Elasticity and Absorption Approaches' (1961) pp. 912–36, reproduced in Cooper (ed.) Chapter 6, pp. 135–64.

But we may, perhaps, identify four main channels of response arising from a decline in P_A relative to P_B. First, there is the substitution effect, switching expenditure in both A and B to A goods and from B goods. Second, there is the terms of trade effect reducing domestic expenditures in A (as real incomes fall) and raising them in B. Both these serve to increase the volume of A exports and to reduce the volume of B exports, but may not do so sufficiently to improve the current account if the elasticity of substitution in response to relative price changes is low. Thirdly, the increase in export volume in A (decrease in B) will raise investment and consumption expenditures in A (reducing them in B) via the normal accelerator–multiplier mechanism. Fourth, the rise in output in A (fall in B) will reduce the excess supply of labour in A (excess demand in B) and thus lead to a relatively faster increase in costs (and thus prices) in A (vice versa in B). These last two factors will act to brake an improvement in A's current account resulting from an initial decline in P_A relative P_B.

In practice these factors act as a sort of counterpoise. If the elasticity of substitution leads to a large improvement in the current-account balance, the braking forces come into operation more quickly. If the elasticity of substitution, in response to relative price changes, is low, then exports (and import substitutes) will not increase much in volume, so domestic expenditures and employment will remain weak, and there will be continuing downward pressure on wages and prices in the depressed region. This pressure, at some stage, will be further reinforced by financial pressures (discussed already in Section 1). So long as relative price movements do not suffice to restore current-account balance, there will be a continuing drain of financial assets from the area (an increasing indebtedness to other areas). This outflow of financial assets, to finance the current-account imbalance, leads to a reduction in (the rate of growth of) wealth in the area and to a growing indebtedness that ultimately will cause additional deflationary pressure. The lower the elasticity of substitution in response to shifts in relative prices, the greater the decline, at least temporarily, in employment in the disadvantaged region and the greater the long-term adjustments in incomes and wealth, if current-account balance is to be achieved.

Even where the elasticity of substitution of goods between regions is high it may, however, not happen that a decline in the demand for the products of region A and the emergence of regional unemployment would lead to a restorative shift in relative costs and thence in prices. No single group of workers will accede, without a determined struggle, to a collective bargaining agreement which is directly seen to cut their own real wages, particularly since its effect on local employment seems indirect and very likely to the benefit of others unknown.[1] There will, therefore, be resistance to any direct downward pressure on wages, despite any depression in the local economy. Furthermore, concern with parity may impel union leaders to aim for much the same kind of wage increases as have been obtained in other areas. Indeed, this concern with parity in nominal wages could even induce disequilibrating trends in

---

[1] Andrew Crockett once posed the question to me why then unions often encourage short-time working during slumps, in order to spread the reduction in real incomes more evenly among the labour force. In large part the reason for the acceptance of short-time working as contrasted with the refusal to accept wage cuts during slumps depends on differences in information and in the power relationships. If a union accepts a wage cut, it has no power to ensure that the final price is shaded commensurably; the profit margin might be raised instead. And even if final prices are reduced, the union may have little idea what improvement in sales may result from this step; whereas meeting a given reduction in output by short-time working involves little need for additional information and may give the union negotiators more control over the fate of their members than leaving management to declare redundancies. See also the analysis in Chapter 1.

unit labour costs, if productivity in the more prosperous regions was rising relative to that in less prosperous regions.

It is under these conditions, when falls in the demand for the products of an area have not brought about an equilibrating response in relative costs and prices, that countries adopt the expedient of devaluing (regions, of course, do not have this option). The effect of devaluation is to cause a reduction in real wage rates in the devaluing country relative to the price (and cost) levels ruling in other countries. It represents, therefore, an artificial way of introducing an equilibrating adjustment in relative wage costs.

But if the workers (e.g., through their unions) had refused to accept a reduction in (relative) real wages through collective bargaining, why should they accept it when imposed through administrative action? There are several reasons for this. Collective wage bargains affect individual groups of workers who have little information and no guarantee on the outcome of other wage bargains. Devaluation centralises and makes uniform the effect on all workers in the country concerned: but the success of this does depend on labour being prepared to accept some reduction, albeit perhaps temporary, in (the rate of growth of) real wages relative to that in other countries. Otherwise devaluations would only lead to an immediate catch-up in nominal wages and prices restoring the *status quo ante*,[1] except that the pace of inflation would have now accelerated.

Where regions are relatively small, so that the cost of living mainly depends on price fluctuations in imported goods, and social, cultural and political ties with contiguous regions are strong, so that individuals regularly compare their position against their opposite numbers in other regions, devaluation – even should institutional conditions, requiring the existence of separate monetary authorities, permit – would be much less likely to provide a successful and satisfactory adjustment procedure. It may, however, prove possible to overcome such obstacles to regional adjustment, even under these circumstances where variations in exchange rates are not possible (because it is a single-currency system) or impractical (because local wages and prices will rapidly adjust to restore the *status quo ante*), by taking appropriate fiscal action. Among the many fiscal innovations suggested by Kaldor was the idea of regionally varying taxes and subsidies on labour, i.e., the regional employment premium.[2] As has been frequently pointed out, the effect of devaluation on prices of goods being traded is equivalent to the imposition of a set of taxes and subsidies. The regional employment premia and taxes can therefore be adjusted to have the effect of a change in relative parities. It does this, however, without having an immediately disturbing impact effect on the observed relativities of real wage rates between workers in the same industry in different areas.[3] In this respect it could be an *even more* effective adjustment mechanism than allowing each region to maintain a separate currency and vary its exchange rate against its neighbours. Furthermore, the payment of taxes in more active and prosperous regions and subsidies to the less

---

[1] Monetarists argue that this could occur only if the authorities were prepared to validate these higher wage levels by increasing the domestic money supply. If not, the claims for higher nominal wages to restore previous real wage rates would lead initially to unemployment and, thereafter at some point, to a moderation in wage demands.

[2] See, for example, Kaldor, 'The Case for Regional Policies' (1970) pp. 337–48, especially pp. 346–7. Kaldor, however, noted that since the cost of the premia are borne not by the region but by the tax-paying community as a whole, 'it would be politically very difficult to introduce it on a scale that could make it really effective.'

[3] G. E. Wood pointed out to me, in correspondence, that, whereas there need be no impact effect on relative wages, the demand for labour in the various regions would, as indeed intended, alter and this would lead over time to some readjustments in observed relativities.

prosperous regions should, in general, act to improve the distribution of incomes and wealth over the whole community. Indeed, the chances of success in achieving larger politico-economic groupings among states (as in the EEC) may well depend vitally and urgently upon the further extension of such fiscal techniques.[1]

So far we have been considering cases where, owing for example to a fall off in the demand for products of region A, the region has been suffering simultaneously an adverse current-account balance and a depression of domestic incomes and output. To be sure, current-account imbalance can be caused not only by such external shocks but also by domestic developments. A faster rate of domestic expansion, fuelled say by fiscal or monetary stimuli, will worsen the current-account balance in three ways: the higher level of domestic expenditure and output will pull in more imports; the greater pressure on domestic capacity will raise domestic costs and prices relative to those in other regions; the greater pressure on capacity may lead to some rationing (delivery delays) of sales to customers in other regions and at home, who may turn instead to importers. In such cases the effect of devaluation, in switching demand to local producers, will be ineffective in improving the current account, without accompanying steps to reduce total domestic expenditures. Devaluation by itself would place even more pressure on capacity, redoubling inflationary pressure and supply constraints; it could, at best, only improve the current account temporarily at the expense of worsening the diverging trends in regional inflation.

Indeed, *supply* conditions, both in the devaluing country and also in the rest of the world, play a most important role in determining whether devaluation is to be successful in restoring current-account balance. Of course, the overall price elasticity of demand in the markets for the goods traded is an important factor, but if the goods from a devaluing country can reasonably easily displace goods from other countries in these markets, then the price elasticity of demand for that one country's goods should be high irrespective of the aggregate price elasticity of demand. On these grounds, theorists have argued that the price elasticity of demand for the exports of any one country *must* be pretty large (at least greater than unity), unless that country is virtually the sole producer of a good with a price inelastic demand.[2]

On the other hand, the supply response to devaluation, the response of businessmen to the changing opportunities occasioned by devaluation, may be quite slow. Devaluation may make exports to some additional markets notionally more profitable and imports less profitable (to the foreign exporter), but many goods are only traded through established commercial channels. It takes time, effort and confidence in the future to set up such channels, and once established they will not be easily abandoned in the face of a temporary decline in profitability. Such set-up costs reduce supply elasticities, even when there is spare capacity in the devaluing country. So the supply response may for a number of reasons be quite slow.

In my view it is this that helps to explain the experience of apparently sluggish response – upon the current-account balance – to devaluations and revaluations (e.g., the UK devaluation of 1967 and the slow response of the US trade balance to the fall in the value of the dollar after 1985). Given the strong *a priori* arguments that the price elasticities of demand for exports should be high, I believe that this experience reflected slow supply responses rather than low price elasticities.[3]

---

[1] Instead, a significant proportion of fiscal transfers recovered by EEC arrangements, notably resulting from the Common Agricultural Policy (CAP), have had a perverse effect on the intra-EEC distribution of income and wealth.

[2] See, for example, Harberger (1957) reprinted in Cooper (ed.) (1969) pp. 165–90.

[3] Though see Houthakker and Magee, 'Income and Price Elasticities in World Trade' (1969) p. 111–25. They found that 'The price variables do not perform nearly so well [as the income

Appendix: A Framework for the Analysis of Inter-regional Adjustment

The approach adopted here is to concentrate upon the adjustment process in one particular region, region A, treating the rest of the country as region B. The purpose of this appendix is to set out a model of the structure of region A as a guide to examining the inter-regional adjustment process. Presumably both regions could be producing a wide assortment of goods, both consumption and capital goods, which could be traded with the other region, and offering a wide variety of services which could be used by inhabitants of both regions. For simplicity, however, it will be assumed that it is possible to aggregate the goods produced in each region into a composite A and B good respectively, each with its accompanying price level. Although the goods (services) are thus distinguished by the region producing them into A or B goods, this does not exclude the possibility that the bulk of the goods being produced and traded either may be, or could be with relative ease, produced in both regions. With a single currency and (assumed) low transport costs the price of both A goods, P_A, and B goods, P_B, are determined nationally rather than regionally. As a simplifying device it will be assumed that the import content (in both A and B) of all goods whatever their end use, whether for inter-regional export, investment or consumption is the same, and furthermore that the expenditure propensities with respect to all forms of income, whether in the form of returns to capital or to labour, are also the same. This allows the demand for imports, and for consumption, etc., to be expressed as a simple function of income levels without worrying about the distribution of incomes between differing kinds of expenditures or of factor incomes.

In the model five separate assets are identified. Individuals (persons and companies) hold real capital (K), non-monetary financial assets (F), and monetary deposits (M),[1] and borrow from intermediaries on loans (L). Financial intermediaries issue as liabilities both non-monetary financial claims (F) and monetary deposits (M) and hold as per contra assets loans to individuals (L), non-monetary financial claims on other intermediaries, and cash reserves (H, high-powered money). The non-monetary financial claims are assumed, for simplicity, to have a fixed nominal value. Monetary deposits have – again by assumption – a zero nominal yield. For the purposes of this exercise it is assumed that all real capital in any region is entirely owned by the inhabitants of that region, who also maintain all their monetary deposits with local intermediaries (banks); a possible justification for this latter assumption would be on grounds of convenience. Again on

---

variables], with many insignificant estimates and a few incorrect signs ... Even where the estimated price elasticities are significant and negative their standard errors were usually too large to permit a definite stand in the "elasticity pessimism" controversy' (pp. 113–14). However, their study took no account of possible lags in response from the supply side.

---

[1] In this model people do not hold cash; all their money balances are held in the form of demand deposits with financial intermediaries. This assumption helps to simplify the analysis without omitting any vital element of the system.

grounds of convenience, inhabitants of a region will presumably go first to their local financial intermediary to discuss the terms of loan financing, but will shift to more distant external intermediaries if there is a difference in terms offered. Non-monetary financial assets, F, issued in one region are, however, regarded as effectively identical with those issued in another, e.g., a security issued in London is considered to be essentially the same as one issued in Manchester by anyone living in the United Kingdom. Inhabitants (and intermediaries) of both regions (A and B) hold non-monetary financial claims on both A and B intermediaries and buy and sell these in the open market to adjust their asset positions.[1] In the notation used here $_AF_B$ represents a claim issued in B and held in A. Since these assets are regarded as identical, irrespective of issuing region, there will be one nationally-determined interest rate at which these assets are traded. If A is very small relative to the rest of the country, the rate of interest on both financial claims, r_F, and on loans, r_L, will be determined independently of the demand for such instruments by A inhabitants or the supply of them by A intermediaries. Finally, the net balance of the current and capital account of inter-regional transactions results in a positive (surplus) or negative (deficit) balance in monetary clearings between the intermediaries of each region, and these clearing balances are met by transfers of cash reserves (H) by the intermediaries from the deficit to the surplus region.

Having given a brief description of the system, the next stage is to set down the formal structure of the model, starting with certain accounting identities.

(i) Output equals expenditure

$$P_A \cdot Y_A = P_A \cdot X_A - P_B \cdot {}_AX_B + [(1-b)P_A + bP_b](I_A + C_A) - r_F({}_BF_A - {}_AF_B)$$

P_A represents the price of A goods, b is the average propensity to import into A so that $(1-b)P_A + bP_B$ represents a general price index of goods bought in A. Y_A is the production of A goods in A, X_A the export of A goods, excluding interest payments, $_AX_B$ the import of B goods and services in A, I_A investment in additional capital in A,[2] C_A consumption in A, r_F is the national interest rate on non-monetary financial assets, $_BF_A$ are such assets issued by A intermediaries held by B residents, while $_AF_B$ are assets issued in B and held in A,[3] so the final term shows the size and direction of net interest flow between the regions.

(ii) Output equals income

$$P_A \cdot Y_A = \pi_A - [(1-b)P_A + bP_B]K_A + w \cdot Z_A$$

π_A is the rate of return paid to capital in A and K_A the real capital stock in A. The wage rate paid is w; for the moment it will be assumed that the wage rate paid in region A is

---

[1] In this model there is, therefore, portfolio investment – but no direct investment – in the capital account of the inter-regional balance of payments. This treatment differs somewhat from that of Floyd, 'Monetary and Fiscal Policy in a World of Capital Mobility' (1969), who emphasises the role of direct investment in the Canadian capital account. The reason for giving more prominence to portfolio investment here is in order to highlight the role of transactions in financial instruments and the role of financial intermediaries in the adjustment process. In reality direct investment flows can also be very important, but to include them also would further complicate the model.

[2] Capital is assumed not to depreciate. Existing capital and new capital equipment are perfect substitutes and sell at the same price.

[3] There may also be a flow of interest payments on loans made by intermediaries in one region to inhabitants of the other. This term could be easily added also, but would just make the accounting identities even more unwieldy.

determined nationally, say by collective bargaining fixing a single national rate. If region A is small, the state of the labour market in A will have a relatively small impact on the wage rate determined nationally. Z_A gives the total number of workers employed at wage rate w in A. The demand for workers at this wage rate is always satisfied, either by variations in local unemployment or by inter-regional migration.

(iii) Private-sector wealth is composed of existing assets

$$W_A = M_A + {}_AF_A + {}_AF_B + [(1-b)P_A + bP_B]K_A - L_A$$

W_A is the level of wealth of private-sector residents in A in (nominal terms), M_A is the money stock (bank deposits) held by A residents, ${}_AF_A$ and ${}_AF_B$ are the non-monetary financial claims held by A residents, K_A the real capital stock in A, and L_A are the loans obtained by A residents from their local intermediaries.[2]

(iv) The assets of intermediaries balance their liabilities

$$L_A + {}_{IA}F_B + H_A = M_A + {}_AF_A + {}_BF_A$$

H_A are the intermediaries' cash reserves; ${}_{IA}F_B$ represent the holdings by A intermediaries of non-monetary claims on B intermediaries; ${}_BF_A$ represent non-monetary liabilities issued by A intermediaries to B residents (including intermediaries in B).

The ex-post conditions determining the flow of money into, or out of, region A can now easily be worked out from equations (i) and (iii). Taking the assumption that P_A and P_B are constant, in order to avoid dealing with changes in the current value of existing capital goods, equation (iii) can be written in first-difference form, as

ΔM_A	$= \Delta W_A$	$- \Delta_A F_A - \Delta_A F_B$	$- \Delta K_A$	$+ \Delta L_A$
(increase in money stock)	(increase in wealth)	(*less* purchase of non-monetary financial assets)	(*less* investment in real assets)	(*plus* increase in intermediary loans)

but

	ΔW_A	$= P_A \cdot Y_A$	$- [(1-b)P_A + bP_B]C_A$
	(increase in wealth)	(income)	(*less* consumption)

(i.e., the change in wealth is equal to the value of new savings when there is no change in price levels to produce capital gains.) From equation (i) we have

$$P_A Y_A - [(1-b)P_A + bP_B]C_A = [(1-b)P_A + bP_B]I_A$$

(new saving)   (new investment)

$$+ P_A X_A - P_B \cdot {}_A X_B + r_F({}_A F_B - {}_B F_A)$$

(current-account surplus)

---

[1] In order to limit the number of terms in the accounting identities, it is assumed here that all loans to inhabitants of a region are made by intermediaries situated in that region. There would be no difficulty in relaxing that assumption to take account of borrowing from intermediaries in other regions.

Then collecting terms, and noting that if $P_{A_t} = P_{A_{t-1}}$ and $P_{B_t} = P_{B_{t-1}}$ then $I_A = \Delta K_A$. we have

(v) Factors associated with regional monetary expansion

$$\Delta M_A = P_A X_A - P_B \cdot {}_A X_B + r_F({}_A F_B - {}_B F_A)$$

(increase in money stock)

(current-account surplus)

$$- \Delta_A F_A - \Delta_A F_B \qquad + \Delta L_A$$

(*less* purchase of non- monetary financial assets)

(*plus* increase in loans)

In short, the inhabitants of A can obtain more money either by running a current-account surplus with their neighbours, or by (net) sales of their holdings of non-monetary financial assets, or by borrowing from their local financial intermediaries.

From equations (iv) and (v), it is next easy to set out the conditions determining the flow of the intermediaries' cash reserves (ΔH_A) into, or out of, the region. Putting equation (iv) in first difference form, we have

$$\Delta H_A = \Delta M_A + \Delta_A F_A + \Delta_B F_A - \Delta L_A - \Delta_{IA} F_B$$

(increase in reserves)

(increase in deposits)

(increase in non-monetary liabilities of A intermediaries taken up by A, B residents)

(*less* increase in loans)

(*less* increase in A intermediaries' claims on B intermediaries)

Then collecting terms and substituting into (v), equation (vi) is obtained:

(vi) Factors associated with inter-regional cash reserve transfers

$$\Delta H_A = [P_A X_A - P_B \cdot {}_A X_B + r_F({}_A F_B - {}_B F_A)]$$

(increase in reserves)

(current-account surplus)

$$- \Delta_A F_B - \Delta_{IA} F_B + \Delta_B F_A$$

(*less* A purchases of B's assets)

(*plus* B's purchases of A assets)

(capital account)

So by manipulation of the basic accounting identities one can show that the flow of reserves into, out of, any region has to be exactly that necessary to clear the balance on the current and capital account with neighbouring regions.

All this, however, remains purely definitional. Given the assumptions of the model, these equations are accounting identities that must hold at all times, both in and out of equilibrium. In order to examine the process of adjustment, it is necessary to supplement the accounting identities with sets of relationships, showing the desired relationships between income and expenditure flows, and between wealth and asset holdings, all as functions of relative prices and the relevant budget constraints.

The analysis is complicated by the need to show the connections between the achievement of flow equilibrium and stock equilibrium. Income and expenditure flows, whether or not they are equilibrium flows, may cause changes in quantities and/or prices that disturb the asset equilibrium and, similarly asset adjustments may disturb expenditure flows. The main, and most obvious, linkage between flow and stock relationships, at least in this model, comes in the treatment of real capital. Investment, a change in the stock of real capital, enters the income account as an expenditure *flow*, yet the production function relates the demand for a *stock* of capital to the flow of output (income), and as an element of wealth the demand for capital must be a function of the net wealth of the community, together with the prospective yields and risks on alternative assets.

Following our previous procedure we shall once again set down the behavioural relationships in matrix form, making the normal simplifying assumption of linearity, starting with the adjustment matrix for the inhabitants of region A (other than intermediaries).

	Y_A	W_A	Y_B	P_A	P_B	r_F	r_L	w
$P_B \cdot {}_A X_B$	a_{11}	/	/	a_{14}	a_{15}	/	/	/
$[(1-b)P_A + bP_B]C_A$	a_{21}	a_{22}	/	a_{24}	a_{25}	a_{26}	a_{27}	/
$P_A X_A$	/	/	a_{33}	a_{34}	a_{35}	/	/	/
$[(1-b)P_A + bP_B]K_A$	a_{41}	a_{42}	/	a_{44}	a_{45}	a_{46}	a_{47}	a_{48}
${}_A F_A$	a_{51}	a_{52}	/	a_{54}	a_{55}	a_{56}	a_{57}	a_{58}
${}_A F_B$	a_{61}	a_{62}	/	a_{64}	a_{65}	a_{66}	a_{67}	a_{68}
L_A	a_{71}	a_{72}	/	a_{74}	a_{75}	a_{76}	a_{77}	a_{78}
M_A	a_{81}	a_{82}	/	a_{84}	a_{85}	a_{86}	a_{87}	a_{88}

The sub-matrix below the broken line represents simply another version of our standard asset-portfolio adjustment model, in which the demand for the ith asset is expressed in terms of wealth, the budget constraint, relative prices, and other independent variables (which the inhabitants regard as parameters to which they respond) such as incomes. As before, the sum of column 2 from row 4–8 must add to unity, and – to preserve the balance-sheet identity – the coefficients of rows 4–8 in all other columns must add to zero.

The sub-matrix above the broken line describes the demand for A's exports, imports and consumption flows as a function of incomes, wealth (affecting consumption), incomes in region B (affecting the demand for A's exports), relative prices, and interest rates (affecting consumption). The wage level does *not* affect expenditure flows, since it was assumed that the distribution of income (given the level of income) between returns to capital and to labour had no effect on expenditure propensities.

Considering this matrix in more detail the /s represent coefficients whose value is expected to be zero. Going through the matrix column by column, first taking column 1, a_{11} and a_{21} set out the standard expenditure propensities (marginal assumed to equal average) as a function of incomes. The coefficients a_{41}–a_{81} in column 1 are more interesting, since they show how the inhabitants would want to readjust their assets if income was, say, higher but total wealth was unchanged. Clearly if people hold more of one asset (e.g., real capital) their holdings of some other assets (e.g., financial claims) would, with a given total of wealth, have to be less. The need to produce additional goods and to finance a higher level of transactions suggests that a_{41}, $a_{81} > 0$ and that a_{51}, a_{61}, $a_{71} < 0$ (i.e., that the inhabitants of A will borrow more from banks and run down their other financial claims to finance larger holdings of real capital and of money).

In column 2, a_{22} represents the wealth effect on consumption, $a_{22} > 0$. The coefficients a_{42}–a_{82} sum to unity. All these coefficients will be > 0, except for a_{72} which will possibly be less than zero, as people might increase their financial indebtedness – in order to achieve their preferred time path of consumption – *pari passu* with growing wealth. An increase in income levels in B will raise A's exports, but should have no other effect on A's expenditure propensities or preferred asset balance. An increase in the price of A goods, other prices and wages being constant (by assumption),[1] will cause inhabitants in both A and B to substitute B goods in place of A goods, the extent of the shift depending on the elasticity of substitution between them. In addition the change in P_A will change real incomes in both A and B. If P_A rises, then

$$\frac{P_A}{(1-b)P_A + bP_B}$$

rises, so long as $1 > b > 0$ (i.e., incomes obtained from the production of A goods can now buy more of the desired consumption basket of A and B goods). Similarly, real incomes in B decline. The change in real incomes (for a given Y_A, Y_B) will have an effect on the demand for imports, consumption and exports.

The increase in P_A will have two main effects[2] on the desired asset balance in A. First, by raising the general price level it will raise the general level of money incomes and expenditures, and thus the demand for transactions balances. Second, the increase in P_A will raise the price of capital equipment in A (thus providing capital gains to existing owners of capital) and, with the level of wages (w) held constant, will shift the price of capital relative to the price of labour. With labour becoming relatively cheaper, there would be some substitution of labour for capital. The rate of return on capital in A may either rise or fall, depending on the elasticity of substitution between labour and capital in the production function. The short-run elasticity of substitution is probably quite low, and the return to capital should rise. If the rate of return on capital rises, following a rise in P_A, then the demand for capital (at a given level of wealth) would be greater.[3]

The effect of a change in P_A, *ceteris paribus*, on the demand for money balances will, therefore, be positive, $a_{84} > 0$, but the sign of the effect on the demand for other assets in the portfolio is uncertain without further information about the form of the production function in A (though our expectation would be that $a_{44} > 0$ and a_{54}, a_{64}, $a_{74} < 0$). A rise in P_B will similarly have substitution and income effects on the flow demand for exports, imports and consumption, with substitution effects leading inhabitants in A and B to

---

[1] Since other prices, and wages, are assumed to be constant, the increase in P_A must reflect either increased demand for A goods or attempts by their producers to obtain a larger profit margin.

[2] Abstracting from the possible effect of a change in price levels in influencing expectations of future changes in price levels.

[3] If the shift in reltive factor prices should cause a divergence between rates of return on capital in A and B, then one would also expect to see inter-regional capital flows for direct investment in real assets, but for simplicity this model excludes such capital flows. An increase in rates of return in A (relative to B) should raise investment and thus incomes and imports in A and so worsen A's current account in the short run. This may be to some extent offset, even within the context of the present model, by the rise in returns on real capital in A causing portfolio-investment flows into A, as A inhabitants and intermediaries sell financial assets to B residents in order to take up more real capital. None the less, the capital account offset to the worsening current account in such circumstances is likely to be considerably less in the absence of direct inter-regional investment flows. In the longer run, however, the investment in A should help to make As products more competitive and thereby generate a sufficient export surplus to redeem the previously incurred.

purchase A goods instead of B goods when P_B rises, and income effects resulting in a fall in real incomes (and expenditures) among A inhabitants as the price of B goods rises. The substitution effect of an increase in P_A relative to P_B must be the same whether the differential occurs as a result of a change in P_A or P_B; but the income effect will vary depending on the weight of A and B goods in the overall consumption basket. Therefore the sub-matrix

$$\begin{bmatrix} a_{14} & a_{15} \\ a_{34} & a_{35} \end{bmatrix}$$

will not in general be symmetrical. Nevertheless, the effect of a rise in P_B on these expenditure flows (exports, imports, consumption) will be of the opposite sign to that of a rise in P_A. The effect of a rise of P_B on asset demands (with Y_A and W_A given) is, however, more like a similar, but slighter,[1] reflection of a change in P_A. A rise in P_B raises the average price level of transactions, and with w constant raises the price of capital relative to that of labour. In this case, however, the rate of profit on the production of A goods must fall, since revenue $(P_A \cdot Y_A)$ remains, by assumption, unchanged, while the price of a capital import has risen; so $a_{45} < 0$, $a_{85} > 0$ and the sign of the other asset coefficients is ambiguous.

An increase in the rate on non-monetary financial assets, r_F, or loans, r_L, raises the yield on that asset relative to the yield on all other assets. On the usual assumption that all assets are substitutes in a sector's portfolio, a rise in the yield on the ith asset will have a positive effect on the demand for that asset and a negative effect on the demand for other assets. Thus a_{56}, $a_{66} > 0$, and a_{46}, a_{76}, $a_{86} < 0$; similarly $a_{77} > 0$ and a_{47}, a_{57}, a_{67}, $a_{87} < 0$ (i.e., in this latter case where loans are a liability – a negative asset – a rise in bank loan rate will make people want to diminish their liability on bank loans, $a_{77} > 0$, and they will obtain the finance to do so by running down their holdings of real capital, non-monetary financial assets and money, a_{47}, a_{57}, a_{67}, $a_{87} < 0$). As noted previously in Chapters 10 and 12, a change in interest rates may make people revise their consumption plans. A rise in interest rates will cause a substitution effect in favour of future consumption (current saving), which will generally be supported by a wealth effect (as market values of existing assets fall), but may be offset by an income effect as the rise in rates allows current incomes to have a greater command over the desired consumption basket of current and future goods. Theoretically, therefore, the sign of the coefficients a_{26}, a_{27} is ambiguous, but it would probably command general assent to treat them as mildly negative.

With Y_A, W_A, P_A and P_B given, and on the assumption that the distribution of incomes between labour and capital has no effect on expenditure propensities, a change in wage rates would have no effect on $_AX_B$, C_A or X_A. Nor with Y_A, P_A and P_B given, would money incomes change in response to the shift in wage rates, so the demand for money balances would be unaltered. The main effect – under these circumstances – of a fall in w would be to alter the price of capital relative to the price of labour but, as noted already, the effect of this on the demand for real capital (with a consequential effect on other assets, to retain the wealth constraint) is not certain, though we would expect in practice to see at least an initial increase in demand for capital. In reality, of course, a change in wage rates would probably bring forth an accompanying change in the prices of goods, including capital equipment, i.e., the assumption of P_A constant in the face of a change in w is implausible. How far a change in wage rates would be reflected in a general shift in all prices, leaving relative factor prices as before, and how far a change in wage rates would lead to a shift in relative factor prices is a matter outside the scope of this appendix.

Having discussed the likely response of the inhabitants in A to shifts in the economic parameters facing them, we may set out the signs of these responses in the coefficients of the previous matrix: a double sign (+ + or − −) suggests a relatively large response, a (?) implies a weak and/or uncertain response.

---

[1] Assuming $0 < b < 0.5$.

	Y_A	W_A	Y_B	P_A	P_B	r_F	r_L	w
$P_B \cdot {}_A X_B$	+	/	/	+	−	/	/	/
$[(1-b)P_A + bP_B]C_A$	+	+	/	+	−	−?	−?	/
$P_A X_A$	/	/	+	−	+	/	/	/
$[(1-b)P_A + bP_B]K_A$	+	+	/	+?	−	−	−	?
${}_A F_A$	−	+	/	−?	?	++	−	?
${}_A F_B$	−	+	/	−?	?	++	−	?
L_A	−	−	/	−?	?	−	++	?
M_A	+	+	/	++	+	−	−	?

The range of choice open to intermediaries is relatively circumscribed in comparison with the much wider range available to individuals. On our assumptions, the interest rate offered on monetary deposits is fixed at zero, and the rates to be offered on non-monetary financial instruments (F) and loans (L) are determined nationally, and are treated by the intermediaries in each region as parameters. The intermediaries may have some leeway to deter, or to encourage, loan business at the going rate by varying non-rate terms (e.g., the requirements for collateral) but basically they have to accept all deposits, both monetary and non-monetary, and undertake all reasonable, credit-worthy loan business at the going rates. The only margin of freedom which this leaves them, with the volume of their liabilities and of their loans and advances exogenously determined, is the ability to adjust their liquid assets (in this case cash reserves, H, and claims on financial intermediaries in other regions) in such a way as best to distribute the balance of the portfolio between liquidity and earning assets.[1] The available choice set open to intermediaries in A can then be described in terms of the following simple matrix

	r_F	$M_A + F_A - L_A$
H_A	b_{11}	b_{12}
${}_{IA}F_B$	b_{21}	b_{22}

Here $M_A + F_A - L_A$ represents total available liquid assets, that is the budget constraint, which is exogenously determined; b_{12} and b_{22} are both > 0 and must together add to unity. The rate of interest on financial intermediary claims, r_F, determines the relative yield obtained on the two alternative liquid assets, since the rate of interest on reserves is assumed equal to zero, so $b_{21} = -b_{11}$.

Possibly the condition that the levels of interest rates, particularly on rates for non-monetary deposits, is nationally determined may be excessively restrictive, especially in a large country. If intermediaries in one region are short of liquidity they may be in a

---

[1] On this, see White, 'Some Econometric Models of Deposit Bank Portfolio Behaviour in the UK, 1963–70' in Renton (ed.) (1975).

position to respond by raising the rates which they bid for funds above the level bid in other areas, thus opening up an inter-regional differential. In a single country, where the liabilities of intermediaries in different regions are treated as effectively identical, the establishment of a small differential should cause a large shift in desired holdings of that asset by inhabitants of all regions towards those liabilities issued by the region now offering the higher return. In this case it becomes necessary to distinguish between r_{FA} and r_{FB}. The choice matrix for the intermediary then becomes

$$
\begin{array}{c|ccc}
 & r_L & r_{FB} & M_A + F_A - L \\
\hline
H_A & b_{11} & b_{12} & b_{13} \\
{}_{1A}F_B & b_{21} & b_{22} & b_{23} \\
r_{FA} & b_{31} & b_{32} & b_{33}
\end{array}
$$

and the probable nature (sign) of the responses are as shown below

$$
\begin{array}{c|ccc}
 & r_L & r_{FB} & M_A + F_A - L \\
\hline
H_A & + & - & + \\
{}_{1A}F_B & - & + & + \\
r_{FA} & + & + & -
\end{array}
$$

If the loan rate rises, with a given volume of liquid assets, the intermediary will probably respond by raising rates offered on liabilities in order to obtain additional funds to make the higher earning loans. With higher earnings on the loan portfolio, the intermediary is likely to seek additional liquidity, at the expense of earnings, in the liquid-assets portfolio, so $b_{11} > 0$ and $b_{21} < 0$.

Furthermore, if r_{FA} can differ from r_{FB}, this will introduce an additional price in response to which private-sector individuals will have to adjust their asset holdings. Generally a rise in r_{Fi}, relative to r_{Fj} ($i \neq j$) will cause a large increase in the demand for non-monetary claims on i intermediaries, financed largely by running down similar claims on j intermediaries, but also partly by running down other assets.

At this stage it would be possible to give some numerical examples of the adjustment of the system in response to disturbances. However, I shall restrict myself to illustrating the simple case set out at the start of Section 2, in which all prices and interest rates are taken as constant: for it seems hardly worthwhile to put much weight on such limited models, especially when one does not give empirical content to the coefficients, and where the dynamic process in conditions of limited information is difficult to discern and to specify. In the case of this model, apart from these drawbacks, the model as set out does not allow one to study the interaction between regions A and B, since the economic position of region B is taken as given, and even certain important elements in region A (viz., a separate company sector, or a regional fiscal authority able to vary local taxes and expenditures) are lacking. Rather, the model in this appendix should be regarded basically as a prolegomenon to the analysis in the text, showing in a more formal and compressed way how the main elements in the system fit in together.

Anyhow, in the case posited at the start of Section 2 all prices, interest rates, etc., are taken as constant, and the effects of financial asset readjustments on inter-regional interest payments – and thus on the regional current-account balance – are ignored, that is to say P_A, P_B, b, w, r_F, r_L are all taken as constant and $r_F(_BF_A - _AF_B)$ is assumed to equal zero throughout. So from equation (i)

$$Y_A = X_A + I_A + C_A - _AX_B$$

Then substituting from the private sector's adjustment matrix

$$Y_{At} = a_1 + a_{33}Y_{Bt} + a_{41}(Y_{At} - Y_{At-1}) + a_{42}(W_{At} - W_{At-1})$$
$$+ a_{21}Y_{At} + a_{22}W_{At} - a_{11}Y_{At}$$

Collecting terms,

$$(1 - a_{41} - a_{21} + a_{11})Y_{At} = a_1 + a_{33}Y_{Bt} - a_{41}Y_{At-1} + (a_{42} + a_{22})W_{At} - a_{42}W_{At-1} \qquad \text{(vii)}$$

Similarly, from the previous accounting identities (with prices constant)

$$W_{At} - W_{At-1} = X_A - _AX_B + I_A$$

Substituting from the adjustment matrix gives

$$W_{At} = a_2 + a_{33}Y_{Bt} - a_{11}Y_{At} + a_{41}(Y_{At} - Y_{At-1}) + a_{42}(W_{At} - W_{At-1}) - W_{At-1}$$

Collecting terms again,

$$(1 - a_{42})W_{At} = a_2 + a_{33}Y_{Bt} + (a_{41} - a_{11})Y_{At} - a_{41}Y_{At-1} + (1 - a_{42})W_{At-1} \qquad \text{(viii)}$$

In a stationary equilibrium $W_{At} = W_{At-1}$ and $Y_{At} = Y_{At-1}$: assuming that $a_1 = a_2 = 0$, then from equation (viii) above it follows that in such an equilibrium it is necessary that $a_{33}Y_{Bt} = a_{11}Y_{At}$ (i.e., that exports equal imports; otherwise, even when $Y_{At} = Y_{At-1}$ there would be changes in wealth). Then from equation (vii) it follows that, with $a_{33}Y_{Bt} = a_{11}Y_{At}$, and wealth constant, it is necessary for $Y_{At} = a_{21}Y_{At} + a_{22}W_{At}$ (i.e., that domestic income is exactly matched by domestic consumption, in order to maintain incomes at a constant level).

Given the values of the coefficients in the adjustment matrix and the value of Y_B, it is then possible to calculate the equilibrium stationary values for the variables in region A and the time paths of these variables. Let us take a numerical example, with $a_1 = a_2 = 0$, and the coefficients in the remaining, reduced-size adjustment matrix having the following values

	Y_A	W_A	Y_B
$_AX_B$	0.2	/	/
C_A	0.60	0.05	/
X_A	/	/	0.1
K_A	0.2	0.35	/

and let the initial value of Y_B be 4000. Then the stationary equilibrium requires that $a_{33}Y_{Bt} = 0.1 \times 4000 = a_{11}Y_{At} = 0.2 \times Y_{At}$; so $Y_{At} = Y_{At-1} = 2000$, and $X_A = _AX_B = 400$. Similarly, domestic income must be exhausted by domestic consumption in stationary equilibrium, so $Y_{At} = 0.6 \times Y_{At} + 0.05 \times W_{At}$; with $Y_{At} = 2000$, $W_t = W_{t-1} = 16,000$, and $C_t = 2000$. The constant capital stock (there being no depreciation) equals 6000.

If Y_B should increase from 4000 to 4200, then in order to restore a stationary equilibrium Y_A should rise to 2100 and W_A to 16,800. However, in this postulated system the variables will not adjust monotonically from one equilibrium state to another. Equations (vii) and (viii) represent a couple of simultaneous difference equations,[1] which in this case have the following numerical coefficients

$$0.4 Y_{At} = 420 - 0.2 Y_{At-1} + 0.40 W_{At} - 0.35 W_{At-1}$$
$$0.65 W_{At} = 420 - 0.2 Y_{At-1} + 0.65 W_{At-1}$$

Starting from the previous equilibrium position with $W_{At-1} = 16,000$ and $Y_{At-1} = 2000$ the time paths of the variables, following a rise in Y_B in period 1, are as shown in Table 16.1.

TABLE 16.1

	W	Y	$_A X_B$	C	I	X
$t = 0$	16,000	2000	400	2000	0.0	400
1	16,031	2081	416	2050	26.92	420
2	16,037	2019	404	2013	−10.21	420
3	16,061	2070	414	2045	18.75	420
4	16,071	2032	406	2023	−4.25	420
5	16,092	2064	413	2043	13.60	420
6	16,103	2041	408	2030	−0.65	420
7	16,121	2061	412	2042	10.34	420
8	16,133	2047	409	2035	1.48	420
9	16,150	2060	412	2043	8.24	420
10	16,162	2051	410	2039	2.73	420
11	16,177	2060	412	2045	6.86	420
12	16,189	2055	411	2042	3.42	420
13	16,203	2060	412	2046	5.94	420
14	16,216	2058	412	2045	3.77	420
15	16,229	2061	412	2048	5.29	420
16	16,241	2060	412	2048	3.92	420
17	16,253	2062	412	2050	4.82	420
18	16,264	2062	412	2050	3.95	420
19	16,276	2064	413	2052	4.46	420
20	16,287	2064	413	2053	3.89	420

In the first round when Y_B increases, the increase in exports causes an increase in Y_A and thus, through the accelerator mechanism, an increase in investment. In the next round, however, with Y_B constant, there is no further stimulus to incomes from rising exports.

---

[1] The system has the general form

$$Y_{At} = a_1 u_t + a_2 Y_{At-1} + a_3 W_{At} + a_4 W_{At-1}$$
$$W_{At} = b_1 v_t + b_2 W_{At-1} + b_3 Y_{At} + b_4 Y_{At-1}$$

where u and v are (vectors of) exogenous variables.
In this case the conditions for stability are

$$-1 < \frac{a_4 b_4 - a_2 b_2}{1 - a_3 b_3} < 1$$

and

$$-1 < \frac{a_2 + b_2 + a_3 b_4 + a_4 b_3}{1 + a_2 b_2 - a_3 b_3 - a_4 b_4} < 1$$

I am grateful to J. P. Burman and D. Williams for help with the mathematics of this system.

Without a continuing stimulus, however, investment and incomes must fall back from previous levels; wealth, however, continues to rise, since the cut back in investment is offset by the improved current-account balance. Given these values for the coefficients, Y_4 oscillates in an increasingly damped manner from one period to the next under the influence of the investment accelerator; wealth, however, converges steadily and monotonically to the new equilibrium position, since the fluctuations in investment and in the trade balance offset each other.

XVII
International Monetary Relations – 1: Exchange Rate Regimes

Summary

There are two main factors determining whether the balance of payments adjustments of some geographic area would be more easily handled as a region within a common currency area or as an independent country with a separate currency and a potentially variable exchange rate. The first of these is size. The smaller the size of the region, the easier it is for it to adjust within a common currency area and the greater the difficulty of making an independent command over monetary and exchange-rate policies effective. Larger countries may enjoy certain economies of scale (for example in government itself) and the existence of large currency areas does eliminate the need for continuous currency exchanges within the area. On the other hand, a region which cannot adjust its exchange rate in response to external shocks will have to bear additional adjustment costs in terms of disturbances to labour markets (e.g., migration and unemployment) and large shifts in incomes and wealth. If the prime goal is internal stability, it would seem that the greater the number of separate currencies the better. However, simple observation shows that single currency areas range from huge countries down to very small states. This diversity suggests that the costs of diverging from the optimally-sized currency area are not sufficient to outweigh other more powerful forces shaping political boundaries.

Indeed the second, and more important, factor determining the optimal extent of currency areas is the existence of social and political unity between the regions of the area. If this exists, fiscal transfers (and migration) will ease, and possibly resolve, regional disparities, and allow the burden of adjustment to disturbances to be amicably shared. It is, however, possible to find counter-examples of countries linked together in a single currency area without the support of a (partially) centralised fiscal authority. One such example was provided by the earlier fixed relationship between the Irish and UK currencies before Ireland joined the Exchange Rate Mechanism (ERM) of the European Monetary System (EMS) while the UK did not (1979). Another more famous example is provided by the Gold Standard.

The maintenance of *permanently*-fixed exchange rates virtually implies the abandonment of autonomous control over domestic monetary policy. Otherwise the more inflationary country, within a fixed exchange-rate system, would not only obtain command over additional goods and services, but would also pass on unwanted inflation to its partners. No such system can, therefore, persist without some discipline over the monetary policies of the countries involved. But, in the modern world, powerful, independent nations are not likely to submit themselves to the external constraints of automatic rules. The discipline and decisions necessary to run a fixed exchange-rate system will nowadays have to depend on political harmony.

The political scene today gives few grounds for optimism on the prospects for establishing a permanently-fixed exchange-rate system over the Atlantic community. The world system will continue to contain a number of countries (currency areas) with separate currencies whose value in exchange can, and will, vary. The question, addressed in Section 2, is how such adjustments are best carried out; in particular we examine whether the exchange rate should be allowed to float entirely freely or whether its movements should be managed by the authorities; and if the decision is to manage the exchange rate, whether this should be by maintaining (temporarily) fixed but adjustable parities or by intervening to moderate the rate of change of the exchange rate.

I doubt whether it would be desirable to leave the exchange rate entirely at the mercy of market forces. In the short run devaluations often seem to worsen the trade account, probably because of lags in adjustment to price changes (the *J*-curve syndrome), while speculation is also usually on too short run a basis to provide a stabilising influence. So a regime of freely floating rates may lead to considerable 'overshooting' and unnecessary instability. Moreover, when external balance is disturbed, not by an external shock, but by some impulse from domestic conditions, reliance on flexible exchange rates to restore external balance will tend to exaggerate the initial divergence from internal balance. Supporters of flexible exchange rates have a liberal optimism in the perfectability of domestic policy making.

On the other hand, once an exchange rate is pegged it ceases to insulate the economy from external shocks. If the authorities are not driven from their internal objectives – and the whole idea is to prevent that happening – an external imbalance will develop over time. The existence and direction of this imbalance will generally become obvious, opening up one-way options to speculators. If the authorities try to peg the rate for any length of time, the change in the rate ultimately necessary to restore equilibrium will become larger. Large, abrupt, occasional changes in market conditions tend to impose greater adjustment costs than small, continuous changes. Furthermore, the longer a rate is forcibly held at some disequilibrium level the harder it may be to see what the appropriate level at which to re-fix might be.

For all these reasons my own conclusion has been that the authorities should intervene in exchange markets, but that their concern should not be to pick and to defend any particular level of rates, but to control the *rate of change* of parities, managing this rate of change to see that it never becomes too large (e.g., under the influence of low short-run elasticities and destabilising market speculation) to become a disruptive force.

1. Optimal Currency Areas

From the analysis of Chapter 16 we should now be able to extract and to identify the main features which differentiate the international from the inter-regional adjustment process. The most obvious difference, of course, is that regions share a single common currency, whereas each nation maintains a separate currency, autonomously controlled, which can in principle vary in value against the currencies of other independent states.

In certain ways the adjustment problem for the region is easier than for the larger state which contains it. Being smaller, and also producing a smaller range of goods, its marginal propensity to import will be higher. So, in those cases when there are no equilibrating relative price–cost movements, it would take a lesser variation in incomes and wealth to restore equilibrium in the region, as compared with the country. In any case the region will be part of a single currency area with, presumably, an integrated capital market; in this market there should be a high degree of substitution between financial assets of similar kinds issued in the various regions. So each region should be able to finance fluctuations in its current account with considerable ease; so much so that the financial problems that do arise will appear rather in the guise of concern over the future viability of local industries than in the forms which concern separate nations, with their recurring worries over the level of official reserves and their persistent efforts to identify and to influence the channels of international capital flows.

Finally, and perhaps most important, social unity between regions provides the popular support for fiscal centralisation which should, given the usual schedules of benefits and taxes, provide a flow of funds from the more active and the more prosperous regions to the depressed and poorer parts of each country; this should ameliorate imbalances and disparities. Furthermore, sympathy with the plight of the less fortunate regions may cause the central government to act directly to improve the competitiveness of the depressed regions by encouraging the development of new industries there, by improving the capital infrastructure (transport, communications, etc.), by special efforts to train and to educate the local labour force, etc. And, as has been already noted, the central government does also have at hand the fiscal tools, in the form of regional employment premia and taxes, to cause divergences between final prices and wage costs in the various areas, which can act as a surrogate for exchange-rate changes. Finally, even if the government does not, or cannot, act effectively to prevent disparities between prosperous and depressed regions developing and persisting, social unity between the regions of the country, encompassing and depending on such matters as language and accent, common legal institutions, etc., would facilitate easier migration between regions, which would also serve to ease the situation.[1]

The main difficulty confronting regions in their attempts to adjust to imbalances, which usually show themselves in a decline in the demand for local products, is their comparative inability to induce an equilibrating movement in relative costs and prices. Moreover, a fairly small region often concentrates upon the production of a few goods, coal say, or textiles, or cars, so that its balance is bound to be frequently disturbed by minor variations in taste, in technology or in foreign competitiveness, while the larger country should find some of these somewhat random developments offsetting each other.[2] It is not only that regions cannot formally devalue, or revalue, against other regions; the very social unity between one region and another leads to concern over parity of (real) incomes, with wage negotiations undertaken on a national basis, so that market-based wage changes in response to local excess-supply conditions may be suppressed. In these circumstances a decline in activity in some region is less likely to lead to a relative reduction in wages and prices there. On the

---

[1] Migrants tend to be young adult males. So emigrations may worsen the dependency ratio of the home region and push its rate of growth of productivity down further. It is far from clear whether the longer-term regional problems of areas which have experienced large-scale emigration, e.g., Ireland, Southern Italy, have been greatly eased by such migration. On this see Whitaker, 'Monetary Integration: Reflections on Irish Experience' (1973) pp. 4–21, especially p. 16.

[2] A point emphasised by Kenen in his paper on 'The Theory of Optimum Currency Areas: An Eclectic View', in Mundell and Swoboda (eds) (1969) pp. 41–60.

other hand, social cohesion should limit the emergence and development of disequilibrating movements in wages and prices in the first place.[1]

Even if a very small area did obtain monetary autonomy, and was able to vary its exchange rate, it is dubious whether this would be nearly as successful as in the case of a larger country. To be sure the elasticity of demand for a small region's exports should be usually higher; despite a greater concentration on a few products it will provide a smaller proportion of world supply and should, therefore, find it easier to displace other suppliers.[2] On the other hand, the high propensity to import of a small region, its openness,[3] will cause any variation in exchange rates to be rapidly reflected in a nearly equivalent (inverse) shift in prices. Such a larger and more obvious effect of devaluation on real wage rates and living standards may call forth greater resistance on the part of labour. This will be greater the more that social unity between contiguous areas encourages a comparison between living standards and prompts people in similar occupations in differing regions to demand similar real living standards. Furthermore, the large weight of imported goods in consumption, and therefore the crucial significance of the terms of trade between local wages and import prices, may make labour and others prefer to have their receipts specified, and their assets denominated, in terms of foreign prices.[4] In these circumstances the ability of the local monetary authorities to undertake an independent monetary policy or to vary the rate of exchange with the stronger foreign currency may be severely curtailed.

There appear to be two common factors here determining whether the balance-of-payments adjustments of some geographical area would be more easily solved as a

---

[1] I am indebted to John Williamson for reminding me of this point.

[2] If this were not so, the high propensity to import of a small area might make deflation a cheaper method – in terms of the absorption of goods given up – of adjustment to a deficit than a devaluation, *assuming* for the moment that such a devaluation could succeed in reducing real wages in the small region. Formally, on the assumption also of completely elastic supplies of goods, though this is implausible particularly for the small region, deflation would be preferable to devaluation if

$$1 + \frac{1}{m} < \frac{\eta_x + \eta_m}{\eta_x + \eta_m - 1}$$

where m is the marginal propensity to import, η_x the external elasticity of demand for the small region's exports, and η_m its elasticity of demand for imports.

I am grateful to W. A. Allen for pointing this out to me. Although m will be higher in a small region, so also will η_x normally be. The value of m is bounded, but η_x can rise to infinity: the higher external elasticity of demand for the exports of a small region should, in my view, normally outweigh the effect of the greater propensity to import, thus making devaluation, *on these assumptions*, the more preferable option for the very small region.

[3] McKinnon emphasised the importance of this factor in determining whether it would or would not be advantageous for a region to become part of a wider single-currency area, in his paper on 'Optimum Currency Areas' (1963) pp. 717–25.

[4] Corden, in his pamphlet on 'Monetary Integration' (1972) criticises the choice of the extent of 'openness' of an economy as an indicator of the likely advantages of monetary union on the grounds that exchange-rate movements can still allow even a small open economy to be insulated from variations in external prices feeding through into import prices. This is so, but living standards can also be protected from imported inflation by relating domestic wage rates to import prices. Relating local wages to wages and prices in neighbouring areas may give the inhabitants of a small, open region a greater feeling of certainty than reliance on the vagaries of the foreign-exchange market, which in the case of a small country would be a narrow market.

region within a common-currency area or as an independent country with a separate currency and a potentially-variable exchange rate. These are size, and social unity with surrounding, contiguous regions. The smaller the size of the region, the easier it is for it to adjust within a common currency area and the greater difficulty it will have, as a small, open economy, in making its supposed independent command over monetary policy and exchange rates effective. One can point to examples of independent countries which are too small to maintain an effective independent monetary policy; nevertheless, even tiny countries by the standards of the giants (e.g., Russia, the United States) do operate independent monetary policies.[1] The more important factor is social unity: if this exists, fiscal transfers (and migration) will on the one hand ease and even possibly solve regional disparities, while on the other hand concern for parity may suppress equilibrating movements in relative costs and prices, whether market-based or induced by exchange-rate variations.

Frankly it is difficult to believe that size is the most crucial variable determining the boundaries of the 'optimal' currency area, or even a particularly important variable once the minimum size necessary to support effective independence has been attained. Simple observation shows that the basic single-currency areas, i.e., the independent nation states, vary from vast giants (e.g., China, Russia, the United States) whose administrative regions (e.g., the States of California, New York, Texas, etc.) are much larger on any criterion than the majority of independent nations, right down to relatively tiny nation states. If size were so very important, surely economic pressure would encourage separatist movements in the larger countries and attempts at mergers and unification among groupings of smaller countries, with a convergence towards some common size for each single national-currency area. There is little evidence of this occurring, or of its having occurred in the past. The economic advantages of a larger grouping of small principalities (and among these economic considerations the ease of balance-of-payments adjustments was itself a minor issue) played some role in the unification of Germany and possibly of other countries also, but historical experience suggests that if there are adjustment costs involved in maintaining single-currency areas greater or less than some 'optimum' size, these costs are too slight[2] to affect seriously the historical process determining their size. This great diversity in the size of existing common-currency areas should cause a certain hesitance in putting forward the thesis that there is a well-defined optimally-sized currency area, or that adjustment costs increase significantly as the size of the area diverges markedly from the optimal (i.e., that size is, or should be, an important determinant of the boundaries of a common currency area).

The additional adjustment costs (in terms of extra unemployment, forced migration and reduced incomes and wealth) that may arise when a region cannot adjust its exchange rate, in order to shift relative (wage) costs and prices, seem clear and obvious; the offsetting gains of having a larger currency area seem generally more nebulous.[3] As a result several authors on this topic have found themselves virtually

---

[1] Practical experience suggests that Luxembourg may be too small, but Denmark is large enough, to operate an effective independent monetary policy. Eire appears to be on the borderline.

[2] This is not to say that these costs are in fact negligible. It is rather that they are hard to visualise and are outweighed by other stronger political forces.

[3] See, for example, the assessment of the 'pros' and 'cons' of monetary unification within the European Economic Community by Fleming, 'On Exchange Rate Unification' (1971) pp. 467–88.

forced into the position of arguing in favour of currency regions which are as small as feasible (i.e., just large enough still to allow for effective independence of monetary policy and for variable exchange rates to be a useful instrument). Mundell, for example, argued:

> If then, the goals of internal stability are to be rigidly pursued, it follows that the greater is the number of separate currency areas in the world, the more successfully will these goals be attained. .... But this seems to imply that regions ought to be defined so narrowly as to count every minor pocket of unemployment arising from labour immobility as a separate region, each of which should apparently have a separate currency.[1]

He went on to note, however, that besides the stabilisation argument, which pointed to having a plethora of currency areas, there were costs associated with the maintenance of many currency areas. These were that it reduced the usefulness of each independent money as a medium of exchange, that it would lead to excessively narrow exchange-rate markets, and that in small regions with high import propensities the community might not accept the changes in real incomes brought about by exchange-rate variations for the reasons we have already mentioned. Nevertheless, these costs cannot have bulked high with him, since he concluded[2] 'If the world can be divided into regions within each of which there is factor mobility and between which there is factor immobility, then each of these regions should have a separate currency which fluctuates relative to all other currencies'.

Again Kenen[3] argued that the less diversified are a region's products, the more necessary it is for that region to maintain a flexible exchange rate. '*Ex ante*, diversification serves to average out external shocks and, incidentally, to stabilise domestic capital formation. *Ex post*, it serves to minimise the damage done when averaging is incomplete'.[4] But the smaller the area, the more likely that it will be concentrating on the production of a limited number of goods. This principle appears to lead to the curious conclusion that the smaller the region, the greater the need for an independent monetary policy and flexible exchange rates.

There must be something wrong with that. In my view these authors are placing too much weight on the effects of size, with its implications for openness and diversity, as a determinant of the costs of adjustment within a single-currency area and too little on the role of social unity. If there is social unity throughout a country, irrespective of size, the authorities could, and should, introduce fiscal measures that will ease adjustment costs as, or perhaps even more, effectively as exchange-rate changes. Moreover, in such conditions labour migration will be easier, and relative wage–price adjustments harder to bring about under any exchange-rate regime.

If people in the prosperous regions of a single-currency area, say in the south-east of England, feel that everyone in the country deserves the same treatment as them, they will not resent a continuing transfer of funds, through the fiscal mechanism,[5] to

---

[1] Mundell, 'A Theory of Optimum Currency Areas' (1961) p. 662.
[2] Mundell (1961) p. 663.
[3] In 'The Theory of Optimum Currency Areas: An Eclectic View', in Mundell and Swoboda (eds) (1969) pp. 41–60.
[4] Mundell and Swoboda (eds) (1969) p. 54.
[5] They will, no doubt, complain about the level of taxation, but they are not likely to resent the fact that there are net fiscal transfers to other regions.

the less prosperous regions, say in Scotland or the north-east.[1] Equally the fiscal redistribution should soften the impact of current-account imbalances on activity and incomes in the lagging regions and, perhaps, lessen the attraction of political separatism. On the other hand, any attempt to impose an exchange-rate union on a set of areas without an underlying social unity can lead rapidly to disaster. If the members of the more prosperous regions (e.g., Germany and Holland in the EEC) should object to providing a potentially very large flow of funds for an indefinite time period to the less prosperous regions (e.g., Ireland and Italy), on the grounds that these foreigners are different and should be content with different treatment, then the adjustment costs and separatist pressures within the single-currency area could easily become intense. The 'optimal' currency area is a function not so much of geography but rather of social psychology.

Indeed, as far as one can observe, the problems of maintaining balance between regions in a single-currency area do not seem qualitatively that much harder in vast countries such as the United States or Russia than in much smaller countries such as the United Kingdom, Italy or Sweden. The disparity between economic conditions in West Virginia and, say, New York does not seem qualitatively so much worse than, say, the difference between parts of Scotland and the south of England, or between the south and north of Italy. The extent, severity and persistence of regional disparities do not seem to be very closely correlated with the size of the currency area.

The costs of maintaining a common-currency area (due to the prevention of the use of exchange-rate variations among the constituent regions as an instrument of adjustment to imbalances) are not – we have argued – particularly closely related to the size, the extent, of that area. Are there, perhaps, any gains, any advantages, on the other hand, to be obtained from having larger currency areas? If so, with no significant additional costs but real advantages, one would advocate having common-currency areas among all those regional groups with sufficient social unity to make them work well.

The most obvious benefit from having a larger currency area is that it eliminates the need for currency exchanges within the area and also uncertainty about likely future exchange rates. Consider the additional time and effort that would have to be devoted to currency exchanges by all travellers and businessmen, as well as the further employment of specialised exchange brokers with their attendant equipment, if every state among the fifty United States had its separate currency and exchange rate. Even worse, there would be a multiplication of Central Banks and Central Bankers, each with its staff of bureaucrats and its printing press, churning out fifty different currencies. Or think of the extra bother if each county in the United Kingdom tried to run an independent monetary system. Alternatively, imagine the advantages, in ease and simplicity, of having a single currency all over the world.[2]

These exchange costs are largely incurred because of uncertainty about the future relative values of the separate currencies. If everyone knew exactly what the exchange rate of the pound and franc was going to be at every point of time, people would

---

[1] Within most industrialised countries the fiscal mechanism transfers considerable sums from the more to the less prosperous regions without there being much fuss or bother about it. Yet the provision of development aid to very much poorer people in foreign countries runs into much political opposition and resentment. One of the few cases of really large-scale transfers beyond political frontiers was Marshall Aid, but that was in special circumstances and is continuously cited as an exceptional case.

[2] On this subject see Wood, 'European Monetary Union and the U.K. – A Cost-Benefit Analysis' (1973).

accept either currency equally readily.[1] In part this uncertainty can be reduced, at a cost, by obtaining extra information, e.g., reading the newspaper to see what current exchange rates are, or by hedging future foreign-exchange commitments in the forward market. But there are limits to the extent that uncertainty can be overcome, whether by the acquisition of extra information or by operations in forward markets.

This uncertainty about exchange rates is one of the major factors, alongside difficulties of communication over long distances, separate languages, differing legal institutions, etc., which raise barriers to trade in goods and assets. A single common-currency area aids the integration of markets, which should improve allocative efficiency, allowing capital to move with greater flexibility to those areas where it can offer the highest return. For example, one of the major benefits of a move towards a common European currency should be the impetus this would give to the development of an integrated capital market.[2]

It is, however, unrealistic to discuss 'optimal' currency areas without giving explicit consideration to the close links between control of the currency and national sovereignty. As noted in Chapter 2, the right to issue legal-tender currency is one of the most important, and prized, aspects of independent, sovereign power. Monetary independence entails the power also to change the exchange rate of the country *vis-à-vis* the currencies of other areas. If, say, British Columbia, or Florida, or Scotland, was given a separate Central Bank, a separate currency and the power to vary its exchange rate *vis-à-vis* the Canadian dollar, or US dollar or English pound, how much would be, or could be, left of national union between the two areas? Not only monetary policy, common currencies and integrated markets would have gone, but it is also extremely difficult to see how it would be possible to maintain any coherent common fiscal policy between the two areas.[3]

---

[1] Or almost so. The payment of money generally leaves the recipient's asset balance out of equilibrium, i.e., he will want to use most of these monetary receipts to buy goods or services or financial assets. If there is a lag between the receipt of the money and his ability to redistribute it, he will prefer to receive the currency which will appreciate in this interval.

[2] In their pamphlet on *European Monetary Integration* (1972), Magnifico and Williamson saw one of the main advantages of establishing a new European currency (the 'Europa') that it could 'fill the role that the Euro-dollar has performed for the past decade in acting as an instrument for the creation of unified European money and capital markets' (p. 9); see also pp. 7–10, 20.

There is always, however, a possibility of conflict between efficiency and equity. It could well be that, at the moment, the marginal return to capital is higher in Germany than in Italy. An integrated capital market would then direct investment even more towards Germany, thus raising total EEC output obtainable from a given total of factor inputs, but at the expense of exaggerating intra-EEC disparities. This provides a further indication of the vital importance of an appropriate fiscal and regional policy in the EEC.

[3] Many of the arguments here resemble the question of precedence of the chicken or the egg. The establishment of a successful monetary union may well require support from a strong, centralised, or at least inter-regionally co-ordinated, fiscal (and regional) policy to ease the complications of regional adjustment. Yet it is very difficult to establish a centralised fiscal authority unless there is a monetary union, a single currency, throughout the area. In order to establish conditions conducive to the successful working of a single-currency area the constituent regions need to exhibit social unity, but the existence of different currencies is one of the factors tending to divide and separate groups of people. The problems involved in moving, through a process of political agreement, from a system consisting of several independent currencies to a single-currency area are extremely difficult and delicate. In my view the Werner Report (1970), on the attainment of economic and monetary union with the EEC, failed to give adequate attention to the complexities of the course which it was charting.

Thus Kenen asked:[1]

> How would taxes be collected if a single fiscal system were to span a number of currency areas, each of them entitled to alter its exchange rate? How would a treasury maintain the desired distribution of total tax collections? Suppose that the treasury levied an income tax to be paid in each resident's regional currency and that the West was printing money faster than the East, causing a more rapid rise in prices and incomes. Unless the West's currency were to depreciate *pari passu* with the faster rise in money incomes, the West would come to pay a larger fraction of the tax (and if the tax were graduated, might also have to furnish a larger share of the goods and services absorbed by the government, as its tax payments would rise faster than its prices). The same problem would arise even more dramatically if the treasury relied on property taxation. Property values and property assessments might not keep pace with money incomes, and even if the difference in rates of inflation were exactly matched by the change in the exchange rate, there could be a significant redistribution of the tax burden. In which currency, moreover, would the central government pay for goods and services? Which one would it use to pay its civil servants? And what may be the thorniest practical problem in which currency should the central government issue its own debt instruments?

Neither he, nor Corden,[2] were prepared to go so far as to claim that these problems were insurmountable, but they are clearly very difficult. If social and political unity is sufficient to solve amicably the problems of fiscal redistribution when a central budget is disturbed by exchange-rate variations, the necessary conditions surely also exist for the successful establishment of a single-currency area. Alternatively, if pressures within an area are such as to require the establishment, or maintenance, of separate currency areas, there is unlikely to be much agreement forthcoming on the transfer to a central authority of local fiscal powers, or on how such powers as it has been granted should be exercised. Fiscal and monetary harmonisation will march together, or not at all.

If separate currency areas do entail separate fiscal areas, then all the main economic powers have been devolved. Groupings of such areas, each with its own independent fiscal policy, monetary policy and exchange rate, may form a confederation or an alliance, but hardly a union, much less a united country. It is extremely difficult, perhaps impossible, for a unified country to extend over more than one currency area. If so, possible economies of scale that may appertain to larger countries (e.g., in defence, administration, etc.) require the establishment of large currency areas. To put it bluntly, if each state in the Union had retained its own independent currency after the War of Independence it is doubtful whether they would now form part of a set of United States.

I have argued both that a single-currency area requires a strong, centralised fiscal authority,[3] ready and able to ease regional adjustment problems, and also that it will be difficult to establish any effective centralised fiscal authority covering areas with independent, separate currencies (i.e., both that a single-currency area cannot cover several, independent, unco-ordinated fiscal areas, and the converse that an integrated

---

[1] (1969) p. 46.

[2] (1972) p. 38.

[3] Simple inspection shows that it is not necessary for *all* fiscal operations to be centralised within a single-currency area. Within sovereign countries there is often a considerable devolution of the right to levy taxes and to determine expenditures to the local, State, county, township level. How much fiscal centralisation is necessary to keep a single-currency area working smoothly is a matter for conjecture.

fiscal area cannot extend over several independent currency areas). There are no doubt exceptions to both rules but the weaker claim, on historical experience, seems to be that a currency area requires strong centralised fiscal support. Without reaching too far back in time, the success of the Gold Standard in the period from 1890 to 1914 shows that it has been possible for countries to establish virtually a common-currency area, an apparently permanent, fixed exchange-rate system, without the support of fiscal policy.[1]

How then did the Gold Standard system work so well in these years, while nowadays, we have argued, any system of permanently-fixed exchange rates would need help from fiscal measures to ease regional adjustments? Of course, the countries on the Gold Standard did enjoy several of the benefits of a single-currency area. The establishment of an integrated capital market in London, together with confidence in the maintenance of the parity of the major industrial countries,[2] did allow large-scale accommodating (short-term) capital flows. As discussed in the previous chapter (Section 1), a high elasticity of substitution among financial assets enables current-account imbalances to be settled with little monetary disturbance. Furthermore, the continued strong balance-of-payments position of the United Kingdom (with a large surplus on invisibles more than offsetting a trade deficit) prevented the growth of short-term sterling liabilities, claims on London, relative to the stock of UK gold reserves from becoming a serious problem.[3] But this only helps to explain how the

---

[1] A second, more up-to-date, counter-example was to be found in the case of the fixed exchange rate between sterling and the Irish pound prior to that link being broken in 1979, when Ireland joined the Exchange Rate Mechanism (ERM) of the European Monetary System (EMS) and the UK did not do so. Irish fiscal policy is certainly independent; yet there did not seem to be any serious strains in maintaining the fixed parity. The factors responsible for this state of affairs were analysed by Dr T. K. Whitaker, the Governor of the Central Bank of Ireland, in his paper on 'Monetary Integration: Reflections on Irish Experience' (1973) pp. 4–21. These include a very open economy, with a high proportion of trade conducted with the United Kingdom; free and easy migration between Ireland and the United Kingdom; considerable integration of the financial system, and indeed of many of the other economic institutions, between the two countries; the continued ability of the Irish to use tariffs, export subsidies, etc. in lieu of exchange-rate variations, which, as Dr Whitaker notes (p. 20), calls into question the association often posited in the EEC context between establishing a customs union and a monetary union.

[2] This confidence developed in the particular historical circumstances of the period. It is not, however, producible by design; certainly not by assertions of intent from political leaders.

[3] Gold does not offer an interest rate; sterling balances did, and were also exchangeable for gold. Apart from the atavistic desires of certain Central European Central Banks to build up 'war chests' of gold in their own vaults, sterling balances were a relatively more attractive investment. Foreign holdings of claims on London almost certainly increased over these years, 1890–1914, far more than UK gold reserves. This did cause London bankers a lot of worry at the time, particularly in the foreseen context of an outbreak of hostilities, with 'enemy' countries possibly making a financial raid on London by withdrawing all their funds and thus endeavouring to bring about a financial collapse there. There were several papers on this subject delivered by prominent London bankers at the time, see for example Schuster, 'Our Gold Reserves' (1907); see also the discussion on the gold holdings of the London banks in Goodhart (1972) pp. 100–7.

Nevertheless, the growth of foreign claims on London, relative to UK reserves, never caused the same instability in the system, as did the growth of foreign claims on the United States during the 1950s and 1960s, see Triffin (1960), because the underlying balance-of-payments position of the United Kingdom in the 1900s was much stronger than that of the United States in the 1960s.

system was able to finance current-account imbalances;[1] it still leaves unanswered the central question of how these imbalances themselves were resolved, in a fixed-rate system, without apparently causing unacceptably large-scale fluctuations in employment, incomes and wealth.[2] What makes the Gold Standard period particularly interesting is the puzzle of trying to decipher its adjustment mechanism. A partial explanation may be found in the fact that the nineteenth century, including the years up till 1914, was characterised by enormous, cyclic migration flows;[3] standard analysis suggests that migration should mitigate some of the economic effects of regional imbalance. Other economists have suggested that prices (and wages) responded sufficiently flexibly to regional conditions of excess or insufficient demand (whether induced by a monetary multiplier mechanism or by a Keynesian foreign-trade multiplier)[4] to restore equilibrium. It may, therefore, have been the greater stickiness of (real) wage rates and prices since 1914 which is partially to blame for the subsequent failings of fixed exchange-rate systems.[5] Certainly if all wages–prices were completely flexible, the only (weak) economic argument for abandoning a one-world single-currency system would be that different countries (regions) had preferences for different rates of price inflation (an issue touched on again in the next section).

The maintenance of permanently fixed exchange rates does, however, practically imply the abandonment of independent control over the domestic money supply,[6] a step with major political connotations. To illustrate why this is so, consider a counter-example, in which two countries agree to accept each other's currencies in payment at par (fixed exchange rates) but both retain their freedom to expand, or to contract, their own money stock. The country that has the faster monetary expansion will experience a relative increase in domestic expenditures and prices, sucking in imports and non-monetary financial assets from abroad, paid for by exports of money balances accepted in the other country, by assumption, at par. So the more inflationary country not only obtains command over additional assets (or the services of assets),[7] but also passes on much of the additional inflation to its partner. Clearly no fixed exchange-rate system can persist without some discipline over the monetary

---

[1] Another factor was the willingness of Central Banks to bend the rules of the Gold Standard system in order to ease financial adjustments; on this see Bloomfield (1959).

[2] In that period people had less faith in the ability of governments to manage the economy; so they did not attach quite so much blame to governments for economic misfortunes, nor expect them to find answers to all economic problems. To that extent the fluctuations in incomes, prices, etc., that were politically acceptable then may have been larger than they are now.

[3] See Thomas (1954).

[4] Monetarists tend to emphasise the importance of monetary flows as a factor causing price adjustments, see for example Friedman and Schwartz (1963) p. 141. Keynesians, on the other hand, often argue that accommodating capital flows allowed the money stock in the major countries to adjust to demand, and that it was the variations in foreign demand for the domestic products that led directly to price changes, via the foreign-trade multiplier.

[5] The turmoil and disruptions caused by the First World War and the subsequent erratic plunges of government policies in the 1920s and 1930s threw far more pressure on the adjustment mechanism than it had had to cope with before 1914. Whether the mechanism really had become significantly less responsive after 1914 remains doubtful.

[6] Ignoring the theoretical possibility of using variable exchange controls to reconcile fixed exchange rates with an independently-determined money supply.

[7] In so far as interest is paid on money balances, the additional command over current output enjoyed by the more inflationary country will involve a subsequent offset in transfers required to service the interest payments.

policies of the countries involved.[1] One way of maintaining such a discipline is for the monetary authorities in each country to commit themselves to relate their domestic monetary creation to their international reserve holdings, and to settle international deficits (surpluses) by transferring (titles to) such reserves. Then the more inflationary country loses reserves as it expands, and this forces it to check its monetary expansion.

Any asset which is in fairly inelastic supply and of sufficient uniformity to serve as 'money' without requiring extensive investigation in transfer (see Chapter 2, Section 2) could do in principle as the international reserve base – gold, oil, corn, cows, SDRs. The use of a commodity reserve money, such as gold or oil or cows, suffers certain serious disadvantages. The growth of such reserves, affecting the overall rate of change of prices in the system, is largely dependent on erratic shifts in supply technology and on changes in the nature of demand for purposes other than monetary reserves for the commodity. The increased demand for these objects, to add to monetary reserves, encourages the use of scarce resources in their production[2] but the stocks amassed for such reserve purposes sit unused and unhelpfully, say in the vaults of the Federal Reserve Bank of New York.[3] Anyone observing the settlement of international imbalances by the transfer of a gold bar from a pile marked, say, Germany and placing it on a pile marked, say, Japan in a vault under a bank in New York, cannot be other than struck by the ridiculous nature of the whole proceedings.

There are better ways to maintain monetary discipline within a fixed exchange-rate area. One method is to replace commodity money as the international reserve by a financial asset (e.g., SDR or Bancor), thus avoiding the waste of scarce resources, supply uncertainties, etc. This does require political agreement on the distribution and creation of international reserves – perhaps more than is required to adhere to a commodity standard – but under modern conditions it seems unlikely that, unless there is sufficient political harmony to agree on the methods of providing the international financial reserve base, there would be sufficient social unity to devise

---

[1] The tenor of much European criticism of US international economic policy in the years before 1973 was basically that the United States played the role of the more inflationary country in the above example, because it accepted no external discipline over its domestic monetary policy. The US reply appears to have been that the system of fixed exchange rates, at existing parities, was maintained at the behest of the Europeans, not of themselves; so they saw no need to accept a discipline to maintain a system which they did not particularly wish to preserve. They argued that the Europeans could always have revalued to avoid any inflationary pressures emanating from US monetary expansion. Indeed, they claimed that the Europeans wanted to have their cake, of an undervalued exchange rate making their exports competitive, and eat it, by escaping the inflationary consequences of the resulting export surpluses and monetary inflows.

In turn the various European countries argued that their own individual exchange rates were not out of line with those of other countries, except for the United States. Thus no individual European country would wish to revalue unilaterally. The main imbalance was between the United States and the rest, and that could be most easily cured by action by the United States.

And so the argument went on, until the Bretton Woods system finally broke down in 1973.

[2] The additional demand for such commodities in their role as monetary reserves also affects the terms of trade between areas with a comparative advantage in their production and those without.

[3] In some respects it would be much more sensible to use cows rather than gold as monetary reserves. The cows, unlike the gold bars, need not be barren and could provide milk to thirsty bankers while acting as reserves. If everything King Midas touched had turned to beef he would have been a much happier man.

means of overcoming adjustment strains (e.g., by inter-area transfers) within a
(permanently) fixed exchange-rate area. Large individual countries cannot, in the
modern world, be forced willy-nilly into particular forms of balance-of-payments
adjustment by the scarcity of some selected international reserve asset.

Although a financial asset base, instead of a commodity base, to international
reserves should allow a planned overall rate of growth of reserves,[1] the monetary
authorities must still abide by certain rules (of the game) if a (permanently) fixed
exchange-rate system is to work. Adherence to these rules may often involve stress. It
is dubious whether independent countries, especially large powerful ones, are likely
to submit to the external constraints of automatic rules. It seems unlikely then that a
fixed exchange-rate system can be maintained on any permanent basis until political
harmony and social agreement allow the division of burdens within the area and the
direction of policy in each major part of the system to be decided by an accepted
central *political* process. Once that stage has been reached the next step, to a more
efficient single-currency area, eliminating the need for separate currencies, exchange
transactions, etc. should be simple.

2. Monetary Relationships Between Currency Areas

There are a number of benefits, therefore, that can be obtained from the establishment of a large-scale currency area; it facilitates the development of more efficient
integrated markets, eliminates the costs and uncertainties connected with internal
exchange transactions, and allows the establishment of larger governmental units in
those fields where they may be considerable economies of scale. But except in
circumstances, now probably rare, where local wage rates and prices vary sufficiently
flexibly, relatively to each other, to maintain activity and employment in each region,
the maintenance of a system of completely fixed exchange rates, as in a single-
currency area, may well impose considerable strains of adjustment in the face of trade
imbalances among the constituent regions.[2] Even when confidence in the permanence

---

[1] Problems with the *composition* of international reserves may arise under either a commodity
or a financial asset reserve-base system. If a country, especially one whose currency is much
used in international transactions, offers a liquid asset with a more attractive yield than the
basic reserve asset (e.g., bills on London, US Treasury bills), other countries may prefer to hold
these rather than the basic reserve assets, treating them as the equivalent of reserves. Thus a
very slight increase (or even a fall) in basic reserves may be consistent with a very rapid increase
in perceived reserves. But in that case the ratio of claims on this reserve-centre country to its
own holdings of basic reserves may reach a point which raises doubts about the fundamental
international liquidity of its liabilities. At this stage attempts by holders to cash in their claims,
exercising their convertibility rights, only precipitates the crisis. On this see Triffin (1960).

Nevertheless, even disregarding the possibility of political agreement to limit the use of
claims on other countries as part of official reserves, the adoption of a financial asset base
reserve should, in principle, help to solve this problem, since it should prove possible to devise
means of paying, and varying, interest on the base financial asset in order to influence the
composition as well as the total of official reserve assets.

[2] Even if wages/prices were sufficiently flexible to cope with all problems of adjustment –
though this is not the case in reality – it might still be argued that a single-currency area would
impose a single rate of price change over its whole extent, whereas differing groups within the
area might have differing 'tastes for inflation'. And it is true that some countries have in the last
couple of decades experienced significantly differing rates of inflation. The differences in
inflation rates that have been observed (e.g., between the United Kingdom and Germany) may

of the fixed-rate system allows imbalances to be *financed* with the minimum of fuss and difficulty, inability to induce an equilibrating move in relative costs and prices can allow marked disparities in incomes and wealth to develop, and lead to significant differences in regional unemployment rates and/or large-scale 'forced' migration.

These adjustment problems can, in my view, be overcome within the confines of a fixed exchange-rate system, even under conditions where relative real wages are slow to adjust. To do so, however, requires the adoption of 'appropriate' fiscal policy, which would probably involve a large-scale, and often long-continued, transfer of real resources from the more prosperous to the disadvantaged regions (e.g., through the provision of unemployment benefits, direct expenditure, regional employment premia for the disadvantaged regions, financed through the collection of income (or property) taxes imposed centrally at rates harmonised over the whole area). The decision to provide such transfers of resources between regions is essentially political; whether people will accept such inter-regional transfers depends on their feelings of social unity.

The political scene today gives few grounds for believing that there is sufficient harmony among peoples to establish a permanently-fixed exchange-rate system, or even better a single-currency area, on such a basis over the Western world, or even among the industrialised countries of the Atlantic community. It is not possible to establish a 'one-world' system, or solution, to international monetary relationships, in a world effectively divided among independent powers. Indeed, it is difficult enough to forge a monetary union between a small number of like-minded neighbouring countries. So the international monetary system is likely to remain fissile. Independent countries, or perhaps wider currency areas, will seek to retain control over their own domestic monetary policies and exchange rates in order to follow their perceived self-interests.

Thus, whether or not the next decade sees a continuing trend towards the successful emergence of currency areas embracing several countries, the world system will still contain a number of countries (currency areas) maintaining separate currencies whose value can vary in exchange (i.e., can be adjusted in relation to those of other countries). The question then becomes to decide how these exchange-rate adjustments can best be carried out in order to maintain prosperity and stability for the countries involved.

Should the exchange rates between these separate areas be freely determined in the market place (i.e., flexible or 'floating' rates) or should they be managed, controlled, by the respective monetary authorities? And if the exchange rates are to be managed, how should the authorities seek to do this, by *ad hoc* interventions to influence an otherwise freely-determined exchange rate (i.e., managed floating), by setting limits to the extent that the free market price can move from day to day, but allowing the rate to vary freely (or almost so) within these limits (i.e., gliding or crawling parities),

---

owe *something* to a differing weighting (trade-off) among the populace in each country with respect to the relative pain of unemployment and inflation, though other factors (e.g., the elasticity of supply of foreign workers in Germany) have no doubt also been responsible. Indeed the Germans have consistently had both lower inflation and lower unemployment than the British. But whatever the cause of the faster inflation in the United Kingdom, it is hardly due to an *absolute* preference among the British for a higher rate of inflation.

by pegging the rate but allowing frequent small moves or occasional large moves (pegged but adjustable rates)?

The basic reason why countries feel the need to retain the ability to vary their exchange rate is because external developments (e.g., a fall in foreign demand for domestic products or increasing inflation abroad) threaten the maintenance of internal balance. For example, an attempt to prevent the domestic economy inflating in response to foreign-generated inflation by domestic deflationary measures will under a fixed-rate system only serve to worsen the external imbalance and draw in more money from abroad, with probably only very limited success on the home front. Expressions of preference among alternative exchange-rate regimes are likely, therefore, to hang mainly on the issue of which allows the smoothest domestic adjustment to external shocks.

In this respect adoption of a regime of freely-floating exchange rates has a number of apparent advantages. If the authorities maintain some particular level of domestic demand (i.e., if the volume of domestic output and the level of domestic prices are fixed) then, with a given set of external, foreign economic conditions,[1] there will be, in general,[2] one, and only one, exchange rate that will allow the maintenance of external balance consistent with the chosen internal balance. The authorities do not have the information, indeed no one has, to enable them to tell what this rate may turn out to be. If they try to pick a rate to support, it will turn out to be more or less far from the 'equilibrium' rate as defined above, and this will cause problems of varying severity – depending on how far out the selection was – in maintaining both internal and external balance. If the chosen rate differs sufficiently from this 'equilibrium', so that the external imbalance becomes too severe and/or persistent to finance by an acceptable variation in reserve levels or in interest rates[3] (relative to those abroad), then either domestic demand may have to be varied from the desired level in order to maintain external balance, or controls of one kind or another placed on international transactions (e.g., import quotas or exchange controls) to buttress the exchange rate, or the rate itself abandoned.

In theory at least, the acceptance of market-determined, flexible exchange rates should allow the authorities to concentrate on the exercise of achieving a proper level of internal balance, allowing the exchange rate to act as a buffer to absorb external shocks. And, again in theory at least, adoption of flexible exchange rates should lessen the incentive to resort to direct controls over international transactions, which interfere with allocative efficiency, and should reduce the need for, and public and political concerns with, international reserve holdings. Finally, if the domestic monetary authorities are not trying to manipulate their exchange rate with another country, but are responding passively to market developments, a direct conflict of objectives between governments is somewhat less likely to arise than if both sets of authorities are seeking directly to manage their exchange rates.

---

[1] Including among such prior conditions the existing set of restrictions (tariffs, quotas, exchange controls, etc.) on international transactions.

[2] Though not in all cases. As Professor Hahn has noted, in his review article on Kornai's book (1971) entitled 'The Winter of our Discontent' (1973b) p. 324, the student of Arrow–Debreu general equilibrium theory 'would note at once not only that there may be no equilibrium level, but also that if there is one such level there may be very many.'

[3] Recall the criticism in Chapter 14 of Mundell's ingenious suggestion for using monetary and fiscal policy in tandem to maintain external and internal balance under fixed exchange-rate regimes.

At the end of Chapter 16 it was argued, on *a priori* grounds, that the *long-term* price elasticity of demand for any one country's exports should be significantly greater than unity. The long-run change in the exchange rate required to adjust to an external shock – given the level of domestic demand – should, therefore, be quite small. But for a number of reasons, many of them depending on lags and rigidities in the response of suppliers (even when there is 'spare capacity' in the devaluing country) to relative price changes, the short-run price elasticity of demand for a country's exports may seem much lower; indeed so much so that in the short run, for a few quarters, the effect of a devaluation may be to worsen the trade balance. This has now been termed the *J*-curve effect, since the shape of the capital letter *J* mimics the initial decline in the balance followed, after a lapse of time, by an even larger improvement.

If the elasticities are so low in the short run that the trade balance may even temporarily deteriorate after a devaluation, complete reliance on movements in exchange rates to maintain external balance, while keeping a constant level of internal demand, would not be viable, *unless* the fall in the exchange rate should induce a capital inflow. If there was no sustaining capital inflow, and no action by the authorities to support the rate in one way or another, then over any short period the exchange rate would be unstable; a reduction in the sterling exchange rate would lower the demand for pounds.

Even if the situation does not actually become unstable because the elasticities are not that low, or because there are countervailing capital flows, the lower short-run price elasticities could, in an exchange market without official intervention, force the exchange rate to overshoot the long-term equilibrium level. Excessive short-run variations in exchange rates, in relation to the adjustment needed in the longer term, would have a number of serious consequences. In the first place large fluctuations in exchange rates complicate the authorities' task of maintaining internal balance. A large fall in the exchange rate will raise domestic prices and shift incomes, at least in the short run, quite sharply towards profits and away from wages. This is bound to make the efforts of the authorities to restrain inflation that much harder. If the devaluation was caused by an external shock (say, a decline in foreign demand for domestic products), so that in the absence of the devaluation domestic incomes and output would have declined from the desired level, this effect of the overshoot – if not too exaggerated – might be tolerable. But if the devaluation was caused by a perhaps unforeseen expansion of domestic demand, any such overshoot would seriously intensify the problems of domestic demand management.

Secondly, exaggerated fluctuations in exchange rates, again in the sense that they exceeded the long-run adjustment required, could cause large swings in the profit margins obtainable in the production of tradeable goods. Profits would be more variable, uncertainty would be increased, it would be more difficult to plan ahead and there would be less stability in industrial activities. The greater instability would, one may assume, lead to more planning errors. Specific investment in human and non-human capital would be more likely to be wasted.

It is admitted by most proponents of completely flexible exchange rates that the price elasticities may be fairly low in the short run: they would have us put our trust then in countervailing capital flows to stabilise the exchange rate in the short run and prevent any large-scale 'overshooting'.[1] The argument runs as follows: suppose a

---

[1] See, for example, Friedman, 'The Case for Flexible Exchange Rates' (1953) especially Part ii, Section C on 'Flexible Exchange Rates and the Timing of Adjustment', pp. 182-6; also Brittan (1970) pp. 67–8.

country's exchange rate is depreciating. The price elasticities are larger in the long run; *ergo* the exchange rate should not need to depreciate very far in the longer term to achieve the required adjustment. If the (long-term) forward rate should fall below the actual rate expected to rule at this time, then speculators, acting on their expectations about the appropriate, or 'equilibrium', rate in the longer-term future, should buy forward. A fall in current spot rates, relative to these forward rates, pegged by speculators' expectations, opens up a profit on covered inward interest arbitrage; that is an investor switching funds into temporary investment in the depreciating country can buy the currency spot cheaper than he can sell it forward, and so will enjoy an additional safe return on the switch. The demand for spot currency to undertake such interest arbitrage (i.e., the capital inflow) should prevent its price falling far from its expected longer-term future level.

There are a number of reasons for entertaining doubts about this suggested story. First, the estimation, indeed the concept, of an appropriate, or 'equilibrium', level of exchange rates at some future date does depend on making some assumption about the expected future level of domestic output and prices. If these are taken as given, or at least as predictable, then speculators have some basis for working out their expectations of future equilibrium rates. But, as has already been noted, a devaluation may complicate the task of internal demand management, especially when it was itself caused by internal expansion. How is the speculator to be reasonably sure that internal demand management will be conducted well enough over the long run in order to feel confident about the maintenance of any 'long-run equilibrium' exchange rate?[1]

The second reason for doubting whether such 'stabilising' speculation will materialise is that the time scale is too long. No one has any clear idea exactly how long it takes for the major part of the adjustment to an exchange-rate variation to work through the system, but eighteen months to two years would not be regarded as excessive.[2] That is a long period of time in a market context. In that period there may be economic and political crises or wars involving any number of countries. Uncertainty about the state of the world in two years' time will discourage people

---

[1] One way of giving speculators the necessary confidence is for the authorities to signal their determination not to allow domestic conditions, especially inflation, to deteriorate by accompanying any depreciation with overt steps to reduce domestic claims on resources. This can, however, cause difficulties, because the authorities – as for example in the immediate aftermath of the 1967 devaluation – may feel that any such steps are unnecessary or even damaging domestically. Yet in such cases, without such signals of intent, it would hardly be surprising to find speculators uncertain about the long-term future of the exchange rate.

[2] 'As to the timing of trade effects, collective wisdom, based mainly on intuition rather than empirical study, put the time it would take for most of the effects of the Smithsonian realignment to work through at somewhere between eighteen months and two years. However, there are reasons why one might expect the adjustment to take longer than that', Junz and Rhomberg, 'Price Competitiveness in Export Trade among Industrialized Countries' (1973) p. 412. Indeed, they conclude (p. 418), 'The response of trade flows to relative price changes quite clearly seems to stretch out over a rather longer period than has generally been assumed, perhaps around four to five years.'

There have been other research studies of the lags in adjustment (e.g., by Minford for the United Kingdom, unpublished, and by Clark 'Some Early Estimates of the Price and Quantity Effects of the Smithsonian Agreement on the U.S. Trade Account', presented to the annual meeting of the Econometric Society (1973) which go to support the findings of Junz and Rhomberg of even longer lags than 'collective wisdom' had appreciated.

from trying to visualise a state of long-term equilibrium (a condition which is never achieved), or from backing their predictions with money. In any case the long-term forward market is very thin. Much more action takes place in the one- and three-month forward exchange market. Here, at least, speculators may feel that they have more hard information to bite on. But, given the low short-term elasticities, the short-term information that speculators will receive, and act on, is that a depreciating currency is likely to depreciate more in the coming quarter, unless the authorities do something to check the short-term worsening of the trade balance.[1] If this is so, the inherent problems of short-run instability in a freely-floating exchange-rate system may well be exacerbated by the action of speculators with short planning horizons.

Experience in this respect has been mixed. The Canadian experiment with floating exchange rates during the years 1950–62 was assessed by several observers[2] as broadly successful. There were few signs of serious short-term instability or of destabilising speculation.[3] On the other hand, initial experience in 1971–3 of a more general system of floating rates was less happy (subsequent experience is reviewed in the final Chapter). During the years 1972–3 there were continuous bouts of speculation driving the exchange rate of the dollar down and that of certain European currencies (especially the DM) upwards. It is difficult ever to make a sure judgement about what the 'long-term equilibrium' relativities might be, but many observers felt that some of these movements in exchange rates did represent considerable 'overshooting'.[4] There are a number of qualifications that may be made about the role of speculation in this period, e.g., that the initial starting point for exchange rates in 1971 was so badly out of line that it was harder to estimate appropriate relativities, that some of the fluctuations in rates were due to the authorities' actions (e.g., the tight German

---

[1] 'Those who rely on market forces fail to recognise that most foreign exchange operators are concerned with the future only over a short interval of time – very few with more than six or nine months. On the other hand, an exchange rate depreciation frequently begins by exercising a perverse influence on the basic balance of payments . . . It usually takes quite a long time for the volume effects to outweigh the price effects . . . The foreign exchange operators are therefore right to exercise a downward pressure on the value of the currency. If they are so perspicacious as to realise that, within the short space of time that concerns them, this depreciation will worsen the balance of payments, they will carry the depreciation far further than would have been called for to restore the competitive position', Kahn, 'The International Monetary System' (1973) p. 182.

[2] 'The general conclusion of the research efforts into the Canadian experience of 1950–62 is that a flexible exchange rate system can be made to operate successfully if those setting monetary and other economic policies understand its implications . . . The potential benefits of a flexible exchange rate for the Canadian economy as a whole and for policy makers in particular, are sizable', Dunn (1971) pp. 67, 74.

Dunn gives a list of economists who studied the Canadian experience (p. 60), including Wonnacott, Mundell, Marsh, Plumptre and Yeager and concludes, 'Virtually all of the students of Canada's history with a flexible rate conclude that the difficulties of 1958–62 were not the fault of the system, but instead grew out of a series of unfortunate or perhaps disastrous policy decisions in Ottawa'.

[3] For models of the working of the Canadian economy under the two exchange-rate regimes, see Rhomberg, 'Canada's Foreign Exchange Market: A Quarterly Model' (1959–60) pp. 439–56, and his later paper, 'A Model of the Canadian Economy under Fixed and Fluctuating Exchange Rates' (1964) pp. 1–31.

[4] 'The exchange market is apt to push a weak floating currency too far down, and a strong floating currency too far up' *National Institute Economic Review*, No. 67 (February 1974) 'Appraisal', p. 5.

monetary policy) not to speculation, and that anyhow the speculators were largely concerned with trying to predict the authorities' short-run policy moves. But, however you may qualify it, the conclusion of many observers[1] remained that speculation during this period did not assist, in balance, in stabilising the international monetary system.

Basically there seem to be two main arguments emerging from this discussion that militate against complete acceptance of freely-floating exchange rates. The first is that if external balance is disturbed not by an external shock but by some change in domestic *internal* conditions, then reliance on flexible exchange rates to restore external balance will exaggerate the initial divergence from internal balance. Internal deflation will raise the exchange rate, thus depressing domestic activity even more. Flexible rates, therefore, buffer the economy from external shocks, but exaggerate internal shocks. Following the same line of analysis as outlined in Chapter 14 (Section 2) in the discussion on stabilisation policy under uncertainty, the extent to which one should wish to keep exchange rates fixed, or flexible, depends on the relative likelihood of domestic or foreign disturbances.[2] Given that the possibility of internal economic disturbances is greater than zero, there is on these grounds a case for some limits to the complete market-determined flexibility of rates.

The second argument, which has been outlined in more detail, is that a regime of freely-flexible exchange rates may involve greater short-term variations in rates, a tendency towards 'overshooting', than is necessary for long-term adjustment of the external balance. On these grounds as well there is a case for some limitations to be imposed on the extent of short-run movements in rates.

There are, therefore, reasons for trying to temper the extent of short-run movements in exchange rates, for managing the exchange market to avoid unfavourable internal repercussions and unnecessary instability.[3] But how far along this road

---

[1] Take, for example, the remarks of H. J. Witteveen, Managing Director of the International Monetary Fund, at the World Banking Conference in London, 15 January 1974:

Experience has shown us, however, that floating rates can be subject to wide fluctuations, and rate movements can be exaggerated beyond what is consistent with underlying adjustment needs. When this happens, countries may with good reason wish to engage in intervention to prevent rates diverging unduly from a pattern considered to be conducive to the achievement of equilibrium (*Press Release*, pp. 1 and 2).

Private markets sometimes over-react to changes in underlying conditions, whether because of a failure to appreciate fully the lags involved in the adjustment process, or because of purely speculative factors (*Press Release*, p. 3).

Also see the statement of the Managing Director, in presenting the 28th Annual Report of the Executive Directors to the Board of Governors of the International Monetary Fund, in Nairobi, on 24 September 1973, *Press Release No. 3*, final paragraph.

[2] So, in a sense, support for a system of flexible exchange rates can be construed as a vote of confidence in the authorities' ability to handle domestic policy effectively, and preference for fixed exchange rates as a vote of no confidence. Seen in this light the usual line-up of supporters and opposers of a move to more flexible exchange rates often has an ironic appearance. Though to be fair, supporters of flexible exchange rates usually add the caveat that the domestic economy should at the same time be run according to their own precepts.

On this general point see Brittan (1970) Chapter 7, especially pp. 61–7.

[3] Moreover, whether or not you accept these reasons for official intervention in the exchange market, most countries will in practice seek to manage their rates, whenever exchange-rate movements seem to threaten their objectives. If some countries do this, others will feel defensively compelled to follow, and this provides a case for establishing certain 'rules of the game'.

should one go? Remember that we claimed that the basic reason why countries retained the right to vary their exchange rate (and to maintain an independent monetary policy) was to be able to insulate their domestic economy from external shocks. The objective is to allow variations in the exchange rate to maintain external balance, while the authorities concentrate on achieving the desired level of domestic demand.

If the exchange rate is pegged it is not going to be doing this job. If the authorities are not driven to abandon their internal objectives – and the whole idea was to prevent this happening – then an external imbalance will develop, and often grow over time, as the 'equilibrium' rate diverges from the pegged rate (e.g., under the influence of differing trend rates of inflation among the various countries). For a time such imbalances may, perhaps, be financed by acceptable fluctuations in reserve holdings or by relatively small variations in interest rates *vis-à-vis* other countries. There are, however, fairly narrow bounds to the extent that this is possible, particularly in support of a rate that appears to be overvalued.[1] Reserves are limited[2] and there can be difficulties in arranging large-scale international borrowing on acceptable terms. The main problem, however, is that such financing of itself does nothing to correct the imbalance caused by the divergence between the pegged and the 'equilibrium' exchange rate. At some point of time there will, therefore, be pressures on the authorities to correct the external imbalance by adjusting the exchange rate. It will generally be obvious under such conditions which way the exchange rate must move, if it moves at all: there is only a 'one-way option'. This 'one-way option' encourages speculation against the pegged currency, and such speculation will cause large-scale flows of capital out of the country which is seen as a devaluation candidate into the country which is seen as a revaluation candidate.[3] The volume of such flows was much increased, but *not caused,* by the development of an efficient, large-scale, international money market[4] in the shape of the euro-dollar market.

---

[1] This asymmetry between the problems of financing a large deficit, as compared with a large surplus, in the balance of payments may account for the bias towards devaluations which some observers have claimed to discern in the working of the Bretton Woods system of fixed but adjustable rates.

[2] The widespread feeling of shortages of reserves is often regarded as the consequence of an insufficient supply of new reserves. Conferences are arranged to discuss the process of creating an adequate flow of additional international reserves. Such fluctuations in supply do affect the *short-term* adequacy of reserves, but over the *longer term* the 'adequacy' of reserves will be determined by the relative incentive to hold reserve assets compared with the return on other assets. If the reserve asset offers a low yield, governments will economise on their holdings of reserve assets, in order to allow the economy to enjoy a current greater command over goods and higher-yielding assets. A faster growth in the supply of gold, or SDRs, would then simply encourage more expenditure and higher prices, ultimately leaving the 'shortage' of reserves exactly as it was. When considering the optimum quantity of money, the key issue is not how many notes should be printed, but what is the appropriate rate of interest to offer on money. Exactly analogously, in the international field it is only now beginning to be realised that the key issue is not how many SDRs to create but what rate of return they should bear (and how this can be financed). On this subject see Johnson (1972) pp. 86–8.

[3] The volume of such flows would no doubt redouble if countries were *required* to devalue or to revalue in response to some presumptive indicator which speculators could anticipate and observe.

[4] The efficiency of this market increases the response to a given incentive to redistribute funds, but is not itself responsible for the emergence of such an incentive.

During the course of the last three decades, the volume of mobile private capital that could, and would, move in response to the emergence of an apparent imbalance – a divergence between the pegged and 'equilibrium' rate – seems to have expanded enormously. The size of short-term capital flows now can swamp the reserve positions of most countries in a flash, as was seen in June 1972 when sterling was forced to float after a speculative flurry lasting only about a week. Thus, even if it should be a sensible policy in the first place, the scope now open to a country to finance an imbalance, without taking other steps to correct it, is becoming increasingly attenuated.

If the authorities are willing neither to sacrifice internal balance to the dictates of the external position, nor to allow the exchange rate to vary in response to external pressures, and they are not in a position to finance an external imbalance for long, what instruments have they got left to control their external position? The answer, of course, is to be found in direct controls on external transactions, controls on both trade flows and flows of financial assets, capital flows. As Corden, for example, pointed out,[1] the likely concomitant of the establishment of a system of firmly pegged, but ultimately adjustable, exchange rates (in his terms, a 'pseudo-monetary union') is a growing proliferation of controls over international transactions, a result hardly in keeping with endeavours of statesmen in other areas to ensure freer movement of goods and capital from country to country.

Even such controls are palliatives, to disguise and to cloak the existence of imbalance rather than to cure it. Apart from the increasing allocative inefficiency that such controls are likely (but not certain) to cause, direct controls over trade flows are liable to cause international antagonism and, perhaps, retaliation, while controls over capital flows, though less unpopular, are equally less easy to enforce. In a world of multi-national companies there are many loopholes open through which capital can be transmitted from country to country. Controls may work for a time, but in the longer run they cannot prevent the need for a more fundamental adjustment.

Thus a persistent current-account imbalance must ultimately force a country to readjust its exchange rate. Can one claim that a longer retention of a fixed parity, *vis-à-vis* other currencies, a less frequent occurrence of parity changes imparts a net benefit to the community? It would seem doubtful. The less frequent are the parity changes, the larger they are likely to be. The larger the parity changes, the more disruptive they will probably be, causing sharp changes in relative profitability between industries, sharp changes in price levels and in income distribution.[2] Moreover, the uncertainty engendered by a system of occasional large changes in parity would seem likely to be greater than that of a system involving more frequent small steps. Markets, especially forward markets, ought to be able to adjust to coping with regular, small price movements, but the prospect of a really major change may paralyse them. Finally, the longer a parity has been pegged, the more difficult it probably becomes to see how great the underlying imbalance really is. The occasional large parity change is likely to leave the country still some way from a position of long-run balance. Although the situation is bedevilled by slow, lagged adjustments to relative price changes, at least more frequent exchange-rate revisions provide an opportunity for correcting obvious mistakes, in a situation where lack of information

---

[1] In his pamphlet on 'Monetary Integration' (1972) especially pp. 21–4.

[2] Moreover, in the intervening period larger distortions in the allocation of resources build up, so there will be both static and dynamic costs.

is virtually bound to make the authorities pick a more or less inappropriate level of rates.

The conclusion, to which we are drawn by this discussion, is that the authorities charged with running the international monetary system, as set up at Bretton Woods, kept their eye fixed on the wrong measure. They were usually concerned with parity *levels* and controlling, pegging, or adjusting these levels. But they do not, and cannot, know what levels are correct; their attempts to maintain such levels led to the imposition of distortions on the world economy (e.g., via direct controls); and the occasional large-scale jumps in exchange rates to rectify an impossible situation were disruptive. Instead their concern ought to have been with the *rate of change* of parities, and controlling and managing this rate of change to see that it is never too large (e.g., under the influence of low short-run elasticities) to represent a disruptive force.

On this issue my sympathies are closely in line with the band of international monetary economists[1] who have proposed various schemes for 'gliding' or 'crawling' parities, for these are in essence methods for imposing some control over the rate of change of parities rather than over their level. It may be, however, that such intervention to limit the rate of change of parities is better done on a discretionary than on any automatic basis. Central Banks have lost so much of their power to control rates, given the development of the international money markets, etc., that they could, perhaps, be knocked off even more modest targets for limiting the rate of change of rates. For example, could a system of 'crawling' or 'gliding' rates have been maintained in the face of a severe disruption such as the energy crisis of 1973–4? Discretionary Central Bank intervention does have a role, since they are (or should be) better informed of economic prospects and more capable of taking a long view than are private speculators; Central Banks should have the opportunity to stabilise exchange rates and make a profit in so doing.

Nevertheless, it is not the details of these schemes to manage the rate of change of parities that matter yet (e.g., whether the authorities' intervention should be automatic, determined by the rules of the game, or discretionary) but the basic principle. There remains dissension between those who believe in absolutely free exchange markets, those who want to peg exchange-rate levels, and those who want to manage the rate of change of exchange rates, and the aim of this Section bas been to try to convince you that the last of these alternatives is the best.

---

[1] The general idea of a moving parity of this kind was first put forward by J. Black of Merton College, Oxford, in an unsigned note in *The Economist* of 4 November 1961, and was then taken up with various refinements by several other economists, notably Cooper, 'Flexing the International Monetary System: The Case for Gilding Parities', (1970); Meade, 'Exchange-Rate Flexibility', (1966), pp. 3–27; Williamson, 'The Crawling Peg' (1965).

XVIII
International Monetary Relations – 2: The Turbulent Float

Summary

After the final collapse of the Bretton Woods system in 1973, the exchange rates of the major countries of the world floated relatively freely against each other. In Section 1, we recount the disturbed record of this float. Prior to 1973, it had been expected that the nominal exchange rate would respond quite sensitively to nominal (relative price) shocks, leaving the real exchange rate more stable than under the previous adjustable peg system. Those hopes were dashed. Real exchange rates fluctuated widely and over long periods, causing major misalignments which had severe adverse effects on tradeable goods sectors and national and world economies.

We turn next in Section 2 to the not-very-successful attempts of economists to model these developments. Much of the volatility of exchange rates appeared to spring from massive capital movements. In line with this, exchange rate models shifted from Keynesian-type flow models, emphasising current account adjustments, to more monetarist stock-adjustment models, emphasising capital flows to restore asset equilibrium. The simple monetary-approach-to-the-balance-of-payments models, assuming instantaneous Purchasing Power Parity (PPP), could not, however, account for 'overshooting'. The development by Dornbusch of 'sticky-price' versions of the monetary-approach models could explain overshooting. But there were several aspects of forex market developments (e.g., the behaviour of forward rates) that the Dornbusch model could not explain. More complex portfolio balance models proved little better able to explain these facts. Some recent theories have suggested that the interplay between speculators using different analytical approaches (e.g., fundamental analysis vs Chartism) may help to explain events, but this last approach is in its infancy.

Given the discomforts of the floating exchange rate system, it was inevitable that commentators would see some advantages in returning to a more managed regime. Recent efforts in that direction are surveyed in Section 3. Particularly with the intervention reserve funds available to Central Banks being dwarfed by the size of potential capital flows, the achievement of greater exchange rate stability requires $n-1$ countries in an n country exchange rate system to predicate their monetary policy primarily to that end, thereby giving up at least some domestic autonomy. The European Monetary System has been the foremost regional system of adjustable pegged exchange rates and we examine the various reasons advanced to explain its comparative success. In the early 1980s, American and English politicians tended to doubt the wisdom of co-operative official intervention. Even since opinions changed around 1985, attempts to establish a basis for international monetary co-operation have not gotten far or achieved much. There has been too much national political discordance owing to differences in national perceptions and preferences. The prospects for improved international co-operation in the future are not bright.

1. The Experience of Floating Exchange Rates Since 1973

The scepticism expressed in Chapter 17, virtually unchanged since the original 1973 version, on the equilibrating properties of flexible exchange rates proved all too prescient. Let us compare how one might have expected flexible exchange rates to have worked in practice with how they worked in reality. Again, let us start with the assumption of perfectly flexible markets and instantaneous price adjustments, an assumption that will, of course, be dropped in due course.

A necessary consequence of the prior behavioural assumption of rational, profit-maximising agents is that profitable riskless arbitrage will always be undertaken. Accordingly, if a good is selling in one country at a price greater than its price in another (when translated by the appropriate current foreign exchange forward rate), by more than enough to cover the costs of shipment, insurance, etc. (plus risks of price changes during the period of shipment), then agents will import the good from the cheap country to sell in the more expensive. This leads on to the Law Of One Price (LOOP) whereby, expressed in a common currency, a tradeable good should sell at the same single price world-wide (abstracting, of course, from tariffs, quotas, etc.).

There are numerous qualifications to the assumptions leading to this result, notably perfect clearing markets, non-existence of tariffs, quotas, low transport costs, etc. so LOOP will hold only to an approximation. Nevertheless, the basic validity of LOOP has been thought to be sufficiently strong that, given a nominal domestic shock in country *A* which raises the general level of its prices *vis à vis* other countries, its exchange rate would have to depreciate *pro rata*. Otherwise, goods would flow into country *A* in increasing volume, depressing its current account balance.

At the limit, real exchange rates, i.e., nominal exchange rates adjusted for relative prices–costs,[1] should be unaffected by purely nominal, monetary shocks. This does not mean that real exchange rates should be expected to remain *constant* since these would be affected by real shocks (e.g., by changes in natural endowments, such as the discovery of North Sea oil, by changes in comparative rates of underlying productivity, by changes in tastes, etc.). Nevertheless, with the *possible* exception of certain energy discoveries (e.g., North Sea Oil in the UK and Norway and natural gas in the Netherlands), the size of real, supply-side shocks in most developed countries has generally been perceived as small in comparison with the scale of nominal shocks, as

[1] The practical question of which set of price–domestic cost indices to utilise in order to estimate the level of 'real' exchange rates has had much detailed study, particularly from the IMF during the 1970s, see Rhomberg 'Indices of Effective Exchange Rates (1976), pp. 88–112 and International Monetary Fund, *IFS Supplement on Exchange Rates* (No. 9) (1985). Ordinary consumer price indices, such as the CPI or RPI, include a proportion of direct foreign prices, whereas the appropriate index should include purely domestic prices–costs. The same was true, but even more so, for business input costs. The GNP deflator was theoretically a better series but it suffered from several statistical weaknesses, being a somewhat artificial construct, difficult to comprehend, with a considerable lag before appearance and subject to sizeable revision. After considerable experimentation the IMF settled on relative unit labour costs, or such costs adjusted for estimated cyclical fluctuations in productivity, as their measuring rod for calculating comparative national trends in relative nominal values and, hence, for computing real exchange rates.

inflationary pressures built up at different rates between countries and were then met by varying national contra-inflationary measures. The expectation would thus have been that *nominal* exchange rates should have shown much more variation than *real* exchange rates; in addition, the latter might have been expected to remain relatively stable.

Moreover, one might have expected real and nominal shocks to be independent of each other. Thus, whatever might have been happening to the real exchange rate, one would have expected the nominal exchange rate to be responding to relative domestic price fluctuations in such a way as to dampen (depending on the speed of adjustment) the effect on the real exchange rate.

These expectations were strongly held at the outset of the period of floating in the 1970s. Yet, they appeared in some large part to have been falsified by the facts, at least over the period 1973–86. Whereas the expectation was that floating exchange rates would allow real exchange rates to remain relatively stable relative to nominal rates, frequently the reverse happened over this period with real exchange rates varying by more than nominal rates. The two most extreme cases of this were the appreciation of the real value of the pound (1976–81) and of the dollar (1979–85), when the respective nominal exchange rates appreciated sharply despite unit labour costs in these countries growing faster than in their main competitors (see Figure 18.1 (A) and (B)).

Even more striking, one would have expected that bilateral nominal exchange rates would have adjusted over time to movements in relative price levels. Since we may assume nominal shocks to be uncorrelated (otherwise they would be predicted and hence not shocks at all), the individual series for the nominal exchange rate and relative price movements may each approximate to a random walk. Yet, one would have expected them to be 'cointegrated'[1] in the sense that the residuals (u_t) from the equation,

$$x_t = a + by_t + u_t,$$

where x is a nominal bilateral exchange rate and y is an index of relative price levels, should be a stationary, mean-reverting series. In his paper, 'An Empirical Examination of Long-Run Purchasing Power Parity Using Cointegrating Techniques' (1987), Mark Taylor runs this test on 'data on relative prices and nominal exchange rates against the US dollar ... for the UK, West Germany, France, Canada and Japan'. He fails 'to find cointegration between the nominal exchange rate and relative prices for any of the countries examined ... Thus, rather than finding evidence of stable, long-run proportionality between exchange rates and prices, we were unable to reject the hypothesis that they tend to drift apart without bound'.[2] Thus, the time series[3] data for this period show little evidence of bilateral nominal exchange rates among the

---

[1] Analysis of whether variables are 'cointegrated' or not became a fashionable exercise in econometrics in the mid-1980s; for a reference to this methodology, see Engle and Granger, 'Cointegration and Error Correction: Representation, Estimation and Testing' (1987) pp. 251–76).

[2] Taylor's results supported similar findings from time series studies (e.g., by Darby 'Movements in Purchasing Power Parity: The Short and Long Runs', in Darby *et al.* (eds.) *International Transmission of Inflation* (1980) and Adler and Lehmann, 'Deviations from Purchasing Power Parity in the Long Run' (1983) pp. 1471–87).

[3] Cross-section data (e.g., comparing changes in a wide number of US bilateral exchange rates, including LDCs, against changes in relative price–cost levels) appear to be more favourable to the PPP hypothesis, as some unpublished work by Professor L. Summers indicates.

industrialised, developed countries adjusting in response to movements in relative price–cost levels, even in the long run. While it remains, *a priori*, almost impossible for me to believe that LOOP and purchasing power parity (PPP) can be infringed beyond some limit, such ranges remain apparently far wider under a regime of flexible exchange rates, allowing much greater fluctuations in real exchange rates, than most would have believed likely or even possible, *ab initio*.

It had always been recognised that flexible exchange rates would be likely to exhibit more *short-run* volatility than in the case of exchange rates that were pegged within narrow margins. Indeed, the extent of short-run (high-frequency) exchange rate volatility did increase with the onset of floating in 1973.[1] However, the growing availability of, and familiarity with, forward and future[2] exchange rates meant that for regular and professional operators in forex markets – if not for tourists and small traders – such short-term volatility was potentially only a minor nuisance and not a serious barrier to trade.[3]

As already noted, however, it had been expected that flexible exchange rates would allow real exchange rates to remain more stable and to adjust relatively smoothly to such real shocks as did occur. When there were real shocks (e.g., the discovery and exploitation of North Sea Oil) it was recognised that adjustment would be necessary. Given a sudden new endowment of valuable energy resources, the real exchange rate of the UK and Norway would have to appreciate to restore the balance of payments.[4] This adjustment would be painful for the manufacturers of tradeable goods, which would find themselves becoming less competitive as the exchange rate rose in response to the improved current account balance.

If it had been believed that the extraordinary gyrations of the real exchange rate had been due to a (remarkably autocorrelated) sequence of real shocks in recent years, then the resulting painful fluctuations in the real competitiveness of tradeable goods might have been accepted with more equanimity. But it is not widely believed that this has been the case. Instead, something is thought to have gone very wrong with the working of the flexible exchange rate system itself. Even in the UK case (1979–81), when some sizeable proportion of the pound's appreciation was due to the revaluation of North Sea Oil, much of the appreciation has had to be attributed to other (non-oil) factors.[5]

---

[1] See Vaubel, 'Real Exchange-Rate Changes in the European Community: The Empirical Evidence and Its Implications for European Currency Unification' (1976) pp. 429 70 and Artus and Young, 'Fixed and Flexible Exchange Rates: A Renewal of the Debate' (1979) pp. 654–98.

[2] A forward exchange rate bargain is made between agents for a particular, tailormade, amount and date, though the forward market for particular future dates (e.g., one month and three months) is much broader and more liquid than for 'broken' dates. The futures market involves a *standardised* date, contract size, etc. and, owing to such standardisation, can provide even broader and more liquid markets with lower transactions costs.

[3] For tests of the proposition that foreign exchange volatility reduces trade, see International Monetary Fund, *Exchange Rate Volatility and World Trade* (1983) and Cushman, 'Has Exchange Risk Depressed International Trade? The Impact of Third Country Exchange Risk' (1986).

[4] It remains surprising that so little notice appears to have been taken of the implications of North Sea Oil for the UK exchange rate prior to 1979.

[5] Trying to discriminate between the factors that may have led to the 1979–81 appreciation of the pound is impossible to do accurately, but most of the various studies on this suggest that North Sea Oil was probably responsible for less than half of it. For a recent assessment, see Bean, 'The Macroeconomic Consequence of North Sea Oil' in Dornbusch and Layard (eds) (1987a). For earlier attempts at this exercise, see among others, Niehans, 'The Appreciation of

442

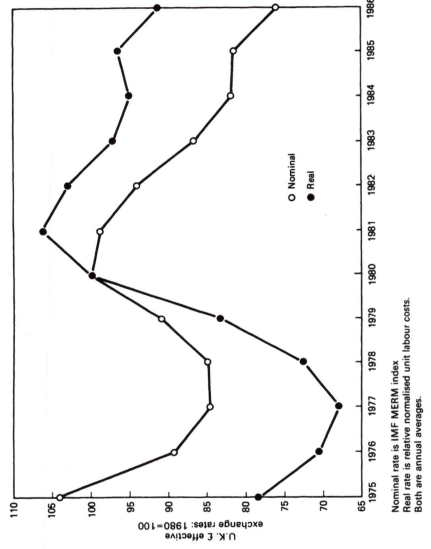

Nominal rate is IMF MERM index
Real rate is relative normalised unit labour costs.
Both are annual averages.

FIG. 18.1(A)

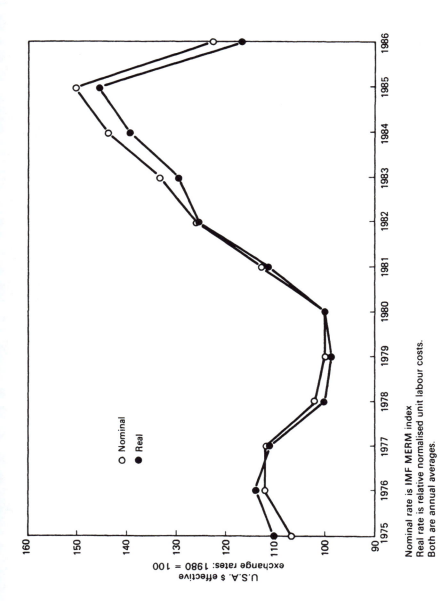

Nominal rate is IMF MERM index
Real rate is relative normalised unit labour costs.
Both are annual averages.

FIG. 18.1(B)

Source: IFS Supplement on Exchange Rates (1985); *IFS Yearbook* (1987).

Unlike the relatively minor, nuisance effects of short-term volatility in the forex market, these major misalignments in real exchange rates, as shown in Figure 18.1, have had an extremely severe, even devastating, effect on the competitiveness, profitability and viability of the tradeable goods industries[1] in the countries concerned. Between end-1976 and January 1981, the pound appreciated by no less than 32 per cent in real terms; by comparison, the real appreciation of the pound required to return to the Gold Standard in 1925, of which Keynes had been so critical[2] and which has been held to account for the dismal performance of the UK economy in the late 1920s, amounted to only about 10 per cent. The pound appreciation (1979-81) and the US$ appreciation (1981-5) left whole industries in those countries non-viable. The decline in manufacturing output in 1979-81 in the UK was worse than in any earlier (non-war) period of similar length. Given that the massive appreciations then eventually reversed themselves, in the UK between 1981 and 1984 and in the US between 1985 and 1988, the enormous dislocation, disruption, and loss of valuable resources in the form of both human and fixed capital appears to have been a major failing in the working of the economic system.[3]

Apart from the actual disturbances to the economies involved, the failure of the foreign exchange market to provide reasonably stable real exchange rates made the forward planning of industrial location, and hence the efficient exploitation of international comparative advantage, much more difficult. How could one decide, say, to concentrate on cloth in the UK and wine production in Portugal, when the gyrations of real exchange rates were such as to make *both* either extraordinarily profitable or calamitously loss-making in either country? These massive, unpredictable, fluctuations in real exchange rates increased the risk of concentrating production where it seemed comparatively most profitable at any one moment and led most multi-national manufacturing companies to adjust their productive capacity more closely to the size of each (geographically distinct) market, as a way of trying to reduce the exchange risk.

How did all this happen?

2. Why Were Flexible Rates so Unstable?

At the end of Chapter 17, we noted that the relative elasticities of demand and supply for tradeable goods might be so low, in the short run at least, that the current account would be slow to respond beneficially to a devaluation, the so-called *J* curve effect. This continued to be observed in practice, with the US trade balance, for example,

---

Sterling – Causes, Effects, Policies' (1981); Goodhart and Temperton, 'The UK Exchange Rate, 1979-81: A Test of the Overshooting Hypothesis' (1982); Sheffrin and Russell 'Sterling and Oil Discoveries: The Mystery of Nonappreciation' (1983).

---

[1] See, for example, Buiter and Miller, 'Changing the Rules: Economic Consequences of the Thatcher Regime' (1983) pp. 305–65.

[2] 'The Economic Consequences of Mr. Churchill (1925)', Volume 9, Chapter 5 in *The Collected Writings of John Maynard Keynes* (1972).

[3] The costs involved are not just immediate and contemporaneous but persist over time (e.g., because once an industry disappears, there are considerable set-up costs involved in re-starting it). For a discussion of these so-called 'hysteresis' effects – i.e., where the current equilibrium level is affected by the previous time-path of development – see Bean, 'Sterling Misalignment and British Trade Performance' (1987b).

being agonisingly slow to improve following the decline in the dollar exchange rate (1985–8). Yet the behaviour of the current account balance in response to exchange rate fluctuations was not better nor worse than had been foreseen in 1973 and noted in Chapter 17. In particular, the most extreme misalignment of the period – the real appreciation of the US dollar (1981–5) – was not caused by any malfunctioning of the US trade or current account balance. Similarly, the appreciation of the pound in 1979–81 led, as expected, to a sharp worsening in the non-oil trade balance.

Until the 1960s at least, international capital flows had been directly constrained by exchange controls so that pressures on the exchange rate usually reflected shifts in the balance of trade and 'leads and lags' in trade financing. The current account balance, in turn, reflected relative competitiveness and demand pressures in the countries involved. In a pegged exchange rate system, such pressures would be reflected, initially at least, in a requirement to use the nation's foreign exchange reserves to maintain the balance of payments at the fixed exchange rate; in a floating exchange rate system, such pressures would be reflected in changes in exchange rates. Taking the latter case as our example and labelling the variables of the Rest of the World by an *, we can construct the kind of Keynesian exchange rate equation typical of that period as:

$$e = f(P/P^*, y - y^*, i - i^*)$$

where e is the exchange rate, P the price level, y the level of real output, and i the nominal interest rate, and the partial derivatives with respect to the three arguments are negative (indicating depreciation) with respect to the first two and positive for the last one.

The relative level of nominal interest rates enters since it influences trade financing decisions and such other capital flows as were permitted, and/or occurred, under the exchange control regulations.

Increasingly, however, during the last two decades the barriers to capital flows, whether by official constraints (exchange controls) or from the natural limitations of information and transactions costs, have been tumbling.[1] As a result, the volume of transactions in the foreign exchange market representing speculative capital transactions have increasingly become a large multiple of the volume related to visible and invisible trade.[2] The foreign exchange market shifted from basically responding to current account flows to reacting to asset holders' decisions on which currency in which to hold their *stock* of wealth.

In particular, the exchange rate defines the relative price of two moneys; thus, the pound–dollar exchange rate showed the number of dollars obtained in return for £1. So, the stock approach to the balance of payments (and foreign exchange rate) began by analysing the foreign exchange market in terms of the relative money demand and supply in the countries concerned (two countries when considering bilateral exchange rates). The assumptions initially made were that:

---

[1] There still seem to remain considerable imperfections, frictions and barriers to international capital substitution, as witnessed for example in the widely differing price–earning ratios in the Tokyo and New York Stock Exchanges in 1987. Also see Feldstein and Horioka, 'Domestic Saving and International Capital Flow' (1980) pp. 314–29.

[2] In the surveys of foreign exchange turnover in London and New York carried out by the Bank of England and FRBNY in March 1986, only about 10 per cent of banks' total foreign exchange business was directly with final customers (and much of the latter would also have represented capital-account rather than current-account transactions).

1. The exchange rate is freely floating, i.e., no intervention.
2. Each country determines the level of its own domestic money stock as a policy-determined variable.
3. There is perfect substitution between national capital markets, so real interest rates are the same in both.
4. There are perfectly clearing goods/factor markets in both countries.
5. Purchasing power parity (PPP) holds continuously.
6. Nominal interest rates equal real rates plus the expected rate of inflation (the Fisher effect).

Then, with a demand-for-money function in both countries of the form:

$$M_d = P.f(y, i),$$

and M_s given by policy, we can write:

$$P = M_s/f(y, i).$$

but, since (from 3 and 6 above)

$$i = \bar{r} + E\dot{P}$$

and $\bar{r}$, the world level of real interest rates is the same in all countries and (from 5 above),

$$e = P/P^*,$$

we can write:

$$e = (M - M^*, y - y^*, E\dot{P} - E\dot{P}^*),$$

where the partial derivatives are negative (i.e., the exchange rate depreciates in response to an increase in the variable) for the first and third argument and positive for the second.

Note that the exchange rate is now expected to *depreciate* in response to an increase in interest rates arising from worsening fears about inflation; with the money stock policy-determined, a rise in interest rates reduces the demand for money and hence, with prices perfectly flexible by assumption, also depreciates the exchange rate. Again, the exchange rate appreciates following a rise in domestic real output, because with a given M_s this must imply a fall in P.

The next stage is to incorporate rational expectations into the model. In this case, the forward rate for period t determined in period $t-1$ will already incorporate all available information about M_s, y and $E\dot{P} - E\dot{P}^*$. So the difference between the spot rate that actually transpires at period t and the forward rate, set at $t-1$ and applicable to period t, will reflect surprises in actual monetary growth, output levels and changing price expectations.

Hoffman and Schlagenhauf put this quite neatly in their useful survey-type article, 'The Impact of News and Alternative Theories of Exchange Rate Determination' (1985) pp. 328–46, where they write pp. 331–2 that:

> In the mid-1970s the monetarist model of exchange rate determination emerged as an alternative exchange rate model. The foundation of the monetary approach is a domestic and foreign money demand function. Each country's demand for money

depends on domestic income and the domestic nominal interest rate. If the money demand functions are combined with the assumptions of purchasing power parity and uncovered interest rate parity, the spot exchange can be written as a function of relative money supplies, relative income, and differences in expected inflation rates. This suggests that the appropriate form of the excess returns equation for this model is:

$$s_t - f_t|_{t-1} = g[(m_t/m_t^*) - E(m_t/m_t^*), \ (y_t/y_t^*) - E(y_t/y_t^*), (\dot{p}_t^e/\dot{p}_t^{e*}) - E(\dot{p}_t^e/\dot{p}_t^{e*})],$$

where $g_1 > 0$; $g_2 < 0$; $g_3 > 0$ [note that $g > 0$ implies depreciation of the exchange rate here]; and m, y and $\dot{p}_t^e$ represent the money supply, the income level, and expected inflation, respectively. The derivation of this equation appears in numerous papers. [Perhaps the best source is Frankel 'Monetary and Portfolio-Balance Models of Exchange Rate Determination' in Bhandari and Putnam (eds) (1983)]. Hence, an unanticipated increase in the domestic nominal money supply relative to the foreign money supply results in an increase in domestic prices relative to foreign prices, which, in turn, causes an unexpected depreciation in the domestic currency. A surprise increase in either the domestic income level or domestic expected inflation rate relative to the corresponding foreign variable alters the domestic demand for money relative to foreign demand. The former increases the demand for domestic currency leading to an unanticipated appreciation while the latter increase results in a decrease in money demand and unexpected depreciation.

A variant of this model assumes price expectations are rational. When the money demand equations and the assumptions of purchasing power parity and interest parity are combined with the assumption of rational expectations, the spot exchange rate, as noted by Bilson [in 'The Monetary Approach to the Exchange Rate: Some Empirical Evidence' (1978) pp. 48–75], can be written in terms of current and future relative money supply and income. If the variables can be modelled as $AR(1)$ processes [i.e., as random walks], as in Hoffman and Schlagenhauf ['Rational Expectations and Monetary Models of Exchange Rate Determination' (1983) pp. 247–60], the spot exchange rate can be shown to depend only on the current relative income and money supply. The news version of this model is

$$s_t - f_t|_{t-1} = g[(m_t/m_t^*) - E(m_t/m_t^*), \ y_t/y_t^* - E(y_t/y_t^*)],$$

where $g_1 > 0$, and $g_2 < 0$.

One notable feature of the monetary approach to the balance of payments is that it implies that increases in interest rates would (normally) be associated with a depreciation in the exchange rate, in contrast to the appreciation predicted in the standard Keynesian flow model. The evidence here is very mixed.[1] In the 1970s, it was common for interest rate increases to be associated with exchange rate depreciations; this may have been due to a Central Bank reaction function where the authorities raised interest rates in response to a weakening exchange rate (see Chapter 10), as well as, or rather than, worsening inflationary fears causing both movements. In the

---

[1] As is made clear by the assessment of the empirical evidence in Hoffman and Schlagenhauf (1985) and in Hacche and Townend 'Exchange rates and monetary policy: Modelling sterling's effective exchange rate, 1972–80' in Eltis and Sinclair (eds) (1981).

early 1980s, however, when the UK and USA were giving greater emphasis to monetary targetry (see Chapter 15), the empirical relationship tended to reverse, with a rise in interest rates being associated with an appreciation in the exchange rate.

Given the assumptions of perfect clearing markets, instantaneous PPP and rational expectations, the model was not able to account for the most notorious feature of the flexible exchange rate regime, i.e., the tendency for exchange rates to 'overshoot' their equilibrium values and to become misaligned. Dornbusch[1] found a way both to incorporate greater realism into the model, by assuming *short-run* price stickiness so that PPP only held in the long-run, and, by so doing, to provide an explanation of such overshooting.

Given *long-run* PPP and rational expectations, long-run forward rates will still reflect the fundamental determinants of the equilibrium exchange rate, i.e., future expected paths of monetary growth and real output. However, with short-run prices being sticky, nominal and real interest rates[2] would be temporarily driven down by a (once-for-all) monetary expansion in order to restore equilibrium in the money market. Assuming that covered interest parity, whereby

$$f_{t+1} - s_t = i_t - i_t^*$$

is maintained, a once-for-all expansion in M_s depreciates f_{t+1} by an amount determined by fundamentals but also lowers i_t, so that s_t must drop by more than f_{t+1} (i.e., must 'overshoot' its fundamental equilibrium value). The time paths of e, i, and P are shown below in Figure 18.2 for an economy with instantaneous PPP holding throughout and also with short-term sticky prices and long-term PPP.

One immediate criticism could be that, in the event, expansionary monetary surprises during the period of monetary targetry were followed by increases (not falls) in interest rates, as already noted in Chapter 15. This finding, however, was explained by the policy reaction hypothesis, whereby the monetary expansion was expected to make the authorities tighten monetary policy and to reduce monetary growth in future periods. Meanwhile, Dornbusch's sticky-price monetary model had the virtues of explaining misalignments primarily in terms of capital flows, occasioned largely by interest rate differentials in a world of slowly adjusting prices–wages, all of which seemed to square with the major stylised facts of the period.

Another criticism of the Dornbusch model was that it implied 'jump' overshoots in response to monetary news. Yet, the actual time path of exchange rates did not appear to exhibit many obvious 'jumps' of this kind, even in response to major news items; instead, the actual time path of the dollar – on the basis of this model – would appear to have required 'news' over the 1980–6 period to have exhibited a pattern of serial correlation that belies its definition.[3] One answer to such criticism is that a

---

[1] See 'Expectations and Exchange Rate Dynamics' (1976) pp. 1161–76; 'Flexible Exchange Rates and Interdependence' (1983) pp. 3–38, reprinted in *Dollars, Debts and Deficits* (1986); and 'Exchange Rate Economics: 1986' (1987) pp. 1–18.

[2] Superficially, this might seem inconsistent with the assumption of perfect international capital market substitution, assumption 3 above, but it is not so. The inhabitants in country A, following the monetary expansion, now face a lower real interest rate whether they invest in their own country *or abroad* since the higher foreign nominal rate will be offset by the predicted depreciation of the foreign exchange rate over the life of the investment. Similarly, the non-resident will enjoy a relatively higher but constant real interest rate whether he invests in Country A or elsewhere.

[3] See Koromzay, Llewellyn and Potter (1987) and also Goodhart, 'The Foreign Exchange Market: A Random Walk with a Dragging Anchor' (1988).

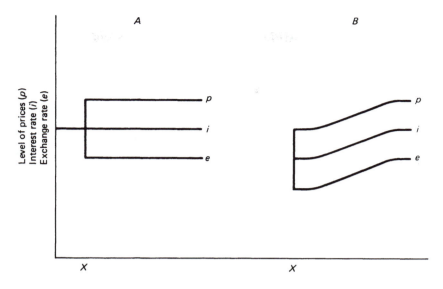

FIG. 18.2

X — once for all monetary expansion

A — instantaneous PPP

B — short term sticky prices and long-term PPP

combination of prior anticipations of events, slow assimilation of new information, and even slower accretion of public credibility to governments' policy announcements can help to transform immediate 'jumps' into a more serially correlated time series with some apparent inertia without destroying the main elements of the analysis.

In most models of this genre, relative prices and hence, via PPP, the exchange rate, are set in the longer run by comparative expected rates of growth of the money stock and of real output. With rational expectations, the forward rate should be an unbiased predictor of the future path of spot rates. As noted earlier, not only is the tendency for a reversion to long-term PPP weaker than most economists might have expected but, even more seriously, the evidence clearly indicates that the forward rate is not an unbiased efficient predictor of future spot rates.[1] That this latter finding must be so can be easily inferred from two well-established stylised facts in the forex market. First, the spot exchange rate approximates closely to a random walk over periodicities of up to three months;[2] this would imply that the best estimate of the future spot rate should be its present value. Second, the forward rate actually diverges from the present spot rate by an extent equal to the current interest differential, in

[1] See Boothe and Longworth, 'Foreign Exchange Market Efficiency Tests: Implications of Recent Empirical Findings' (1986) pp. 135–52.

[2] See Mussa 'Empirical Regularities in the Behavior of Exchange Rates and Theories of the Foreign Exchange Rates' (1979) pp. 9–57, and various articles in the *Journal of International Money and Finance*, Vol. 5, No. 2 (June 1986).

order to maintain covered interest arbitrage. Even worse, however, was to follow. In his article, 'Forward and Spot Rates',[1] Fama demonstrated that, in the equation

$$S_{t+1} - S_t = a + b(f_t - S_t)$$

where S_t is the current rate and f_t is the forward rate applicable at time $t + 1$, b was frequently *negative* and significantly different from its expected value of 1. Moreover, the explanatory power of the forward rate in predicting future changes in spot rates was just about zero.[2]

One response to this finding was to claim that the deviation of the forward rate from the best statistical expectation must be due to risk aversion. The assumption of perfect international capital substitution inherent in the monetary model (assumption 3 in the list above) implied that there was no risk perceived (or that agents were risk-neutral) in holding more or less wealth in one currency or the other. This assumption, like most of the others involved in this model, almost certainly did not hold exactly.

Hoffman and Schlagenhauf (1985), note that 'for many, the assumption that domestic and foreign bonds are perfect substitutes is unrealistic'. They then list a number of economists who

> have developed asset market models where the perfect substitutes assumption is relaxed. In these models the exchange rate adjusts to ensure that the demand for assets (typically foreign and domestic bonds) balances with predetermined supplies. An interesting aspect of these models is that current account developments affect the exchange rate without reverting to the traditional flow model [i.e., because they alter the balance of the outstanding stock of foreign assets].

> Portfolio balance models can be classified according to assumptions made regarding portfolio preferences of residents in different countries. In his review article on exchange rate models, Frankel (1983) presents a model that embodies various assumptions on asset preferences. In this model, the spot exchange rate is determined by the interest rate differential, the net supply of U.S. bonds to the private sector, and the net supply of foreign-bonds to the foreign private sector, the net supply of foreign bonds to the U.S. private sector, and the net supply of U.S. bonds to the foreign private sector. This would suggest that unanticipated changes in the spot exchange rate are due to unanticipated changes in the same set of variables.

> Time series data on various countries' holding of domestic bonds and foreign bonds are not readily available. However, these data limitations need not preclude tests of the portfolio balance model in news form. Since announcements on the stock of bond holdings are not made, it may be argued that market participants respond to announcements that indicate or are suggestive of bond holding changes. Frankel argues that the supply of a given country's bonds available to the private sector is made up of that country's government debt, the cumulative sales of its foreign-denominated assets in foreign exchange intervention, its assets held by other central banks, and its monetary base. The supply of foreign bonds available to a country (under flexible exchange rates) can be measured as the accumulation of its current account position plus sales by other central banks of foreign assets for its currency less its central bank purchase of foreign assets in foreign exchange intervention.

> These definitions suggest that fiscal deficits should be an important factor indicating changes in a country's supply of bonds, while current account developments signal

---

[1] *Journal of Monetary Economics*, Vol. 14 (December 1984) pp. 319–38.

[2] These results have now been frequently replicated, see Boothe and Longworth (1986) and Goodhart (1988).

possible changes in the supply of foreign bonds available to a country. Therefore, unanticipated changes in each country's current account, fiscal deficits, as well as the interest rate differential should be correlated with unanticipated changes in the spot exchange rate.

Unfortunately, the use of these supplementary variables (e.g., on comparative levels of externally-held debt or changes in such levels) to help to explain either changes in exchange rates or the spot–forward divergence have so far had relatively little success. Unless it is possible to give an adequate explanation for the factors causing 'time-varying risk premia' in forward exchange rates, categorising the divergences between forward and future spot rates as due to such premia is vacuous.

Again, worse was to follow. The risk premium argument, suggesting why forward rates diverged from the best statistical (approximately random walk) expectations, implied that the true ('underlying') expectation of the future spot rate would be nearer the current level of the spot rate than was the forward rate. But when actual survey data of market participants' expectations were examined, such expectations – especially longer-term expectations – were more frequently found to be *further* away from the current spot rate than the forward rate,[1] implying 'risk premia' of the *opposite* sign to those offered as a possible explanation of the original results of exercises like those in Fama's (1984) article.

Both Frankel and Froot, 'The Dollar as an Irrational Speculative Bubble: A Tale of Fundamentalists and Chartists',[2] and Goodhart, 'The Foreign Exchange Market: A Random Walk with a Dragging Anchor', have interpreted these results as suggesting that there are heterogeneous groups of speculators in the forex market, some basing their expectations on an analysis of longer-term fundamentals, others relying on the shorter-term random walk property of spot exchange markets, and yet others using 'Chartist' analysis. The shifting balance of influence of these groups within the market, as their respective predictions are falsified or not, largely by unanticipated events, can lead to apparent overshooting and misalignment.

Operators in the forex market are thus not basing their expectations/predictions on just one model, even that preferred by the majority of economists at any moment, but on a variety of differing models. The interplay of beliefs, views and events then drives the exchange rate.

Although this latter formulation seems much more realistic than the earlier monetary or portfolio-balance models, it is at a very early stage of development. It also relies heavily on the use of survey data on expectations which have traditionally been treated with much suspicion in empirical work. If, then, the question is asked whether the economics profession can currently provide a satisfactory, broadly accepted, answer to current puzzles in the forex market (e.g., the massive misalignments; the comparative weakness of PPP; the failure of forward rates to be unbiased, efficient estimators of future spot rates), the answer would have to be 'no'.

---

[1] See Frankel and Froot, 'Interpreting Tests of Forward Discount Bias Using Survey Data on Exchange Rate Expectations' (1986), extensively revised into the paper, 'Using Survey Data to Test Standard Propositions Regarding Exchange Rate Expectations' (1987) pp. 133–53.

[2] *The Marcus Wallenberg Papers on International Finance*, Vol 1, No. 1 (1987) pp. 27–55, also 'Understanding the US Dollar in the Eighties: The Expectations of Chartists and Fundamentalists', *Economic Record*, special issue (1987) pp. 24–38.

3. Attempts to Establish a More Stable Regime

The discomforts caused by the major misalignments of foreign exchange rates under the floating regime were not lessened by the inability of economists to come up with convincing answers for the causes of them, except that the fault probably lay primarily in the determinants of massive capital flows. However, just as the instability of real exchange rates led commentators to hanker after a more controlled system, so did the overwhelming pressures of capital flows indicate that such control would be increasingly difficult to implement. In particular, the potential size of capital flows, especially when unhindered by exchange controls, dwarfed the size of reserves that Central Banks had available for intervention.

Additional reserves could, of course, be created, virtually instantaneously and on a practically limitless scale, if Central Banks were prepared to swap claims[1] or borrow from other Central Banks. In practice, however, Central Banks were hesitant to borrow reserves on a massive scale, in part because the decision whether or not to accept an adjustment in exchange rates (which would, of course, decisively affect the cost of such borrowing), was not entirely in their own hands but was largely determined by unpredictable events, foreigners and politicians (in increasing order of unreliability). Similarly, Central Bankers were unwilling to lend to deficit countries without limit for a variety of reasons, among which was that the use of such reserves by the deficit country would tend to increase monetary growth in the surplus countries. So, although *in theory* an almost limitless extra volume of reserves could have been conjured up at the drop of a hat by Central Bankers, in practice they limited themselves to the use of their wholly-owned reserves supported by some discreet borrowing, usually arranged when their credit was good because they had no immediate need for the reserves thus created! Accordingly, the potential extent of Central Bank intervention was quite small compared to the potential size of capital flows and the effectiveness of intervention as an instrument was reduced.

The effectiveness of intervention was even less when the effects of such intervention on domestic monetary growth, to reduce (increase) it in the deficit (surplus) country, were 'sterilised' by offsetting open market operations. Indeed, the mercurial *masse de manoeuvre* of internationally mobile capital was so large that financial–monetary measures beyond mere sterilised intervention formed an essential part of any attempt to stabilise the major currencies. This caused an essentially 'political' problem, in that, in any system to control the extent of variation of n exchange rates, at least $n-1$ countries' political autonomy over monetary policy–domestic interest rates had to be given up to some greater or less extent since such policy would be predicated to the maintenance of exchange rate stability.

As already discussed in Chapter 17, a fixed exchange rate system works better, and the abandonment of domestic control over monetary policy appears less of a problem, where there is political and fiscal cohesion. There was little or no advance in that latter direction during the last two decades. Indeed, the decline in the supremacy of the United States and the rise of Europe, under the leadership of West Germany, and of Japan as economic powers of almost similar magnitude, led to some further erosion of international consensus on economic policy issues. As considered briefly in

---

[1] Thus, the Fed and the Bank of England could simultaneously provide each other with x billion of pounds and dollars respectively, exchanged at a given spot rate and with the interest rates and forward rate at which the deal would be unwound (unless rolled over) established to provide covered interest parity.

Chapter 15, the likelihood of any of the major countries reverting to a gold or a commodity standard is currently minuscule. Similarly, political divergences in perceptions, preferences and policies made it implausible to envisage Japan and West Germany totally subordinating their own monetary policies to that of the United States to the extent necessary to restore absolutely fixed exchange rates.

One may ask whether there is not room for some middle-way or compromise between absolute abandonment of domestic monetary control and fixed exchange rates on the one hand, and complete domestic monetary sovereignty and freely floating exchange rates on the other. Many of the recent efforts to restore some modicum of official direction over the exchange rate regime have represented an effort to find such a middle-way.

The best known experiment of this kind in recent years has been the European Monetary System (EMS) or, to be pedantic, the Exchange Rate Mechanism (ERM) of the EMS.[1] This was formed in 1979 precisely to try to provide an island of exchange rate stability in the turbulent sea of floating exchange rates. It was recognised at the outset that the various countries participating in the ERM were sufficiently diverse in their natures, and sufficiently unwilling to give absolute priority to maintaining a fixed exchange rate, to make the latter a permanent commitment. Instead, if there were excessively divergent pressures from unaligned policies or different labour cost trends, the central parities could be revised through an agreed process of political discussion and compromise. This meant that the EMS was not a firmly fixed exchange rate system but an adjustable peg system which – as we noted in Chapter 17 – was described by Corden as a 'pseudo-monetary union'.

As noted in Chapter 17, such pegged and adjustable systems have a number of disadvantages. In recent decades, the ranking of most countries in terms of their comparative resistance or susceptibility to inflation has remained relatively constant; Italy and the UK have thus been more susceptible than France, which in turn has been more prone to inflation than West Germany. Accordingly, the question has rarely been 'whether' France or Italy would depreciate its exchange rate against West Germany but just 'when'. As such, if a depreciation becomes increasingly probable in the prospective near future, it provides a great incentive for capital to move to the country that will (if changed) appreciate. This is what is known as a 'one-way option' for speculators. The incentive, arising even from a quite low probability of a small actual depreciation[2] to shift funds to the appreciating country, could be very large and therefore require an equivalently large variation in short-term interest rates to restrain such capital movements.

In the event, the EMS has been rather more successful in maintaining exchange

---

[1] The UK has been a member of the EMS from the outset, playing a full role in the EMS' various other functions (e.g., pooling reserves and exchanging these for European Currency Units (ECUs), etc.); the UK, however, did not subsequently join the ERM.

[2] A 10 per cent probability of a 5 per cent change in actual exchange rates within the month would provide an expected immediate gain of $\frac{1}{2}$ per cent, or at an annual rate of gain, of over 6 per cent per annum. But note that the permitted margin around the central parity becomes very important in such calculations. If the margin was $\pm 2\frac{1}{2}$ per cent and the actual rate was at the bottom of its band before the revaluation and at the top thereafter, it would be theoretically feasible to shift central parties by 5 per cent with no change in the actual exchange rate at all. The wider the bands around the central parity, the greater the flexibility in coping with capital flows – and the less serious would be 'one-way options' – but equally, the less would be the stability and monetary discipline achieved by such looser union.

TABLE 18.1

Changes in EMS Central Rates

	Dates of realignments											
	24/9 1979	30/11 1979	22/3 1981	5/10 1981	22/2 1982	14/6 1982	18/5 1983	21/3 1983	21/7 1985	7/4 1986	4/8 1986	12/1 1987
Belgian franc	0.0	0.0	0.0	0.0	−8.5	0.0	+1.5	0.0	+2.0	+1.0	0.0	+2.0
Danish kroner	−2.9	−4.8	0.0	0.0	−3.0	0.0	+2.5	0.0	+2.0	+1.0	0.0	0.0
German mark	+2.0	0.0	0.0	+5.5	0.0	+4.5	+5.5	0.0	+2.0	+3.0	0.0	+3.0
French franc	0.0	0.0	0.0	−3.0	0.0	−5.75	−2.5	0.0	+2.0	−3.0	0.0	0.0
Irish punt	0.0	0.0	0.0	0.0	0.0	0.0	−3.5	0.0	+2.0	0.0	−8.0	0.0
Italian lira	0.0	0.0	−6.0	−3.0	0.0	−2.75	−2.5	−7.8	−6.0	0.0	0.0	0.0
Dutch gilder	0.0	0.0	0.0	+5.5	0.0	+4.25	+3.5	0.0	+2.0	+3.0	0.0	+3.0

Source: Artis, M. and Taylor, M. (1987) *Exchange Rates and the EMS: Assessing the Track Record*, paper presented at the Money Study Group Conference, Oxford (September) Table 1.

rate stability than the early pessimists, including myself, had expected. There were twelve realignments between 1979 and 1987 but several of these involved only one or two of the member countries resetting their central parities (see Table 18.1). The central parities remained pegged for long enough periods to provide a meaningful modicum of nominal exchange rate stability. Many studies have estimated[1] that exchange rates (both nominal and real) of the EMS countries exhibited greater stability after the formation of the EMS and in relation to non-EMS countries (see Radaelli, 1987, Table 1).

How did the EMS countries achieve such comparative stability? One reason *could* have been that the $n-1$ peripheral countries abandoned any attempt at domestic monetary autonomy, and allowed their domestic monetary policies to be adjusted in line with the central (nth) country, in this case West Germany, so as to give top priority to exchange rate stability. In fact, the evidence, both qualitative and quantitative, appears to be that this did *not* happen. In the first few years, there appeared to be only limited economic convergence between the EMS countries, see Rogoff (1985). In the later years, there *was* more convergence on a conservative fiscal retrenchment, counter-inflationary policy but such convergence was not noticeably greater than in the case of non-EMS countries.

Another factor that has often been mentioned is that for much of the period, the US dollar was strengthening (i.e., during the years 1980–5). The main European alternative to the dollar is the Deutschemark, so a strong dollar tends to mean a weak Deutschemark. Since the Deutschemark is fundamentally the strongest currency in the EMS, external forces that serve to weaken the Deutschemark may allow other EMS currencies to retain their existing peg more easily. While this argument has some plausibility, I have not seen any serious empirical test of its validity.

A third line of argument has been that the EMS has consisted essentially of two separable parts: first, a cohesive extended West German market area including the Netherlands, Denmark, Austria and Switzerland, even though these latter two are

---

[1] Radaelli, 'EMS Stability, Capital Controls and Foreign Exchange Market Intervention' (1987); Artis and Miller, 'On Joining the EMS' (1986); Padoa-Schioppa, 'Policy Cooperation and the EMS Experience', Chapter 8 in Buiter and Marston (1985) and Rogoff 'Can exchange rate predictability be achieved without monetary convergence? Evidence from the EMS' (1985) pp. 93–115.

not EMS members and, second, the other peripheral countries (e.g., Belgium, France and Italy) which protect themselves from capital flows by exchange controls. The markets for goods, labour and capital were both so interpenetrated and dominated by West Germany in the first group that the junior partners *had* effectively abandoned most, if not all, of their monetary policy to the leadership of the Bundesbank. When the Bundesbank forced a discrete step change in money market rates, the Nederlandsche Bank often followed within the day.

The extent of reliance of France and Italy on exchange controls can be documented by the divergence between domestic money market rates, protected by exchange controls, and euro-deposit rates for the same currencies, set in free, uncontrolled international markets. As shown by Giavazzi and Pagano,[1] this divergence was often large at times of tension and of expectations of realignments in central parities. Certainly, exchange controls allowed the authorities to withstand market pressures for short periods of time, and allowed them leeway to conduct the political process of realignment at a measured pace.

Whether this limited degree of control over capital flows was of major importance in permitting the relatively smooth adjustments of the EMS may shortly be seen. The EEC is encouraging, and France and Italy are permitting, a dismantling of exchange controls with the intention of providing a truly unified European market, including within that a unified capital market, by 1992. Furthermore, the comparatively smooth working of the EMS may be even more severely tested by the possible future adherence of the UK to the ERM. With its independent policies, a financial centre as large as that in West Germany and no exchange controls, the entry of the UK could introduce much larger and potentially destabilising capital flows into the context of the EMS.

The proponents of these latter policy changes believe that increasing policy convergence, itself stimulated by market unification and the successful operation of the EMS, will enable the pegged exchange rate system to survive and prosper, despite the dismantling of exchange controls and the possible entry of the UK. Sceptics note the failure of the EEC to develop successful supranational fiscal or political centralisation. The main policy choices are still primarily made at the national level and EEC decisions are the results of debates–disputes between national governments. The centrifugal forces affecting national currencies will still be great, so that the imposition of such extra pressures on the EMS could well destroy it, rather than reinvigorate it. In due course, we shall discover the outcome.

Although the EMS has worked rather better to stabilise exchange rates than pessimists had expected, it remains, of course, an experiment in *regional* stabilisation. Attempts to find some workable compromise between completely fixed and floating rates have so far proved less successful at the world level (i.e., between USA, Japan and West Germany (Group of Three, G3), plus France and UK (G5), plus Canada and Italy (G7)). This resulted partly because economic policy was in the hands of those in the USA and in the UK between 1980 and 1985 who believed that the outcome of an uncontrolled, perfectly free, foreign exchange market would be, *ipso facto*, optimal, and that any official attempts to manage exchange rates were misguided. Eventually, the combination of the experience of the misaligned dollar, together with the changeover in US Secretaries of the Treasury from Regan to Baker, brought a change of heart and allowed the question of possible international policy co-operation towards managing the exchange rate to return to the agenda.

---

[1] See Giavazzi and Pagano, 'Capital Controls and Foreign Exchange Legislation' (1985).

The first fruits of this became apparent following the Plaza accord (22 September 1985), when finance ministers of G5 agreed to co-ordinate intervention in order to bring about an orderly depreciation of the dollar. The effect of this co-operative venture was then given somewhat exaggerated credit for the subsequent continuing (and *not* notably orderly) decline of the dollar; 'exaggerated' since the peak in the dollar's value had already occurred in February–March 1985 and official intervention was going with the existing grain (the underlying trend) in the market. As already noted, official intervention by itself, especially when sterilised, was widely reckoned to be a weak reed. Subsequent agreements again allowed for co-ordinated intervention to maintain exchange rates within unpublished bounds, but both the extent of actual co-ordination – with differing Central Banks intervening on widely differing scales – and their success in achieving their exchange rate objectives remained unclear. At times, the intervention was massive, as in the spring of 1987 when for several months official (largely Japanese) intervention financed the whole of the US current account deficit. Intervention on this scale will surely have had *some* impact but whether it greatly changed the underlying direction or potential long-term equilibrium of the exchange rate remains uncertain.

Given the weakness of intervention as an instrument, co-operation – if it was to mean anything – implied that some of the major countries would have to be prepared to adjust their monetary or fiscal instruments in the pursuit of exchange rate stability when they would *not* have done so anyway on independent, domestic grounds. But which countries should adjust, and why and how? Little or no progress has been made towards answering these questions. Meanwhile, the major countries continue to decide their own domestic policies independently, noting their own individual international co-operative spirit when their decision happens to promote international exchange rate stability as a side-effect and ignoring the international aspect when it does not do so. The major countries criticise each others' policies (too much fiscal expansion in the US, too little in Japan and West Germany), partly to place the onus for adjustment on the other countries.

Various suggestions have been made for establishing a set of objective criteria that a body such as the IMF might apply to give some guidance as to which country was diverging from plan and should adjust.[1] It is almost impossible to undertake such an exercise objectively, however, especially when the economic analysis and modelling is so uncertain and national political perceptions remain so different.

Perhaps the most operational proposal was that advanced by McKinnon[2] – to build on the basis of existing national monetary targets. The monetary targets of the US, West Germany and Japan would be set domestically within the context of a co-ordinated, agreed set of reference range (bilateral) exchange rates. Then, if the bilateral exchange rate moved beyond that intended range, the appreciating country would be expected to raise its target by an agreed proportionate coefficient (e.g., an X per cent higher monetary growth target in response to a 10 per cent appreciation above the range), and vice versa for the depreciating country. This scheme could have been quantified and monitored in a straightforward manner. Alas, the scheme also depended on the stability of domestic demand-for-money functions and the continued use of monetary targets as a central policy plank. When these collapsed in the

[1] See Frenkel and Goldstein, 'A Guide to Target Zones' (1986) pp. 633–73.
[2] McKinnon, *An International Standard for Monetary Stabilization. Policy Analyses in International Economics: 7* (1984).

mid-1980s, so effectively did the McKinnon scheme, even though the idea still receives occasional support.

As of mid-1987, the prospect is not encouraging. This is primarily a political failure due to the continuing supremacy of national political power and the limited transfer of allegiance, and power to supranational bodies. In this political context, proposals that are primarily economic in content are unlikely to prove successful.

Yet, the world economy *is* being unified by technological developments, continuously reducing the costs of transferring information, capital, goods and people from place to place. At its most fundamental level, the volatility of exchange rates may be regarded as the outcome of the interaction between increasingly unified economic systems with persistently national political systems. There are, perhaps, three possible outcomes, in ascending order of likelihood:

1. Increasing political unification.
2. Intervention to limit market unification (e.g., by exchange controls, tariffs, etc.), and to make the boundaries of the market again coincident with that of the nation state.
3. Trying to cope with continuing – even worsening – exchange rate volatility.

Bibliography

Acheson, K. and Chant, J. (1973) 'Bureaucratic Theory and the Choice of Central Bank Goals', *Journal of Money, Credit and Banking* 5(2) (May).

Adler, M. and Lehmann, B. (1983) 'Deviations from Purchasing Power Parity in the Long Run', *Journal of Finance*, 38(5) (December).

Aharony, J. and Swary, I. (1983) 'Contagion Effects of Bank Failures: Evidence from Capital Markets', *Journal of Business*, 56(3).

Ahmad, S. (1970) 'Is Money Net Wealth?', *Oxford Economic Papers*, 22(3), (November).

Akerlof, G. (1970) 'The Market for "Lemons", Qualitative Uncertainty and the Market Mechanism', *Quarterly Journal of Economics*, 84(3) (August).

———— (1979) 'Irving Fisher on His Head: The Consequences of Constant Threshold-Target Monitoring of Money Holdings', *Quarterly Journal of Economics*, 93(2) (May).

Akhtar, M. and Harris, E. (1987) 'Monetary Policy Influence on the Economy—An Empirical Analysis', *Federal Reserve Bank of New York Quarterly Review* (Winter).

Alchian, A. A. (1970) 'Information Costs, Pricing, and Resource Unemployment', in E. S. Phelps (ed.) *Microeconomic Foundations of Employment and Inflation Theory* (New York: Macmillan).

———— and Demsetz, H. (1972) 'Production, Information Costs and Economic Organisation', *American Economic Review*, 62(5) (December).

———— and Klein, B. (1973) 'On a Correct Measure of Inflation,' *Journal of Money, Credit and Banking*, Vol. 5, No. 1, Pt 1 (February).

Aliber, R. B. (1986) Comment on R. Cooper's Paper, 'A Monetary System Based on Fixed Exchange Rates', in C. C. Campbell and W. R. Dougan (eds), *Alternative Monetary Regimes* (Baltimore: Johns Hopkins University Press).

Amihud, Y. *et al.* (1985) 'Alternative Views of Market Making', in *Market Making and the Changing Structure of the Securities Industry* (Lexington, Mass.: Lexington Books).

Andersen, L. and Carlson, K. (1970) 'A Monetarist Model for Economic Stabilization', *Federal Reserve Bank of St Louis Review*, 52(4) (April).

———— and Jordan, J. (1968) 'Monetary and Fiscal Actions: A Test of Their Relative Importance in Economic Stabilization', *Federal Reserve Bank of St Louis Review*, 50(11) (November).

Anderson, G. J. and Hendry, D. F. (1984) 'An Econometric Model of United Kingdom Building Societies', *Oxford Bulletin of Economics and Statistics*, 46(3) (August).

Andrew, A. P. (1908) 'Substitutes for Cash in the Panic of 1907', *Quarterly Journal of Economics*, 22(4) (August).

Argy, V. and Polak, J. J. (1971) 'Credit Policy and the Balance of Payments', *IMF Staff Papers*, 18.

Aronson, J. R. (1968) 'The Idle Cash Balances of State and Local Governments: An Economic Problem of National Concern', *Journal of Finance*, 23(3) (June).

Arrow, K. J. (1963) 'Uncertainty and the Welfare Economics of Medical Care', *American Economic Review*, 53(5) (December).

———— (1973) 'Social Responsibility and Economic Efficiency', *Public Policy*, 21(3) (Summer).

458

Artis, M. and Lewis, M. (1976) 'The Demand for Money in the United Kingdom, 1963–73, *Manchester School Journal*, 44(2) (June).
———— and Miller, M. H. (1986) 'On Joining the EMS', *Midland Bank Review*, (Winter).
———— and Nobay, A. R. (1969) 'Two Aspects of the Monetary Debate', *National Institute Review*, 49 (August).
———— and Taylor, M. (1987) *Exchange Rates and the EMS: Assessing the Track Record*, paper presented at the Money Study Group Conference, Oxford (September).
Artus, J. and Young, J. (1979) 'Fixed and Flexible Exchange Rates: A Renewal of the Debate', *IMF Staff Papers*, 26(4) (December).
Axilrod, S. (1983) 'Monetary Policy, Money Supply, and the Federal Reserve's Operating Procedures' in P. Meek (ed.), *Central Bank Views on Monetary Targeting*, (Washington: Federal Reserve Bank of New York).
———— and Beck, D. (1973) 'Role of Projections and Data Evaluation with Monetary Aggregates as Policy Targets', in *Controlling Monetary Aggregates II: The Implementation*. (Boston: Federal Bank of Boston).
Azariadis, C. and Stiglitz, J. (1983) 'Implicit Contracts and Fixed Price Equilibria', *Quarterly Journal of Economics*, 98(3), Supplement.
Azzi, C. F. and Cox, J. C. (1976) 'A Theory and Test of Credit Rationing: Comment', *The American Economic Review*, 66(5) (December).
Bagehot, W. (1873, reprinted 1962) *Lombard Street* (Homewood, Ill.: Richard D. Irwin).
Baillie, R. and McMahon, P. (1987) 'Rational Forecasts in Models of the Term Structure of Interest Rates', in C. Goodhart, D. Currie and D. Llewellyn (eds) *The Operation and Regulation of Financial Markets* (London: Macmillan).
Baltensperger, E. (1980) 'Alternative Approaches to the Theory of the Banking Firm', *Journal of Monetary Economics*, 6(1) (January).
Bank of Canada (1973) *Bank of Canada Annual Report for 1973*.
Bank for International Settlements (1980) *The Monetary Base Approach to Monetary Control* (Basle: BIS) (September).
———— (1986) *Recent Innovations in International Banking* (Basle: BIS), see also Cross, S. *et al.* (1986).
Bank of England (1971) 'Competition and Credit Control', *Bank of England Quarterly Bulletin*, 11(2) (June).
———— (1982a) 'The supplementary special deposits scheme', *Bank of England Quarterly Bulletin*, 22(1) (March).
———— (1982b) 'The composition of monetary and liquidity aggregates and associated statistics', *Bank of England Quarterly Bulletin*, 22(4) (December).
———— (1984a) 'The Role of the Bank of England in the Money Market', in *The Development and Operation of Monetary Policy: 1960–1983* (Oxford: Clarendon Press).
———— (1984b) *The Development and Operation of Monetary Policy 1960–1983* (Oxford: Clarendon Press).
———— (1984c) 'Funding the public sector borrowing requirement, 1952–83', *Bank of England Quarterly Bulletin*, 24(4) (December).
———— (1986) Speech by Governor of Bank, on 'Financial Change and Broad Money', *Bank of England Quarterly Bulletin*, 26(4) (December).
———— (1987a) 'Measurement of broad money', *Bank of England Quarterly Bulletin*, 27(2) (May).
———— (1987b) 'The Instruments of Monetary Policy', *Bank of England Quarterly Bulletin*, 27(3) (August).
Barnett, W. A. and Spindt, P. A. (1982) 'Divisia Monetary Aggregates: Their Compilation, Data and Historical Behaviour', *Federal Reserve Board Staff Study*, No. 116.
Baron, D. (1982) 'A Model of the Demand for Investment Banking and Advising and Distribution Services for New Issues', *Journal of Finance*, 37(4) (September).

Barro, R. J. (1970) 'Inflation, the Payments Period, and the Demand for Money', *Journal of Political Economy*, 78(6) (November–December).

———— (1971) 'Inflation, the Payments Period and the Demand for Money', [Abstract of PhD Thesis] *Journal of Finance*, 36(3) (June).

———— (1974) 'Are Government Bonds Net Wealth?', *Journal of Political Economy*, 82(6) (November).

———— (1977) 'Unanticipated Money Growth and Unemployment in the United States', *American Economic Review*, 67(2) (May).

———— (1978) 'Unanticipated Money, Output and the Price Level in the United States', *Journal of Political Economy*, 86(4) (July).

———— (1983) 'Inflationary finance under discretion and rules', *Canadian Journal of Economics*, 16(1) (February).

———— (1986a) 'Rules vs Discretion', Chapter 1 in C. C. Campbell and W. R. Dougan (eds), *Alternative Monetary Regimes* (Baltimore: Johns Hopkins University Press).

———— (1986b) 'Recent Developments in the Theory of Rules Versus Discretion', *Economic Journal*, 96, Supplement.

———— and Gordon, D. B. (1983b) 'A Positive Theory of Monetary Policy in a Natural Rate Model', *Journal of Political Economy*, 91(4) (August).

———— (1983a) 'Rules, discretion and reputation in a model of monetary policy', *Journal of Monetary Economics*, 12(1) (July).

———— and Santomero, A. M. (1972) 'Household Money Holdings and the Demand Deposit Rate', *Journal of Money, Credit and Banking*, 4(2) (May).

Baumol, W. J. (1952) 'The Transactions Demand for Cash: An Inventory Theoretic Approach', *Quarterly Journal of Economics*, 66 (November).

Beales, J. H., III (1980) 'The Economics of Regulating the Professions', in R. D. Blair and S. Rubin (eds), *Regulating the Professions* (Lexington, Mass.: Lexington Books).

Bean, C. R. (1987a.) 'The Macroeconomic Consequence of North Sea Oil', in R. Dornbusch and R. Layard (eds), *The Performance of the British Economy* (Oxford: Oxford University Press).

———— (1987b) 'Sterling Misalignment and British Trade Performance', *Centre for Economic Policy Research Discussion Paper Series*, 177 (May).

Becker, G. S. (1965) 'A Theory of the Allocation of Time', *Economic Journal*, 75 (299) (September).

Benham, L. and Benham, A. (1980) 'The Informers' Tale', in *Regulating the Professions*, R. D. Blair and S. Rubin (eds) (Lexington, Mass.: Lexington Books).

Bennett, A and Grice, J. (1984) 'Wealth and the Demand for £M3 in the United Kingdom, 1963–1978', *The Manchester School*, 52(3) (September).

Benston, G. J. (ed.) (1983) *Financial Services: The Changing Institutions and Government Policy* (Englewood Cliffs, N. J.: Prentice-Hall).

————, Eisenbeis, R. A., Horvitz, P. M., Kane, E. J. and Kaufman, G. G. (1986) *Perspectives on Safe and Sound Banking: Past, Present and Future* (Cambridge, Mass.: MIT Press).

Bernanke, B. S. (1983) 'Non-monetary Effects of the Financial Crisis in the Propagation of the Great Depression' *American Economic Review*, 73, (3) (June).

———— and Gertler, M. (1985) 'Banking in General Equilibrium', *NBER Working Paper*, 1674.

Bester, H. (1985) 'Screening vs Rationing in Credit Markets with Imperfect Information', *American Economic Review*, 75(4) (September).

Bhandari, B. (1983) *Economic Interdependence and Flexible Exchange Rates*, in B. Bhandari and D. Putnam (eds) (Cambridge, Mass.: MIT Press).

Bilson, J. (1978) 'The Monetary Approach to the Exchange Rate: Some Empirical Evidence', *IMF Staff Papers*, 25(1) (March).

Black, F. (1970) 'Banking and Interest Rates in a World Without Money: The Effect of Uncontrolled Banking', *Journal of Bank Research*, 1 (Autumn).

Black, J. (1961) unsigned note, *The Economist* (4 November).

Blair, R. D. and Kaserman, D. L. (1980) 'Preservation of Quality and Sanctions within the Professions', in R. D. Blair and S. Rubin (eds), *Regulating the Professions* (Lexington, Mass.: Lexington Books).

Blanchard, O. and Summers, L. (1984) 'Perspectives on High World Real Interest Rates', *Brookings Papers on Economic Activity*, 2.

Bloch, E. (1984) 'The Benefits of Multiple Regulators', paper presented at the Conference on Market Making and the Changing Structure of the Securities Industry (May).

Bloomfield, A. I. (1959) *Monetary Policy Under the International Gold Standard, 1880–1914* (monograph, Federal Reserve Bank of New York).

Boothe, P. and Longworth, D. (1986) 'Foreign Exchange Market Efficiency Tests: Implications of Recent Empirical Findings', *Journal of International Money and Finance*, 5(2) (June).

Bordo, M. D. (1986) 'Explorations in Monetary History – A Survey of the Literature', *Explorations in Economic History*, 23(4) (October).

Boschen, J. and Grossman, H. (1982) 'Tests of Equilibrium Macroeconomics Using Contemporaneous Data, *Journal of Monetary Economics*, 10(3) (November).

Brillenbourg, A. and Khan, M. (1979) 'The Relationship Between Money, Income and Prices: Has Money Mattered Historically?', *Journal of Money, Credit and Banking*, 11(3) (August).

Brittan, S. (1970) *The Price of Economic Freedom: A Guide to Flexible Exchange Rates* (London: Macmillan).

Bronfenbrenner, M. and Mayer, T. (1960) 'Liquidity Functions in the American Economy', *Econometrica*, 28 (October).

Brunner, K. (1971) *A Survey of Selected Issues in Monetary Theory*, Reprint no. 2 of the Research Project in Monetary Theory and Monetary Policy at the University of Konstanz (University of Konstanz).

———, Cukierman, A. and Meltzer, A. (1983) 'Money and Economic Activity, Inventories and Business Cycles', *Journal of Monetary Economics*, 11(3) (May).

——— and Meltzer, A. (1964) 'Some Further Investigations of Demand and Supply Functions for Money', *The Journal of Finance*, 19(2), Pt 1 (May).

——— (1967) 'Economies of Scale in Cash Balances Reconsidered', *Quarterly Journal of Economics*, 81 (August).

——— (1971) 'The Uses of Money: Money in the Theory of an Exchange Economy', *American Economic Review*, 61(5) (December).

——— (1972) 'Money, Debt, and Economic Activity', *Journal of Political Economy*, 80(5) (September–October).

——— (1976) *The Phillips Curve and Labor Markets*, Carnegie-Rochester Conference Series on Public Policy, 1 (Amsterdam: North Holland).

Buiter, W. H. and Miller, M. H. (1983) 'Changing the Rules: Economic Consequences of the Thatcher Regime', *Brookings Papers on Economic Activity*, 2.

Burman, J. P. and White, W. R. (1972) 'Yield Curves for Gilt-edged Stocks', *Bank of England Quarterly Bulletin*, 12(4) (December).

——— (1973) 'Yield Curves for Gilt-edged Stocks: Further Investigation', *Bank of England Quarterly Bulletin*, 13(3) (September).

Buse, G. (1967) 'The Structure of Interest Rates and Recent British Experience: A Comment', *Economica*, 34(135) (August).

Cagan, P. (1956) 'The Monetary Dynamics of Hyperinflation', in M. Friedman (ed.), *Studies in the Quantity Theory of Money* (Chicago: University of Chicago Press).

——— (1965) *Determinants and Effects of Changes in the Stock of Money, 1875–1960*, National Bureau of Economic Research, Studies in Business Cycles, 13 (New York: Columbia University Press).

——— (1986) 'The Conflict between Short-run and Long-run Objectives', comment on Barro's paper, 'Rules versus Discretion' in C. C. Campbell and W. R. Dougan (eds), *Alternative Monetary Regimes* (Baltimore: Johns Hopkins University Press).

Calvo, G. A. (1978) 'On the Time Consistency of Optimal Policy in the Monetary Economy', *Econometrica*, 46(6) (November).

Cameron, R. (1967) *Banking in the Early Stages of Industrialisation* (London: Oxford University Press).

Campbell, C. C. and Dougan, W. R. (eds) (1986) *Alternative Monetary Regimes* (Baltimore: Johns Hopkins University Press).

Cargill, T. and Mayer, R. (1972) 'A Spectral Approach to Estimating the Distributed Lag Relationship Between Long- and Short-Term Interest Rates', *International Economic Review*, 13(2) (June).

Carr, J. and Darby, M. (1981) 'The Role of Money Supply Shocks in the Short-run Demand for Money', *Journal of Monetary Economics*, 8(2) (September).

————, Darby, M., and Thornton, D. (1986) 'Monetary Anticipations and the Demand for Money', *Journal of Monetary Economics*, 16(2).

Carruth, A. and Oswald, A. (1987) 'On Union Preferences and Labour Market Models: Insiders and Outsiders', *Economic Journal*, 97 (June).

Chant, J. (1987) 'Regulation of Financial Institutions – A Functional Analysis', *Bank of Canada Technical Report*, 45 (January).

Chase, S. B. (1978) 'Introduction to The Symposium on Bank Regulation', *The Journal of Business*, 51(3) (July).

Chick, V. (1989) 'On the Place of *Value and Capital* in Monetary Theory', in *The Monetary Economics of John Hicks* (London: Macmillan) (forthcoming).

Chirinko, R. (1986) 'Business Investment and Tax Policy: A Perspective on Existing Models and Empirical Results', *National Tax Journal*, 39(2) (June).

Chossudovsky, M. (1972) 'Optimal Policy Configurations under Alternative Community Group Preferences', *Kyklos*, 25(4).

Chouraqui, J. C. and Driscoll, M. (1987) 'The Effects of Monetary Policy', *OECD Research Paper* (mimeo) (February).

Chowdhury, G., Green, C. J. and Miles, D. K. (1986) 'An empirical model of company short-term financial decisions: evidence from company accounts data', *Bank of England Discussion Paper*, 26.

Christ, C. F. (1968) 'A Simple Macroeconomic Model with a Government Budget Restraint', *Journal of Political Economy*, 76(1) (January–February).

———— (1976) 'A Short-run Aggregate-Demand Model of the Interdependence and Effects of Monetary and Fiscal Policies with Keynesian and Classical Interest Elasticities', *American Economic Review*, Papers and Proceedings, 57 (May).

Clark, P. W. (1973) ' Some Early Estimates of the Price and Quantity Effects of the Smithsonian Agreement on the U.S. Trade Account', presented to the Annual Meeting of the Economic Society (28–30 December) (New York) (mimeo).

Clayton, G., Gilbert, J. C. and Sedgwick, R. (eds) (1971) *Monetary Theory and Monetary Policy in the 1970s, Proceedings of the 1970 Sheffield Money Study Group Seminar* (Oxford: Oxford University Press).

Clower, R. W. (1965) 'The Keynesian Counterrevolution: a Theoretical Appraisal', from F. H. Hahn and F. Brechling (eds), *The Theory of Interest Rates* (London: Macmillan).

———— (1967) 'A Reconsideration of the Microfoundations of Monetary Theory', *Western Economic Journal*, 6 (December).

———— (1971) 'Theoretical Foundations of Monetary Policy', from *Monetary Theory and Policy in the 1970s*, ed. C. Clayton, J. C. Gilbert and R. Sedgwick (Oxford: Oxford University Press).

———— (1984) Collected essays, in D. Walker (ed.), *Money and Markets: Essays by Robert W. Clower* (Cambridge: Cambridge University Press).

Coase, R. H. (1937) 'The Nature of the Firm', *Economica*, New Series, 4 (November), reprinted in *Readings in Price Theory*, American Economic Association Series (London: Allen & Unwin, 1953).

———— (1964) 'The Regulated Industries – Discussion', *American Economic Review*, 54(3), Papers and Proceedings of the AEA (May).

Cohen, B. C. (1976) 'The Demand for Money by Ownership Category', *National Banking Review*, 4(3) (March).

Congdon, T. (1981) 'Is the provision of a sound currency a necessary function of the State?', *National Westminster Quarterly Review* (August).

Cooper, I. (1986) 'Innovations: New Market Instruments', *Oxford Review of Economic Policy*, 2(4) (Winter).

Cooper, R. N. (ed.) (1969) *International Finance* (Harmondsworth: Penguin Books).

———— (1970) 'Flexing the International Monetary System: The Case for Gliding Parties', *The International Adjustment Mechanism*, Federal Reserve Bank of Boston, Proceedings of a Conference held in October 1969, Conference Series No. 2.

Cootner, P. (ed.) (1967) *The Random Character of Stock Market Prices* (Cambridge, Mass.: MIT Press).

Copeland, T. and Galai, D. (1983) 'Information Effects on the Bid Ask Spread', *Journal of Finance*, 38(5) (December).

Corden, W. M. (1972) 'Monetary Integration', *Essays in International Finance*, 93 (April) (International Finance Section of the Department of Economics of Princeton University).

Corner, D. and Mayes, D., (eds) (1983) *Modern Portfolio Theory and Financial Institutions* (London: Macmillan).

Cornell, B. (1983) 'The Monetary Supply Announcement Puzzle: Review and Interpretation', *American Economic Review*, 73(4) (September).

Cramp, A. B. (1967) 'The Control of Bank Deposits', *Lloyds Bank Review*, 86 (October).

Cramton, R. C. (1964) 'The Effectiveness of Economic Regulation: A Legal View', *American Economic Review*, 54(3), Papers and Proceedings of the AEA (May).

Cross, S. *et al.* (1986) *Report on Recent Innovations in International Banking* (Basle: BIS).

Culbertson, J. M. (1957) 'The Term Structure of Interest Rates', *Quarterly Journal of Economics*, 71 (November).

———— (1965) 'The Interest Rate Structure: Towards Completion of The Classical System', in F. H. Hahn and F. Brechling (eds), *The Theory of Interest Rates* (London: Macmillan).

Currie, D. (1985) 'Macroeconomic Policy Design and Control Theory – A Failed Partnership?', *Economic Journal*, 95 (June).

Cushman, D. (1986) 'Has Exchange Risk Depressed International Trade? The Impact of Third Country Exchange Risk', *Journal of International Money and Finance*, 5(3) (September).

Cuthbertson, K. and Taylor, M. (1987) 'Buffer Stock Money: An Appraisal', in C. Goodhart, D. Currie and D. Llewellyn (eds), *The Operation and Regulation of Financial Markets* (London: Macmillan).

Darby, M. R. (1980) 'Movements in Purchasing Power Parity: The Short and Long Runs', in M. R. Darby *et al.* (eds), *The International Transmission of Inflation* (Chicago: University of Chicago Press).

———— and Karni, M. (1973) 'Free Competition and the Optimal Amount of Fraud', *Journal of Law and Economics*, 16(1) (April).

Davidson, J. (1987) 'Disequilibrium Money: Some Further Results with a Monetary Model of the UK', Chapter 6 in C. Goodhart, D. Currie and D. Llewellyn (eds), *The Operation and Regulation of Financial Markets* (London: Macmillan).

Davidson, P. and Weintraub, S. (1973) 'Money as Cause and Effect', *The Economic Journal*, 83(332) (December).

Davis, R. G. (1971) 'Short-run Targets for Open Market Operations', *Open Market Policies and Operating Procedures – Staff Studies* (Federal Reserve Board).

———— (1973) 'Implementing Open Market Policy with Monetary Aggregate Objectives', *Federal Reserve Bank of New York Monthly Review*, 55(7) (July).

Deaton, A. (1981) *Essays in the Theory and Measurement of Consumer Behaviour* (Cambridge: Cambridge University Press).

———— (1972) 'Production, Information Costs and Economic Organisation', *American Economic Review*, 62(5) (December).

Demsetz, H. (1968) 'The Cost of Transacting', *Quarterly Journal of Economics*, 82(1) (February).

Dhrymes, P. *et al.* (1984) 'A Critical Reexamination of the Empirical Evidence on the Arbitrage Pricing Theory', *Journal of Finance*, 39(2) (June).

Diamond, D. W. (1984) 'Financial Intermediation and Delegated Monitoring', *Review of Economic Studies*, 51(3) (July).

———— and Dybvig, P. H. (1983) 'Bank Runs, Deposit Insurance, and Liquidity', *Journal of Political Economy*, 91(3) (June).

Dickens, R. R. (1987) 'International Comparisons of Asset Market Volatility: A Further Application of the ARCH Model', *Bank of England Discussion Papers*, Technical Series, 15 (February).

Dixon, R. (1982–3) 'On the new Cambridge School', *Journal of Post Keynesian Economics*, 5(2) (Winter).

Dornbusch, R. (1976) 'Expectations and Exchange Rate Dynamics', *Journal of Political Economy*, 84(6) (December).

———— (1983) 'Flexible Exchange Rates and Interdependence', *IMF Staff Papers*, 30(1) (March), reprinted in Dornbusch, R., *Dollars, Debts and Deficits* (Cambridge, Mass.: MIT Press).

———— (1987) 'Exchange Rate Economics: 1986', *Economic Journal*, 97(385) (March).

———— and Layard, R. (eds) (1987) *The Performance of the British Economy* (Oxford: Oxford University Press).

Dowd, K. (1987) 'Automatic Stabilising Mechanisms Under Free Banking', University of Sheffield Working Paper (March).

Duck, N., and Sheppard, D. (1978) 'A Proposal for the Control of the UK Money Supply', *Economic Journal*, 88 (March).

Dunn, R. M., Jr (1971) *Canada's Experience with Fixed and Flexible Exchange Rates in a North American Capital Market* (Canadian–American Committee, sponsored by National Planning Association (USA) and Private Planning Association of Canada).

Dutton, D. S. and Gramm, W. P. (1973) 'Transactions Costs, the Wage Rate and the Demand for Money', *American Economic Review*, 63(4) (September).

Easton, W. W. (1985) 'The importance of interest rates in five macroeconomic models', *Bank of England Discussion Paper*, No. 24 (October).

Edwards, J., Franks, J., Mayer, C. and Schaefer, S. (eds) (1986) *Recent Developments in Corporate Finance* (Cambridge: Cambridge University Press).

Eltis, W. and Sinclair, P. (eds) (1981) *The Money Supply and the Exchange Rate* (Oxford: Oxford University Press).

Elzinga, K. G. (1980) 'The Compass of Competition for Professional Services', Chapter 6 in R. D. Blair and S. Rubin (eds), *Regulating the Professions* (Lexington, Mass.: Lexington Books).

Engle, R. F. and Granger, C. W. J. (1987) 'Cointegration and Error Correction: Representation, Estimation and Testing', *Econometrica*, 55(2) (March).

Fama, E. F. (1971) 'Risk, Return and Equilibrium', *Journal of Political Economy*, 79(2) (January–February).

———— (1975) 'Short-term Interest Rates as Predictors of Inflation', *American Economic Review*, 65(3) (June).

———— (1976) *Foundations of Finance* (New York: Basic Books).

———— (1980) 'Banking in the Theory of Finance', *Journal of Monetary Economics*, 6(1) (January).

———— (1984) 'Forward and Spot Rates', *Journal of Monetary Economics*, 14 (December).

Fand, D. I. (1967) 'Some Implications of Money Supply Analysis', *American Economic Review*, 57 (May).

Federal Reserve Board (1971) *Open Market Policies and Operating Procedures – Staff Studies* including papers by Axilrod, Davis, Andersen, Pierce, Friedman, Poole and Kareken (Washington: Federal Reserve Board).

———— (1981) *New Monetary Control Procedures*, Vols 1, 2, Board of Governors of the Federal Reserve System (February).

Federal Reserve Board, Boston (1969) *The International Adjustment Mechanism*, Conference Series No. 2 (Boston: Federal Reserve Bank of Boston) (October).

Federal Reserve Board, Chicago (1986) *Proceedings of a Conference on Bank Structure and Competition*, Federal Reserve Bank of Chicago (May).

Feige, E. (1964) *The Demand for Liquid Assets: A Temporal Cross Section Analysis* (Englewood Cliffs, NJ: Prentice-Hall).

———— and Parkin, M. (1971) 'The Optimal Quantity of Money, Bonds, Commodity Inventories, and Capital', *American Economic Review*, 61(3), Pt 1 (June).

Feldstein, M. and Horioka, C. (1980) 'Domestic Saving and International Capital Flow', *Economic Journal*, 90(358) (June).

Fellner, W. (1979) 'The Credibility Effect and Rational Expectations: Implications of the Gramlich Study', *Brookings Papers in Economic Activity*, 1.

Fischer, S. (1975) 'The Demand for Index Bonds', *Journal of Political Economy*, 83(3) (June), also reprinted as Chapter 9 in *Indexing, Inflation and Economic Policy* (1986).

———— (1977a) 'Long-Term Contracts, Rational Expectations and the Optimal Money Supply Rule', *Journal of Political Economy*, 85(1) (February).

———— (1977b) 'On the Nonexistence of Privately Issued Index bonds in the US Capital Market', originally published in E. Lundberg (ed.), *Inflation Theory and Anti-Inflation Policy* (London: Macmillan), reproduced as Chapter 10 in *Indexing, Inflation and Economic Policy* (1986).

———— (1977c) 'Wage Indexation and Macroeconomic Stability', originally published in *Stabilization of the Domestic and International Economy*, Carnegie–Rochester Conference Series on Public Policy, 5 (Amsterdam: North-Holland), reproduced as Chapter 5 in *Indexing, Inflation and Economic Policy* (1986).

———— (1980) 'Activist Monetary Policy with Rational Expectations', in S. Fischer (ed.), *Rational Expectations and Economic Policy* (Chicago: University of Chicago Press), reproduced as Chapter 14 in *Indexing, Inflation and Economic Policy* (1986).

———— (1986) *Indexing, Inflation and Economic Policy* (Cambridge, Mass.: MIT Press).

———— and Huizinga, J. (1982) 'Inflation, Unemployment and Public Opinion Polls', originally published in *Journal of Money, Credit and Banking*, 14(1) (February), reproduced as Chapter 4 in *Indexing, Inflation and Economic Policy* (1986).

———— and Modigliani, F. (1978) 'Toward an Understanding of the Real Effects and Costs of Inflation', *Weltwirtschaftliches Archiv*, 114(4), reproduced as Chapter 1 in *Indexing, Inflation and Economic Policy* (1986).

———— et al. (eds) (1986) *Macroeconomics and Finance: Essays in Honor of Franco Modigliani* (Cambridge, Mass.: MIT Press).

Fisher, D. (1964) 'The Structure of Interest Rates: A Comment' – Grant, J., 'A Reply', *Economica*, 31(124) (November).

———— (1966) 'Expectations, The Term Structure of Interest Rates, and Recent British Experience', *Economica*, 33(131) (August).

———— (1967) 'Reply' to A. Buse, 'The Structure of Interest Rates and Recent British Experience: A Comment', *Economica*, 34(135) (August).

Fisher, G. and D. Sheppard (1972) *Effects of Monetary Policy on the United States Economy*, Organisation for Economic Co-operation and Development Occasional Studies (Paris: OECD) (December).

Fisher, I. (1930) *Theory of Interest* (London: Macmillan).

Fleming, J. M. (1971) 'On Exchange Rate Unification', *Economic Journal*, 81(323) (September).

Flemming, J. (1989) 'Three Points on the Yield Curve' in A. Courakis and C. Goodhart (eds), *The Monetary Economics of John Hicks* (forthcoming).

Floyd, J. E. (1969) 'Monetary and Fiscal Policy in a World of Capital Mobility', *Review of Economic Studies*, 86(108) (October).
———— (1973) 'A Reply', *Review of Economic Studies*, 40(122) (April).
Flux, A. W. (1911) 'The Swedish Banking System', from *Banking in Sweden and Switzerland*, National Monetary Commission, 42 (Washington: Government Printing Office).
Foley, P., Shaked, A. and Sutton, J. (1981) *The Economics of the Professions: An Introductory Guide to the Literature* (ICERD) (London School of Economics).
Frankel, J. (1983) 'Monetary and Portfolio-Balance Models of Exchange Rate Determination', in B. Bhandari and D. Putnam (eds), *Economic Interdependence and Flexible Exchange Rates* (Cambridge, Mass.: MIT Press).
———— and Froot, K. A. (1986) 'Interpreting Tests of Forward Discount Bias Using Survey Data on Exchange Rate Expectations', *NBER Working Paper*, 1672.
———— (1987a) 'Using Survey Data to Test Standard Propositions Regarding Exchange Rate Expectations', *American Economic Review*, 77(1) (March).
———— (1987b) 'The Dollar as an Irrational Speculative Bubble: A Tale of Fundamentalists and Chartists', *The Marcus Wallenberg Papers on International Finance*, 1(1).
———— (1987c) 'Understanding the US Dollar in the Eighties: The Expectations of Chartists and Fundamentalists', *Economic Record*, Special Issue.
Freimer, M. and Gordon, M. J. (1965) 'Why Bankers Ration Credit', *Quarterly Journal of Economics*, 79(3) (August).
Frenkel, J. and Johnson, H. G. (eds) (1976) *The Monetary Approach to the Balance of Payments* (London: Allen & Unwin).
———— and Goldstein, M. (1986) 'A Guide to Target Zones', *IMF Papers*, 33(4) (December).
Friedman, M. (1953) The Case for Flexible Exchange Rates', *Essays in Positive Economics* (Chicago: University of Chicago Press).
———— (1956) 'The Quantity Theory of Money – A Restatement', in M. Friedman (ed.), *Studies in the Quantity Theory of Money* (Chicago: University of Chicago Press).
———— (1959a) 'The Demand for Money: Some Theoretical and Empirical Results', *Journal of Political Economy*, 67 (August).
———— (1959b) *Programme for Monetary Stability* (New York: Fordham University Press).
———— (1969a) *The Optimum Quantity of Money and Other Essays* (Chicago: Aldine).
———— (1969b) 'Money and Business Cycles', in M. Friedman, *The Optimum Quantity of Money and Other Essays* (1969).
———— (1970) 'A Theoretical Framework for Monetary Analysis', *Journal of Political Economy*, 78(2) (March–April).
———— (1971a) 'A Monetary Theory of Nominal Income', *Journal of Political Economy*, 79(2) (March–April).
———— (1971b) 'Government Revenue from Inflation', *Journal of Political Economy*, 79(4) (July–August).
———— (1972) 'Comments on the Critics', *Journal of Political Economy*, 80(5) (September–October).
———— and Meiselman, D. (1964) 'The Relative Stability of Monetary Velocity and the Investment Multiplier in the United States, 1897–1958', Research Study No. 2, in *Stabilization Policies: Commission on Money and Credit* (Englewood Cliffs, NJ: Prentice-Hall).
———— and Schwartz, A. J. (1963) *A Monetary History of the United States, 1867–1960*, National Bureau of Economic Research (Princeton: Princeton University Press).
———— (1969) 'The Definition of Money: Net Wealth and Neutrality as Criteria', *Journal of Money, Credit and Banking*, 1(1) (February).
———— (1982) *Monetary Trends in the United States and the United Kingdom: Their Relation to Income, Prices, and Interest Rates, 1867–1975* (Chicago: University of Chicago Press).

Fry, M. (1981) 'Government Revenue from Monopoly Supply of Currency and Deposits', *Journal of Monetary Economics*, 8(2) (September).

———— (1982a) 'Models of Financially Repressed Developing Economies', *World Development*, 10(9) (September).

———— (1982b) 'Analysing Disequilibrium Interest Rate Systems in Developing Countries', *World Development*, 10(12) (December).

Gale, D. (1982) *Money: In Equilibrium* (Cambridge: Cambridge University Press).

———— (1983) *Money: In Disequilibrium* (Cambridge: Cambridge University Press).

———— and Hellwig, M. (1985) 'Incentive-compatible Debt Contracts: The One-Period Problem', *Review of Economic Studies*, 52(4) (October).

Gardener, E. P. M. (ed.) (1986) *UK Banking Supervision: Evolution, Practice and Issues* (London: Allen & Unwin).

Garvy, G. and M. Blyn (1969) *The Velocity of Money* (New York: Federal Reserve Bank of New York).

Giavazzi, F. and Pagano, M. (1985) 'Capital Controls and Foreign Exchange Legislation', Occasional Paper, *Euromobiliare* (June).

Glasner, D. (1983) 'Economic Evolution and Monetary Reform', mimeographed working paper (March).

Glosten, L. R. and Milgrom, P. R. (1985) 'Bid, Ask and Transaction Prices in a Specialist Market with Heterogeneously Informed Traders', *Journal of Financial Economics*, 14(1) (March).

Goldfeld, S. (1973) 'The Demand for Money Revisited', *Brookings Papers*, 3.

———— (1976) 'The Case of the Missing Money', *Brookings Papers*, 3.

———— and A. S. Blinder (1972) 'Some Implications of Endogenous Stabilisation Policy', *Brookings Papers on Economic Activity*, 3.

Gold Standard Commission (1982) *Report to the Congress of the Commission on the Role of Gold in the Domestic and International Monetary Systems* (Washington: US Government Printing Office).

Goodhart, C. A. E. (1969) *The New York Money Market and the Finance of Trade, 1900–1913* (Cambridge, Mass.: Harvard University Press).

———— (1972) *The Business of Banking 1891–1914*, London School of Economics Research monograph (London: Weidenfeld & Nicolson).

———— (1984a) *Monetary Theory and Practice: The UK Experience*, (London: Macmillan).

———— (1984b) 'Bank Lending and Monetary Control', Chapter IV in C. A. E. Goodhart, *Monetary Theory and Practice*.

———— (1985) *The Evolution of Central Banks: A Natural Development?* (London School of Economics, STICERD monograph).

———— (1986a) 'Why do we need a Central Bank?', Banca d'Italia temi di discussione, 57 (1 January).

———— (1986b) 'How Can Non-Interest-Bearing Assets Co-exist with Safe Interest-Bearing Assets', *British Review of Economic Issues*, 8(19) (Autumn).

———— (1986c) 'Financial Innovation and Monetary Control', *Oxford Review of Economic Policy*, 2(4) (Winter).

———— (1987a) 'Why do Banks Need a Central Bank?', *Oxford Economic Papers*, 39 (March).

———— (1987b) 'The Economics of "Big Bang"', *Midland Bank Review* (Summer).

———— (1988) 'The Foreign Exchange Market: A Random Walk with a Dragging Anchor', *Economica*, 55 (220) (November).

———— and Bhansali, R. J. (1970) 'Political Economy', *Political Studies*, 18(1) (March).

———— and A. Crockett (1970) 'The Importance of Money', *Bank of England Quarterly Bulletin*, 10(2) (June).

————, Currie, D. and D. Llewellyn (eds) (1987) *The Operation and Regulation of Financial Markets* (London: Macmillan).

———— and Gowland, D. (1977) 'The Relationship between Yields on Short and Long-

Dated Gilt-edged Stocks', *Bulletin of Economic Research*, 29(2) (November).

————, Gowland, D. and Williams, D. (1976) 'Money, Income, and Causality: The U.K. Experience', *American Economic Review*, 66 (June).

———— and Smith, R. (1985) 'The Impact of News on Financial Markets in the United Kingdom', *Journal of Money, Credit and Banking*, 17(4) (November).

———— and Temperton, P. V. (1982) 'The UK Exchange Rate, 1979–81: A Test of the Overshooting Hypothesis', Bank of England mimeo.

Gordon, R. J. (1984) 'The Short-Run Demand for Money: A Reconsideration', *Journal of Money, Credit and Banking*, 16(4) (November).

Gould, J. P. and Verrecchia, R. E. (1985) 'The Information Content of Specialist Pricing', *Journal of Political Economy* 93(1) (February).

Governor of the Bank of England (1986) 'Financial Change and Broad Money', *Bank of England Quarterly Bulletin*, 26(4) (December).

Gower, L. C. B. (1984) *Review of Investor Protection*, Cmnd 9125 (London: HMSO) (January).

Gowland, D. and Goodhart, C. (1978) 'The Relationship between Long-dated Gilt Yields and Other Variables', *Bulletin of Economic Research*, 30(2) (November).

Gramlich, E. (1971) 'The Usefulness of Monetary and Fiscal Policy as Discretionary Stabilization Tools', *Journal of Money, Credit and Banking*, 3(2) (May).

Granger, C. (1969) 'Investigating Causal Relations by Econometric Models and Cross Spectral Methods', *Econometrica*, 37 (July).

Grant, J. (1964) 'Meiselman on the Structure of Interest Rates: A British Test', *Economica*, 31(121) (February).

Greenfield, R., and Yeager, L. (1983) 'A Laissez-faire Approach to Monetary Stability', *Journal of Money, Credit and Banking*, 15(3) (August).

Grier, K. (1986) 'A Note on Unanticipated Money Growth and Interest Rate Surprises: Mishkin and Makin Revisited', *Journal of Finance*, 41(4) (September).

Grossman, S. and Shiller, R. (1981) 'The Determinants of the Variability of Stock Market Prices', *American Economic Review*, Papers and Proceedings, 71 (May).

———— and Stiglitz, J. (1980) 'On the Impossibility of Informationally Efficient Markets', *American Economic Review*, 70(3) (June).

Grunewald, A. E. and Pollock, A. J. (1985) 'Money Managers and Bank Liquidity', *Federal Reserve Bank of Chicago Conference Proceedings* (1–3 May).

Gurley, J. and E. Shaw (1960) *Money in a Theory of Finance* (Washington: The Brookings Institution).

Hacche, G. (1974) 'The demand for money in the United Kingdom: experience since 1971', *Bank of England Quarterly Bulletin*, 14(3) (September).

———— and Townend, J. (1981) 'Exchange rates and monetary policy: Modelling sterling's effective exchange rates, 1972–80', in W. Eltis and P. Sinclair (eds), *The Money Supply and the Exchange Rate* (Oxford: Oxford University Press).

Hahn, F. H. and Brechling, F. (eds) (1965) *The Theory of Interest Rates*, F. H. Hahn and F. Brechling (London: Macmillan).

———— (1973a) 'On the Foundations of Monetary Theory', in M. Parkin (ed.), *Essays in Modern Economics* (London: Longman).

———— (1973b) 'The Winter of our Discontent', *Economica*, 40(159) (August).

Hall, M. J. B. (1986) 'Financial Deregulation in the UK: the Prudential Issues', mimeo.

———— (1987) 'UK Banking Supervision after the Johnson Matthey Affair', in C. Goodhart, D. Currie and D. Llewellyn (eds), *The Operation and Regulation of Financial Markets* (London: Macmillan).

Hall, R. E. (1982) 'A Review of *Monetary Trends in the United States and the United Kingdom* from the Perspective of New Developments in Monetary Economics', *Journal of Economic Literature*, 20 (December).

———— (1984) 'The Short-Run Demand for Money: A Reconsideration', *Journal of Money, Credit and Banking*, 16(4) (November).

———— (1986) 'Optimal Monetary Institutions and Policy', Chapter 5 in C. Campbell and W. Dougan (eds), *Alternative Monetary Regimes* (Baltimore: Johns Hopkins University Press).

Hamburger, M. J. (1971a) 'Expectations, Long-Term Interest Rates and Monetary Policy in the United Kingdom', *Bank of England Quarterly Bulletin*, 11(3) (September).

————— (1971b) 'The Lag in the Effect of Monetary Policy: A Survey of Recent Literature', *The Federal Reserve Bank of New York Monthly Review*, 53(12) (December).

————— (1973) 'The Demand for Money in 1971: Was there a Shift?', *Journal of Money, Credit and Banking*, 5(2) (May).

————— (1977) 'Behaviour of the Money Stock: Is there a Puzzle?', *Journal of Monetary Economics*, 3(3) (July).

————— and Platt, E. (1973) 'The Expectations Hypothesis and the Efficiency of the Treasury Bill Market', mimeo (New York: Federal Reserve Bank of New York).

Hansen, B. (1973) 'On the Effects of Fiscal and Monetary Policy: A Taxonomic Discussion', *American Economic Review*, 63(4) (September).

Harberger, A. C. (1969) 'Some Evidence on the International Price Mechanism', *Journal of Political Economy*, 65 (1957), reprinted in R. N. Cooper (ed.), *International Finance* (Harmondsworth: Penguin Modern Economics).

Hardouvelis, G. (1985) 'Exchange Rates, Interest Rates, and Money-Stock Announcements: A Theoretical Exposition', *Journal of International Money and Finance*, 4(4) (December).

Hart, O. D. (1983) 'Optimal Labour Contracts under Asymmetric Information: An Introduction', *Review of Economic Studies*, 50(1) (January).

Hayashi, F. (1982) 'Tobin's Marginal q and Average q: A Neoclassical Interpretation', *Econometrica*, 50(1) (January).

Hayek, F. A. (1976) *Denationalisation of Money* (London: Institute of Economic Affairs).

————— (1978a) *Denationalisation of Money*, 2nd edn (London: Institute of Economic Affairs).

————— (1978b) *Denationalisation of Money – The Argument Refined* (London: Institute of Economic Affairs).

Hendry, D. and Ericsson, N. R. (1983) 'Assertion without empirical basis', an econometric appraisal of *Monetary Trends . . . in the United Kingdom* by Milton Friedman and Anna Schwartz', *Bank of England Panel of Academic Consultants Panel Paper*, 22.

————— and von Ungern Sternberg, T. (1981) 'Liquidity and Inflation Effect on Consumers' Expenditure', in A. Deaton, *Essays in the Theory and Measurement of Consumer Behaviour* (Cambridge: Cambridge University Press).

Hester, D. and Britto, D. (1973) 'Stability and Control of the Money Supply', presented at a meeting of the Money Study Group at the London School of Economics.

Hicks, J. R. (1937) 'Mr. Keynes and the "Classics": A Suggested Interpretation', *Econometrica* (April).

————— (1965) *Capital and Growth* (London: Oxford University Press).

————— (1967) 'The Classics Again', Chapter 8 in J. R. Hicks, *Critical Essays in Monetary Theory* (Oxford: Clarendon Press).

High, J. (1983–4) 'Knowledge, Maximizing and Conjecture: A Critical Analysis of Search Theory', *Journal of Post Keynesian Economics*, 6(2) (Winter).

Hilton, K. and Crossfield, D. (1970) 'Short-run Consumption Functions for the U.K., 1955–66', in K. Hilton and D. Heathfield (eds), *The Econometric Study of the United Kingdom* (London: Macmillan).

————— and Heathfield, D. (eds) (1970) *The Econometric Study of the United Kingdom* (London: Macmillan).

Hirshleifer, J. (1970) *Investment, Interest and Capital* (Englewood Cliffs, N.J.: Prentice-Hall).

————— (1976) 'Comment on Peltzman's Toward a More General Theory of Regulation', *Journal of Law and Economics*, 29(2) (August).

—————— and Riley, J. (1979) 'The Analytics of Uncertainty and Information – An Expository Survey', *Journal of Economic Literature*, 17(4) (December).

Ho, T. and Saunders, A. (1981) 'The Determinants of Bank Interest, Margins: Theory and Empirical Evidence', *Journal of Financial and Quantitative Analysis*, 16(4) (November).

Hodgman, D. (1960) 'Credit Risk and Credit Rationing', *Quarterly Journal of Economics*, 74 (May).

—————— (1963) *Commercial Bank Loan and Investment Policy* (University of Illinois Bureau of Economic and Business Research).

Hoffman, D. and Schlagenhauf, D. (1983) 'Rational Expectations and Monetary Models of Exchange Rate Determination', *Journal of Monetary Economies*, 11(2) (March).

—————— (1985) 'The Impact of News and Alternative Theories of Exchange Rate Determination', *Journal of Money, Credit and Banking*, 17(3) (August).

Holbrook, H. (1972) 'Optimal Economic Policy and the Problem of Instrument Instability', *American Economic Review*, 62(1) (March).

Holmes, A. and Meek, P. (1972) 'Open Market Operations and the Monetary and Credit Aggregates – 1971', *Federal Reserve Bank of New York Monthly Review*, 54(4) (April).

Horowitz, I. (1980) 'The Economic Foundations of Self-Regulation in the Professions', Chapter 1 in R. D. Blair and S. Rubin (eds) *Regulating the Professions* (Lexington, Mass.: Lexington Books).

Houthakker, H. S. and Magee, S. P. (1969) 'Income and Price Elasticities in World Trade', *Review of Economics and Statistics*, 51(2) (May).

Hume, D. (1898) 'Of the Balance of Trade', from *Essays Moral, Political and Literary*, 1, (London: Longmans Green), reprinted in R. N. Cooper (ed.), *International Finance* (Harmondsworth: Penguin Books).

Humphrey-Hawkins Act (1978) 'Full Employment and Balanced Growth Act', *United States Statutes at Large* (Washington: US Government Printing Office, 92(2)).

Ingram, J. C. (1962) 'Some Implications of Puerto Rican Experience', from *Regional Payments Mechanism: The Case of Puerto Rico* (Chapel Hill: University of North Carolina Press), reprinted in R. N. Cooper (ed.), *International Finance* (1969).

—————— (1969) Comment on P. B. Kenen's paper 'The Theory of Optimum Currency Areas: An Eclectic View', in R. A. Mundell and A. K. Swoboda (eds), *Monetary Problems of the International Economy* (Chicago: University of Chicago Press).

International Monetary Fund (1983) *Exchange Rate Volatility and World Trade*, IMF Occasional Paper, 28 (July).

Jacklin (initial unknown) (1985) 'Essays in Banking', Stanford Graduate School of Business, PhD Thesis.

Jaffee, D. M. (1971) *Credit Rationing and the Commercial Loan Market* (New York: Wiley).

—————— and Modigliani, F. (1969) 'A Theory and Test of Credit Rationing', *American Economic Review*, 59(5) (December).

—————— and Russell, T. (1976) 'Imperfect Information, Uncertainty and Credit Rationing', *Quarterly Journal of Economics*, 90(4) (November).

Jao, Y. C. (1984) 'A Libertarian Approach to Monetary Theory and Policy', *Hong Kong Economic Papers*, 15.

Jensen, M. (1972) 'Capital Markets: Theory and Evidence', *The Bell Journal of Economics and Management Science*, 3(2) (Autumn).

Johnson, H. G. (1962) 'Monetary Theory and Policy', *American Economic Review*, 52 (June), reproduced as Chapter 1 in R. S. Thorn (ed.), *Monetary Theory and Policy* (New York: Random House).

—————— (1969) 'Inside Money, Outside Money, Income, Wealth and Welfare in Monetary Theory', *Journal of Money, Credit and Banking*, 1(1) (February).

—————— (1972) *Inflation and the Monetarist Controversy* (Amsterdam: North-Holland).

—————— (1973) 'The Monetary Approach to Balance-of-Payments Theory, in M. B.

Connolly and A. K. Swoboda (eds), *Further Essays in Trade and Money* (London: Allen & Unwin).
————— (1974) 'The Monetary Theory of Balance of Payments Policies', included in J. Frenkel and H. G. Johnson (eds), *The Monetary Approach to the Balance of Payments* (London: Allen & Unwin).
Jones, R. (1976) 'The Origin and Development of Media of Exchange', *Journal of Political Economy*, 84(4) (August).
Jonson, P. D., Moses, E. R. and Wymer, C. R. (1977) 'The RBA 76 Model of the Australian Economy', in W. E. Norton (ed.), *Conference in Applied Economic Research, December 1977* (Sydney: Reserve Bank of Australia).
Jonung, L. (1985) 'The Economics of Private Money: The Experience of Private Notes in Sweden 1831–1902', *Nationalekonomiska Institutionen*, mimeo (September).
Jordan, W. A. (1972) 'Producer Protection, Prior Market Structure and the Effects of Government Regulation', *Journal of Law and Economics*, 15(1) (April).
Judd, J. and Scadding, J. (1981) 'Liability Management, Bank Loans and Deposit "Market" Disequilibrium', *Federal Reserve Bank of San Francisco Economic Review* (Summer).
————— (1982) 'The Search for a Stable Money Demand Function: A Survey of the Post-1973 Literature', *Journal of Economic Literature*, 20(3) (September).
Junz, H. B. and Rhomberg, R. R. (1973) 'Price Competitiveness in Export Trade Among Industrialised Countries', *American Economic Review*, 63(2) (May).
Kahn, R. (1973) 'The International Monetary System', *American Economic Review*, 63(2) (May).
Kaldor, Lord N. (1955) 'Alternative Theories of Distribution', *Review of Economic Studies*, 23(61).
————— (1970) 'The Case for Regional Policies', *Scottish Journal of Political Economy*, 17(3) (November).
————— (1980) 'Memorandum of Evidence on Monetary Policy to the Select Committee on the Treasury and Civil Service', *Treasury and Civil Service Committee, Memoranda on Monetary Policy*.
Kane, E. J. (1972) 'Regulatory Structure in Futures Markets: Jurisdictional Competition among the SEC, the CFTC, and Other Agencies', National Bureau of Economic Research (NBER), Working Paper 1331 (April).
————— (1985) *The Gathering Crisis in Federal Deposit Insurance*, (Cambridge, Mass: MIT Press).
Kareken, J. (1981) 'Deregulating Commercial Banks: The Watchword Should Be Caution', *Federal Reserve Bank of Minneapolis Quarterly Review*, 5(2) (Spring–Summer).
————— (1984) 'Bank Regulation and the Effectiveness of Open Market Operations', *Brookings Papers on Economic Activity*, 2.
————— (1987) 'Deposit Insurance Reform or Deregulation is the Cart, Not the Horse', *Federal Reserve Bank of Minneapolis Quarterly Review*, 7(2) (Spring).
————— and Wallace, N. (1972) 'The Monetary Instrument Variable Choice: How Important?', *Journal of Money, Credit and Banking*, 4(3) (August).
————— (1978) 'Deposit Insurance and Bank Regulation: A Partial-Equilibrium Exposition', *The Journal of Business*, 51(3) (July).
Karni, E. (1973) 'The Transactions Demand for Cash: Incorporation of the Value of Time into the Inventory Approach', *Journal of Political Economy*, 81(5) (September–October).
Kaufman, G. G. (1987) 'The Truth About Bank Runs', Staff Memoranda, Federal Reserve Bank of Chicago, SM-87-3 (April).
Keating, G. (1984) 'The Financial Sector of the London Business School Model', mimeo, presented to the Centre for Economic Policy Research (May).
Kenen, P. B. (1969) 'The Theory of Optimum Currency Areas: An Eclectic View', in R. A.

Mundell and A. K. Swoboda (eds), *Monetary Problems of the International Economy* (Chicago: University of Chicago Press).

Keran, W. (1970a) 'Monetary and Fiscal Influences on Economic Activity: The Foreign Experience', *Federal Reserve of St Louis Review*, 52(2) (February).

———— (1970b) 'Selecting a Monetary Indicator – Evidence from the United States and Other Developed Countries', *Federal Reserve of St Louis Review* 52(9) (September).

Kessel, R. (1965) 'The Cyclical Behavior of the Term Structure of Interest Rates', *NBER Occasional Paper*, 91 (New York).

Keynes, J. M. (1972) *The Economic Consequences of Mr. Churchill (1925)*, 9(5) in *The Collected Writings of John Maynard Keynes* (London: Macmillan).

Khan, M. S. (1973) 'A Note on the Secular Behaviour of Velocity within the Context of the Inventory-Theoretic Model of Demand for Money', *The Manchester School Journal*, 2 (June).

King, R. C., Plosser, C. I. and Rebelo, S. T. (1987) 'Production, Growth and Business Cycles', working paper, presented at the Money Study Group Conference (September).

Kinley, D. (1901) 'Credit – Currency and Population', *Journal of Political Economy*, 10(1) (December).

Kleidon, A. W. (1986) 'Variance Bound Tests and Stock Price Valuation Models', *Journal of Political Economy*, 94(5) (October).

Klein, B. (1974) 'The Competitive Supply of Money', *Journal of Money, Credit and Banking*, 6(4) (November).

Klein, J. J. (1970) Discussion of Fand's paper on 'A Monetarist Model of the Monetary Process', *The Journal of Finance*, 25(2) (May).

Kochin, L. A. (1972) 'Judging Stabilisation Policy', mimeo (New York: Federal Reserve Bank of New York).

Kohli, V. and Rich, G. (1986) 'Monetary Control: The Swiss Experience', *The Cato Journal*, 5(3) (Winter).

Kornai, J. (1971) *Anti-Equilibrium: On Economic Systems Theory and the Tasks of Research* (Amsterdam and London: North-Holland).

Koromzay, V., Llewellyn, J. and Potter, S. (1987) 'The Rise and Fall of the Dollar: Some Explanations, Consequences and Lessons', *Economic Journal*, 97(385) (March).

Kydland, F. E. and Prescott, E. C. (1977) 'Rules rather than discretion: The inconsistency of optimal plans', *Journal of Political Economy*, 85(3) (June).

Laffer, A. (1970) 'Trade Credit and the Money Market', *Journal of Political Economy*, 78(2) (March–April).

———— and Ranson, R. D. (1971) 'A Formal Model of the Economy', *Journal of Business*, 44 (July).

Laidler, D. (1969a) 'The Definition of Money', *Journal of Money, Credit and Banking*, 1(3) (August).

———— (1969b) *The Demand for Money – Theories and Evidence* (International Textbook Co.).

———— (1972a) 'Thomas Tooke on Monetary Reform', in M. Peston and B. Corry (eds), *Essays in Honour of Lord Robbins* (London: Weidenfield & Nicolson).

———— (1972b) Review of Orr's 'Cash Management and the Demand for Money', *Economica*, 39(156) (November).

———— (1973) 'Expectations, Adjustment, and the Dynamic Response of Income to Policy Changes', *Journal of Money, Credit and Banking*, 5(1), Pt 1 (February).

———— (1984) 'The "Buffer Stock" Notion in Monetary Economics', *Economic Journal Supplement*, 94.

———— (1988) 'Some Macroeconomic Implications of Price Stickiness', *The Manchester School*, 56(1) (March).

Lane, T. (1984) 'Instability and Short-term Monetary Control', *Journal of Monetary Economics*, 14(2) (September).

Laurent, R. (1979) 'Reserve Requirements: Are They Lagged in the Wrong Direction?', *Journal of Money, Credit and Banking*, 11(3) (August).

Layard, R. (1986) *How to Beat Unemployment* (Oxford: Oxford University Press).
───── and Nickell, S. (1986) *Unemployment in Britain*, Centre for Labour Economics, Discussion Paper No. 240 (London School of Economics).
Leamer, E. (1985) 'Vector Autoregressions for Causal Inference', *Carnegie-Rochester Conference Series on Public Policy* (Amsterdam: North Holland).
Lee, T. H. (1966) 'Substitutability of Non-Bank Intermediary Liabilities for Money: The Empirical Evidence', *The Journal of Finance*, 21(3) (September).
Leeuw, F. de and Gramlich, E. (1969) 'The Channels of Monetary Policy', *Federal Reserve Bulletin Staff Economic Study*, 55(6) (June).
Leijonhufvud, A. (1968) *On Keynesian Economics and the Economics of Keynes* (London: Oxford University Press).
───── (1981) 'Inflation and Economic Performance', University of Stanford, California, mimeo.
───── (1984) 'Constitutional Constraints on the Monetary Powers of Government', in *Constitutional Economics: Containing the Economic Powers of Government* (Lexington, Mass.: Lexington Books).
───── (1986) Comment on Barro's paper entitled 'Rules with Some Discretion', in C. Campbell and W. Dougan (eds), *Alternative Monetary Regimes* (Baltimore: Johns Hopkins University Press).
Leland, H. E. and Pyle, D. H. (1977) 'Information Asymmetries, Financial Structure and Financial Intermediaries', *Journal of Finance*, 32(2) (May).
Lerner, A. P. (1944) *The Economics of Control* (New York: Macmillan).
Leroy, S. F. (1982) 'Expectations Models of Asset Prices: A Survey of Theory', *Journal of Finance*, 37 (March).
Levine, P. and Currie, D. (1987) 'Does International Macroeconomics Policy Coordination Pay and Is It Sustainable? A Two Country Analysis', *Oxford Economic Papers*, 39(1) (March).
Levy, H. and Sarnat, M. (1984) *Portfolio and Investment Selection: Theory and Practice* (Englewood Cliffs, N. J.: Prentice-Hall International).
Lewis, M. K. (1986) 'Banking as Insurance', mimeo (Nottingham University).
Lindsey, D. (1986) 'The Monetary Regime of the Federal Reserve System', Chapter 5 in C. Campbell and W. Dougan (eds), *Alternative Monetary Regimes* (Baltimore: Johns Hopkins University Press).
Lippman, S. and McCall, J. (1976) 'The Economics of Job Search: a Survey', *Economic Inquiry*, 14(1) (June), (2) (September).
Lipsey, R. and Parkin, M. (1970) 'Incomes Policy: a Re-appraisal', *Economica*, 37(146) (May).
Litterman, R. and Weiss, L. (1985) 'Money, Real Interest Rates, and Output: A Reinterpretation of Postwar U.S. Data', *Econometrica*, 53(1) (January).
Lucas, R. Jr (1972) 'Expectations and the Neutrality of Money', *Journal of Economic Theory*, 4(1) (February).
───── (1973) 'Some International Evidence of Output-Inflation Trade-Offs', *American Economic Review*, 63(3) (June).
───── (1976) 'Econometric Policy Evaluation: a Critique', in K. Brunner and A. Meltzer (eds), *The Phillips Curve and Labour Markets*, Carnegie-Rochester Conference Series on Public Policy, 1 (Amsterdam: North-Holland).
───── (1983) 'Corrigendum', *Journal of Economic Theory*, 31(1) (October).
Luckett, D. (1967) 'Multi-period Expectations and the Term Structure of Interest Rates', *Quarterly Journal of Economics*, 81(2) (May).
Macaulay, F. (1938) *Some Theoretical Problems Suggested by the Movements of Interest Rates, Bond Yields and Stock Prices in the United States Since 1856*, 33, National Bureau of Economic Research (New York).
Machlup, F. (1943) *International Trade and the National Income Multiplier* (Philadelphia: The Blakiston Co., reprinted 1950).
MacKinnon, J. and Milbourne, R. (1984) 'Monetary Anticipations and the Demand for Money', *Journal of Monetary Economics*, 13(2) (March).

Magnifico, G. and Williamson, J. H. (1972) *European Monetary Integration* (A Federal Trust Report).

Malkiel, B. G. (1966) *The Term Structure of Interest Rates* (Princeton: Princeton University Press).

———— and Kane, E. (1967) 'The Term Structure of Interest Rates: An Analysis of a Survey of Interest-Rate Expectations', *The Review of Economics and Statistics*, 49(3) (August).

Mankiw, G. and Summers, L. H. (1984) 'Do Long-Term Interest Rates Overreact to Short-Term Interest Rates?', *Brookings Papers on Economic Activity*, 1.

Manuelli, R. E. (1986) 'Modern Business Cycle Analysis: A Guide to the Prescott-Summers Debate', *FRB Minneapolis Quarterly Review* (Fall).

Marais, D. A. J. (1979) 'A Method of Quantifying Companies' Relative Financial Strength', *Bank of England Discussion Paper*, 4 (July).

Marris, R. and Wood, A. (1971) *The Corporate Economy* (London: Macmillan).

Marshall, A. (1930) *The Pure Theory of Foreign Trade; The Pure Theory of Domestic Values* (London School of Economics Reprints of Scarce Tracts in Economics and Political Science, No. 1) (London).

Marsh, T. and Merton, R. (1986) 'Dividend Variability and Variance Bounds Test for the Rationality of Stock Market Prices', *American Economic Review*, 76 (June).

Marty, A. L. (1969) 'Inside Money, Outside Money and the Wealth Effect', *Journal of Money, Credit and Banking*, 1(1) (February).

Mascaro, A. and Meltzer, A. (1983) 'Long- and Short-term interest rates in a risky world', *Journal of Monetary Economics*, 12(4) (November).

Masera, R. S. (1972a) *The Term Structure of Interest Rates* (Oxford: Clarendon Press).

———— (1972b) 'Properties of a Monetarist Model for Economic Stabilization: Comment on Andersen', from K. Brunner (ed.), Proceedings of the First Konstanzer Seminar, Supplement to *Kredit und Kapital* (Berlin: Duncker & Humboldt).

McCallum, B. (1985) 'Bank Deregulation, Accounting Systems of Exchange, and the Unit of Account: A Critical Review', *Carnegie–Rochester Conference Series*, 23.

———— (1986) 'On "Real" and "Sticky-Price" Theories of the Business Cycle', *Journal of Money, Credit and Banking*, 18(4) (November).

McCloskey, D. and Zecher, R. (1976) 'How the Gold Standard Worked, 1880–1913', in J. Frenkel and H. Johnson (eds), *The Monetary Approach to the Balance of Payments* (Toronto: University of Toronto Press).

McCulloch, J. H. (1986) 'Beyond the Historical Gold Standard', Comment on A. J. Schwartz, 'Alternative Monetary Regimes: The Gold Standard', in C. Campbell and W. Dougan (eds), *Alternative Monetary Regimes* (Baltimore: Johns Hopkins University Press).

McKinnon, R. I. (1963) 'Optimum Currency Areas', *American Economic Review*, 53(4) (September).

———— (1984) *An International Standard for Monetary Stabilization, Policy Analyses in International Economics: 7* (Washington: Institute for International Economics).

McLeod, A. N. (1962) 'Credit Expansion in an Open Economy', *Economic Journal*, 72(287) (September).

Meade, J. E. (1986) 'Exchange-Rate Flexibility', *The Three Banks Review*, 70 (June).

Meek, P. (1981) *New Monetary Control Procedures*, 1, 2, Federal Reserve Staff Study, Board of Governors of the Federal Reserve System (February).

———— (ed.) (1982) *US Monetary Policy and Financial Markets* (New York: Federal Reserve Bank of New York).

Meiselman, D. (1962) *The Term Structure of Interest Rates* (Englewood Cliffs, NJ: Prentice-Hall).

Melton, W. (1985) *Inside the Fed: Making Monetary Policy* (Homewood, Ill.: Dow Jones-Irwin).

Meltzer, A. (1986) 'Size, Persistence and Interrelation of Nominal and Real Shocks', *Journal of Monetary Economics*, 17(1) (January).

Merton, R. (1986) 'On the current state of the Stock Market Rationality Hypothesis', in S. Fischer *et al.* (eds), *Macroeconomics and Finance: Essays in Honor of Franco Modigliani* (Cambridge, Mass.: MIT Press).

Milbourne, R. (1987) 'Re-examining the Buffer-Stock Model of Money', *Economic Journal*, Supplement, 97 (Conference).

Milde, H. (1974) 'Informationskosten, Anpassungskosten und die Theorie das Kreditmarktes', *Kredit und Kapital*, 7(4).

Miller, M. H. , and Orr, D. (1966) 'A Model of the Demand for Money by Firms', *Quarterly Journal of Economics*, 80(3) (August).

———— (1968) 'The Demand for Money by Firms: Extensions of Analytic Results', *The Journal of Finance*, 23(5) (December).

Miller, Marcus and Sprenkle, C. M. (1980) 'The Precautionary Demand for Narrow and Broad Money', *Economica*, 47(188) (November).

Mills, T. C. (1981) 'Unobserved components, signal extraction and relationships between macroeconomic times series', *Bank of England Discussion Paper*, No. 19 (December).

———— (1983a) 'Composite Monetary Indicators for the United Kingdom; Construction and Empirical Analysis', *Bank of England Technical Series Discussion Paper*, No. 3 (May).

———— (1983b) 'The Information Content of the UK Monetary Components and Aggregates', *Bulletin of Economic Research*, 35(1) (May).

Minford, P. (1983) 'Labour Market Equilibrium in an Open Economy', *Oxford Economic Papers* (November).

———— *et al.* (1983) *Unemployment: Cause and Cure* (Oxford: Martin Robertson).

Mishkin, F. (1982) 'Does Anticipated Monetary Policy Matter? An Econometric Investigation', *Journal of Political Economy*, 90(1) (February).

Modigliani, F. and Shiller, R. (1973) 'Inflation, Rational Expectations and the Term Structure of Interest Rates', *Economica*, 40(157) (February).

———— and Sutch, R. (1966) 'Innovations in Interest Rate Policy', *American Economic Review*, 56(2) (May).

———— (1967) 'Debt Management and the Term Structure of Interest Rates: An Empirical Analysis of Recent Experience', *Journal of Political Economy*, 75(4) (August).

Monti, M. (1971) 'A Theoretical Model of Bank Behaviour and its Implications for Monetary Policy', *L'Industria Revista di Economica Politica*, 2.

Moore, B. J. (1968) *An Introduction to the Theory of Finance* (New York: The Free Press).

———— (1972) 'Optimal Monetary Policy', *Economic Journal*, 82(325) (March).

Morrison, G. R. (1966) *Liquidity Preferences of Commercial Banks* (Chicago: University of Chicago Press).

Moran, M. (1984) *The Politics of Banking* (London: Macmillan).

Mundell, R. A. (1961) 'A Theory of Optimum Currency Areas', *American Economic Review*, 60(4) (September).

———— (1962) 'The Appropriate Use of Monetary and Fiscal Policy for Internal and External Stability', *International Monetary Fund Staff Papers*, 9 (March).

———— and Swoboda, A. (eds) (1969) *Monetary Problems of the International Economy* (Chicago: University of Chicago Press).

Murphy, A. E. (1972) 'The Nature of Money – with Particular Reference to the Irish Bank Closure', mimeo (Dublin: Trinity College).

Mussa, M. (1979) 'Empirical Regularities in the Behavior of Exchange Rates and Theories of the Foreign Exchange Rates', *Carnegie–Rochester Conference Series on Public Policy*, 11 (Autumn).

Muth, R. (1961) 'Rational Expectations and the Theory of Price Movements', *Econometrica*, 29 (July).

Newlyn, W. T. (1962) *The Theory of Money* (Oxford: Clarendon Press).

———— (1964) 'The Supply of Money and its Control', *The Economic Journal*, 74 (June).

Niehans, J. (1969) 'Money in a Static Theory of Optimal Payments Arrangements', *Journal of Money, Credit and Banking*, 1(4) (November).

————— (1971) 'Money and Barter in General Equilibrium with Transactions Costs', *American Economic Review*, 61(5) (December).

————— (1978) *The Theory of Money* (Baltimore: The Johns Hopkins University Press).

————— (1981) 'The Appreciation of Sterling – Causes, Effects, Policies', unpublished manuscript, SSRC Money Study Group Discussion Paper, Volkswirtschaftliches Institute (University of Bern) (February).

Nobay, R. and Johnson, H. (eds) (1974) *Issues in Monetary Economics* (Oxford: Oxford University Press).

Nordhaus, W. (1975) 'The Political Business Cycle', *Review of Economic Studies*, 42(2) (April).

————— and Wallich, H. (1973) 'Alternatives for Debt Management', a paper given at the Federal Reserve Bank of Boston Conference on 'Issues in Federal Debt Management' (June).

Norton, W. E. (1969) 'Debt Management and Monetary Policy in the United Kingdom', *Economic Journal*, 79(315) (September).

Okun, A. (1981) *Prices and Quantities: A Macroeconomic Analysis* (Washington: The Brookings Institution).

Orr, D. (1970) *Cash Management and the Demand for Money* (New York: Praeger).

————— (1972) 'Cash Management and the Demand for Money', *Economica*, 39(156) (November).

————— and Mellon, W. G. (1961) 'Stochastic Reserve Losses and Expansion of Bank Credit', *American Economic Review*, 51 (September).

Ostroy, J. M. (1973) 'The Informational Efficiency of Monetary Exchange', *American Economic Review*, 63(4) (September).

Padoa-Schioppa, T. (1985) 'Policy Cooperation and the EMS Experience', in W. Buiter and R. Marston (eds), *International Economic Policy Cooperation* (Cambridge: Cambridge University Press).

Page Committee (1973) *Committee to Review National Savings*, Cmnd 5273 (London: HMSO).

Paish, F. (1968) 'How the Economy Works', *Lloyds Bank Review*, 88 (April).

Parkin, M. (1986) 'The Output Inflation Tradeoff When Prices are Costly to Change', *Journal of Political Economy*, 94(1) (February).

————— Barrett, R. and Gray, M. (1975) 'The Demand for Financial Assets by the Personal Sector of the U.K. Economy', in G. A. Renton (ed.), *Modelling the Economy* (London: Heinemann Educational Books).

————— and M. Gray (1973) 'Portfolio Diversification as Optimal Precautionary Behaviour', in M. Morishima *et al.* (eds), *Theory of Demand: Real and Monetary* (Oxford: Clarendon Press).

Peltzman, S. (1976) 'Toward a More General Theory of Regulation', *Journal of Law and Economics*, 19(2) (August).

————— (1984) 'Constituent Interest and Congressional Voting', *Journal of Law and Economics*, 27(1) (April).

Pepper, G. (1973) Monetary Bulletin (17), mimeo (London: Greenwell) (October).

Peretz, D. (1971) 'Thirty-five Years of Change for the Financial System', *Futures*, 3(4) (December).

Perlman, M. (1971) 'The Roles of Money in an Economy and the Optimum Quantity of Money', *Economica*, 38(151) (August).

Pesek, B. and Saving, T. (1967) *Money, Wealth and Economic Theory* (New York: Macmillan).

Peston, M. (1972) 'The Correlation between Targets and Instruments', *Economica*, 39(156) (November).

Phelps, E. S. (1972) *Inflation Policy and Unemployment Theory, The Cost-Benefit Approach to Monetary Planning* (London: Macmillan).

————— (ed.) (1970) *Microeconomic Foundations of Employment and Inflation Theory* (New York: Macmillan).

Pierce, D. and Haugh, L. (1977) 'Causality in Temporal Systems: Characterizations and a Survey', *Journal of Econometrics*, 5(3) (May).

Pierce, J. and Thomson, T. (1973) 'Some Issues in Controlling the Stock of Money', *Controlling Monetary Aggregates II: The Implementation*, proceedings of a Conference held in September 1972 (Boston: Federal Reserve Bank of Boston).

Podolski, T. (1986) *Financial Innovation and the Money Supply* (Oxford: Basil Blackwell).

Polak, J. J. (1957–8) 'Monetary Analysis of Income Formation and Payments Problems', *International Monetary Fund Staff Papers*, 6.

Poole, W. (1968) 'Commercial Bank Reserve Management in a Stochastic Model: Implications for Monetary Policy', *Journal of Finance*, 23(5) (December).

————— (1970) 'Optimal Choice of Monetary Policy Instruments in a Simple Stochastic Macro Model', *Quarterly Journal of Economics*, 84(2) (May).

————— (1971) 'Alternative Paths to a Stable Full Employment Economy', *Brookings Papers on Economic Activity*, 1971:3 (Washington: The Brookings Institution).

————— and Kornblith, E. (1973) 'The Friedman–Meiselman CMC Paper: New Evidence on an Old Controversy', *American Economic Review*, 63(5) (December).

Prescott, E. G. (1977) 'Should Control Theory Be Used for Economic Stabilization?', *Carnegie–Rochester Series on Public Policy*, Supplement to the *Journal of Monetary Economics*, 7.

————— (1986) 'Theory ahead of Business Cycle Measurement', *FRB Minneapolis Quarterly Review* (Fall).

Radaelli, G. (1987) 'EMS Stability, Capital Controls and Foreign Exchange Market Intervention', mimeo, Chase Manhattan Bank (London) Working Paper in Financial Economics, No. 2, paper presented at Money Study Group Conference (Oxford) (September).

Radcliffe Report (1959) *The Committee on the Working of the Monetary System: Report*, Cmnd. 827 (London: HMSO).

Ramakrishnan, N. and Thakor, A. (1984) 'Information Reliability and a Theory of Financial Intermediation', *Review of Economic Studies*, 5(3) (July).

Rayner, A. C. (1969) 'Premium Bonds – The Effect of the Prize Structure', *Bulletin of the Oxford University Institute of Economics and Statistics*, 31(4) (November).

Reid, M. (1982) *The Secondary Banking Crisis, 1973–75* (London: Macmillan).

Renton, G. A. (ed.) (1975) *Modelling the Economy* (London: Heinemann Educational Books).

Rhomberg, R. R. (1959–60) 'Canada's Foreign Exchange Market: A Quarterly Model', *International Monetary Fund Staff Papers*, 7.

————— (1964) 'A Model of the Canadian Economy under Fixed and Fluctuating Exchange Rates', *Journal of Political Economics*, 72(1) (February).

————— (1976) 'Indices of Effective Exchange Rates', *IMF Staff Papers*, 23(1) (March).

Rhymes, T. K. (1986) 'Further Thoughts on the Banking Imputation in the National Accounts', *The Review of Income and Wealth*, 32(4) (December).

Rich, G. and Beguelin, J. P. (1985) 'Swiss Monetary Policy in the 1970s and 1980s', *Monetary Policy and Monetary Regimes*, A Symposium Dedicated to Robert Weintraub, Graduate School of Management, University of Rochester Center Symposia Series, CS-17.

————— and Kohli, U. (1986) 'Monetary Control: The Swiss Experience', *The Cato Journal*, 5(3) (Winter).

Robinson, J. (1951) 'The Rate of Interest', *Econometrica*, 19(2) (April).

Rockoff, H. (1974) 'The Free Banking Era: A Reexamination', *Journal of Money, Credit and Banking*, 6(2) (May).

————— (1985) *The Free Banking Era: A Reconsideration* (New York: Arno Press).

Rogoff, K. (1985) 'Can exchange rate predictability be achieved without monetary convergence? Evidence from the EMS', *European Economic Review*, 28, (1–2) (June–July).

Rothschild, M. (1973) 'Models of Market Organisation with Imperfect Information: A Survey', *Journal of Political Economy*, 81(6) (November–December).

Rousseas, S. W. (ed.) (1968) *Inflation: Its Causes, Consequences and Control, A Symposium* (New York: New York University Press).

Samuelson, P. (1965) 'Proof that Properly Anticipated Prices Fluctuate Randomly', *Industrial Management Review*.

Sandler, T. and Tschirhart, J. (1980) 'The Economic Theory of Clubs: An Evaluative Survey', *Journal of Economic Literature*, 43(4) (December).

Santomero, A. (1984) 'Modeling the Banking Firm: A Survey', *Journal of Money, Credit and Banking*, 16(4) (November).

Sargent, J. A. (1986) 'Pressure Group Development in the EC: The Role of the British Bankers Association', Chapter 7 in E. P. M. Gardener (ed.), *UK Banking Supervision: Evolution, Practice and Issues* (London: Allen & Unwin).

Sargent, T. (1972) 'Rational Expectations and the Term Structure of Interest Rates', *Journal of Money, Credit and Banking*, 4(1) (February).

————— (1973) 'Rational Expectations, the Real Rate of Interest, and the Natural Rate of Unemployment', *Brookings Papers on Economic Activity*, 2.

————— (1982) 'Beyond Demand and Supply Curves in Macroeconomics', *American Economic Review Papers and Proceedings* 72(2) (May).

————— and Wallace, N. (1975) ' "Rational" Expectations, the Optimal Monetary Instrument, and the Optimal Money Supply Rule', *Journal of Political Economy*, 83(2) (April).

Schuster, F., Sir (1907) 'Our Gold Reserves', *Journal of the Institution of Bankers* (January).

Securities and Investments Board (SIB) (1986) *Drafts Relating to Rules, Regulations, Orders and Directions to be made by the Securities and Investments Board as Designated Agency under the Financial Services Bill* (London: SIB).

Shackle, G. L. S. (1949) *Expectations in Economics* (Cambridge: Cambridge University Press).

————— (1955) *Uncertainty in Economics* (Cambridge: Cambridge University Press).

————— (1967) *The Years of High Theory: Invention and Tradition in Economic Thought 1926–1939* (Cambridge: Cambridge University Press).

Shaked, A. and Sutton, J. (1982) 'Imperfect Information, Perceived Quality, and the Formation of Professional Groups', *Journal of Economic Theory*, 27(1) (June).

Sharp, C. (1981) *The Economics of Time* (Oxford: Martin Robertson).

Sheffrin, S. M. and Russell, T. (1983) 'Sterling and Oil Discoveries: The Mystery of Nonappreciation', University of California, Davis, Working Paper Series, No. 6 (September).

Sheppard, D. K. and Barrett, C. R. (1965) 'Financial Credit Multipliers and the Availability of Funds', *Economica*, 32(126) (May).

Shiller, R. J. (1979) 'The Volatility of Long-Term Interest Rates and Expectations Models of the Term Structure', *Journal of Political Economy*, 87(6) (December).

————— (1985) 'Conventional Valuation and the Term Structure of Interest Rates', *NBER Working Paper*, 1610 (April).

—————, Campbell, J. and Schoenholtz, K. (1983) 'Forward Rates and Future Policy: Interpreting the Term Structure of Interest Rates', *Brookings Papers on Economic Activity*, 1.

Shubik, M. (1973) 'Commodity Money, Oligopoly, Credit and Bankruptcy in a General Equilibrium Model', *Western Economic Journal*, 9(1) (March).

Shughart, W. and Tollison, R. (1983) 'Preliminary Evidence on the Use of Inputs by the Federal Reserve System', *American Economic Review*, 73(3) (June).

Siegel, J. (1985) 'Money Supply Announcements and Interest Rates: Does Monetary

Policy Matter?', *Journal of Monetary Economics*, 15(2) (March).

Silber, W. (1971) 'Monetary Policy Effectiveness: The Case of a Positively Sloped IS Curve', *Journal of Finance*, 26(5) (December).

Sims, C. A. (1972) 'Money, Income and Causality', *American Economic Review*, 62 (September).

Smith, B. D. (1984) 'Private Information, Deposit Interest Rates, and the "Stability" of the Banking System', *Journal of Monetary Economics*, 14(3) (November).

Smith, R. and Goodhart, C. (1985) 'The Relationship Between Exchange Rate Movements and Monetary Surprises: Results for the United Kingdom and the United States Compared and Contrasted', *Manchester School Journal*, 53(1) (March).

Smith, V. and Marcis, R. (1972) 'A Time Series Analysis of Post Accord Interest Rates', *The Journal of Finance*, 27(3) (June).

Solow, R. (1968) 'Recent Controversy on the Theory of Inflation: An Eclectic View', in S. W. Rousseas (ed.), *Inflation: Its Causes, Consequences and Control, A Symposium* (New York: New York University Press).

Spencer, P. D. (1986) *Financial Innovation, Efficiency and Disequilibrium: Problems of Monetary Management in the United Kingdom 1971–1981* (Oxford: Clarendon Press).

Spencer, R. and Tohe, W. (1970) 'The "Crowding Out" of Private Expenditures by Fiscal Policy Actions', *Federal Reserve Bank of St Louis Review*, 52(10) (October).

Sprenkle, C. (1969) 'The Uselessness of Transactions Demand Models', *Journal of Finance*, 24(5) (December).

———— (1971) 'Effects of Large Firm and Bank Behavior on the Demand for Money of Large Firms', American Bankers' Association, mimeo.

———— (1972) 'On the Observed Transactions Demand for Money', *Manchester School of Economic and Social Studies*, 3 (September).

Starrett, D. A. (1973) 'Inefficiency and the Demand for "Money" in a Sequence Economy', *Review of Economic Studies*, 40(4) (October).

Stewart, K. (1972) 'Government Debt, Money and Economic Activity', *Federal Reserve Bank of St Louis Review*, 54(1) (January).

Stigler, G. J. (1970) 'The Optimum Enforcement of Laws', *Journal of Political Economy*, 78(3) (May–June).

———— (1971) 'The Theory of Economic Regulation', *Bell Journal of Economics and Management Science*, 2(1) (Spring).

———— and Friedland, C. (1962) 'What can Regulators Regulate? The Case of Electricity', *Journal of Law and Economics*, 5(1) (October).

Stiglitz, J. (1972) 'Some Aspects of the Pure Theory of Corporate Finance: Bankruptcies and Take-overs', *The Bell Journal of Economics and Management Science*, 3(2) (Autumn).

———— (1985a) 'Equilibrium Wage Distributions', *Economic Journal*, 95 (September).

———— (1985b) 'Information and Economic Analysis – A Perspective', *Economic Journal*, Supplement, 95(5).

———— and A. M. Weiss, (1981) 'Credit Rationing in Markets with Imperfect Information' *American Economic Review*, 71(3) (June).

———— (1983) 'Incentive Effects of Terminations: Applications to the Credit and Labor Markets', *American Economic Review*, 73(5).

———— (1986) 'Credit Rationing and Collateral', in J. Edwards *et al.* (eds), *Recent Developments in Corporate Finance* (Cambridge: Cambridge University Press).

Stoll, H. (1985) 'Alternative Views of Market Making', in Amihud, Y. *et al.*, (eds) *Market Making and the Changing Structure of the Securities Industry* (Lexington, Mass.: Lexington Books).

Summers, L. H. (1986a) 'Some Skeptical Observations on Real Business Cycle Theory', *FRB Minneapolis Quarterly Review* (Fall).

———— (1986b) 'Do We Really Know that Financial Markets are Efficient?', in J. Edwards *et al.*, (eds) *Recent Developments in Corporate Finance* (Cambridge: Cambridge University Press).

————— and Poterba, J. (1987) 'Mean Reversion in Stock Returns: Evidence and Implications', LSE Financial Markets Group, Discussion Paper No. 5.

Svensson, L. (1985) 'Money and Asset Prices in a Cash-in-Advance Economy', *Journal of Political Economy*, 93(5) (October).

Tanner, J. E. (1969) 'Lags in the Effects of Monetary Policy: A Statistical Investigation', *American Economic Review*, 59(5) (December).

Taylor, J. B. (1983) 'Comments', on R. J. Barro and D. B. Gordon, 'Rules, discretion and reputation in a model of monetary policy', *Journal of Monetary Economics*, 12(1) (July).

Taylor, M. (1987) 'An Empirical Estimate of Long-Run Purchasing Power Parity Using Cointegrating Techniques', Bank of England, mimeo.

Tew, B. (1969) 'The Implications of Milton Friedman for Britain', *The Banker*, 119(522) (August).

Thomas, B. (1954) *Migration and Economic Growth* (Cambridge: Cambridge University Press).

Thompson, E. A. (1986) 'A Perfect Monetary System', UCLA, mimeo (March).

Thomson, T. and Pierce, J. (unpublished) 'A Monthly Econometric Model of the Financial Sector', Federal Reserve Board Staff Studies.

————— and Pierce, J. (date unknown) 'A Monthly Money Market Model', Federal Reserve Board, mimeo.

Thorn, R. S. (ed.) (1966) *Monetary Theory and Policy* (New York: Random House).

Thygesen, N. (1971) *The Sources and the Impact of Monetary Changes, an Empirical Study of Danish Experience, 1951–68* (Studies from the Copenhagen University Economic Institute, 17 (Copenhagen)).

Timberlake, R. (1978) *The Origins of Central Banking in the United States* (Cambridge, Mass.: Harvard University Press).

Tobin, J. (1947) 'Liquidity Preference and Monetary Policy', *Review of Economics and Statistics*, 21 (May).

————— (1958) 'Liquidity Preference as Behavior Towards Risk' *Review of Economic Studies*, 25(67).

————— (1963) 'Commercial Banks as Creators of "Money"', in D. Carson (ed.), *Banking and Monetary Studies* (Homewood, Ill.: Irwin).

————— (1965) 'The Theory of Portfolio Selection', in F. Hahn and F. Brechling (eds), *The Theory of Interest Rates* (London, Macmillan).

————— (1969) 'A general equilibrium approach to monetary theory', *Journal of Money, Credit and Banking*, 1(1) (February).

————— (1970) 'Money and Income: Post Hoc Ergo Propter Hoc', *Quarterly Journal of Economics*, 84(2) (May).

————— (1972) 'Inflation and Unemployment', Presidential Address, *American Economic Review*, 62(1) (March).

————— (1980) *Asset Accumulation and Economic Activity* (Oxford: Basil Blackwell).

————— (1985) 'Financial Innovation and Deregulation in Perspective', *Bank of Japan Monetary and Economic Studies*.

————— and Buiter, W. (1982) 'Fiscal and Monetary Policies, Capital Formation, and Economic Activity', in *Essays in Economics* (Cambridge, Mass: MIT Press).

Tower, E. (1972) 'Monetary and Fiscal Policy in a World of Capital Mobility: a Respecification', *Review of Economic Studies*, 39(119) (July).

Treasury, HM (1980) 'Monetary Control', HM Treasury (London: HMSO (March).

————— (1980) 'Financial Statement and Budget Report 1980–81' (London: HMSO) (March).

Triffin, R. (1960) *Gold and the Dollar Crisis* (New York: Yale University Press).

Tsiang, S. C. (1961) 'The Role of Money in Trade-Balance Stability: Synthesis of the Elasticity and Absorption Approaches', *American Economic Review*, 51(5) (December).

———— (1972) 'The Rationale of the Mean-Standard Deviation Analysis, Skewness Preference, and the Demand for Money', *American Economic Review*, 62(3) (June).

———— (1989) 'Sir John Hicks's Contributions to Monitoring Theory and What We Would Like to Expect of Him', in *The Monetary Economics of John Hicks* (London: Macmillan: forthcoming).

Tucker, D. P. (1966) 'Dynamic Income Adjustment to Money Changes', *American Economic Review*, 56(3) (June).

United States (1912–13) *Investigations of the Financial and Monetary Conditions in the United States*, House of Representatives' Subcommittee on Banking and Currency, under House Resolutions 429 and 504, 2(29) (Washington: Government Printing Office).

Vaubel, R. (1976) 'Real Exchange-Rate Changes in the European Community: The Empirical Evidence and Its Implications for European Currency Unification', *Weltwirtschaftliches Archiv*, 112(3).

Walker, P., (ed). (1984) *Money and Markets: Essays by Robert W. Clower* (Cambridge: Cambridge University Press).

Wallace, N. (1983) 'A Legal Restrictions Theory of the Demand for "Money" and the Role of Monetary Policy', *Federal Reserve Bank of Minneapolis Quarterly Review*, 7(1) (Winter).

———— and Sargent, T. (1985) 'Interest on Reserves', *Journal of Monetary Economics*, 15(3) (May).

Wallich, H. (1984a) 'Recent Techniques of Monetary Policy', Midwest Finance Association (Chicago, Ill.) mimeo (5 April).

———— (1984b) 'A Broad View of Deregulation', paper presented at the FRB San Francisco Conference on Pacific Basin Financial Reform, mimeo (December).

Walters, A. (1965) 'Professor Friedman on the Demand for Money', *Journal of Political Economy*, 73(5) (October).

Weingast, B. R. (1980) 'Physicians, DNA, Research Scientists, and the Market for Lemons', in R. D. Blair and S. Rubin (eds), *Regulating the Professions* (Lexington: Lexington Books).

Weiss, A. M. (1986) 'Credit Rationing and Collateral', in J. Edwards *et al.*, (eds) *Recent Developments in Corporate Finance* (Cambridge: Cambridge University Press).

'Werner Report' (1970) [1982 in Selection of Texts concerning Matters of the Community from 1950 to 1982, European Parliamentary Committee on International Affairs] (Luxembourg: Office for Official Publications of the European Communities).

Whitaker, T. K. (1973) 'Monetary Integration: Reflections on Irish Experience', *Moorgate and Wall Street* (Autumn).

White, E. N. (1983) *The Regulation and Reform of the American Banking System 1900–1929* (Princeton, N.J.: Princeton University Press).

White, L. H. (1983) 'Competitive Money, Inside and Out', *Cato Journal* 3(1) (Spring).

———— (1984a) Competitive Payments Systems and the Unit of Account', *American Economic Review*, 74(4) (September).

———— (1984b) *Free Banking in Britain: Theory, Experience and Debate (1800–1845)* (Cambridge: Cambridge University Press).

———— (1986) 'Accounting for Non-Interest-Bearing Currency: A Critique of the "Legal Restrictions" Theory of Money', New York University, mimeo.

White, W. H. (1981) 'The case for and against "Disequilibrium" money', *IMF Staff Papers*, 28(3) (September).

White, W. R. (1971) 'Expectations, Investment and the U.K. Gilt-Edged Market – Some Evidence from Market Participants', *Manchester School of Economic and Social Studies*, 4 (December).

———— (1974) 'The Term Structure of Interest Rates – A Cross-Section Test of a Mean-Variance Model', in R. Nobay and H. Johnson (eds), *Issues in Monetary Economics* (Oxford: Oxford University Press).

—————— (1975) 'Some Econometric Models of Deposit Bank Portfolio Behaviour in the UK, 1963–1970', in G. A. Renton (ed.), *Modelling the Economy* (London: Heinemann Educational Books).

Whiteman, C. (1986) 'Analytical Policy Design under Rational Expectations', *Econometrica*, 54(6) (November).

Whittaker, J. and A. J. Theunissen (1986) 'Why does the Reserve Bank set the Interest Rate', University of Cape Town, mimeo (October).

Wicksell, K. (1898/1936) *Interest and Prices*, trans. R. F. Kahn (London: Macmillan).

Wilcox, J. B. (1985) 'A Model of the Building Society Sector', *Bank of England Discussion Paper*, 23 (August).

Williams, D. , Goodhart, C. and Gowland, D. (1976) 'Money, Income, and Causality: The U.K. Experience', *American Economic Review*, 66 (June).

Williamson, J. G. (1964) *American Growth and the Balance of Payments* (Chapel Hill: University of North Carolina Press).

Williamson. J. H. (1965) 'The Crawling Peg', in *Essays in International Finance*, 50 (December), International Finance Sections, Department of Economics, Princeton University.

—————— (1971) 'On the Normative Theory of Balance-of-Payments Adjustment', in G. Clayton, J. Gilbert and R. Sedgwick (eds), *Monetary Theory and Policy in the 1970s* (Oxford: Oxford University Press).

Williamson, O. (1971) 'Management Discretion, Organisation Form, and the Multi-Division Hypothesis', in R. Marris and A. Wood (eds), *The Corporate Economy* (London: Macmillan).

Witteveen, H. J. (1974) remarks at the World Banking Conference in London (15 January).

Wojnilower, A. (1973) talk on 'A New Monetary Environment' (The First Boston Corporation, New York) (16 November).

—————— (1980) 'The Central Role of Credit Crunches in Recent Financial History', *Brookings Papers on Economic Activity*, 2.

Wood, G. E. (1973) 'European Monetary Union and the U.K. – a Cost-Benefit Analysis', *Surrey Economic Papers*, 9 (July).

Wood, J. (1963) 'Expectations, Errors, and the Term Structure of Interest Rates', *Journal of Political Economy*, 71(2) (April).

Wooley, J. (1984) *Monetary Policy: the Federal Reserve and Politics of Monetary Policy* (Cambridge: Cambridge University Press).

Yeager, L. (1985) 'Separated Functions in Monetary Reform', mimeo, (December).

Yellen, J. (1984) 'Efficiency wage models of unemployment', *American Economic Review*, Papers and Proceedings, 74(2) (May).

Index

Made in the USA
Coppell, TX
05 January 2020